Women, Science, and Myth

Gender Beliefs from Antiquity to the Present

SUE V. ROSSER

EDITOR

A B C • C L I O

Santa Barbara, California   Denver, Colorado   Oxford, England

Library of Congress Cataloging-in-Publication Data

Rosser, Sue Vilhauer.
Women, science, and myth : gender beliefs from antiquity to the present / Sue V. Rosser.
p.   cm.
Includes bibliographical references and index.
ISBN 978-1-59884-095-7 (hardcover : alk. paper)
1. Sex role—Research.   2. Sex differences—Research.
3. Sex customs.   I. Title.
HQ1075.R674   2008
305.4—dc22   2008009359

12 11 10 9 8   1 2 3 4 5 6 7 8 9 10

Editorial Manager: David Tipton
Submission Editors: Alex Mikaberidze and Kim Kennedy White
Production Editor: Kristine Swift
Production Manager: Don Schmidt
Media Editor: Ellen Rassmussen
Media Production Coordinator: Ellen Brenna Dougherty
Media Resources Manager: Caroline Price
File Management Coordinator: Paula Gerard

This book is also available on the World Wide Web as an eBook.
Visit www.abc-clio.com for details.

ABC-CLIO, Inc.
130 Cremona Drive, P.O. Box 1911
Santa Barbara, California 93116-1911

This book is printed on acid-free paper ∞
Manufactured in the United States of America

Contents

Introduction

Sue V. Rosser

Both gender and science represent pervasive, powerful, and determining factors in 21st-century U.S. society, just as they do in most countries today and have in most cultures since antiquity. A number of myths and beliefs surround both gender and science.

Everyone has a gender. Typically the first question asked about a healthy baby when born is the sex, assuming that the parents don't know this already from prenatal tests. One of the myths is that biological sex determines gender. As the entry in this volume on sex/gender describes, it need not do so, since many opportunities occur for disconnections between sex and gender. Because biological sex typically correlates with gender roles, expectations, and stereotypes in the particular culture, the response to this question sets off a series of reactions and behaviors in parents, relatives, friends, health care workers, and others to the newborn baby.

If the baby is a girl, in addition to receiving a pink cap and diapers with different reinforced padding than that given to boys, the adults will talk more to her and describe her as smaller with finer features than they would the same baby if told he was a boy. These responses suggest the initiation of a series of behaviors, expectations, and stereotypes that will determine parameters and norms for whom that baby is likely to marry, what career she is more likely to have, and a probable series of other likes, interests, and outcomes for her life. If the baby is a boy, he'll be described as larger, be talked to less, and be given more visual stimulation. The adults will also anticipate gender determinations based on his sex such as falling in love with a woman and being more likely to become an engineer than a nurse. These determinations result from the beliefs that masculinity and femininity are associated with particular roles and behaviors in a particular culture, time, or society.

Just as everyone has a gender that exerts a powerful influence in determining social behaviors, career choice, and choice of life partner, science also exerts a powerful and determining influence on most people's lives. In our society, for most people, science provides the explanation for why the physical world operates as it does, causes of health and disease in the human body, and even for much psychological and social behavior. Because we believe that science accurately explains and helps us to negotiate our world, we may change our behavior because we trust the results of scientific research. For example, many people stopped smoking when the scientific evidence demonstrated a link correlating smoking with lung cancer and other diseases. Because most people now believe the mounting evidence for global warming, U.S. consumers have begun to push for fuel efficiency and alternatives to fossil fuels.

Myths and beliefs also represent powerful forces held by everyone that partially determine their behavior. The dictionary defines myth first as a traditional story focusing on the deeds of gods or heroes, often in explaining some natural phenomenon such as the origin of the sun; the fifth definition states that myth is a false opinion, belief, or idea. The definition of belief overlaps with that of myth. The first definition, "acceptance of the truth or actuality of anything without certain proof," is followed by "something held to be true or actual." Belief denotes "acceptance with or without proof or strong emotional feelings."

Women, Science, and Myth: Gender Beliefs from Antiquity to the Present explores the interactions between gender and scientific research both over time and in relationship to particular topics or themes. The first section of the volume uses a chronological historical approach; the second examines gender and science thematically.

Chronological Section: Changes in Myths of Gender over Time

Myths and beliefs about gender expectations and stereotypes have changed over time and vary today in different cultures. In the 18th-century United States, most secretaries were men; today most secretaries are women. As pointed out in "Gender and Occupational Interests," in the 1960s in the former Soviet Union, most physicians were women, while in the United States at that time, most physicians were men. Today, less than 50 years later in the United States, 50 percent of medical students are women. As discussed in "Gender/Sex—How Conjoined," although the association of gender with particular occupations and stereotypes of characteristics attributed to each gender may differ among cultures, one universal constant remains: whatever men do holds higher value and prestige in a particular culture, although what they do in that culture may be done by women and associated with lower pay and prestige in another culture.

Myths and beliefs about science have also changed over time and differ somewhat today in various cultures. Before Galileo, people believed that the earth was the center of the universe and that the sun revolved around it. Aristotle believed that women were "weaker and colder than men." As described in "Antiquity," "According to Aristotle, femaleness should be considered 'a deformity, though one which occurs in the ordinary course of nature.' From the very beginning, he explains, males and females develop differently. Although while in the womb the female takes longer to develop than the male, the process reverses after the child is born. Everything is speeded up in the female—she reaches puberty, maturity, and old age sooner" (Aristotle, *De generatione animalium I.* 20728a 18–29; 4.6775a 13–15).

Myths and beliefs also surround gender and science, both historically and today. One of the most persistent beliefs is that only men can be scientists. As Caroline Herzenberg points out in "Medieval Era," in the Middle Ages science was not a profession as we think of it today. Educated members of the upper class held most scientific knowledge and undertook most experiments. Since very few women had access to education, they did not become scientists. Because the Christian Church played a central role in scholarly activities, including science, some nuns practiced medicine; Abbess Hildegaard of Bingen also wrote significant scientific treatises on cosmology, botany, medicine, and natural history.

As Cindy Klestinec underlines in "Renaissance," Francis Bacon laid the architecture for early modern science. Bacon rejected the excessive reliance on the works of the ancients, proposing observation and experimentation as means to scientific knowledge. Although he ridiculed the Church's emphasis on scholasticism, he retained its views on the subordinate position of women. Women did not even qualify as witnesses able to validate scientific experiments, let alone as experimenters.

In "The 18th Century," as Marilyn Ogilvie emphasizes, this notion that only men could be scientists was reinforced by the belief that men and women had radically different natures. Women who did receive an education in the 18th century, either at home or in boarding schools, followed curricula that emphasized music and fine arts, reflecting the belief that their nature differed from the male nature; males were taught a curriculum that included science.

As Narin Hassan points out in "The 19th Century," Romanticism challenged the more mechanical notions of science but did not lead to substantial increases in women's participation in scientific fields. In "Women's Education," Amy Bix suggests that women did not begin to receive educations in science until the women's colleges and public land-grant institutions were established in the late 19th century in the United States, although most were encouraged to pursue nonscientific courses of study.

The entries "Early 20th Century" and "Discrimination" underline the struggles of women to become scientists and to have their work accepted by their male colleagues as valid science. Today, as described in "Gender and

Occupational Interests," women have reached parity in degree attainment only in some of the social sciences and in the biological or life sciences. In computer science, engineering, and some of the physical sciences, women receive less than one quarter of the degrees. Despite increases in women's degrees, educational attainment for women has not translated into equal employment opportunities for women scientists in government, industry, or academia. A dearth of women scientists persists, particularly in powerful leadership and decision-making positions in all sectors.

Why does the myth or belief persist that women shouldn't be scientists? Is it discrimination, historical legacy, biological difference, or choice? An equally interesting question is, As most scientists are men, what impact does this have on the kind of science produced? Evelyn Fox Keller asked, Does gender matter for science? (Keller 1985).

Does Gender Matter for Science?

As outlined by Chris Cuomo in "Critiques of Science," the scientific method emphasizes objectivity, autonomy, and distance of observer from the object of study. Keller (1985) used object relations theory to explain that having women as primary caretakers for most children in our society may result in the encouragement of more boys to be separate, distant, and autonomous from the female caretaker from whom the boys are distinguishing their gender identity, compared to girls who are permitted to remain closer and more dependent. More males than females will feel comfortable with scientific approaches and careers because of this socialization; the science they create will in turn reflect those same characteristics of objectivity, autonomy, and separation.

Engineering represents a significant example of the conjoining of masculinity with technology. As Amy Bix points out in "Technology," the military, until recently, included only men, and men built roads and bridges and developed much technology; therefore, engineering, the military, and masculinity became tightly conjoined.

Equally frequently, science and technology have been used to explain gender differences. This volume illustrates that the scientific explanations of gender differences have changed over time. For example, Aristotle described women as intellectually inferior and attributed this inferiority to their colder nature. In the 19th century, the "science" of craniometry emerged. Craniometric measurements uncovered differences in overall size and particular parts of the brain considered the seat of intelligence between men and women and between White and non-White men. These differences justified the superior position of White men over all women and men of other races. Today, neuroscientists use fMRI to reveal the degree of lateralization and functional specificity of differences between men's and women's brains. As "The Brain" and "Nature/Nurture" emphasize, these gender differences are assumed to result from genetic and hormonal differences between males and females rather than from environmental effects.

Co-Evolution of Myths of Gender and Science

Scientific beliefs about gender differences have changed over time, just as beliefs about women as scientists have changed. The chronological arrangement of the first part of this encyclopedia charts the co-evolution of the myths and beliefs of gender and scientific research from antiquity through the 20th century. These myths and beliefs have co-evolved because changes in beliefs about women and gender roles might affect the expression of scientific theories in a particular era. In *Gender and Boyle's Law of Gases* (2001), Elizabeth Potter showed that Boyle's conservative political and religious beliefs, including his notions of gender, influenced his choice of theoretical model to explain his law of gases. Potter recreates the historical period of the civil war that raged in England in the 1640s during which Boyle conceived his law and undertook his experiments. At this time, radicals threatened not only the absolute monarchy and decision-making authority and wealth of the king, Church, and upper classes but also of men. The petitions presented by women claimed political equality with men and led to the establishment of civil marriage. Potter claims that Boyle, an upper-class male, was personally threatened by and opposed to the radicals; therefore, he rejected the animism that he saw as linked with radicalism. He chose the mechanistic model because (1) it comported well with the data and (2) it supported proper religion, monarchy, and the status quo with regard to class and gender. The same data could have been used to support an alternative law offered by Boyle's contemporary Franciscus Linus. Boyle did not clearly refute Linus's hypothesis on methodological or experimental grounds.

Just as beliefs about gender may influence scientific theories or interpretations of data, a new scientific approach, tool, or technique might reveal new information that destroys a particular myth or belief about gender. For example, with several thousand years of distance, most scientists admit that Aristotle's experiments, in which he counted fewer teeth in the mouths of women than men, were biased by views that women are inferior to men (Arditti 1980). Although not a Christian himself, Galen incorporated the Judeo-Christian creation belief into his science of anatomy. He claimed that men had one less rib on one side than the other since a rib had been used to create Eve. This anatomical inaccuracy was perpetuated throughout the Dark Ages and was not corrected until the early Renaissance when dissection of bodies was permitted.

The numerous examples of co-evolution of myths and beliefs of gender and scientific research over time reveal one constant. Each of the six chronological periods in the first section of the volume documents that myths and beliefs about gender prevented women from full participation in science and that scientific research served as a significant source to explain gender differences. Although the particular myths and beliefs about gender and the particular scientific research used to buttress those myths and beliefs has changed over time, the emphasis on gender differences and the use of science to support those differences and exclude women has not.

Thematic Section: Concepts of Gender in Different Contexts

The second part of the volume uses a different approach to explore gender and myths and beliefs of scientific research. Instead of focusing on a chronological period, each entry centers on a particular theme, subject, discipline, or perspective to explore and compare myths of gender and scientific research across time periods and in different contexts.

Disciplines

Scientific disciplines have emerged at different times, typically branching from a previously established discipline when sufficient new information or approaches developed that warranted distinction as a separate discipline. As Barbara Whitten points out in "Physics/Astronomy," physics emerged as a discipline distinct from mathematics in the 17th century with Newton's publication of *Principia Mathematica,* while computer science did not separate from mathematics until the 20th century. Each of the science disciplines has a somewhat different relationship to myths and beliefs of gender that varies based on the time and social/cultural context in which the discipline became established and the content of the discipline. The participation of women as scientists/practitioners also varies significantly among disciplines. For example, as Barbara Whitten shows in "Physics/Astronomy," at the time physics became established as a separate discipline in 1686, women did not participate in science. Although Émilie du Châtelet translated Newton's work and helped to reconcile Newton's and Leibniz's versions of mechanics in the early 18th century, in the 21st century, just over 20 percent of U.S. undergraduate degrees in physics go to women (National Science Foundation 2004); less than 10 percent of physicists in the United States are women, although in France, the proportion is 27 percent (Hartline and Li 2002).

The content of physics, mathematics, astronomy, computer science, and even chemistry does not include gender or gender differences since these subjects focus on the properties of physical, nonliving aspects of the world. However, as Keller suggested, the extremely large proportion of men in these disciplines may be reflected in their choice of questions asked, approaches to data collection, analysis, and theories and conclusions drawn from the data. Masculinity may have become synonymous with good science in those fields. Alternative approaches might have been rejected by the scientific community since men dominated the discipline and did not perceive their masculine bias. Prevailing notions of gender may also have influenced the specific theoretical explanations proposed and accepted at a particular time, as Potter illustrated in the case of Boyle's Law.

More women scientists populate the disciplines that focus on life and particularly on humans. Although discrimination, quotas, and gender stereotypes prevented women from entering medicine, biology, and psychology in the past, women now receive half of the degrees in the life sciences and over 70 percent of the degrees in psychology. A predominant feature that stands out in the many studies exploring what attracts women to become scientists is that women especially want to study living beings and to use science to help people (Rosser 1997). Because of their focus on living beings, biology, health, medicine, and psychology also constitute the disciplines from which much of the scientific research emanates that is used to support myths and beliefs of gender. The 19th-century "science" of craniometry provided data on differences in size of different parts of male and female brains just as fMRIs and brain lateralization studies are used in the 21st century to explain gender differences in visuospatial abilities, aggression, and depression.

Aspects of Human Biology and Behavior

A significant portion of the second part of the volume explores the evolution of myths of gender and scientific research about specific aspects of human biology, behaviors, or abilities over time. In "Nature/Nurture," Muriel Lederman underlines a theme that reverberates in entries on biological topics ranging from endocrinology/hormones, menstruation/menopause, through the brain to race and gender/sex: scientific research has often been used to "prove" or overstate the case for the effects of anatomy, hormones, or genes as the basis for gender and racial differences in behaviors and abilities that may be environmentally determined or strongly influenced. For example, in "Gender/Sex—How Conjoined," I document that even in something as fundamental as sex/gender determination, environmental factors may play a role. Although genetic sex of XX usually is correlated with female internal and external genitalia, several conditions such as congenital adrenal hyperplasia (CAH) can interfere with this biologically determined path, resulting in female internal genitalia but male external genitalia, while androgen insensitivity results in genetic males (XY) with testes but female external genitalia.

In a similar fashion, throughout history, scientists have searched for biological bases as the causes for gender differences in mental illness, personality types, and cognitive abilities. As Susan Nolan underlines in "Mental Illness," although gender differences exist in higher rates of some mental illnesses such as depression, anxiety, and eating disorders in women and substance abuse in men, it becomes difficult to disentangle the substantial contribution of environmental influences to the illness. For example, for many women, depression may result as much from their realization of their poor economic and social position in a society where a woman earns $.59 for every dollar earned by a man and where wealth and salary earned have as significant an impact upon prestige, power, and position as does biology. The current emphasis on neuroscience and brain chemistry has pushed research on behaviors and abilities further toward biological determinism; biological causes rather than environmental forces are sought increasingly to explain gender and racial differences in occupational choices and cognitive abilities as well as sexual orientation.

Institutions

Institutions serve as a primary means through which disciplines build their boundaries, form group identities, and transmit knowledge. Educational institutions become the site where research generates new knowledge and where education is transmitted to the next generation. At the university and sometimes even in high school, departments correspond to the disciplines, so that individuals major in physics, chemistry, mathematics, or psychology. In the United States the government shapes much of scientific research through agendas and funding. It also carries out substantial research through the national laboratories, National Institutes of Health (NIH), and agencies such as the National Aeronautics and Space Administration (NASA). Corporations conduct some basic research and substantial amounts of applied research, technology transfer, and product development. Professional societies decide what constitutes a profession and who can be members of that profession. Most of the scientific professional societies form around disciplines, such as the American Chemical Society (ACS), aggregates of scientific disciplines such as the American Association for the Advancement of Science (AAAS), or subdisciplines such the Society for Molecular Biology.

Less clear than the role institutions play in scientific research is their role with regard to gender. Through advising and teaching, faculty and staff in educational institutions may transmit gender stereotypes and/or direct students toward particular disciplines or majors. At coeducational institutions, physics and engineering become stereotyped as male majors; psychology and English as female majors.

Government policies and funding in the United States have directly or indirectly influenced numbers of women in particular scientific disciplines. For example, until recently, the all-male draft and the requirement that most pilots have military flight experience epitomized the conjoining of the military with engineering, keeping many women out of engineering, especially aerospace engineering. In contrast, as Daryl Chubin outlines in "Federal Agencies," the programs to attract women to science, especially those funded by the National Science Foundation (NSF), have provided positive incentives to both individuals and educational institutions to increase numbers of women scientists. Similar programs funded by corporations encourage women scientists to enter industry. Currently, as Cecilia Marzabadi documents in "Chemistry," in some disciplines such as chemistry, women scientists view industry as more female friendly than academia.

Historically, professional societies have served as particularly severe gatekeepers of gender and science. In Europe, women were not permitted to be members of the societies where scientific work and experimental results were presented, verified, published, and rewarded. The first female members of the Royal Society in England were not elected until after World War II. Neither Marie Curie nor her daughter Irene Joliot-Curie became members of the French Academy of Sciences, despite repeated nominations (Tang 2006). Although women are no longer strictly prohibited from becoming members of scientific societies, the small percentages of women admitted to the most prestigious societies and the few women receiving major awards suggest that the professional societies continue to play a significant role in supporting the belief that women do not do scientific research that ranks on a par with that done by men. In 2007, only nine of 72 members elected to the National Academy of Sciences were women, making the total percentage around 10 percent (Brainard 2007). In "Nobel Laureates," Joyce Tang documents that since its inception in 1901, 4 percent (33 of 768) of Nobel Prizes in all areas have gone to women. She details the lives of the 11 women who have won the Nobel Prize in science or medicine; she also discusses the significant issue of why so few women have won this prestigious professional award.

Discrimination

Discrimination against women scientists and the use of scientific research to provide justification for women's inferiority become threads that run through many of the entries. In addition, "Nobel Laureates" and "Discrimination" as well as the entries on education, government, industry, and women as leaders document active or covert discrimination against women scientists. Although discrimination does not serve as the primary focus for either the chronological essays or for the entries devoted to disciplines, it emerges in most of those entries as an underlying theme.

Other Perspectives on Gender and Myths and Beliefs in Scientific Research

In some senses, discrimination might be viewed as a perspective on gender and myths and beliefs in scientific research. Gender discrimination implies that women have not received equal access, opportunity, or treatment either as scientists or in scientific research compared to men. Notions of equity as a corrective to discrimination emanate from the perspective of universalism, associated with the Enlightenment and liberalism. This encyclopedia concludes with a series of entries that provide critiques of gender and myths and beliefs of scientific research from a variety of perspectives. Chris Cuomo, in "Critiques of Science," provides a philosopher's critiques of concepts such as universalism, positivism, and objectivity that underpin scientific research, particularly with regard to gender. "Race, Postcolonial Gender, and Science" and "Marxism/ Socialism and Feminism/Gender" suggest where race-based and class-based critiques overlap and differ from gender-based critiques of scientific research. "Science Fiction" by Lisa Yasek provides insights of alternatives to currently held myths of gender and scientific research from the world of fiction.

Because feminism and feminists place women and gender at the center of their critiques and approaches, the impact of feminism on diverse science disciplines provides insights into future directions for gender and myths of scientific research. Feminist biologists and primatologists have revealed both the biases that emanate when females are excluded from research and the expansion of theories and conclusions that can be reached when females are included in research. Ecofeminists and cyberfeminists have documented destructive impacts of male dominance on both the natural and virtual environments and feminist visions that would ultimately lead to better lives for men and women in both environments.

Feminist historians of science reveal the patterns over time in the co-evolution of the myths and beliefs surrounding women as scientists and of the scientific research on gender. Feminist science studies use all the perspectives, combining class, race, postcolonial orientations, and varieties of feminist approaches to expose the myths and beliefs that support the scientific research in relationship to the social structures in modern culture.

In some sense, the entries on perspectives, particularly Mary Wyer's "Feminist Science Studies," might be read as the 21st-century chronological entry. Just as myths and beliefs of gender and scientific research co-evolved in prior centuries and eras, in this century, gender and scientific research interact to produce cultural and societal beliefs about what constitute both science and gender. This volume explores these historical and thematic interactions of gender myths and beliefs in scientific research.

References and Further Reading

Arditti, Rita. "Feminism and Science." In *Science and Liberation*. Edited by Rita Arditti, P. Brennan, and Steve Cavrak. Boston: South End Press, 1980.

Aristotle. *De generatione animalium I. The Basic Works of Aristotle*. Translated by R. McKeon. New York: Random House, 1941.

Brainard, Jeffrey. "National Academy Elects Fewer Women." *Chronicle of Higher Education* 53 (36) 2007: A36.

Hartline, Beverly, and Dong Qi Li. *Women in Physics: The IUPAP International Conference on Women in Physics, Paris, France, 2002*. Melville, NY: AIP Press, 2002.

Keller, Evelyn Fox. *Reflections on Gender and Science*. New Haven, CT: Yale University Press, 1985.

National Science Foundation. *Women, Minorities, and Persons with Disabilities in Science and Engineering 2004*. (NSF 00–327.) Arlington, VA: National Science Foundation, 2004.

Potter, Elizabeth. *Gender and Boyle's Law of Gases*. Bloomington: Indiana University Press, 2001.

Rosser, Sue V. *Re-engineering Female Friendly Science*. New York: Teachers College Press, 1997.

Tang, Joyce. *Scientific Pioneers: Women Succeeding in Science*. Lanham, MD: University Press of America, 2006.

Chronological Section: Changes in Myths of Gender over Time

Antiquity

MARILYN OGILVIE

Since cultures are not homogeneous, it is impossible to generalize about the contributions of women in science, technology, and medicine in antiquity. However, some cultures and chronological periods were more friendly than others to the activities of women in the scientific enterprise. Although women are seldom mentioned as engaging in scientific work, it is possible to select representative protoscientific or scientific cultures and describe how the rare woman whose name is mentioned fits into the contemporary scientific enterprise. However, the apparent absence of women scientists in a specific culture does not necessarily mean that women did not engage in scientific activities. Because of the paucity of reliable sources, it is almost impossible to ensure that information about early science is trustworthy. The material that is available suggests that there are two ways by which we can learn about the contributions of women to the scientific endeavor in antiquity, neither of which is totally satisfactory. The first includes contextual extrapolation from what is known, or assumed, about the social and cultural milieu in which a person or event exists. The second involves fragmentary descriptions of events or people in classical sources of different genres. An additional caveat should be mentioned. Many accounts of women in antiquity can be traced to a single secondary source, and all subsequent secondary accounts are based on the earliest account.

The societies of Mesopotamia and Egypt illustrate the contextual approach. Both produced two tools of science: writing and mathematics, developed as responses to specific practical problems. Although direct evidence is lacking, the social structure of Mesopotamia was such that the participation of women in these activities was unlikely. The great legal code of Hammurabi (*fl.* 1792–1750 BC) pronounced a girl the legal property of her father until sold to her husband—hardly a hospitable situation for encouraging a woman to produce science. A different situation existed in Egypt where women traditionally owned property, and it was the mother's name that was listed in genealogies. Even after the Semitic influence of the 19th Dynasty strengthened patriarchal societal elements, the woman's right to property persisted until later. Among her other qualities, the goddess Isis was honored as the greatest of physicians whose medical disciples were often women. Isis's qualities trickled down to other women, many of whom were literate. In this society, women were allowed to attend either medical school with men or their exclusively female school at Säis, which specialized in obstetrics and gynecology. Although there is no direct evidence that Egyptian women participated in other areas important to science, the high level of education that Egyptian women physicians received suggests that this society was one in which women might have been able to participate in the science of the time.

Equality with men is not necessarily a condition for the development of science among women. If this were the case, the city-state of Sparta, with its liberal attitude toward women's rights, should have produced women scientists. The Spartan lawgiver, Lycurgus (ninth century BC) suggested that women should be encouraged to engage in all of the physical sports of men such as wrestling and throwing the javelin. However, the reason for the strenuous activity was to prepare women for the rigors of childbirth. Spartan culture was lacking in scientific thinkers of either sex. In contrast to Sparta, the city-state of Athens did not pretend to allow women the same rights as men for any reason. The great Athenian statesman, Pericles (ca. 495–429 BC), considered the ideal woman one who is never talked about for any reason by men (Thucydides *History of the Peloponnesian War* 2.45). However, Socrates (ca. 470–399 BC) disagreed with Pericles' view of women, and it is through the work of his distinguished disciple Plato that we are able to glimpse his ideas on the role of women in society (Ogilvie 1986).

Plato (ca. 428–348/347 BC)

Although not a scientist himself, Plato had an extraordinary influence on science. Born at the end of the Periclean Age, Plato was in his late twenties when his friend and mentor, Socrates, was executed. According to legend, he prudently left town for 12 years of travel. In about 387 BC, he returned to Athens and began to teach. He established a school on a piece of ground that was associated with the hero Academus; thus the school was known as the Academy. At the Academy, Plato taught that a reality exists beyond the objects we observe. The objects of our senses are merely imperfect copies of an ideal reality that exists in a suprasensible world of forms or ideas. In Book VII of the *Republic,* he states that the true value of astronomy is found in its ability to direct the attention of the soul not to any visible objects but to invisible realities. The ideas are the reality. Even though Plato knew that the senses could not be trusted, he realized that he possessed an instrument by which he could examine the world in the most minute detail—his mind.

Plato not only used his mind to assess the nature of the universe but he also used it to visualize the ideal state. Always looking beyond the obvious, he reasoned that the guardians of the ideal state and their wives should have similar educations. In the *Republic,* Plato's mouthpiece Socrates argues with those who think that men and women have radically different natures and consequently should receive different educations. He insisted that no difference in the intellectual natures of men and women had been demonstrated. If either male or female is superior in any "art or pursuit," then the task should be assigned to the most fit. However, if both men and women are equally capable of pursuing a given task, they should both be educated to perform it. Using an analogy from the animal kingdom, Socrates points to animal societies to justify the equal education of boys and girls. He asks, Are dogs "divided into hes and shes" or do they share equally in "hunting and in keeping watch and in the other duties of dogs?" Do only the males care for the flocks while the females remain at home "under the idea that the bearing and suckling of their puppies is labor enough for them"? Extrapolating to humans, Socrates concludes that if women are to share the responsibilities of the state with men, they must have the same "nurture and education" (Plato *Republic* 5.3.45I). Given Plato's ideas about the importance of educating women in the ideal state, it is reasonable to accept the statements by Diogenes Laertius that Plato had two female disciples who dressed as men in their role as his students. These two women were Axiothea of Phlius (*fl.* 350 BC) and Lasthenia of Mantinea (fifth century BC). Although we know nothing about their actual contributions, it was significant that women, whether actually or apocryphally, were considered a part of the entourage of Plato, one of the most significant contributors to the form of modern science. Societies and individuals who accepted Plato's view of the importance of educating women were much more apt to produce women scientists than those who followed the views of Plato's student Aristotle (Ogilvie 1986).

Aristotle (384–322 BC)

Like Plato, Aristotle was a philosopher but, unlike Plato, he was also a scientist and codifier of scientific knowledge. He left behind an enormous body of written material covering a wide range of knowledge, including scientific knowledge. From Plato, Aristotle absorbed the importance of discerning the nature of reality. Unlike Plato, he did not find reality in the concepts or the ideals but in the objects of the senses. This is not to say that concepts were unimportant to him, but he emphasized the reality of both phenomena and the objects of the world more than had Plato.

Aristotle had little patience with Plato's ideas about women. He wrote in the *Politics* that the inequality between the sexes is permanent. By his very nature the man is more fit to command and the woman to obey. The source of female passivity was biological, for "the female, in fact, is female on account of inability of a sort, viz., it lacks the power to concoct semen." According to Aristotle, femaleness should be considered "a deformity, though one which occurs in the ordinary course of nature." From the very beginning, he explains, males and females develop differently. Although while in the womb the female takes longer to develop than the male, the process reverses after the child is born. Everything is speeded up in the female—she reaches puberty, maturity, and old age sooner because females are "weaker and colder in their nature" (Aristotle *De generatione animalium* 1.20.728a.18–29, 4.6.775a.13–15). Aristotle's ideas dominated much of the thinking about women during subsequent periods. Clearly, it would be surprising to find women scientists among those who accepted Aristotle's ideas (Pomeroy 1975; Horowitz 1976; Ogilvie 1986).

Early Women in Medicine

From the earliest times, women have been involved in the healing professions. Names of specific women have come down to us in references from classical authors. Little is known of them, and the information that we have may be apocryphal. However, in antiquity, it was important for women to be healers and have expertise in the medical arts.

Agamede (12th century BC)

One of the first reports appears in Homer's *Iliad,* which describes an early Greek physician, Agamede, who lived before the Trojan War "when the Pylians and th' Epeans met." This epic identifies her as the "yellow-hair'd" eldest daughter of Augeas, king of the Epeans in Elis, the son of Helios whose husband was the "bold spearman, Mulius," killed by Nestor in battle. Myth and reality merge in the *Iliad;* however, the statement that a woman was skilled in the use of plants for healing purposes and that she "all the virtues knew of each medicinal herb the wide world grows" indicates the existence of a specific woman with knowledge of the medicinal properties of plants (Homer *Iliad* II.740).

Agnodike (last third of fourth century BC)

Agnodike, according to the *Fabulae* of Hyginus, was an Athenian maiden who disguised herself as a man and studied under the physician Herophilus.

In Athens during the fourth century BC, slaves and free-born Athenian women were forbidden to practice medicine. As their modesty kept them from consulting male physicians, many of them died in childbirth and from "private diseases" because of these restrictions. Agnodike, attempting to help a woman in labor, was thrust aside by the patient until Agnodike assured her that she too was a woman. For transgressing the law she was tried and convicted by the Aereopagus. Throngs of women protested her conviction, and the judge recanted his former position, replacing the old law with one that allowed women to practice medicine on their own sex; it even gave stipends to those who "did it well and carefully" (Hyginus *Fabulae* 274.25–35).

Elephantis (first century BC)

Pliny the Elder in his *Natural History* reported on the contributions of several women physicians. However, his accounts cannot be accepted unconditionally. For example, the woman Elephantis was mentioned by both Galen and Pliny as a physician. However, the name Elephantis was used commonly in classical times by the *hetaerae* who often adopted animal names. It is possible that the Elephantis mentioned by Galen and Pliny was a courtesan and also may be a blend of two or more people of the same name. Galen noted her ability to cure baldness and Pliny her skills as a midwife. Pliny also discussed a conflict that she had with another midwife, Laús.

Laús (first or second century BC)

Laús's work was also described by Pliny the Elder, the only source for her practice of medicine. Laús developed treatments for rabies and "intermittent fevers" (malaria), which could be "cured by the flux on wool from a black ram enclosed in a silver bracelet" (Pliny 28.23.80–82). He notes that she and Elephantis disagreed about abortives. The two physicians also clashed about the effect of eating grains of barley contaminated with menstrual blood. One said that this process produced fertility whereas the other claimed it caused barrenness. Pliny concluded that it is best not to believe either of them.

Salpe (first century BC)

Pliny the Elder is the single source for our knowledge of the Greek midwife Salpe. Saliva and urine were Salpe's favorite remedies for numerous disorders. Saliva could restore sensation to a numbed limb if one would spit "into the bosom or if the upper eyelids are touched by saliva." Weak eyes could be strengthened by an application of urine. Urine was also helpful for sunburn, particularly if mixed with the white of an egg (preferably of an ostrich) and rubbed on the skin. As had Laús, Salpe suggested remedies for rabies and malaria. Since we are forced to rely on Pliny for knowledge of Salpe's "scientific" accomplishments, it is difficult to ascertain whether she had other ideas more acceptable to modern readers. We do know that she was a midwife and must have had practical skills.

Metrodora (first or second century BC)

Even less is known about Metrodora than other early midwives, although the potential to learn more is present in an extant manuscript in Florence entitled *Extracts from the Works of Metrodora Concerning the Diseases of Women*. According to Pauly, it consists of 263 leaves of parchment.

Olympias (first century BC)

Olympias of Thebes was a practicing midwife who wrote of her experiences. There is evidence that the herbalist Dioscorides (b. ca. AD 20) knew of her work. Pliny the Elder reported that Olympias could cause abortions by mixing mallows with goose grease and cure barrenness by bull's gall, serpents' fat, copper, rust, and honey "rubbed on the parts before intercourse."

Sotira (first century BC)

According to Pliny the Elder, Sotira was able to affect marvelous cures. She may be the author of a manuscript, *Gynaecia,* found in Florence.

Saint Nicerata (fourth century AD)

The Christian martyr, physician Saint Nicerata, reputedly cured Saint John Crysostom of a stomach ailment. Nothing else is known about her medical contributions, but she is representative of a class of Christian women who took care of the medical needs of the poor.

Saint Theodosius (fifth century AD)

Numerous female Christian saints and nuns are known for their medicinal skills. Saint Theodosius, a Christian martyr who practiced medicine in Rome and was killed during the persecutions of Diocletian, represents this group of female physicians.

Fabiola (d. 399 AD)

Fabiola was the daughter of a patrician Roman family. When she was 20 years old she converted to Christianity and became one of the 15 followers of Saint Jerome who practiced medicine and offered their services free to the indigent.

Aspasia (first century AD)

The confusion between two Aspasias indicates the difficulty in understanding the women of antiquity. Aspasia, the celebrated *hetaera* of Pericles, is often conflated with Aspasia, the physician who lived in the first centuries of the Common Era. The *hetaera* Aspasia often appears as the physician and the physician Aspasia as the *hetaera*.

Aspasia the Physician (first century AD)

Although nothing is recorded about Aspasia's life, fragments cited by a physician to an emperor of Byzantium indicate that she was a physician whose major medical contributions were in the areas of obstetrics and gynecology. Her contributions were practical, not theoretical. She apparently developed an important technique for rotating the fetus in a breech presentation. Her discussion of preventive medicine during pregnancy was based on a common-sense approach, not on the consideration of an abstract principle.

Aspasia of Miletus (d. ca. 401 BC)

Athenian men who found their dutiful spouses insufficiently entertaining and inadequately informed frequently turned to foreign women called *hetaerae* (companions). These women, often Ionians, occupied a position between that of an Athenian lady and that of a prostitute. It was from these ranks that Pericles found the educated Milesian Aspasia. She reputedly influenced men such as Plato, Xenophon, Cicero, and Plutarch and apparently held a popular salon frequented by Anaxagoras and Euripides. Early sources often provide contradictory information about her. The most reliable seems to be Plutarch in his *Life of Pericles*. As a member of the *hetaerae,* Aspasia could participate

Aspasia, a highly educated Greek woman and companion to the statesman Pericles, was recognized by Socrates as one of the best intellects of Athens. She was able to converse with men and move in public circles, which was unusual for Athenian women of the time. (Araldo de Luca/Corbis)

in the intellectual and social life of Athens. Her union with Pericles presumably produced a son. She later supposedly married an Athenian politician, Lysicles, and produced a son by him.

Allegedly, Aspasia wrote some of Pericles' best speeches, including his famous funeral oration for those who died in the battle of Potidaea. Plato's dialogue, the *Menexenus,* includes a funeral oration said to be written by Aspasia. However, the account in the *Menexenus* is filled with historical misstatements. Aspasia was certainly not a scientist but apparently was an influential advocate for women's rights. If she taught Socrates, as Plato claimed, she was a highly respected scholar and her views may have influenced those expressed by Plato in the *Republic* regarding women. Clearly, she was an important figure in fifth-century Athens. Although she left no books of her own she was satirized in Greek comedy and was considered an important personage in Greek philosophical dialogue (Lipinska 1900, 1930; Hurd-Mead 1938; Ogilvie 1986; Mozans 1991).

Women in Mathematics and Astronomy

Although medicine was the scientific endeavor most often pursued by women, they also reputedly participated in other areas of the scientific enterprise.

Aglaonike (fl. fifth century BC)

We know of the existence of the Greek astronomer Aglaonike from two classical sources: Plutarch and the scholiast of Apollonios of Rhodes. She was regarded by her contemporaries as a sorceress because she supposedly possessed the occult power traditionally attributed to certain Thessalian women to make the moon disappear at will. Plato, Horace, and Virgil all mention this. However, Aglaonike's abilities may have gone beyond the purely magical realm into the area of eclipse prediction. Apparently she was familiar with the periodic recurrence of lunar eclipses. The prediction of the general time and the general area in which a lunar eclipse would occur was an ancient skill and not one that Aglaonike originated. However, it is likely that she had mastered the skill of predicting eclipses and was interested in celestial astronomy (Ogilvie 1986).

Hypatia of Alexandria (ca. AD 355–415)

Hypatia captured the imagination of 18th-century writers because of her brutal murder at the hands of an Alexandrian mob. These writers derived their information from a small number of sources from late antiquity and the Middle Ages. Most of the material comes from Socrates Scholasticus, a fifth-century historian of Constantinople, and two compilations—the 10th- or 11th-century *Suidas,* a lexicon-encyclopedia containing excerpts from early Greek writers; and the *Bibliotheca* of the ninth-century theologian Photius. Other sources for these 18th-century accounts were the Byzantine chronicler Malalas, whose material was notoriously inaccurate, and the *Ecclesiasticae historiae* by Niceporus Callistus. Later accounts were loosely based on the earlier culturally biased material. For example, John Toland, an ardent Protestant, published an essay (1720) on Hypatia blaming the Alexandrian clergy for her death. Voltaire asserted Enlightenment values by also blaming her death on religious fanaticism. Hypatia appears in E. Gibbon's *The Decline and Fall of the Roman Empire,* in Henry Fielding's *A Journey from This World to the Next* (1743), two poems by Leconte de Lisle (1847, 1874), and a novel, *Hypatia* (1853), by Charles Kingsley. During the second half of the 19th century, positivists found that Hypatia satisfied their needs for elevating science over superstitious

religion. The life, work, and death of Hypatia have continued to fascinate literary and religious writers, artists, and scientists in the 20th century. However,
scholars may never be able to arrive at an entirely satisfactory evaluation of
her life and works.

Hypatia's father was Theon of Alexandria, a mathematician attached to the
museum at Alexandria. Although Theon is described in some reports as the
director of the museum, there is no consensus about this position. Most accounts assume that Hypatia's early education was in mathematics and astronomy at the Museum. However, it is uncertain where she received her training
as a Neoplatonist, although most sources assume that she was educated in the
Neoplatonic school at Alexandria since she became a teacher in this school.
The *Suidas* asserts that she assumed the directorship of the school in AD 400
when she was 31 years old.

Socrates Scholasticus proclaimed that Hypatia was not only well known in
her native land but that her fame was widespread, attracting students from far
away. Synesius, later bishop of Ptolemais, was one of her most famous students. She carried on an extensive correspondence with him, and he became
an excellent public relations agent for her. The best evidence indicates that
Hypatia never married, although there are reports to the contrary.

The report of Hypatia's death recorded in the *Suidas* says that "she was
torn apart by the Alexandrians and her body was outraged and scattered
throughout the whole city." The same source blames this atrocity on Bishop
Cyril of Alexandria, envious over "her wisdom exceeding all bounds and especially in the things concerning astronomy" (*Suidas* 166:644). Most of the
sources agree on the circumstances of her death but differ as to the reason
for it, depending on their biases. Several, like the *Suidas,* blame her death on
the jealousy of Bishop Cyril. Others cast Hypatia as a victim of political ri-
valry between the Roman prefect Orestes, who was a great admirer of Hypatia, and Cyril, who wanted to extend his authority over secular as well as
religious areas. Additional accounts blame the murder on the unruly nature
of the Alexandrians, which caused them to riot at the slightest provocation.
Later writers continued to speculate on the part that Cyril and the Church
played in her murder. Catholic partisans insisted that Cyril was completely
innocent and unjustly maligned by biased reporters. Protestant writers were
equally vehement in denouncing Cyril as the instigator of her death.

Tradition assumes that Hypatia wrote books on mathematics, lectured on
a variety of subjects, and invented mechanical devices. It has generally been
accepted that although she wrote commentaries on Apollonius of Perga, Diophantus, and Ptolemy, none of these works survived. However, scholar Alan
Cameron postulates that editions of Ptolemy (Theon's commentary on the third
book of the Almagest and *Handy Tables* now available) were actually codified

and arranged by Hypatia. He also presents the possibility that certain commentaries on Diophantus's work were also made by Hypatia.

Synesius refers to two mechanical devices, a hydrometer and a silver astrolabe, that he and Hypatia invented.

Hypatia's life will undoubtedly continue to be shrouded in uncertainty. The terse early accounts of her life and death are often ambiguous and lend themselves to a variety of interpretations. Reputedly a brilliant, beautiful woman, her fame was assured by her martyrdom (Alic 1986; Ogilvie 1986; Dzielska 1995).

Lilovati (or Leelavati) (fl. 12th century AD)

The status or even the existence of Lilovati (or Leelavati) is more uncertain than that of Hypatia. According to one tradition, she was the daughter of the well-known Hindu mathematician Bhaskaracharya or Bhaskara II (born AD 1114), who taught her arithmetic. Bhaskaracharya is best known for his *Siddhânta Siromani,* a mathematical work, basically a textbook, divided into four parts: Lilavati (arithmetic), Bijaganita (algebra), Goladhyaya (celestial globe), and Grahaganita (mathematics of the planets). It is immediately evident that the first section of the *Siddhânta Siromani,* the Lilavati, shares its name with Bhaskaracharya's daughter. According to C. N. Srinivasiengar in *The History of Ancient Indian Mathematics,* Lilavati or Leelavati was a popular girl's name. Why did Bhaskaracharya choose this name for the first part of his mathematical work? According to one story, he named it after his daughter. As a good astrologer, Bhaskaracharya studied her horoscope and concluded that Lilavati would become a widow. However, this disaster could be avoided if the couple married on a specific date at a specific time. To ensure that they would be married at exactly the propitious time, he constructed a "sand glass," a device that measured time in a fixed interval by controlling the flow of sand from one vessel to another beneath it through a small hole. However, Lilovati, overcome with curiosity, examined the instrument; as she leaned over it, a pearl fell in the sand from the ornament in her nose. The pearl slowed the motion of the sand; consequently, the marriage took place after the ideal time fixed by astrological calculations. Her husband died shortly after the marriage and to console her, the story goes, her father taught her arithmetic and named his work for her.

According to Srinivasiengar, this often-told story has no basis in fact. He writes that "the concluding stanza of the *Leelavati* is a pun on language, and would bear evidence to the statement that the name is one of fancy" (Srinivasiengar 1967, 80–81). He continues with reasons for his skepticism, including the presence of other books pertaining to different subjects, also named Lee-lavati (Srinivasiengar n.d.).

Theano (latter part of sixth century BC)

The historical position of Theano, while better documented than that of Lee-lavati, is still elusive. Although some sources consider her the wife of Pythago-ras, others consider her a Cretan woman, the daughter of Pythonax. Still others place her as a Crotonian, the daughter of Broninos or Brotinos, Pythagoras's successor. Another tradition indicates that she is not the wife of Pythagoras but his student. Still another claims that she is Pythagoras's daughter and Bron-tinos's wife. If she was indeed the wife of Pythagoras, the number and names of the children attributed to Theano and Pythagoras vary with the sources.

No writings of Theano are extant, although an apocryphal literature under her name has emerged. The earliest of these writings probably appeared from the fourth to the third century BC and consist of a collection of apothegms. This first group and the second, consisting of seven letters and based on the apothegms, do not show characteristics of Pythagoreanism. The third group, however, contains a mathematical pseudo-Pythagorean literature in Theano's name. According to tradition, medicine was another of her fields of expertise.

It is difficult to determine which works attributed to Pythagoras actually represented his ideas. Because of the cult of secrecy surrounding Pythagore-anism, the practice arose of assigning all important ideas to Pythagoras himself. This practice carried over to Theano. Since the Pythagorean-mathematical apocrypha appeared much later than the apothegms, it cannot be assumed that they expressed the words or even the ideas of Theano. It is often claimed but not confirmed that Theano continued the school of Pythagoras after his death. We can only conclude that, according to tradition, Theano was a math-ematician, a physician, and an administrator—someone who kept alive an important training ground for future mathematicians (Alic 1986; Ogilvie 1986).

Women in Alchemy

Alchemy has always been surrounded by mystery; consequently, it is diffi-cult to extricate the factual from the fanciful in the works of the ancient al-chemists. To ensure their own exalted positions, they couched their works in symbolic and metaphorical terms. They also appropriated historical names such as Moses, Cleopatra, and Adam. According to one tradition, Cleopatra was a physician of the fifth century BC mentioned in the Hippocratic writings. An-other suggested that she was an alchemist who was a follower of Mary the

Jewess. During the Middle Ages the traditions became confused and a third complication was added: Queen Cleopatra of Egypt's name was linked with the work of both Cleopatra the physician and Cleopatra the alchemist. However, both women's and men's names were associated with early alchemy.

Mary the Jewess (first or second century AD)

Mary the alchemist assumed the name of the sister of Moses and is known variously as Mary, Maria, or Miriam the Jewess. Enough reports of her writings are extant to establish her historicity. In Alexandria where she worked, the presence of mystery cults, Christianity, and the liberalization of the strict patriarchal attitudes of rabbinical Judaism toward women provided a perfect climate for the existence of a woman alchemist.

As Mary understood it, alchemy represented a fusion of the rational, the mystical, and the practical. This hybridization, which would have been impossible in classical Greece, would be expected in an eclectic Hellenistic society. Mary produced a three-part still, described by the alchemist Zosimos, illustrating the practical technological facet of her alchemy. She merged this invention with the imagery of the "above and below" that suffused the mystical Hermetic philosophy. It is not for her theoretical contributions that Mary is remembered but for the invention or elaboration of apparatuses that proved basic for the development of chemistry. These contributions include the three-armed still, the *kerotakis,* the hot ash bath, the dung bed, and the water bath (the last bears her name to this day, the *bain-marie*). This name was first applied by Arnald of Villanove in the 14th century. Mary was one of the few women in antiquity to attempt to incorporate the empirical-sensory elements of science within an explanatory-theoretical framework (Ogilvie 1986).

Conclusion

Science and myth are inextricably combined when the contributions of women to the scientific activity are considered. However, women were clearly involved in these activities to various degrees from the very beginning of recorded history. Women have a history as scientists and physicians and their names appear in the works of the classical writers. Although we may never be able to collect more factual information about these women because their existence is buried so deeply in the morass of history (a history that did not value their contributions), from the slim material that is available we know that women as well as their brothers always were interested in explaining their environment and improving human life. (*See* Early Modern Health)

References and Further Reading

Adler, Ada, ed. *Suidas. Lexicographi Graeci,* vol. 1, parts 1–4. Stuttgart: Teubner, 1971, 166–644.

Alic, Margaret. *Hypatia's Heritage: A History of Women in Science from Antiquity through the Nineteenth Century*. Boston: Beacon Press, 1986.

Aristotle. *De generatione animalium* [*Generation of Animals*], 1.20.728a.18–29, 4.6.775a.13–15. Translated by A. L. Peck and edited by T. E. Page. Loeb Classical Library. Cambridge, MA: Harvard University Press, 1953.

Dzielska, Maria. *Hypatia of Alexandria*. Cambridge, MA: Harvard University Press, 1995.

Henry, Madeleine M. *Prisoner of History: Aspasia of Miletus and Her Biographical Tradition*. New York: Oxford University Press, 1995.

Homer. *Iliad* II. 740.

Horowitz, Maryanne Cline. "Aristotle and Woman." *Journal of the History of Biology* 9 (Fall 1976): 183–213.

Hurd-Mead, Kate Campbell. *A History of Women in Medicine: From the Earliest Times to the Beginning of the Nineteenth Century*. Haddom, CT: Haddom Press, 1938.

Hyginus. *Fabulae* 274.25–35.

Lipinska, Melina. *Histoire des femmes médecins. Depuis l'antiquité jusqu'à nos jours*. Paris: G. Jacques, 1900.

Lipinska, Melina. *Les femmes et le progress des sciences médicales*. Paris: Masson, 1930.

Mozans, H. J. *Woman in Science*. 1913. Reprint, University of Notre Dame Press, 1991.

Ogilvie, Marilyn Bailey. *Women in Science. Antiquity through the Nineteenth Century. A Biographical Dictionary with Annotated Bibliography*. Cambridge, MA: MIT Press, 1986.

Ogilvie, Marilyn, and Joy Harvey, eds. *The Biographical Dictionary of Women in Science. Pioneering Lives from Ancient Times to the Mid-20th Century*. 2 vols. New York: Routledge, 2000.

Pauly, August Friedrich von. *Paulys Real-Encyclopädie der classischen Altertumswissenschaft*. Edited by G. Wissowa. Stuttgart: J. B. Metzler, 1894–1919.

Plato. *Republic,* Book 5, 5.3.451C ff. Translated by Paul Shorey and edited by G. P. Goold, 1982. Loeb Classical Library. Cambridge, MA: Harvard University Press, 1982.

Pliny the Elder. *Natural History,* 28.23.80–82. Translated by W. H. S. Jones and edited by T. E. Page. Loeb Classical Library. Cambridge, MA: Harvard University Press, 1963.

Pomeroy, Sarah B. *Goddesses, Whores, Wives, and Slaves. Women in Classical Antiquity*. New York: Schocken Books, 1975.

Srinivasiengar, C. N. *The History of Ancient Indian Mathematics*. Calcutta: World Press, 1967.

Medieval Era

Caroline L. Herzenberg

Introduction

Until about a generation ago, women's achievements in science were, with few exceptions, largely ignored in the historical record, and both scholarly and popular writings left the impression that women did not participate in science before relatively modern times. In fact, women have been practicing science and the precursors of science throughout the entire history of science and technology.

The last great scientist of antiquity was Hypatia of Alexandria; her birth in the year 370 was roughly contemporary with the burning of much of the great library of Alexandria, which resulted in great loss of the knowledge of antiquity. From the perspective of science, these events together may be regarded as marking the concluding era of late antiquity, which was followed by the Early Middle Ages.

The Middle Ages, or medieval era, is the period in European history between classical antiquity and the Renaissance, usually considered as running from the late fifth century to about 1350, with some authors extending this period to as late as 1500—a time span of about 1,000 years. Most of the records that we have of women's participation in the practice of science during the Middle Ages refer to science in Western Europe, although there is also evidence of women engaged in theoretical and applied science in Asia, principally in Islamic, Indian, and Chinese cultures, and possibly even in the Western Hemisphere.

The medieval period was an age of faith and feudalism; European society as a whole was organized around feudal economic structures and the structure of the Christian Church. Throughout the medieval period, life was bitterly hard for most people and especially hard for women. Only members of the upper economic classes, primarily members of the feudal nobility and the hierarchy of the Church, had significant access to education or the leisure time to engage in scholarly activities. In the patriarchal society of the Middle Ages, gender-based discrimination, coupled with the social, cultural, and economic barriers, especially limited access and participation of women in higher education and scholarly activities.

During the Middle Ages, the whole body of scientific and technical knowledge was much smaller that it is today so that educated individuals could be conversant with many fields of knowledge. Thus, most of the individuals whom we recognize and classify as scientists were members of the upper classes who engaged in many activities and interests, of which science was only one. Science was not a profession then in the sense that it can be at present, and much of the practice of science was in the hands of individuals whom we might regard as amateurs, albeit very talented and well-informed amateurs. Furthermore, science was in an earlier stage, with the practice of chemistry conflated with alchemy and the knowledge and practice of astronomy included within astrology.

Throughout the entire Middle Ages only limited progress took place in science and mathematics, but investigations in the sciences and particularly medicine continued, and some technological progress occurred.

Early Middle Ages

The Early Middle Ages began with the final disintegration of the Roman Empire in Europe during the 400s. The decline of the Roman civilization with the accompanying loss of the imperial social order left a breakdown of society and limitation of intellectual life through much of Western Europe. Throughout the Early Middle Ages, the knowledge of science was preserved and flourished mainly in Arabic culture; knowledge of the science of antiquity survived only precariously during these centuries in Western Europe.

After the disintegration of the Roman Empire, medicine in Western Europe was mostly folk medicine, although some knowledge of Greek medicine and even the gynecological tradition of the second century survived. During the Early Middle Ages, many of the women who have been identified as participating in science and science-related activities were working in medicine. Many were herbalists and passed the traditions of herbal medicine within their families. Throughout the Middle Ages, medicine remained one of the very few channels for the scientific interests of medieval women.

During the Early Middle Ages, notable individual women included the Empress Theodora (500–548), who rose from plebian origins to become Empress of the Eastern Roman Empire in Constantinople and the most powerful woman in Byzantine history. She appears to have had serious interests in philosophy, mathematics, and science as well as poetry. She is credited as one of the earliest rulers who recognized the rights of women; she passed laws to prohibit prostitution of young girls and altered the divorce laws and property owner-ship laws to benefit women.

Other aristocratic women of this period included the Empress Eudocia (396–460), a classical scholar who had skill in medicine and founded a great hospital in Jerusalem; her interests also included astronomy and mathematics. The Empress Julia Anicia (472–512) was deeply interested in medicine; her illustrated codex of Disocorides' herbal has survived; it is the earliest known complete medical manuscript. Although there are few records of individual women, illustrations have survived that show medieval Arabic women dealing with obstetrics and gynecology as well as Arabic women and men engaged in alchemy.

During the Early Middle Ages in Western Europe, the Christian Church had a central role in both education and scholarly activities. Religious institutions such as monasteries and nunneries provided the milieu for most science and science-related activities. Such religious institutions were located throughout Western Europe, and many of the women involved with science during the Early Middle Ages were associated with these religious institutions. Included among these women were Saint Briget of Ireland (453–525), who was a physician; the Abbess Hilda of Whitby (614–680), who was an English physician and surgeon and educator; Abbess Berthildis of Chelles (652–702), who was a French scholar and physician; and German Abbess Mathilda of Quedlinburg (895–968), who also practiced medicine.

Other notable women active in Western Europe included Radegonde (513–587), who practiced medicine in France. Hroswitha of Gandersheim (935–1000) was a German nun who by the standards of her time was learned in mathematics and medicine as well as being a playwright and poet and one of the first outstanding female literary figures in Europe. In addition to these and other women whose names have come down to us from the Early Middle Ages, there were also less well-known women who worked in medicine and related fields such as pharmacy, as indicated in sculpture and other visual records as well as written references.

High Middle Ages

The historical period known as the High Middle Ages began around 1000 and lasted to roughly 1300. At that time, Europe still remained a backwater compared to other civilizations such as those of Islam or China. In the early 11th century in Europe, knowledge of science was largely limited to fragments of the science of antiquity, but progress soon became more rapid. Cultural changes came partly as a result of the Crusades, which started in the 11th century and continued through the 15th century. Contact with the Arabic culture allowed

Europeans to access preserved Greek and Roman texts as well as Arabic commentaries and texts, and large numbers of Greek and Arabic works on medicine and the sciences were translated and widely distributed throughout Europe. Alchemy was introduced into Europe at the time of the Crusades. Also, because the Crusades contributed to spreading diseases through Europe and the Middle East, the need for hospitals and physicians increased; hospitals were built along the Crusaders' routes, some staffed largely by women, and many women practiced medicine.

Around AD 1000, the number of women scientists for whom we find records begins to increase, concurrent with the rise of European science. This increase in the population of women scientists started in Italy and gradually spread to Northern Europe, as did science in general. During the High Middle Ages, more women seemed to have been practicing science than at any previous period of history.

Role of the Religious Communities

During medieval times, convents and monasteries played a very important role in preserving and disseminating knowledge, and a significant number of scientists, both men and women, belonged to religious communities. Medieval convents provided women with opportunities for education and scholarly research. Throughout most of the medieval period in most of Europe, women scientists were frequently members of religious orders, and they studied and practiced science within convents.

The most outstanding woman scientist of this period was the Abbess Hildegard of Bingen (1098–1179). Her prolific writings included treatments of various scientific subjects, including medicine, botany, and natural history, and she authored what have been called the greatest scientific works of the Middle Ages. Historian of science George Sarton has referred to Hildegard as the most distinguished naturalist of this period and also as the most original 12th-century philosopher in Western Europe. Hildegard was a visionary but also a politically powerful person. Her interests included cosmology, and she put forward the idea of a heliocentric solar system as well as other revolutionary scientific ideas in her writings. Her major work was the *Scivias,* completed in 1151. Her ideas continued to affect the direction of scientific thought throughout the Late Middle Ages and into the Renaissance.

Another outstanding woman of this period was Herrade of Landsberg, a contemporary and possibly also a friend of Hildegard. Herrade, the abbess of Hohenburg in Alsace and a prominent scholar, author, and educator, was born early in the 12th century and died in 1195. During the 12th and 13th centuries in Europe there was a marked increase in the rate of new inventions,

Illustration from Scivias (Know the Ways of the Lord), *by the German nun and mystic Hildegard von Bingen. This illustration shows Hildegard's vision of the universe as a cosmic egg.* (Erich Lessing/ Art Resource)

innovations in the ways of managing traditional means of production, technological advances, and a surge in economic growth. Herrade had a very extensive knowledge of the technology in use during the Middle Ages, and she recorded this for posterity. Herrade's encyclopedic works covered not only history, religion, and philosophy but also geography, astronomy, natural history, medical botany, and the technology of the Middle Ages, with descriptions and depictions of many inventions, such as mills powered by wind and water. For centuries, Herrade of Landsberg's encyclopedic works were a major source of information, and it is from them that we have derived most of our present knowledge of the technology of the Middle Ages.

Another exceptional woman of the medieval period was Héloïse (1101–1164). She was a scholar of languages as well as a philosopher and logician with a reputation for outstanding intelligence and insight. Her relationship with her mentor, the scholar Pierre Abelard (a principal figure in early scholasticism), provided one of the earliest and best-known records of romantic love. Later in life Héloïse became an abbess. She was one of the foremost intellectuals of medieval times and has been described as an outstanding mathematician and the most learned woman physician of France of the 12th century.

Hildegard, Herrade, and Héloïse were among the last of the scholarly abbesses. As time went on, the prestige and power of abbesses were reduced; in some cases these women became subordinated to abbots. More nuns became cloistered, and many convents that had previously shared facilities with monasteries were subsequently separated from them.

Cathedral schools had been introduced near the beginning of the High Middle Ages to improve the education of the clergy. These new schools were open only to males training for the clergy and did not admit women. The effect was to exclude women from the mainstream of education and learning through much of the rest of the Middle Ages. While some women continued to have access to education in nunneries, the educational divide between men and women increased to the disadvantage of medieval women. As time went on, abbey schools were closed, and by the 13th century, educational opportunities in the convents had been seriously reduced.

Role of the Universities

An important development in the revival of learning during the Middle Ages was the rise of the first universities in Europe, which started with the medical schools of Italy. These universities aided in the translation, preservation, and propagation of earlier learning and started a new infrastructure that could support scientific communities. During the Middle Ages in Italy, a number of women scientists were associated with the universities.

During the 11th century in Italy, a major revival of Western medicine began at the medical school at Salerno. Salerno seems to have been the first medieval medical center independent of the Church; it also seems to have become the first European university. In view of the limited access to education generally afforded to medieval women, the early tradition of female medical students and faculty members at Salerno was significant. One of the earliest and most famous of these medieval women was Trotula of Salerno (d. ca. 1097) who was a widely acclaimed professor of medicine at the medical school in Salerno during the 11th century. With the field of medicine dominated by men, Trotula recognized the need for medical knowledge and medical care specific to women's needs and became a leading specialist in obstetrics and gynecology. She also was known for her practice in dermatology and epilepsy, and she was recognized for her departure from tradition in methods of diagnosis, which included both questioning the patient and discussing the patient's condition with the patient. Trotula was the author of medical treatises that were widely used throughout Europe during the Middle Ages. Her most famous work was *Passionibus mulierum curandorum* (*The Diseases of Women*), which dealt with menstruation and pregnancy from conception to childbirth, as well as general diseases and treatments. Among her innovations was her suggestion that opiates be provided for women during childbirth in direct defiance of the Church's teachings. She also seems to have pointed out that physiological defects of men as well as women could affect conception; this was a dangerous claim to make during the Middle Ages in

Europe since it implied that men could be responsible for infertility, an idea not easily accepted in a patriarchal culture. She taught many Italian women of the nobility, a group sometimes referred to as the "Ladies of Salerno," who became widely known as physicians and medical scholars.

The 12th century saw the beginnings of a renaissance in learning. This came about in part as a result of the growth of towns with literate upper classes. In part it came from contacts with more advanced Islamic culture. The influence of Arab science first became evident in Italy and Spain, the areas of Europe that had the most contact with the Moslem civilization. This interaction led to the introduction of Arabic science and the rediscovery of the works of Aristotle, Ptolemy, and Galen in Western Europe during the 12th and 13th centuries. Greek scientific treatises were translated from Arabic into Latin, and Europeans began rediscovering the science of antiquity as it had been preserved and extended by the Arabs. Arabic numerals were introduced into Europe around 1200.

The period 1100–1400, and particularly the 13th century, was known as the age of scholasticism, the system of thought that integrated philosophy and theology during the Middle Ages. This approach sought to combine the secular understanding of the ancient world, particularly as exemplified by Aristotle, the authority in philosophy, with the doctrines of the Church.

The most striking intellectual development of the 13th century was the rise of the universities, with several (including Bologna, Paris, and Oxford) founded around 1200. These new institutions of higher education were in many cases outgrowths of the cathedral schools, and women, as a result, were most often excluded.

In France early in the 12th century, women studied privately and taught medicine at Montpellier, but subsequently women were excluded from French universities. With the exception of institutions in Italy, universities seem to have been closed to women throughout Europe during much of this period, an exclusion that became a significant drawback to women with scientific interests. Because women were largely prohibited from universities, they were effectively barred from participating in the revival of philosophy and mathematics that took place during the High Middle Ages. This situation was also disadvantageous to women in medicine, since medicine was becoming a profession requiring a university education. As a result, the hierarchy of medicine became more and more dominated by male physicians. Laws against women healers were introduced and enforced, and women who would have qualified as physicians in the 13th century would be treated as charlatans and witches in the 14th and 15th centuries.

An example was Jacobina Félicie (*fl.* 1300s), who was born in Florence about 1280 and who, after private study, had practiced medicine very successfully in Paris. However, in 1322, the dean of the medical faculty at the University of Paris brought charges against her for practicing medicine without a license, citing an edict dating back to 1220 that prohibited anyone not a member of a faculty of medicine from practicing medicine. Eventually the charges were withdrawn and the prosecution was dropped, but this set a precedent against women practicing medicine in France until the 19th century.

A number of other women were involved in scientific activities during the High Middle Ages including Anna Comnena (AD 1083–1148), daughter of the emperor of Constantinople, a scholar who was a well-known historian. She seems to have been the first woman historian whose writings have survived, and she also engaged in mathematics, astrology, and the practice of medicine.

During the 1200s in Italy, Maria di Novella was a prominent educator and mathematician and a professor of mathematics. At the age of 25 she became head of the department of mathematics at the University of Bologna.

Persian Princess Gevher Nesibe (ca. 1200) had an interest in medicine and was responsible for the founding of the historic Gevhar Nesibe Hospital, the oldest hospital in Anatolia.

Well-known medieval physicians of this period included Saint Elizabeth of Hungary (1207–1230); Elizabeth of Aragon (1271–1336), who practiced medicine in Spain and Portugal; Agnes of Bohemia (d. 1282), who practiced medicine in what is now the Czech Republic and Slovakia; Saint Clara of Assisi (1194–1253), a physician in Italy during the 1200s; and Mechthild of Hackecdorn (1212–1282), who was a German physician.

Late Middle Ages

The age of scholasticism in the 1200s was followed by the historical period known as the Late Middle Ages (1300–1500). During this period, power was shifting from the religious establishment to the towns and the middle classes, and some limited educational opportunities for women opened in the towns. The first half of the 14th century was initially promising for science, with a decline in scholastic debates and further attention devoted to searching for natural explanations of phenomena that directed the way toward experimental science.

But this was a time of rapid change and turmoil. Some centuries of relative prosperity in Western Europe were brought to an end by a series of events referred to collectively as the Crisis of the Late Middle Ages. A factor contributing to the crisis was the onset of a period of cooler climate known as the Little Ice Age, which set in around 1350 and lasted for some 500 years; this was a time of hard winters, violent storms, and droughts. There were also plagues and severe famines. The Black Death, a form of bubonic plague, arrived in Europe around 1350, spread over Europe, and killed an estimated one quarter to one third of the population during the 1300s. The impact of the plague was especially severe in the crowded towns, where much of the intellectual activity took place. Recurrences of the plague and other disasters caused a continuing decline of population and difficult times for about a century. These circumstances in turn led to severe economic problems, associated financial collapse, social unrest, and endemic warfare. The Hundred Years' War, actually a series of wars between England and France, extended from 1337 to 1453. Other societal events contributing to the societal crises toward the end of the Middle Ages included the Spanish inquisition, started around 1478 during the transition to the Renaissance. All of these circumstances may have contributed to a reduction in the level of scholarly and scientific activities.

One additional societal crisis that started during the Late Middle Ages and was probably uniquely important to the participation of women in science was the horrific persecution of women as witches that occurred throughout Europe starting around 1300; it began turning into a frenzy during the late 1400s and extended into the 1600s. Accusations of witchcraft were notably directed against women herbalists, natural healers, and midwives. Probably the worst peril that women in medicine were exposed to from the 1300s onward was the accusation of witchcraft. The pursuit of witches reached such intensity in the 1600s that by some estimates at least 40,000 women accused of witchcraft were executed and many more were tortured. Women in other sciences and even engineering also suffered in the witchcraft frenzy.

But a countervailing effect to the disastrous events in Late medieval and early Renaissance Europe were provided by the invention of printing: during the middle years of the 1400s, the then-recent invention of printing with movable type contributed to the democratization of learning, allowed a faster propagation of new ideas, and made it possible for scientific publications to become much more widely available than ever before.

During the Late Middle Ages, there was some early feminist activity with women challenging the male hegemony over education and scholarly activities. In Western Europe at this time, a number of literate upper-class women were writing on behalf of women and promoting women's education. One of the most prominent of these was Christine de Pisan (1363–1431), an early and active feminist who challenged academic misogyny; she became Europe's first woman who earned a living as a professional writer. She was an important French scholar, philosopher, poet, historian, and author. Born in Venice, the daughter of a professor of medicine and alchemy and astrology, she apparently had an interest in medicine and the sciences although she does not seem to have worked actively in these fields. She wrote several books dealing with the importance of women and equal rights, including *Le Livre de la cite des dames*.

Medieval illustration depicting Christine de Pisan presenting a manuscript to Isabella of Bavaria. (Historical Picture Archive/Corbis)

The University of Bologna had allowed women to attend lectures from its inception in 1088 and subsequently had women on the faculty. The study of anatomy had been in stasis for over 1,000 years since the time of Galen, but it was revived at the University of Bologna. Alessandra Giliani, an anatomist who lived in Italy during the early 1300s, was the dissector and assistant to the anatomist Mondino de Luzzi at the anatomy school at the University of Bologna. She is credited with devising the technique of injecting dye into the blood vessels of cadavers so that the locations of the blood vessels could be traced in dissection studies.

Women professors who taught at the famous medical school at Salerno during the 1300s included the notable medieval Italian physician and educator Abella of Salerno, the author of two lost medical treatises, *De atrabile* and *De natura seminis humani;* Rebecca Guarna, also a medical author whose writings on topics including urine and embryos have been lost; and Mercuriade, whose writings on topics including crises in fevers and the cure of wounds also did not survive. Another woman involved in science during the 1300s was Perenelle Flamel (d. 1413), a French alchemist who worked with her more famous husband, the alchemist Nicholas Flamel.

An interesting feature of the practice of medicine in medieval Europe was the significant number of Jewish women physicians. The educated Jewish population was able to contribute to bridging the gap between European and Arabic culture, helping to provide continuity in the knowledge of Galen and other Roman and Greek physicians. Medieval Jewish women physicians included the previously mentioned Jacobina Félicie. Others were Virdimura, a physician in Sicily who was licensed to practice medicine in 1376; Salome of Cracow, who was a physician in Poland during the 1200s; Sarah de Saint Gilles, who was a physician and educator in Montpellier in France around 1300; Sarah la Mirgesse, who taught and practiced medicine in Paris in 1292; and Sarah of Wurzburg, who practiced medicine successfully in Germany in the 15th century.

Among the women engaged in scientific work during the 1400s was Dorotea Bocchi (1360–1436). She succeeded her father as professor of medicine and moral philosophy at the University of Bologna and remained in that position for 40 years. While she held the chair of medicine at Bologna, she had students from all over Europe. Constanza Calenda, daughter of an Italian professor of the 14th century, studied medicine at the University of Salerno and lectured at the University of Naples.

In Italy, Cassandra Fidelis (1465–1558) was the most renowned woman scholar in Italy and was a physician; also, the scholar Laura Ceretta (1469–1499) studied mathematics and astronomy and lectured on philosophy.

The Middle Ages gradually came to an end, as the 15th century saw the rise of the cultural movement of the Renaissance. Women active in science during this period included the Spanish nun Beatrix Galindo (1473–1535), who was a physician as well as a philosopher and scholar; Countess Margaret Beaufort (1443–1509), an English scholar and medical practitioner; and Isabella Losa (1473–1546), a Spanish physician.

In spite of the impediments during these difficult times, a number of women continued to work in science during the Late Middle Ages and early Renaissance. Isabella d'Este (1474–1539) became one of the leading women of the Italian renaissance and was involved in archaeological investigations. Many women became interested in and practiced alchemy, a precursor of chemistry. We know from visual and written records that women worked in the medieval equivalent of industrial laboratories and also in private laboratories. Somewhat later, during the 1500s, Anna Electress of Saxony (1532–1587), a member of the Danish royal family, built her own private laboratory, which was the largest laboratory in Europe at that time.

Conclusion

With the increased revival of Greek science, early Renaissance scholars to some extent repudiated medieval science. However, the medieval sciences provided transitional knowledge during the millennium between antiquity and the Renaissance.

During all of the Middle Ages, only about 200 women have been specifically identified as participating actively in scientific work. (We may presume that many additional, less prominent women must have been present but their names have not come down to us.) Since the Middle Ages represents a period of about 1,000 years, this corresponds on average to some 20 prominent women per century (scattered over all of Europe, with a few in the Middle East). Lifetimes were typically shorter during the medieval period and travel extremely difficult; accordingly, few of these women would ever have had the opportunity of meeting each other, let alone mentoring or collaborating with one another.

We can also examine the number of identified women scientists as a function of time during the Middle Ages, bearing in mind that the numbers are so small that such assessments are at best semiquantitative and subject in interpretation to many biasing effects. From the end of antiquity, the number of women in scientific pursuits dropped from about 10 per century to none at all identified during the 800s, then rose rapidly through the 1100s and 1200s, peaked during the 1300s, and dropped off appreciably during the 1400s, at least partly in response to the trends and causative factors already discussed.

Thus, after a decline in numbers after late antiquity, followed by a promising rise in the participation of women in science during the High Middle Ages, the Middle Ages ended in a period of increased exclusion of women from education and from participation in the sciences. However, some brilliant women would continue to practice science during the Renaissance. (*See also* Early Modern Health; Medicine; Universities)

References and Further Reading

Alic, Margaret. *Hypatia's Heritage: A History of Women in Science from Antiquity to the Late Nineteenth Century*. London: Women's Press, 1986.

Ehrenreich, Barbara, and D. English. *Witches, Midwives, and Nurses: A History of Women Healers*. Old Westbury, NY: Feminist Press, 1973.

Enciclopedia Biografica de la Mujer. Barcelona, Spain: Edicions Garriga, S.A., 1967.

Herzenberg, Caroline L. *Women Scientists from Antiquity to the Present: An Index*. West Cornwall, CT: Locust Hill Press, 1986.

Herzenberg, Caroline L. "Women in Science during Antiquity and the Middle Ages." *Journal of College Science Teaching* (November 1987): 124–127.

Herzenberg, Caroline L., Susan V. Meschel, and James A. Altena, "Women Scientists and Physicians of Antiquity and the Middle Ages." *Journal of Chemical Education* 68 (1991): 101–105.

Høyrup, Else. *Women of Science, Technology, and Medicine: A Bibliography.* Roskilde, Denmark: Roskilde University Library, 1987.

Hurd-Mead, Kate Campbell. *A History of Women in Medicine from the Earliest Times to the Beginning of the Nineteenth Century.* Haddam, CT: Haddam Press, 1938. Reprint, Dover, NH: Longwood Press, 1978.

Mozans, H. J. *Woman in Science.* New York: D. Appleton, 1913. Reprint, Cambridge, MA: MIT Press, 1974.

Ogilvie, Marilyn Bailey. *Women in Science: A Biographical Dictionary with Annotated Bibliography.* Cambridge, MA: MIT Press, 1986.

Rebiere, A. *Les Femmes dans la science.* Paris: Nony, 1897.

Wayley-Singer, Dorothea. "Les Femmes de Science." *La Femme dans La Société.* Edited by Margaret Mead, Helene Deutsch, Henri Perruchot, Micheline Murin, Dorothea Singer, and Paul Lorenz. Paris: Editions Lidis, 1965.

Renaissance

Cynthia Klestinec

Until recently, it was assumed that women, largely undereducated, did not play a significant role in the cultural developments of the Renaissance. In many ways, however, women were important to the literary, political, and scientific developments of this period. Some gained access to print—the most important technology of the day—reading books as well as writing them. They became astoundingly well educated, establishing themselves among the elite and shaping the intellectual, humanist traditions of scholarship. Others sought to develop their own communities, traditions of communication, and beliefs. In direct and indirect ways, women helped to shape the cultural programs of the Renaissance, including those associated with the Scientific Revolution.

From 1450 to 1650, Europe witnessed profound changes in technological capacity, political landscape, social customs, and literary traditions. This period saw the rise of print, the flourishing of humanist and civic culture, and the expansion of trade in urban centers across the continent and with "the rest of the world" (a phrase that could only appear, as Mary Louise Pratt has shown, when Europe had an idea of itself as something different from and often opposed to non-European others, which was another development of the Renaissance). These changes were both guides and sources of inspiration for the Scientific Revolution; and like the Scientific Revolution itself, the history of these sweeping changes depends on the ideas, activities, and communities of men and women alike.

Print Culture and Humanism

In Mainz, Germany, around 1450, printing with movable type was perfected, and while the invention has been attached variously to the names of Johann Gutenberg and Johann Fust as well as Peter Schöffer, the year 1450 provides a useful marker for the beginning of the Renaissance. Matched perhaps only by the Internet today, the printing press was to have the most profound impact of any innovation on European culture. Books became more affordable and more pervasive, and their accessibility changed educational institutions, intellectual practices, and reading habits. At universities, students could afford small, roughly made editions, sometimes with extra pages at the end for note taking; and instead of relying wholly on lectures and the oral traditions of education, students began to rely on the scripted traditions of books: encyclopedias, dictionaries, monographs, and illustrated volumes. Students as well as noblemen and merchants also began to amass books—the first library at the university in Padua, Italy, was begun by German students—and to read silently. This shift to silent reading hints at the radical impact of movable type and the technology of print on the development of the individual.

The rapid spread of printed material encouraged alternative political and religious opinion. After 1517, when Martin Luther openly criticized the corruption of the Catholic Church, the fervor for alternative religious views and communities began to take shape with the help of vernacular Bibles, pamphlets, and other literature. Indeed, in England, before Henry VIII broke with the Catholic Church, the government attempted to censor and prevent these publications, actions that attest to the power of this new technological resource.

The spread of print also helped to shape a new set of intellectual practices among elite, learned Europeans (those who knew Latin) and the unlearned or "un-Latined" people, including barbers, surgeons, midwives, and artisans. As scholars were freed from the painstakingly slow work of producing manuscripts (literally, texts "written by hand"), they recognized the value of print and began to work on editions of classical texts of both Greek and Roman origin. Renaissance means "rebirth," and these scholars set out to recover and revive the ideas and eventually the practices of the classical age, for which they were called humanists and their program, humanism (a later term derived from *studia humanitatis*). Humanism sought to appropriate Greek and Latin learning, focusing on the disciplines of grammar, rhetoric, and poetics to transform students into active, politically engaged, and ethically responsible citizens. Humanism, these pedagogues argued, prepared students for the lively world of political debate by training them in legal constructs of argument and in eloquence. While the 15th century (1400s) witnessed a gradual spread of humanistic inquiries and educational initiatives, the 16th century (1500s) reveals the fruits of those efforts.

In 1513, Niccolò Machiavelli (1469–1527), author of *The Prince,* wrote a letter to Francesco Vettori in which he associated the book as much with the development of liberal thought as with the image of a noble humanist: "When evening comes, I return home, and I enter into my study; and at the door I take off my everyday dress, full of mud and dirt, and I put on royal and courtly clothes; and decently dressed I enter into the ancient courts of ancient men . . . [and] for four hours at a time I feel no boredom. I forget all trouble, I do not fear poverty, death does not frighten me. I put myself completely at their disposal" (93–95). Withdrawing from the world and taking refuge in the private, silent space of his library, Machiavelli read the works of the ancients, reconstituted their dilemmas, and sought to learn equally from their successes and their failures. The book, the library, the resonance between ancient and contemporary courts—these features became part of the material culture of the Renaissance. They signified not only material wealth but also the noble spirit that humanists first celebrated. They would be duplicated and adapted by men and by women, for soon women humanists emerged in various European cities and courts.

Women Writers

In a now famous essay, "Did Women Have a Renaissance?" Joan Kelly-Gadol suggested that medieval women enjoyed a range of liberties, including sexual ones, that were not extended to women in the Renaissance. Some medieval women had access to property ownership if spouses and fathers died; other medieval women, such as Marie de France, were sophisticated poets, gifted at articulating their desires in a language that blended the eroticism of Scripture with that of court culture. Medieval women writers were not merely the objects of male desire or of the chivalric narratives of conquest; rather, women helped to shape the literary traditions of their day, using the clichés or conventions of romance to transform the heroine from a passive object into an agent in hot pursuit of her beloved. Writing before many of the texts of Renaissance women had been discovered, Kelly-Gadol focused on the texts of medieval women writers, illuminating early developments in women's history. Following her lead, subsequent scholars have recovered the writings of Renaissance women, demonstrating the many ways that these women responded to the social and political forces that served to constrain them.

One Renaissance text that encouraged women to write or that seems to have demanded a response from its female audience was *The Book of the Courtier* (1528) by Baldesar Castiglione (1478–1529). *The Courtier* provided a nuanced representation of court culture, specifically the court of Urbino. Written as a dialogue, the courtiers set out to describe the ideal courtier. Written as a dialogue between courtiers and courtesans, the text begins with the question of what constitutes the ideal courtier. The ideal courtier was supposed to embody the aspect of *sprezzatura,* a certain graceful nonchalance, and to possess extensive knowledge of the classics. Castiglione modeled his courtier on the Renaissance humanist and made humanist learning the means of attaining power and prestige at court. When the interlocutors discuss the relationship between the ideal courtier and the courtesan, they struggle with

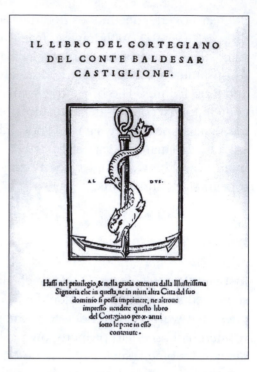

IL LIBRO DEL CORTEGIANO
DEL CONTE BALDESAR
CASTIGLIONE.

Haffi nel priuilegio, & nella gratia ottenuta dalla Illuftriffima
Signoria che in quefta, ne in niun'altra Citta del fuo
dominio fi poffa imprimere, ne aitroue
impreffo uendere quefto libro
del Cortegiano per.x. anni
fotto le pene in effo
contenute.

Title page of Baldasar Castiglione's The
Book of the Courtier, *1528.* (Lebrecht
Music & Arts/The Image Works)

hierarchy and complementarity. Was the courtesan ideally subordinate to the
courtier or a complement? And if a complement, then how learned should
she be? As they explore the question of women's education, it becomes clear
that the ideal courtesan was based on more than humanist learning. If she is
learned, the courtiers wonder, should her learning have consequences—for
policy making or advising the prince—or should it be merely ornamental, a
testament to the wealth and nobility of the court itself? While much debate
ensues and several comments about equality emerge, one interlocutor seals
the fate of women. If the courtesan is to have knowledge of all things, will
she then go on to govern cities? His question allowed the anxiety around the
publicly accessible female, the appropriately humanist courtesan, to crystal-
lize. Although the conversation turns in another direction, the issue would
emerge repeatedly in the texts of Renaissance women writers.

The question of whether a woman could or should govern joined questions
about whether women were capable of intellectual inquiry; these questions
were subsumed by the broader debate on women's natural inferiority. Known
in its literary manifestation as the *querelle des femmes,* the "Woman Question,"
this debate was wide ranging, attracting European and English authors and
eliciting various responses. Veronica Franco (ca. 1546–1591), a Venetian courtesan, published a collection of letters and poems that established her presence
among Venetian noblemen, especially those responsible for the governance

of that city-state. Her writing displayed her humanist education; it also turned the traditions of love poetry to her favor. Condemning a critic of hers, she transformed the language of chivalry into her own, poetic defense.

> As if jolted awake from sweet sleep all at once,
> I drew courage from the risk I'd avoided,
> though a woman, born to milder tasks;
> and, blade in hand, I learned warrior's skills,
> so that, by handling weapons, I learned
> that women by nature are no less agile than men
> (*Poems and Selected Letters,* Capitoli 16)

Franco indicated that her "blade" was, in fact, her pen, which she used to negotiate the humanist world of Venetian nobility, to establish and defend her authority as an independent, learned woman.

A similarly critical edge is visible in the work of Moderata Fonte (Modesta Pozzo, 1555–1592). A Venetian noblewoman rather than a courtesan, Fonte operated under different constraints. Like most Venetian noblewomen, she was supposed to remain indoors, sheltered and away from public scrutiny. For Fonte, this became the context of her dialogue, *The Worth of Women* (1600). Like Castiglione's work, Fonte's dialogue included several interlocutors, debates on a range of issues, and witty exchange. Unlike Castiglione, however, Fonte made all of her interlocutors female, stressing the different perspectives that unmarried virgins, wives, and widows brought to the topic of the worth of women. Fonte, that is, transformed the traditional or conventional nature of the dialogue to her advantage, using it to explore the issues that faced Renaissance women and to expose the nature of inequality.

Like other learned women, Fonte obtained her education under atypical circumstances. When her brother returned home from school, she would beg him to explain to her the many things he'd learned that day. Her brother's sympathy in these early years became open support in later years when he helped to connect her to noblemen interested in her publishing career. The themes of education for women and the intellectual inferiority of women occupy much of Fonte's dialogue. Early in Fonte's dialogue, one interlocutor explains: "This pre-eminence [of men] is something they have unjustly arrogated to themselves. And when it's said that women must be subject to men, the phrase should be understood in the same sense as when we say that we are subject to natural disasters, diseases and all the other accidents of this life: it's not a case of being subject in the sense of obeying, but rather of suffering an imposition; not a case of serving them fearfully, but rather of tolerating them in a spirit of Christian charity, since they have been given to us by God as a spiritual trial. But they [men] take the phrase in the contrary sense and set themselves up as tyrants over us, arrogantly usurping that dominion over women that they claim is their right, but which is more properly ours" (59). So bold and direct, Fonte's prose startles and reminds us that Renaissance women, even in the rich, cosmopolitan context of Venice, were severely limited in terms of their access to the public sphere, to political agency, and to social mobility. Equally, however, her remarks reveal that Renaissance women were highly articulate about their situation and about the possibility of change.

If Moderata Fonte set up her dialogue among women to dramatize the merits of a female community and to highlight by contrast the faults of the existing male community, Lucrezia Marinella (1571–1653) produced a polemical tract that sought to effect change more directly. Marinella was the daughter of a physician, learned in literary traditions and, one must imagine, in medical ones. Her work, *The Nobility and Excellence of Women and the Defects and Vices of Men* (1600) was written as a forceful and immediate response to a misogynist tract by Giuseppe Passi. In her chapter on the nature and essence of the female sex, Marinella rehearsed the arguments in favor of female superiority, but she also added a catalogue of classical and contemporary philosophical and literary sources that served as evidence for her point. Finally, she transformed the typical discussion of beauty—women could serve as ornaments to a society or a court because they were beautiful—into a sustained discussion of the inherent link between beauty and nobility: because they are more beautiful than men, women are also more noble in spirit; that is, a woman's body is beautiful because it is the vessel for her noble spirit. The debates on the nature of women were also reflected in the Renaissance medical and scientific traditions, for as female practitioners such as midwives began to write treatises on medical care, they made powerful arguments in favor of the superior inclinations and capabilities of women.

Women and Vernacular Science

Like learned women, who resisted and responded to a range of social and political constraints through writing, women practitioners and professionals similarly responded to these restrictions in writing. Nowhere is this as clear as in the evolving relation between midwives, surgeons, and physicians. While the early Renaissance saw midwives as the appropriate and often expert practitioners of the birthing chamber, the midwife's authority was slowly eroded. This erosion was in part due to the educational disparities between physicians and midwives, between practitioners trained at the university (a learned culture) and those trained typically by long apprenticeships with other midwives (a vernacular culture). In the 16th century, moreover, many city ordinances instructed midwives to call for a physician or a surgeon if there were any problems with a delivery. Both the exclusion from university education and the new scientific study of childbirth helped to deteriorate the image of the successful, female midwife. In the midst of this development, however, female midwives took up their pens, writing sophisticated and polemical treatises in favor of female birth attendants and female expertise.

The importance of print to these developments should not be overlooked. Women chose to write and to seek publishing opportunities just as female readers became a more important segment of the book market. Vernacular readers, especially women, were interested in books that responded to issues of health. An array of medical manuals was available ranging over such diverse topics as how to read urine, how to treat insomnia and cramps to the salutary effects of mineral baths and separate herbals for boils, fistulas, and bad breath. Female readers, in particular, were familiar with technical writing that dealt with domestic technologies such as cooking and silkworm propagation, and household "physick" as well as midwifery. In England, for example, between 1475 and 1575, the 85 practical guides directed to women generated 290 editions. Indeed, the numerous editions on technical subjects indicate that the expansion of the book trade depended on a thirst for practical—not just literary or historical—works, suggesting that technical manuals constituted a major part of the public reading culture during the period.

Appealing to this market, Louise Bourgeois (1563–1636) wrote *Various Observations concerning sterility, miscarriages, fertility, births and diseases of women and newborn children* (1626), a midwifery manual that celebrated her skill and experience as well as her learning. Married to a surgeon and living in Paris, Bourgeois had access to a great deal of technical, medical education; she became the midwife for the royal court and eventually to Marie de Medici. Written at the height of her successful career, her manual combines technical education with hands-on expertise, two features that were to become standard themes in subsequent midwifery publications.

In her *Midwives Book* (1671), Jane Sharp, a London midwife, emphasized her experience and her learning, especially her awareness of contemporary, academic debates about anatomy. Sharp, however, was inclined to privilege her experience, which consisted of more than 30 years of successful practice. She celebrated the art of midwifery alongside her own diligence, dedication, and success. For Sharp, female expertise in the birthing chamber depended on experience (and proper training) as well as the natural inclinations of the female sex. Sharp also highlighted various problems with academic medicine. She presented an image of learned medicine that was fractured, argumentative, and incapable of arriving at a consensus. In direct contrast, Sharp created an image of a female-dominated community of birthing experts, a community that was coherent, integrated, lively, and in agreement on many issues concerning birth and the health of both mother and child. Like Jane Sharp,

Justine Siegemund (1636–1705), a German midwife, took up her pen to argue forcefully for the expertise and authority of female midwives. In *The Court Midwife* (1690), she claimed that she acquired her special skills because she was a woman. Initially a successful strategy, this eventually was used to criticize and dismantle her authority (and the authority of many midwives).

Kept from the more scientific study of childbirth, midwives were less practiced with the tools of child birthing, such as the forceps. Frequently used by surgeons, the forceps allowed practitioners to deliver babies who would not be deliverable using the hands alone. The tool was invented by Peter Chamberlen (1560–1631) in early 17th-century England. Surgeons began to develop a reputation for expertise and technological skill in the birthing chamber and this allowed them to encroach on the midwife's clientele. In the 18th century, the debates continued. Favoring female attendants, many authors relied on norms about modesty—that it was improper for a man to examine a woman's body—and on the notion that women, because they were female, were inherently better at caring for other women. Those favoring male attendants, though, emphasized formal education and technological skill. It was the issue of who could guarantee safe delivery of mother and child that eventually carried more weight than moral arguments about modest behavior. Thus, while medical men gained the experience that traditionally only midwives possessed, midwives did not in turn come to be regarded as medical practitioners.

Women, Men, and Learned Science

In the 16th century, vernacular or popular writings proliferated; women began to publish literary works and medical treatises. While these changes were afoot, the learned cultures of the Renaissance were also changing. Responses to humanism began to take shape. Andreas Vesalius (1514–1564), an anatomist working in Bologna and Padua in the 1540s, set out to recover the anatomical studies of the ancient anatomist, Galen (second century AD). In 1543, he published *The Fabric of the Human Body,* a monumental textbook with exquisite woodcuts of dissected bodies and anatomical parts. Vesalius sought to "raise from the dead" the ancient art of dissection, which Galen had first perfected. But Vesalius went one step further. He lamented the ways that anatomists and medical humanists depended more on books than on cadavers and other specimens; they, he said, "croak away" about things they have read but never seen "with their own eyes" (dedication). As a Renaissance humanist, Vesalius resuscitated Galen's works, but by the 1540s, that resuscitation was openly critical of many humanist practices. So characteristic of late-humanist thought, that opposition marked a new direction that was to be instrumental to the Scientific Revolution.

The desire for change is also clearly evident in the work of Francis Bacon (1561–1626), often called the architect of the New Science. In his first major work, *The Advancement of Learning* (1605), Bacon ridiculed the medieval, intellectual traditions of scholasticism and attacked the syllogism as the key example of circular, repetitive reasoning. Like Vesalius, Bacon distinguished himself from humanists who merely parroted the words of the ancients. He depicted scholasticism as stale, repetitive, and traditional and highlighted to a greater extent the failures of the humanist enterprise. In the treatise on blood circulation (1628), William Harvey (1578–1657) followed this path, insisting that observations rather than books should form the basis for claims about anatomical and physiological processes. Vesalius and Bacon also reflect a misogynist approach to the study of nature. As recent research has shown, the female body became the very symbol of nature; as the study of nature developed, the role of the natural philosopher (scientist) was to penetrate the "secrets of nature," a phrase originating from the tradition of the "secrets of women." Fantasies of penetration and even rape would later combine with the rhetoric of imperial conquest, signaling the darker sides of scientific inquiry and progress.

The rhetoric of innovation began to oppose the practices of humanism. In the introduction to *On the Revolution of the Heavenly Spheres,* Nicolaus Copernicus (1473–1543) referred to classical mathematics in order to pave a new road for mathematical study in the realm of astronomy (traditionally seen as theoretical rather than practical inquiry). By the late 16th and early 17th century, however, the tone was more confrontational. Galileo Galilei (1564–1642), the famous astronomer, celebrated his new observations of the moon's uneven, jagged surface so that he could unsettle part of the foundation of Aristotelian natural philosophy—namely, that the universe was perfect in form. If the moon's surface was uneven and more like the Earth's surface, it was then clear that the universe was not formally perfect. In this and other ways, Galileo argued forcefully against the older, Aristotelian plan of the universe.

Other disciplines began to explore questions that lay beyond the strict bounds of humanist thought. Rene Descartes (1596–1650) composed the *Discourse on Method* (1637) and *Meditations on First Philosophy* (1641) around the idea that he could overcome doubt with the principle "I think, therefore I am" or better, when I am thinking, I exist. Descartes argued that the mind and the body were distinct. In the *Discourse,* he claimed to abandon the study of letters and pursue his personal desire for new, more solid foundations. Tellingly, he noted that only mathematicians were able to demonstrate "certain and evident" reasoning. Abandoning the humanist enterprise, the study of letters, and hinting at the new role attributed to mathematics, Descartes embodied the sentiments most closely associated with the Scientific Revolution.

While Descartes' ideas would lay the groundwork for rationalism and be heavily criticized by Thomas Hobbes and others, the reception of his ideas among female readers is intriguing. Women were attracted to ways that Descartes' split between the mind and the body served to place the mind above the body. This hierarchy of intellect and reason over nature presented women with a system or a set of ideas that freed them from the linked relationship between woman, body, and nature. The proper use of a woman's mind was revealed through her reason, her serious engagement with the world, rather than her ability to be an ornament to that world. Women, that is, could be more than social butterflies.

Although 17th-century women did not employ Descartes' ideas in an orthodox way, they did use his ideas to elaborate the theme of the worth of women, particularly the worth of women's mental faculties. Mary Astell (1668–1731) wished to extend the role of a woman beyond that of wife, mother, and nun; she proposed an institution that would operate like a secular convent where women could live, study, and teach. Margaret Cavendish (1623–1673) recognized these themes in her writing; she also sought to penetrate the male world of science. Cavendish, the Duchess of Newcastle, published several works that ranged from literary to historical to philosophical or natural philosophical (scientific). She drew attention to the poor education that women received at public institutions; she noted that they were subordinated within the home and limited by the demands associated with childbirth; and she explored and lamented the vision of woman as incompetent, unintelligent, and irrational. However, she also indicated that these views were due to the few contributions made by women, implying that this was not because of educational disparity but rather inherent capability. Difficult to assess, her works are openly critical of institutional inequality and of women themselves. Her enthusiasm for science was reflected in her focus on the smallness of atoms and her ability to imagine alternative worlds within this world, an idea that captures her creativity and poetic potential as well as her interest in the developments of science and her ongoing commitment to political debate.

By the mid-17th century, scientific inquiry began to occur not only at universities but also at meetings held by learned societies. These societies appeared across Europe and in England. The Royal Society of London held regular meetings at which members would debate recent findings, share the results of their research, and conduct live (sometimes spectacular) experiments. In this semiprivate context, Robert Boyle (1627–1691) conducted his experiments with the air pump, built largely by Robert Hooke (1635–1703). In addition to building experimental apparatuses, Hooke is well known for his work with the microscope and his published study, *Micrographia* (1665). Even at this late date, science was open to its surrounding culture, for Hooke described the "new worlds" that he viewed in the microscope and the scientist's mandate to "conquer" them. In doing so, he echoed overtly the discovery of non-European lands, marking an early instance of the close relationship between science and imperialism.

Isaac Newton (1642–1727), mathematician and natural philosopher, studied the work on optics done by Boyle and Hooke as well as Descartes. He conducted his work at Cambridge University, but it was not until 1715 that he published his research on optics, forced to wait until his critics were dead. In the area of mathematics and cosmology (the structure of the universe), Newton published his major study, the *Mathematical Principles of Natural Philosophy,* in 1687. There, Newton demonstrated the principle of gravitation. In addition, while Newton contributed to many areas of mathematical study, he is best known for his solutions to the contemporary problems in analytical geometry of drawing tangents to curves and quantifying the areas bounded by those curves, which are known today as differentiation and integration. In 1675, Gottfried Wilhelm Leibniz (1646–1716) set out his first principles of differential calculus. Though Newton indicated these as early as 1676, Leibniz seems to have evolved them independently. An active debate ensued, however, with Newton's friends and Leibniz's friends seeking to claim priority.

Leibniz received a great deal of support from his friend, Sophia Charlotte of Hanover (1668–1705), first Queen of Prussia. Leibniz was her tutor, but in later years, she became an advocate for his work, persuading her husband to provide financial support to the Berlin academy of sciences where Leibniz worked and thrived. Even earlier, however, in 1697, Sophia Charlotte suggested the building of an astronomical observatory at Lützenburg, which Leibniz used to promote his proposals for a full-scale scientific society. The proposals were eventually accepted; the Society received a charter in 1700, and Leibniz was made president. According to the letters exchanged between them, Leibniz also gave support and encouragement to Sophia Charlotte, for it was no secret that Sophia's husband kept a mistress at court and that this mistress, unlike Sophia, was less interested in intellectual matters. Judging from her letters, Sophia turned with relief and delight to discussions of philosophy and theology with Leibniz and others.

While the period began with Machiavelli, who escaped daily toil by withdrawing into his library where he could engage in a conversation of sorts with the classical philosophers and historians of ancient Greece and Rome, it may be said to end with Sophia Charlotte, who surrounded herself with learned men so that she—sensitive, learned, and inquisitive—might escape the domestic difficulties of her marriage and engage the burgeoning world of Enlightenment science and letters. While the Renaissance witnessed so many changes in the political, social, and technological terrain of Europe, it did so with the industry, perseverance, and desire of women as different as Veronica Franco and Margaret Cavendish, women who are now being appreciated for the full impact of their work. (*See also* Early Modern Health)

References and Further Reading

Dear, Peter. *Revolutionizing the Sciences: European Knowledge and Its Ambitions, 1500–1700*. Princeton, NJ: Princeton University Press, 2001.

Fissell, Mary. *Vernacular Bodies: The Politics of Reproduction in Early Modern England*. Oxford: Oxford University Press, 2004.

Fonte, Moderata (Modesta Pozzo). *The Worth of Women: wherein is clearly revealed their nobility and superiority to men*. Translated by Virginia Cox. Chicago: University of Chicago Press, 1997.

Franco, Veronica. *Poems and Selected Letters*. Translated by Ann Rosalind Jones and Margaret Rosenthal. Chicago: University of Chicago Press, 1998.

Grafton, Anthony, and Eugene Rice. *The Foundations of Early Modern Europe, 1460–1559*. New York: W. W. Norton, 1994.

Grosz, Elizabeth. *Volatile Bodies: Toward a Corporeal Feminism*. Bloomington: Indiana University Press, 1994.

Jones, Kathleen. *A Glorious Fame: The Life of Margaret Cavendish, Duchess of Newcastle, 1623–1673*. London: Bloomsbury, 1998.

Kelly-Gadol, Joan. "Did Women Have a Renaissance?" *Women, History, and Theory: The Essays of Joan Kelly*. Chicago: University of Chicago Press, 1984.

King, Margaret. *Women in the Renaissance*. Chicago: University of Chicago Press, 1991.

Machiavelli, Niccolò. *The Prince*. Edited by Quentin Skinner and Russell Price. Cambridge: Cambridge University Press, 1988.

Pratt, Mary Louise. *Imperial Eyes: Travel Writing and Transculturation*. New York: Routledge, 1992.

Shapin, Steven, and Simon Schaffer. *Leviathan and the Air Pump: Hobbes, Boyle, and the Experimental Life*. Princeton, NJ: Princeton University Press, 1985.

Sheridan, Bridgette. "At Birth: The Modern State, Modern Medicine and the Royal Midwife Louise Bourgeois in Seventeenth-Century France." *DYNAMIS* 19 (1999): 145–166.

Vesalius, Andreas. *The Fabric of the Human Body*. Basel: Oporinus, 1543.

The 18th Century

MARILYN BAILEY OGILVIE

Eighteenth-century intellectuals accepted, articulated, expanded, and clarified the idea that men and women had radically different natures. One of the most enigmatic and influential philosophers of this time was Jean-Jacques Rousseau.

Jean Jacques Rousseau (1712–1778)

Rousseau's mother died shortly after his birth, and he was raised by his aunt. Although Rousseau did not have a formal education, his profligate watchmaker father, Isaac, taught his son to love books, music, and ideas. At first apprenticed to the city notary or registrar and second to a young engraver, Rousseau despised them both. After working for only three years of a five-year contract, Rousseau left the second apprenticeship and worked at various menial jobs (Damrosch 2005). He was befriended by Baronne de Warens, who further exposed him to books and ideas.

In spite of his background, Rousseau became one of the Enlightenment's most original thinkers. Noted for his political philosophy expressed in *The Social Contract,* he influenced the American Founding Fathers and the French Revolutionaries. His *Confessions* provide us with a record of his life through his own eyes and were important in establishing the genre of autobiography. His own personal life was chaotic and his recollections of it, written much after the fact, reflect his own obsessions and fears. His views concerning women are somewhat contradictory. While he put women on a pedestal to be worshipped, his view as to their place in society was inimical to their success in intellectual pursuits. Rousseau was a mass of contradictions. In his book on education, *Émile,* he stated that children should be allowed to develop according to their natural abilities. But he put his own children in a foundling home as soon as they were born. While making an inspired case for social equality, he formed close friendships with aristocrats and endorsed female subservience.

Rousseau wrote in *Émile* that "a perfect woman and a perfect man ought not to resemble each other in mind any more than in looks" (Rousseau 1979, 358). It is the nature of man and woman to complement each other with man being the strong, rational partner and woman the weak, sensuous one. Going against nature would be futile. "Boys seek movement and noise: drums, boots, little carriages. Girls prefer what presents itself to sight and is useful for ornamentation: mirrors, jewels, dresses, particularly dolls. The doll is the special entertainment of this sex. This is evidently its taste, determined by its purpose" (Rousseau 1979, 367). The difference in temperament should dictate the kind of education that each receives. "Once it is demonstrated that man and woman are not and ought not to be constituted in the same way in either character or temperament, it follows that they ought not to have the same education" (Rousseau 1979, 363). Rousseau wrote that a girl's education should provide her with the skills that would make her an asset to a man. Women should please and be useful to men and make themselves loved and esteemed by them. They should educate boys when they are young and take care of them when grown up. They should advise, console, and render men's lives easy and agreeable (Rousseau 1979, 365). This view of women was shared by many 18th-century intellectuals, but not by Mary Wollstonecraft, who had an entirely different view of the capabilities of women.

Mary Wollstonecraft (1759–1797)

Wollstonecraft in her *Vindication of the Rights of Woman* complained that men were not content with being physically superior to women but encouraged them to pursue the trivial. When women complied, the men whom they sought to please were upset because they appeared shallow and uninteresting. In a culture such as this one, it was difficult for women who wanted to engage in scientific pursuits to find ways to do so. In spite of the effort involved, some women defied the stereotype of woman as a frivolous creature without the interest or the ability to pursue difficult science.

Wollstonecraft had a miserable childhood with a father who drank too much and who beat his wife. Mary, the second of seven children, was self-educated except for a short stay at a day school in Yorkshire. Her tyrannical father had a difficult time supporting his family at farming, and they moved many times hoping to find success. In 1778 Mary took a position as a companion to a Miss Dawson in Bath. After two years in this job, she shared quarters with her childhood friend, Fanny Blood. After Mary's sister Eliza left her husband and child because of an unhappy marriage, she moved in with Mary and Fanny. The three women established a school at Newington Green. Al-

An 18th-century British writer and educator, Mary Wollstonecraft lived a short, bold life filled with interesting companions and revolutionary ideas. (Library of Congress)

though the school failed, Mary's experiences there formed the basis for the educational theories espoused in *Thoughts on the Education of Daughters* (1787) (Flexner 1972).

Wollstonecraft's friend Fanny Blood married, became pregnant, and moved to Lisbon, and Wollstonecraft went to Lisbon to assist her. However, both Fanny and her child died, and Wollstonecraft returned to England. She accepted a job as a governess in Ireland, where she wrote a novel, *Mary, a Fiction.* After she was dismissed from her position, she decided to pursue a literary vocation. Among her many writings was her *Vindication of the Rights of Men* (1790), a radical work replying to Burke's *Reflections on the Revolution in France.* In 1792, she published the even more radical feminist tract, *A Vindication of the Rights of Women*—a work that had a profound effect on the education of women. Enamored with the French Revolution, she went to France in 1792, where she met with other English supporters of the Revolution, including Tom Paine. In 1793 she published *An Historical and Moral View of the French Revolution,* the same year that she began an affair with a former officer in the American Revolutionary Army, Gilbert Imlay. This relationship was a disaster. Imlay abandoned her to care for their child, Fanny, who was born in 1794. Upon discovering Imlay's infidelity Wollstonecraft twice attempted suicide. She worked for the publisher Joseph Johnson, for whom she had previously worked, for a second time in 1796 in London, where she met William Godwin, whom she married after she became pregnant. Ten days after the birth of their daughter Mary (later Mary Shelley), she died of puerperal fever (Flexner 1972).

Wollstonecraft's arguments in the *Vindication of the Rights of Women* challenged Rousseau's ideas on female intellectual inferiority and claimed that women should have opportunities for equal education, employment (for single women), and an open relationship with men. As a polemicist, she focused the attention of her society on social and sexual inequalities; however, most people looked with horror at her ideas.

Erasmus Darwin (1731–1802)

In the 18th century, most girls were educated at home, but a smaller group attended boarding schools. Many of these schools stressed ladylike accomplishments such as drawing, music, and embroidery, whereas others included modern and classical languages. Science, however, was largely ignored in the curriculum. Two of the three influential writers on contemporary education (Hannah More and John Burton) did not include science when they discussed curricula. The third writer, Charles Darwin's grandfather, Erasmus Darwin, in his book *A Plan for the Conduct of Female Education in Boarding-Schools* (1797) included science and mathematics within the curriculum. He considered zoology, botany, chemistry, applied science, mathematics, and shorthand suitable subjects for young women to study (Ogilvie 1986).

Erasmus Darwin was a doctor by profession (George III tried to convince him to become his personal physician) and a scientific revolutionary, developing a concept of biological evolution 50 years before publication of *On the Origin of Species* by his grandson. He was also a social revolutionary, supporting both the American (he was a good friend of Benjamin Franklin) and French revolutions. During his lifetime he gained fame as a poet. A group of his friends including some of the more interesting people in England christened themselves the Lunar Society of Birmingham and met once a month during the time of the full moon. This group expanded and was influential in Darwin's life (King-Hele 1977).

Darwin's first wife was Mary Howard. After many years of ill health and a marriage of 13 years, she died leaving three sons, Charles, Erasmus, and Robert. Alcoholism was a factor in her death. After Mary's death Darwin had a liaison with a Miss Parker who bore him two daughters, Susan (b. 1772) and Mary (b. 1774). The two girls spent their childhood in Darwin's house and were treated like his children born in wedlock. He married Elizabeth Pole in 1781, who had three children of her own plus the illegitimate son of her dead husband. Erasmus and Elizabeth had six children together. With this large family it is not surprising that Erasmus Darwin was interested in educational reform (King-Hele 1977).

Unhappy with traditional education, Darwin decided to set up two of his 14 children (Susan and Mary Parker) in a school of their own where they could try out some of his ideas on education. In 1793, Darwin's friend Sir Brooke Boothby offered him a house at Ashbourne, 15 miles northwest of Derby. Darwin bought the house, which had previously been a pub, and converted it into a "ladies' seminary." The school opened in 1794. The first pupils in the school were his own children and the children of his friends. Before long, the school had 30 pupils and had gained a good reputation. Darwin's little book *A Plan for the Conduct of Female Education in Boarding-Schools* was written at the request of Susan and Mary when they set up the school. He opposed the idea that girls were unable to master difficult subjects. He begins the book by highlighting the importance of physical education for girls. Exercise and air should be emphasized; music and dancing are stressed too much in the usual seminary curriculum. Modern languages, not Latin and Greek, and the sciences should be a part of the program. His reforms covered most aspects of life in the school. This school was a success and represented an early step toward sexual equality. Although many of the leading families in the Midlands sent their children to Ashbourne, his innovations were not widely accepted elsewhere. Only two schools, Margaret Bryan's school at Blackheath and Mrs. Florian's at Epping Forest, followed his program (King-Hele 1977).

Women were increasingly involved in the scientific enterprise during the 18th century. Their participation covered a variety of fields, but few of them are well known. For example, the French anatomist, Marie Catherine Biheron (1719–1786) turned her artistic skills to preparing anatomical models from wax. The models were so realistic that a contemporary mentioned that all that they lacked was the odor of the original. Her models were used by midwives to teach their students. Another woman, Italian anatomist Anna Morandi Manzolini (1716–1774), was also an expert in making wax models. A skilled craftsperson, she did careful dissections that resulted in anatomical discoveries, including the termination of the oblique muscle of the eye.

An expert in the Linnean sytem, Jane Colden (1724–1766) was an American botanist whose work involved classification and cataloging of plants. She made large collections of plant specimens and exchanged them with correspondents. French illustrator Marie Anne Pierrette Paulze (1758–1836) was the wife of the chemist Antoine Laurent Lavoisier who used her artistic skills to make sketches of experiments and experimental apparatuses. She drew the diagrams for Lavoisier's treatise *The Elements of Chemistry* (1789) and her illustrations are scattered throughout his laboratory notebooks. She translated Richard Kirwan's work *Essay on Phlogiston* (1787) along with a commentary by her husband. After Antoine Lavoisier was executed, she married the physicist Sir Benjamin Thompson, Count Rumford. The marriage was not a success and the couple separated. German astronomer Maria Margaretha Winkelmann Kirch (1670–1720) was the wife of Gottfried Kirch. Marrying Kirch increased her chance to pursue her astronomical interests as her husband's assistant. The couple's children, Christfried (1694–1740), Christine (ca. 1696–1782), and Margaretha (b. ca. 1700) became astronomers as well (Ogilvie and Harvey 2000).

Scientific didactic writings were common during this century. For example, Priscilla (Bell) Wakefield (1751–1832) was a British writer for children on botany and natural history. In her botany book Wakefield used the correspondence between two teenage sisters to introduce children and young people to botany. She explained the Linnean classification system and presented basic essentials of plant morphology. Probably the most important didactic writing on natural philosophy was written by Jane Haldimand Marcet (1769–1858). With the encouragement of her physician husband, Alexander Marcet, she was able to indulge the taste for popular science that had developed during the 18th century. Her *Conversations on Chemistry* (1809) was enthusiastically received and was followed by other "Conversations" books. Michael Faraday (1791–1867) praised *Conversations on Chemistry* throughout his life and claimed that it introduced him to electrochemistry. It is evident that 18th-century women were delving into many branches of science. Maria Agnesi was one of the more important and better-known examples (Ogilvie and Harvey 2000).

Maria Gaetana Agnesi (1718–1799)

Maria Agnesi was a child prodigy whose father encouraged his gifted daughter in her intellectual pursuits. By the age of five she spoke French fluently and had an excellent command of Latin by age nine. When she was 11, her competence in Italian, Latin, French, Greek, Hebrew, German, and Spanish earned her the title of the "Seven-Tongued Orator." She gained a reputation as a scholar and debater, with disputations ranging over a wide subject area including logic, physics, mineralogy, chemistry, botany, zoology, and ontology. Her father took advantage of every opportunity to show off his brilliant daughter by inviting groups of people to their home for performances by Maria. In 1738, at one of these events, she defended 190 theses as a finale for her studies. A compilation of these arguments, published as the *Propositiones philosophicae,* did not contain any of her purely mathematical ideas. However, other documents indicate that she had an early interest in mathematics and that by the time she was 14 she was solving difficult problems in ballistics and geometry (*The Contest for Knowledge,* 2005).

Agnesi's physical and mental health suffered from the strain of always needing to appear perfect to her father. She pursued her studies with an obsessive zeal and in 1730 contracted a stubborn illness that her physicians blamed on an overabundance of study and a sedentary life. The prescribed treatment, dancing and horseback riding, was unsuccessful because she was unable to pursue even these activities with moderation. After the publication of *Propositiones philosophicae* (1738), she shocked her father and teachers by announcing that she planned to enter a convent. Her distressed father convinced her to reconsider. She promised him that she would not enter the order if he would agree to three conditions: she must be permitted to dress simply and modestly, to go to church whenever she wanted, and to abandon secular activities such as dancing and the theater (Frisi 1979).

No longer burdened with social obligations, Agnesi began a work on an integrated discussion of algebra and analysis, emphasizing the mathematical concepts that were new to her day. The resulting work was the two-volume *Instituzioni analitiche ad uso della gioventù,* dedicated to Empress Maria Theresa of Austria, who responded by sending her a diamond ring and a letter in a crystal case. She also received laudatory letters from scientists and mathematicians and was even praised by Pope Benedict XIV. He sent her a gold medal and a wreath containing precious stones set in gold. Even more unusual was her appointment, at Benedict's request, to the chair of mathematics and natural philosophy at the University of Bologna. Although she never taught at Bologna, Agnesi accepted the position as an honorary one (Anzoletti 1900; Ogilvie and Harvey 2000).

The praise that she received for this book would seem to have presaged a sterling career for this woman mathematician. However, her physical and mental health began to decline again and she turned away from mathematics and became even more involved with the Church. She reported that the doctors had forbidden her to study because of a persistent headache. Rather than pursuing mathematics, she spent much of her time working at the Parish hospital. When she was at home she separated herself from the rest of her large family, having persuaded her father to give her rooms in a remote part of the house. After her father's death in 1752, Agnesi increased her isolation from the world, refusing to correspond with or visit men from the academic world. Her life became completely focused on the Church. She gradually gave away her inheritance to the poor, including the ring given to her by Maria Theresa. When her own resources were exhausted she begged money from others to help the indigent. In 1783 she founded the Opera Pia Trivulzi, a charitable home for the aged in Milan and lived there for the rest of her life as its director. Shortly before her death she became obsessed with the state of her soul, worrying that in senility she might forget to say her prayers (Anzoletti 1900; Ogilvie and Harvey 2000).

Agnesi clearly had the aptitude for great achievements in mathematics. Her personal demons interfered with her attaining this promise. Her major mathematical publication, the *Instituzioni analitiche,* was written to provide a handy compilation for students, and its merit was recognized universally. Although it has sometimes been said that this book contained many new ideas, most critics suppose that while some of her methods were original, the work contains no original discoveries. Even the so-called Witch of Agnesi, the cubic curve with an equation of $x^2y = a^2 (a - y)$ usually credited to Agnesi, had actually been formulated by Pierre de Fermat (1601–1665) and the name *versiera* (meaning "versed sine curve," but also the Italian for witch) had been used for it by Guido Grandi in 1703. Maria Agnesi's reputation for brilliance convinced her contemporaries that women were capable of abstract thought (Ogilvie and Harvey 2000).

Laura Maria Caterina Bassi (1711–1778)

Like Maria Agnesi, Italian anatomist and natural philosopher Laura Bassi was a child prodigy. Bassi, too, was well educated by tutors and paraded before Italian intellectuals, family, and friends to show her mastery of the traditional scholastic disputational form. She became a popular curiosity, discussing and debating philosophical questions. Academic scientists were convinced by semi-public displays of her skills (some involving scientific experiments) to admit her to the Academy of Science (March 20, 1732). As did Agnesi, she benefited from Pope Benedict's patronage. While still Cardinal Lambertini, he arranged for her a public disputation in the Hall of the Elders. After her successful performance, Lambertini informed her that she would be eligible for a doctoral degree and a professorship at the university. She was awarded a doctorate after a second formal degree examination. The third disputation resulted in a professorship in philosophy, a handsome honorarium of 100 *scudi* annually, and a medal with her portrait and a motto. Later, Agnesi was awarded an honorary chair in mathematics even though she lacked a degree (Ogilvie and Harvey 2000).

On February 6, 1738, Bassi married Giuseppe Verati, a young physician. The couple had at least eight children (some sources say 12) and, as did Agnesi, Bassi suffered from poor health throughout much of her life.

Laura Bassi was important to the scientific culture of Enlightenment Italy; however, few of her works have survived. She published only four works during her lifetime and they tell us little about her experimental and pedagogical activities. Paula Findlen cites an additional work published posthumously that places Bassi as a centerpiece linking the university, the salon, and the urban patricians (Findlen 1991). Since the Bolognese professors hesitated to allow a woman to give regular lectures at the university, she did most of her experiments and teaching at home. Her family responsibilities also made this necessary. Supplying the apparatuses herself, she offered daily, well-attended classes in experimental physics. Charles de Brosses (1709–1777) and Joseph-Jérome Le Française de Lalande (1732–1807) attended her classes when they visited from France. According to de Brosses, she occasionally presented public lectures wearing her robe and ermine mantle.

Bassi had every advantage in her early life. She was brilliant, came from a wealthy family that provided her with the best possible education, and enjoyed the patronage of Cardinal Lambertini. However, even with this auspicious beginning, Bassi's letters imply that she encountered numerous professional obstacles because of her sex. One incident involved the nomination of 20 *pensionari* each year to give dissertations. Although Bassi was not selected, she devised a solution whereby she, as a member of the university, was selected as a supernumerary member.

Gabrielle-Émilie Le Tonnelier de Breteuil, Marquise du Châtelet (1706–1749)

Émilie du Châtelet at first glance might have appeared to be the kind of frivolous woman about whom both Rousseau and Wollstonecraft complained. However, in spite of her reputation among some circles as spoiled and self-indulgent, she was intelligent, insightful, and diligent. She was important in French intellectual history as both a popularizer and translator of Newton. Her role in the integration of Newtonian and Leibnizian ideas in dynamics is significant. Like Agnesi and Bassi, Émilie, the youngest child of Louis-Nicolas Le Tonnelier de Breteuil, was surrounded by the best available governesses and tutors. Her marriage to Florent-Claude, marquis du Châtelet, was turbulent. After the birth of her third and last child by du Châtelet when she was 27 years old, Emilie began to study mathematics seriously. She became reacquainted with Voltaire, who had been a guest in her family's household when she was a child, and her mathematical interests were tweaked again. After spending time in England, Voltaire returned to France saturated with the physics of Newton and the philosophy of John Locke. Official France was incensed by the ideas expressed in his newly completed *Lettres philosophiques* (1733) and banned the work. Madame du Châtelet not only shared Voltaire's interest in science but was able to provide him with a retreat from hostile officials. She and Voltaire retired to the tolerant Marquis du Châtelet's estate at Cirey. Since the marquis was often away, he allowed Voltaire to manage his estate in his absence. Occasionally, all three of them were in residence at the same time. Numerous petty intrigues, lawsuits, brilliant fêtes, and dramatic

productions characterized Émilie's 16 years at Cirey. Behind all of the frivol-
ity, however, was a background of study and creativity (Zinsser 2006; Ogilvie
and Harvey 2000).

The affection between Voltaire and du Châtelet remained after their physical relationship ended. They each fell in love with someone else. Émilie became pregnant by a young officer, Jean-François, marquis de Saint-Lambert,
and she and Voltaire conspired to get the Marquis du Châtelet to visit Cirey.
When he departed three weeks later he was convinced that he was to be a
father again. She spent her confinement in the palace of Stanislas I, former
king of Poland, at Lunéville where she worked frantically to complete her translation of Newton's *Principia* begun in 1744. Complications occurred after the
baby's birth and Mme. du Châtelet died. The baby died a few days later.

Although physics and mathematics were her major intellectual interests,
du Châtelet shared Voltaire's interests in metaphysics and ethics. In the first
half of the 18th century, thinkers considered the systems of Leibniz and Newton incompatible. Voltaire had introduced her to Newtonian thought. While
she remained impressed with Newton's analyses, she was less than satisfied
with his failure to relate theories in physics and metaphysics. After meeting
Samuel König, a disciple of Leibniz's interpreter Christian von Woff (1679–
1754), she accepted his suggestion that agreeing with Leibnizian metaphysics
did not preclude accepting Newtonian physical theories if one postulated
that these theories were only involved with the phenomena. This realization
led Mme. du Châtelet to accept a compromise between the two systems. She
published this compromise in a textbook for her son, the *Institutions de
physique,* published anonymously in 1740. König and du Châtelet quarreled
over this book, with König complaining that she had merely published a
collection of his essays. Du Châtelet's appeal to the secretary general of the
Académie des Sciences was futile. William H. Barber examined the question
of the originality of this book and concluded that although the first chapters
were rewritten after her conversion to Leibnizianism, she had not plagiarized
König's works (Besterman 1969).

Before du Châtelet became involved in the Newton-Leibniz debate, she produced an essay on the nature of fire in response to a contest announced by
the Académie des Sciences on that subject. Voltaire had arranged for a small
chemistry laboratory to be built at Cirey so that he could do research for the
prize. He was unaware that du Châtelet was also using the laboratory and
entering the competition. Neither won the prize but Voltaire arranged for their
essays to be published with those of the winners in 1739. By the time of publication, du Châtelet had modified her Newtonian ideas with Leibnizian ones.
Although she petitioned the Academy to published a revised version, it refused,
allowing her, however, to add a series of errata that reflected her new views.
A revised version was published in 1744.

Du Châtelet's work represents a solid contribution to the history of science. Her most important contributions were her translation of the *Principia* and the integration of Newtonian and Leibnizian mechanics (Besterman 1969).

Catherine Littlefield Greene (1755–1814)

Catherine Littlefield Greene is best known as a patron of inventor Eli Whitney. She may have provided design assistance to him, but the extent and nature of her contributions are not clear. Rhode Island–born Catherine was the third of five children of John and Phebe (Ray) Littlefield. Catherine married Nathanael Greene, who became a general under George Washington in 1774. She accompanied her husband during most of his campaigns including the Valley Forge winter of 1777–1778. Three of their five children were born during the Revolutionary War years. General Greene was rewarded for his service in the war with an estate on the Georgia side of the Savannah River. The family settled on a plantation on this estate, but Greene died less than a year after the move, leaving his wife with debts and five young children. Her husband was a close friend of the Marquis de Lafayette, and the marquis took their oldest son to Paris for his education.

Greene met Eli Whitney through Phineas Miller, formerly the children's tutor who became the manager of the plantation. Whitney was a recent Yale graduate and Miller had recruited him as a tutor for a neighboring family. This position fell through, but Catherine Greene asked him to stay on to devise a machine that would strip the seeds from short-staple cotton. This is the stage where the record becomes murky. Was Greene merely a patron and Whitney's muse, or did she, as is sometimes reported, invent the cotton gin herself? If the latter is correct, then she would have been one of the most important inventors of the 18th century. The reports that she is the inventor or the co-inventor of the cotton gin cannot be confirmed. Whitney did not credit Greene with the invention, but he did pay her royalties from her patent. These facts do not prove that her help went beyond suggestions. Autumn Stanley summarizes the three approaches to Greene's contributions to the invention of the cotton gin. The first view insists that Greene was the actual inventor and Whitney merely her model maker; the second that he was the actual inventor, but she solved a crucial problem with the first model; and finally that the story of Greene as the inventor is just fantasy. She concludes that we would not be correct in replacing Eli Whitney's name with Catherine Greene's as the inventor. Nevertheless, she probably did make the intellectual leap that caused Whitney to replace the traditional brushes with a bristled brush. Without her help, the traditional brushes would have continued to become hopelessly clogged and the resulting gin would not have been useful. Although there is some evidence for all of these positions, there may never be a definitive answer (Stanley 1995).

During the time that Whitney and Greene were working on the invention, Greene's eldest son, who had just returned from France, drowned in the Savannah River. Still, as soon as Whitney had finished a working model (1793), Greene publicized it among her neighbors. Before Whitney and his partner Phineas Miller could secure a patent and begin large-scale production, copies of the machine had already begun to appear. The patent litigation continued for over 10 years, and Greene committed all of her resources to the struggle. Eventually Whitney was able to reestablish title to the invention, but he did not profit from it.

Catherine Greene married Phineas Miller in 1796, but legal expenses had forced them to sell the plantation. They moved to another plantation on the Greene estate. Phineas Miller died of a fever in 1803 and Catherine also died of a fever in 1814 (Stanley 1995; Ogilvie and Harvey 2000).

Caroline Lucretia Herschel (1750–1848)

Caroline Herschel was born in Hanover, Germany, but moved to England to work with her organist and orchestra leader brother, William, as a vocal soloist. Caroline's father, Isaac, was an oboist with the Hanoverian Foot Guards. Although he lacked formal schooling himself, Isaac stressed the importance of education to his six children. Her mother, on the other hand, saw no advantage in education. Although she grudgingly accepted the fact that the four boys could receive an education, she was adamantly opposed to giving the same advantages to her two daughters. The older daughter (23 years older than Caroline) was content with her mother's values. To her mother's dismay, Caroline was more interested in joining the lively discussion of ideas by Isaac and her brothers than in honing her skills in embroidery and cooking. An admirer of astronomy, her father introduced her to the night skies.

From 1757 to 1760 Isaac Herschel was away from home with the Hanoverian army fighting the French. During this time Caroline's brother William emigrated to England to pursue a career in music. Left under the tutelage of her mother, Caroline was miserable. She spent much of her time knitting stockings for her brothers and father and writing letters for her illiterate mother. She also wrote letters for soldiers' wives. When Isaac Herschel returned in 1760 his health was broken; he died in 1767. William, her favorite brother, had become an organist and an orchestra leader in Bath. After hearing of Caroline's plight (she was treated as an unpaid servant by her mother and older brother), he brought her to England to train as a professional singer. Caroline left Hanover for England in 1772 (Ogilvie 1986).

England was a disappointment to Caroline, largely because William had little time to devote to her. Her English was almost nonexistent and she was dependent on her brother for everything. He served as her tutor in English, singing, arithmetic, and bookkeeping. One of her favorite occupations was to relax with William and talk about astronomy. Caroline had William's undivided attention at their 7:00 a.m. breakfast. He gave her lessons in mathematics, "Little Lessons for Lina." They progressed through algebra, geometry, and trigonometry. Caroline acquired sufficient skill in spherical trigonometry to put it to practical use but showed no interest in progressing further into abstract mathematics.

William's hobby, astronomy, occupied increasing amounts of his time. Interested in the little-studied stellar regions, he needed to equip himself with a proper telescope. He required Caroline's help in grinding and polishing mirrors, copying catalogues and tables, and providing assistance in a variety of tasks. She was not altogether pleased with these unasked-for jobs, which stole time from her music. The erstwhile musician, William Herschel, was catapulted into fame when he discovered what he first thought was a new comet. This "comet" turned out to be the seventh planet from the sun. Herschel first named the body *Georgium sidus* after George III of England, but it is now known as Uranus. This discovery netted him a stipend of 200 pounds a year, enabling him to give up his music; Caroline's short career as an oratorio singer also ended with the discovery of Uranus.

Her musical career at an end and encouraged by William, Caroline became more involved in astronomy. Using a telescope provided by William, Caroline swept the heavens looking for comets. She discovered three new nebulae in 1783. William provided her with a new telescope, her "Newtonian small sweeper," as a reward for her diligence. When William was home, Caroline had little opportunity to use her new telescope for his demands superseded her own work. She noted that she could not expect to find comets when she was sitting by his side recording his observations or running to the clock. Comets were not to be found in the part of the sky where she swept.

William occasionally was away from home, and it was at these times that Caroline had time to work on her own observations. She discovered eight comets over the period 1786–1797. She became popular with the astronomical community and her growing fame resulted in a salary of 50 pounds per year from the king in 1787 for her work as William's assistant.

Caroline Herschel's world was turned upside down in 1788 when William married Mary Pitt. She apparently wrote disparaging comments about Mary in her journal that she later regretted and destroyed all of the entries from this period.

Caroline Herschel's qualities of perseverance, accuracy, and attention to detail bore fruit when she was asked to update the star catalogue of the first

Astronomer Royal, John Flamsteed (1646–1719). Flamsteed's catalogue was difficult to use because the original observations were published in a volume separate from the catalogue. William Herschel had discovered numerous discrepancies between the catalogue and his own observations. Although he needed a cross-index to trace these differences, he was unwilling to devote the necessary time to the project. He asked Caroline to take on the grueling task of providing this index, which was published by the Royal Society in 1798. It contained an index to every observation of every star noted by Flamsteed. This publication included a list of over 560 stars that were not in the original catalogue as well as an enumeration of errata.

After years of failing health, William Herschel died in 1822. Concerned that England without William would be insufferable, Caroline decided to return to her native Hanover, a decision that she immediately regretted for she found that she had more friends in England than in Germany. John Herschel, William's son, was the only person who could compete with William for Caroline's affections. Caroline took a great interest in John's career as he progressed in astronomy, physics, and chemistry. She looked forward to his letters and visits from England and compiled a new catalogue of nebulae for his use. Arranged in zones, it amassed material from William's multivolume "Book of Sweeps" and "Catalogue of 2,500 Nebulae." Although the catalogue was indispensable to John's investigations, it was never published. The Royal Astronomical Society rewarded her for this work with a gold medal in 1828.

Caroline Herschel became a legend among her scientific contemporaries. Eminent scientists felt compelled to visit her when they were in Hanover. She and Mary Somerville became the first women to be awarded honorary memberships in the Royal Society. She was elected to membership in the Royal Irish Academy in 1838 and received a gold medal for her accomplishments in science from the King of Prussia. Herschel lived to the age of 97 years and 10 months and was buried with a lock of her beloved William's hair (Herschel 1876; Lubbock 1933; Ogilvie and Harvey 2000; Hoskin 2003).

Herschel made important contributions to observational astronomy, including the discovery of eight comets (five of which can be properly credited to her), and located several new nebulae and star clusters. Her contributions also included skilled, accurate transcription and reduction of astronomical data.

Mary Fairfax Greig Somerville (1780–1872)

Mary Fairfax, the fifth of seven children of Vice Admiral Sir William Fairfax and his second wife, Margaret Charters, was one of the most important women scientists of the late 18th and early 19th centuries. She spent her early childhood in a seaport town, Burntisland, across the Firth of Forth from Edinburgh.

Mary Somerville was one of the most important women scientists of the late 18th and early 19th centuries. (Library of Congress)

Perhaps her later curiosity about the natural world was spawned during this time when little attention was given to her education, and she spent much of her time freely exploring and roaming around the countryside. This idyllic existence did not last past her ninth year. When her vice admiral father returned to Scotland after one of his frequent long absences for sea duty, he was appalled by his daughter's ignorance. She was unable to write and read badly with a strong Scots accent. His first remedy was a forced reading program; however, he concluded that Mary needed more structured instruction and sent her to Miss Primrose's fashionable boarding school at Musselburgh. Utterly miserable during that year, she was made to wear a contraption that included steel stays so that she would be forced to sit up straight at her desk. According to Mary, she successfully avoided learning during that year. The next year, Mary's mother rented a small apartment for the winter in Edinburgh where Mary attended a writing school to improve her penmanship and learn basic arithmetic. By the time she returned to Burntisland she had acquired a taste for knowledge and enjoyed reading and studying French. She even taught herself some Greek and Latin. She also engaged in the accepted feminine accomplishments such as practicing the pianoforte, painting, doing needlework, cooking, and reading poetry. Her uncle, the clergyman and historian Thomas Somerville, was one of the few people who approved of her intellectual interests, even going so far as to read Virgil with her.

When 14-year-old Mary was reading a "lady's magazine" that included pictures of fashionable dresses as well as charades and puzzles, she encountered a problem containing x's and y's. When she inquired about their meaning, she was told that they were algebraic symbols. This different form of mathematics fascinated her, as did geometry. After overhearing her drawing teacher, Alexander Nasmyth, telling two women that to learn about perspective as well as astronomy and the mechanical sciences it was important to study Euclid's *Elements,* she was able to acquire copies of *Elements* and Bonnycastle's *Algebra* from her younger brother Henry's tutor. Mary's father, however, found algebra and geometry improper studies for a young woman and forbade her to study mathematics, forcing her to proceed in secret.

Mary Fairfax married Samuel Greig, a captain in the Russian navy and a cousin on her mother's side, who had a low opinion of the intellectual capabilities of women. Although Mary was unable to continue her mathematical studies during her three-year marriage, Captain Greig died leaving Mary with two small sons, one of whom died in infancy. She and her son returned to her parents' home in Edinburgh. Here the young widow became popular in intellectual circles, becoming friends with the liberal statesman and educational reformer, Henry Brougham (1778–1868); the scientist, John Playfair (1748–1810); and the author of the Waverley novels, Sir Walter Scott (1771–1832). During this time, she was tutored in mathematics by William Wallace, who later became professor of mathematics at the University of Edinburgh. She also struggled through Newton's *Principia.*

Her second marriage to her first cousin, William Somerville, was much more successful. Her army doctor husband approved of education for women and supported Mary in her mathematical and scientific work. In 1816 William was appointed to the army medical board and the couple moved to London. Mary flourished in this energizing intellectual and social climate. The Somervilles became popular hosts, associating with such scientists as John Herschel (1792–1871), Thomas Young (1773–1829), Roderick Murchison (1792–1871), Charles Babbage (1791–1871), and William Wollaston (1766–1828). During a tour of Europe in 1817 she met several other important scientists including Dominique Arago (1786–1835), Jean Baptiste Biot (1774–1862), Georges Cuvier (1769–1832), Joseph Gay-Lussac (1778–1850), Pierre Simon, Marquis de Laplace (1749–1827), and Augustin de Candolle (1778–1841).

It is amazing that Mary Somerville found the time to write, read, and experiment because of her varied domestic and social duties. As a mother of six, two by her first husband and four by the second, she was constantly involved in their care. Only one son, Woronzow Greig, and two daughters, Martha and Mary Somerville, survived to maturity. As was befitting a wife, when Mary's physician husband accepted a new post at the Royal Hospital in Chelsea, Mary followed him to this less convenient location on the outskirts of London. She found time to attend the theater and the opera and gave numerous dinner parties. In spite of her hectic life, she produced a series of works on astronomy, physics, mathematics, chemistry, and geography that earned her the respect of her contemporary scientists.

Mary was self-conscious about her scientific abilities. Her first work was presented to the Royal Society by her husband in 1826 and published in the *Philosophical Transactions*. Even though this work "On the Magnetizing Power of the More Refrangible Solar Rays" was well received, she was diffident when Henry Brougham asked her to provide an English version of Laplace's *Mécanique céleste* for the library of his Society for the Diffusion of Useful Knowledge. The resulting *The Mechanism of the Heavens* (1831) was an immediate success and served as a textbook for almost 100 years. Its reception encouraged her to publish other works of scientific exposition including *On the Connexion of the Physical Sciences* (1834) and an article on comets in the *Quarterly Review* (December 1835), *Physical Geography* (1848), and *On Molecular and Microscopic Science* (1869). She also wrote two more papers on the results of her experiments with light rays (1836 and 1845).

The Somervilles moved to Italy in 1838 for William Somerville's health. Mary outlived most of her friends and relatives—her husband died in 1860 and her son in 1865. She remained active intellectually, and when she was 92 years old in 1872 wrote that although she was very deaf and her memory for ordinary events was failing she was still able to read books on higher algebra for four or five hours and could even solve mathematical problems. She was engrossed in a study of two recent mathematical texts, William Hamilton's *Lectures on Quaternions* and Benjamin Peirce's *Linear Associative Algebra*, at the time of her death.

In spite of her insistence that she lacked scientific originality, her ability to comprehend and synthesize the work of her contemporaries made her a very important contributor to the scientific enterprise. She made science understandable to both general readers and more advanced students. Somerville's pleasant personality made her a favorite of her scientific associates, and they gladly critiqued her work and happily supplied her with new information. (*See also* Mathematics; The 19th Century; Physics/Astronomy)

References and Further Reading

Anzoletti, Luisa. *Maria Gaetana Agnesi*. Milan: L. F. Cogliati, 1900.

Besterman, Theodore. *Voltaire*. New York: Harcourt Brace and World, 1969.

The Contest for Knowledge: Debates over Women's Learning in Eighteenth-Century Italy. Maria Gaetana Agnesit and the Accademia de' ricovrati. Edited and translated by Rebecca Messbarger and Paula Findlen. Chicago: University of Chicago Press, 2005.

Damrosch, Leo. *Jean-Jacques Rousseau*. Boston: Houghton Mifflin, 2005.

Findlen, Paula. "Science as a Career in Enlightenment Italy: The Strategies of Laura Bassi." *Isis* 82 (1991): 510–519.

Flexner, Eleanor. *Mary Wollstonecraft*. Baltimore: Penguin Biijsm, 1972.

Frisi, Antonio Francesco. *Elogio storico di Maria Gaetana Agnesi, Milanese. Dell'instituto delle scienze, e lettrice onoraria di matematiche nella Università di Bologna*. Milan: Giuseppe Galeazzi, 1979.

Herschel, Mary Cornwallis. *Memoir and Correspondence of Caroline Herschel*. New York: Appleton, 1876.

Hoskin, Michael, ed. *Caroline Herschel's Autobiographies*. Cambridge: Science History Publications, 2003.

King-Hele, Desmond. *Doctor of Revolution. The Life and Genius of Erasmus Darwin*. London: Faber and Faber, 1977.

Lubbock, Constance A. *The Herschel Chronicle: The Life-Story of William Herschel and His Sister Caroline Herschel*. Cambridge: Cambridge University Press, 1933.

Neeley, Kathryn A. *Mary Somerville. Science, Illumination, and the Female Mind*. Cambridge: Cambridge University Press, 2001.

Ogilvie, Marilyn Bailey. *Women in Science. Antiquity through the Nineteenth Century. A Biographical Dictionary with Annotated Bibliography*. Cambridge, MA: MIT Press, 1986.

Ogilvie, Marilyn Bailey, and Joy Harvey, eds. *The Biographical Dictionary of Women in Science. Pioneering Lives from Ancient Times to the Mid-20th Century*. New York: Routledge, 2000.

Rousseau, Jean Jacques. *Emile or On Education*. Translated by Allan Bloom. New York: Basic Books, 1979.

Stanley, Autumn. *Mothers and Daughters of Invention: Notes for a Revised History of Technology*. New Brunswick, NJ: Rutgers University Press, 1995.

Wollstonecraft, Mary. *Letters Written during a Short Residence in Sweden, Norway, and Denmark*. London: J. Johnson, 1796.

Zinsser, Judith P. *La Dame d'Esprit. A Biography of the Marquise Du Châtelet*. New York: Viking, 2006.

The 19th Century

Narin Hassan

The Industrial Revolution, the expansion of empire and national progress, and the rise of institutions were conditions that made the 19th century a period of immense ideological, social, and cultural change. The Industrial Revolution impacted not only the kinds of work people did but also where and how they did it. The transformation of the landscape; the shift to an urban from a largely agrarian culture; and the rise of a new, largely professional middle class created sharper divisions between the public and private realms that affected gender roles significantly since women were largely responsible for maintaining domestic harmony in an increasingly active, male-dominated public world. This division of public and private made it a more challenging time for women to enter the world of science since the ideals of femininity often required women play the role of wife and mother during this time when the family was becoming restructured as a symbol of middle-class life. Thus, while science was becoming more institutionalized and connected to largely male-dominated universities and professional societies, domestic roles were ascribed to women, and family life was itself increasingly socially structured and monitored.

Within this period of rapid growth and change, the nature and representation of scientific work was shifting. Formerly, science had been a domain open to the privileged "gentlemen of science," but the popularization of science and the growth of new fields began to develop a broader and more complex population of scientists; increased cultural interest in science meant that new debates about what constituted science and what it meant to be a scientist were being heard. During this period, the growth and expansion of the publishing industry encouraged the production and dissemination of a range of new written documents. The industrial revolution and progress in paper technology, printing, and marketing allowed for a new mass market of texts and a much broader literate audience. Conduct manuals, medical guides, scientific treatises, garden magazines, novels, and newspapers flooded the marketplace and presented the increasing numbers of literate individuals with a range of material both representing and constructing new images of science and technology. Newspapers and weekly journals allowed individuals to learn about the global, political, social, and cultural changes taking place, and these textual forms meant that scientific knowledge could be distributed much more widely and rapidly. Thus, scientific authority progressed with the rise of a broader reading culture. With the increased urbanization and industrialization that took place in the 19th century, reading became a central mode by which a rising middle class could gain knowledge, and books shaped 19th-century understanding of the role of the individual in an increasingly fast-paced, global, and more modern world.

The growth in publishing also resulted in couplings of science and literature; a range of 19th-century texts engaged questions about the nature of scientific work, and as the century progressed, novels not only represented the shaping of new scientific fields but also took on a more scientific form through their intensely empirical and realist attention to detail and use of scientific metaphor. Such examples include George Eliot's *Middlemarch* (1871), a novel tracing the career of an ambitious doctor that reveals shifts in the field of medicine, and Thomas Hardy's *Two on a Tower* (1882), which features a central character with a passion for astronomy.

The growth of new scientific disciplines and specializations, and of related disciplines including anthropology and sociology, had a cultural impact on gender roles. Science served as a tool to both manipulate and identify roles for men and women, and as scientific discourse gained influence within the period, it merged with larger political, social, and cultural dialogues surrounding marriage, education, women's work, and appropriate behaviors for men and women. What was termed in the 19th century "The Woman Question"—a range of debates, representations, and concerns that dominated discussions of gender within the period—intersected quite often with the scientific and medical knowledge that flourished during this time. Within this exciting culture of change and newness, women both gained and struggled; progress brought new opportunities for women on the one hand and stifled them further on the other. Scientific discourses provided multiple ways to imagine women and men, but with the growing institutionalized nature of fields like medicine and with stronger divisions between the public and private realms, women were often relegated to the private sphere as the domestic ideal of *angel in the house*. This term, which appeared initially in a British poem by Coventry Patmore, became a common phrase describing the unrealistic and often unattainable ideal for 19th-century women.

The Early to Mid-19th Century: Romantic Ideals, Nature, and the Growth of Scientific Inquiry

In Western Europe, a rising intellectual and philosophical movement termed Romanticism originated in the 19th century as a countermovement to the

Enlightenment. Understanding nature and recognizing the human relation-ship to nature were central to this movement; in this way, Romanticism chal-lenged a more mechanical approach to science and embraced an immersion in the understanding of the natural world as the path to scientific knowledge. Central figures of this period included Friedrich Schelling (1775–1844), who in *Naturphilosophie* first defined a Romantic conception of science as the union of man with nature, and Jean Baptiste Lamark (1744–1829), who began to es-tablish the science of biology as an independent discipline. Lamarck studied botany and medicine and was one of the early figures of the period to de-velop evolutionary theories. His *Philosophy Zoologique,* published in 1809, examined the gradual change of organisms as they began to interact with and become adapted to their environments; Lamarck set forth the idea that or-ganisms slowly but constantly "improved" from one generation to the next. While Lamarck was establishing this evolutionary theory in France, Erasmus Darwin (Charles Darwin's grandfather) was exploring similar work in England and had already published his first formal theory, *Zoonomia, or, the Laws of Organic Life* in 1794–1796. The interests of Romantic intellectuals in the sci-ence of nature allowed for the fields of cosmology, geology, mineralogy, and biology to emerge and flourish during this period.

This era of Romantic inquiry also allowed the birth of what we would now consider pseudo-sciences, including, for example, phrenology and physiog-nomy. These popular fields often opened up questions about what actually constituted science, since they became quickly popular and accessible to the public. Further, interest in the nature and origins of life produced popu-lar literary works that examined the relationship of scientific discovery to humanity. The most notable of these, written by Mary Shelley (1797–1851), is *Frankenstein* (1818), a work that stresses the importance of human respon-sibility in light of scientific progress and raises questions about the relation-ship of science to religion. Although Shelley was not trained as a scientist herself, her novel addressed natural philosophy and the romantic interest in chemistry, electricity, and anatomy. Other women writers of the period who engaged with new scientific ideas of the period were Jane Loudon (1807–1858), the wife of John Claudius Loudon who was a well-known botanist and gardener. Jane Loudon became a well-known naturalist, illustrator, and writer herself, producing botanical manuals and gardening guides for women. In her popular narrative, *The Young Naturalist's Journey* (1840), a fictional young girl and her mother explore the British Isles discovering and learning about exotic animals. Barbara T. Gates has argued that through this narrative, Loudon gave readers an opportunity to learn the thrills of natural history, dis-cover wider worlds, and examine animal adaptation. Loudon also produced an early science fiction novel, *The Mummy,* which explored new scientific and technological ideas by representing the reanimation of a mummy with a gal-vanic battery. Set in the year 2126, Loudon's novel introduced readers to an

Illustration of Echinacea *by Jane Loudon, from* The Ladies' Flower-Garden of Ornamental Perennials*, 1844.* (The LuEsther T. Mertz Library, NYBG/Art Resource)

imaginary future filled with the wonders of expanding technology. While these scientific ideas colored Loudon's fictional work, she was also recognized for her authoritative botanical treatises that included *Ladies Flower Garden of Ornamental Annuals* (1840) and *British Wild Flowers* (1846).

A number of political revolutions marked the rise of the Romantic period. The French and American revolutions of the late 18th century produced philosophical works that increasingly examined the "rights" of people and questioned the "natural" generational shifts of political power within monastic systems. Thus, political and social writers were, like scientists, interested in interrogating the natural order of things. Questions surrounding the rights of individuals, particularly women, within this new Romantic era had been raised by figures including Mary Wollstonecraft and William Godwin (who were Mary Shelley's parents). Wollstonecraft's *A Vindication of the Rights of Women,* which had been published in 1792, questioned the limitations of women and argued that women were not naturally inferior to men but simply lacked the education and resources available to men.

By the mid-19th century, John Stuart Mill, among others, built on the ideas initiated by figures like Wollstonecraft to argue that gender was largely a social category, not a biological one. In his *Subjection of Women* (1869), Mill claimed: "what is now considered the nature of women is an eminently artificial thing"—nurture shaped character more than nature ever could (148). This was a sharp challenge to 19th-century patriarchal society, and Mill's argument spurred responses by scientists, most notably Charles Darwin (1809–1882). At the time, Darwin was at work on *The Descent of Man* (1871), which emphasized that male and female nature was rooted in biology. Darwin emerged as one of the most influential scientists of the period, shaping the field of science to engage the question of "man's place in nature," which involved establishing hierarchies in nature based on both gender and racial categories. Natural and sexual selection were central to Darwin's understanding of evolution. Darwin, born in Shrewsbury, Shropshire, England, was one of six children and the son of a wealthy doctor and financier. He became interested in natural history when he went to medical school in Edinburgh, but instead of following a traditional path of medical education, he became involved with the Plinian society, a student group that studied the natural history of figures like Lamarck and Erasmus Darwin. Darwin spent some time at a clergymen's college but eventually gained a position as an unpaid naturalist on the HMS *Beagle* that was beginning an expedition to South America. It was during this five-year voyage that Darwin began to examine the geological features, animals, and peoples he encountered during the voyage, and his notes from this study (from 1831 to 1836) formed his published journal, *The Voyage of the Beagle*. His contact with native peoples aroused interest in both race and sex and helped shape the ideas surrounding evolution and sexual difference that appeared in his later work, *Descent of Man*. The most popular of Darwin's work alluding to evolution, and the publication that put him in the spotlight as a premier scientist of his age, was *On the Origin of Species by Means of Natural Selection, or the Preservation of Favoured Races in the Struggle for Life* (published in 1859 and abbreviated as *The Origin of Species*). This publication was popular not only with the scientific community but with the public as well, and it sparked a range of debates and dialogues surrounding the nature of man. It impacted Victorian popular social, cultural, and scientific ideas and placed scientific writing alongside other popular texts and discourses. Other prominent figures who addressed the questions of evolution and inheritance and dealt with the field of natural history during this time included Alfred Russell Wallace (1823–1913) in England and the German-born Gregor Johann Mendel (1822–1884).

While Darwin's scientific texts emerged as some of the most influential and debated of this age, the question of woman's nature was explored in a number of textual forms. The domestic manual, or guide to household management, became a popular form engaging questions of gender, as did the health guide, which often traced the cycles and natures of male and female bodies. Manuals for women increasingly focused on the phases of femininity based on biology. For example, Albert Naphey's *Phases of Womanhood* established, as the title suggests, femininity through cycles of puberty and adolescence, marriage and motherhood, and menopause. Thus, through such manuals, the female body was represented more and more through biological norms and conditions such as motherhood. The increasingly frantic nature of the public world (associated with masculinity) was then imagined to be calmed and tended by a private, domestic world relegated to women. This division of spheres that marked much of the culture of mid-19th-century Western Europe and the United States was upheld through a number of literary and social guides that established women as "angels in the house."

Gender and the Rise of Professional Medicine: Nursing and the Pioneers of Female Medical Education

In this environment, women with ambition had to seek avenues to challenge the idea that femininity was best suited for domesticity. They sought to build occupations for women highlighting women's roles as caregivers that would make them suitable for certain professions. Many women became involved in charity and reform work that involved helping the poor in the growing slums or aiding the victims of disease outbreaks. In the mid-19th century, although respectable categories of work outside the home were almost non-existent for middle- and upper-class women (women of these classes who needed to work would often gain positions as governesses and teachers), one figure who clearly built a new field based on natural "feminine" modes was Florence Nightingale (1820–1910). Born into a well-connected and wealthy family, Nightingale was inspired to pursue nursing by what she called a "divine calling"; although she was driven by a religious passion to help others, her parents forbade her to pursue nursing and instead encouraged her to seek marriage and build a family. Resistant to this plan, Nightingale announced that she would enter nursing in 1845—a time when the field was filled with poorer women and in need of reform. Nightingale received her nursing training in Germany and then returned to London where she worked at the Institute for the Care of Sick Gentlewomen; she received some financial support from her family during this time that allowed her to live comfortably and decline proposals for marriage, which she believed would interfere with her work and pursuit of a career in nursing.

Nightingale redefined the field of nursing and gained much recognition for her work during the Crimean War when she worked with a staff of volunteer nurses and cared for wounded soldiers under horrific conditions. It was here that Nightingale began to establish her ideas about sanitation and ventilation that would mark a huge transformation in nursing. She recognized that poor ventilation in hospitals, generally poor living conditions, and the lack of sanitary supplies and foods for soldiers impacted mortality rates. When Nightingale returned to Britain she contributed to the Royal Commission on the

Health of the Army and was recognized for her work with the development of a Nightingale Fund to support the training of nurses. Her biographer, Cecil Woodham-Smith (1951), claims that her 1859 book outlining the importance of higher standards of cleanliness and sanitation, *Notes on Hospitals,* "was a success; it went into three editions, and after its publication she was constantly asked for advice on Hospital Construction" (226).

Nightingale built a legacy around her work in nursing—she reshaped what had been a largely disorganized and unrecognized field to a more professional and respectable one—but she also impacted the debates surrounding women's work in general. Along with her *Notes on Nursing* (1860), her treatise on the methodologies of the field that highlighted the importance of sanitation and ventilation, Nightingale also published *Cassandra,* which highlighted the constraints many women felt because of the "separate spheres" that relegated women to be domestic angels. She argued that such confinement resulted in helplessness, illness, and invalidism. Further, Nightingale's own position as traveler and nurse (she visited not only Germany and the Crimea but also Egypt, publishing her journal entries and letters about this Middle Eastern country) provided women a model of female mobility that challenged the domestic ideal for women in the period.

While the emergence of figures like Florence Nightingale impacted the interest of women in medical fields, the area of medicine itself was being reshaped during this time to establish the doctor as the authoritative voice in medicine and the hospital as the center for medical care. This new medical model was established in France, which became a center for medical education and patient care based on a clinical, administrative model. John Harley Warner and others have shown the importance of Paris in attracting doctors and medical students from the United States and European nations during this period; Paris emerged as an exciting and dynamic center for medicine. A number of shifts occurred during the 19th century that professionalized medicine and the place of doctors in it. Emerging specializations, including gynecology, obstetrics, and surgery, created new standards for care; new technological tools and instruments, such as the speculum, developed and gained popularity; new discoveries, such as chloroform and anesthesia, changed the nature of medical care; and an increasing number of medical societies and associations—populated largely by men—became venues where medical ideas were shared and shaped. A number of scholars, including Ornella Moscucci, Barbara Ehrenreich, Dierdre English, and G. J. Barker Benfield, have shown how the rise of specializations like gynecology and obstetrics impacted not only medical practice but also the culture of women's health and reproduction. In the past, midwives had been the primary caregivers of women and dealt with issues surrounding pregnancy in the home—largely passing on knowledge through practice and oral tradition. In the 19th century, however, such events in women's lives were increasingly managed and monitored by doctors; knowledge was received in medical institutions and distributed through written medical manuals. Further, a shift occurred so that the emphasis on women's health was not through touch and interaction (a model that dominated traditional midwifery) but through an increasing focus on the visual and observational nature of scientific inquiry.

In the United States, one of the central figures responsible for shaping the field of gynecology and obstetrics was J. Marion Sims (1813–1883). Born in South Carolina, Sims built his career in Alabama through a range of innovative surgeries and tools that he developed through work with his patients, many of whom were slave women and Irish women who were operated on in his backyard without their consent. As Terri Kapsalis and other critics have noted, Sims's legacy is thus intertwined with the legacy of racism and slavery. Sims earned the title Father of Gynecology through his invention of the speculum, a tool he developed through his experimental surgical procedures. He moved to New York in 1853 and established the first hospital for women in the United States.

Sims gained the attention of a then-emerging woman doctor, Elizabeth Blackwell (1821–1910). In a letter to her sister, she wrote that she wished to learn more about the special treatments developed by Marion Sims and hoped he would help her pursue work in the field of gynecology and obstetrics: "He seems to be in favour of women studying medicine. I think I shall help him in any way I can" (Blackwell 1895, 201). Blackwell was the first woman to receive a medical degree in the United States in 1849 from Geneva Medical College in New York State. She was born in Bristol, England, and her family moved to the United States when she was a child. She became interested in medical education, but since no models existed for women to pursue such a field, she convinced family friends who were physicians to allow her to read with them. She applied to several medical schools and gained admission to Geneva Medical College in 1847 after the faculty asked the all-male student body to vote on her admission. They voted "yes" largely as a joke, thinking it was impossible that she would really attend, but she received her M.D. degree two years later. Blackwell also studied and worked in clinics in Paris and London, and then returned to New York where initially she struggled to build a practice. Her efforts to expand female medical education and support women's health were achieved when she, with the help of her sister Emily Blackwell, established the New York Infirmary for Women and Children in 1857. The institution included a medical college for women and provided practical training for its students through the infirmary. Blackwell influenced other new female physicians, including Maria Zakrzewska (1829–1902), who helped her organize and build the New York Infirmary. Born in Berlin, Zakrzewska emigrated to the United States in the 1850s. She had already received practical training as a midwife—a field in which her mother was trained—and wanted to pursue medical training. She was admitted to Cleveland's Western Reserve College in 1854. After graduating and working with Blackwell in New York, she eventually gained a position as professor of obstetrics at New England Medical College.

While these and other women in the United States were struggling to establish themselves in the male-dominated field of medicine, they had more freedoms and opportunities than their counterparts in Britain; it would take another decade, and much debate, before women in Britain could gain admission to medical programs. Prior to the 1860s, British women, restricted from medical education in England, traveled to the United States or France to study and practice. In 1865, Elizabeth Garrett Anderson (1836–1917) passed the examination of the Society of Apothecaries and became a central figure in the move toward women's admission to medical programs. Garrett Anderson, the sister of Millicent Fawcett (an important figure in the British suffragette movement), was refused admission to medical schools and not allowed to sit for medical examinations after private study, but she was able to gain a license for apothecaries that placed her on a medical register. In 1873 she gained membership in the British Medical Association. She worked tirelessly to develop medical programs for women and build hospitals in London. Like her sister, Garrett Anderson was active in the suffragette movement and also a lively contributor to dialogues surrounding female education.

The *Fortnightly Review* of 1874 records a debate between Henry Maudsley of the University College of London and Elizabeth Garrett Anderson that exemplifies arguments both for and against the education of female doctors. This pivotal debate over medical education reveals Victorian engagement with categories of biological difference and displays the perplexity and instability with which the categories were sustained. Garrett provided published responses to Maudsley's claim that women were biologically unfit for medical work and needed to devote their energies to maternity. Several other medical journals of the period were questioning the role of women in medicine and focused largely on popular ideas regarding femininity to argue that medicine was a male field. These anxieties were not limited to Britain; Regina Morantz-Sanchez (1987) has pointed out that throughout the 1850s the *Boston Medical and Surgical Journal* published articles opposing the entrance of women into the profession. Quoting from the journal, she describes the belief that women's "physiological condition, during a portion of every month, disqualifies them for such grave responsibilities" of medical work (58).

Thus, although women had been traditionally viewed as healers and commonly prepared home-based remedies, their professional entry into medicine was viewed as unnatural and unnecessary. Although, as Catherine Judd (1998) has argued, in England and the United States, "hygiene was symbolically, and often literally, a female province," medicine assumed an increasingly distinct, less domestic, and more administrative space during the 19th century (20). The rise of hospital-based care, available even for the middle classes, prompted the shift of medical practice from domestic to public spaces. As medicine gained institutional authority during this period, it incorporated rigid domestic ideologies and was associated with masculinity in a number of ways. The association of medical practice with "rational," scientific ideas and the growth in various forms of experimentation increasingly separated professional medical practice from popular home-based notions of healing. Large anatomical theaters, the dominant sites for medical training with their structure as public performance spaces, were seen as potentially dangerous and improper spaces for female viewers, as was the work of surgery and the structure of medical knowledge with its increased focus on concepts of vision and experimentation. Medical discourses and practices often positioned the male doctor as viewer and female patient as the subject of study.

Within this period of struggle, Sophia Jex-Blake (1840–1930) emerged as a pioneer. Influenced by Elizabeth Garrett Anderson and motivated by her vocal and practical efforts at reform, Jex-Blake was accepted into the University of Edinburgh as part of a small group of women who formed the first generation of women seeking medical degrees. They were consequently denied actual degrees and offered "certificates of proficiency." Jex-Blake then received her medical degree in Berne and became licensed through the College of Physicians in Ireland (Porter 1999, 358). Eventually, the Medical Act of 1876 enabled women to receive medical licenses and facilitated the admission of women to the University of London. Edith Petchey was another woman doctor who studied with Jex-Blake in Edinburgh; she eventually traveled overseas to practice medicine and opened one of the first women's hospitals in India.

Venturing abroad became increasingly common for women seeking professional opportunities. For women who were eventually allowed to receive medical training, one of the biggest obstacles was the lack of clinical training. It became easier for women to gain admission to programs, study from medical textbooks, and sit for various examinations, but they lacked practical medical interaction with actual patients because of continued anxieties about women as practicing physicians. The absence of clinical study in Britain prompted women to see foreign countries as offering an access to clinical practice and opportunities to enjoy more professional freedoms than they would have at home. In this age of imperial expansion, women could serve larger colonial interests and form specific relations with native subjects that were not possible for male doctors because of cultural and/or religious traditions that often segregated men from women. Thus, the 19th century, with its technological advancements, improvements in travel, and imperial interests, opened up opportunities for women to seek a wider sphere for their medical ambitions.

Mary Scharlieb (1845–1930) was one of the first women to take advantage of her role outside Britain and impact women's health in India. She was admitted to the Madras Medical College in India—the first female allowed to do so—and then, upon her return to England in 1878, she studied at Elizabeth Garrett Anderson's new London School of Medicine for Women. Scharlieb was especially interested in the field of gynecology because native women in India often refused to be seen by male doctors. She was encouraged by Queen Victoria to continue her involvement in Indian health care for women, and she became active in the development of women's clinics and hospitals in India. Scharlieb developed a successful practice in London and also gained a position as a chair of gynecology and midwifery in the Medical School. She produced a number of publications including *The Seven Ages of Woman* (1915) and *Motherhood and Race Regeneration* (1912); the latter presented her ideas about eugenics and population control.

Gender and Nature: Botany, Geology, and Natural History

In the case of nursing and medical care, women could argue that their roles as caregivers within domestic realms provided the ideal background for pursuing medical work. In other areas of science, women needed to articulate ways that scientific knowledge was compatible with the ideals of femininity. One area where women progressed during the 19th century was scientific botanical culture. Once again, the expansion of empires and of a more modern, global culture encouraged this field of scientific inquiry; increased travel and colonial expansion allowed scientific specimens from all over the world to be brought into Europe and the United States. Through their exhibition, individuals could see, read about, and interact with the wonders of nature.

The fields of botany and geology grew as sciences in the 19th century, and while scientific expeditions pursued by men provided the groundwork, women's interest in geography and natural history also flourished closer to home. Thus, the gardening manuals produced by women like Jane Loudon enjoyed popular readership, and since activities like gardening could be pursued at home, many women became amateur botanists while others were recognized for their work in this realm. Botany became viewed as a respectable pastime for women. Some of the notable botanists of the 19th century include Anne Pratt (1806–1893). She authored the five-volume *Flowering Plants and Ferns of Great Britain* (1889) and several botanical books for women including *Wild Flowers* (1852). Thus, Pratt, like the well-known children's writer Beatrix Potter, combined her knowledge of flora and fauna with the publication of

books for children—incorporating the scientific with the domestic and introducing natural history in children's education.

While the study of botany and the practice of botanical illustration became
an increasingly popular and respectable pastime for many women, it also encouraged some to expand their interests to a more global pursuit of scientific
knowledge. Going beyond the borders of home, women could often establish themselves as European authorities in native lands—this way they gained
the respect often afforded exclusively to men. Marianne North (1830–1890)
is the best-known British woman who traveled the world extensively to discover plants and paint them. Her autobiography, *Recollections of a Happy
Life,* reveals how escape from the confines of Europe provided her with the
energy and freedom to research flora and fauna and record them through her
art. Although North was not trained as a botanist, she formed friendships with
figures including Charles Darwin, and her detailed, highly realistic, and scientifically accurate paintings contributed to readers' understanding of the natural world around the globe. North's travels took her to Java, Borneo, Brazil,
South Africa, the United States, India (where she spent a full year), and Australia and New Zealand (at Darwin's suggestion).

Illustrations were also crucial in the books produced by Charles Lyell
(1797–1875), whose *Principles of Geology* (1830–1833) helped to establish
him as the premier British geologist of his time. Lyell was a contemporary of
Charles Darwin and supported much of his work. As Barbara Gates (1998)
has noted, "like Darwin's, Lyell's work was highly visual, but its sights were
set less on detail and more on the larger picture. Lyell liked to envision the
scope of things, to play with images that worked as museum-like panoramas
or cross sections, sending the reader's eye back through time or downward
through the unseeable layers of the earth's crust" (53). Readers, then, were
observers of Lyell's broad scientific vision of geology that most importantly
set forth his notion of Uniformitarianism—the idea that the shape of the earth
was formed by forces slowly over time—unlike the biblical idea of earth
coming to being through sudden, cataclysmic events. His secretary, Arabella
Buckley (1840–1929), became well known for her work after Lyell's death in
1875. She wrote the scientific entries about him in the *Encyclopedia Britan-
nica* and published books including *A Short History of Natural Science* (1876)
and *The Fairy Land of Science* (1879) in which she instructs children in the
wonders of science (Gates 1998, 51–52).

Eleanor Anne Ormerod (1828–1901) was another British woman enticed by
the wonders of nature. She was born in Sedbury Park, Gloucestershire, on
an estate that gave her ample opportunity to nurture her interests in insect
life. In 1868, when the Royal Horticultural Society was collecting insects from
her farm, she became involved with the project and began writing pamphlets
on pests and injurious insects. Her work captured attention from both the Royal

Horticultural Society (she earned the Flora medal) and the Royal Agricultural Society. She was appointed a consulting etymologist to the latter and eventually built a career around lecturing and writing, Her published works include *The Injurious Insects of South Africa* (which gained her acclaim outside England) and *Handbook of Insects Injurious to Orchard and Bush Fruits* (1898).

Women in the Fields of Astronomy and Mathematics

While medical work and natural history dominated the areas in which women pursued scientific interests, two important figures emerged in the expanding fields of astronomy and mathematics: Maria Mitchell (1818–1889) and Sofia Kovalesky (1850–1891). Maria Mitchell was the first American woman elected to the American Academy of Arts and Sciences, the first woman member of the American Association for the Advancement of Science, and the first woman professor of astronomy. As these honors reveal, she managed to cross the barriers that often hindered women from entering the professional institutions of science in the 19th-century United States, becoming a member of numerous male societies. Part of Mitchell's introduction to scientific education was through her father, William Mitchell, who was an active observer and calculator in Nantucket and who introduced her to astronomers at Harvard. Mitchell received recognition for her work quite early in life; in 1848, she was cited by Lucretia Mott at the Seneca Falls Women's Rights Convention—this was soon after she had discovered a comet in 1847. Of this discovery, Sally Gregory Kohlstedt (1987) has noted, "her calculations of its exact position at the time of discovery brought her a gold medal from the King of Denmark and led to her membership in the American Society of Art and Science 'in spite of being a woman'" (130). Mitchell believed that scientific education was central for women and gained a position at Vassar where she worked to advance women's higher education and build opportunities for women in science.

Sofia Kovalesky was born in Moscow, Russia, and was educated in Berlin, Germany. She was the first major Russian female mathematician and established an international reputation, winning several awards and honors. Among these were the Prix Bordin of the French Academy of Sciences, the Oscar Prize of the Swedish Academy of Sciences, and an academic position at Stockholm University in Sweden, where she became the chair of her department. She grew up at a time when social and political reform in Russia opened up questions of equality and produced a range of efforts to build women's rights. This, along with family support (her father provided her with a mathematics tutor) for her ambitions, allowed her to develop her natural talent for mathematics and the natural sciences to her full potential. She received her Ph.D. at the University of Goettingen in 1874, and her research involved applying

*Maria Mitchell (seated) and Mary Whit-
ney inside the observatory dome of Vassar College with an equatorial telescope
and ladder, 1889.* (Special Collections,
Vassar College Libraries)

the theory of differential equations to the study of the shape of the rings of
Saturn. Although Kovalesky led an unconventional life, she did marry and
have a child—although her marriage with her husband, Vladimir Kovaleski,
has been termed a "fictitious marriage"; it was largely a way for her to obtain freedom to travel since at the time women could obtain passports only
through their fathers or husbands, and she spent some time living apart from
her husband.

Kovalesky's experience of negotiating family life with a career reflects what
was a common conflict for women in the 19th century. Many women who
succeeded in building their careers did so by avoiding the cultural demands
to build a family; the roles of wife and mother were often seen as incompatible with the desire to work, and for much of the 19th century women
continued to be defined not through their own successes but through their
positions as wives, mothers, and daughters. Much of the literature of the period reflects the struggles of women who chose to work. Nineteenth-century
American novels representing the desires and struggles of women as doctors
or scientists include Elizabeth Phelps's *Doctor Zay* and Sarah Orne Jewett's *A
Country Doctor;* several British novelists, such as Charles Reade and Arabella
Kenealy, built their plots around the woman with scientific ambitions. In the
works of these two writers, women pursuing science are often imagined as
being "unsexed" spinsters. As issues of sexuality became a part of the public
discourse and as increasing debates about women emerged (along with in-

creased publicity around women who pursued careers), one way to imagine these women's successes was to represent the women themselves as less feminine.

The Late 19th Century: The Rise of Sexology and Psychology

Michel Foucault has argued that although the 19th century appears to be a period of repression around issues of sexuality, it is instead, ironically, the period in which discourses of sex flourished; thus, while notions of respectability and Victorian prudery may have reigned in certain contexts, the period was deeply invested in shaping and defining ideas about sexuality through new professional and scientific discourses. In his book, *The History of Sexuality,* Foucault (1978) describes the "great archive of the pleasures of sex" that was built during this period (64). A number of prominent figures in the late 19th century built their careers in the field of sexology and established a professional vocabulary around the nature of sexuality. Among these early scholars of sexuality, Henry Havelock Ellis (1859–1939) and Richard von Kraft-Ebbing (1840–1902) were the most influential and representative, although they often had contrasting viewpoints. Kraft-Ebbing was born in Mannheim, Baden, Germany, and was trained in psychiatry. His *Psychopathia Sexualis* (1886) concentrated on exploring conditions of perversity and abnormal sexuality as distinct from so-called normal sexual phenomena. He is recognized for coining the terms *sadism* and *masochism* and for establishing the concept that sexuality that did not lead to procreation was "perverse." Much of his research also explored the nature of homosexuality; he suggested that it originated in a biological sexual inversion of the brain.

Although Kraft-Ebbing's title and his use of scientific terminology was aimed at physicians and specialists, his book became highly successful and popular with the reading public; thus his text revealed how scientific and professional writing on matters of sex dominated the understanding of these aspects of identity and became part of the larger culture. Scientific constructions of sexuality replaced other popular myths and conceptions of sexual desire and activity. The confessional letters and testimonials that Kraft-Ebbing received after publication also revealed the public's engagement with the text and the need for individuals to share and reveal their own relationship to sexuality.

One of the most important English responses to his work came from Havelock Ellis in his *Studies in the Psychology of Sex* (1898). Ellis reorganized Kraft-Ebbing's categories of "abnormal" sexual behavior to establish a broader spectrum of "normal" sexual activities; thus, while he recognized that abnormal behaviors existed, he liberated some of the aspects of deviancy that formed Kraft-Ebbing's theories and superimposed aspects of the abnormal on the normal. Unlike Kraft-Ebbing, Ellis aimed to uncover hidden truths regarding sex for the public and the common individual. He addressed homosexuality in *Sexual Inversion,* a study co-authored with John Addington Symonds. His approach was more sociological, and by discussing a broad range of examples and cases of homosexuality he suggested that homosexuality was not a diseased or criminal condition. Both Kraft-Ebbing and Ellis contributed to dialogues regarding female sexuality and the nature of women in contradictory ways, since for both the issue of a female sexual drive did not coincide neatly with Victorian mores of male and female behaviors.

It is apt that studies regarding sexuality and psychology increased in popularity during the late 19th century and engaged issues of gender, since during this period the concept of the middle-class family and the conditions of the individual had become part of the social imagination. While the ideals of the middle-class household and roles of men and women within it had been established by the end of the century, an interest in the conflicted nature of the relationships within this nucleus and the ongoing tensions between the social and biological conditions of such relationships could be merged through these new fields.

Conclusion

The 19th century was a crucial era in the development of scientific ideals. Throughout this period of invention and progress, there emerged a desire to understand and explore the "newness" of things, their natures, and their relationships. Within this era, a continued struggle between a biological basis for the nature of individuals—particularly in terms of gendered and racial identities—and a social understanding of them continued, and science became immersed in the cultural debates surrounding these issues. By the end of the century the enduring "Woman Question" had to deal with the "New Woman," a figure shaped by the new educational and professional activities opening to women. Although, by the end of the 19th century, men still dominated the sciences, an influential legacy of women's work allowed for a new set of role models to emerge; dialogues about sexuality and female biology forced the public to complicate its vision of ideal masculinity and femininity. As the century progressed, women participated increasingly in the scientific culture that had become part of everyday life, and while the women highlighted here stand out as the exceptional pioneers in the expanding fields of science, many women, yet undiscovered, played crucial roles as educators, observers, and explorers of scientific knowledge.

By the end of the 19th century, life had changed drastically because of the scientific developments that emerged and the ways scientific knowledge could be read, viewed, and analyzed. New technological innovations, including photography, x-ray, and a vast range of new tools and instruments, changed the nature of scientific work and the way it was recorded. Thanks to such innovations, the progress of this period can continue to be analyzed and interpreted. Perhaps what is most significant about this period of scientific growth is that the models of empiricism, objectivity, and truth that are so embedded in science were built into not only the scientific professions that emerged but also the culture itself. It is here that the 19th century may have produced its most potent and enduring mark, since our visions of science continue to be influenced by the discourses produced at this time and we continue to address many of the debates that so deeply engaged 19th-century readers. (*See also* Medicine; Women's Education)

References and Further Reading

Abir-Am, Pnina G., and Dorinda Outram, eds. *Uneasy Careers and Intimate Lives. Women in Science 1789–1979.* New Brunswick, NJ: Rutgers University Press, 1987.

Barker-Benfield, G. J. *The Horrors of the Half-Known Life.* New York: Harper and Row, 1976.

Bell, E. Moberly. *Storming the Citadel. The Rise of the Woman Doctor.* London: Constable, 1953.

Blackwell, Elizabeth. *Pioneer Work in Opening the Medical Profession for Women.* New York: E. P. Dutton, 1895.

Bynum, W. F. *Science and the Practice of Medicine in the Nineteenth Century.* Cambridge: Cambridge University Press, 1994.

Ehrenreich, Barbara, and Dierdre English. *Complaints and Disorders: The Sexual Politics of Sickness.* New York: Feminist Press, 1973.

Foucault, Michel. *The History of Sexuality.* Vol. 1. New York: Vintage Books, 1978.

Garrett Anderson, Elizabeth. "Sex and Mind in Education: A Reply." *Fortnightly Review* 21 (1894): 582–584.

Gates, Barbara. *Kindred Nature. Victorian and Edwardian Women Embrace the Living World.* Chicago: University of Chicago Press, 1998.

Jex-Blake, Sophia. *Medical Women. A Thesis and History.* London: Hamilton, Adams, 1866.

Jordanova, Ludmilla. *Sexual Visions. Images of Gender in Science and Medicine between the Eighteenth and Twentieth Centuries.* Madison: University of Wisconsin Press, 1989.

Judd, Catherine. *Bedside Seductions. Nursing and the Victorian Imagination 1830–1880.* New York: St. Martin's Press, 1998.

Kohlstedt, Sally Gregory. "Maria Mitchell and the Advancement of Women in Science." In *Uneasy Careers and Intimate Lives. Women in Science 1789–1979.* Edited by Pnina G. Abir-Am and Dorinda Outram. New Brunswick, NJ: Rutgers University Press, 1987.

Lutzger, Edith. *Edith Pechey-Phipson, M.D. The Story of England's Foremost Pioneering Woman Doctor.* New York: Exposition Press, 1958.

Mill, John Stuart, and Harriet Taylor Mill. *Essays on Sex Equality.* Edited by Alice S. Rossi. Chicago: University of Chicago Press, 1970.

Morantz-Sanchez, Regina. "The Many Faces of Intimacy: Professional Options and Personal Choices among Nineteenth and Early Twentieth Century Women Physicians." In *Uneasy Careers and Intimate Lives. Women in Science 1789–1979.* Edited by Pnina G. Abir-Am and Dorinda Outram. New Brunswick, NJ: Rutgers University Press, 1987.

Moscucci, Ornella. *The Science of Woman. Gynaecology in England, 1800–1929.* Cambridge: Cambridge University Press, 1990.

Peterson, M. J. *The Medical Profession in Mid-Victorian London.* Berkeley: University of California Press, 1987.

Porter, Roy. *The Greatest Benefit to Humankind: A Medical History of Humanity.* New York: W. W. Norton, 1999.

Russet, Cynthia. *Sexual Science. The Victorian Construction of Womanhood.* Cambridge, MA: Harvard University Press, 1989.

Warner, John Harley. *Against the Spirit of the System. The French Impulse in Nineteenth-Century American Medicine.* Baltimore, MD: Johns Hopkins University Press, 1998.

Woodham-Smith, Cecil. *Florence Nightingale* 1820–1910. New York: McGraw Hill, 1951.

Early 20th Century

MARILYN OGILVIE

By the early 20th century, political situations and educational reforms begun in the 19th century had come to fruition, making it more likely that women might become scientists. Suffrage movements and opportunities for higher education for women were important 19th-century developments. These movements appeared in different guises in diverse places throughout much of the Western world. A previously unthinkable concept, a voting woman, was contemplated in several parts of the world during the mid-19th century. In the United States, the organized women's movement is usually considered to have originated in the 1848 Seneca Falls Convention. In 1840 at the World Anti-Slavery Convention in London, Lucretia Mott and Elizabeth Cady Stanton discussed the possibility of a convention that would address the problems of women. They, after meeting with Jane Hunt, Mary Ann McClintock, and Martha Coffin Wright (Lucretia Mott's sister), on July 13, 1848, proceeded to call a woman's rights convention the next week on July 19 and 20. After a two-day debate, the *Declaration of Sentiments,* modeled on the *Declaration of Independence,* was adopted and signed by 100 people. In Europe, reform movements arose at about the same time (Cullen-DuPont 2000).

Educational reforms fell in lockstep with political ones. By the early 20th century, women were active in most fields of science, although certain areas such as the biological and the human sciences were better represented than the physical sciences and mathematics.

Annie Jump Cannon (1863–1941)

Annie Cannon's career in astronomy became possible because of the changes in educational opportunities for girls born in the last half of the 19th century. Born in Dover, Delaware, she received her early education in the Dover public schools. Annie was the oldest of three siblings in a household that included four other half-siblings. Her shipbuilder father, Wilson Cannon, was the Democratic state senator who broke with the Democratic Party at the outbreak of the Civil War and cast the deciding vote against secession. Her mother was interested in astronomy and she and Annie had a makeshift observatory in the attic where they watched the heavens. After public school, Cannon attended the Wilmington Conference Academy. After she graduated from the Academy, Cannon had the opportunity to profit from the 19th-century advances in women's education through the Seven Sisters colleges. Wellesley College was only five years old when Cannon decided to matriculate there in 1880. At Wellesley, Cannon studied with astronomer Sarah Whiting and became interested in the new study of spectroscopy. After graduation in 1894, Cannon did not immediately try to enter the job market or graduate school but returned home where she was involved in Dover social activities. After her mother's death, she returned to Wellesley as a graduate student working under Whiting, earning her M.A. degree in 1907. From 1895 to 1897 she was a graduate student at Radcliffe, another of the Seven Sisters, or early Eastern women's colleges, that is, Vassar, Wellesley, Smith, Bryn Mawr, Radcliffe, Mount Holyoke, and Barnard.

Women astronomers were not totally unheard of in the early 20th century. Observational astronomy was a study that a woman amateur could pursue at home without breaching the two-spheres concept. However, paid positions for women in astronomy were very difficult to obtain. Nevertheless, low-paid jobs as computers at the Harvard College Observatory and the Royal Greenwich Observatory provided women with jobs. Harvard College Observatory director Edward Pickering found well-educated women astronomers excellent employees because astronomy was moving away from observational work and into the new field of photographic astrophysics. The adoption of cameras and spectroscopes had great implications for women since it required a different labor force. Pickering needed fewer observers (men's work) and many more assistants (women's work) to classify as cheaply as possible the thousands of photographic plates his equipment was generating.

Cannon became an assistant at the Observatory in 1896 along with Williamina Fleming (1857–1911) and Antonia Maury (1866–1952). Cannon worked at the Observatory until her retirement in 1940, succeeding Fleming as curator of the Observatory's photographs. In 1938 she was made William Cranch Bond Astronomer at Harvard University—one of the first appointments of women by the Harvard corporation. Most of her career involved the observation, classification, and spectroscopic analysis of stars. The volume of her work on spectral classification is notable. In addition to her major work on classification (she classified 350,000 stars), *The Henry Draper Catalogue* and *The Henry Draper Extension,* she published nine smaller catalogues and many short papers. She was especially fascinated by variable stars.

Cannon received a number of awards including six honorary degrees, an honorary membership in the Royal Astronomical Society, the Draper Medal of the National Academy of Sciences, and the Ellen Richards Prize of the Society to Aid Scientific Research by Women.

Home Economics

By choosing fields that could be considered "women's work," women had the opportunity to infiltrate science. In the 19th century when the "two spheres" concept was so popular, woman's sphere was the home and man's the public arena. Home economics seemed especially suitable for women because of its proximity to the private sphere and best of all, its lack of interest to the public-sphered male. Home economics' founder was Ellen Swallow Richards (1842–1911), the wife of an engineering professor at MIT; she volunteered her services and about $1,000 annually to support the Women's Laboratory at that institution. In 1880, she began to stress the value of chemistry to the homemaker. Although home economics as "women's work" successfully provided women with jobs, its "facts" were not valued nearly as highly as were those created by men in the "hard sciences." The very success of women's work on major campuses helped to harden the gender separation for future generations. Rather than being accepted for other scientific employment once the pioneers had shown that women could handle this work, women found themselves more restricted than ever to "women's work." Since women were finding such good opportunities in the field, many persons (including the first vocational counselors, a new specialty around 1910) urged ambitious young women interested in science to head for home economics. It was the only field in which a woman scientist could hope to be a full professor, department chair, or even dean in the 1920s and 1930s (Rossiter 1982; Ogilvie and Harvey 2000).

Alice Hamilton (1869–1970)

Alice Hamilton followed a long tradition of women in health-related fields. Born to an intellectually vibrant family in Fort Wayne, Indiana, she and her three sisters and brother learned languages, literature, history, and some mathematics informally from their parents and occasionally from tutors. After preparing for medical school she attended the co-educational medical school of the University of Michigan, where she received her degree in 1893. After interning at the Hospital for Women and Children in Minneapolis and at the New England Hospital for Women and Children near Boston, she went to Germany

Dr. Alice Hamilton was a pioneer in the field of industrial medicine, arousing public concern about occupational diseases and the safety of workers on the job. (Library of Congress)

where she received additional training in bacteriology and pathology—fields in which she would spend her entire working life.

After returning to the United States, Hamilton studied at the Johns Hopkins Medical School until she received an appointment at the Woman's Medical School of Northwestern University. On arriving in Chicago, she boarded at Jane Addams' Hull House, where she came in contact with prominent Chicagoans as well as the often poverty-stricken, lower-class individuals who frequented Hull House. Hamilton not only taught but also engaged in research in pathology and bacteriology. Her interest in social service inspired her to establish Chicago's first baby health center. After the Woman's Medical School closed in 1902, she went to Paris to study for a year at the Pasteur Institute. Upon returning to Chicago, she went to work for the Memorial Institute for Infectious Diseases as assistant to the pathologist. At this time, Chicago was in the throes of a typhoid epidemic, and Hamilton conducted investigations for the Chicago Health Department to determine causes and treatments. Her recommendations resulted in a major reorganization of the department. Hamilton investigated other public health problems in the Chicago area. She found that many immigrant workers became sick from inhaling poisonous fumes from their jobs in foundries, factories, and steel mills and she became an active crusader in investigating and alleviating the causes of occupational diseases. She became the managing director of the Illinois Occupational Disease Commission. After Hamilton read a paper at the International Congress on Occupational Accidents and Diseases in Brussels, Belgium, her work was brought to the attention of the United States Commissioner of Labor (Department of Commerce) who asked her to undertake a national survey. This post, although unsalaried, allowed her to travel throughout the country. She was also active in the International Congress of Women at the Hague (1915), a group that attempted to avoid the impending war. However, after the United States entered the war, she served her country and the world by studying the munitions industry and observing the effects of several new poisons on workers.

After the war, Hamilton was appointed assistant professor at Harvard University's new Department of Industrial Medicine. Because of her previous participation in the surveys, she was the only person qualified for the job. As a woman she was excluded from the Harvard Faculty Club and could not march in the graduation procession. She taught at Harvard for 16 years but never received a promotion. Her teaching responsibilities were only for six months out of the year; the other six months were spent working for the federal government. She completed numerous important projects, including a study of the new rayon industry, silicosis and other diseases common to miners, lead toxicity in bathtubs and paint, toxicity of nitrous fumes inhaled by workers in the explosives industry, and the occupational hazards of certain positions on maternal and fetal health. Her work was not confined to the United States. As the only female member of the League of Nations Health Committee she went abroad and studied various conditions. Hamilton's accomplishments were recognized by numerous awards and honorary degrees (Sicherman 1984; Ogilvie and Harvey 2000).

Karen Clementine Danielsen Horney (1885–1952)

Perhaps because psychology and psychoanalysis were relatively new fields and did not have a long history of male domination, women were increasingly influential in these developing studies. Karen Horney, as one of these early psychoanalysts, accepted many of Freud's views but rejected his theory that biological and sexual factors were primary in personality relations. She rebuked the developers of psychoanalysis for their male-centered views. Instead, she averred that cultural factors, not women's feelings of inferiority, were more important in perpetuating the idea that females were subordinate to males in society.

Born in Hamburg, Germany, Karen Danielsen was the daughter of a Norwegian sea captain and a Dutch mother. Although her father did not approve of education for women, her mother was supportive. The couple separated, and after the separation Karen Danielsen moved to Freiburg, where she attended the university and excelled both academically and socially. She met the hand-some and brilliant economics major, Oskar Horney, at Freiburg, and eventually both entered the University of Göttingen where they were married. Success-fully combining marriage with work, she eventually received her medical de-gree in 1915. During the time that she was in medical school she had three daughters. She also became interested in psychoanalysis and joined the Berlin Psychoanalytic Society headed by Karl Abraham. Between 1922 and 1929, Horney wrote her most important papers on feminine psychology in which she theorized that young women did not envy males their penises but rather the superior position of men in society.

Horney and her husband separated in 1926, and between 1926 and 1932 she focused on personal conflicts. During this time she published six papers on marital problems and also considered the importance of raising adoles-cents. Horney immigrated to the United States in 1932 after she was offered a job as assistant director of the Institute for Psychoanalysis in Chicago. Two years later she moved to New York City to work at the New School for Social Research and at the New York Psychoanalytic Institute. Here she wrote her most significant and most controversial books, *The Neurotic Personality of Our Time* (1937) and *New Ways of Psychoanalysis* (1939). Her reinterpreta-tion of Freudian ideas created professional pandemonium with the result that she resigned from the New York Psychoanalytic Society in 1941. However, that same year she became one of the founders of the Association for the Ad-vancement of Psychoanalysis and of the American Institute of Psychoanalysis, where she served as dean until she died of abdominal cancer in 1952. Her contributions to theories in various fields are legion; she opened the door to holistic thinking and freedom from mechanistic structures (Rubens 1978).

Emily Noether (1882–1935)

Mathematician Emily Noether elected a field of study that few early 20th-century women chose. Born into a distinguished German-Jewish family of scientists, mathematicians, and musicians, Emmy Noether decided to study mathematics at the University of Erlangen where her father was a research mathematician. However, she was admitted only as an auditor, for women could not yet matriculate at the university. She stayed at Erlangen for two years but left to attend the University of Göttingen, again as a nonmatriculated student. However, after she had spent one semester at Göttingen, Erlangen changed its policy and allowed women to matriculate and take examinations with the same privileges as men. At Erlangen, she studied under the algebraist Paul Gordan and in 1807 received her doctorate, summa cum laude, for a disser-tation on algebraic invariants. Even with a doctorate it was almost impossible for a woman to obtain a paid position. Consequently, from 1908 to 1915 Noether worked without pay at the Mathematical Institute at Erlangen. David Hilbert, the mathematician, invited her to Göttingen to lecture in 1915 and tried unsuccessfully to obtain a university appointment for her. Finally (1922) she was given the title of "unofficial associate professor" and a small salary. She remained at Göttingen until 1933 when she (and other Jewish faculty members) received a communication that withdrew from her the right to teach at this university. She accepted an offer to teach at Bryn Mawr College partly because of its tradition of eminent female mathematicians, including Charlotte Scott and Anna Pell Wheeler. In the United States she lectured and did research at both Bryn Mawr and the Institute for Advanced Study at Princeton, New Jersey. However, after two years she died after undergoing surgery for an ovarian cyst.

Emmy Noether was an original and creative mathematican. Mathematicians now speak of the "Noether school" of mathematics because her work in abstract algebra in which she concentrated on formal properties such as associativity, commutativity, and distributivity has inspired so many successors (Ogilvie and Harvey 2000).

Beatrix Potter (1866–1943)

Beatrix Potter is remembered more for her children's stories than for her science. In many ways her accomplishments as a British natural historian hearken back to an earlier period when women could only pursue science at home. Her family was well-to-do but aloof, and she spent most of her time isolated in a third-floor nursery with her brother Bertram. After Bertram went away to school, Beatrix received a minimal education with a governess, studying French, German, and needlework. Her more formal studies were completed with a Miss Cameron with whom she studied from ages 12 to 17 and completed the Art Student's Certification, second grade, in July 1881.

Painfully shy, Beatrix took comfort in drawing natural history objects. She kept careful notes on her collections and drew them in great detail. With Bertram she skinned dead rabbits and boiled them until only the bones remained. She then drew the skeletons. She also caught and tamed rabbits, bringing them back to London as pets. Her shyness only grew worse as she got older. At age 19, she visited the British Museum and drew many of the objects in the collections there. On family vacations to Scotland she became interested in fungi, and she drew and described numerous specimens in a coded journal. Her uncle tried unsuccessfully to have her accepted to study at the Royal Botanic Gardens. She shared her research on the germination of spores with the Linnaean Society of London. However, after the keeper of botany at the

Museum of Natural History disparaged her work on fungi, she returned to the picture letters that she had sent to the children of her last governess, Annie Moore. These letters were the basis for what became *The Tale of Peter Rabbit*. This children's story, based on her own rabbit, Benjamin Bouncer, was rejected by a series of publishers. Finally the Frederick Warne publishing company suggested that she publish the letters in color. She did so, and the books were a success. She became engaged to Norman Warne, her editor, but he died suddenly at the age of 37.

After her aging parents died, Potter bought a farm where she continued to write children's stories. After buying additional land she married the solicitor in her land purchases when she was 47 years old. For the last 30 years of her life, Potter was a farmer.

Potter's research on fungi did not get the attention that it deserved. She described the symbiotic relationship between algae and fungi in lichens. Although a Swiss botanist had previously described lichens as consisting of two organisms, British botanists did not accept his theory. Potter's manuscript using the term *symbiosis* was burned after her death. However, when her encoded notebooks were deciphered, her theory became available. Even though her uncle had introduced her to the director of the Royal Botanic Gardens at Kew, Sir William Turner Thiselton-Dyer, he was uninterested in her ideas on symbiosis and claimed that her drawings were "too artistic" to meet scientific criteria (Ogilvie and Harvey 2000).

Margaret Higgins Sanger (1879?–1966)

Margaret Sanger is important in the social history of science. Known for her advocacy of birth control, she became an activist in support of her ideas. As the sixth of 11 children she saw the relationship between poverty and overpopulation very clearly. After the death of her tubercular mother whom she had cared for, Sanger trained as a nurse. She married architect William Sanger in 1902 and the couple produced two sons and a daughter. The daughter died of pneumonia when she was five years old. The life of a housewife never appealed to Sanger. She became involved with radical politics and took a position as a home nurse on the Lower East Side of New York City. As an activist in the International Workers of the World (IWW), one of her first causes was organizing textile workers in the Northeast. She soon recognized the connection between the issues of economic and social justice and feminist demands for the right of women to control their own bodies. Without sexual reform for women, the ability to command higher wages simply would not happen.

Her radical political activities weakened her marriage. Sanger and her husband began to grow apart during the second decade of the 20th century. She

BIRTH CONTROL REVIEW

$1.50 A Year   Fifteen Cents

JULY

How Shall
We Change
The Law?

—Page 8

Dedicated to Voluntary Motherhood

Must She Always Plead in Vain?

"You are a nurse—can't you tell me? For the children's sake—help me!"

—Hard Facts page 19

The July 1919 cover of the Birth Control Review. *The magazine was published by the American Birth Control League, led by contraception activist Margaret Sanger.* (Special Collections, New York Public Library)

began publishing articles in the socialist weekly, *The Call,* disseminating information on venereal diseases, the dangers of abortion, and contraception. However, these efforts were thwarted because of the provisions of the Comstock Act of 1873 banning materials from the United States mail considered obscene, including information on contraception and abortion. Attempting to eliminate the stigma of obscenity from contraception, she went to Europe (1914) with its more accepting environment to study methods of female-controlled contraception. When she returned to the United States full of information, she began to fight for the legalization of birth control through the publication of her journal *The Woman Rebel.* The dissemination of this publication caused her to be indicted for violating the Comstock Act. Her response was to leave again for Europe. While she was gone, her pamphlet *Family Limitation* was distributed by her followers. During this second visit she learned about the spring-controlled diaphragm. While she was in Europe her husband William was arrested by a Suppression of Vice agent for handing out *Family Limitations* and their daughter died of pneumonia. Back in the United States, Sanger embarked on a nationwide tour disseminating the knowledge she had gained in Europe. She and her younger sister opened the Brownsville clinic in New York and counseled almost 500 Brooklyn women before the clinic was closed and Sanger was arrested and put in jail. This highly publicized event led to the clarification of the New York law that forbade the distribution of birth control information, resulting in what Sanger considered a mandate for physician-staffed birth control clinics.

While Sanger was in Europe, she had met Havelock Ellis, who suggested that she separate herself from militant feminism and concentrate on social and eugenic arguments for birth control. She gained financial support from prominent people, allowing her to organize the American Birth Control League which later became the Planned Parenthood Federation of America.

William Sanger had problems with Margaret's sexually liberated views and actions. She railed against the double standard for sexual behavior and found it offensive. However, they stayed together until 1920 when Sanger divorced him. She married millionaire J. Noah Slee in 1922 after he agreed to respect her autonomy and fund her cause. Her later accomplishments included opening the first doctor-staffed birth control clinic in the United States: Birth Control Clinical Research Bureau, New York City (1923); forming the Committee on Federal Legislation for Birth Control; and helping to found the International Planned Parenthood organization (1952). One of her most important lobbying efforts came after a long legal battle to reverse the Comstock Act's classification of birth control as an obscenity. Her eventual success led to the American Medical Association's recognition of contraception as a legitimate medical service and one that should be taught in medical schools. After this 1937 success, Sanger moved to Tucson, Arizona, for her and her husband's retirement. Never fully retiring, Sanger brought the work of biologist Gregory Pincus to the attention of Katherine Dexter McCormick, who partially subsidized the birth control pill. In 1960, Sanger died of congestive heart failure at a Tucson nursing home (Ogilvie and Harvey 2000).

Nettie Maria Stevens (1861–1912)

Nettie Maria Stevens, who, along with Edmund Beecher Wilson, is credited with discovering the chromosomal determination of sex, was born in Cavendish, Vermont, to Julia (Adams) and Ephraim Stevens, a carpenter. She had only one sister, Emma Julia, who survived to maturity. Stevens's early education was in the public schools of Westford, Massachusetts, and later the Westford Academy. After her graduation from Westford in 1880, she attended the Westfield (Massachusetts) Normal School. To save money for her future education, following graduation from Westfield (in 1883), she taught Latin, English, mathematics, physiology, and zoology at a high school in Lebanon, New Hampshire; worked as a librarian at the Chelmsford (Massachusetts) Free Public Library; and taught at the Howe School, Billerica, Massachusetts.

In 1896 Stevens had saved enough money to enter Stanford University where she matriculated as a special student. In January 1897, she was awarded regular freshman standing and in March of that year was admitted to advanced standing. Although during her first year at Stanford, Stevens proposed to major in physiology under Oliver Peebles Jenkins, in 1897–1898 she became a student of Frank Mace MacFarland and began to concentrate in histology. After receiving a bachelor's degree in 1899 she remained at Stanford as a graduate student, obtaining a master's degree in 1900. Her M.A. thesis, *Studies on Ciliate Infusoria,* was published in 1901. While she was a student at Stanford, Stevens spent four summer vacations at the Hopkins Seaside Laboratory at Pacific Grove, California, pursuing histological and cytological research.

In 1900, Stevens returned to the East to study at Bryn Mawr College. This institution was a fine choice for a potential cytologist or histologist because two well-known biologists, Edmund B. Wilson and Thomas Hunt Morgan, were on its faculty. Although Wilson had left before Stevens arrived, his reputation remained at the school. Wilson corresponded with Morgan who became one of Stevens's teachers. When she first came to Bryn Mawr she worked with Joseph Weatherland Warren on the physiology of frog contractions, but shortly thereafter she began to work with the geneticist Thomas Hunt Morgan whose interests at that time were in cytology and regeneration. Morgan did not accept a chromosomal theory of heredity until much later. After six months at Bryn Mawr, Stevens was awarded a fellowship to study abroad. Her work at the Naples (Italy) Zoological Station and at the Zoological Institute of the University of Würzburg, Germany, resulted in several papers. After her year abroad (1901–1902) Stevens returned to Bryn Mawr and was awarded the Ph.D. degree in 1903. Her dissertation, *Further Studies on the Ciliate Infusoria, Licnophora and Boveria,* was published in the same year.

Stevens retained an affiliation with Bryn Mawr College for the rest of her life. She became a research fellow in 1902 and remained in that position until 1904. Her research in 1903–1904 was funded by a Carnegie Institution Grant. From 1904 to 1905, Stevens was a reader in experimental morphology and from 1905 to 1912, an associate in experimental morphology. It seemed as if she would finally be rewarded for her excellent research work when the trustees of Bryn Mawr created a research professorship for her; unfortunately, she died of breast cancer before she could occupy it.

During her lifetime, Stevens published at least 38 papers, most of which were cytological in nature, although some were in experimental physiology. All of these papers were exquisitely conceived and executed, but one particular set of research results assured her place in the history of cytogenetics. During the years of her Carnegie Foundation research work, she demonstrated that sex is determined by a specific chromosome.

During the late 19th and early 20th centuries, the behavior of the chromosomes during cell division had been described, but their connection with Mendelian heredity had not been confirmed. No trait had been traced from the chromosomes of the parent to those of the offspring, nor had a specific chromosome been linked with a specific characteristic. Hints existed, however, that the inheritance of sex might provide the sought-after link, for if sex were shown to be inherited in a Mendelian fashion, a chromosomal basis for heredity would be supported.

Stevens was one among several investigators interested in the problem of chromosomes and sex determination. By 1903, when she applied to the Carnegie Institution for a grant, she described one of her research interests as "the histological side of the problems of heredity connected with Mendel's Law" (Stevens, Letter to the Secretary of the Carnegie Institution, July 19, 1903). While Stevens was doing her research, Columbia University professor Edmund Beecher Wilson was working on the same problem. Both Wilson and Stevens concluded that sex was determined by a specific chromosome, raising the question of which of the scientists made the discovery first. Until recently, Wilson was credited with this discovery, but recent research has indicated that the two arrived at their conclusions independently. While studying spermatogenesis in five insect species from four different groups, Stevens observed that two species had an extra or "accessory" chromosome in the male. The common mealworm, *Tenebrio molitor*, was especially interesting because the size of one chromosme differed in males and females. In 1905, Stevens established that male mealworms have 19 large chromosomes and females 20 large ones. She tentatively concluded that this situation represented a case of sex determination by the particular pair of differently sized chromosomes, for she assumed that the spermatozoa containing the small chromosome determine the male sex and those containing 10 large chromosomes the female. Neither Stevens nor Wilson stated their conclusions unequivocally, for the situation in different insect groups was extremely varied. Clearly, however, Stevens recognized the significance of the chromosomal differences between males and females, and she continued investigation in a number of different species in an attempt to establish a pattern (Ris 1973; Ogilvie and Choquette 1981; Maienschein 1990; Ogilvie and Harvey 2000).

Conclusion

The achievements of these women and many others were possible because of the political and educational changes made in the previous century. Although women were still at a decided disadvantage, as the century progressed they had the opportunity to earn college degrees, to participate in professional organizations, and (more rarely) to use their education to earn a living. Ellen Swallow Richards and home economics became a model for an acceptable career for women. But it was not only "women's work" that women scientists were engaged in. They were active in astronomy (Annie Jump Cannon), medicine and bacteriology (Alice Hamilton), psychology and psychoanalysis (Karen Horney and Melanie Klein), mathematics (Emily Noether), scientific illustration (Beatrix Potter), social science (Margaret Sanger), and cytogenetics (Nettie Maria Stevens). These women represent a new generation of creative women scientists. Bryn Mawr–educated Nettie Stevens, for example, produced a major theoretical breakthrough in her hypothesis on sex determination by chromosomes. Annie Jump Cannon was able to take advantage of her education at Wellesley and Radcliffe to become an assistant at the Harvard College Observatory. Horney and Klein made creative contributions to the new study of psychoanalysis. Although she had a difficult time finding a paid position after she obtained her Ph.D. from the University of Göttingen, Emmy Noether demonstrated that women could be creative in mathematics. Although Beatrix Potter was never able to transcend her environment to be accepted in British natural history circles, her skills at drawing and writing reflected her knowledge. Margaret Sanger was not a theoretical scientist but she was totally committed to publicizing the dangers of overpopulation and was effective in educating the public. Thus, during the early 20th century, women were involved in most aspects of science, both theoretical and practical. (*See also* Women's Education)

References and Further Reading

Cullen-DuPont, Kathryn, ed. *Encyclopedia of Women's History in America*. 2nd ed. New York: Facts on File, 2000.

Maienschein, Jane. "Stevens, Nettie Maria." *Dictionary of Scientific Biography*. Edited by Frederic L. Holmes. Vol. 18, Supplement II, 867–869. New York: Charles Scribner's Sons, 1990.

Ogilvie, Marilyn Bailey. *Women in Science. Antiquity through the Nineteenth Century. A Biography with Annotated Bibliography*. Cambridge, MA: MIT Press, 1986.

Ogilvie, Marilyn Bailey. "The 'New Look' Women and the Expansion of American Zoology: Nettie Maria Stevens (1861–1912) and Alice Middleton Boring (1883–1955)." In *The Expansion of American Biology*. Edited by Keith R. Benson, Jane Maienschein, and Ronald Rainger. New Brunswick, NJ: Rutgers University Press, 1991.

Ogilvie, Marilyn Bailey, and Clifford J. Choquette. "Nettie Maria Stevens (1861–1912): Her Life and Contributions to Cytogenetics." *Proceedings of the American Philosophical Society* 125 (August 1981): 292–310.

Ogilvie, Marilyn Bailey, and Joy Harvey, eds. *Biographical Dictionary of Women in Science*. 2 vols. New York: Routledge, 2000.

Ris, Hans. "Stevens, Nettie Maria." *Notable American Women 1607–1950. A Biographical Dictionary*. Edited by Edward T. James. Vol. 3, 372–373. Cambridge, MA: Belknap Press of Harvard University Press, 1973.

Rossiter, Margaret. *Women Scientists in America. Struggles and Strategies to 1940.* Baltimore, MD: Johns Hopkins University Press, 1982.

Rubens, Jack. *Karen Horney: Gentle Rebel of Psychoanalysis.* New York: Dial Press, 1978.

Sicherman, Barbara. *Alice Hamilton: A Life in Letters.* Cambridge, MA: Harvard University Press, 1984.

Stevens, Nettie M. Letter to the Secretary of the Carnegie Institution, July 19, 1903.

Thematic Section:
Concepts of Gender
in Different Contexts

Disciplines

Chemistry

Cecilia H. Marzabadi

Background

Women have practiced chemistry since the beginnings of recorded time. However, the reports of women's roles in chemistry are limited. In part, this is because prior to the end of the 19th century, women lacked access to formal education. It was not until the universities opened their doors to female students in the late 1800s that women began to be recognized for their achievements in chemistry.

The first woman to gain admittance to any school of science and technology in the United States was Ellen Swallow Richards in 1870 (WIST, APA Web site). As a condition for her admittance at the Massachusetts Institute of Technology, there was an understanding "that her admittance did not establish a precedent for the general admission of females." Three years later, she received a bachelor of science degree in chemistry from MIT as well as a master of arts degree from the women's college, Vassar. She continued to study at MIT and would have been awarded the school's first doctoral degree, but the faculty rescinded her degree, unwilling to have a woman receive this distinction.

Certain fields of chemistry proved early to be more hospitable to women than did others. In particular, women tended to fare better in the fields of crystallography, radioactivity, and biochemistry (Rayner-Canham 1996, 2001). These three areas were seen as relatively uncharted, on the fringe of science, and with uncertain prospects for success. But importantly, some of the early men in these fields were receptive to mentoring female students.

Crystallography

Two early crystallographers were William H. Bragg (Royal Institution, London) and William L. Bragg (University of Manchester, England). In 1923, three of

W. H. Bragg's students were women. In subsequent years, seven additional women worked with him. W. L. Bragg's first research student was Lucy Wilson from Wellesley College, joined later by many other women.

Kathleen Yardley (Lonsdale) was the first female crystallographer to gain prominence. She received her master of science degree in 1924 and her doctor of science degree in 1927 from University College under the direction of W. H. Bragg. She is best known for her work on the structure of benzene, which gave her international recognition. Yardley married Thomas Lonsdale in 1927 and had three children. He was an extremely supportive spouse. At one time Yardley Lonsdale had considered quitting work to become a traditional housewife but Lonsdale insisted he had not married to have a free housekeeper and encouraged her to continue working. She had difficulty finding an academic post for many years, but at the age of 43 she finally received a position at University College where she remained for many years (Rayner-Canham 2001).

By far, the most famous of all female crystallographers was Dorothy Crowfoot Hodgkin. This prominent scientist received the Nobel Prize for her work on the structures of penicillin, vitamin B_{12}, and insulin.

Whereas Hodgkin's life was full of successes, another female colleague, Rosalind Franklin, never received the recognition she deserved for her contributions to structural elucidation of DNA. The photograph of DNA that Franklin had obtained was "leaked" to James Watson and Francis Crick; this led to the publication of their famous *Nature* paper on the structure of DNA, and Watson and Crick subsequently received a Nobel Prize (in 1962) for this work.

Radioactivity

Many of the women who excelled in this area of chemistry came from three famous research groups—French, British, and Austro-German (Rayner-Canham 1996, 2001). One of the reasons for the great success of women from these institutions is due in part to the collaborative efforts among these research groups and the opportunities provided for informal socialization among the women.

One well-known woman from the French group was Marie Curie. Parisians saw the famous Madame Curie as the role model for women. However, Curie did not seem to act in any mentoring role; instead, some have hypothesized that because of her rapid fame she accepted more readily the values of the male society than those of the women who struggled for success.

Biochemistry

As in the other two fields discussed, biochemistry also had less-defined pre-requisites for entry into its study and also had its share of supportive mentors (Rayner-Canham 1996, 2001).

The founder of modern biochemistry, F. Gowland Hopkins, is often credited with initiating the female-friendly nature of this area of study. Hopkins in the United Kingdom at Cambridge University and Lafayette Mendel at Yale University in the United States provided the environment that allowed many early female biochemists to succeed.

One notable biochemist to come from Mendel's group was Icie Macy Hoobler. Hoobler devoted more than 30 years of her life to studying women's health and nutrition-related issues. Other accomplished biochemists from this era included Rachel Fuller Brown, who was credited with the discovery of the anti-fungal compound, nystatin; Gerty Cori, who investigated the metabolism of carbohydrates; and Gertude Elion, the co-discoverer of several potent antiviral drugs, including acyclovir. The latter two women were also recipients of the Nobel Prize.

Women in Industrial Chemistry

In addition to women's lack of access to advanced chemical studies, once they had been trained, they still faced barriers in their professional lives. One such barrier was opposition to their membership in professional chemical societies. For example, both the Chemical Society of London and the American Chemical Society excluded women from participation until the early 1890s (Rayner-Canham 1996). In spite of this additional discouragement, women were determined to enter the profession of chemistry. It took the events of World War I to begin to open the doors of industrial chemistry to them. World War I (1914–1918) is often called the "Chemists War" because of the increasing demand for explosives, poison gases, dyes, and pharmaceuticals (Rayner-Canham 2001). Many of the male chemists of the time were drafted, and more and more women began to enter the workplace out of necessity. Many of these women were unskilled workers. The proportion of women in many chemical companies during this time was as high as 88 percent.

The work was often quite dangerous and women were paid about two thirds of men's salaries. The health effects from working with toxic compounds were often quite severe. In particular, tetranitrotoluene (TNT) poisoning gave a particular yellowish coloring to the skin and a green color to hair. The women who worked with this compound were called the "Canary Girls."

Other women during this period took jobs painting radium onto the faces of watch dials; the decay of the radium caused the numbers to glow in the dark, a glowing watchface being useful during night warfare (Kovarik 2002). This activity was also dangerous, but to make it even more hazardous, many of the workers licked the tips of the paintbrushes in order to get a fine line on the watch face. The "Radium Girls" developed many lip and mouth cancers, and many eventually died from this exposure. Five women in particular are famous for this title because they sued their employer, the United States Radium Corporation, because of the health effects they experienced.

Post–World War I

Once the war was over, the job situation for women became much worse. Many were asked to resign to free up positions for the men returning from the war. There were other arguments against the employment of women in the chemical industry. Some commented that women generally marry, have children, and leave the profession. Others believed that often the nature of industrial work was unsuitable for women because it frequently involved physically arduous tasks. Still others questioned the scientific proficiency of women, claiming that women did not have the "research type of mind" or were concerned with thinking about "womanly things."

World War II

The employment situation for industrial women chemists remained stagnant until World War II when women were again recruited to fill vacancies left when the male chemists went to war. Not only were these openings temporary but the demand for female chemists was not as great as expected, with many employers hiring women "only as a last resort." Reasons given for the underemployment of women included the need to provide women's washrooms and the impingement on privileges of the male workers (i.e., being able to wear their undershirts when it was hot or to swear).

At the end of the war, women were afraid to fight for their jobs. Some advocated "the cheerful acceptance" of their demotion after the men returned. Some believed that women should just seek other niches in which they could excel (i.e., microanalysis, which required delicate manipulations of small amounts of materials, or library science). After World War II, the situation was far from hopeful for women in the industrial sector.

Today's Situation in the Industrial Workforce

The number of women entering the industrial workforce has increased steadily over the last several decades. However, at the highest levels of training women are employed in numbers below the pool of available graduates. For example, in the year 2000, the percentage of women holding bachelor's level industrial positions was 33.5 percent; at the master of science degree level, 28.9 percent of the positions were held by women; and for those positions requiring a doctoral degree, only 15.1 percent were filled by women.

The salaries of women surveyed in the year 2000 averaged 75–80 percent of the salaries received by men in similar positions. Women from this group were also more likely than their male counterparts to work part-time or hold temporary positions. Finally, the positions held by women differed from those held by the men in this group. Women were less likely than were men to have management positions (12% versus 88%). Women continued to be employed in high numbers in niches such as chemical information (librarians), analytical services, and training functions (Women Chemist Committee 2001).

Women in Academic Chemistry

The number of women enrolled in baccalaureate programs in the sciences continues to increase. In fact, women today constitute more than 50 percent of the bachelor degree recipients in chemistry in the United States and more than 30 percent of the chemistry doctorates awarded at the schools ranked by the National Research Council as the top 50 (Marzabadi 2006).

The 1960s and Title IX

One of the largest periods of growth in the number of women receiving advanced science degrees occurred in the period 1963–1970. This followed a huge surge in federal funding that followed the launch of Sputnik by the Soviet Union in 1957. Also instrumental to the increase in women achieving advanced degrees were the Civil Rights Act of 1964 (Title VII) and Title IX.

Women in the Professoriate

The last 20 to 30 years has also shown a steady increase in the number of women teaching at four-year colleges. Between 1990 and 2000 the percentage of women who were full professors at these institutions increased from 6.7

percent to 11.8 percent. Increases over this same time were also seen at the associate and assistant professor levels (18.0 percent to 25.8 percent, and 25.2 percent to 34.2 percent, respectively). However, the number of women on the faculties at Ph.D.-granting institutions has increased much more slowly. In 2006, only 10 percent of full professors at top 50 U.S. schools were women; 22 percent of the associate professors and 21 percent of the assistant professors were women (Marasco 2006).

The MIT Report and comments by former Harvard President Larry Summers reveal discrimination and discouragement for women scientists, especially at these elite institutions. In addition, women's personal choices for a balanced lifestyle may also contribute to the lack of parity observed in academic chemistry.

The Future

Although the number of women participating in chemistry at all levels is increasing compared to men, attrition of women occurs at each subsequent level of higher education. Senior female women in industrial and academic positions are scarce.

It is clear from the preceding historical perspective that both subtle and overt discrimination practices in the chemical workplace have impeded women's progress. More effort must be made to promote women to leadership positions within the field of chemistry and to recognize them for their accomplishments. (*See also* Discrimination; Nobel Laureates)

References and Further Reading

Kovarik, B. "The Radium Girls." *Mass Media and Environmental Conflict,* 2002. http://www.runet.edu/~wkovarik/envhist/radium.html.

Marasco, C. A. "Women Faculty Gain Little Ground." *Chemical and Engineering News* 84 (2006): 58–59.

Marzabadi, C. H. "Findings from the American Chemical Society Career Continuity Survey: Elucidating Gender Patterns in Training and Career Paths." In *Are Women Achieving Equity in Chemistry? Dissolving Disparity and Catalyzing Change.* ACS Symposium Series 929. Edited by C. H. Marzabadi, V. J. Kuck, S. A. Nolan, and J. P. Buckner, 89–106. Washington, DC: American Chemical Society, 2006.

Rayner-Canham, M. F., and G. W. Rayner-Canham. "Women's Fields of Chemistry: 1900–1920." *Journal of Chemical Education* 73 (1996): 136–138.

Rayner-Canham, M. F., and G. W. Rayner-Canham. *Women in Chemistry. Their Changing Roles from Alchemical Times to the Mid-Twentieth Century.* Edited by A. Travis and O. T. Benfey. Philadelphia, PA: Chemical Heritage Foundation, 2001.

Women Chemist Committee, Committee on Economic and Professional Affairs. *Women Chemists 2000*. Washington, DC: American Chemical Society, 2001.

Women in Science and Technology (WIST). "Timeline of Historical Highlights." American Psychological Association. http://www.apa.org/science/wist/time-line.html (Accessed March 1, 2007).

Physics/Astronomy

Barbara L. Whitten

Physics

Anyone who looks at the history of science sees that there have always been women in science, no matter how high the barriers they faced. Physics began as a distinct discipline with the publication of Newton's *Principia Mathematica* in 1686. Émilie du Châtelet (1706–1749) made the first French translation of this central work and helped to reconcile Newton's and Leibniz's versions of mechanics. The only woman scientist many people know about is physicist Marie Curie, the discoverer of radium and first scientist to win the Nobel Prize twice. Two other women physicists have also won the Nobel Prize: Irène Joliot-Curie, Marie's daughter, for synthesizing new radioactive elements, and Maria Goeppert Mayer, for inventing the shell model of the nucleus. Many believe that two other women physicists should have been Nobel Laureates: Lise Meitner, co-discoverer of nuclear fission, and Chien-Shiung Wu, who performed the difficult experiment to show parity nonconservation. The Web site "Contributions of 20th Century Women to Physics" (http://cwp.library.ucla.edu/) describes the work of many other eminent women.

But despite this wealth of role models, physics remains a male-dominated field. In an early study of women in science and engineering, Stephen Brush called physics "the coldest science" for women (Brush 1991). Figure 1 shows that physics lags significantly behind the other sciences in participation by women. In the last 30 years many physicists have made significant efforts to increase the diversity of the physics community, and the participation by women in physics has increased sharply. The percentage of women in receiving Ph.D.s in physics rose from 3 percent in 1972 to 18 percent in 2003. Essentially all of these women are white; the participation of women of color in physics is vanishingly small. From 1997 to 2003, an average of fewer than three Hispanic women and African American women earned Ph.D.s in physics each year (Ivie and Ray 2005).

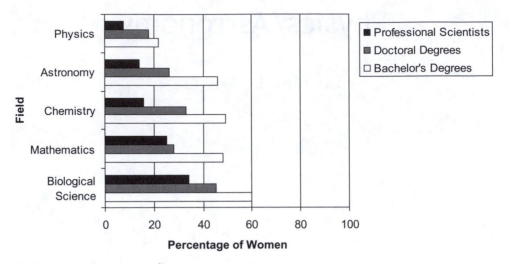

Figure 1. Partcipation of women in American science.

It is not clear why physics is so unfriendly to women, but we can rule out a few common explanations. The rapid rise in the participation of women in recent decades argues against the suggestion, made by Larry Summers and others, that women lack innate talent. Others propose that the material of physics is inherently unattractive to women, an explanation rendered unlikely by the much higher participation of women in closely related disciplines like mathematics and chemistry. The participation of women in physics in different countries varies wildly, from 8 percent in Japan to 27 percent in France (Hartline and Li 2002) without any clear pattern, which suggests that some of the explanation is cultural.

Figure 1 shows that the participation of women in physics decreases at every step up the academic ladder. This is often called the "leaky pipeline," and much attention in the physics community is devoted to plugging leaks, that is, to encouraging women in physics to continue. The pipeline metaphor has recently come under criticism because it assumes that the only path to a faculty position in physics is to decide in high school and never deviate from that decision. This misrepresents the complexities of women's career paths; perhaps women do (or could) drop in to physics at other points. They may have left physics and wish to return, or they may decide on a career in physics in college or later. It is difficult to measure the size of these pools of women, but Xie and Shauman (2003) studied paths of scientists through college. They found that men are more likely to choose the "path of persistence," never deviating from their initial choice of a science major. More women decide on a science major *after* coming to college. This path into physics is made more difficult by the undergraduate physics major, with its tightly interlocking mathematics and physics prerequisites. It might be useful to consider ways to make the physics major more flexible. We might learn from historically Black colleges, which often arrange their curriculum so that there is more than one starting point for students with different backgrounds.

Recruiting and retaining women in physics requires different approaches at different points in a career path. For precollege students, there are many programs to encourage girls' interest in science in general; few are focused on physics. At the undergraduate level, efforts have addressed both curriculum and department culture. The first year of science courses has been singled out as unattractive to students in general and women and minorities in particular. Seymour and Hewitt (1997) argue that the impersonal structure of introductory science classes is unnecessarily discouraging to young women, who drop out in larger numbers than men, even with performance as good as that of men. The structure of physics classes was designed largely by male professors for students like them and is more likely to be amenable to male learning styles.

The physics community has made major efforts in recent years to reform the introductory physics class; one of the stated goals is to make the course more attractive to underrepresented students. This has resulted in more active pedagogy that emphasizes interactive classes, peer learning, and more exploratory exercises. See, for example, *Workshop Physics,* developed by Priscilla Laws and collaborators (Jackson, Laws, and Franklin 2002). Many physics faculty find that an atmosphere of cooperation rather than competition, both inside and outside the classroom, encourages women students.

Other work has focused on department culture. Whitten et al. (2003) found that a warm department that offers many opportunities for students and faculty to interact informally is vital to a female-friendly atmosphere. Other important components include tutorial programs staffed by majors, a student lounge, seminars, department parties, and outreach activities to the community.

The American Physical Society Committee on the Status of Women in Physics has studied the climate for women in graduate programs. They also find that a warm department culture encourages women students and recommend activities that give students and faculty an opportunity to interact informally. The first year is critical for graduate students, and the committee recommends that departments offer good teaching and advising to first-year graduate students. More senior graduate students appreciate better career advice.

Career-family conflicts are the most important barrier to career advancement for postdocs and junior faculty in the early stages of their career. Xie and Shauman (2003) suggest that geographical mobility early in a scientific career is important to success. Because so many more women than men are married to other scientists, and because young people are also establishing their families during this time, lack of mobility can be very detrimental to women's careers. Mason and Goulden (2004) show that 70 percent of men with tenure are married with children, compared to only 44 percent of women. Women are often forced to choose between their career and family in a way that men are not.

Finally, the MIT report (MIT 1999) found that senior women scientists at MIT have smaller lab space, less access to internal funds and graduate students, fewer nominations for prizes and invited speakers, and other perks of a successful scientific career than their equally accomplished male colleagues. It is helpful to remember that this is how discrimination works in the 21st century. Blatant discrimination has been against the law for decades and rarely occurs. But more subtle forms of discrimination, much harder to measure and harder to fight, accumulate over a lifetime and keep these distinguished women from the prestige and rewards that equivalent male scientists accept as a matter of course. It is encouraging that elite institutions are beginning to recognize and address these issues.

Astronomy

Though astronomy is often grouped with physics, it is a distinct science with its own methods and its own culture, which is much more friendly to women. This may be because of the presence of very well-known women in astronomy, beginning with astronomer Maria Mitchell, probably the most famous American woman scientist of the 19th century. She discovered a comet at the age of 28 when she was working as a librarian on Nantucket; she went on to a distinguished career at the newly established Vassar College, where she involved students in her research and inspired generations of students. Sarah Frances Whiting, though less well known, played a similar role at Wellesley College. Edward Pickering, the director of the Harvard College Observatory, hired a number of women to perform what he thought of as mundane tasks such as sorting and classifying stellar spectra and maintaining star catalogues. This became an acceptable form of "women's work" and gave women scientists a new role in astronomy (Rossiter 1982).

This legacy stands today, of many important astronomers being women, including, for example, Vera Rubin, who discovered the existence of dark matter, and Jocelyn Bell Burnell, who found the first pulsar as a graduate student. Of the 87 astronomers in the National Academy of Sciences, 10 are women. Figure 1 shows that women participate in astronomy at all levels at a rate higher than in physics. The higher participation by women has some positive effects on the astronomy community; American Astronomical Society meetings, for example, unlike physics meetings, offer child care.

Astronomer Jocelyn Bell Burnell. (The Open University/Courtesy AIP Emilio Segre Visual Archives)

Some physics programs use the attractiveness of astronomy to recruit students into the physics major. This is particularly noticeable in women's colleges, where faculty work hard to recruit students into the major. Astronomy lends itself to student-faculty research and to outreach programs using observatories and planetariums, two important components of a female-friendly program.

Much work remains to be done at all levels to encourage young girls to be interested in physics, to recruit women into physics, and to support those women who have opted into a physics career. In her 1875 presidential address to the Association for the Advancement of Women, Maria Mitchell said, "How much science needs women" (Rossiter 1982, 15). These words are echoed by Donna Shalala, chair of the committee that produced the recent report by the National Academy of Science on women in science and engineering. "Women are capable of contributing more to the nation's science and engineering research enterprise, but bias and outmoded practices governing academic success impede their progress almost every step of the way. . . . The United States should enhance its talent pool by making the most of its entire population" (Shalala 2006). (*See also* Discrimination; Nobel Laureates)

References and Further Reading

Brush, Stephen G. "Women in Science and Engineering." *American Scientist* 79 (1991): 404–419.

Hartline, Beverly K., and DongQi Li. *Women in Physics: The IUPAP International Conference on Women in Physics,* Paris, France, 2002. Melville, NY: AIP Press, 2002.

Ivie, Rachel, and Kim Nies Ray. 2005. "Women in Physics and Astronomy, 2005." AIP report R-430.02. http://www.aip.org/statistics/trends/gendertrends.html. (Accessed November 15, 2006.)

Jackson, David P., Priscilla W. Laws, and Scott V. Franklin. *Explorations in Physics: An Activity-based Approach to Understanding the World.* New York: Wiley, 2002.

Mason, Mary Ann, and Marc Goulden. "Do Babies Matter? (Part II) Closing the Baby Gap." [Electronic version.] *Academe* (November–December 2004). http://www.aaup.org/publications/Academe/2004/04nd/04ndmaso.htm. (Accessed November 15, 2006.)

Massachusetts Institute of Technology. "A Study on the Status of Women Faculty in Science at MIT." *MIT Faculty Newsletter* 11(4) (March 1999). http://web.mit.edu/fnl/women/women.html#The%20Study. (Accessed November 15, 2006.)

Rossiter, Margaret. *Women Scientists in America: Struggles and Strategies to 1940.* Baltimore, MD: Johns Hopkins University Press, 1982.

Seymour, Elaine, and Nancy M. Hewitt. *Talking about Leaving: Why Undergraduates Leave the Sciences.* Boulder, CO: Westview Press, 1997.

Shalala, Donna. "Broad National Effort Urgently Needed to Maximize Potential of Women Scientists and Engineers in Academia." National Academy of Science press release. http://www8.nationalacademies.org/onpinews/newsitem.aspx?RecordID=11741. (Accessed November 15, 2006.)

Whitten, Barbara L., Suzanne R. Foster, Margaret L. Duncombe, Patricia E. Allen, Paula Heron, Laura McCullough, Kimberly A. Shaw, Beverley A. P. Taylor, and Heather M. Zorn. "What Works? Increasing the Participation by Women in Undergraduate Physics." *Journal of Women and Minorities in Science and Engineering* 9 (2003): 239–258.

Xie, Yu, and Kimberlee A. Shauman. *Women in Science: Career Processes and Outcomes.* Cambridge, MA: Harvard University Press, 2003.

Mathematics

ABC-CLIO

A common belief is that there are few women in mathematics. Some statistics about science and technology reinforce this view, and others counter it. For example, in the United States:

Women earn 18 percent of Ph.D.s in physics, but 46 percent of Ph.D.s in biological sciences.

Women represent 18 percent of network and systems administrators, but 62 percent of accountants and auditors.

Women are 39 percent of computer game players, but over 50 percent of Internet users.

It is hard to infer much about women's participation or interest in mathematics from these figures (Commission on Professionals in Science and Technology 2006). One reason is that the figures concern fields related to mathematics—not mathematics itself. However, women's participation in mathematics is difficult—if not impossible—to characterize by any one statistic. It has varied and still varies considerably with time and place.

Inside Mathematics: A Brief History

Gaps in the historical record make it difficult to know the extent of women's intellectual activities in any discipline. However, what is known suggests that differences in national practices can influence women's participation—and documents women's interest and determination in intellectual pursuits. It may come as a surprise that several firsts for women in mathematics and physics are also firsts for women in academe.

For example, in the 17th and 18th centuries, a few women could study and lecture at Italian universities. Elena Cornaro Piscopia, the first woman to earn a doctorate of philosophy anywhere, was granted her degree in 1678 at the

University of Padua. Laura Bassi, the first woman to hold an official university position, was awarded a doctorate in 1732 at the University of Bologna and became a professor of physics there. In 1749, the University of Bologna offered an honorary chair of mathematics and natural philosophy to Maria Agnesi. Agnesi did not accept this offer, and in 1776 Bassi became the first woman to hold a university chair (Findlen 1999).

German universities, which developed a new research-based approach to science in the 19th century, did not allow women to matriculate until 1902. But in the 1880s, women began to audit courses at German universities. One such auditor was Sonia Kovalevsky, who was granted (in absentia and as an exception) a doctorate in mathematics summa cum laude from Göttingen in 1874, becoming the first woman to earn a Ph.D. in mathematics. In 1889, Kovalevsky accepted a position at the University of Stockholm, becoming the first woman in modern Europe to hold a chair at a research university. She was followed at Göttingen by Grace Chisholm who earned a Ph.D. in mathematics in 1895, becoming the first woman to earn a Ph.D. from a Germany university through the normal procedure—after getting official permission from the German government (Case and Leggett 2005, 40).

Agnesi, Kovalevsky, and Chisholm were all celebrated for their mathematical achievements, which differ according to the mathematical activities of their times. Agnesi was internationally known for her book on differential and integral calculus. Kovalevsky's and Chisholm's achievements reflect the modern emphasis on research in academic mathematics. Kovalevsky became the first woman to be on the editorial board of a major scientific journal (*Acta Mathematica*), received the prestigious Prix Bordin from the French Academy of Sciences, and was the first woman elected as a corresponding member of the Russian Imperial Academy of Sciences (Koblitz 1999, 216–217). Chisholm did not hold a university position but was known internationally for her research (Case and Leggett 2005, 39–45).

Mathematics: Current Situation

Since the 19th century, women's participation in mathematics has continued to grow worldwide (Case and Leggett 2005). However, there is considerable variation by country and by university. As in many professions, one widespread trend is that the proportion of women decreases as rank and status increase. Statistics collected by European Women in Mathematics in the 1990s show a wide variation in percentages of women in mathematics departments but follow this trend. In Portugal and Macedonia, about 45 percent of mathematicians were women, but women were only 5 percent and 8 percent, respectively, of full professors of mathematics. In Italy, 13 percent of full professors of mathematics were women, but in Sweden there were none.

In the United States, women are now 31 percent of tenure-eligible professors of mathematics. They hold 16 of approximately 300 tenured positions at the "top ten" mathematics departments, yet Harvard (one of the top ten) has never hired a woman for a tenured or tenure-eligible position. Women earned 27 percent of the Ph.D.s in mathematics granted to citizens in 2006, up from 24 percent in 1990 and 18 percent in 1980. For over 20 years, women have earned between 40 percent and 48 percent of undergraduate degrees in mathematics granted by U.S. universities, about twice the proportion of the 1950s (Commission on Professionals in Science and Technology 2006).

In the United States, high school course-taking patterns have changed. National transcript studies indicate that in 1982, 5.7 percent of male high school graduates and 4.4 percent of female graduates took calculus. That increased in 2000 to 12.2 percent of males and 11.1 percent of females. In 2000, mathematics courses other than calculus were taken by larger percentages of females than males. Similarly, a 2001 California study called "Who's Lagging Now?" found that in high school, female enrollment in college preparatory courses was greater than that of males—except for computer science.

Mathematics achievement as measured by the National Assessment of Educational Progress shows little gender difference. In contrast, the gap favoring men on the mathematics portion of the SAT has not changed, although test-taker demographics have changed: the percentage of women taking this test is now larger than the percentage of men. (Interestingly, the SAT items that produced the largest gender differences for U.S. students produced none for Japanese and Chinese high school students.) Women, however, tend to earn better grades in high school and college than men—overall and in mathematics courses.

To summarize, in the United States, there is little overall gender difference in current college and precollege participation and achievement. Other measures show gender differences: high school and college grades favor women, but SAT scores favor men. Women's proportion of Ph.D.s and faculty positions has increased. These proportions vary considerably by country and university, but the proportion of women in faculty positions diminishes as rank and status increase.

This rather complicated picture is not reflected in findings that receive wide publicity outside mathematics. We now turn to discussion of one such finding.

Outside Mathematics: Popular Media

In 1980, the psychologists Camilla Benbow and Julian Stanley published "Sex Differences in Mathematical Ability" in *Science,* reporting large gender differences in "mathematical reasoning ability." Their evidence was scores on the mathematics SAT taken by seventh and eighth graders as part of a talent search for a program at Johns Hopkins University. In a sample of about 10,000, collected between 1972 and 1979, the distribution of boys' scores differed greatly from the distribution of girls' scores. For example, 1,817 boys and 675 girls scored above 500. In their conclusion, Benbow and Stanley explicitly favored (their word) "the hypothesis that sex differences in achievement in and attitude towards mathematics result from superior male mathematical ability . . . [which] is probably an expression of a combination of both endogenous and exogenous variables," thus including the possibility of social and environmental factors.

This carefully worded conclusion was not reflected in headlines such as "Do Males Have a Math Gene?" (*Newsweek*), "Boys Have Superior Ability, Study Says" (*Education U.S.A.*), or "The Gender Factor in Math" (*Time*). Although discussion and criticisms of Benbow and Stanley's data and interpretations were published in *Science,* these received little, if any, notice in mainstream media.

Benbow and Stanley's 1980 and 1983 findings, without discussion of their limitations or later talent search statistics, are still mentioned in the mainstream press (e.g., "Academy of P.C. Sciences," *New York Times* 2006), and cited in popular works (e.g., *Boys and Girls Learn Differently!* 2001).

Outside Mathematics: Psychologists and Psychological Research

As noted previously, Benbow and Stanley's findings in *Science* concerned talent search ratios. They reported that in talent searches in 1980, 1981, and 1982, about 13 boys to every 1 girl scored above 700 on the mathematics SAT. Over the three years, two separate searches were conducted: nationwide (total sample size approximately 24,000) and at Johns Hopkins (total sample size 39,820).

Benbow wrote in a 1988 *Behavioral and Brain Sciences* article, "the ratio is 12.9 to 1 for the 278 cases reported in [the 1983 *Science* article]. When in November 1983 SMPY had temporarily completed its national search . . . the ratio remained around 12 to 1." Later she stated, "From 1980, the [talent search] samples, have indeed been selected by the same criteria. During this time period there is no evidence for a decrease [in sex difference], rather the opposite." (Particulars about this change such as sample size and change in ratio are not given.) She concluded, "it is clear after the testing of several hundred thousand intellectually talented 12- to 13-year-old students nationwide over a 15-year period that there are *consistent* [emphasis added] sex differences favoring males in mathematical reasoning ability (or more specifically in SAT-M scores). These differences are pronounced at the highest levels of that ability."

Between 1988 and 2000, the 13 to 1 ratio was reported in journal articles by Benbow and her colleagues (*Psychological Science* 2000). In 2000, Lubinski, Benbow, and Morelock gave the 13 to 1 ratio in the *International Handbook of Giftedness and Talent,* indicating that comparable ratios had been replicated across the United States in a number of talent searches.

Other psychologists used this ratio in works such as *Male, Female* (Geary 1998), *The Blank Slate* (Pinker 2002), or *Gender Differences in Mathematics* (Gallagher and Kaufmann 2005); none mentions later talent search ratios. This might suggest that these ratios have not changed since 1983. However, this is not the case. In Johns Hopkins talent search statistics collected between 1984 and 1991, the average over-700 ratio was 5.7 to 1. The sample size was 243,428, considerably larger than the earlier samples (Brody, Barnett, and Mills 1994). Talent searches conducted by Duke University between 1981 and 1992 produced an average over-700 ratio of 5.6 to 1. The sample size was 308,397. In 2005, Brody and Mills reported in *High Ability Studies* that the over-700 ratio had dropped to 3 to 1. In 2006, Benbow reported it as 4 to 1 in a personal communication (see Valian's essay in Ceci and Williams 2007).

Discussion. Psychologists in general appear to be unaware of the later talent search findings, perhaps because they appeared in publications regarding gifted children rather than in mainstream psychological journals. More complex aspects of the talent search statistics are just beginning to receive discussion among psychologists (Ceci and Williams 2007; Gallagher and Kaufmann 2005). Some major limitations are the following:

The samples are not random.
Testing conditions are not described.
Connections between SAT scores and mathematical proficiency or ability
    are not clear.

Conclusion

History and national comparisons suggest that women's participation in mathematics is influenced by social and cultural practices. In the United States, most measures associated with mathematical proficiency show few gender differences, and some favor women (Hyde and Linn 2006; Linn and Kessel 2002). Women's participation in mathematics has increased—in the United States and worldwide. Yet, as Susan Chipman notes (Gallagher and Kaufmann 2005, 18), the actual facts have little impact on stereotypes about women and mathematics. Heavy reliance on one measure and one finding help to explain how stereotypes are perpetuated about women, mathematics, and their interaction. This reliance may be, in part, due to a cultural propensity to focus on gender differences—in the media and among scientists. (*See also* Cognitive Abilities; Discrimination; Physics/Astronomy; Women's Education)

References and Further Reading

Benbow, Camilla P., and J. Stanley. "Sex Differences in Mathematical Ability: Fact or Artifact?" *Science* 210 (12) (1980): 1262–1264.

Benbow, Camilla P., and J. Stanley. "Sex Differences in Mathematical Reasoning Ability: More Facts." *Science* 222 (1983): 1029–1031.

Benbow, Camilla P., D. Lubinski, D. Shea, and H. Eftekhari-Sanjani. "Sex Differences in Mathematical Ability at Age 13: Their Status 20 Years Later." *Psychological Science* 11 (6) (2000): 474–480.

Brody, Linda E., Linda B. Barnett, and Carol J. Mills. "Gender Differences among Talented Adolescents: Research Studies by SMPY and CTY at Johns Hopkins." In *Competence and Responsibility: The Third European Conference of the European Council for High Ability*. Edited by Kurt A. Heller and Ernst A. Hany. Seattle: Hogrefe and Huber, 1994.

Case, Bettye Anne, and Anne Leggett, eds. *Complexities: Women in Mathematics*. Princeton, NJ: Princeton University Press, 2005.

Ceci, Stephen, and Wendy Williams, eds. *Why Aren't More Women in Science? Top Researchers Debate the Evidence*. Washington, DC: American Psychological Association, 2007.

Commission on Professionals in Science and Technology. *Professional Women and Minorities: A Total Human Resources Data Compendium*. 16th ed. Washington, DC: CPST, 2006.

Findlen, Paula. "Science as a Career in Enlightenment Italy: The Strategies of Laura Bassi." In *History of Women in the Sciences: Readings from Isis*. Edited by Sally Gregory Kohlstedt. Chicago: University of Chicago Press, 1999.

Gallagher, Anne, and James Kaufmann, eds. *Gender Differences in Mathematics*. New York: Cambridge University Press, 2005.

Hyde, Janet S., and Marcia C. Linn. "Gender Similarities in Mathematics and Science." *Science* 314 (2006): 599–600.

Koblitz, Ann Hibner. "Science, Women, and the Russian Intelligensia." In *History of Women in the Sciences: Readings from Isis*. Edited by Sally Gregory Kohlstedt. Chicago: University of Chicago Press, 1999.

Linn, Marcia C., and Cathy Kessel. "Gender Differences in Cognition and Educational Performance." In *Encyclopedia of Cognitive Science*. Edited by Lynn Nadel. New York: Macmillan, 2002.

Lubinski, D., C. P. Benbow, and M. Morelock. "Gendered Differences in Engineering and the Physical Sciences among the Gifted: An Inorganic-organic Distinction." In *International Handbook for Research on Giftedness and Talent*. 2nd ed. Edited by K. A. Heller, F. J. Mons, R. J. Sternberg, and R. F. Subotnik. Oxford: Pergamon Press, 2000.

Pinker, Steven. *The Blank Slate: The Modern Denial of Human Nature*. New York: Viking, 2002.

Computer Science

Rebecca Scheckler

Computer science is an excellent example of a field with clearly defined roles and job paths that not only differentiate between female and male roles but whose gendered roles reflect a difference between empowered users and creators of digital technology and disempowered users and construction line builders of computers. This awareness of gendered roles did not occur initially. First there was a belief that computer science was not gendered—in line with the belief that all technology was genderless and certainly gender blind.

Computer Science Follows the Lead of Science and Gender Research

Computer science has not been at the forefront of gender research. Rather, it has reflected research on gender in math and science. This essay presents a historical account of gender beliefs in computer science; how it is entwined with gender research in other science, math, engineering, and technology fields (SMET); and how computer science reflects gender beliefs in these other fields. Computer science has a recent history but one lengthy enough to demonstrate changes in conceptualization of gender and one that parallels gender myths and beliefs in other fields.

The first, second, and third waves of feminism are described by Lorber (2005) as Gender Reform Feminisms, Gender Resistance Feminisms, and Gender Rebellion Feminisms, respectively. In computer science, where these waves can be found but lag behind other fields, wave one (1990–2005) is interpreted as when the field recognized that women were absent and something needed to be done. Wave two represents the current phase of women either struggling to become more like men to fit into the already constructed male computer science departments or resisting these stereotypes and being left to feel like inadequate women. Finally, phase three represents the future of computer science when the field changes to encompass women and other previously excluded groups.

Another useful framework for computer science gender change through time was articulated by Sue Rosser (1997), who described six phases of gendered transformation in science to which I can also compare the progress of computer science. In Rosser's phase theory there is a progression from (1) recognizing the absence of women in science, to (2) recognizing that most scientists are male, to (3) identifying the barriers to "not men," to (4) searching for women's contributions to demonstrate the possibility of women doing science, to (5) science being done by women, to (6) finally, science changing to include women (Rosser 1997, 3–5). Computer science has progressed through the first two stages but is still trapped somewhere in stage three, with four, five, and six hoped for in the future.

Research in science and technology studies (STS), such as work using actor network theory done by Bruno Latour (1987), demonstrated that social aspects of life transact with the technical aspects of life leaving neither one unchanged. This threshold in the study of technology allowed an understanding that the development of technology was much more than a trajectory off on its own. The development of technology such as computers was driven by social forces and also drives social changes. For instance, the invention of word processors has changed the way we write; similarly, the creation of word processors is affected by our stated needs for technology. If computer science and other technological fields were socially constructed, they could be deconstructed and then reconstructed to include those who were previously excluded by these fields. This insight had a huge effect on those who were currently excluded since they could now theorize places for themselves in science and technology.

Unfortunately, Latour and other STS researchers did not recognize gender as an important component of the social context of science and technology. It was left to feminist scholars such as Judy Wajcman, Cynthia Cockburn, and Susan Ormond to bring an awareness of gender into the social construction of technology (Ormrod 1995; Wajcman 1991). An early gender myth in technology and computer science, that technology was gender blind and gender neutral, was debunked by the gendered STS work (Wajcman 2004). This critical research unfortunately remains ignored in much current computer science and gender research.

Definitions

Computer science has been driven by gender beliefs and gender myths but also contributes evidence to different conceptualizations of gender. Definitions of gender are fluid. This essay utilizes Bryson and de Castell's discussion of gender as progressing generally from constructed as positivistic based on sex, to a social construction, then to an ideological construction, and finally as an ongoing construction and reconstruction known as the postmodern conceptualization of gender (Bryson and de Castell 1997). Gender is defined as a social construction that is created at birth and partially reinforced by power hierarchies and the desire for some to dominate others. This definition allows gender to be redefined so that a male field such as computer science need not remain a male field.

The following definition of computer science is particularly interesting since it comes from a U.S. government source, and because it functionally cuts off most women's interactions with computers:

"The systematic study of computing systems and computation. The body of knowledge resulting from this discipline contains theories for understanding computing systems and methods; design methodology, algorithms, and tools; methods for the testing of concepts; methods of analysis and verification; and knowledge representation and implementation" (http://www.nitrd.gov/pubs/bluebooks/1995/section.5.html, accessed 3/4/07; Interagency Working Group on Information Technology Research and Development 1995).

This definition excludes most women since it excludes the users of computers whether by office workers, teachers, help desk employees, or nurses and also excludes the construction line workers doing the dangerous and tedious jobs of building computers with dangerous materials and tiny components. This second grouping is composed of women and men who were mainly born outside the United States. It limits computer science to a very theoretical conceptualization of the field—indeed, the one maintained by the largely male academic departments that largely consider themselves gender neutral. While this definition supposes a gender neutrality, it really means that male has become normal and natural and therefore does not need to be mentioned in terms of computer science.

A Brief Chronology

Before there was a field of computer science there were many women literally "computing" by hand and with slide rules and mechanical adding machines such essential war-related figures as the trajectory of rockets for World War II field commanders. When electronic computing machines replaced and enhanced this hand computing, women continued their role as programmers and operators of these machines. This employment of women in the early field of computer science was further enhanced by the flow of men to the battlefields of the war.

Once computer science became a formal discipline, first at Purdue University in 1962 and then increasingly at other technological and later liberal arts schools, women were not absent—at least as students. The number of women in the computer science major gradually increased from about 10 percent undergraduates in 1967 to a high of about 37 percent in 1984 (Cohoon and Aspray 2006, x) and has since been declining to 28 percent or lower (Bae et al. 2000). It was in the late 1980s and onward when the number of women declined steadily that researchers began to notice the absence of women in the field.

On a Web site describing the history of computer science, the only women mentioned are Ada Augusta Byron, Countess of Lovelace, who first conceptualized programming, and Grace Murray Hopper, a navy officer who conceptualized the idea of computer compilers (Shallit 1995). There were certainly many other women involved in the early years of computer science but they were invisible to the author of this online history. The cover of Alison Adam's fine book, *Artificial Knowing: Gender and the Thinking Machine*, illustrates some of the early female workers (Adam 1998).

This absence of women from the computer science major was first blamed on math phobias, lack of encouragement, inadequate preparation in middle and high school, and insufficient exposure to computers. Interventions were devised to include more girls in computer programs by just "including more girls." The number of girls in advanced math classes increased, girls participated in computer summer camps and weekend programs, and they used computers more at home—but they did not go into the field of computer science. At the same time, the Internet grew and flourished. Online communications brought many girls into contact with computers. Women used computer networks for radical goals like marketing products, organizing social justice causes, supporting abused women and children, and linking up needy people with resources such as affordable prescription drugs and mental health professionals. However, the number of women in computer science majors did not increase but continued to decline.

The American Association of University Women report, *Tech Savvy*, came out in 2000 and described interviews with many girls who said "we can do it but we do not want to do it." This suggested "that the culture of computing needs to catch up with the girls rather than the girls needing to catch up with computing" (American Association of University Women 2000, ix).

Gender stereotypes in computer science also seem to be part of a struggle to maintain disciplinary boundaries. Larger numbers of women were involved in computer science before the field was institutionalized as departments in universities. At that transition point, power hierarchies in computer science meant controlling departments rich in students and grants and the stakes became higher to be in power. As in other fields such as medicine, education,

Grace Hopper created the first compiler and invented the computer language that became the basis for COBOL. She also served in the navy, retiring with the rank of admiral in 1986. (U.S. Department of Defense)

and law, men took power, created a male-centered environment, and made it uncomfortable or impossible for women to participate.

What is peculiar to computer science is that through these historical and developmental phases, stages, and reconceptualizations, the numbers of women have dropped, not increased as in most other disciplines after recognizing the nonparticipation of women. Why is this so? How does computer science differ from other predominantly androcentric disciplines, and why does it differ? Why are gender myths so tenacious in computer science?

Currently there is no good answer, but we do see some interesting developments. Applied computer science majors are being introduced in many first-tier universities, second-tier universities, and community colleges. These majors range from business information technology, educational technology, bioinformatics, educational technology, nursing informatics, to applied computer science, Web design, and game design. These applied computer science majors have attracted more women than the more theoretical computer science or computer engineering majors although much less than 50 percent. Perhaps these majors will be the lever to wrest power from the computer science boy's club. There is currently no indication that the graduates from these applied majors are doing worse in the job market than the more theoretical computer science majors and in some cases they seem more employable in our global computerized society.

A recent study at a historically Black university reports an equal number of women and men in the computer science major there. This finding strongly indicates that an appropriate educational context makes it comfortable for women to persist in the computer science major.

The decline of women in computer science is mainly a North American and European phenomenon and does not affect many women born abroad whether educated in the United States or in their countries of birth. Women in developing countries in Africa and Asia are participating in computer science in large and growing numbers

The past research suggests that institutional factors such as school climate, pedagogy, degree of diversity, and support for women are more important than individual differences such as previous experiences with computers, math interest, or previous skill in programming in recruiting and retaining women in computer science departments.

Conclusion

Research on gender and computer science has been slowed by assumptions of gender myths. The first was that computers as tools and the field of computer science are not gendered. The second was that if they were gendered there needed to be changes in the individual to make her more "suitable" for the field. These myths persist even though much research has been done demonstrating the gendered nature of computers and computer science and the necessity for institutional changes rather than individual changes to engage women in the field. Sadly, these myths also live in other fields such as science, math, architecture, law, medicine, and education, although computer science seems to be one of or even the most resistantly gendered field. (*See also* Discrimination; Historians of Science and Technology Who Focus on Feminism; Technology)

References and Further Reading

Adam, Alison. *Artificial Knowing: Gender and the Thinking Machine*. London: Routledge, 1998.

American Association of University Women. *Tech-savvy: Educating Girls in the New Computer Age*. Washington, DC: AAUW Educational Foundation Commission on Technology, Gender, and Teacher Education, 2000.

Bae, Yupin, Susan Choy, Claire Geddes, Jennifer Sable, and Thomas Snyder. *Trends in Educational Equity of Girls and Women*. Washington, DC: National Center for Education Statistics, 2000.

Bryson, Mary, and Suzanne de Castell. "En/gendering Equity: Paradoxical Consequences of Institutionalized Equity Policies." In *Radical In<ter>ventions*. Edited by S. de Castell and M. Bryson. Albany: State University of New York Press, 1997.

Cohoon, J. McGrath, and William Aspray, eds. *Women and Information Technology: Research on Underrepresentation*. Boston: MIT Press, 2006.

Interagency Working Group on Information Technology Research and Development. Guide to the NITRD Program: FY 2004–FY 2005: Supplement to the President's Budget, 1995. http://www.nitrd.gov/pubs/bluebooks/1995/section.5.html. (Accessed March 4, 2007.)

Latour, Bruno. *Science in Action*. Cambridge, MA: Harvard University Press 1987.

Lorber, Judith. *Breaking the Bowls: Degendering and Feminist Change*. New York: W. W. Norton, 2005.

Ormrod, Susan. "Feminist Sociology and Methodology: Leaky Black Boxes in Gender/Technology Relations." In *The Gender-Technology Relation: Contemporary Theory and Research*. Edited by K. Grint and R. Gill. London: Taylor and Francis, 1995.

Rosser, Sue V. *Re-engineering Female Friendly Science*. New York: Teachers College Press, 1997.

Shallit, Jeffrey O. "History of Computer Science." 1995. http://www.cs.uwaterloo.ca/~shallit/Courses/134/history.html. (Accessed May 31, 2007.)

Wajcman, Judy. *Feminism Confronts Technology*. University Park: Pennsylvania State University Press, 1991.

Biology

Mary Wyer

The field of biology has played a uniquely central role in research on women and gender in science because of extensive research at individual, social, and symbolic levels of analysis (Harding 1986). Historically, women were systematically excluded from formal higher education in the biological sciences and medicine in Western culture. This exclusion was justified by an ideology that proclaimed men as intellectually and physiologically superior to women. As a result, knowledge about human biology has been biased by the notion that a male body is the normal human body. In recent years, social and political initiatives focusing on women's health have begun to correct and advance biomedical knowledge to provide a more comprehensive understanding of human biology (Schiebinger 1999). Growing awareness about social biases in scientific research has prompted many researchers to discard simplistic theories about the relationship between biology and intellectual ability. More complex theories about human physiology and behavior now posit dynamic interactions between biological, psychological, and cultural influences to explain individuals' abilities, interests, and performance in social and historical contexts. Though this has helped to decrease gender biases in women's professional opportunities and in knowledge about women's biology, it has also opened up a new set of questions about objectivity and taken-for-granted "facts." Feminist theories have advanced the idea that social biases are deeply rooted in and sustained by the organization and frameworks of the ideas, perspectives, and facts that are accepted as legitimate (Harding 1986). Thus, the process of developing and reconstructing knowledge about human biology that is informed by critiques of gender bias has just begun.

Increasing Numbers of Women in Biology

At the individual level of analysis, it is clear that women have the interest, ability, and talent to pursue training in the biological sciences. Biology as a field has seen dramatic increases in the representation and participation of women. In the 1960s, only one in 10 doctoral degrees in the biological sciences were awarded to women. Forty years later, women are receiving nearly half of the doctoral degrees in the biological sciences. By 2004, at the undergraduate level, women received six out every 10 bachelor's degrees in the biological sciences (NSF 2006). In the interim, and facing a national shortage of scientists, the U.S. Congress had passed the Equal Opportunities in Science and Technology Act (1980) to direct the National Science Foundation to develop programs to ensure that girls and women had equal opportunities in education, training, and employment in the sciences. Educational researchers identified a wide variety of individual-level factors at play in discouraging girls and women from excelling in science. Particularly influential in diverting girls from their science interests were primary and secondary educational experiences (Sadker and Sadker 1994). Political will and employment opportunities thus converged with educational concerns to cultivate increasing numbers of women who choose biology as a career. Women now constitute over 40 percent of the workforce in the biological sciences. However, representation of women at the highest ranks has lagged. For instance, only 20 percent of faculty in the biological sciences are women, and women's achievements are underrecognized among those who receive the most prestigious awards.

Research on Women's Biology

At the level of social practices and processes, women in biology have been at the forefront of challenging the myth that women are incapable of becoming scientists. They have also played a key role in focusing attention on the need for unbiased research about women's biology. The idea that the imperatives of human evolution have defined women as caretakers and men as wage-earners was promoted in 19th-century European patriarchal beliefs about sex differences. The inequality of women in social, political, and economic life was said to be a product of natural, universal, and immutable sex differences. These ideas emerged in the context of evolutionary theory and social Darwinism, in particular in the work of sociologist Herbert Spencer. The roots of research on human sex differences are notorious for providing historical evidence of biases in the underlying assumptions of scientific research, including in particular the history of research about dimorphic "sex hormones" (Fausto-Sterling 2000). Contemporary studies of the relationship between biology and intellectual ability reveal that measured cognitive and performance differences between women and men are very small and often nonexistent.

However, the biology of female bodies is understudied, since women have long been excluded from medical research. With the rise of the modern women's movement in the 1970s and 1980s came increased concern about the quality, content, and priorities of medical research about women. National efforts such as the Boston Women's Health Book Collective and the Black Women's Health Movement, and local initiatives such as the Mound Bayou Community Health Clinic organized and educated the public to challenge medical research and training that ignored, devalued, or marginalized women. For instance, the 1958 Baltimore Study of Aging, a grounding study of human aging, included no women even though two thirds of those over 65 years old are women (Schiebinger 1999). Heart disease is the leading cause of death in women, and yet many of the foundational national studies of heart disease included no women. Examples such as these prompted advocates for women's health to lobby the federal government to require that women be included in medical testing and research. The absence of women, and women's bodies, from research populations impoverished the data, interpretations of the data, applications of research findings, and delivery of care to women as consumers of medicine.

Gender Bias in Language and Symbols

Some have argued that biological knowledge also embeds gender bias at the symbolic level (Keller 1992). The exclusion and marginalization of women as biologists and the exclusion and marginalization of women's biology from scientific knowledge are evidence that the culture of science is influenced by the larger society. Social theorists have argued that because all scientific knowledge is constructed through human action and activity, biological knowledge by extension is not so much "fact" as "contested territory" (Haraway 1991). This means that social values, conflicts, and priorities are represented by the language, topics, methods, and interpretations offered through scientific inquiry. Nature, in this perspective, is not transparently revealed to scientists through the use of the scientific method. Rather, scientists formulate theories in historical and social context, utilizing language that necessarily taps a widely shared repertoire of meanings and metaphors. What is known about nature in general, and biology in particular, reveals as much about the knowledge makers as about the natural world. For instance, descriptions of the relationship between the egg and the sperm have drawn upon conventional stereotypes about how women and men relate to one another (Martin 1991). Narratives of heterosexual courtship and marriage have influenced terminology in a wide variety of biological sciences, including cell biology, genetics, botany, and bacteriology (Schiebinger 1999). This influence goes beyond merely borrowing terms because it informs what questions can and cannot be asked, and which answers are considered legitimate to offer. For instance, some have described the preeminence of genetics in biology as an example of technical machismo that reflects competitive and capitalist, rather than cooperative and caring, applications of scientific expertise (Shiva 1995). Others have argued that a focus on the dynamics of competition in the natural world distorts scientific knowledge itself, promoting a willful blindness to the complexities and interactions that define natural phenomena (Subramaniam 2001).

Conclusion

The topic of biology in relation to women and gender is complex. Contemporary fields within human biology cover a wide variety of topics (muscles, nerves, blood, brains, bones, reproduction, sexuality, sex similarities and differences, to name a few). The people who have created that knowledge, the process of creating that knowledge, and the knowledge itself all spring from human activity in social and historical contexts. In Western history, biased research about the capabilities and interests of women have shaped, and been shaped by, many of our social, economic, political, educational, and scientific practices and priorities. Because the study of biology has been influenced by these biases, using a perspective that includes women and gender promises to have a positive impact on human health and well-being. (*See also* Feminist Science Studies; Gender/Sex—How Conjoined; Nature/Nurture; Women's Health Movement; Nobel Laureates; Biologists Who Study Gender/ Feminism)

References and Further Reading

Fausto-Sterling, A. *Sexing the Body: Gender Politics and the Construction of Sexuality*. New York: Basic Books, 2000.

Haraway, D. *Simians, Cyborgs, and Women: The Reinvention of Nature*. New York: Routledge, 1991.

Harding, S. *The Science Question in Feminism*. Ithaca, NY: Cornell University Press, 1986.

Keller, E. F. *Secrets of Life, Secrets of Death: Essays on Language, Gender, and Science*. New York: Routledge, 1992.

Martin, E. "The Egg and the Sperm: How Science Has Constructed a Romance Based on Stereotypical Male-Female Roles." *Signs: Journal of Women in Culture and Society* 16 (1991): 485–501.

National Science Foundation (NSF). *Women, Minorities, and Persons with Disabilities*. Washington, DC: U.S. Government Printing Office, 2006.

Sadker, M., and D. Sadker. *Failing at Fairness: How America's Schools Cheat Girls.* New York: Charles Scribner's Sons, 1994.

Schiebinger, L. *Has Feminism Changed Science?* Cambridge, MA: Harvard University Press, 1999.

Shiva, V. "Democratizing Biology: Reinventing Biology from a Feminist, Ecological and Third World Perspective." In *Reinventing Biology.* Edited by L. Birke and R. Hubbard, 50–71. Bloomington: Indiana University Press, 1995.

Subramaniam, B. "The Aliens Have Landed! Reflections on the Rhetoric of Biological Invasions." In *Making Threats: Biofears and Environmental Anxieties,* 135–148. New York: Rowman & Littlefield, 2001.

Psychology

Janine P. Buckner and Susan A. Nolan

The role of women in psychology, as in most fields, has changed greatly over its history. In the early years, psychology was focused on men, with respect both to those who practiced and studied within the field and the topic of study. In line with this, many early findings were biased against women. For example, when the intellect was thought to reside in the frontal lobes, women were "found" to have smaller frontal lobes than men, and when that theory was revised to place the intellect in the parietal lobes, women were then "found" to have larger frontal lobes and smaller parietal lobes than men (e.g., Matlin 2004).

The participation of women within the field has steadily increased. In the early 1900s, a female researcher, Helen Thompson Woolley, was among the first working to diminish bias against women. She reported that women and men had similar levels of intelligence and that, in fact, women outscored men in some intellectual arenas (Matlin 2004).

Since Woolley's pioneering research, there have been several movements within the field that have spearheaded overall change. Among these were organizations dedicated to forwarding women in the field and encouraging research on women. Most prominent among these is the Society for the Psychology of Women, Division 35 of the American Psychological Association (APA).

APA: Division 35

The APA has a number of divisions dedicated to specific areas within the field of psychology. Division 35 is the Society for the Psychology of Women. Founded in 1973, Division 35's goal is "to promote feminist scholarship and practice, and to advocate action toward public policies that advance equality and social justice." Among the division's activities is the maintenance of a heritage Web site dedicated to preserving and disseminating information about the history of women in the field of psychology (http://www.psych.yorku.ca/femhop/).

Division 35, however, was pre-dated by the Association for Women in Psychology (AWP), an organization founded in 1969 at one of the annual meetings of the APA. Activist members of AWP protested at an APA board meeting, expressing concern that there was no official APA organization dedicated to women. Their protests and actions led to the creation of Division 35. Since this establishment, Division 35 and AWP continue to work together to advance the goals of female psychologists and to promote gender-fair research within psychology. Both organizations have recruited many women and men to assist with these goals. In fact, APA's Division 35 is one of the largest subdivisions within the overall structure of the organization.

Melanie Klein

Division 35's heritage Web site provides information on female psychologists who have made lasting contributions to the field. A number of these are women who studied and practiced in the field of psychoanalysis and have been pioneers in raising consciousness about women's issues. Psychoanalysis, although now subject to a great deal of criticism due to its perceived lack of empiricism, was an important early arena within psychology, one that paved the way for much of the work that succeeded it. Several female psychoanalysts, including Anna Freud, Nancy Chodorow, and Karen Horney, are well known, and yet a greater contribution was made by a little known female psychoanalyst, Melanie Klein.

Melanie Klein was the founder of object-relations theory, a branch of psychoanalysis in which the relationship between a mother and child is viewed as central to a child's development (Donaldson 2002). In addition, Klein was the first to use psychoanalysis with children and to develop a theory of psychoanalysis for use with children. The approach, which she derived from her theories, has been incorporated into what is now often referred to as play therapy. Much of this work was included in her book, *The Psychoanalysis of Children,* published in 1932. In addition to her influence on therapeutic techniques for children, many of the techniques of psychoanalysis for adults that came later were couched in the language of Klein's theory. Moreover, Klein's work influenced many prominent psychologists who followed her, including John Bowlby. In fact, her writing on depressive and anxiety-producing mechanisms in childhood commanded the most respect and harshest criticisms from colleagues across the field, and across time. But even though there is disagreement about Klein's theory, there is consensus that her ideas left their mark on developmental psychology (Donaldson 2002).

Klein's influence was evident during her lifetime. Her theories were often referred to as Kleinianism, and debates of her time focused on whether Kleinianism was different from or the same as Freudianism. Klein became quite prominent in European psychiatric circles through both her theories and writing and her participation in the training of psychoanalysts (Donaldson 2002). Although psychoanalysis has gone out of favor among most research psychologists today, Melanie Klein's early contributions were important for their groundbreaking nature and her willingness and courage to challenge the establishment within psychology. She died from cancer in 1960.

Jean Baker Miller and the Stone Center

The contributions of psychiatrist and psychoanalyst Jean Baker Miller to the advancement of women have been described as efforts to "de-pathologize" women's behavior and shape a rational view of women (Woolf 2006). Her theory, called the relational-cultural approach (RCT), has become widely applied in psychotherapeutic practice and is also used to explain individuals' everyday behaviors and relationships. A hallmark of this approach is the subscription to a developmental model that views all humans as having a central need to connect to others in intimate ways rather than striving toward independence and moving away from significant others throughout development. With respect to psychotherapy, Miller's key to therapeutic change in individuals' lives is to correct relational disconnections; thus, the approach of RCT includes ways of fostering emotionally invested roles for both the client and therapist in the course of their relationship, rather than centering the therapist in an authoritative role as impartial or objective. Miller's model also focuses on the strengths of women's relational styles and the buffering effects that connections to others may provide them. In this context, Miller's work elaborates the developmental models by fostering growth in relationships, and thus within the self.

In 1986, Jean Baker Miller became director of the Elizabeth Stone Center for Developmental Services and Studies at Wellesley College, a major aim of which is to provide alternative treatments for individuals who would otherwise be hospitalized in psychiatric facilities. In 1995 the work of Miller fostered the foundation of the Jean Baker Miller Training Institute. The Institute, which is part of the Stone Center, trains professionals in the relational-cultural approach in psychotherapy and research. In effect, the aim of the Institute is to increase awareness regarding the myths of gender and to change the ways individuals make personal decisions as well as to influence the design and support of policies that are applied to society more generally.

Researchers, community leaders, therapists, and business executives have benefited from their associations with the Institute. Research symposia, training

Psychiatrist Jean Baker Miller. (Courtesy Jean Baker Miller Training Institute)

programs, and manuscripts based on the Institute's work continue to shape the course of scholarship and practice. Such well-known scholars as Carole Gilligan, Jean Kilbourne, and Judith Herman have been closely associated with the work of the Institute.

Miller's contributions to the field of psychology also include the book *Toward a New Psychology of Women* (Miller 1976), a groundbreaking text on developmentally emergent gender differences and cultural implications for these differences. Under the direction of Jean Baker Miller, both the Stone Center and the Institute have shaped the course of many women and the organizations that serve them.

Women's Ways of Knowing

The inauguration of important organizations for women in psychology, such as Division 35, did much to advance the roles of women within psychology. These groups have overseen the promotion of more equitable gender-related research within psychology as well as the advancement of women more generally in society. Despite the import of this work, however, progress was perceived to be slow (a continuing observation). As a response to this per-ception, four psychologists—Mary Field Belenky, Blythe McVicker Clinchy, Nancy Rule Goldberger, and Jill Mattuck Tarule—wrote a critically acclaimed book, *Women's Ways of Knowing*. Its impetus was the need for a more com-prehensive explanation of the feeling expressed among women in the United States that they have not achieved equality and remain stifled in family, school, and work settings. Based on extensive interviews with 135 women, the authors posit a theory that elaborates a feminist perspective of "voice." In modern cultures, women's perceptions and perspectives are often "silenced" by more powerful ("masculinized") views. From this vantage, "voice" repre-sents a form of power given or constructed within interpersonal contexts. In negotiating through relationships, women develop one of five ways of know-ing from which they perceive themselves and approach the world (Belenky et al. 1986).

The five ways of knowing demonstrated by women range from healthy exploration and expression of self and one's values or beliefs to a silent or muted and unexplored notion of self that leads to a lack of confidence and a deference toward authority. For instance, women whose cognitive style is characterized by "silence" do not actively explore or express their own per-spectives but instead follow prescribed stereotypes. With such a stifled un-derstanding of identity, they will not—and cannot—engage in productive behaviors that benefit themselves. A second cognitive style, received know-ing, portends that women attend to the voices of significant others in their lives and therefore will tend to conform to social stereotypes and expectations. In a different way of knowing (subjective knowing), the self is most actively involved in interpreting experiences; this style reflects a tendency to avoid others' directions or perceptions and "listen" only to one's own voice. In pro-cedural knowledge, women are invested in learning and applying objective procedures for obtaining and communicating knowledge. Still another way of knowing is constructed knowledge, where one balances and integrates in-trapersonal knowledge and styles of cognition with those that fit best with the information valued by the external world. This style is perhaps the most likely to predict successful management of personal goals within a broader set of community or workplace objectives.

Drawing on these ways of knowing, therapists, mentors, and researchers can design interventions or practices that best support and encourage women to lead healthy, successful lives. They also may be used to describe why in-dividuals fail to thrive or grow in culturally valued arenas of life.

This book and the theory it proffers have been widely read and lauded by the lay public and by psychology professionals. *Women's Ways of Knowing* was awarded the Distinguished Publication Award by the AWP (in 1987).

Psychology of Women Now

The field of psychology of women has progressed greatly since the days of Helen Thompson Woolley. As one measure of change, a researcher (Worell 1996) identified 589 published works on gender and psychology in 1983, and about five times as many—2,782—just 10 years later in 1993. As Women's Studies programs are renamed and repurposed as Gender Studies programs, so too are textbooks on the psychology of women renamed and revised as the psychology of gender, a shift both political and practical in purpose.

In addition, researchers who focus on gender and psychology are realizing more and more that neither women nor men can be described solely by their gender, and that other characteristics such as race, sexual orientation, country of origin, and education are also important predictors of behavior. Moreover, researchers and practitioners have become increasingly aware that gender similarities far outweigh gender differences. In many cases, the focus on gender differences within psychological literature has led to the search for gender differences instead of similarities. Unfortunately, this preference to describe and discuss differences rather than similarities has led to much research on gender differences. It seems that Division 35 and its sister organizations still have a role to play in furthering efforts to expand the awareness of women's and men's issues. (*See also* Early 20th Century; Gender/Sex—How Conjoined)

References and Further Reading

Belenky, Mary F., B. M. Clinchy, N. R. Goldberger, and J. M. Tarule. *Women's Ways of Knowing: The Development of Self, Voice, and Mind.* New York: Basic Books, 1986.

Donaldson, G. "Melanie Klein, Psychoanalyst (1882–1960)." *The Feminist Psychologist,* newsletter of the Society for the Psychology of Women, Division 35 of the American Psychological Association, 2002, 29. http://www.psych.yorku.ca/femhop/Melanie%20Klein.htm. (Accessed on November 7, 2006.)

Matlin, M. W. *The Psychology of Women.* 5th ed. Belmont, CA: Wadsworth, 2004.

Miller, Jean B. *Toward a New Psychology of Women.* Boston: Beacon Press, 1976.

American Psychological Association. "Society for the Psychology of Women." http://www.apa.org/divisions/div35/. (Accessed on November 6, 2006.)

Division 35, American Psychological Association. "Society for the Psychology of Women Heritage Site." http://www.psych.yorku.ca/femhop/. (Accessed on November 6, 2006.)

Woolf, Linda M. "'Jean Baker Miller' Women's Intellectual Contributions to the Study of Mind and Society." http://www.webster.edu/~woolflm/women.html. (Accessed on November 8, 2006.)

Worell, J. "Opening Doors to Feminist Research." *Psychology of Women Quarterly* 20 (1996): 469–485.

Medicine

Amy Bix

Since ancient times, the theory and practice of medicine have been influenced by assumptions, generalizations, and myths about the differences between men and women. Across cultures and many centuries, folk medicine promoted superstitions about gender, such as a popular belief that the female body was connected to the lunar cycle.

Antiquity

In the fourth century BC, followers of Hippocrates, the "father of medicine," sought to separate medicine from magic and wrote numerous books analyzing female anatomy, women's illnesses, and childbirth. Hippocratics argued that in their natural balance of the body's four essential humors (blood, phlegm, yellow bile, and black bile), women were "colder" and "wetter" than men and therefore more emotional and more sexual. Women's looser-textured flesh supposedly retained more moisture, and the Hippocratics warned that without regular menstruation to purge this surplus fluid, women could suffer mental distress, physical illness, or even death. Virgins at the onset of puberty were considered particularly vulnerable to mental disorders, stemming from menstrual irregularity before the womb had been "opened" via sexual relations, and some observers prescribed marriage as the "cure." Without a woman's regular menstruation or intercourse, humoral imbalances could dislocate the uterus from its proper place, and this "wandering womb" would cause headaches, pain, or other symptoms as it moved around the body. Physicians recommended enticing the womb back to its proper place with sweet scents, believing that the womb, like an animal, reacted to smells. This belief in the uterus as a primary source of women's illnesses and strange weaknesses continued for centuries and led to the concept of "hysteria" (the word derived from the Greek for "uterus") (Tuana 1993).

Writing about natural philosophy, Aristotle started from the premise that men were more biologically advanced than women, who had less "vital heat" and were therefore weaker physically, mentally, and emotionally. Aristotle asserted that in almost all species, females were smaller, less courageous, and more deceptive. Aristotle defined a fundamental dichotomy between males as active and rational, and females as passive and emotional. He portrayed the male as the true and superior form of nature, the female as a departure from that ideal. Such biological characterizations accorded well with patriarchal Greek life, which excluded women from citizenship, and Greek mythology that portrayed women's existence as punishment for men. Building on such arguments, the influential physician Galen maintained that male and female genitals were structurally identical, but women's lack of vital heat prevented theirs from emerging from the body, the final step in development. The assumption that women had less vital heat than men shaped theories about reproduction. Aristotle argued that women contributed only raw material to make new life, while men created the higher spirit by passing on soul and intellect.

Europeans followed the writings, prescriptions, and assumptions of Aristotle, Hippocrates, and Galen as unchallenged expertise through the medieval era, when Christian doctrine reinforced biological ideas of women's weakness and inferiority. Church leaders insisted on clerical celibacy and monastic seclusion, denouncing women as the devil's temptation. Some theologians maintained that childbirth pains represented God's ongoing punishment for Eve's responsibility in the fall of man. Theologians' assessment of women as weak and wicked corresponded with both medicine and superstition. Biblical rules for women's ritual cleansing linked menstruation to contamination, while physicians warned that intercourse during menstruation would result in a malformed child. Menstrual blood itself was considered either dangerous or magical, and popular rumor held that a menstruating woman could cause cows to stop giving milk.

Thomas Aquinas (1225–1274) accepted Aristotle's assumption about women having less vital heat and lent the Church's weight to reinforce generalizations about women as biologically inferior to men. Church authorities fed the witchcraft scare of the 1500s and 1600s that spread across Europe and America, suggesting that women's inherent mental and emotional weakness made them especially susceptible to Satan's lures.

Through the Middle Ages, medical students were taught by rote recitation of Galen or Hippocratic work, and social, religious, and legal regulations generally prohibited human dissection. Physicians thus clung to inaccurate anatomical ideas; some textbooks showed a uterus divided into seven chambers or treated the uterus as an independent creature that could be irritated or calmed. Respected writers repeated tales of women who gave birth to 20 children in just two pregnancies.

Renaissance

Renaissance medical advances offered a new approach to anatomy. Leonardo da Vinci (1452–1519) produced voluminous sketches of muscles, organs, and other bodily components out of interest and a desire to make his artistic depictions more accurate and graceful. But while his notes and drawings revealed greater understanding of anatomy than any before, Leonardo's journals and studies were not published or made widely accessible for many decades. Before then, Andreas Vesalius (1514–1564) avidly undertook dissections (at great risk, due to religious scruples and civil prohibitions against violating bodily integrity). In *The Structure of the Human Body* (1543), Vesalius opened a new era for studying the human body and corrected some, though not all, errors in older notions about the structure of the female reproductive system.

18th Century

By the 18th century, scientific biology had encouraged reevaluation of ideas about female nature. Rather than regarding women's anatomy as an incomplete distortion of man's, experts instead portrayed women's reproductive system as unique. The uterus represented the perfect tool for pregnancy, letting women fulfill their main function in life, while men's greater physical and intellectual strength matched the demands of their public and military leadership. Anatomical illustrations often exaggerated sex differences, highlighting women's larger pelvis, and anatomists deliberately selected models who represented the ideal masculine or feminine build, thereby both reflecting and reinforcing cultural values (Schiebinger 1989).

Behind the supposedly objective science, assumptions about women's inferiority persisted, as shown in 19th-century studies of the brain. Observers realized that while overall men had larger brains than women, women's skulls were proportionately larger to their bodies. Craniologists suggested that women's large skulls actually proved their biological immaturity, placing them on an anatomical parallel with children, who have relatively large heads and delicate bone structure (Russett 1989).

Despite tangible advances in the practice of European and American medicine, 19th-century medical theories and treatments revealed the persistence of gendered assumptions (Haller and Haller 1974). Just as Greek physicians blamed the "wandering womb" for many female illnesses, Victorian physicians believed that the uterus was directly connected to the nervous system and thus could cause disease throughout a woman's body. Like the Greeks, they emphasized the dangers posed to young women by the onset of menstruation.

Even as 19th-century observers measured women's nature and life options in terms of reproductive capacity, they characterized the female reproductive system as inherently pathological, causing all sorts of physical, mental, and emotional complications. Reflecting what historians have called the ideology of "separate spheres," authorities defined men's role as public life, politics, and business, and women's role (at least among the middle and upper classes) as children and household. Novels and advice books promoted this "cult of domesticity," characterizing the true woman as submissive, pure, and self-sacrificing. Among some upper-class women, romanticized invalidism even became stylish, and corsets made it hard to eat, sit, or even breathe normally. Women expected to collapse during every menstrual period, and experts cautioned women against dancing, riding, or shopping at "that time of the month." "Hysteria" represented an ultra-emotional extreme of delicate woman-hood. Historians have suggested that for some women, hysteria became a means of claiming attention, fighting social control, or escaping family de-mands. The "rest cure" for mental breakdown confined patients to a dim room without visitors, a lack of stimulus meant to sink the brain into inactivity.

Impact on Education

Even as medical thought seemingly justified assumptions that women's bio-logical cycle, from menstruation to menopause, kept them fragile and unfit for social roles beyond the home, women after the mid-1800s pursued wider concerns and interests. In the United States, coeducational state land-grant colleges offered women increasing opportunity to pursue advanced degrees, as did private women's colleges. By 1891, over 10,000 women were enrolled in higher education, yet observers worried that education made women too mannish. Prominent doctors, including Harvard professor Edward Clarke, warned that higher education posed substantial medical risk for young women. Physicians argued that the human body, like an economic system, contained only finite resources and that women who devoted too much energy to the brain would drain away sustenance for vital reproductive organs. Clarke cau-tioned that especially during menstruation, women who studied as hard as men risked nervous collapse, physical breakdown, or future infertility. Many experts worried about indications that female graduates had lower marriage rates and fewer children than the noncollege female population. Officials at women's colleges defended the appropriateness of female education, pro-moting exercise and healthy habits among their students and collecting data to prove female graduates' good health.

Further controversy arose as women sought to enter the modern medical profession. Historically, women across cultures had long served as family healers and midwives, skilled with herbal cures and folk medicine. But with increasing professionalization, especially in urban areas, doctors strove to exert gatekeeping authority and tighten requirements for the right to practice. Many passionately opposed giving women access to medical education, suggesting that no decent woman should want to learn about topics such as venereal disease and that women lacked the stamina to handle long hours. Revealingly, few cited physical stress as reason to oppose having female nurses, who were not perceived as threats to male doctors, at least as long as they remained in a subordinate station. Elizabeth Blackwell became the first woman to earn an American medical degree in 1849, after she was admitted to medical school as a fluke. Because almost all 19th-century medical schools continued to reject female students, supporters opened medical schools just for women. Meeting varying degrees of criticism and opposition, women doctors gradually established themselves as part of the profession and contributed substantially; Alice Hamilton pioneered the field of industrial medicine, earning a position at Harvard Medical School (Morantz-Sanchez 1985).

20th Century

But while the 20th century brought numerous changes in women's political, economic, legal, and social conditions, gendered assumptions about women's nature continued to affect medical thinking. Especially after World War II, with suburbanization and the baby boom, social scientists reasserted the centrality of traditional gender roles. Freudian psychology, postwar corporate advertising, and American popular culture glorified marriage and presented domesticity as women's natural calling. Experts warned that ambitious girls who rejected womanly instincts and competed with men for paid employment risked unhappiness, spinsterhood, frigidity, infertility, or homosexuality.

By the 1960s and 1970s, feminism turned many medical matters into political issues, fighting old stereotypes and encouraging new questions about the biology of gender. The feminist health movement organized to help women better understand their own bodies and gain the courage to demand nonpaternalist, nonjudgmental, and satisfactory medical treatment. Activists protested that the male-dominated medical establishment devalued women, with gynecological textbooks that promoted sexist stereotyping and encouraged doctors to patronize female patients. They denounced a lack of respect for women's physical autonomy that led doctors to perform unnecessary hysterectomies and turned childbirth into hypermedicalized, assembly line torture.

Greater female representation gradually created noticeable changes in the look and outlook of the medical system, at least in some aspects. In 2006, women outnumbered men in medical school applications (though male admissions remained a bare majority). However, women entering macho specialties such as surgery still complained about discrimination and harassment from the "boys' club" (Rosser 1993).

Recent research seeks to address unsolved questions about biological sex differences. For such reasons, it is essential to continue thinking about the history and persistence of gender assumptions in medicine. (*See also* Antiquity; Women's Education; The 18th Century; Medieval Era; The 19th Century; Renaissance; Women's Health Movement)

References and Further Reading

Haller, John S., and Robin M. Haller. *The Physician and Sexuality in Victorian America*. Champaign: University of Illinois Press, 1974.

Morantz-Sanchez, Regina. *Sympathy and Science: Women Physicians in American Medicine*. Oxford: Oxford University Press, 1985.

Rosser, Sue V. *Women's Health: Missing from U.S. Medicine*. Bloomington: Indiana University Press, 1993.

Russett, Cynthia Eagle. *Sexual Science: The Victorian Construction of Womanhood*. Cambridge, MA: Harvard University Press, 1989.

Schiebinger, Londa. *The Mind Has No Sex? Women in the Origins of Modern Science*. Cambridge, MA: Harvard University Press, 1989.

Tuana, Nancy. *The Less Noble Sex: Scientific, Religious, and Philosophical Conceptions of Woman's Nature*. Bloomington: Indiana University Press, 1993.

Technology

Amy Bix

Gendered questions about technology depend on that word's definition. "Technology" often signifies machinery, images of race cars, robots, or military weapons that play to a macho love of power and speed. But once we broaden the concept of technology to include baby bottles, contraceptive devices, sewing patterns, and cell phones, gender connotations change. Furthermore, historians define technology not just as hardware but, equally important, as knowledge about making or doing things. This understanding opens discussion about technology to include skills such as cooking, weaving, and nursing (Lerman, Oldenziel, and Mohun 2003).

Technological assumptions often follow a dichotomy that men build machines while women use them, gendering engineering (active) as male and consumerism (passive) as female. But in reality, women maintain complex relationships to technology, not just as consumers but also as inventors, producers, and workers (Horowitz and Mohun 1998).

Technology itself carries gendered meanings, both deliberate and unintended (Wosk 2001). If asked to assign gender to inanimate objects, most Americans will color a typewriter pink and a jet engine blue. But the relationship is not static; women have actively chosen to accept, reject, or reshape technologies to fit their needs and desires.

Automobiles

"Women's technology" is seen as less valuable, as illustrated in the early 1900s, when buyers could choose between electric, steam, and gasoline-powered automobiles. Experts presumed women were too high-strung to handle noisy, dirty gasoline cars and too weak to manage the difficult, exhausting ignition cranking. Manufacturers of electric cars marketed their easy push-button start as naturally suited to female drivers. Heavy batteries limited electrics' range to 50 miles, but women who roamed too far were controversial anyway; when

Theodore Roosevelt's daughter's long solo drives drew criticism, the president allegedly commented that he could run the country or control Alice, not both. Even Henry Ford bought an electric car for his wife to make calls around town. But once quiet, clean, electric cars became associated with female drivers, men scorned them for sportier gasoline models (Scharff 1991).

While assuming men to be natural drivers, skeptics disparaged women as easily distracted, nervous, and unable to react rapidly in emergencies. Early racer Joan Cuneo suggested that cautiousness and responsibility actually made women better drivers. But when a female driver had an accident, critics held her mistakes against her entire sex.

Ironically, female drivers' presumed inferiority opened one opportunity. To convince potential customers that automobiles weren't just fads, promoters staged long-distance trips to demonstrate their machines' practicality. In 1909, manufacturers sponsored Alice Ramsey's cross-country 41-day drive across primitive roads. The publicity stunt signaled to men, "What are you worried about? Even a woman can handle this!"

Despite criticism, hundreds of women soon adopted automobiles. Suffragists made driving tours to promote women's voting rights; cars drew attention, covered ground rapidly, and made an important statement. In breaking from old notions of ideal womanhood, the suffragists' comfort with technology fostered an alternate vision of gender roles, the independent "New Woman." During World War I, dozens of British, French, and American women (including Gertrude Stein and Alice B. Toklas) volunteered to transport wounded soldiers, bring supplies to battlefield hospitals, and evacuate refugees. Ambulance driving took women into areas under fire and across destroyed roads where women had to repair breakdowns themselves.

Aviation

In aviation, many flying instructors initially refused to teach women, calling them emotionally unreliable and incapable of mastering mechanical details. America's first licensed female pilot, Harriet Quimby, flew the English Channel in 1912, and subsequently, female pilots beat male competitors in high-profile air races. The 1929 Women's Air Derby required female aviators to carry male navigators, outraging Amelia Earhart. Earhart promoted her flying records (including the first Atlantic Ocean solo since Charles Lindbergh) as proving women's ability to succeed in all areas of life. In the 1930s, at least 700 women held American pilot's licenses, but "ladybirds" and "sweethearts of the air" were expected to look pretty even following exhausting flights. Photographs of Earhart in both flying helmet and pearl necklace underlined expectations of femininity.

Elizabeth L. Gardner, a WASP (Women's Airforce Service Pilot), of Rockford, Illinois, prepares for takeoff. The WASPs flew noncombat missions during World War II. (National Archives)

Airplane manufacturers hired female pilots as public representatives, as their demonstrations made aviation look glamorous and easy enough for a woman. But airlines refused to hire women as commercial pilots, figuring that 1920s passengers already felt nervous about flying without the additional worry of having a female pilot. In 1934, Helen Richey beat seven men in tests for air mail employment, but male pilots forced her to resign by pressuring the Commerce Department into forbidding Richey from flying in bad weather (and possibly grounding her during menstruation). While airlines excluded female pilots until the 1970s, they welcomed all-American girls as stewardesses to pamper passengers.

Just as World War I made female drivers valuable, so the manpower shortage of World War II temporarily opened flying opportunity to women. Women's Airforce Service Pilots (WASPs) delivered military planes, tested planes after repairs, and towed gunnery targets for artillery crew training (with live ammunition). But the government refused to grant WASPs official status, and the program was canceled once the military found male pilots to replace the women. Russia's female pilots actually flew in combat, conducting night bombing raids on German positions and airlifting supplies to stranded troops.

WASP performance indicated that women had high endurance for isolation, pain, and temperature extremes, supporting the National Aeronautics and Space Administration's (NASA) 1960 move to consider female pilots as astronauts. Despite women's excellence in physical and psychological testing, the program was abruptly canceled after critics (including John Glenn) warned that the sideshow of training female astronauts might cost the United States the space race. Women didn't fit the "right stuff" test-pilot model, and the government feared the political ramifications if female astronauts got killed. NASA did not name female astronauts until 1978, under pressure to offer equal opportunity to women.

Bicycles

While female aviators offered curiosity value, women's more common relationship to technology, as consumers, also threatened to disrupt "separate spheres" ideology. Although women (and many men) hesitated to tackle tricky high-wheeled bicycles, the safety bicycle developed in the 1890s appealed particularly to women. Appearance presented issues; for practicality, many female riders adopted divided skirts or knickers. Pointed humor caricatured female bicyclists as either revoltingly muscular or helplessly fragile. Experts encouraged female riders to acquire technical competence, learning to maintain and fix their own machines. Medical experts warned about physical consequences of overexertion, while moralists worried about women cycling alone or worse, with men. Jokes about women riding off, leaving husbands with chores and child care, masked real concerns about women abandoning demure domesticity.

Consumers and Home Economics

Even as women were bicycling, entering college, and agitating to vote, early 20th-century experts hoped new technologies could reinforce traditional roles. The discipline of home economics aimed to lure women back to their "natural" domestic role by teaching them to become more scientific, more efficient, and thus happier homemakers. High school and college home ec instructors, women's magazines, and extension workers emphasized the advantages of modern kitchen equipment, following corporations in promoting a vision where electrified homes meant big business.

Some industries reshaped technologies to court female consumers. Early 20th-century men and boys tinkered with homemade radios in garages, but when commercial broadcasting began in the 1920s, radio moved into living rooms. Manufacturers designed sets resembling elegant furniture, and networks created soap operas and cooking shows to attract female audiences. But other businesses overlooked or devalued the women's market. Early telephone systems promoted business communication and condemned wasteful female chatting before belatedly recognizing the financial potential of leisure calling.

Homemakers were not passive recipients of technology. To make women technically informed purchasers, home economists taught students to inspect appliances down to the seams. Defying helpless housewife stereotypes, classes studied the construction of refrigerators by literally taking them apart. Nor did women automatically obey messages about technology reinforcing traditional roles. Farm life experts praised rural electrification as enabling women to leave fieldwork to men and return to their "natural" domestic place. Yet farmwomen resisted this urban gender ideal and continued driving tractors and running milking machines, which felt more interesting and important than full-time homemaking.

Machine Age toys both reflected and reinforced traditional roles. Model airplanes were intended to inspire the next Orville Wright, while Erector Sets taught civil engineering. Girls' toys also scaled down new adult technology: their mothers' kitchen appliances. Given this indoctrination, 25 percent of American boys in the 1920s planned to become engineers versus 3 percent of girls.

Technologies in the Workforce

Gendered assumptions also dictated how workplaces incorporated technology. Establishing his 1820s textile mills, Boston merchant Francis Cabot Lowell avoided Britain's horrors of child labor by recruiting New England farmers' daughters eager to earn money before marriage. While men repaired machines and supervised, women tended looms for long hours under exhausting, unhealthy conditions. Female employees lived in company-run boardinghouses under paternalistic rules aimed at protecting femininity and maintaining order. But women proved less than compliant; when factories cut wages, female workers walked out on strike and owners turned to children and immigrants for cheap labor.

Similarly, when boys initially hired as telephone operators proved rowdy and rude to callers, companies replaced them with girls socialized to be polite. The Bell System became America's largest employer of women; generations of "telephone girls" soothed frustrated customers and provided personalized convenience (including prearranged wake-up calls). While advertisements idealized this feminine "Voice with a Smile," the Bell System began installing automatic dialing in the 1930s, pushing operators into technological unemployment.

Workplace machinery itself, particularly office equipment, became gendered. Most 1870s clerical workers were male, and men were first to use the new typewriters. But soon observers portrayed women as naturally superior typists, with smaller hands and manual dexterity developed through sewing and piano-playing. By 1930, women made up 95 percent of all typists, and adding machines also became associated with female operators. Critics warned that the rough, immoral business world might destroy femininity, and they complained about secretaries giggling, crying, and being incapacitated by monthly periods. But employers could hire women at half men's salaries, and secretaries presented a pleasant face in the office, offering bosses sympathetic (almost wifely) support.

Technology became devalued when assigned to women. Early 20th-century nurses assumed responsibility for using clinical thermometers and ensuring their accuracy. Though taught to recognize abnormal temperature variations, nurses were chided not to diagnose patients, which remained physicians' specialty. As thermometers became symbols of nurses' work, the prestige formerly attached to that instrument disappeared. Doctors reserved stethoscopes for themselves, convinced that their use required special perceptual skills and training beyond nurses' ability.

Stereotypes questioned women's ability to handle equipment bigger than typewriters, but wartime manpower shortages proved women able to operate nontraditional machines. World War I metal-working factories that hired women reported their productivity equaled or exceeded men's; one munitions plant found women 50 percent more productive than men working drill presses and milling machines. Unions feared female labor would lower male status and wages; men refused to work alongside women, calling this inappropriate, and regulations subsequently barred women from heavy labor. World War II, however, brought millions of women into shipyards and airplane manufacturing. Government praised "Rosie the Riveter" as essential to victory, and media images portrayed Rosie as strong (yet still feminine), willing to learn new skills, but always at a technical disadvantage.

Engineering

Assumptions linking men with technical mastery long kept women out of engineering (Oldenziel 1999). Most pre-1900 engineers were trained in the military, the field, or the machine shop, routes closed to most women. Among the few exceptions, Lillian Gilbreth (1878–1972) conducted time-and-motion studies with her efficiency-expert husband while raising a huge family (immortalized in *Cheaper by the Dozen*). After Frank's early death, Lillian had trouble, as a woman, securing engineering consulting jobs. After remarketing herself as a household efficiency specialist, she won employment, numerous honorary degrees, and the nickname "the First Lady of Engineering."

But leading American technical schools, including Georgia Tech and Caltech, refused to enroll women until after World War II. Male students, faculty, and alumni ridiculed the notion of female engineers, drawing cartoons of women getting their hair tangled in equipment or using machinery to crack nuts. Women who insisted on entering engineering were oddities; by definition, a female engineer was not a typical engineer and not a typical woman. This defiance of norms created social and sexual tensions, with cracks about women in engineering just looking for husbands. Administrators considered teaching women a waste of time, as they inevitably dropped careers to marry. Psychologists labeled female engineers abnormal, unhealthily competing with men and rejecting identification with their mothers. The Society of Women Engineers blamed such attitudes for scaring away girls and campaigned to show that female engineers were both professionally capable and wholesomely feminine. Yet many late 20th-century female engineers continued to encounter negative comments, sexual harassment, or job discrimination.

The default "engineer" remained male; female engineers complained about office visitors mistaking them for secretaries. Similarly, the image of "inventor" remained male. Although women historically held few patents (in part due to expensive, time-consuming legalities), women created countless innovations over the centuries, in both household devices and more unexpected directions. Women devised better butter churns and dishwashers, baby carriages, sewing machine accessories, surgical instruments, fire escapes, shoemaking and metalworking equipment, elevator improvements, railroad couplings, computer languages, even military technology (actress Hedy Lamarr helped develop a World War II anti-jamming torpedo system). California farmer Harriet Strong created a working model for water storage dams, but analysts later misclassified her patent as culinary equipment, undoubtedly reflecting assumptions about women's narrow interests (Stanley 1993).

The 21st century still equates high-tech with male despite the prevalence of computers and other technologies in women's workplaces and private life. Men are considered and position themselves as computer experts, ready to tinker, and as "early adopters" in love with the latest gadgets. "Geek" or "hacker culture" remains intensely male. Boys in computer classes boast about how easy they find programming; when they imply that computing comes naturally to men, less-confident girls may switch majors. Video game makers have drawn criticism for depicting highly eroticized women and passive damsels in distress. Research suggests that degrading female representations, along with extreme violence, discourage some women from gaming. Attempts to design games appealing to girls often also play to stereotypes, as with "Barbie Fashion Designer."

In many ways, critics suggest, the technological world remains less than female friendly. Car airbags initially were engineered to protect bodies of typical male height and weight, posing dangers to women, children, and smaller men. Yet women have proven ingenious in adapting technologies such as the Internet to their own purposes, leaving much scope for discussion about gender and technology. (*See also* Computer Science; Early 20th Century)

References and Further Reading

Horowitz, Roger, and Arwen Mohun, eds. *His and Hers: Gender, Consumption, and Technology*. Charlottesville: University Press of Virginia, 1998.

Lerman, Nina E., Ruth Oldenziel, and Arwen P. Mohun, eds. *Gender and Technology: A Reader*. Baltimore, MD: Johns Hopkins University Press, 2003.

Oldenziel, Ruth. *Making Technology Masculine: Men, Women, and Modern Machines in America, 1870–1945*. Amsterdam: Amsterdam University Press, 1999.

Scharff, Virginia. *Taking the Wheel: Women and the Coming of the Motor Age*. New York: Free Press, 1991.

Stanley, Autumn. *Mothers and Daughters of Invention: Notes for a Revised History of Technology*. Metuchen, NJ: Scarecrow Press, 1993.

Wosk, Julie. *Women and the Machine: Representations from the Spinning Wheel to the Electronic Age*. Baltimore, MD: Johns Hopkins University Press, 2001.

Aspects of Human Biology and Behavior

The Brain

PATRICIA MILLER AND SUE V. ROSSER

Scientific research focused on differences between the brains of men and women can be traced back to antiquity. Although the specific focus of the research has varied from overall size to size of particular parts to functional differences, depending upon the era and technology available, the overarching thrust has been to demonstrate the relationship of brain size or function to intelligence and performance of tasks. Typically, in an attempt to justify a particular social stance or agenda, the evidence demonstrated that the brains of women were inferior to those of men.

Aristotle noted that the brains of women were smaller than the brains of men; he used this size difference to argue that women were less intelligent than men and therefore naturally inferior (Aristotle 1913, 809b). In the early 19th century, this same basic argument of the smaller size of women's brains was used by the phrenologists who claimed that mental functions could be assessed by measurement of the size and shape of the skull. Since women's skulls were smaller, women were assumed to be less intelligent.

Craniometry

By the late 19th century, phrenology had morphed into craniometry, used initially to provide a biological basis for slavery and colonization. Demonstrating that the European "races" had larger brains than the "races" they colonized meant that the inferior colonials could benefit from subjugation. The data collected through the science of craniometry also permitted the colonizers to better understand the colonials and how to govern them.

Although race, not gender, served as the impetus, data on sex differences were also collected and typically reported in a way to show women's inferiority. For example, when craniometrists discovered that women's brains were relatively larger than men's, proportional to their overall body size, this was used to describe women as infantile and childish (Vogt 1864).

The leading craniometrist, de Broca, believed that women's smaller brain size made them less intelligent than men. However, de Broca insisted that brain size was affected by intelligence, so that the sex differences may have resulted from women's lack of use of their brains for intellectual purposes. Feminists of the late 19th century used this argument for the reason that women should have more access to education. During the late 19th century, the debate also centered on sex differences in size of particular parts of the brain (Sayers 1982). Originally, the frontal lobes were discovered to be relatively larger in men while the parietal lobes were relatively larger in women. Later in the century, scientists reversed their findings to indicate that the parietal lobes were larger in men and the frontal lobes smaller. After this reversal, they also switched their decision about which part was the site of intelligence, claiming the parietal lobes as the site, rather than the frontal lobes (Patrick 1895, 212).

Brain Organization

By the middle of the 20th century, the focus of sex differences research had shifted to brain organization. Finding sex differences in the size of the corpus callosum that links the two halves of the brain, and correlating these with differences in language and visuospatial ability in so-called split-brain patients (individuals who had had their corpus callosum severed), researchers attempted to explain sex differences in performance on verbal and mathematical tests as well as occupational choice. Ironically, the same data were used by different researchers to argue that women's brains were more lateralized, the Buffery-Gray Hypothesis, or less lateralized, the Levy Hypothesis. Because hormones, either prenatally or at puberty, were thought to be the cause of the sex differences in brain organization, much as in the 19th century, the biological determinists argued that this biological difference explained women's lower performance on visuospatial tests and absence in professions such as science, architecture, and engineering.

Feminists, in contrast, have critiqued the studies on brain lateralization, hormones, and brain anatomy. They demonstrated flaws in experimental design, assumptions based on limited experimental data, and unwarranted extrapolation of data from rodents to humans as well as problems with conversion of hormones from estrogens to androgens within the body. They also emphasized that genetic, hormonal, and structural effects of the brain on behavior cannot be separated from the effects of learning and socialization in the environment on behavior, even before birth. For example, malnutrition both before and after birth in rats results in a decrease in the number and size of neurons in the brain. Human infants dying of malnutrition during the first year of life also have smaller than normal brains with a reduced number and size of neurons (Bleier 1984).

In the last half of the 20th century, attempts to tie brain organization and lateralization to male superiority ran into contradictions. "Left brain thinking" was supposed to involve reason and critical thinking (male) but it also reflected verbal abilities (female). "Right brain thinking" was supposed to involve emotions and intuitions (female) but it also reflected creativity, imagination, and mathematical brilliance (male). Such simplistic depictions of brains are not useful because most cognitive tasks involve several parts of the brain; a given problem can be solved differently by individuals who draw on different kinds of cognitive skills.

Hormonal Influences

Research documenting similar gender differences in humans and other primates also is taken to support biologically based brain differences in males and females. For example, young vervet monkeys show sex differences in toy preferences that parallel those of young children (Alexander and Hines 2002). Still another influential line of research examines the effects of prenatal hormones by studying CAH (congenital adrenal hyperplasia). In this condition, fetuses are exposed to high levels of androgens due to an enzyme defect. Although females with CAH have ovaries and a uterus and are fertile, they also have masculinized external genitalia to various degrees. They display toy preferences, peer preferences, feelings, behaviors, cognitive abilities, and occupational interests more characteristic of boys than girls. Early studies, though flawed methodologically, were taken as evidence for hormone-influenced differences in the brain development of boys and girls. More recent studies, with improved methodology, report similar results and also fail to support the critique that reactions of parents to their CAH girls, rather than brain differences, might be causing the effects. For example, observations of their parents show that they encourage them to play with girls' toys (Pasterski et al. 2005). Still, parental influences can be subtle, so the nature-nurture issue in this research still is not resolved.

Other hormonal studies also often support the influence of hormones on the brain. For example, circulating estrogens in adolescents and adults enhance verbal ability and memory, whereas increasing females' levels of androgen improves spatial ability. Despite these links between hormone levels and performance on certain cognitive tasks, there is no evidence that this has any influence on performance in school during childhood and adolescence or on occupational success. Clearly, other factors such as motivation and experiences that provide practice may be more promising lines of investigation for our understanding of individual differences in success in science, math, and engineering.

f-MRI

In the early 21st century, much of the research on sex differences in the brain focuses on brain imaging, particularly fMRIs (functional magnetic resonance imaging). By identifying areas of increased blood flow in the brain, cognitive neuroscientists can identify the site of mental activity during various sorts of thinking. That is, fMRIs produce a sort of map of brain activity. A number of studies have found gender differences in fMRIs; when thinking about the same problem, males and females show activity in different areas of the brain. For example, in a task assessing judgments of whether nonsense words rhymed, women used both the left and right inferior frontal gyrus whereas men used only the left, and there was little overlap between males and females in these patterns (Shaywitz et al. 1995). Such brain differences typically are interpreted as being innate and often viewed as reflecting the superiority of male brain organization. Even young boys and girls show differences in brain activity, a finding that bolsters the biological perspective even further. Thus, MRIs encourage an essentialist and reductionist view of gender differences by lumping together "female brains" separate from "male brains." They also downplay the diversity within each sex due to differing experiences, opportunities, and stresses of various races, ethnicities, sexual orientations, countries of origin, and social classes. Because of the availability of federal funding for biomedical research, including cognitive neuroscience, compared to less biological areas of psychology, this line of research is likely to remain quite active in the future.

Claiming innateness in these studies ignores the fact that experiences and behavior cause changes in the brain as much as the brain causes behavior. We are born with numerous synapses (connections among brain cells), and as a result of experience certain ones are strengthened while less used pathways are pruned away. Thus, sex differences in the site of neural activity during a particular task could be explained by differences in childhood experiences such as boys' and girls' preferred play activities. Sex differences in what experiences are *provided* to boys and girls, *permitted* for them, or *sought* by them most likely contribute to gender differences in the brain. For example, when parents talk about emotions more with preschool daughters than preschool sons, this emotion talk may stimulate neural pathways in the parts of the girls' brains that do emotion work. In short, these gender brain differences are created; they do not simply unfold.

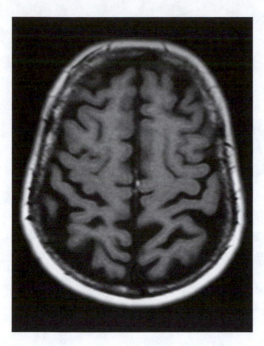

Magnetic resonance image (MRI) of a female brain. (iStockPhoto)

Conclusion

In the early 21st century the notion of "the male brain" persists. For example, the Extreme Male Brain theory of autism spectrum disorders (ASD) (Baron-Cohen and Hammer 1997) hypothesizes that children with ASD have brains that characterize males, especially in being at least average or superior in analyzing and constructing systems and impaired in the ability to identify and respond appropriately to another person's mental state. This theory has been linked to male neuroanatomy and is consistent with the fact that the vast majority of individuals with ASD are male.

The persistent search for brain differences in males and females suggests that society considers such differences important. With each new technology, the bias toward the male brain being the standard is simply expressed in a different way. Focusing on brain differences essentializes males and females and enforces traditional gender roles. This bias also directs attention away from the large variance within gender on any characteristic and from inequities in the environments of females and males such as lesser encouragement for girls to pursue scientific activities or mathematics when they show interest in them. Although prenatal differences in the hormones of males and females are likely to produce brain differences, we know little about the exact developmental pathways from hormone to brain to behavior (and vice versa). These differences are unclear especially in the context of a culture with different expectations regarding the behavior of males and females. (*See also* Cognitive Abilities; Endocrinology and Hormones; Nature/Nurture; The 19th Century; Race)

References and Further Reading

Alexander, G. M., and M. Hines. "Sex Differences in Response to Children's Toys in Nonhuman Primates (Cercopithecus Aethiops Subaeus)." *Evolution and Human Behavior* 23 (2002): 467–479.

Aristotle. "Physiognomonica." *The Works of Aristotle V.* Edited by W. D. Ross. Oxford: Clarendon Press, 1913.

Baron-Cohen, S., and J. Hammer. "Is Autism an Extreme Form of the 'Male Brain'?" *Advances in Infancy Research* 9 (1997): 193–217.

Bleier, Ruth. *Science and Gender: A Critique of Biology and Its Theories on Women*. Elmsford, NY: Pergamon Press, 1984.

Pasterski, V. L., M. E. Geffner, C. Brain, P. Hindmarsh, C. Brook, and M. Hine. "Prenatal Hormones and Postnatal Socialization by Parents as Determinants of Male-Typical Toy Play in Girls with Congenital Adrenal Hyperplasia." *Child Development* 76 (2005): 264–278.

Patrick, G. T. W. "The Psychology of Woman." *Popular Science Monthly* 47 (1895): 209–225.

Sayers, Janet. *Biological Politics: Feminist and Anti-feminist Perspectives*. London: Tavistock, 1982.

Shaywitz, B. A., S. E. Shaywitz, K. R. Pugh, R. T. Constable, et al. "Sex Differences in the Functional Organization of the Brain for Language." *Nature* 373 (1995): 607–609.

Vogt, K. *Lectures on Man*. London: Longman, 1864.

Cognitive Abilities

PATRICIA MILLER

Larry Summers, president of Harvard University, asserted in 2005 that women inherently have poorer cognitive abilities related to science than do men. This event returned to center stage a topic that has a long history: are males inherently more intelligent than females, particularly regarding valued abilities such as logic, mathematical and spatial reasoning, and scientific reasoning?

Early on, claims of male mental superiority were based on the physical brain. Aristotle claimed that women's smaller brains provided evidence of their lesser intelligence. Later, in the early 1800s, phrenologists made the same argument. In the late 1800s, the focus was on the size of particular parts of the brain. By the mid-1900s, neuropsychologists emphasized gender differences in brain organization, such as the degree to which one lobe was specialized toward particular cognitive abilities. In the early 21st century, research focuses on brain function, for example, gender differences in which part of the brain is most active when females or males perform a particular task. In each of these historical stances, whatever characterized males was considered evidence of an innate brain-based superiority. Moreover, the fact that research has focused on brains suggests that researchers have assumed gender differences in cognitive abilities to be caused by biological differences, not differences in experience.

Research on behavior, such as performance on paper-and-pencil tests, followed a parallel history in that whatever characterized males was considered superior. Moreover, when tests (e.g., IQ tests or verbal SAT) showed female superiority, they were adjusted (e.g., certain items were dropped or their content changed) to remove these differences (Caplan and Caplan 1994). Such adjustments typically were not considered necessary when male superiority emerged. More recently, researchers have focused on gender differences in specific cognitive abilities, particularly claims of males' superiority in math and spatial abilities and females' superiority on tests of verbal ability.

The problem for females is that seemingly neutral findings of "difference" seem to lead quickly to claims of "better than." The claim that men are "naturally" better at mathematical and spatial thinking has had a normative function:

it emphasized the differences between women and men, essentialized "female" and "male," and enforced the traditional gender roles. The myth also directed attention away from the large variance within gender on any characteristic, with many females being better than most males in abilities in which males as a group are better. Claims that men are better than women at mathematical and spatial reasoning are not benign; they may reinforce barriers to scientific careers for women and erode the self-confidence of girls and women with interest in such a career.

As further evidence of the influence of beliefs about gender on research, cognitive tasks on which girls excel tend to be interpreted negatively (see Caplan and Caplan 1994 for a review). For example, for years researchers concluded that women were more "dependent" than men. A reexamination of these data showed that this label actually referred to arguably positive cognitive abilities such as looking at other people's faces and accurately interpreting emotion-related messages. In addition, even when females excel on a task with a positive label, this sometimes is turned into something negative, as when females' strong verbal skills are interpreted as indicating they talk too much or indiscreetly.

The following examination of contemporary research on cognitive abilities will address four questions: Are there differences between females and males? If so, do they matter for occupational success in scientific fields? What are the relative contributions of genetics and environment? What's missing from the picture?

Are There Differences?

Maccoby and Jacklin's (1974) influential review of more than 2,000 studies of gender differences across many psychological domains revealed most beliefs about gender differences to be false. They found substantial support for differences in only four areas, three of which were cognitive—verbal ability, visual-spatial ability, mathematical ability, and aggression. Despite this strong evidence of widespread similarities, however, the cultural belief in pervasive gender differences prevailed. As Hyde (2005) pointed out, "secondary reports of their findings in textbooks and other sources, however, focused almost exclusively on their conclusions about gender differences" (581).

Contemporary research, drawing on new statistical techniques, reports few gender differences in cognitive abilities. In 2005, a review of 46 meta-analyses (analyses in which the data from numerous studies are pooled) shows that males and females are similar on most psychological variables (Hyde 2005). Of 39 meta-analytic studies of cognitive abilities, 36 percent found close-to-zero effect sizes and 46 percent found small effects. Only 13 percent found even moderate effects, 5 percent found large effects, and none found very large effects. These results are particularly compelling because the meta-analyses were biased toward finding differences: they examined abilities believed to show gender differences. Still, meta-analytic studies do identify some notable group mean differences. The two meta-analyses reporting large effect sizes found male superiority in mechanical reasoning during adolescence and mental rotation (imagining a viewed three-dimensional figure rotated) at various ages.

Contemporary work on general as opposed to specific cognitive abilities shows no evidence that females are less intelligent overall than males. However, IQ tests are constructed so that there would be no gender differences in overall intelligence. In addition, gender differences on SAT tests are difficult to interpret because of biases in who decides to take them. Thus, these data are not informative.

Critiques of research identify reasons to question any obtained gender differences. First, the content of the assessment task—for example, business or art—affects the results. Second, differences can disappear or even reverse if the context of assessment changes. For example, girls obtain higher scores on the math GRE test when they take it with other girls rather than boys (Inzlicht and Ben-Zeev 2000). Their verbal scores are not affected in this way, and boys' scores are not affected by this manipulation on either the math or verbal tests. In another study (Spencer, Steele, and Quinn 1999), male and female college students with equal math backgrounds were told, in one condition, that the math test had shown a gender difference in the past and in the other condition, that males and females had received equal scores on the test. Females performed more poorly than males in the former condition and performed equal to males in the latter condition. Such findings challenge the generality of any studies showing gender differences in cognitive performance.

Do Differences in Cognitive Abilities, if They Exist, Matter for Occupational Success?

One can question whether it is even productive to examine gender differences in cognitive abilities. This approach has not added much to our understanding of cognitive functioning or how cognition develops. On the practical side, there is no evidence that the few modest differences that seem to hold up have any consequences for occupational success for men or women. Moreover, standardized tests may not even be good at predicting school performance. Although the SAT is intended to predict grades in college, it in fact underpredicts women's grades and overpredicts men's grades in their first year of college. That is, women earn higher grades than their SAT scores would predict and men earn lower grades than their SAT scores would predict. It thus is an inequity that these scores are used for decisions about admission to college and awarding of scholarships. In short, rather than studying gender differences, it may be more productive to create contexts in which the salience of stereotypes is diminished, provide training in specific skills for both males and females who need it, and improve the teaching of science.

What Are the Relative Contributions of Genetics and Environment?

The development of any ability is a complex intertwining of genetic and environmental contributions. A number of findings favor environmental interpretations: the fact that older studies of gender differences in cognitive abilities found larger differences than did more recent studies argues for experiential influences. Demonstrations that scores on spatial ability tests can be improved by training (e.g., Newcombe, Mathason, and Terlecki 2002) also point to experience. The size of a gender difference in a particular cognitive skill often varies substantially from one age to another; differences that grow larger or smaller at different times in the lifespan suggest differential exposure to different tasks and practice. Finally, the effects of context described above clearly argue against innate differences or even any differences at all.

The gender-difference approach in psychology has seemed to assume, historically, that some cognitive differences are inherent in being male or female and thus are mainly innate. Unfortunately, despite the many critiques of this assumption, this perspective continues to bias interpretations of research findings. For example, in the early 21st century, new neuroimaging techniques, such as fMRIs (functional magnetic resonance imaging) that show differences in male and female brains during cognitive activity usually are interpreted as showing innate differences in these brains. However, a large body of research shows that experience affects the organization and functioning of brains. Given the substantial evidence that boys and girls engage in somewhat different sorts of activities and are encouraged or discouraged from entering particular learning environments (e.g., playing on sports teams versus playing with dolls), such brain differences are not surprising. Thus, the interpretation of research has been influenced by cultural beliefs.

Males and females obviously do differ innately in many physical ways, particularly in the hormonal differences operating even prenatally. The unresolved issue, though, is whether these differences matter for cognition or whether all differences are mediated by societal norms concerning gender.

What's Missing from the Picture?

The focus of research on differences in abilities valued by a society based on masculine values (e.g., math, science, mechanical, and spatial skills) leads to a very unbalanced account of human cognition. Focusing on cognitive abilities required for activities typically associated with females in our culture would lead to a broader, more complete, theory of cognition. For example, one could research the cognitive skills needed to do collaborative scientific research to understand biological nonlinear systems composed of complex connections among parts or to conceptualize diversity and variability in nature.

Conclusion

The differences within each sex in any cognitive ability are always greater than the average differences between the genders. Males and females are more alike than they are different. Still, the belief persists that the two genders have vastly different profiles of cognitive strengths and weaknesses. Exaggerated claims about gender differences in cognitive abilities negatively affect women in the workplace. For girls, the myth of their inferiority in math, disproven by meta-analyses and by girls' higher grades in math (Kimball 1989), still remains and may cause mathematically talented girls to be overlooked by adults and cause the erosion of girls' confidence in their math skills (Hyde 2005). President Summers's comments about females' innate inferiority in science-relevant abilities clearly show the differential expectations for women and men in the minds of at least some members of society, including potential employers. (*See also* Gender/Sex—How Conjoined; Mathematics; Nature/Nurture)

References and Further Reading

Caplan, P. J., and J. B. Caplan. *Thinking Critically about Research on Sex and Gender*. New York: Harper Collins, 1994.

Hyde, J. S. "The Gender Similarities Hypothesis." *American Psychologist* 60 (2005): 581–592.

Inzlicht, M., and T. Ben-Zeev. "A Threatening Intellectual Environment: Why Females Are Susceptible to Experiencing Problem-solving Deficits in the Presence of Males." *Psychological Science* 11 (2000): 365–371.

Kimball, M. M. "A New Perspective on Women's Math Achievement." *Psychological Bulletin* 105 (1989): 198–214.

Maccoby, E. E., and C. N. Jacklin. *The Psychology of Sex Differences*. Stanford, CA: Stanford University Press, 1974.

Newcombe, N. S., L. Mathason, and M. Terlecki. "Maximization of Spatial Compe-
tence: More Important than Finding the Cause of Sex Differences." In *Biology, So-
ciety, and Behavior: The Development of Sex Differences in Cognition*. Edited by
A. McGillicuddy-De Lisi and R. De Lisi, 183–206. Westport, CT: Ablex, 2002.
Spencer, S. J., C. M. Steele, and D. M. Quinn. "Stereotype Threat and Women's Math
Performance." *Journal of Experimental Social Psychology* 35 (1999): 4–28.

Mental Illness

Susan A. Nolan

Gender differences in the prevalence and experience of mental illness have long been observed by both clinicians and researchers. A number of studies, mostly in Western countries (and primarily in the United States), have documented patterns in psychopathology related to gender. It appears that men and women have very similar overall rates of psychopathology (e.g., Kessler et al. 1994); however, there are differences in prevalence rates and in symptomatic expression of a number of disorders. In particular, there is a fairly consistent gender disparity in the spectrum of mood, anxiety, somatoform, and eating disorders (e.g., Kessler et al. 1994). For most disorders in these categories, rates are higher among women than among men. One of the categories for which the gender difference is reversed is substance abuse; men are more likely than are women to abuse alcohol and other drugs, a pattern that might be changing as women become more likely to use substances than in the past. Among the most severe of mental disorders, such as bipolar disorder and schizophrenia, there does not seem to be a significant gender difference.

Disorders that Afflict More Women than Men

Anxiety Disorders

Women are more likely than are men to experience anxiety disorders. More specifically, women are anywhere from 1.8 to 2.5 times as likely to suffer from specific phobias, panic disorder, generalized anxiety disorder, and post-traumatic stress disorder (e.g., Kessler et al. 1994). (Some have noted a smaller gender difference in the same direction for social phobia and obsessive-compulsive disorder, although others have not observed a gender difference in their prevalence rates.) With some of the more debilitating anxiety disorders, the preponderance of women is even more pronounced; 80 to 90 percent of people suffering from severe agoraphobia are women.

Mood Disorders

For the vast majority of the lifespan, women have higher rates of depression than men. Until age 12, boys seem to have slightly higher rates of depression than girls, and after age 65, there appears to be no gender difference. However, from ages 12 to 65, depression is approximately twice as common in women as in men.

Somatoform Disorders

Somatoform disorders are those in which an individual complains of a physical problem in the absence of a medical or physical explanation (APA 2000). There are several somatoform disorders and the gender pattern varies from disorder to disorder. Although there is no apparent gender difference in hypochondriasis (unreasonable fears that one has a physical illness), there are large differences in somatization disorder (reporting a range of physical problems that have no apparent organic explanation) and the similar but more specific somatoform pain disorder. Women are 10 times as likely as men to have this disorder. Somatoform disorders are less common than but frequently co-occur with mood disorders and anxiety disorders.

Eating Disorders

Both anorexia nervosa, in which an individual refuses to eat, and bulimia nervosa, in which an individual binge-eats and then often purges that food, occur more often among women than men. Rates among women have been reported to be from six to 10 times the rates in men. Eating disorders are less common than but frequently co-occur with mood disorders and anxiety disorders.

Explanations for the Gender Differences in Depression and Anxiety

The bases for the observed gender differences in rates of anxiety disorders and depressive disorders have been investigated much more frequently than have factors contributing to gender differences in other mental illnesses, and numerous explanations have been proposed (e.g., Nolen-Hoeksema 1990). Some of these explanations might be applicable to gender differences in other disorders, but more research is needed to generalize many of these ideas beyond mood and anxiety disorders.

An oft-cited explanation is that there is no actual gender difference and that the perceived difference is due to an artifact. For example, perhaps women are more likely than men to seek help for symptoms of depression and anxiety because such admissions are gender congruent for women but not for men. In line with this suggestion, some have proposed that men have the same underlying symptoms as women but exhibit different behaviors. Men might present with issues related to substance abuse or anger; both are seen as more gender appropriate for men. Research, however, does not support this explanation. Studies have assessed the presence of disorders using a range of measures and techniques and in a range of contexts (community, medical, outpatient psychiatric, and inpatient psychiatric settings), and the gender difference is consistently present. Moreover, there is little or no evidence that the underlying cause of substance abuse and depression is the same. The artifactual explanation for gender differences in depression and anxiety appears to be merely a myth.

A second artifactual explanation focuses on gender biases of therapists. That is, some suggest that women are more likely to be diagnosed with mood, anxiety, somatoform, and eating disorders than are men, even though they may present with similar symptoms. Because of gender stereotypes, clinicians (as do nonclinicians more generally) expect to see higher rates of these disorders among women than men (e.g., Madden, Barrett, and Pietromonaco 2000). A woman exhibiting even some of these symptoms is likely to be diagnosed with one of the disorders whereas a man exhibiting the same level of symptoms might not receive such a diagnosis.

Most commonly, researchers and clinicians have cited social and psychological explanations for the gender difference. Researchers have suggested that women are more likely to display symptoms of anxiety and depression because such symptoms are deemed appropriate expressions of emotion, according to cultural prescriptions for women (e.g., Madden, Barrett, and Pietromonaco 2000). This hypothesis implies that women learn a repertoire of responses that includes depression and anxiety. Men, on the other hand, display their symptoms in other ways. Some suggest that men display negative affect through anger, aggression, or substance abuse. This explanation is related to the artifactual explanation above. The difference is that the artifactual explanation indicates a more conscious decision of what symptoms to present whereas the psychological explanation purports that women and men internalize what they learn and the resulting disorders are not artifactual but are real.

Other psychological explanations focus on the role of women in society. Women, some theorists suggest, are depressed and anxious because their life experiences are more likely to include negative life events that appear beyond their control. Women are more likely than men to experience discrimination, poverty, a career/family imbalance, and abuse within relationships (e.g., Madden, Barrett, and Pietromonaco 2000). Research suggests that such negative life experiences are associated with increased risks for depression (e.g., Nolen-Hoeksema 2002).

A third psychological explanation involves girls' responses to the biological changes that occur in puberty (e.g., Hankin and Abramson 2001). During adolescence, girls accumulate more body fat, and tend to become more dissatisfied with their bodies, which puts them at greater risk for developing body image problems; on the other hand, boys accumulate muscle tissue in puberty and tend to be happy with the physical changes that are occurring. Given that cultural standards value slenderness in girls and muscular physiques for boys, gendered expectations for appearance seem to be more detrimental for girls than for boys and might contribute to the greater likelihood of mood, anxiety, and eating disorders that we see in adolescence.

Another explanation, one specific to depression, is women's tendency to ruminate in the face of a negative mood (e.g., Nolen-Hoeksema 2002). Women who are depressed tend to focus their thoughts and actions on the depression itself—for example, listening to sad songs or thinking about why they are depressed. Men, on the other hand, tend to distract themselves by engaging in activities or behaviors unrelated to their depressed mood. It appears that rumination exacerbates depression whereas distraction ameliorates it.

Other psychological mechanisms have been proposed to work in conjunction with each other to lead to higher rates of depression for women than men (e.g., Hankin and Abramson 2001). Rumination and higher levels of negative life events might combine with a pessimistic attributional style. Specifically, people who attribute their own negative life experiences to negative traits in themselves—in effect, blaming themselves when bad things happen—seem to have higher rates of depression. This combination of mechanisms appears to pose a particular risk for girls as they enter adolescence and might explain why it is at this point in development that girls are more likely than boys to be depressed.

Others have proposed biological explanations for gender differences in psychopathology, but researchers typically have not found strong support for biological hypotheses (e.g., Nolen-Hoeksema 2002). Hormones, for example, have been studied for their possible role in the gender differences in depression and anxiety. Overall, data indicate that fluctuations in hormones that occur naturally across women's lifetimes do not appear to cause depression among most women; however, it is possible that hormones might play a causal role for small numbers of women at high risk for depression. Overall, however, the common belief that hormones lead to depression in women appears to be a myth.

Similarly, there does not seem to be support for hypotheses that genetic differences lead to gender differences in psychopathology. Interestingly, the disorders viewed as most biologically rooted, including bipolar disorder and schizophrenia, do not demonstrate the gender differences that we see among disorders that appear to have sociocultural roots.

Consequences of the Gender Difference

Some have proposed that there are gender issues at a meta-level with respect to psychopathology. For example, there are arguments that the organization of the diagnostic structure, the *Diagnostic and Statistical Manual of Mental Disorders,* published by the American Psychiatric Association, is inherently biased. Some have suggested that the criteria for diagnoses are written in such a way as to pathologize aspects of women's behavior that occur naturally. This accusation was particularly strong when researchers suggested the inclusion of post-luteal phase disorder, a disorder that many likened to a pathologizing of premenstrual syndrome.

Many have argued that including such questionable disorders, even if there is possibly an overly high rate of women receiving diagnoses, is useful in that the disorders are viewed as "real" and that insurance companies are then willing to reimburse for treatment. On the other hand, some worry that the stigma that all too often accompanies diagnosis with a mental disorder outweighs the benefits of arbitrarily including diagnoses that might be artificially constructed.

The stigma that affects women who exhibit depression- and anxiety-related emotions is often subtle. Such symptoms are viewed more positively among women than among men, but nonetheless those who display them are viewed as more emotional and less rational. The perception of being less rational may lead women who display such symptoms to be viewed as less capable—as weaker—than others (Madden, Barrett, and Pietromonaco 2000).

Finally, it is important to realize that our internalized gender-related stereotypes affect even what we choose to study. Clinicians and researchers choose to look for and publish findings related to gender differences (Madden, Barrett, and Pietromonaco 2000). Because of this bias, the emphasis in the research and clinical literature is on aspects of psychopathology in which women and men vary rather than on aspects in which they are similar. We may have inadvertently highlighted—or exaggerated—differences at the expense of similarities. Moreover, as with gender differences across the field of psychology, gender differences reflect *average* differences. When there is a difference between women and men, it is between the means for women and men. There is always a great deal of overlap between the distributions for women and men, and knowing that a gender difference exists does not provide information about any specific individual. The way that psychopathology research and the ensuing literature have been structured might perpetuate the very biases they purport to help us understand. (*See also* Gender/Sex—How Conjoined; Personality/Rationality/Emotionality; Women's Health Movement)

References and Further Reading

American Psychiatric Association (APA). *Diagnostic and Statistical Manual of Mental Disorders: DSM-IV-TR*. Washington, DC: American Psychiatric Association, 2000.

Hankin, B. L., and I. Y. Abramson. "Development of Gender Differences in Depression: An Elaborated Cognitive Vulnerability-Transactional Stress Theory." *Psychological Bulletin* 127 (2001): 773–796.

Kessler, R. C., K. A. McGonagle, S. Zhao, C. B. Nelson, M. Hughes, S. Eshleman, H. U. Wittchen, and K. S. Kendler. "Lifetime and 12-Month Prevalence of DSM-III-R Psychiatric Disorders in the United States: Results from the National Comorbidity Survey." *Archives of General Psychiatry* 51 (1994): 8–19.

Madden, T. E., L. F. Barrett, and P. R. Pietromonaco. "Sex Differences in Anxiety and Depression: Empirical Evidence and Methodological Questions." In *Gender and Emotion: Social Psychological Perspectives*. Edited by Agnetta H. Fischer, 277–298. London: Cambridge University Press, 2000.

Nolen-Hoeksema, S. *Sex Differences in Depression*. Stanford, CA: Stanford University Press, 1990.

Nolen-Hoeksema, S. "Gender Differences in Depression." In *Handbook of Depression*. Edited by I. H. Gotlib and C. L. Hammen, 492–509. New York: Guilford, 2002.

Personality/Rationality/ Emotionality

Janine P. Buckner

Personality

Everyday stereotypes about being male or female include beliefs regarding the kind of individual one should be; preferences, activities, personality attributes, and emotional behaviors are all parts of stereotyped identities that we ascribe to others and apply to ourselves. As early as two years of age, children expect different kinds of interactions with women and men, and they assume that different personal qualities "belong" to these kinds of people. Both girls and boys describe men as confident, strong, aggressive, dominant, and even cruel, whereas women are characterized as being delicate, emotional, gentle, weak, and affectionate. These beliefs expressed by children expose the cultural expectations that shape their knowledge and lead them to view gender as being represented along a single continuum of personality traits—with masculinity on one end of the spectrum and femininity at the other.

Typically, stereotypes for masculinity describe features focused on a concern about one's own interests and success, a concept described as *agency*. Such qualities as self-confidence, competitiveness, dominance, and leadership are included in this set of masculine traits. Stereotypes for femininity, on the other hand, prescribe the "opposite" features and are characterized as representing a connectedness to others, or *dependence* (Tannen 1990). As such, women are expected to be more socially attuned: relational rather than rational; emotional and collaborative rather than competitive; nurturing rather than selfish; weak and yielding rather than strong and assertive.

As children become adults, assumptions about the bipolarity of gender continue to shape perceptions of self and interpretations of experience. Indeed, when adults are asked to select traits that are most like themselves, men rate high agency-type features and infrequently endorse communal/dependent traits; however, women more often select features associated with social identities (caring, friendly, emotional) rather than qualities of agency (Bem 1993).

Translating Gendered Personalities into Expectancies

The agency and assertive ideals of masculinity are not necessarily viewed as negative qualities. In many cultures, such traits as rationality and persistence afford individuals opportunities for success. For example, those most likely to excel in the workplace are described as individuals who put great importance on autonomy and confidence and who strive for personal success. These characteristics are valued even in traditional theories of development, where maturity is "evidenced" by one's logical or analytic skills, individuation, personal responsibility, and autonomy. Women and girls, quite differently, are often evaluated by their compliance and the relationships they create, maintain, and nurture (Gilligan 1982). Thus, women who aim to "discover themselves" and achieve personal goals or who are seen as "driven" are viewed in a less than positive light—by men *and* women.

Although it is currently more acceptable than in times past for women to value and embody typically "masculine" traits (particularly in employment contexts), women who display these qualities are viewed by themselves and others as being masculine women (a negative image) rather than as pioneers of a positive-shifting stereotype for women. But both men and women are less apt to tolerate men who display female-typical qualities than women who display "masculine" qualities.

Gender stereotypes for personality and emotionality are not supported by cognitive or behavioral data because in reality differences between men and women are small, inconsistent, and context-specific at best. Yet stereotypes still credit men as more mathematical, scientific, and analytical than women and women as more verbally precocious. And while men continue to have more rigid boundaries around their gender roles, they are nonetheless advantaged by their roles, given the cultural preferences for masculine traits.

Emotionality

Gender stereotypes of personality include characterizations about emotion; that is, they describe gender differences in the experience and expression of emotion. Emotion behaviors, like stereotypes for personality, appear to be largely shaped by gender socialization practices within families, communities, schools, and other social institutions. Like personality, emotional stereotypes for masculinity and femininity may be implicitly taught and reinforced. And the effects of this socialization of emotion, though not readily apparent, may lead to different cognitive styles that men and women use to interpret experience and to process different details of an experience (whether explicitly or implicitly emotional in nature). According to such a view, "his and hers" theories of emotion perception suggest that socialization may play different roles in the experience of affect. Men's perceptions may be shaped to attend to physical or neurological cues for emotion whereas women may instead learn to focus upon emotion as an emergent quality of social interaction (see Brannon 2005 for a review).

The Experience and Expression of Emotion

The debate regarding gendered emotion is not at its core about whether men and women have similar experiences of emotion. Myriad studies suggest that women and men have similar emotional responses to stimuli; moreover, the findings appear to be culturally universal. Although men show greater neurological responses (galvanic skin measures) to anger and other emotions than women, more general measures of emotional reactivity reveal similarities in men's and women's affective states (Fischer and Manstead 2000). Interestingly, the specific pattern of gender differences observed in emotionality depends on the particular emotion investigated. Whereas women are apt to respond emotionally to a wider number of situations than men (and with more broadly defined emotional behaviors), men appear more likely to internalize their reactions. (Note, however, that women are more likely than men to be diagnosed with mood, anxiety, or eating disorders, all presumed to be internalizing disorders related to emotional responses.)

These differences notwithstanding, Matlin (2004) and others have argued that beliefs in gender polarization may have led to exaggeration of any small differences that are empirically observed in men and women. In short, more differences lie within the gender groups than between them. Disparity in emotional behaviors and cognitions of men and women may be more an artifact of experience than of biology.

Perceptions of Emotional Experience

Rather than take issue with the experience of emotion per se, researchers and theorists tend to focus on *expressions* of emotion—that is, how women and men respond to these internal emotional experiences. Cultural gender roles portray women as having more emotional reactions *and* more emotional intensity than men, even for similar experiences. Theorists and researchers must contend with these distinctions between emotional frequency and emotional intensity.

Although there is some evidence that displays of emotion differ between women and men, usually these differences are artifacts of observational contexts. For instance, research indicates that smiling behaviors vary with the degree of tension in a situation or the familiarity of others in a social setting. Likewise, women are purported to smile more frequently than men and to demonstrate more visible mouth movements than men in response to a wider set of contexts and individuals. However, conclusions about this social smiling must be qualified; in situations where there is a power differential, women are more likely to smile when they are subordinate than are men (who typically show no smile). Moreover, women are reported to smile more frequently than men when they experience negative affect or social tension.

Self-reports of Emotionality

Women do report different rates of experiencing affect than do men, particularly in social contexts. The majority of affective states appear to be recognized, expressed, and reported more frequently (and even remembered in more detail) by women than by men. The caveat to this pattern is that anger appears to be behaviorally (and verbally) expressed more by men than women, whereas sadness is more frequently and elaborately expressed by women than men (for a review see Fivush and Buckner 2003). Even within indirect measures of self-reports, such as when counting the number of emotion words used in conversations, gender difference may be discovered. Whether within a developmental study (such as in parent-child discussions about the past) or in interviews with college students or older adults, men and women often choose different words and labels when characterizing the same emotional concepts and feeling states. Other studies report differences in the ways men and women relate the nuances of their emotional experiences. For instance, women and their conversational partners may use more synonyms for the feelings they talk about. Women may also discuss other emotions in addition to the target feelings about which they converse, whereas men are more apt to center the content of their talk on the specific feeling they are discussing.

These differences in emotion expression correlate with socialization practices that emphasize a boyhood culture of dominance, rationality, and non-emotion. In this culture, boys (and men) are encouraged to be calm, cool, and collected, or rational and controlled (that is, emotionally restrained). From this perspective, they would not be expected to talk much (if at all) about their feelings and would not be given much practice to do so. Conversely, women who "grow up" in a culture that prescribes their roles as dependent and connected to others would be encouraged to be sociable and emotional. As such, girls (and women) would be expected to express a broad set of emotions in a wide range of contexts. Oft encountered throughout life, these kinds of messages can become internalized beliefs that serve to guide individuals' own thoughts, decisions, and actions with respect to emotionality.

Perceptions of Others' Emotion

Another way to investigate emotional stereotypes is to examine the feelings that individuals ascribe to others (emotional decoding). Studies of emotional decoding often require participants to report the emotions displayed by others that are usually displayed on gender-ambiguous faces or in filmed vignettes with gender-neutral individuals. The targets shown to participants can be babies, children, or adults. Sometimes individuals are informed of the gender of the targets as they view the emotional displays. In studies where targets show "upset" expressions or behaviors, men and women are both more likely to ascribe sadness or guilt to female targets whereas anger is attributed to faces and filmed behaviors of male targets. And even when participants are not told the gender of the target individuals, women and men make the same attributions based on their assumptions or beliefs about the target's gender. Male and female participants each attribute "sadness" to a visibly upset target when they believe the target is female and describe the targets as "angry" when they believe they are observing a male target. Such findings indicate how effective conventions and stereotypes are in inducing conformity to social stereotypes; more to the point, these stereotypes are applied unilaterally when one explains one's own behaviors or those of other individuals.

The "Whens" and "Wheres" of Feelings Matter

Given the contextually dependent nature of gender and gender roles, reasonable explanations for gender differences in emotionality and personality must avoid assumptions that they are founded in essential differences between men and women. Indeed, empirical evidence suggests that the disparities observed between male and female emotion behaviors are likely not due to an innate or hormone-dependent affect system but to beliefs learned from and reinforced by other members of our cultural settings. Thus, social stereotypes about emotionality are largely the result of perceptual differences, which emerge out of experience. Consequently, an individual's degree of conformity to gender-prescribed roles is usually a better predictor of emotional expressions in a given context than is the sex of that individual. Therefore, the best approach to understanding gender differences in emotionality and personality traits is to address the ways individuals come to perceive experiences.

For instance, although individuals identify common experiences of anger, what most angers women are behaviors of individuals familiar to them whereas men are most angered by strangers. The issue is not that men do not have emotional reactions and women have too many—instead, the issue may be the need to explain the circumstances in which (and with whom) individuals acknowledge and display their emotions in particular ways. (*See also* Gender/ Sex—How Conjoined; Mental Illness)

References and Further Reading

Bem, Sandra L. *The Lenses of Gender: Transforming the Debate in Sexual Inequality.* New Haven, CT: Yale University Press, 1993.

Brannon, Linda. *Gender: Psychological Perspectives.* 4th ed. Boston: Allyn and Bacon, 2005.

Brody, Leslie R., and Judith A. Hall. "Gender, Emotion, and Expression." In *Handbook of Emotions.* Edited by M. Lewis and J. M. Haviland-Jones, 338–349. New York: Guilford Press, 2000.

Fischer, Agnetta H., and Anthony S. R. Manstead. "Gender Differences in Emotion across Cultures." In *Gender and Emotion: Social Psychological Perspectives.* Edited by Agnetta H. Fischer, 91–97. London: Cambridge University Press, 2000.

Fivush, Robyn, and Janine P. Buckner. "Constructing Gender and Identity through Autobiographical Narratives." In *Autobiographical Memory and the Construction of a Narrative Self: Developmental and Cultural Perspectives.* Edited by Robyn Fivush and Catherine Haden, 140–168. Hillsdale, NJ: Erlbaum, 2003.

Gilligan, Carole. *In a Different Voice.* Cambridge, MA: Harvard University Press, 1982.

Matlin, M. W. *The Psychology of Women.* 5th ed. Belmont, CA: Wadsworth, 2004.

Tannen, Debra. *You Just Don't Understand: Women and Men in Conversation.* New York: HarperCollins, 1990.

Endocrinology and Hormones

Sue V. Rosser

The use of hormones to reinforce gender myths and of gender myths to establish hormonal differences between the sexes stands as an addition to the lengthy tradition of biological determinism; the use of biological differences among races, sexes, classes, and species in anatomy, hormones, and genes provides biological justifications for social, behavioral, and psychological inequalities. The biological determinism tradition predates the 19th century, and works by Gould (1981) and Sayers (1982) elegantly trace the roots connecting the 19th-century tradition to its pre-19th-century antecedents as well as its successors in the 20th century. More recently, research has emphasized the connections between hormones and differences between the sexes in brain lateralization, anatomy, and function and behavioral traits such as visuospatial ability and aggression correlated with men's success in science and mathematics.

Because of the linkage between hormones and anatomical differences in males and females, it is not surprising that endocrinological research has put much effort into searches for differences between the sexes. The terminology of male hormones (commonly used to describe testosterone and its derivatives) and female hormones (frequently used for both the estrogen-related hormones and the progestins) is a telling example of the emphasis on sex differences. In fact, the so-called male hormones and female hormones are found in both males and females.

The major difference is in the levels or amounts produced in the two sexes, not in their presence in one sex or the other. There are also differences in the major anatomical sources of these hormones in the adults of the two sexes (ovaries in the female, testes in the male, and adrenal glands in both males and females) and their cyclicity of production. There are also many different forms of estrogens, progestins, and androgens, all closely related to each other in chemical structure. The basic structure of all is the four carbon rings of cholesterol, a steroid, with the main difference among them being in one or two of the side chains having oxygen (O) or hydrogen (H). In various body

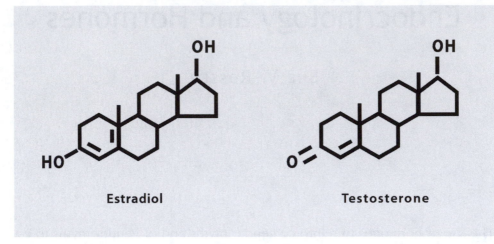

Molecular structures of estradiol and testosterone.

tissues of both sexes, cholesterol is normally metabolized to progesterone, which is metabolized to testosterone, the major androgen, which is metabolized to estradiol, the major estrogen. There are many other circulating metabolic forms of the three steroids, each with unique physiological effects, present all of the time in varying levels in females and males, with constant conversions from some forms to others. However, use of the terms *male* and *female* hormones obscures these true differences in amount and cycle of production and suggests incorrectly to the layperson that men produce only "male hormones" and that women produce only "female hormones."

Flaws in Interpretation of Endocrine Research

Some endocrinological research and the way it is conducted suggest fuzziness and flaws in understanding the relationship between hormones and sex:

1. Some work assumed that the cyclical nature of the female reproductive pattern made female rodents and primates unsuitable as experimental subjects for tests of hormones or other chemicals. Tests for drugs run only on male subjects, either rodent or human, may yield "cleaner" data, but it is more limited. The cyclicity of hormones in females may yield differing results or interactions with drugs, depending on the stage of the cycle. Thus, extrapolation of results from male populations only to females frequently is not appropriate. In addition, tests of blood hormone levels reveal episodic rather than steady patterns of secretion of virtually all hormones in both males and females.

2. Because "male hormones" and "female hormones" occur in both sexes and are closely related biochemically, biochemical conversions between hormones may occur within the body. An injection of testosterone may be converted to estrogen or another derivative before it reaches the brain. Therefore, research purporting to demonstrate that testosterone makes males more aggressive or faster at running mazes may be flawed because the testosterone injected may or may not have been converted to other derivatives before it reaches the operative organs.

3. In addition to problems with biochemical conversions of hormones after injection, behavioral effects induced in one species do not ensure similar effects in a different species. Biochemical traits in one species cannot necessarily be extrapolated to another species, nor can changes in hormone levels be assumed to be the cause of behavioral or other performance differences between the sexes.

4. Behavioral and biological factors may be relatively inseparable and interactive. Environmental physical or psychological stress factors such as position in the dominance hierarchy have been shown to be both the cause and the effect of higher or lower levels of testosterone in primates.

Sociobiology

Unfortunately, hormone differences between the sexes have in some cases been used to explain differences in behavior, aptitude, and position between men and women. Sociobiology, the late 20th-century version of biological determinism, added genes to the 19th-century factors of anatomical and hormonal differences that might justify social inequalities between human sexes, races, and classes.

Sociobiology is the study of the biological basis of behavior. Some sociobiologists such as Barash (1977) and Wilson (1975) state that behavior is genetically determined, that genes determine hormones, and that differences between males and females in role, status, and performance are biologically based. Critiques of sociobiology have centered around criticisms of the assumption that behaviors such as aggression, homosexuality, promiscuity, selfishness, and altruism are biologically determined through genes and hormones and the problems involved with anthropomorphism in animal behavior studies. However, despite critiques, the most renowned sociobiologists have continued to assume that genes do determine behavior and that the behaviors described as aggression, homosexuality, rape, selfishness, and altruism in animals are equivalent to those behaviors in humans.

Sometimes the scientific controls and experimental design in these studies have not met the rigor required to draw such conclusions. Researchers must guard against confounding correlation of changing hormone levels and behavioral manifestations with cause and effect. This confounding is particularly likely to occur when the biological results correlate well with the social status quo and accepted notions of gender-appropriate behavior and roles in a particular society. (*See also* Nature/Nurture)

References and Further Reading

Barash, David. *Sociobiology and Behavior.* New York: Elsevier, 1977.
Gould, Stephen Jay. *The Mismeasure of Man.* New York: W. W. Norton, 1981.
Sayers, Janet. *Biological Politics.* New York: Tavistock, 1982.
Wilson, Edward O. *Sociobiology.* Cambridge, MA: Harvard University Press, 1975.

Menstruation/Menopause/PMS

SUE V. ROSSER

Menstruation serves as a visible marker that distinguishes men from women. Since it also signals the potential for physical, reproductive capability for a woman, it becomes a defining stage in the female life cycle. Because it begins at puberty and ceases at menopause, menstruation provides an outward manifestation of a complex interaction among the brain, hormones, ovaries, and uterus occurring each month in most women from adolescence through middle age.

The Greeks believed that women's balance of humors made them "colder and wetter" and also more emotional and sexual than men. Without regular menstruation to eliminate the surplus fluid, women could suffer physical and/or mental illness. In the absence of regular menstruation and intercourse, the uterus was believed capable of wandering around the body, causing a variety of physical or mental ailments. These Greek notions of fragility during menstruation and links to mental imbalances endured into the 19th and early 20th centuries as *hysteria* (the Greek term for uterus) when delicate, upper-class Victorian women experienced breakdowns that necessitated bed rest. Too much studying was also thought to drain sustenance to the brain from the uterus, making college-educated women less fertile and more mannish.

Anthropological studies suggest that menstruation is a cultural event, experienced in different ways by individual women in different societies. Thus, it is not surprising that myths have historically surrounded the science of this marker of gender differences and that the "natural" processes surrounding menstruation and menopause have become increasingly medicalized today.

One motivation for such medicalization may be men's interest in controlling reproduction. The current medical structure in the United States segregates issues of women's reproduction, and virtually all aspects of women's health, into the specialty of obstetrics/gynecology. Medical models of menstruation, premenstrual syndrome (PMS), and menopause reflect negative images of women and their bodies through their depiction of menstruation as failed reproduction, PMS as raging hormones, and menopause as diminished production of estrogen. Physicians prescribe synthetic hormones and drugs to cure and control the hormonal changes.

Menstruation

The medical model of menstruation describes day one of the cycle (in a normative 28-day model) as the first day of menstruation. At this time, the uterine lining is being sloughed off (because of failed implantation of a fertilized egg) and low levels of estrogen and progesterone produced by the ovary circulate in the blood and are detected at the hypothalamus in the brain. By approximately the end of menstruation (days 5–7), one or more follicles in the ovary begin to prepare to be released (ovulated) at mid-cycle and also release estrogen and some progesterone. A few days later (8–12) during this estrogen-dominated follicular phase, the uterine lining begins to rebuild (proliferatory phase) and the cervical mucus is thinner. In response to increasing levels of estrogen, an egg is ovulated from the ovary on day 14.

After the egg is released at ovulation, the follicle turns into the corpus luteum, which produces increasing amounts of progesterone and less estrogen. The uterine lining thickens and becomes prepared to receive a fertilized egg for implantation. In the absence of fertilization and implantation, the corpus luteum decreases its output of progesterone and estrogen. Falling levels of estrogen and progesterone cause the uterine lining to be sloughed off (menstruation), signaling day one of the next cycle.

PMS

Following this medicalized model of menstruation, in which hormones and physiology predominate in a context of failed reproduction, loss, and sloughing off, premenstrual syndrome (PMS) is ascribed primarily to hormonal and physiological causes. Although the medical literature acknowledges that PMS constitutes a group of social, psychological, behavioral, and physiological symptoms that vary widely among women and within the same woman and that the timing and severity of the symptoms also vary, physical, rather than psychological and social reasons, are sought to explain the syndrome. For example, inadequate levels of progesterone relative to estrogen become the underlying hypothesis to explain a number of social, psychological, and physical symptoms common to PMS ranging from breast tenderness, weight gain, irritability, and depression as a result of water retention promoted by excessive estrogen relative to progesterone.

Under this medical model, hormones (progesterone) and/or drugs such as bromocriptene or antidiuretics become the cures to alleviate both physical and psychological symptoms. An extreme version of this medical model, advocated by British physician Katharina Dalton, led not only to the prescription of progesterone to counteract the excessive estrogen in women with PMS but also the use of PMS as a defense to have women acquitted of charges of murder. The model has also been used to keep women out of high-paying leadership positions under the guise that fluctuations in hormones during PMS render them incapable of making rational decisions. Nondrug alternatives—such as changes in diet by decreasing salt, caffeine, alcohol, and sugar or increasing exercise—fit the medical model because they serve as natural sources or enhancers of synthetic hormones and drugs.

Although many women taking hormones and drugs report alleviation of PMS symptoms, no drug or hormone has been shown to be effective in a double-blind study. This failure, coupled with questions about whether it is appropriate to give a label such as PMS or Late Luteal Phase Dysphoria (LLD) to a variable, vague group of symptoms that as many as 70 to 90 percent of women experience (Reid and Yen 1981), challenges the medical model as the most useful depiction of normal life cycle events for women such as menstruation, PMS, and menopause.

Menopause

The medical definition of menopause can be traced to developments in sex endocrinology research from the early 20th century when sexuality, reproduction, and various aspects of human sexual behavior became tied to the effects of fluctuating sex hormones, and estrogen was defined as the "female sex hormone." The medical view saw menopause as the result of decreasing ovarian production of estrogen. This absence or decline led to the definition of menopause as a disease that might be treated through the therapy of replacement by commercially prepared estrogen. Dr. Robert Wilson popularized the use of estrogen replacement therapy to treat the disease of menopause and diminished femininity through his 1966 book *Feminine Forever.*

Until the Women's Health Initiative begun in 1992, very little research on women's menopausal experience existed. As the baby-boom generation ages, the pharmaceutical companies developed an extreme interest in capturing the market of consuming women approaching menopause. These companies redefined menopause as a disease that required hormones to cure it and made large amounts of money by selling hormone replacement therapy (HRT) to women before, during, and after menopause.

Most women expressed rage against the pharmaceutical companies and health care industry after the announcement in 2002 that HRT increased the risk of stroke, breast cancer, and blood clots and did not prevent heart attacks or Alzheimer's. Immediately, over 6 million women stopped taking hormone therapy and demanded to know more about the research and policies that had encouraged them to take it (Pearson 2006). They asked why they had been given HRT before such research had been completed and began to question seriously the medicalization of menstruation, PMS, and menopause. (*See also* Endocrinology and Hormones; Women's Health Movement)

References and Further Reading

Pearson, Cynthia. "Menopause Hormone Therapy and Age of Initiation: Reasonable Theory or Marketing Hoax?" *The Women's Health Activist* (March/April). Washington, DC: National Women's Health Network, 2006.

Reid, Robert, and S. S. Yen. "Premenstrual Syndrome." *American Journal of Obstetrics and Gynecology* 139 (1981): 86.

Wilson, Robert. *Feminine Forever.* New York, 1966.

Early Modern Health

Narin Hassan and Cynthia Klestinec

Ideas about health are derived from a variety of sources, practices, and institutions. While hospitals and public health reforms existed in the early modern period and especially in urban environments, health was not limited to the absence of disease, nor was it the only goal of the physician. Disease, a condition inseparable from and known through the body it affected, and illness, the perception of a lack of health or well-being, help to illuminate the category of health as it was managed and experienced in the early modern period.

Lasting into the 18th century, the system of the four humors structured both medical diagnoses and treatments. Each humor, moreover, was associated with an element: black bile with water, yellow bile with fire, blood with earth, and phlegm with air. Accordingly, illness was due to an imbalance of humors. Health was understood as the maintenance of a balance, difficult to achieve but constantly sought after. Treatments accounted for the condition and the patient's disposition: men tended to be hotter and drier; women, colder and moister. In contrast to modern understandings of the body as composed of solid organs and processes such as blood circulation, early modern people imagined the body as a complex system of humors, liable to be put in a state of imbalance and capable of directing attention to a person's temperament (e.g., melancholic if phlegm was more prominent, sanguine if blood was). It was through this system that ideas about health were constituted, a system that blended rather than divided the mental and the physical.

Treating illness depended on several principles, not only on the oppositions between watery or dry humors. For example, the principle of sympathy indicated that a disease could be expelled if it were transferred from the body to other objects. Mary Lindemann (1999) records that as late as the 18th century, peasants brought sheep into the bedroom of patients suffering from fever so that the fever could be transferred from human to beast. For the most part, illnesses were treated with attempts to restore balance through laxatives and bloodletting as well as sleep and waking, food and drink, rest and exercise, excretion and retention, and the passions or emotions. Both lay and learned people took some direction from astrological medicine (which was not superstitious but formally a part of astronomy), which sought harmony between the microcosm, the body, and the macrocosm, the universe; the stars, that is, could influence the human body, bringing the humors into balance or knocking them out of balance. In the middle of the 18th century, the humoral system was given a stronger environmental component. Joining older beliefs, newer ideas about the effect of climatic and environmental factors entered the picture: long periods of rain, for example, could cause illnesses related to an abundance of phlegm.

What were the illnesses that our modern eyes can detect in the historical record? Childhood diseases included smallpox, whooping cough, infantile diarrheas, and tuberculosis. Adding to mortality figures were plague and typhus. Diseases that affected a larger segment of the demographic included plague, leprosy, and St. Anthony's fire (gangrenous ergotism), influenza, tuberculosis, malaria, and typhus. Diseases of old age included cancer, heart disease, circulatory problems, and gout (Park 1992). In addition, worm infestations, eye infections (causing blindness), and poor nutrition (stunted growth and caused glandular tuberculosis known as scrofula) contributed to many health concerns. Finally, environmental factors, related to food, housing, and war, helped to determine the incidence of many diseases. Were the food sources sufficient or deficient in nutrients? Was housing properly ventilated or overcrowded? Was sanitation adequate or a source for typhosoid fevers, dysentery, and body vermin? As every government knew, moreover, war brought about makeshift housing, overcrowding, inadequate sanitation, which were all sources of concern for public health.

Early modern public health did not revolve solely or even initially around the hospital. Rather, in an attempt to deal with the epidemic proportions of plague (ca. 1348) as well as postwar development, governments throughout Europe (but first in Italy) instituted boards of health, which sought to regulate everything from sanitation—such as the collection of manure (for farming) that was moved outside the city walls—and prostitution to trade and the implementation of quarantines and other isolation techniques to limit the spread of disease.

The hospital eventually responded to public health concerns. In its late medieval and early Renaissance incarnation, though, it was an institution devoted to charity, to the health and healing of a wide range of people and especially the poor. In the medieval period, health fell to religious healers, shrines, and other locations of miraculous healing; midwives; barber-surgeons; and physicians. In the early modern period, however, such variety diminished as the market for health care providers developed a clear hierarchy. Medical schools, for example, began to adopt specific procedures for training, licensing, and practice. Academic medicine, moreover, found its way to broader society; surgeons as well as physicians were able to obtain medical information from lessons or lectures as well as printed texts or manuals in the vernacular (not only in Latin). This helped to standardize (and hierarchize) approaches to healing; and this feature foreshadows the rise of the hospital and its transition from a charitable institution to an embodiment of scientific authority.

Hospitals also adopted regulatory procedures that were identified most closely with public health concerns. They designated space for quarantine and converted old units to leprosaria, which were then used for people considered to be chronically ill (such as the insane). In addition to these institutional developments, the relationship between the practitioner and the patient, formerly one of mutual respect and equality, shifted to a hierarchical interaction between practitioner (a superior) and patient (an inferior). These changes reflected the growing authority of science and its embodiment in institutions. As scientific ideas about health emerged, the universal "body" took the place of a specific patient's body; with that, the male body became the standard while the female body became important in the sole area of reproductive health.

Health and the Rise of Modernity

In the 18th and 19th centuries, social and medical reforms encouraged public health to evolve into a discipline. The hospital established itself as the center for medical care. Through its institutional presence, medicine gained authority, and health care entered the public realm, retreating from the domestic one. Hospitals also became the centers of teaching and research, where major diseases were studied more fully. In the 19th century, the hospital became a site of reform. Further, as Bruce Haley (1978) has revealed, the discovery of physiological systems, a growing interest in the relationship of mind to body, and a belief that education and physical training could impact the body changed the ways that attaining good health was imagined.

One of the most dangerous contagious diseases of this period was smallpox, and one of the groundbreaking achievements was the discovery that inoculation and vaccination could prevent it. Although Edward Jenner is celebrated for his development of the smallpox vaccine, a woman traveler, Lady Mary Wortley Montagu, is responsible for popularizing the idea of inoculation in England in the early 18th century. After having her son inoculated in Turkey, she worked to spread this practice in England several years before Jenner's experiments. Thus, she, like many other women of the period, played a role in the educational and social dissemination of ideas surrounding health.

Lady Mary Wortley Montagu. (Paston, George. *Lady Mary Montagu and Her Times,* 1907)

In 1797, Jenner revealed that tiny amounts of cowpox could create resistance to smallpox; published, his research caused vaccination to spread quickly around the globe as a form of disease prevention. Vaccination ushered in the idea of preventative care and encouraged a dialogue on public health issues.

While the Enlightenment had encouraged a search for the causes of ill health and disease, 19th-century reformers began to transform public institutions such as the hospital into disease prevention units. Florence Nightingale revealed how poor ventilation and sanitation in hospitals actually promoted disease; with her influence, hospitals were restructured to promote new ideas about healthy healing environments. Because disease was linked to larger social systems, moreover, health warranted political and national concern. New scientific fields such as statistics encouraged the management of populations and their health. Urban development, moreover, had produced slums where disease outbreaks spread quickly and where sanitation and environmental conditions required reform. Freidrich Engels (1958), in his *The Condition of the Working Class in England,* noted that industrialization and capitalism produced unhealthy urban environments; and Thomas Carlyle (1904) proposed that the state should invest in the health of its population. In Britain, the Age of Reform had begun, and it included figures like Edwin Chadwick who produced the *Sanitary Report* of 1842, which calculated the illnesses and detailed the conditions of poor and working-class life. As Mary Poovey (1995) notes, "Chadwick declared that unsanitary living conditions increased poor rates to unnatural levels . . . more government intervention in the realm of public health would free the economy to govern itself." Other figures, like John Snow, discovered that cholera spread in industrial neighborhoods through the water supply; his epidemiological work heightened the awareness of the relationship between bodies and their environment.

Other discoveries, such as germ theory and bacteriology, created a culture focused on the isolation and containment of disease. Female bodies were increasingly under surveillance because knowledge about sexually transmitted diseases increased. Yet, prostitution remained one of the only choices for survival for poor or "fallen" women. In Britain, the Contagious Diseases Act of 1864 allowed authorities to arrest prostitutes and force them to have medical examinations and treatments. But the sanctions applied only to women, not to men.

In the 20th century, such state-led management and surveillance of bodies around issues of health became the norm, as the field of public health grew and as influential governmental and global agencies emerged. Two of the most important of these are the World Health Organization (WHO) and the Centers for Disease Control (CDC). Such institutions developed programs, such as the 1958 Smallpox Eradication Program (WHO), an early example of the move toward global immunization and standardization of health care initiatives.

With the emergence of large-scale public health movements and the expansion of preventative care, the male body was posited as the universal model. Women's health focused on the reproductive capacities of women. Issues surrounding maternity and sexual diseases built the field of women's health, but research in almost all other aspects of illness concentrated on the ways diseases impacted men. Thus, gender stereotyping and bias often shaped health care policy, and it continues to do so. Tracing the current conditions of gender and health policy in the United States, Kary Moss (1996) argues that institutional bias restricts the entry of women into the United States health care system since they are often excluded from clinical trials and drug treatments, as many programs do not address the needs of women.

While health in the early modern period was understood in light of various communities, institutions, and ideas about the body, modern health has been increasingly understood and managed by institutions like the WHO and CDC. Gender biases, however, continue to pervade these governing bodies and other medical institutions. The recognition of gender as well as class, race, and ethnic differences constitutes a crucial component of new research in the areas of health.

References and Further Reading

Carlyle, Thomas. *The Works of Thomas Carlyle*. New York: Charles Scribner's Sons, 1904.

Chadwick, Edwin. *Report on the Sanitary Condition of the Labouring Population of Great Britain*. 1842. Reprint, Edinburgh: Edinburgh University Press, 1965.

Cipolla, Carlo. *Fighting the Plague in Seventeenth-Century Italy*. Madison: University of Wisconsin Press, 1981.

Engels, Frederick. *The Condition of the Working Class in England 1844–5*. Reprint, London: Basil Blackwell, 1958.

Haley, Bruce. *The Healthy Body and Victorian Culture*. Cambridge, MA: Harvard University Press, 1978.

Lindemann, Mary. *Medicine and Society in Early Modern Europe*. Cambridge: Cambridge University Press, 1999.

Moss, Kary, ed. *Man Made Medicine. Women's Health, Public Policy, and Reform*. Durham, NC: Duke University Press, 1996.

Park, Katharine. "Medicine and Society in Medieval Europe, 500–1500." In *Medicine and Society: Historical Essays*. Edited by Andrew Wear, 59–90. Cambridge: Cambridge University Press, 1992.

Poovey, Mary. *Making a Social Body. British Cultural Formation 1830–1864*. Chicago: University of Chicago Press, 1995.

Gender/Sex—How Conjoined

Sue V. Rosser

For most of history, people believed that biological sex determined sexual orientation, social roles, and even occupational abilities, such as who could become a scientist. This belief led to much scientific research examining the biological bases for sex differences and deviations. Gayle Rubin (1975) explicitly described the sex/gender system, distinguishing the biology of sex from the cultural/social construction of gender to reveal the male-centered social processes and practices that constrain and control women's lives. Rubin built on the implications of *The Second Sex* by Simone de Beauvoir (1948), who initiated the second wave of the women's movement. She provided the philosophical origins of existentialist feminism by suggesting that women's "otherness" and the social construction of gender rest on society's interpretation of biological differences (sex).

Rubin articulated the connection between the biological sex and the social construction of masculinity and femininity that result in superiority being attached to what was labeled masculine and in discrimination against what was defined as feminine across various societies. Although the definition of what tasks, roles, and behaviors were considered masculine and feminine varied among societies, the lower status ascribed to feminine and femininity remained consistent across societies. Rubin's articulation of the operation of the sex/gender system in a variety of contexts within a society and across societies provoked ethical questions about unequal treatment based on sex/gender in all arenas, including science and technology. Her explication of the sex/gender system led to questions about whether sex/gender biases had permeated science and engineering on a variety of levels.

Flexibility of Biological Sex

Aware of the fluidity of biological sex among a variety of species in the animal kingdom, including humans, biologists explored the definition of biological sex. They examined inappropriate direct links from the simplistic, binary categories of biological male and female to gender identities of masculine and feminine as well as inappropriate assumptions to links with particular sexual orientations. At the time of birth, attendants categorize newborns into the binary categories of male or female despite numerous clinical examples in humans demonstrating that biological sex can be disaggregated into genetic, hormonal, internal anatomical, and external anatomical components. Typically a genetic male (XY) will produce some testosterone prenatally that will lead the undifferentiated fetus to develop internal organs such as testes and external structures such as the penis, normally associated with males. Breakdowns or changes at any level may cause development to take a different path. For example, individuals who are genetic males (XY) with androgen insensitivity (testicular feminization) have testes but female external genitalia; individuals with Turner's syndrome (genetic X0) have the anatomy of females at birth (although their genitals may remain immature after puberty and they may or may not have ovaries) but do not have the XX sex chromosomes associated with "normal" females.

After birth, it was assumed that an individual categorized as male would produce increased levels of testosterone at puberty that would lead to the development of secondary sex characteristics such as facial hair and a deeper voice, while a female would develop breasts and begin menstruating in the absence of testosterone and in the presence of estrogen and progesterone. Clinical conditions such as congenital adrenal hyperplasia (CAH) demonstrated further breakdown in the uniformity of biological sex. The absence of the enzyme C-21-hydroxylase in CAH results in genetic females (XX) with female internal genitalia but male external genitalia.

These breakdowns demonstrating that a genetic male did not always result in an individual with functioning male anatomy and secondary sex characteristics undermined the binary sex categories of male and female. They also led scientists to question biologically deterministic models that linked the male sex with male gender identity, role development, and heterosexual identity. Statistical and interview data from the Kinsey Reports coupled with clinical studies revealed difficulties with binary categories and assumptions of cause and effect. For example, the studies of Money and Erhardt (1972) explored so-called ambiguous sex or babies born with external genitalia "discrepant" with their sex chromosomes and internal genitalia (i.e., genetic females [XX], with ovaries, but an elongated or "penoclitoris," or genetic males [XY], with testes, with androgen insensitivity).

Many of the babies in these studies were genetic females who had ambiguous external genitalia at birth resulting from their mothers having been given synthetic progestins to prevent miscarriage during the pregnancy. Money and Erhardt concluded from these studies that operations and hormone treatments to remove ambiguity would not prevent "normal" gender identity development congruent with the assignment of sex based on construction of external genitalia, as long as such reassignment occurred before the baby was 18 months of age. Even at the time of these studies, assumptions that Money and Erhardt made about appropriate gender identities and roles were questioned. For example, people questioned whether exposure to androgens had resulted in the higher IQ of these genetic females and whether the parents of sexually reassigned individuals treated them in ways that would influence them to develop "appropriate" gender identity. In recent years, more emphasis has been placed on the ethics of using surgery and hormones to provide conformity between the biological sex and the socially constructed gender roles. As adults, the patients themselves have raised questions about who made the decisions to do the sexual reassignments, who decided what was "appropriate" gender identity, and in many cases, why they had never been told that these medical and psychological interventions had been done to them.

Transsexual surgery was described as a solution for individuals who have always felt that they were trapped in a body of the wrong sex. A medical intervention became popular during the 1970s to make the socially constructed gender identity of individuals congruent with their biological sex. Although large numbers surfaced almost immediately of "dissatisfied" or "problematic cases" of individuals who had undergone transsexual surgery, the broader medical and mainstream community took longer to realize that sex and gender were not the same and that binary categories of male and female, as well as masculinity and femininity, might be too limited and constraining. Philosopher Jan Raymond in her 1979 book *The Transsexual Empire* pointed out that transsexual surgery would not be needed in a society that did not force people to conform to very constricted, dichotomous gender roles based on their sex, but not until the late 1990s did the transgender movement begin. In *Transgender Warriors* (1996), Leslie Feinberg discusses how the social construction of gender allows her to assume a male gender role/identity without ever intending to undergo transsexual surgery; Feinberg understands and wishes to challenge the notion that biological sex determines the social construction of gender.

Impact of Sex/Gender in Scientific Theories/Experiments

The statistical data demonstrating the dearth of women in science, especially the physical sciences and engineering, led Evelyn Fox Keller (1982) to explore the very interesting question of whether the small number of women has led to the construction of a gendered science that examines nature from a male perspective. Keller coupled work on the history of early modern science, demonstrating that women were purposely excluded and not permitted as valid "witnesses" to scientific experiments, with theories of object relations for gender identity development. Keller applied object relations theory to show how women as primary caretakers of children during gender role socialization leads more men to choose careers in science. Since women may encourage boys to differentiate by pushing them to be distant, autonomous, and separate from them as caretakers, this may result in science becoming a masculine province that excludes women and causes women to exclude themselves since women are encouraged to remain connected and less separate. Science is a masculine province not only because it is populated mostly by men but because this leads men to create science and technology that reflect masculine approaches, interests, and views of the world that are distant, objective and separate.

This gender-biased or masculinized science led to several flaws or biases in scientific theories and results in both life sciences/medicine and physical sciences/technology:

1. Exclusion of females as experimental and design subjects led to flawed medical research. Research protocols for large-scale studies of cardiovascular diseases failed to assess gender differences. Women were excluded from clinical trials of drugs because of fear of litigation from possible teratogenic effects on fetuses.

   Dominance of men in engineering and the creative design sectors may result in similar bias, especially in technology design and user bias. The air bag fiasco suffered by the U.S. auto industry serves as an excellent example of gender bias reflected in design. Would women engineers on the design team have prevented this fiasco, recognizing that a bag that implicitly used the larger male body as a norm would be flawed when applied to smaller individuals, killing rather than protecting children and small women?

2. Androcentric bias in the choice and definition of problems to be studied resulted in subjects concerning women receiving less funding and research. After the 1985 U.S. Public Health Service survey recommended that the definition of women's health be expanded beyond reproductive health, in 1990, the Government Accountability Office (GAO) criticized the National Institutes of Health (NIH) for inadequate representation of women and minorities in federally funded studies.

   Having large numbers of male engineers and creators of technologies also often results in technologies that are useful from only a male perspective (i.e., these technologies fail to address important issues for women users). In addition to the military origins for the development and funding of much technology that makes its civilian application less useful for women's lives, men designing technology for the home frequently focus on issues less important to women users.

3. Androcentric bias in the formulation of scientific theories and methods resulted in those that coincide with the male experience of the world becoming the "objective" theories that define the interpretation of scientific data and use of technology. Excessive focus on male research subjects and definition of cardiovascular diseases as "male" led to underdiagnosis and undertreatment of these diseases in women. The male-as-norm approach in research and diagnosis, unsurprisingly, was translated into bias in treatments for women. Women exhibited higher death rates from coronary bypass surgery and angioplasty.

In equally direct ways, androcentric bias has excluded women as users of technology. Military regulations often apply Military Standard 1472 of anthropometric data so that systems dimensions use the 95th and 5th percentile of male dimensions in designing weapons systems; the result is that the cockpits of airplanes are designed to fit the dimensions of 90 percent of male military recruits (Weber 1997). In the case of the Joint Primary Aircraft Training System (JPATS), used by both the Navy and Air Force to train its pilots, the application of the standard accommodated 90 percent of males but only approximately 30 percent of females. The policy decision to increase the percentage of women pilots uncovered the gender bias in the cockpit design that excluded only 10 percent of male recruits by dimensions but 70 percent of women recruits. The officers initially assumed that the technology reflected the best or only design possible and that the goal for the percentage of women pilots would have to be lowered and/or the number of tall women recruits would have to be increased. This initial reaction, representing the worldview of men, changed. When political conditions reinforced the policy goal, a new cockpit design emerged reducing the minimum sitting height from 34 to 32.8 inches, thereby increasing the percentage of eligible women (Weber 1997).

Awareness and understanding of sex/gender biases raise the fundamental question of how these androcentric biases in scientific methods and theories occur if the scientific method is objective. Are gender and all aspects of science and technology socially or culturally constructed and nonobjective? Can scientists and engineers be objective? More importantly, is good science objective and gender free? (*See also* Endocrinology and Hormones; Homosexuality; Technology; Women's Health Movement)

References and Further Reading

De Beavoir, Simone. *The Second Sex*. Translated and edited by H. M. Parshley. New York: Vintage Books, 1948.

Feinberg, Leslie. *Transgender Warriors: Making History from Joan of Arc to Dennis Rodman*. Boston: Beacon Press, 1996.

Keller, Evelyn F. "Feminism and Science." *Signs* 7 (3) (1982): 589–602.

Money, John, and Anke Erhardt. *Man and Woman, Boy and Girl: The Differentiation and Dimorphism of Gender and Identity from Conception to Maturity*. Baltimore, MD: Johns Hopkins University Press, 1972.

Raymond, Janice. *The Transsexual Empire: The Making of the She-male*. Boston: Beacon Press, 1979.

Rubin, Gayle. "The Traffic in Women: Notes on the 'Political Economy' of Sex." In *Toward an Anthropology of Women*. Edited by Rayna Reiter, 157–210. New York: Monthly Review Press, 1975.

Weber, Rachel. "Manufacturing Gender in Commercial and Military Cockpit Design." *Science, Technology and Human Values* 22 (1997): 235–253.

Homosexuality

Sue V. Rosser

Definition of Homosexuality

In 1869, in an anonymous pamphlet distributed in Germany advocating the repeal of the country's sodomy law, the term *homosexuality* first appeared (Miller 2006). Defined in contrast to heterosexuality, homosexuality is the sexual orientation or attraction to individuals of the same sex. Although technically, homosexuals include both men and women, the term *lesbian* more typically distinguishes women. Originally, "gay" usually meant a male homosexual, but more recently, both male and female homosexuals identify with "gay" and "queer" culture.

Some people confuse homosexuals with transsexual or transgender individuals. Transgender individuals believe that their gender identity does not conform with their primary and secondary sexual characteristics. For example, a biologically male body may house someone who feels like a female and identifies as feminine and female. Some individuals may seek transsexual surgery to make their external genitalia agree with their gender identity; after surgery, these individuals may be referred to as transsexual. Other individuals identify as transgender. Although they may take hormones, may dress to conform with their gender identification, and may even have some minor surgeries, they do not complete transsexual surgery to make their external and internal genitalia conform with their gender identity.

Other confusion exists about distinctions among transvestites, transsexuals, and homosexuals. Transvestites are individuals who cross-dress or wear clothing typically associated with the opposite sex/gender in a particular culture. For example, men who wear skirts in the 21st-century United States, unless they are clerics, belong to certain American Indian tribes, or are participating in Scottish rites, would be cross-dressing, particularly if they receive sexual pleasure from cross-dressing. Although most transgender and presurgery transsexual individuals cross-dress, their reason for doing so is to conform with their gender identity. Some homosexuals, such as male drag queens, cross-dress, but most homosexuals are not transvestites. A significant proportion of transvestites are heterosexuals who receive sexual pleasure from, and enjoy, cross-dressing.

Male homosexuality has been accepted in some cultures (Bullough 1976; Katz 1992) or time periods as normal, as a higher form of sexual relationship than male heterosexuality, or as a form of bisexuality. Since the 16th century in America, homosexuality has been defined in terms of deviation from the heterosexual male norm. In *Gay American History: Lesbians and Gay Men in the USA,* Katz (1992) delineates four periods in gay American history: homosexuality defined by theologians as a sin; by legislators as a legal problem or crime; by medical entrepreneurs as a biological anomaly; and finally by psychiatrists/psychologists as a psychic disturbance.

Emergence of Gay History

On June 28, 1969, in Greenwich Village in New York City, what came to be called the Stonewall riots ushered in the birth of the gay rights movement. Gay American history emerged in the 1970s along with women's history, Black history, and the reemergence of socialist history. Recognizing another group whose voices and experiences were missing from the traditional accounts of history, scholars of gay history revealed sexist bias and homophobia in such accounts. Since lesbians are often ignored by or are invisible to the rest of society, the volume of data documenting male homosexuality was substantially greater than that for lesbians. This dearth of evidence, combined with the fact that most individuals undertaking the first research were gay men, led to the initial parameters for research and theories and conclusions drawn from the documents to be based on the gay male experience.

Evidence of lesbianism can be found to correspond to each of the four periods defined for gay males. Although not ignored, the history of lesbians is again defined against a male norm—that of the male homosexual. Lesbian history based on the experiences of lesbians rather than as a subdiscipline within women's history or gay history remains an understudied field only now beginning to emerge in its own right.

Throughout history, explanations have been sought for the causes or reasons for homosexuality. Because this volume focuses on myths of gender and scientific research, the last two periods of homosexuality Katz delineated—defined by medical entrepreneurs as a biological anomaly and by psychiatrists/psychologists as a psychic disturbance—form the centerpiece of this essay.

Search for Biological Differences

Typically, scientists applied the dominant scientific explanation or active research approach of the era to study homosexuality. In the 19th century, the study of anatomy formed the basis for much of medical and scientific research. Not surprisingly, during this era, researchers looked for anatomical differences between the anatomy of homosexuals and "normal" or heterosexual individuals. The German lawyer Karl Heinrich Ulrichs, himself a homosexual, published a pamphlet in 1864 in which he claimed that homosexuals constituted a third sex:

> Ulrichs developed his theory in the wake of the belief at the time that the human embryo possessed both male and female sex organs, losing one as it develops in the uterus. He theorized that male homosexuality came about when the embryo shed the female sex organ, but the same change did not occur in the part of the brain that regulates the sex drive. (Again, the situation was reversed in the case of female homosexuality.)
>
> Ulrichs assumed that because male homosexuals had a female soul in a male body, they therefore possessed the personality characteristics of women. Likewise, female homosexuals had the personality characteristics of men. According to him, homosexuality was not just an "inversion" in the choice of sexual object but an "inversion" of one's broader gender characteristics as well. This idea did not originate with Ulrichs, to be sure. But his theory of the "third sex" gave these gender stereotypes a quasi-scientific basis, confounding sexual orientation with gender and confusing homosexuals with hermaphrodites. (Miller 2006, 15)

With later scientific discoveries, these differences were documented as other phenomena. For example, individuals with both male and female internal genitalia are not homosexuals; they are hermaphrodites. Individuals with a "penoclitoris" or enlarged external genitalia are not homosexuals. These enlarged genitalia result from conditions such as corticoadrenohyperplasia (CAH) or exposure of a female fetus to testosterone in utero. In short, homosexuals have no known anatomical differences from heterosexuals.

Although Ulrichs contended that homosexuality was hereditary and benign, in France, this genetic trait was viewed as a symptom of degeneration. Homosexuality, along with insanity, poverty, and alcoholism, was seen as transmissible from one generation to the next. Initially, a Viennese professor of psychiatry, Richard von Krafft-Ebing, also promoted the degeneracy theory in his 1886 book *Psychopathia Sexualis*. In the 200 case studies in the book, he emphasized gender stereotypes in his description of homosexuals, attributing characteristics of the opposite sex to homosexuals and viewing this as evidence of the degeneracy theory. In later works, he described "inversion" as a congenital anomaly only and no longer promoted degeneracy.

The British sexologist Havelock Ellis borrowed von Krafft-Ebing's methodology of the case study and also concurred in his belief that homosexuality was inherited. In contrast, Ellis did not find "gender stereotypes" with regard to males. However, he did continue to attribute character inversion to lesbians (Miller 2006).

By the late 19th and early 20th centuries, the discovery of hormones shifted the focus of research on homosexuals from anatomy to a search for hormonal differences between homosexuals and heterosexuals. Researchers assumed that major hormonal differences in treatments designed to turn homosexuals into heterosexuals would succeed.

Jeffrey Weeks writes that in 1898 an asylum in the U.S. state of Kansas reported that 48 men had been castrated; castration was used on sex offenders and homosexuals in Switzerland in the early years of the century and in the 1930s in Denmark. Hormone treatments and aversion therapies were later adopted (Miller 2006, 23).

Some claims of hormonal differences between homosexuals and heterosexuals continue in the research literature today, especially in the areas of neuroscience and brain research. For example, in her 2006 book, Louann Brezindine states the following:

> Sexual orientation does not appear to be a matter of conscious self-labeling but a matter of brain wiring. Several family and twin studies provide clear evidence for a genetic component to both male and female sexual orientation. We know that prenatal exposure to an opposite-sex hormonal environment, like testosterone in a genetically female brain, leads the nervous system and brain circuits to develop along more male-typical lines. This prenatal hormonal environment has enduring effects on behavioral trains like rough-and-tumble play and sexual attraction. (Brezindine 2006, 186)

Since genes now constitute the primary level at which current biomedical research focuses, it is not surprising that research on homosexuality has also shifted to the genetic level. After announcing differences in the brain structure of homosexual and heterosexual men in 1991, Simon LaVay in 1996 surveyed the evidence for "gay genes" in *Queer Science*. Since then, the research has become more complex, with the possibility of several genes suggested as possible causes for homosexuality. These gay genes, turning off and on hormones, are proposed to account for the brain differences:

> The female brain is only half as likely to be wired for same-sex attraction as is the male brain. Therefore men are twice as likely as women to be gay. Bio-

logically, genetic variations and hormone exposure in both male and female brains are thought to lead to same-sex attraction, but the origins in women appear to be different than in men. Most brain studies have been done on the differences between gay and straight males, and only recently have studies on females begun to emerge. Sexual orientation in females occurs along more of a continuum than in males, with females reporting more bi-sexual interests. (Brezindine 2006, 185–186)

Genes and their effects on behavior represent an emergent, rapidly developing area of research now. As this volume goes to press, it is difficult to evaluate definitively the claims that a gene or several genes "cause" homosexuality. The 19th- and 20th-century history of anatomical and hormonal research suggests that caution proves wise in accepting biologically deterministic arguments for homosexuality.

Search for Psychological Differences

Just as over time the changing dominant biomedical area of active research became the explanation of the cause for the "biological anomaly" of homosexuality, the primary trend in psychology/psychiatry at a particular time became the accepted explanation for the "psychic disturbance of homosexuality." Sexuality has traditionally been defined using a white, male, upper-middle-class heterosexual norm. In contrast to the situation in some other cultures and in previous historical periods, sexuality in late 19th- and 20th-century United States was defined biologically. For example, in addition to the central role given to procreation, Freud's "anatomy is destiny" (1968, 18) characterized women's sexual development based on what women lacked compared to the male norm.

Freud's use of the single concept of penis envy to explain the development of sexuality, normal gender development, and neurotic conflict in women was repudiated quickly by female psychoanalysts of the day. Karen Horney (1933) challenged penis envy, ascribing femininity to female biology and awareness of the vagina, not disappointment over lacking a penis. Thompson suggested that the major sexual dilemma for women was not penis envy but acknowledging their own sexuality in this culture. Other women (de Beauvoir 1974) stated that what women envied was men's power, not their penises.

Freud did not ignore lesbian sexuality but subsumed it under female heterosexuality as an immature state in which the woman failed to make the clitoral-to-vaginal transfer. Lesbian sexuality was defined as doubly removed (first as female, then as failed heterosexual) from the male heterosexual norm.

Psychiatrist Karen Horney, an early feminist, challenged much of Sigmund Freud's male-oriented psychology. (Bettmann/Corbis)

By the middle of the 20th century, the American Psychological Association (APA) had classified homosexuality as a mental illness. Homosexuals were frequently institutionalized because of their illness, received electroshock, aversion therapy, or other treatments to cure their illness. In the early 1970s a group of lesbian/gay activists in New York City protested the APA's classification of lesbianism/homosexuality as a mental illness. They threw buckets of chicken blood on psychiatrists and psychologists attending APA meetings to symbolize the gay and lesbian blood that psychiatrists had on their hands. In April 1973, the APA decided that homosexuality by itself did not constitute a mental illness. In 1986, the APA removed all references to homosexuality in the *Diagnostic and Statistical Manual of Mental Disorders (DSM)*–III-R. With the current research interest in the brain and neuroscience, considerable attention and resources in psychology focus on use of fMRI (functional magnetic resonance imaging) and brain scans to discern possible brain differences between homosexuals and heterosexuals.

Impact on Health

The overemphasis on biology rather than behavior in scientific research and homosexuality has introduced some flaws in medical research that hurt both homosexual and heterosexual men and women. For example, when the symptoms of the disease we now know as acquired immune deficiency syndrome (AIDS) first appeared in this country, the categorization of the disease and research focused on groups of people rather than risk behaviors. Despite the strong evidence and history of heterosexual transmission of AIDS in Africa, AIDS was initially characterized in the United States as a gay male disease, with subsequent inclusion of intravenous (IV) drug users and Haitian immigrants. Designation by group identity rather than risk behavior led to a large number of problems resulting in lack of funding and study of AIDS and its transmission and diagnosis in many populations (Shilts 1987). This led the general public to believe that being a homosexual, rather than engaging in certain risk behaviors, causes AIDS. Even today, men who have sex with other men but who do not identify as homosexual may underestimate their risk for AIDS.

Similarly, public health campaigns to educate women about health promotion and disease prevention need to be oriented toward risk behaviors with the recognition that women have diverse sexual orientations. Public service announcements that encourage every woman to have an annual Pap smear or to be vaccinated against the human papilloma virus (HPV) causing cervical cancer do not focus on risk behaviors. They assume that all women engage in heterosexual activity and inadequately convey to the public the risk behavior responsible for cervical cancer, transmissible through heterosexual intercourse. These announcements repeat for public information the mistakes in identifying by group rather than risk behavior.

Conclusion

U.S. and European society from the 19th century to the present have viewed homosexuality as deviant from the heterosexual norm biologically and psychologically. Because of the emphasis on deviance, scientific research has focused on a search for biological or psychological differences between homosexuals and heterosexuals. This biologically deterministic approach was pursued in the search for differences in anatomy and hormones between homosexuals and heterosexuals in earlier times. Genetic and brain differences represent current areas of focus. The emphasis on nature over nurture in scientific research has introduced some problems in medical research and public health messages. Defining people by categories rather than behaviors conveys false information about risk to both homosexuals and heterosexuals. (*See also* The Brain; Gender/Sex—How Conjoined; Women's Health Movement; Nature/Nurture; The 19th Century)

References and Further Reading

Birke, Linda. *Women, Feminism, and Biology: The Feminist Challenge*. New York: Methuen, 1986.

Brezindine, Louann. *The Female Brain*. New York: Morgan Rood Books, 2006.

Bullough, Vern. *Sexual Variance in Society and History*. New York: John Wiley, 1976.

De Beauvoir, Simone. *The Second Sex*. Translated by H. M. Parshley. New York: Vintage Books, 1974.

Ellis, Havelock. *Sexual Inversion*. 3rd ed. Philadelphia, PA: F. A. Davis, 1915.

Freud, Sigmund. "The Passing of the Oedipus Complex." *Sexuality and the Psychology of Love*. New York: Collier Books, 1968.

Horney, Karen. "The Denial of the Vagina: A Contribution to the Problem of the Genital Anxieties Specific to Women." *International Journal of Psychoanalysis* 14 (1933): 57–70.

Katz, Jay. *Gay American History: Lesbians and Gay Men in the USA*. New York: Meridien, 1992.

LaVay, Simon. "A Difference in Hypothalamic Structure between Homosexual and Heterosexual Men." *Science* 253 (1991): 1034–1037.

LaVay, Simon. *Queer Science*. Cambridge, MA: MIT Press, 1996.

Miller, Neil. *Out of the Past: Gay and Lesbian History from 1869 to the Present*. New York: Alyson Books, 2006.

Shilts, Randy. *And the Band Played On: Politics, People and the AIDS Epidemic*. New York: St. Martin's Press, 1987.

Von Krafft-Ebing, Richard. *Psychopathia Sexualis*. Originally published in 1886. Translated from the 12th German edition by Franklin S. Klaf. New York: Arcade, 1998.

Race

ANNE J. MACLACHLAN

More that any other socially fabricated construct, the concept of race is deeply rooted in myth. The traditional meaning of myth comes from the various creation stories of groups of people who have used these stories to create a shared identity. The variation among creation myths is enormous, but the character of the myth can affect personal identity as well as that of the group. Myth creation is also an ongoing process so that as one group came to dominate another, new myths arose that legitimized the victors while often attempting to reconcile the vanquished by incorporating the useful parts of their mythology into that of the victors. Myth is also associated with social and gender hierarchies that typically legitimate the subordination of women.

In the 21st-century United States, myth still plays a powerful role in group identity and social relationships. "Race" becomes a key means of ascribing a particular identity to groups of people who may share elements of a certain physical appearance or originate from a particular location. African Americans bear particularly heinous historical baggage attached to the concept of race. In the book of Genesis, Noah cursed his son Ham's descendants to be slaves. This myth was used by various European and Arab societies to justify their enslavement of Africans (Goldenberg 2005). While this direct connection to the Old Testament is not necessarily made today, the legacy of this pejorative view survives in ongoing discrimination against African Americans, who continue to be viewed by Whites and many Asians as mentally inferior, decadent, and criminal. These prejudices affect the daily life experiences of African Americans and members of other groups such as Latinos, Native Americans, South East Indians, and Arabs, whose brown skin or other physical attributes set them apart from White Europeans. Consequently, no matter how distinguished intellectually and socially an individual is, the impact of race in daily life is captured in this recent quote by an African American scientist about his experience in graduate school: "Your ethnicity is from society, it affects virtually all your experiences. It is part of American society, it is part of the consciousness of Americans. It influences the nature of your experience in graduate school, how you are perceived. It is impossible for me to separate this from graduate education" (MacLachlan 2004, 1).

While "ethnicity" is more commonly used today as a surrogate for race, its use has not reduced the mythical and historical prejudices embodied in racial concepts. "Race" certainly is not an easy concept. Scientific research has been used since the advent of the "modern" approach to observation of natural phenomena in the 18th century to "prove" the inferiority of the "Negro races." One scientific researcher, Samuel George Morton, a Philadelphia physician, collected over 600 skulls in the first half of the 19th century for the purpose of measuring cranial capacity to settle the discussion about the intelligence of people belonging to different racial groups. His work made him famous because he had "finally presented a large body of objective fact," which proved the intellectual inferiority of both the Negro and the Indian. His work was widely hailed as definitive, and his tables were reprinted throughout the 19th century to serve as a "lynchpin in anthropometric arguments about human racial differences" (Gould 1978, 504). All Morton's published data were later reevaluated by Stephen Jay Gould in the 1970s. Gould found that, far from acting as an unbiased observer, Morton made pejorative remarks about the groups in his study, failed to distinguish between male and female skulls, used faulty methods of measurement, and demonstrated a tendency to round his data upward for Caucasians and downward for all others. In short, Gould found "that [Morton's data] are a patchwork of assumption and finagling, controlled, probably unconsciously, by his conventional *a priori* ranking (his folks on top, slaves on the bottom)" (Gould 1978, 504).

Race continues to be contentious, and scientifically based arguments are still used to attempt to justify racial differences. Much of the scientific community today agrees that "race" has no particular biological basis, even though groups with a long history of interbreeding may have developed particular inheritable diseases such as Tay Sachs or sickle cell anemia. Yet the concept of race is still employed in medicine largely because differences in income have created enormous disparities among those who have access to good medical care, and consequently good health, and those who do not. "Race," however, is a social reality in which individuals descended from African slaves in the United States are mistreated as a result of their appearance and suffer higher rates of heart disease, high blood pressure, and often shorter life spans than members of other groups. The prejudices against African Americans and the discrimination they face in employment, housing, and the criminal justice system ensure that the tension this engenders takes a heavy toll on their health. Troy Duster characterizes this as an aspect of "very complex interactive feedback loops between biology and culture and social stratification" (Duster 2003, 258). His concern is that race as a concept will again be reified in this new paradigm.

Another social construction, gender, like race, fluctuates over time and across different cultures. With gender, the creation myth also significantly influences the allocation of roles to women and girls as a means of maintaining patriarchy. After all, it was Eve who was susceptible to the persuasions of the serpent and so, through her weakness, precipitated the fall from grace of humans and their banishment from the garden of Eden. Interpreted through centuries of Judeo-Christian theology, the appropriate gender role for women is as mother and keeper of the hearth. This traditional view casts women as weak, incapable of leadership, and unable to master intellectual complexity. Simultaneously, women are also viewed as sexual objects, temptresses, corrupt —as modern Jezebels. This myth, mixed with the legal codification of male power monopolies in politics, higher education, religion, and within families, has left a powerful inheritance of negative views about women and their capacities throughout the 20th century. Today, complex forms of bias and discrimination undermine women's full participation in many aspects of life, including the practice of science.

Because of patriarchy in the 21st-century United States, men need to sanction the fact that discrimination against women exists for action to be taken against discrimination. In 1999, the president of MIT, Charles Vest, recognized the bias and discrimination against women scientists when shown the actual differences in salary, research assistance, promotion rates, and allocated lab space between men and women. Vest remarked: "I have always believed that contemporary gender discrimination within universities is part reality and part perception. True, but now I understand that reality is by far the greater part of the balance" (MIT 1999, 2). Subsequently, the National Academies published a report on women in 2006 that discussed discrimination against women in every field of science and engineering. Environments that favor men were blamed along with continuous questioning of women's abilities and commitment to an academic career, in a system that claims to reward based on merit, but instead rewards traits such as assertiveness that are socially less acceptable for women to possess (NAS 2006, 3–4).

When issues of race and gender coincide in the person of a woman of color, multiple forms of bias work to keep her from pursuing a scientific career. Although girls of color are enrolling and graduating from college with bachelor's and master's degrees in substantial excess of boys, at the Ph.D. level more men of color than women earn doctorates. In 2004, only 171 African American, Native American, and Chicana women earned doctorates in natural and physical sciences compared to a total of 9,015 for all U.S. citizens (NSF 2006). The insidious effects of racism begin in school where students of color tend to be tracked into nonacademic courses. Currently, segregation in schools is largely de facto, with pupils of color generally steered into less-well-equipped and staffed schools. Once a woman of color has survived this system to receive a Ph.D., she emerges as a disciplined, dedicated scientist who probably has drawn on many personal resources such as family, friends, religion, and a passion for science. Having mastered so much, she often faces a further trial in securing either a postdoctoral position or scientific employment.

The climate for women and persons of color in a scientific work environment is heavily shaped by inherited beliefs about the objective nature of scientific research and the impartiality of scientists in reporting what they find. The idea of impartiality derives from the beginning of inductive scientific reasoning and its elaboration during the 18th century. Max Weber further popularized the idea with his theory of objectivity and value-free observation at the beginning of the 20th century, while Thomas Merton elaborated the idea for natural and physical sciences during the 1950s. Although contested, these ideas about science still hold some sway in the minds of both male and female scientists. The effect of these ideas, which have acquired almost mythic status, is that women encounter the behaviors described in the recent National Academies of Sciences report (NAS 2006) while many in the scientific environment deny they exist. Moreover, implicit belief in objectivity can substantially corrupt the scientific method when, as graphically illustrated in Morton's research on race, choice of problem, choice of method, and understanding of observations is shaped by bias. More subtly, preconceived ideas about capacity in connection with scientists of color or women scientists lead to undervaluing the accomplishments of members of both groups. Again this has been illustrated by studies of journal submissions. When blind reviewing was instituted, the number of accepted articles written by women increased significantly. The full impact of such beliefs results in qualified scientists of color and women not receiving prestigious academic or other scientific positions at the same rate as White men and not obtaining promotions as quickly or at all. Women's salaries also tend to lag substantially behind those of men.

A further consequence of this belief in the objectivity of the scientific method, when combined with pejorative ideas about women and persons of color, makes change difficult. If scientists consider themselves to be objective and are skeptical of social science research that demonstrates bias and prejudice in the scientific enterprise, change becomes even more difficult. The stratification ramifications of "race" seen everywhere in American society—from Mexican American gardeners and maids to the high proportion of African American youth in jail—reinforce old beliefs about intelligence and criminality and the general inferiority of non-White peoples. The social position of people of color resulting from racist discrimination has created a dynamic that tends to reinforce White ideas about race while supporting the social manifestation of discrimination. Breaking this dynamic requires moving beyond inherited mythical thinking to view each individual person as a member of humanity. (*See also* The Brain; Discrimination; The 19th Century; Race, Postcolonial Gender, and Science)

References and Further Reading

Duster, Troy. "Buried Alive: The Concept of Race in Science." *Genetic Nature/Culture: Anthropology and Science beyond the Two-Culture Divide.* Edited by A. H. Goodman et al. Berkeley: University of California Press, 2003.

Goldenberg, David. *The Curse of Ham: Race and Slavery in Early Judaism, Christianity, and Islam.* Princeton, NJ: Princeton University Press, 2005.

Gould, Stephen Jay. "Morton's Ranking of Races by Cranial Capacity: Unconscious Manipulation of Data May Be a Scientific Norm." *Science* 200 (May 1978).

MacLachlan, Anne. "Developing Graduate Students for the Professoriate in STEM." Berkeley, CA: Center for Studies in Higher Education, 2004.

Massachusetts Institute of Technology (MIT), Gender Equity Project. *Overview of the School of Science Report 1999.* http://web.mit.edu/gep/about.html. (Accessed March 3, 2007.)

National Academies of Sciences (NAS), National Academy of Engineering, and Institute of Medicine. *Beyond Bias and Barriers: Fulfilling the Potential of Women in Academic Science and Engineering.* Washington, DC: National Academies Press, 2006.

National Science Foundation (NSF), Division of Science Resources Statistics. *Science and Engineering Doctorate Awards.* NSF 06–308. Project Officer Susan T. Hill. Arlington, VA: National Science Foundation, 2006.

Nature/Nurture

Muriel Lederman

The nature/nurture debate concerns the relative contributions to a person's characteristics of inherent traits and forces in the environment. Currently in the West, and especially germane to the subject of this volume, this debate can play out in discussions of the influences that determine the achievement of women and certain ethnic minorities in science, especially when success is defined as high status in academia.

In this framework, the mental abilities and activities of those who are involved in science or might want to become scientists are central. This primacy of cognition can be traced back through the centuries to the Cartesian duality of the supremacy of mind over body. During the Scientific Revolution, nature was associated with women and framed as a particular, abstract machine. This worldview separated humans from the objects of their investigation, used mechanical procedures for study, and used the knowledge thus gained to exploit nature for man's advantage (Shapin 1996). It is the ability to engage in the socially constructed descendant of this method for investigation, and solely in these procedures, that has value in the scientific arena.

Measurement of cognitive ability has been attempted for centuries with the goal of developing a unitary, linear, hierarchical scale on which an individual's ranking will denote mental prowess. Over time, the basis for the scale has changed, from physical measurements to the scores on specially designed tests and most recently to biological activities measured by sophisticated medical instruments. In no case is the scale "objective"; its developer has the luxury to decide the factors on which the scale is based. Because White males have been the predominant group with access to the "science" of the day, the parameters on which the scales are based and the resulting hierarchical ranking reinforces the position of those who created the instrument. The correctness of the results is vouched for by the community of researchers and accepted by the society at large because of the high status accruing to scientific work.

In the 18th and 19th centuries, there were many demonstrations of the supremacy of the mental powers of Whites and males. These were based on the

characteristics of body structures, assuming that the larger the physical pa-
rameter, the greater the intelligence. These results agreed with the social conventions of the times and the locations in which these demonstrations took
place. In America in the late 1700s, even abolitionists did not believe in the
mental equality of African Americans. The most prominent naturalist in the
United States in the mid-1800s, Louis Agassiz at Harvard, thought that African
Americans were descended from a different (biblical) Adam than Whites. In
this same period, Samuel George Morton, a Philadelphia physician, measured
the cranial cavities of various races by filling these openings with BB shot; he
concluded that the size of these spaces was greater in Whites than in Indians
and greater in Indians than in African Americans, thereby establishing a hierarchy for these races. Stephen Jay Gould (1996) reexamined his data and
concluded that the results were colored by shifting criteria, subjectivity directed toward prior prejudice, procedural miscalculations, and convenient
omissions. Paul Broca, a French anthropologist, also believed the volume of
the brain was directly correlated with intelligence. He noted the small size
of the female brain, even when corrected for body size, and concluded that
this fact "depends on her physical inferiority and in part upon her intellectual
inferiority" (Gould 1996, 136).

Even though the fallacies in these approaches were exposed, contemporary procedures that analyze the fine structure of the brain or measure brain
activity, functional magnetic resonance imaging studies (fMRI), are their descendants. Differences between men and women are found; females have
more left-brain language and emotion processing while males have greater
right-brain visual-spatial activity, correlating with social sex-role expectations.
These studies reduce high-level functions to a single measure and are the basis for reinforcing old dichotomies. Such correlations become the platform for
seeking a genetic basis for brain structure/function (Geschwind et al. 2002).

Testing to determine cognitive function began in the early 1900s. At the
request of the French government, Alfred Binet developed a set of tests designed to identify students whose classroom performance indicated that they
could benefit from intervention. These tests had multiple components and
were administered by a trained individual. The score was the age associated
with the most complex tasks the child was able to perform, but Binet was aware
that his scale did not really measure "intelligence" and feared its use would
stigmatize students rather than aid them.

There was no such sensitivity when the test came into use in the United
States. Based on the single test that evolved, the score became an indicator
of intelligence, converting intelligence into a material entity seen as heritable
and fixed.

Lewis Terman changed Binet's test into the written Stanford-Binet test, which
became the gold standard for such measures. It was adopted by the United

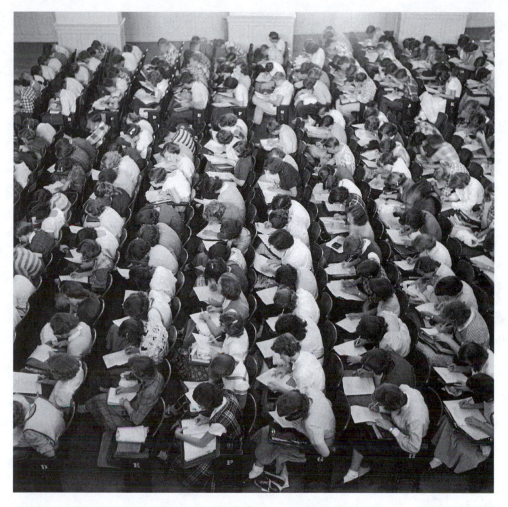

Students take the Scholastic Aptitude Test, 1953. (Genevieve Naylor/Corbis)

States Army to test recruits during World War I; although the resulting data set of the scores of almost 2 million individuals was not of any great benefit to the war effort, it solidified the reputation of psychological testing. At the behest of James Bryant Conant, president of Harvard, the Stanford-Binet test changed yet again into the Scholastic Aptitude Test (Lemann 1999) used by Harvard to democratize its student body by offering full scholarships to public school students who scored well on this measure. Women were not to benefit, since they were not admitted to Harvard and the program did not extend to its sister school, Radcliffe College.

The use of the test became more widespread in part because of the technological advance that allowed the answer sheet to be scored by machine and kept separate from the question booklet. Over time, instead of a measure designed to foster diversity, the SAT became used as the gatekeeper for a meritocracy based on a socially constructed and socially validated instrument. Correlating the scores of SAT, and the IQ test, with various physical traits, such as race, gender, or ethnic origin, became common, leading to a form of biological determinism—that intelligence is fixed and unchangeable. This viewpoint ignores both the social situation of the tests, that is, that the writers introduce a set of unacknowledged biases, and the social situation of the test-takers, some of whom have had less exposure to activities that the test values.

One of the most controversial claims based on IQ test scores was made in *The Bell Curve,* by Herrnstein and Murray (1984). The higher IQs of White Americans compared to Black Americans were alleged to be inborn, hereditary, and unchanging. It is clear that these assertions are inherently political, given the subtitle of the book, "The Reshaping of American Life by Differences in Intelligence," implying that those with lower IQ are inevitably destined for a lower social status and that social intervention will not change this fate. This assessment is confirmed by studies of the IQs of identical twins reared apart (Bouchard et al. 1990). The results of these studies suggest that about 70 percent of the variance in IQ is genetic, with small effects of environmental factors. These individuals are thought to be so psychologically similar because of their genes that they fashion very similar environments for themselves, even when reared apart. These results imply that social intervention to increase achievement would be fruitless, but this conclusion may be based on the false premise that class does not contribute to IQ. Turkheimer et al. (2003) find that "in impoverished families, 60 percent of the variance in IQ is accounted for by the shared environment, and the contribution of genes is close to zero; in affluent families, the result is almost exactly the reverse" (623).

In 1980, Benbow and Stanley published a brief report in the journal *Science* with the provocative title "Sex Differences in Mathematical Ability: Fact or Artifact?" analyzing the scores of seventh and eighth graders at the Study of Mathematically Precocious Youth at Johns Hopkins University who took the SAT test. These students were selected, in part, because they likely had "essentially identical formal instruction in mathematics." Based on these results— showing that boys, on average, had higher scores than girls and that a larger percentage of boys than girls scored over 600 (on a scale of 800)—the authors concluded differential course taking is not likely to account for the differences, nor are the differences caused by the fact that the most able girls chose not to participate in the program. They concluded that males have inherently superior mathematical reasoning ability, perhaps related to superior ability in spatial tasks, and that unspecified environmental influences do not affect inherent ability. Research studies such as these naturalize the heritability of scores on standardized tests, reinforcing the immutable consequences of their results, discounting both negative and positive environmental influences. In contrast, recent critiques of the SAT suggest it may not measure ability for college work, leading some high-profile colleges to stop requiring it for admission consideration.

Negative forces affect the achievement of women and girls in science, mathematics, engineering, and technology (SMET). Some are pervasive in the culture, such as parents encouraging girls to play with dolls and boys with trucks, or fathers teaching male children but not female children how to use tools. Industry reinforces this dichotomy by developing and marketing a Barbie doll that says "math is hard." Unconscious activities of elementary school teachers may negatively impact girls' interest in science and mathematics. Girls with upraised hands were passed over (Sadker and Sadker 1994) when an answer was requested; teachers solved problems for girls instead of encouraging them to work for themselves and made overtly sexist remarks. These biases persist well into college, especially in engineering and computer science programs.

In spite of such barriers, women's achievement in these arenas is equal to or greater than that of males during their education. Hyde and Linn's (2006) meta-analysis of gender differences in mathematics performance shows little difference between the sexes, and women earn 48 percent of the bachelor's degrees in mathematics in the United States. The National Academy of Sciences of the United States has addressed women's abilities and success in the academy, concluding that there are no significant biological differences between the sexes that could account for women's lower numbers in faculty and leadership positions in SMET. Instead, bias, both conscious and unconscious, are contributing factors, as are institutional structures, such as timetables for advancement, which negatively affect women (National Academics Press 2006).

Unfortunately, the discussion of nature versus nurture has not advanced much in three centuries. As in the past, the desire to maintain or gain positions of power and prestige taints the research, in fields such as science and technology, defined by society as essential to its economic and geopolitical supremacy. (*See also* The Brain; Cognitive Abilities; Mathematics; Race, Postcolonial Gender, and Science)

References and Further Reading

Azim, Eiman, Dean Mobbs, Booil Jo, Vinod Menone, and Allan L. Reiss. "Sex Differences in Brain Activation Elicited by Humor." *Proceedings of the National Academy of Sciences USA* 102 (2005): 16496–16501.

Benbow, Camilla Persson, and Julian C. Stanley. "Sex Differences in Mathematical Ability: Fact or Artifact?" *Science* 210 (1980): 1262–1264.

Bouchard, Thomas J. Jr., David T. Lykken, Matthew McGue, Nancy L. Segal, and Auke Tellegren. "Sources of Human Psychological Differences: The Minnesota Study of Twins Reared Apart." *Science* 250 (1990): 223–228.

Geschwind, Daniel H., Bruce L. Miller, Charles DiCarli, and Dorit Carmelli. "Heritability of Lobar Brain Volumes in Twins Supports Genetic Models of Cerebral Laterality and Handedness." *Proceedings of the National Academy of Sciences USA* 99 (2002): 3176–3181.

Gould, Stephen Jay. *The Mismeasure of Man*. New York: W. W. Norton, 1996.

Herrnstein, Richard J., and Charles Murray. *The Bell Curve: The Reshaping of American Life by Differences in Intelligence*. New York: Free Press, 1984.

Hyde, Janet Shibley, and Marcia C. Linn. "Gender Similarities in Mathematics and Science." *Science* 314 (2006): 599–600.

Keller, Evelyn Fox. *Secrets of Life, Secrets of Death*. New York: Routledge, 1992.

Lemann, Nicholas. *The Big Test: The Secret History of the American Meritocracy*. New York: Farrar, Straus and Giroux, 1999.

National Academies Press. "Beyond Bias and Barriers: Fulfilling the Potential of Women in Academic Science and Engineering." http://fermat.nap.edu/books/0309100429/html/10.html. (Accessed November 28, 2006.)

Sadker, Myra, and David Sadker. *Failing at Fairness: How America's Schools Cheat Girls*. New York: Charles Scribner's Sons, 1994.

Shapin, Stephen. *The Scientific Revolution*. Chicago: University of Chicago Press, 1996.

Turkheimer, Eric, Andreana Haley, Mary Walfinaldron, Brian D'Onofrio, and Irving I. Gottesman. "Socioeconomic Status Modifies Heritability of IQ in Young Children." *Psychological Science* 14 (2003): 623–628.

Institutions

Women's Education

Amy Bix

Evolution of the American educational system has been shaped in multiple ways by concepts of appropriate gender roles and the value of different types of learning. In colonial America, while some schools offered boys and girls the same coursework, other teaching both reflected and reinforced gender divisions (Nash 2005). Some towns limited girls' training to basic reading and arithmetic, assuming that academics would prove less valuable to women than domestic skills such as sewing. Even as public high schools began to open over subsequent decades, they similarly focused the education of girls on cultivating them to become good wives and mothers. Poverty and race also determined girls' educational access. And although laws in some parts of the South banned teaching slaves to read and write, some owners cultivated slaves' literacy to enhance their usefulness or enable them to read the Bible.

The post-Revolutionary era provided new justification for educating American women by emphasizing women's responsibility for instilling patriotic duty in their sons and shaping their daughters' character to become good mothers of future citizens. This principle of "republican motherhood" made girls' education less threatening by tying it to maternal influence, the "separate sphere" of the household, and national independence. Reformers such as Judith Sargent Murray argued that girls' intellectual capacity should be nurtured rather than smothered, as a way of giving women confidence and the ability to contribute financially and practically to family, farm, or business success. Such lofty ambitions remained unreachable for many women struggling through a family's immediate economic difficulties, while the ideals of republican motherhood could not apply to African American or native women (Kerber 1980).

By the early 1800s, a large number of private schools had opened, clearly separated by gender in both the subjects of study and the intended purpose of training. Many seminaries prepared boys for professions such as law or the ministry and hence emphasized teaching Greek and Latin. The curriculum at female academies varied widely. Finishing schools stressed "ornamental" subjects such as needlework and etiquette to guide girls (especially from relatively elite families) toward a proper ladylike future. But in 1821, progressive teacher Emma Willard opened the influential Troy Female Academy in New York state (still open in 2007 as a women's university-prep school). In arguing for women's educational rights, Willard wrote a "Plan for Improving Female Education" that won approval from President James Monroe plus former presidents Thomas Jefferson and John Adams. Along with typical feminine instruction in art and behavior, Willard's school offered young women classes not even available to all college-bound boys, such as algebra, chemistry, geography, history, and Greek. Within a decade, enrollment in the Troy Female Academy topped 300 girls. Soon other schools joined in teaching serious subjects to thousands of young women, especially in New England, aiming to make them smart wives, mothers, homemakers, and teachers. Financial troubles forced some academies to close after brief struggles, while the cost of tuition led many would-be pupils to delay or decide against attending. Yet other private schools thrived and soon found new justification for educating women.

Expansion of settlement opened demand for more schoolteachers, as did a sense that literacy was important to the country's future well-being. Women educated to at least certain levels found opportunity for employment as teachers (in part because female teachers could be hired for half a man's pay). Some estimates suggest that as many as one out of every five American-born White women in Massachusetts by the 1850s would have taught school—not usually as a permanent career but at some point in her life. While critics worried whether youthful female instructors could control wild teenage boys, teaching was generally considered acceptable as extending a mother's nurturing instincts. Prominent educational reformer Catharine Beecher, who had co-founded the Hartford Female Seminary in Connecticut in 1823, emphasized that by becoming excellent teachers, women could turn their feminine virtues and moral guidance into valuable service to society. Beecher helped recruit women to teach in frontier schools and supported establishment of teachers' colleges in several midwestern states. Over the years, female teachers across the United States wrote new textbooks, promoted classroom innovations, and worked to earn professional respect.

Racial bias continued to limit educational access for young African American women. During the 1830s, Quaker teacher Prudence Crandall upset her Connecticut neighbors by operating an integrated girls' school. The state then passed a law forbidding the teaching of Blacks from other states. Crandall was put on trial for violating that law, and vandalism and harassment forced her to shut her academy.

Educational conditions during the 19th century varied widely between city and frontier, by class, and between regions. Around the country, pockets of illiteracy remained among segments of the population. Without universally enforced laws for compulsory attendance, high school graduation rates remained relatively low before 1900. In the post–Civil War South, both northern reformers and freed slaves started hundreds of schools for African American boys and girls, but their effectiveness was hampered by poverty, racial tensions, and shortages of teachers. One notable triumph came from Mary McLeod Bethune, daughter of former slaves, who in 1904 founded a Daytona, Florida, school that soon attracted 250 young Black women. Thanks to her energetic fund-raising and devotion, the school Bethune headed for about 20 years thrived, later merging with a Black men's school to remain in existence today as Bethune-Cookman University. For Native Americans, government policy separated girls and boys from their communities, traditions, and tribal knowledge, forcing them to attend boarding schools aimed at assimilation.

Higher Education in Land-Grant Institutions

One of women's first sustained opportunities to pursue substantial degrees beyond high school occurred with the opening of Oberlin as a coeducational college; it issued its first women's degrees in 1842. The principle of coeducation was adopted by the 1860s and 1870s, not by private Eastern universities such as Princeton, Yale, and Harvard, but by state universities, especially in Iowa, Wisconsin, Michigan, and other midwestern areas, along with Maine and Cornell (Solomon 1986).

To take one example, Iowa State College admitted women from the beginning in 1869. After studying the record of Oberlin and a handful of other coeducational colleges, the board of trustees concluded, "If young men are to be educated to fit them for successful, intelligent and practical farmers and mechanics, is it not as essential that young women should be educated to properly understand and discharge their duties as wives of farmers and mechanics?" (Eppright and Ferguson 1971, 4).

President Adonijah Welch argued that Iowa State would do a service to both women and the nation by helping future mothers build "a wide and cultivated intelligence" suited for running a "well-regulated household" and raising new generations of good citizens. Welch discounted any fears that "enlarged intelligence will divert women's attention from domestic life," saying, "Beyond question these are the employments to which her sympathies naturally and usually point. Among her increased facilities for scientific instruction should stand prominent the study of domestic economy." Furthermore, college should prepare women to be self-supporting if necessary and "engage in many suitable employments on a footing equal with man," Welch declared, "because all the faculties of the human mind have, without respect to gender, a natural, unquestionable right to development" (Eppright and Ferguson 1971, 8–9).

President Welch's wife Mary took up the task of creating the new "ladies' course of study" and spent several months in England and at New York's School of Cooking to prepare her course on Domestic Economy. She taught students to cook systematically vegetables, meat, and other plain dishes. Criticizing recipes calling for a "pinch of salt," Welch wrote, "A recipe, to be good for anything, should be as definite as a mathematical statement. The same quantities put together in the same proportions should always produce the same results. Guessing is of no more value in cooking than in science" (Eppright and Ferguson 1971, 34). Women also took lessons blending theory and manual skill in other practical household management chores, including care of children and the sick. In "scrub lab," students practiced ironing one man's shirt per week. But their training was increasingly based on science; by 1904, all female students were required to take two years of chemistry, one year of physics, and one of math. By the 20th century, home economics majors were trained not only to become housewives but also institutional cooking experts, administrators or sales agents with food companies, specialists in development of household technology, household-column journalists, and extension teachers (Stage and Vincenti 1997).

The Seven Sisters and Other Women's Colleges

While the growing field of "domestic science" created many opportunities for women's higher education, a separate important trend arose from the creation of all-women's schools, especially the Seven Sisters (Barnard, Bryn Mawr, Mount Holyoke, Radcliffe, Smith, Vassar, and Wellesley) (Horowitz 1984). In 1837, Mary Lyon established Mount Holyoke in South Hadley, Massachusetts, primarily as preparation for New England schoolteachers. The three-year education plan covered both humanities (English, French, religion and philosophy, geography, history) and sciences (biology, chemistry, math). Holyoke culture emphasized a special connection between students and teachers, intended to reassure parents and potential critics by echoing the mother-daughter link. Holyoke attracted serious, mature women, offering them intellectual discipline and personal growth.

In 1860, Matthew Vassar created the first endowed women's college, supported by more money than Holyoke for the library and instructional equipment, including a medical lecture room, geological collections, and its own astronomical observatory. Vassar hired for its faculty Maria Mitchell, famous for discovering a new comet and the first woman elected to the American Academy of Arts and Sciences. Mitchell maintained that Vassar produced "the best educated women in the world" and said that if anything, women had the potential to be better than men in astronomy because "the perceptive faculties of women are more acute than those of men. Women would perceive the size, form and color of an object more readily and would catch an impression more quickly. The training of girls (bad as it is) leads them to develop these faculties. The fine needlework and the embroidery teach them to measure small spaces. The same delicacy of eye and touch is needed to bisect the image of a star as to piece delicate muslin. The small finders too come into play with a better adaptation to delicate micrometer screws" (author's class notes, Iowa State University 2005). Mitchell encouraged students to pursue interests in science and personally trained practically the entire next generation of America's first female astronomers.

Vassar intended "to build and endow a College for young women which shall be to them what Yale and Harvard are to young men." Such a statement alarmed critics who worried about education "unsexing" women. One called for caution, "lest by too close an imitation of studies of ordinary colleges, we should impair womanliness in our students and encourage the formation of those mannish tastes and manners which are so disgusting to every right mind." Such criticism would continue (Horowitz 1984, 29).

In 1875, Wellesley became the first school to boast from the start female presidents, women trustees, and an all-female faculty. Founder Henry Durant saw female teachers as agents of national reformation and asked, "What would Massachusetts be if our 9000 women teachers were all of them educated Christians? . . . We revolt against the slavery in which women are held by the customs of society—the broken health, the aimless lives, the subordinate position, the helpless dependence, and shams of so-called education. The higher education of women is the cry of the oppressed slave, the assertion of absolute equality, the war of Christ" (Horowitz 1984, 44).

That same year, Sophie Smith created her college, aiming "to furnish for my own sex means and facilities for education equal to those which are afforded now to young men. It is not my design to render my sex any the less feminine, but to develop as fully as may be the powers of womanhood and furnish women with means of usefulness, happiness and honor now withheld from them." The idea was to move women ahead socially, economically, politically, and intellectually while protecting conventional femininity. "It is to preserve her womanliness that this College has been founded. . . . More time will be devoted than in other colleges to aesthetical study, to the arts of drawing and the acquisition of musical skill. . . . What if the same forces which develop all that is most manly in one sex repress and dwarf all that is most womanly in the other?" (Horowitz 1984, 70, 73).

Women's education reached a new peak in 1885 with the founding of Bryn Mawr, where president M. Carey Thomas (herself forced to travel to Europe to obtain her Ph.D.) imported the best ideas of German higher education and opened graduate training for women. Bryn Mawr emphasized ambitious scholarship, with a commitment to innovative modern education.

The final two of the Seven Sisters, Radcliffe (1878) and Barnard (1889), started as the women's annexes to Harvard and Columbia, respectively. There was no chance of the main institutions admitting women, but teaching by some of the same professors allowed nearby women some access to learning.

A significant number of other small but often influential women's colleges opened over subsequent decades, especially in Catholic communities or affiliated with Protestant churches. Segregated female collegiate institutes spread rapidly in the South, where gender-role traditionalism reinforced single-sex education. African American women could attend separate historically black coeducational schools, along with some all-women's colleges, such as Spelman College (1881) in Atlanta.

By 1891, there were over 10,000 American women in college (both coeducational schools and all-women's institutions), over one third of all students enrolled. In 1881, the first generations of female graduates formed a new organization, the Association of Collegiate Alumnae (ACA), to counter their feelings of isolation. These women had defied traditional definitions of femininity (and often defied their parents and friends) by going to college, but they subsequently discovered few ways outside the home in which such equipment of knowledge might be utilized to advantage. The ACA intended to expand opportunities for women college graduates, especially for work in areas of social reform. This valuable network, renamed the American Association of University Women (AAUW), continued to pursue issues of educational equity into the 21st century.

Impact of Education on Health

Yet concern persisted for years about whether it was appropriate for women to attend college. During the 1870s, Harvard doctor Edward Clarke in particular warned that too much concentrated study risked ruining women's health. Nineteenth-century physicians defined women's nature in terms of their reproductive capacity and considered menstruation an especially stressful episode. Analogies compared the body to an economic system with limited resources. Clarke feared that women who tried to compete with men in devoting equal energy to mental work would drain sustaining energy away from their reproductive organs. Clarke declared that he had seen women collapse and even die from too much mental strain (especially during the crucial period each month) or at least ruin their chances of becoming a good wife and mother. One gynecologist wrote in 1901 that a woman "may be highly cultured and accomplished . . . but her future husband will discover too late that he has married a large outfit of headaches [and] backaches . . . instead of a woman fitted to take up the duties of life" (Smith-Rosenberg and Rosenberg 1973, 332–356). Researchers noted with some accuracy that female graduates had lower rates of marriage and childbirth than non-college-attending women, a concern exacerbated by the eugenics movement. One psychologist warned, "Colleges may come to be training stations for the sterile woman—aunt, maiden, nun, schoolteacher or unmarried woman" (Smith-Rosenberg and Rosenberg 1973).

To defend their mission, women's colleges and the ACA conducted research to prove that college women retained good or excellent health (Verbrugge 1988). Women's colleges built large gymnasiums and taught students about proper nutrition, sleep, and dress. A Wellesley graduate described her class as "women who will make the next generation strong, who are strong themselves and able to cope with the struggles of the workaday world" (Verbrugge 1988, 145). Women's colleges soon began fielding basketball, baseball, and rowing teams and encouraging bicycling, golf, and other extracurriculars, saying that sports "develop a young girl's character while she develops her muscles" (Verbrugge 1988, 145). Yet muscles were precisely what critics did not want; too much competitiveness risked making women aggressive and unfeminine. Female sports advocates emphasized moderation and even changed the rules of basketball to minimize dribbling, movement, and ball-stealing.

20th-Century American Women's Education

The early decades of the 20th century brought some significant landmarks in women's education, including greater access to medical, legal, and other professional training (though discrimination in treatment of female students in the classroom and barriers to employment remained). Higher education for American women became increasingly common, though lack of inclusion for poor or minority women remained a problem.

During the years following World War II, social trends favoring the conventional domestic ideal discouraged career ambitions in many women, and those who married and started families at younger average ages frequently delayed or discontinued higher education (Eisenmann 2006). The 1954 Supreme Court ruling in *Brown v. Board of Education of Topeka,* declaring separate schools inherently unequal, set the stage for integration efforts and protests as African American girls and boys sought to attend Little Rock, Arkansas's Central High School and other previously White institutions. After attorney Thurgood Marshall won a legal battle to stop the University of Alabama from turning away Black students, Autherine Lucy enrolled in 1956, only to be expelled three days later for her own safety after threats from rioters.

Starting in the 1960s and 1970s, the feminist movement focused new attention on issues in women's education, including sexual harassment on campus and continued inequities in professional opportunities. As a sign of changing times, most universities that had remained at least partially male-only, such as Harvard, Princeton, and California Institute of Technology, adopted co-education during those decades. Not coincidentally, many women's colleges experienced crises of declining enrollment during the late 20th century, forcing some to admit men; those that escaped closing fought to redefine their social relevance.

New education amendments passed in 1972 included Title IX, a section declaring it illegal to discriminate on the basis of sex in any educational programs or activities receiving federal aid. Over subsequent decades, the aspect of Title IX law that drew the most public attention was the issue of young women's access to athletic opportunities. Subsequent years brought dramatic increases in the number of girls participating in school sports, with tangible benefits for their physical, social, and mental development. Yet problems with enforcement remained, as did controversial accusations that diverting resources to women's teams had forced men's swimming, gymnastics, and wrestling teams to shut down.

Beyond athletics, Title IX covered other forms of educational gender discrimination, including classroom treatment. In 1992, the AAUW issued a report titled *How Schools Shortchange Girls* that accused American school systems of ignoring female gender inequities, such as factors discouraging girls from pursuing math and science (AAUW Educational Foundation 1995). Government agencies such as the National Science Foundation focused attention and resources on creating programs to support and mentor female scientists and engineers, as did many schools and professional organizations. Yet in 2005, then-Harvard president Lawrence Summers downplayed discrimination against women in science and engineering, indicating their underrepresentation might instead be linked to their comparative lack of ability or interest. Those comments spurred a public firestorm contributing to Summers's decision to resign and Harvard's subsequent selection of its first female president, historian Drew Gilpin Faust.

By 1990, women comprised 55 percent of American undergraduates and earned 37 percent of all doctoral degrees. (*See also* Women's Health Movement; Universities)

References and Further Reading

AAUW Educational Foundation. *How Schools Shortchange Girls: The AAUW Report: A Study of Major Findings on Girls and Education*. New York: Marlowe, 1995.

Eisenmann, Linda. *Higher Education for Women in Postwar America, 1945–1965*. Baltimore, MD: Johns Hopkins University Press, 2006.

Eppright, Ercel Sherman, and Elizabeth Storm Ferguson. *A Century of Home Economics at Iowa State University*. Ames: College of Home Economics, Iowa State University, 1971.

Horowitz, Helen Lefkowitz. *Alma Mater*. New York: Knopf, 1984.

Kerber, Linda K. *Women of the Republic: Intellect and Ideology in Revolutionary America*. Chapel Hill: University of North Carolina, 1980.

Nash, Margaret A. *Women's Education in the United States, 1780–1840*. New York: Palgrave Macmillan, 2005.

Smith-Rosenberg, Carroll, and Charles E. Rosenberg, "The Female Animal: Medical and Biological Views of Woman and Her Role in Nineteenth-Century America." *Journal of American History* 60 (September 1973): 332–356.

Solomon, Barbara Miller. *In the Company of Educated Women: A History of Higher Education in America*. New Haven, CT: Yale University Press, 1986.

Stage, Sarah, and Virginia B. Vincenti, eds. *Rethinking Home Economics: Women and the History of a Profession*. Ithaca, NY: Cornell University Press, 1997.

Verbrugge, Martha H. *Able-Bodied Womanhood: Personal Health and Social Change in Nineteenth-Century Boston*. New York: Oxford University Press, 1988.

Motherhood

Laurel Tweed

Motherhood is a concern linked to nearly every feminist issue due to the biological capacity of women to give birth to children and the patriarchal construction of women as naturally inclined to nurturance and caregiving. Feminist viewpoints on motherhood are incredibly variable, some rejecting motherhood as the single basis of women's oppression, others embracing it as an important aspect of women's lives that can be personally enriching and a valuable source of power for women. Motherhood is defined in several different ways. There is traditional motherhood as we normally think of it; one can give birth to a child as a biological mother. Feminism, with the help of modern technology and social science, has broadened this definition to include women who carry a pregnancy for another woman as gestational mothers and those who do the work of mothering with or without any biological connection to a child as adoptive, step-, foster, or grandmothers. In many ways motherhood has been separated from reproduction in feminist thought; therefore, this treatment will consider motherhood as it is practiced rather than as it is produced. There are many different ways of performing motherhood, which historically has been used as a benchmark against which women's validation and worth have been measured. As a result, motherhood (including the choice not to be a mother) overlaps with many other feminist concerns. What a mother is and does changes with cultural and historical contexts and often becomes complicated by race, class, age, and gender.

Historically, practices of motherhood have changed a great deal. Feudal law in the medieval period functioned to favor male children over female children; a woman's value, in many respects, was connected to her ability to deliver a male heir. Children of upper-class families were not raised at home; they were either fostered as children or sent away to school. For example, in 18th-century France, the upper class sent their children to the country to be nursed; they were not returned home until they were ready for education and civilization. In cases such as this, the mother did not perform motherhood as we think of it, beyond giving birth. Following the major flowering of the Industrial Revolution in the 19th century, motherhood changed significantly as fathers left the farms and fields for the industrial plants. In many cases mothers also had to leave home to find work to feed their families. The Victorian Age, which valorized traditional, sacrificial, natural motherhood, may be seen as a reaction to the effects of the Industrial Revolution on the family.

The Myth of "Traditional" Motherhood

Motherhood has long been considered the appropriate and natural role for women in most societies due to their biological capacity to give birth and the assumption that women are naturally inclined to unconditionally love and care for their children. Women were expected to find self-fulfillment in their role as a sacrificing and giving caretaker. Feminist work has attempted to demonstrate that the supposed "unconditional" love that mothers extend to children is not purely instinctual but dependent on many other factors. Anthropologist Sarah Blaffer Hrdy shows in *Mother Nature* (1999) that mothers throughout the species of the world often choose the number of offspring they have and their commitment to them is contingent on "ecological and historically produced circumstances"—the physiological and motivational underpinnings of a "quintessentially pro-choice mammal" are found throughout nature (316–317). The Western concept of "mother love" has been challenged by Elisabeth Badinter (1982), who claims that the existence of mothers who fail to love their children rules out any instinctual basis for mother love. A mother's feelings about children are determined by cultural factors.

Despite feminist attention to the cultural construction of motherhood, dominant trends in childcare and child rearing still focus on the mother as the ideal caretaker. Feminist scholars who write on motherhood in the West today characterize it as guided by dominant rearing practices that demand expert knowledge, intensive labor, and significant expense. Child rearing advice by social scientists and psychologists is overwhelmingly directed toward mothers, with the most popular books reflecting what Sharon Hays (1996) calls a contradictory "ideology of intensive mothering" (57).

Theories of Motherhood: Fundamental Authors and Texts

Adrienne Rich and Of Woman Born: Motherhood as Experience and Institution

Adrienne Rich's *Of Woman Born: Motherhood as Experience and Institution* (1976) was the first major feminist analysis of motherhood as a cultural institution that held important political implications for the second wave women's movement. Rich's text incorporates personal scholarship with her analysis, reflecting on her own experiences with motherhood that contradicted the traditional representations of what a mother should be. Rich's analysis of patriarchal society identified the ambiguity between motherhood as a sacred institution and the degradation of women in a global society produced by men. This fundamental text on motherhood sparked feminist interest in the relationships of mothers to fathers, sons, and daughters as well as a woman's selfhood in relation to her role as a mother, both physically and within her own psyche.

Nancy Chodorow and The Reproduction of Mothering

Nancy Chodorow's *The Reproduction of Mothering* (1978) is foundational feminist theory that provides an account for the social and cultural reproduction of the male-dominant sex-gender system. Chodorow's work has been an influential work for many feminist scholars in many different disciplines, including literary studies, philosophy, sociology, psychology, and anthropology. Chodorow describes how women learn from early in childhood to develop a sense of themselves in relationship to others, in contrast to men's creation of selfhood that denies relation and connection. This psychological development explains how women are constructed socially to be mothers from the very moment of their birth. A mother relates to her daughter as one essentially like her, while sons are considered unlike the mother. Boys and girls internalize this "unconscious maternal communication," which shapes their psychic capacities and desires in gender-specific, culturally acceptable ways that reproduce patriarchal structures in societies. Chodorow's work was one of the first to call for equal parenting, which would function to reverse the psychic structural development of children into rigid gender categories. Equal parenting would provide for a greater involvement of men in the lives of children, opportunities for women outside of the household, and concrete representations of gender roles that are flexible, relational, and equal.

Sara Ruddick and Maternal Thinking

Sara Ruddick's *Maternal Thinking* (1989) is an important social and philosophical theory that describes how the practice of mothering children affects the attitudes, capacities, and values of that those who do it. Beginning with the assertion that all thinking arises from and is shaped by the practices in which one engages, Ruddick examines the practice of motherhood, defines maternal work, and shows how this practice gives rise to a maternal discourse. The work of motherhood is guided by the demands for preservation, growth, and social acceptability. Mothers meet these needs with preservative love, nurturance, and training. Because these demands and the ability of a mother to meet these demands are often in conflict, mothers must think out strategies. Ruddick constructs maternal discourse as a discipline; like any other discipline, mothers establish criteria for determining success and failure, set priorities, and identify virtues that the discipline requires (24). In addition, maternal practice and thought is open to criticism; however, Ruddick asserts that maternal thought, when it has been acknowledged at all in the past, has been recognized by people "interested in interpreting and controlling rather than in listening" (26). Examination of the contradictions of maternal thought by those who develop it by maternal practice, which can be men as well as women, reveals contradictions and inconsistencies within culturally acceptable practices of rearing children. A feminist consciousness combined with maternal thinking provides women with the ability to name and resist the forces within herself and the culture she lives in, to determine the meaning of dominant social values and how they affect her and her children—particularly organized violence and war. Ruddick believes that maternal thinking and political peacemaking have the potential to work hand in hand to challenge "the mythical subdivision between men and women, private care and public defense, that hobbles both maternal and peacemaking endeavors" (244).

Challenges to "Traditional" Motherhood

Women of color have challenged both traditional ideologies of motherhood as well as White feminist critiques of motherhood, by demonstrating that in minority communities it is often not the mother alone who raises children but an extended network of family, neighbors, and friends who work together. Patricia Hill Collins (1990) terms the different experiences of mothering among women of color in America as "divergent" experiences of mothering, which has been expanded by global feminist scholars to analyze the conditions of transnational motherhood by migrant female workers in the global economy.

Feminist analysis of alternative mothering—stepmothering, grandmothering, foster mothering, and mothering by lesbian women—highlights some of the myths of traditional motherhood by demonstrating the role law and politics have played in shaping how children are raised. The existence of successful alternative family structures contradicts the traditional notion that the mother-child relationship is natural and instinctive.

Motherhood and Work

Another way women have challenged the ideology of traditional motherhood is simply by entering the workforce in mass numbers and demanding working conditions that support their efforts outside the home. Childcare, maternity and paternity leave, health care, and fair wages are all important social issues for mothers today, many of whom are single parents or heads of household. Raising children is predominantly women's work, regardless of employment status, and women still are underpaid in the workforce and unpaid in the home. Ann Crittenden (2001) argues that having a baby is the worst financial decision a woman can make and calculates the "mommy tax" on a woman's lifetime earnings to be around 1 million dollars.

Motherhood and Activism

Mothers have a history of social activism in the United States, notably in the creation of the welfare state in the 20th century, and the demand for quality

Hundreds of women whose children disappeared during the armed forces' "Dirty War" in Argentina march from Congress to the palace to demand that the government reveal what happened to as many as 20,000 people who disappeared between 1976 and 1979. (Bettmann/Corbis)

childcare and flexible working conditions for parents in the 21st century. With the decline of the welfare state in the 1990s through the "welfare to work" policy, different strategies for meeting the needs of women who work began to include socialized childcare, universal health care for children, flexible corporate working arrangements for people with children, and fair wages for women. The Internet has created a virtual community of activist mothers fighting for social justice for women and children, including groups such as momsrising.org, motherhoodproject.org, and motherscenter.org—all groups that promote social programs to advance the political and social interests of mothers.

Internationally, women's groups that fight for human rights and women's justice incorporate the concerns of mothers; however, in some cases mothers have grouped together to fight for human rights, such as the Tiananmen Mothers in China and Mothers of the Plaza de Mayo in Argentina, whose children disappeared in Argentina between 1976 and 1983, the years of the military dictatorship in that country. These mothers demanded answers from the Argentine government, which admitted to kidnapping thousands of unaccounted-for children.

In the 21st century, motherhood—specifically the manipulation of motherhood ideology by states, the economic conditions of motherhood in different societies, the safety of motherhood in developing nations, and the demands of mothers for a friendly workplace—will continue to be a concern of women around the world as well as a location from which women can fight for better economic and social conditions. (*See also* Discrimination; The 18th Century; Nature/Nurture; Race, Postcolonial Gender, and Science; Women's Health Movement)

References and Further Reading

Badinter, Elisabeth. *Mother Love*. New York: MacMillan, 1982.

Chodorow, Nancy. *The Reproduction of Mothering*. Berkeley: University of California Press, 1978.

Crittenden, Ann. *The Price of Motherhood: Why the Most Important Job in the World Is Still the Least Valued*. New York: Metropolitan Books, 2001.

Hays, Sharon. *The Cultural Contradictions of Motherhood*. New Haven, CT: Yale University Press, 1996.

Hill Collins, Patricia. *Black Feminist Thought: Knowledge, Consciousness, and the Politics of Empowerment*. New York: Routledge, 1990.

Hrdy, Sarah Blaffer. *Mother Nature: Maternal Instincts and How They Shape the Human Species*. New York: Ballantine, 1999.

Ruddick, Sara. *Maternal Thinking*. Boston: Beacon Press, 1989.

Rich, Adrienne. *Of Woman Born: Motherhood as Experience and Institution*. New York: W. W. Norton, 1976.

Religion

MURIEL LEDERMAN

Religion has long been a force guiding understanding of the humanities' place in the universe. As science became another such force, the two have sometimes clashed and have sometimes complemented each other. Margaret Wertheim (1997) argues that mathematics and physics, the underpinnings of contemporary science, are religious enterprises. Thus, the tenets of both spheres differentially affect men and women; since religion has been historically overwhelmingly male, it should be no surprise that the physical sciences are androcentric and more easily available to men.

Antiquity—Enlightenment

The science of the Greeks placed values on numbers, with the number one being male, heavenly, and immaterial, while the number two was female, earthy, and material, a dichotomy whose influence is felt even today. In medieval times, science and mathematics were practiced in seminaries, which often were headed by an abbess alone or by an abbess and abbot together and were sites of study and scholarship for both men and women. However, two factors worked to remove women from power as heads of these institutions. In the sixth century, Pope Gregory I required celibacy among the clergy to ensure that church property was not split among the heirs of married priests. Charlemagne and other secular rulers of European nations co-opted the churches to consolidate their power. In both cases, monasteries and seminaries became training grounds for those who led the government and the military, and women were prevented from participating. Since women were excluded from these seats of learning, they were consequently excluded from the universities that were their successors.

When natural philosophy emerged in the Enlightenment, it seemed to be quite separate from religion. The universe was seen as a giant mechanism, whose major metaphor was a clock, exemplified by the planetary clock at the

Enlightenment-era planetary clock at Strasbourg Cathedral, France. (B. Didier)

cathedral in Strasbourg, France. Shapin (1996) describes the worldview after the Scientific Revolution as characterized by the mechanization of nature (evidenced by the use of mechanical metaphors), the separation between humans and the objects they investigate, the mechanization of knowledge-making (especially through the use of mathematics), and the use of knowledge in the service of socially defined goals. This change in the nature of knowledge was accompanied necessarily by a change in the conceptualization of Nature. Nature was transformed from an active female or hermaphroditic principle to being inert. With this "Death of Nature" (see Merchant 1980), the female was rendered lifeless and the masculine mind became the route to the unemotional, objective, measured (literally) assessment of the universe. As Susan Bordo says, "the otherness of nature is what allows it to be known" (Bordo 1999, 68). Man could investigate nature with no compunctions but woman could not, since her being the subject of knowing obliterated her as knower.

Some of the characteristics of the new mechanical philosophy were a continuation of the Renaissance Hermetical tradition, in which humans could use their bodies to regulate all things under the influence of their God-given intellect. They also owed much to the changes that occurred during the Protestant Reformation. According to Keller (1992), John Calvin (1509–1564), the Scottish reformer, sought to transfer Nature's intrinsic activity to the control of God. This move foreshadowed and gave permission for the major revolution in worldview described above. The critical step was the movement of "secrets" from God to Nature, giving permission for "science" to investigate these secrets and wrest control of them for the benefit of man. For Sir Francis Bacon (1561–1662), these secrets were to be exploited through technology, to gain mastery over the natural world. Feminist scholars point to the graphic sexual imagery in Bacon's writings as examples of the male domination inherent in androcentric science.

Bacon's desire for control has a religious underpinning. He believed that man had lost dominion over nature during the Fall in the Garden of Eden and it was imperative that sovereignty be regained. This could occur through the application of natural philosophy, which nevertheless was still subservient to God. The Book of Nature was to be read in parallel with the Book of Scripture. It was a duty to read the Book of Nature, to purify religion by ridding it of the superstitions and incorrect notions that had become attached to it in previous times.

The conceptualization of Nature as lifeless was required for both religion and mechanical philosophy. "If you ascribe activity and intelligence to what is properly conceived of as brute nature, you encourage the belief that material nature is self-sufficient, not dependent on external animating agencies for its motions and patterns" (Shapin 1996, 11). The British chemist Robert Boyle (1627–1691) thought that "ascribing to nature [capacities] that belonged to God, have been [a] grand cause of idolatry" (Shapin 1996, 151). Removing the active (female) principle from Nature allowed for the presence of a supernatural being to regulate the universe. The operation of the universe under the direction of God could be explained by the mechanical laws devised by men. Sir Isaac Newton's (1642–1727) computations on the physics of the solar system suggested that it might collapse upon itself. Since it did not, this was taken as proof of the intercession of God in the workings of the natural world.

The mechanistic bent of natural philosophy after the Scientific Revolution was not really at odds with religion. Rather, natural philosophy was to be used to look for evidence of regularity and patterns that testified to God's intelligence, the "argument from design." The vitality and complexity seen in Nature were taken as evidence for the existence of a supernatural rather than as a property intrinsic in Nature. According to Shapin (1996, 150), "Regularities were to be observed in nature and might even be mathematically expressed. Yet it was to be understood that all such regularities were subject to God's pleasure." This "argument from design" has been revived and used to contradict the theory of evolution.

Using 17th-century science to support religion was not a universal program among natural/mechanical philosophers. The Newtonian program abolished the distinction between heaven and earth, since all mathematical laws applied generally, completely throughout the universe. Newton himself hid his fascination with the Paracelsian tradition that flourished prior to the Scientific Revolution (Noble 1992). Rene Descartes (1596–1650) skirted dangerously close to abjuring both a Creator and a "final cause" by his dictum "cogito ergo sum."

The philosopher who most radically eliminated traditional religion from his attempts to understand the universe was Baruch Spinoza. He was born in Amsterdam in 1632 into a community of Portuguese Jews who had hidden their faith during the Inquisition and were reestablishing their religious identity and practice. Spinoza was permanently excommunicated from the community at age 23 for reasons that are mainly unclear but may involve his claim that the Torah is a social construct. His worldview was considered so extreme that his writings were banned in Holland, and his most significant work, *Ethics,* was only published posthumously. Spinoza reversed the position of the early thinkers of the Scientific Revolution who thought that humans could know nature through God. He was an intellectual descendant of Descartes but took Descartes' view that God's existence needed to be proven logically even further; Spinoza's metaphysics gives primacy to reason, not to a deity. "God is immanent in nature, not transcendent. Logic itself is the world. Nature, meaning the laws of nature, needs nothing outside of itself to explain itself" (Goldstein 2006, 52–58). Spinoza's philosophy is considered by some to define modernity, and his ideas have been sustained through centuries. For example, Albert Einstein's views were colored by Spinoza: "the material universe . . . does not lead us to take the step of fashioning a god-like being in our own image. There is neither a will nor a goal nor a must, but only sheer being" (Goldstein 2006, 62). In the view of neurobiologist Antonio Damasio (2003), Spinoza's *Ethics* presaged contemporary research on emotion and feeling. More tellingly, Damasio claims that Spinoza reversed Descartes' separation of mind and body; ironically, this extension of the Cartesian duality goes so far that it returns to the worldview that preceded the Scientific Revolution.

19th Century

Charles Darwin's (1809–1882) *Origin of Species,* published in 1859, changed the perception of humans with regard to their place in the universe and, at least in England, changed the relationship between science and religion. There was no real difficulty reconciling evolution with Scripture, since fundamentalism was not widely accepted. God was no longer needed to account for humans; *natural theology,* the term given in the mid-1800s to the widely accepted theory encapsulated as "the argument from design," was likewise eliminated. "The real challenge of Darwinism for Victorians was that it turned life into an amoral chaos displaying no evidence of a divine authority or any sense of purpose or design" (Browne 2006, 86). Some solved this problem by invoking a force that directed the changes postulated by evolution.

Darwin's *The Descent of Man* (1871) attempted to show the derivation of human traits from animal characteristics. Unfortunately, Darwin was a victim of Victorian beliefs, and his writings reflected prevailing views, such as the superiority of Whites and the superiority of males. He essentialized male dominance and was criticized by contemporary feminists and suffragettes for this stance. "Medical writers understood Darwin to be supporting the assumption that women's brains were smaller and less evolutionarily developed than men's or that the female body was especially prone to disorders if the reproductive functions were denied" (Browne 2006, 113).

21st Century

The relationship between science and religion in the United States in the early 21st century seems unclear. On the one hand, there is a feeling that science should be in service of man and man's faith, when it has traditionally been the scientists who decide on research priorities based on internalist criteria. During the presidency of George W. Bush, a new approach emerged to force science to adhere to religion, specifically to conservative Christian principles. Projects deemed irreligious were quashed by financial starvation; decisions on funding priorities had faith-based ideas and priorities as their foundation rather than the (presumptive) value of the research to humans and the environment. The decision to prohibit federal funding for stem cell research was based on the belief that "Human life is a gift from our Creator—and that gift should never be discarded, devalued or put up for sale" (C-Span.org 2006). Education to prevent HIV/AIDS requires a large portion of the expenditure to stress sexual abstinence. Since this strategy has proved ineffective, state governors turned back funding for this goal. The Bush administration refused to play a political or legislative role in reducing activities that cause global warming, denying its existence and editing scientific reports from the administration's own agencies to align with its policies. One evangelical Christian minister, Dr. Richard Cizek, spoke in favor of action on environmental issues as a requirement of faith. However, he was challenged by mainstream conservatives within his organization, the National Association of Evangelicals, since this concern is a diversion from the great issues of the day, "the sanctity of human life, the integrity of marriage and the teaching of sexual abstinence and morality to our children" (CNN.com 2007).

Simultaneously, during this period, science and religion appear to converge. The dedication of scientific researchers, required for success in the academy, continues to echo a monastic life. The parallel between women's exclusion from the clergy and their difficulty adhering to this androcentric academic standard became evident. The rhetoric surrounding the Human Genome project describes its results as the "Holy Grail" of life.

The Townsend Prize is awarded annually for "discoveries and breakthroughs to expand human perceptions of divinity and to help in the acceleration of divine creativity." Many of the recent recipients have been scientists with an interest in reconciling science and religion. A successful explication of the "Theory of Everything," a mathematical, unified account of nature, perhaps through superstring theory, might lead to knowing God. Margaret Wertheim (1997) realizes that this project is irrelevant to most people's lives and that the mathematical laws of physics are not a transcendent form of knowledge. The mainly unrecognized concordance of religion and science contributes to the androcentrism of the field. Breaking this link would remove a cultural barrier to the participation of women in science. (*See also* The 18th Century; Nature/Nurture; Renaissance)

References and Further Reading

Bordo, Susan. "The Flight to Objectivity." In *Feminist Interpretations of Rene Descartes,* 48–69. University Park: Pennsylvania University Press, 1999.

Browne, Janet. *Darwin's Origin of Species: A Biography*. New York: Atlantic Monthly Press, 2006.

C-Span.org. "President George W. Bush's Address before a Joint Session of the Congress on the State of the Union." January 31, 2006. http://www.cspan.org/executive/transcript.asp?cat=current_event&code=bush_admin&year=2006.

CNN.com. "Global Warming Gap among Evangelicals Widens." March 14, 2007. http://www.cnn.com/2007/POLITICS/03/14/evangelical.rift/index.html.

Damasio, Antonio. *Looking for Spinoza: Joy, Sorrow, and the Feeling Brain*. Orlando, FL: Harcourt, 2003.

Goldstein, Rebecca. *Spinoza Betrayed*. New York: Schocken Books, 2006.

Keller, Evelyn Fox. *Secrets of Life, Secrets of Death*. New York: Routledge, 1992.

Merchant, Carolyn. *The Death of Nature: Women, Ecology and the Scientific Revolution*. San Francisco: Harper and Row, 1980.

Noble, David. *A World without Women: The Christian Clerical Culture of Western Science*. New York: Oxford University Press, 1992.

Schiebinger, Londa. *The Mind Has No Sex*. Cambridge, MA: Harvard University Press, 1989.

Shapin, Steven. *The Scientific Revolution*. Chicago: University of Chicago Press, 1996.

Wertheim, Margaret. *Pythagoras' Trousers: God, Physics, and the Gender Wars*. New York: W. W. Norton, 1997.

Universities

MURIEL LEDERMAN AND BARBARA WHITTEN

Authors' note: This article owes much of its substance to Margaret Rossiter's monumental two-volume work *Women Scientists in America*. Her unique approach is to document the accomplishments and struggles of an entire community rather than to focus on just a few great women. Those interested in a more complete understanding of women scientists in the United States are urged to consult her work.

Women in Early Scientific Institutions

Scientists organize themselves into institutions that foster the practice of science, provide them with resources, and nurture their professional culture. For women to be able to practice science, they must have access to these same resources—the current state of knowledge, necessary materials, and interactions with other scientists. The participation of women in scientific institutions has varied with time and place, but it is rare for women to participate as fully as men.

In classical Greece, some women are believed to have participated in the two most important scientific institutions, the Pythagorean societies and the Academy of Plato. However, the science practiced was androcentric. For example, in Pythagorean number theory, numbers were associated with gender, and the number one was male, heavenly, and immaterial, while the number two was female, earthy, and material, a dichotomy that resonates to this day. In Roman times, Alexandria became a center of learning, and Hypatia was the leader of the Neoplatonist school of philosophy and an important mathematician. She ran afoul of a power struggle between Christians and pagans and was murdered by a fanatical Christian mob.

In medieval Europe, science was kept alive in monasteries, where women could become educated and escape the burdens of household management and childbearing. Many of these were headed solely by abbesses or jointly by an abbess and an abbot. Hildegard von Bingen, for example, a natural philosopher, healer, and visionary, led a community of educated nuns in 12th-century Germany. As religious institutions and secular royalty joined forces, clergy were trained in cathedral schools, which were the direct precursors of universities. The development of universities in the 13th century was beneficial for science and for male scientists; it *decreased* the educational level of women in Europe as they were excluded from universities as students and faculty. Women were not routinely admitted to universities in Europe or the United States until the end of the 19th century.

Despite this exclusion, women found ways to practice science. Some women worked with a male relative, and some participated in informal institutions like the salons of early modern France, where intellectual women discussed the philosophy of Descartes. In Cartesian philosophy, the separation of mind from body is pivotal to the rational, objective nature of science, so Cartesian rules had no sex and offered the hope of a nongendered epistemology. Women embraced and critiqued the work in ways that, according to Harth (1992), foreshadowed standpoint epistemology (Harding 1991). They hoped that a universal discourse would allow their participation in intellectual life but struggled with the embodied differences between men and women; if an identical disembodied mind is made to be the principle of sexual equality, what can be made of embodied difference? Informal salons lost power and credibility with the rise and consolidation of national academies, which were exclusively male. The French Academy of Sciences refused admittance to Marie Curie even in 1911 (its first female member was elected only in 1979) and the science promoted by the academies was androcentric.

Women in American Higher Education—Female Seminaries to Bachelor's Degrees

In the United States, the "common school" movement, led by Horace Mann in the early 19th century, was the first to argue for widespread education. David Noble (1992) claims that religious freedom, one of the founding principles of the United States, was instrumental in shaping the educational system of the United States. An anticlerical stance pervaded the nation through the 19th century; religion was democratically oriented and free from oppressive religious strictures. Women claimed their rightful place in this religious revival, and education was an arena in which they saw the possibility of equality.

Secondary education for women began before the Civil War, due to an ingenious argument called "Republican motherhood" and the efforts of women like Emma Hart Willard. In order to have a strong nation, the argument went, Americans needed good mothers to provide moral training to their sons; this required educated women. This logic worked well enough for Willard to acquire a charter for Troy Female Seminary and to educate several thousand women by the time of her retirement in 1838. The curriculum was far more rigorous than that required for an educated mother and included mathematics, physiology, and physics along with household management and pastry cooking. Graduates often became schoolteachers; female teachers were welcome to tight-fisted school boards because they would work at a fraction of the pay demanded by men. Other female seminaries were founded in the period from 1830 to 1850, most notably Mount Holyoke Seminary. These schools also offered employment to women scientists; Margaret Rossiter (1982) estimates that by 1873 there were 400 women science instructors in the United States.

Female seminaries gradually expanded from secondary to higher education. Oberlin College was coeducational from the time of its founding in 1833, and Vassar College, founded in 1865, was the first educational institution for women to offer a full college curriculum. By 1870, some state schools were also beginning to accept women students; Cornell and the University of Michigan were particularly significant for women in science. Several important women's colleges, including the remaining Seven Sisters—Barnard, Bryn Mawr, Mount Holyoke, Radcliffe, Smith, Vasser, Wellesley—and Spelman College, founded to educate former slaves and the daughters of slaves, were established between 1870 and 1895. At the end of the 19th century, science came to be seen as a resource for capitalism, and scientific education became a way to create practitioners, produce scientific knowledge, and apply this knowledge in practical ways. The Morrill Act, which created the coeducational land-grant universities, further facilitated the inclusion of women in the sciences.

The Importance of Women's Colleges to Women in Science

The importance of these early women's colleges to women in science cannot be exaggerated. At a time when there were very few opportunities for women in science, women's colleges offered rigorous scientific training to students and employed many women scientists. In 1921, for example, *American Men of Science* listed 24 women physicists, of whom 19 were employed at women's colleges. Women's college faculties had a high proportion of women faculty; Wellesley in particular hired essentially all women and created a female intellectual community that may be unique. Women's colleges were also early models of progressive teaching. Sarah Whiting at Wellesley organized one of the very first laboratory-based physics programs in the country (McDowell 1936). Maria Mitchell involved Vassar students in her astronomical research, believing that meaningful scientific work was an important part of science education.

First astronomy class at Vassar College, 1866. Professor Maria Mitchell and 15 female students pose with telescope. (Special Collections, Vassar College Library)

Many very accomplished women scientists, including Mitchell, Cornelia Clapp at Mount Holyoke, and Florence Bascom at Bryn Mawr, spent substantial proportions of their careers as women's college instructors. When, during the Nazi era, the great mathematician Emmy Noether was forced to flee Europe, no coeducational institution was willing to find a place for her. She found refuge at Bryn Mawr for the remainder of her tragically brief life. These women trained other women scientists, leading to multigenerational mentor-protégée chains. For example, Ellen Swallow Richards and Christine Ladd-Franklin were students of Maria Mitchell at Vassar.

Hunter College, a former women's college that is now part of City University of New York (CUNY), provided free education to the daughters of immigrants and nurtured an extraordinary number of eminent scientists; in 1996, 10 of the 86 women in the National Academy of Sciences were Hunter College alumnae (Wasserman 2000). Roman Catholic women's colleges were also founded to serve largely immigrant communities; Our Lady of the Lake University and Incarnate Word University, two formerly women's colleges, are the two institutions in the country most productive of Latina Ph.D.s (Wolf-

Wendel 1998). Spelman College, one of two historically Black women's colleges, is the most productive of African American women scientists (Leggon and Pearson 1997).

In addition, because women's colleges educated more women scientists than they could absorb on their faculties, they created pressure on other institutions to hire women scientists, a phenomenon that Margaret Rossiter calls the "entering wedge."

The Next Steps—Doctoral Degrees and University Positions for Women

In the 1880s and 1890s, science was beginning to be professionalized and colleges and universities began to look for faculty members with doctoral degrees. Although the new graduate programs seemed to indicate that they would be open to both sexes, in practice women were not admitted to most graduate programs. Exceptional women were allowed to attend graduate classes, but obtaining degrees was more difficult. Ellen Swallow Richards and Christine Ladd-Franklin were admitted as "special students" to MIT and Johns Hopkins, respectively. By 1889, 10 colleges and universities, including Syracuse University, Boston University, Smith College, University of Michigan, and Cornell University, had awarded doctoral degrees to 25 women. Yale and University of Pennsylvania and the newly formed Western schools Stanford and University of Chicago followed during the 1890s, and the number of women with advanced degrees increased sharply; by 1900, 56 women had received a Ph.D. in science from American universities. Two thirds of these were from just four schools: Cornell, University of Pennsylvania, Yale, and Chicago.

But a number of prestigious schools in the United States and Europe continued to be closed to women. Christine Ladd-Franklin was instrumental in establishing a graduate fellowship for women, sponsored by the Association of College Alumnae, that gave opportunities to many women who would go on to eminent careers in science, and opened a number of European universities to female graduate students. European universities were more open to foreign women, who would not expect to teach in European universities, but these opportunities were also exploited by European women such as Lise Meitner and Emmy Noether, both of whom received graduate degrees in the early 20th century.

A strategy that Margaret Rossiter calls "coercive philanthropy" was more effective than this gradual approach. Johns Hopkins is a good example; it did not officially open its graduate school to women until 1907 and waited until its 50th anniversary in 1924 to award a degree to Christine Ladd-Franklin. At the age of 79(!), Ladd-Franklin attended the ceremony and received her long-delayed degree. In contrast, the Johns Hopkins medical school began admitting women in 1893, largely due to the requirements of a large bequest by Mary Garrett, heiress to the Baltimore and Ohio Railroad fortune. Johns Hopkins quickly became known for a long line of distinguished women physicians and medical researchers.

When women began to take the natural next step, into jobs at coeducational universities, resistance increased, and women were forced to develop new strategies, often finding new niches that did not threaten the male bastion of the professoriate. The rise of "Big Science" made larger research groups possible and allowed for the creation of research associate positions. Examples included Edward Pickering's group of women "measurers" at the Harvard College Observatory, and museum assistants in a variety of fields.

It was common for scientific women to work with a male colleague, often their thesis adviser or husband. The protection of a powerful man could make research opportunities available for women, but there were drawbacks. It was often assumed that the men had all the ideas, and women had trouble getting credit for their work. Margaret Rossiter (1995, plate following p. 148) shows a photograph of physicist Ann Chamberlain Birge and her husband Robert Birge. The couple was deliberately posed by the photographer with the man standing using the equipment and the woman seated and taking notes, despite the fact that it was *her* equipment and *her* dissertation research.

The Story of Home Economics

Another strategy exploited by women eager to do scientific research was to go into new areas of applied science in "womanly" fields. This approach is exemplified by chemist Ellen Swallow Richards, who created the applied science of home economics almost single-handedly. She stressed the value of chemistry to homemakers, testing water purity and developing low-cost, nutritious meals for the poor. She propagandized for home economics as a field, ran demonstration projects, wrote handbooks, and organized its main activities and professional organizations.

By the time of Richards's death in 1911, the field was well established and moving into a more academic phase. The new agricultural colleges of the Midwest and West formed programs and many young women chose this field as a college major and a profession. Home economics prospered even through the Depression, when so many other academic fields declined.

In 1936, Flemmie Kittrell became the first African American woman to receive a doctorate in home economics. She spent much of her career at Howard University, developing the home economics program into one of international renown. In the late 1940s and 1950s she conducted a "nutritional survey" of underdeveloped African nations and discovered the phenomenon of "hidden hunger," in which a person may be malnourished despite a full stomach. Later she spent a year in India as a Fulbright scholar studying local diets, and she founded a college of home economics there. She also established an exchange program that enabled many Indian students to attend U.S. universities and obtain doctorates.

Home economics and other "womanly" fields tended to be highly feminized, poorly paid, and scorned by many other academics. While they segregated women, they did offer opportunities for academic employment to many women scientists. In many universities the only female full professors, department chairs, and deans were in these "women's" fields. This successful enclave for women scientists was destroyed during another period of "professionalizing" science in the 1950s, when many fine home economics departments were dismantled or replaced by less female-oriented programs. Older women were often brutally expelled from institutions to which they had devoted their careers, to be replaced by younger and better paid men.

Documenting Discrimination

Women tried to document the discrimination and unfair practices that were keeping them from academic jobs. In 1921 Committee W of the American Association of University Professors (AAUP) performed a comprehensive survey of the status of academic women, finding that women had only 4 percent of professorships but 23.5 percent of instructorships, and that 27 of the 100 coeducational schools surveyed had no women faculty at all. Two years later, Marion Hawthorne found that women had lower status and lower pay than men and that this differential could not be explained by advanced degrees or years of experience. She concluded,

> Women with exceptional ability and proper influence testify to the fact that they were able to rise to a position equal to that of male colleagues, but the rank and file of the respondents seem to have developed a defensive attitude bordering on martyrdom, and complained, waxed bitter, and voiced resentment toward the conditions of which they were victims. (Rossiter 1982, 164)

Women who expected anything other than the lowest status, rank, and pay were required to overcome the barriers placed before them and prove themselves equal to the best men in their fields. Those who succeeded in this almost impossible task were quickly labeled "exceptions," so that their outstanding performance did nothing to remove prejudice against other women. Sometimes it even worked against other women; Robert Millikan wrote a letter to the president of Duke University advising against the hiring of German refugee Hertha Ayrton on the grounds that she was not as good a physicist as Lise Meitner. Meitner was at that time one of the most eminent physicists in the world; neither the male physicists at Duke nor any of the male candidates could have met this high standard. The academic community was assumed to be meritocratic, despite obvious inequities, and the dearth of women was taken to be evidence of their lack of ability.

Depression-era cutbacks had a disproportionate impact on women. The development of policies like tenure and antinepotism, while ostensibly gender neutral, worked against women. Antinepotism rules kept Maria Goeppert Mayer and Gerty Cori, both married to other scientists, as volunteer research associates even when they were doing the work that won them each a Nobel Prize. One couple, archaeologists Madeline Kneberg and Thomas Lewis of the University of Tennessee, were so certain that antinepotism rules would end her career that they chose not to marry until they retired.

World War II and the Cold War

Government interest in and support of science increased dramatically during what some have called "the physicists' war," won by radar and ended by the atomic bomb. Women scientists participated in this boom but only as temporary employees. The number of women scientists in academic jobs more than tripled, but tenure was suspended during the war, so their progress was not permanent. Women also made direct contributions to the war effort, most notably on the Food and Nutrition Committee, which advised the government on nutritional needs of fighting men. Ruth Benedict wrote an interpretive work on Japanese culture that was published after the war as *The Chrysanthemum and the Sword*. Some women worked for the Office of Scientific Research and Development and the Manhattan Project, although their contributions were almost invisible.

After the war, serious efforts were made to remasculinize science. The GI Bill made a college education possible for more than a million veterans, but 97 percent of veterans were male, so women barely benefited from this new opportunity. On the contrary, to make room for the returning veterans, many women's colleges began to accept male students, and quotas for women students were instituted at many coeducational schools. Antinepotism policies that had been suspended during the war were reinstated. The needs of the war effort had stretched gender roles, but antifeminism remained strong and women were pushed out of academic institutions at all levels to make room for returning men.

During the postwar period, MacCarthyism and the Cold War made criticism of most institutions subversive. Women lost voice and protest was muted. The

Korean War brought a new concern for scientific manpower, and girls were urged to study science and become teachers and lab workers. Record numbers of women did enroll and complete degrees, despite the discouraging atmosphere.

The period of the middle 1950s through the 1960s was a golden age for science, a time of unprecedented growth and prosperity, but again women did not participate in this boom. The increased research support created many new soft money positions, which often were taken by women scientists. But these positions were low paid and low status and dependent on the project director. The women themselves, together with their hard work and accomplishments, remained invisible. One bright spot, Penn State, upgraded its academic standing by deliberately hiring academic couples and distinguished women.

The Women's Movement and Affirmative Action

The advent of the women's movement in the late 1960s enabled women scientists to find the collective voice and effective strategy that had eluded them for decades. Alice Rossi collected data that showed significant discrimination against women in pay and other important areas. Rather than exhorting women to work harder, Rossi identified discriminatory practices and social pressures that discouraged women from pursuing science. Bernice Sandler filed suit against the University of Maryland for sexual discrimination in hiring under the Civil Rights Act. Until now, universities had been above these laws, but Sandler (advised by her lawyer husband) argued that the university, as a federal contractor, was subject to antidiscrimination legislation. She eventually broadened her suit into a class action lawsuit against 250 colleges and universities. The universities responded by stalling, but this tactic backfired because it increased pressure for more effective legislation.

Representative Edith Starrett Green (D-OR), a member of the House Committee on Education and Labor, appointed Sandler to her staff and used her research to hold hearings on sex discrimination in education. Green's work culminated in the Educational Amendments Act of 1972, which was signed into law by President Nixon in March of that year. Title IX extended the Equal Pay Act of 1963 to higher education and banned sex discrimination in any program of an institution receiving federal funding, including sports, textbooks, and the curriculum.

Affirmative action legislation was certainly significant for women in science. It was now illegal to refuse to hire women or to pay them less than their male colleagues. Hated nepotism rules were finally overturned. But Figure 2 shows that affirmative action did not cause a huge flood of women into science.

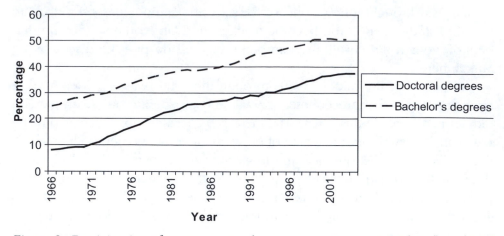

Figure 2. Participation of women in academic science. Source: NSF (2004) and NSF (2007).

Instead, there has been a steady increase of women at all levels of academic science since the mid-1960s. Women were half of all bachelor's degree recipients by 1980 but not half of science bachelor's degrees until 2000. In psychology, women achieved parity by 1974 and in biology by 1995. In the physical and earth sciences, women were still only 42 percent of bachelor's degree recipients in 2004, the most recent year for which the National Science Foundation (NSF) has collected data (NSF 2007). At the doctoral level, progress has been slower. In 2004, women received 37 percent of science doctorates, and only in psychology have women achieved parity. Figure 2 shows clearly that the lower participation by women in science is not due solely to the lack of qualified women. Women have had plenty of time since 1972 to progress into doctoral degrees and academic jobs, but they continue to lag behind; in 2003 women scientists were only 31 percent of all academic job holders (NSF 2007).

While affirmative action is clearly beneficial to women in science, it did not eliminate discrimination as thoroughly as one might have hoped. The overt inequity of antinepotism and pay differentials has been replaced by more subtle forms of discrimination that are often harder to document and fight. Bernice Sandler calls the constant denigration of women and their accomplishments the "chilly climate." This creates a subtle but constant pressure pushing women out of science so that the pipeline continues to leak. Academic women must choose between career and family life in a way that men do not. The incompatibility of the tenure clock with women's biological clocks has been identified as a major reason that women drop out of science. Although the situation is far from ideal, family-friendly policies, such as finding positions for trailing spouses, stopping the tenure clock for both men and women, for pregnancy, adoption, or other family issues, are becoming more prevalent at many institutions.

The closing of many women's colleges was an unanticipated result of Title IX legislation. Women's colleges provide opportunities for women-centered scholarship not available or recognized as valid in androcentric institutions and offer leadership prospects and the presence of female role models, especially in math and science. Mount Holyoke is first among all liberal arts colleges in producing women who went on to receive U.S. doctorates in the life sciences and in the physical sciences from 1966 to 2004. This put it in the top 2 percent of all colleges and universities, some many times its size. There are fewer than 60 women's colleges today in the United States, unfortunately limiting the choices of those who would benefit from this option (Salamone 2007).

In 1997, *Nature* published the results of an analysis of peer review scores in the Swedish Medical Research Council by Christine Wenneras and Agnes Wold; their work showed that peer reviewers overestimated male achievement and underestimated female achievement. And in 1999, Nancy Hopkins, professor of biology at the Massachusetts Institute of Technology, showed significant gender inequalities in salary, research space, start-up packages, resources, and access to graduate students among faculty of equivalent rank. Quickly, representatives of other elite universities found the same situation at their institutions. Indeed, in some departments, statistically significant data on differences between male and female faculty could not be obtained because there were too few women.

In response to these findings, in 2001 the National Science Foundation began the ADVANCE Program (http://www.nsf.gov/funding/pgm_summ.jsp?pims_id=5383) to promote institutional change and increase women's leadership. Previous NSF efforts to encourage women in science had targeted individual women and their research; this is the first effort to change institutions rather than women. For example, the ADVANCE program at the Georgia Institute of Technology (http://www.advance.gatech.edu/) was co-directed by a feminist dean and the provost, a person in a position to promote significant change. This multiyear program incorporates several important elements:

- Termed professorships for senior women professors, equivalent to a chaired professorship, that focuses on mentoring junior women.
- Leadership retreats for women faculty and senior administrators.
- New family-friendly policies.
- Data gathering on recruitment and retention.
- Redesign of the promotion and tenure process to remove bias.

It remains to be seen whether women in leadership positions initiate change or continue long-entrenched policies, and whether five years of funding is sufficient to ensure long-lasting change. One institution has discovered that promises made in connection with an ADVANCE award might be withdrawn by a newly appointed administrator. Nevertheless, many American universities are now trying to ensure equal opportunities for women and to implement family-friendly policies.

Conclusion

Those of us whose careers in science began in the second half of the 20th century often believe that progress for women has been linear, since that has been our experience. But if we look over a longer time, we see that opportunities for women in science have fluctuated. Periods of opportunity are often followed by retrenchment caused by a fear of feminization of science. Opportunities for women often do not parallel those for men. Sometimes when science expands, as during the golden age following World War II, opportunities for women have contracted.

We see a remarkable similarity in strategies by antifeminists seeking to roll back women's progress. In the late 19th century, conservative men argued that higher education made women unfit for motherhood and would damage the reproductive capacity of the nation. This is remarkably similar to the "concern" expressed by contemporary conservatives over the difficulties women have in maintaining both competitive careers and a satisfying family life. The "blame the victim" mentality remains constant. For more than a century, antifeminists have been assuming that science is a meritocracy, ignoring obvious patterns of discrimination against women and explaining that the dearth of women in the upper ranks of scientists must be due to women's lack of talent or interest. Larry Summers was not as original as he imagined.

The counterstrategies of women scientists have also changed little. Many women believed in the meritocracy, kept their heads down, worked hard, and hoped for rewards. For the most part they were disappointed, working many years with low pay, little advancement, and little credit for their work. There were a lucky few exceptions who, because of extraordinary talent and influence, were able to have careers similar to those of male scientists. Some of these lucky women, like Christine Ladd-Franklin, have done significant work to help their less fortunate colleagues. Others who were blind to their own privilege "refused to see any problem." Jessie Bernard, for example, who had generally been well treated at Penn State, blamed the decline of women on academic faculties on a shortage of trained women, and not on discrimination.

Collecting data to document women's accomplishments and discrimination is a standard tactic. From the 1870s, when Maria Mitchell first pointed out that coeducational schools were not hiring very many women, to the statistical report of Committee W of AAUP in 1921 to the MIT Report in 1999, women have attempted to show the effects of discrimination on hardworking and accomplished women. The success of this tactic varies with the political climate; it can convince some powerful men and accomplish change, but all too often results are ignored or blamed on the women themselves.

It is important to appreciate the extent to which women have supported each other. Professional women banded together to form "women in . . ." subgroups of their professional organizations and, denied membership in faculty clubs, formed their own groups. Women's clubs offered prizes and scholarships to women scientists and students. The American Association of University Women (AAUW), for example, established an Annual Achievement Award for a woman scientist or scholar; early winners included Florence Seibert, Ruth Benedict, and Barbara McClintock. The Clare Booth Luce fellowships for women in science, which support both students and faculty, continue this important tradition. Wealthy women (and sometimes men) practiced "coercive philanthropy," forcing academic institutions to include women by providing restrictive bequests. Catherine Naife Kellogg, for example, endowed a chair for a woman scientist at the University of Michigan. The first recipient was noted psychologist Helen Peak, who moved from Connecticut College for Women to one of the largest doctoral programs in the country and became one of the most visible and most honored women in psychology. At MIT, feminist alumna Katherine Dexter McCormick endowed the first women's dormitory (it opened in 1964, 96 years after MIT had become coeducational). Eleanor Roosevelt on several occasions intervened to help women scientists receive equal pay. These efforts helped to remind often-isolated women scientists that there was a supportive community out there. And it helped remind women that highly accomplished women scientists did exist. Women scientists act as role models and mentors to younger women.

We have learned that the political climate matters, that supportive men in positions of power can make significant change, and that women working together can provide a supportive community. Women scientists of the present continue all these strategies to improve our position and provide increased opportunities for younger women. (*See also* Discrimination; Women's Education; Technology)

References and Further Reading

Georgia Institute of Technology. "NSF ADVANCE Program for Institutional Transformation." http://www.advance.gatech.edu/. (Accessed July 5, 2007.)

Harding, Sandra. *Whose Science? Whose Knowledge? Thinking from Women's Lives.* Ithaca, NY: Cornell University Press, 1991.

Harth, Erica. *Cartesian Women*. Ithaca, NY: Cornell University Press, 1992.

Leggon, Cheryl B., and Willie Pearson Jr. "The Baccalaureate Origins of African American Female Ph.D. Scientists." *Journal of Women and Minorities in Science and Engineering* 3 (1997): 213–224.

McDowell, Louise S. "Physics at Wellesley." *The American Physics Teacher* 4 (1936): 57–61.

National Science Foundation. *Women, Minorities, and Persons with Disabilities in Science and Engineering: 2004*. Report 04–317. Arlington, VA: National Science Foundation.

National Science Foundation. *Women, Minorities, and Persons with Disabilities in Science and Technology: 2004*. http://www.nsf.gov/statistics/wmpd/. (Accessed July 5, 2007.)

National Science Foundation ADVANCE Program. http://www.nsf.gov/funding/pgm _summ.jsp?pims_id=5383. (Accessed July 5, 2007.)

Noble, David F. *A World without Women: The Christian Clerical Culture of Western Science*. New York: Oxford University Press, 1992.

Rossiter, Margaret. *Women Scientists in America: Struggles and Strategies to 1940*. Baltimore, MD: Johns Hopkins University Press, 1982.

Rossiter, Margaret. *Women Scientists in America: Before Affirmative Action*. Baltimore, MD: Johns Hopkins University Press, 1995.

Salamone, Rosemary. "A Place for Women's Colleges." *Chronicle of Higher Education* (February 16, 2007): B-20.

Wasserman, Elga. *The Door in the Dream: Conversations with Eminent Women in Science*. Washington, DC: Joseph Henry Press, 2000.

Wolf-Wendel, L. E. "Models of Excellence: The Baccalaureate Origins of Successful European American Women, African American Women, and Latinas." *Journal of Higher Education* 69 (1998): 141–186.

Federal Agencies

Daryl E. Chubin

Recent History

In December 1995, the National Science Foundation (NSF) and Deputy Director Anne Petersen hosted a conference on "Women and Science" in Washington, DC (National Science Foundation 1997). The conference drew 700 participants (90+ percent women scholars, educators, and federal agency administrators). Today, such a gathering sounds unremarkable, but it was remarkable then. NSF had funded several conferences and workshops on gender but had never hosted its own event—determining the agenda and giving the topic agency, and indeed, federalwide visibility.

The concluding panel of the two-day conference, featuring plenary and breakout sessions, was moderated by Director Neal Lane. The panelists were the assistant directors of all NSF directorates. The symbolism was unmistakable. The highest ranking authorities within the agency charged with the support of science and engineering research and education were given minutes each to indicate how their directorates were supporting participation of women in the enterprise. This was, in effect, going on the public record.

To affirm the "field's" reaction to what was being pledged, Director Lane invited comments from the floor. Women converged on the open mikes. Most were laudatory of the event, praising NSF for its forthrightness in providing an opportunity for women to "set their own agenda" and "speak informally in smaller groups" instead of being lectured to and reassured that their concerns were being heard.

To some in attendance, the praise seemed misplaced. This was 1995! NSF should have been "doing the right thing" since at least the 1980 reauthorization that charged NSF with increasing representation of women and minorities in science (see below). What sometimes appears as a milestone might be reconsidered as payment on an overdue account.

Measuring Progress—Slow and Uneven

Now more than a decade later, NSF has the cross-directorate ADVANCE Program that seeks "institutional transformation"—to change the environment for success, not just the behavior of women faculty. The NSF Gender in Science and Engineering Program still awards grants for projects that explore how gender impinges on science education and careers. Other research and development (R&D) agencies and departments cannot but help to see gender as a variable, but few have built programs and dedicated resources to cultivating the talent embodied by more than half of the U.S. population. How have we made progress?

When the National Science Board, the governing body of NSF, revised in 1997 the review criteria to be applied to grant applications, it struck a chord that could be emulated by *all* the R&D agencies. By prescribing the importance of "broader impacts" as a core consideration in decisions to fund science and engineering research and education projects, the Board redefined "excellence" to include the development of human resources as more than a by-product of the knowledge-creation process. In a word, without impacting students (at all levels) or lay publics as an integral part of a project, there can be no excellence (and by implication, no justification for NSF support of it).

The broader impacts criterion, however, did not begin to affect the Foundation's decentralized program-by-program decision making until then-Director Rita Colwell issued a memorandum in 2002 reminding staff and performers alike that the criterion would be enforced. Proposals were expected to explain how those beyond the immediate peer community would benefit from the work conducted under the grant (examples from that memo are posted at NSF 2002).

NSF has a unique role among federal R&D agencies. Operating under the Science and Engineering Equal Opportunities Act of 1980 (revised P.L. 107-368 to include persons with disabilities), which congressionally mandates the agency to increase participation of groups underrepresented in science and engineering, the Foundation deserves credit for spearheading the production of scientists and engineers. But the burden should not fall solely to this one agency.

The reality is that the science and engineering workforce, with women and minorities grossly underrepresented, looks most unlike the nation's overall workforce. This is a legacy of policies that served us in the 20th century (Commission on the Advancement of Women and Minorities 2000). Such policies were fragmented categorically by group, segment of the education system, sector of the economy, institutional type, and so on. The national interest can get lost in the maze of agency missions. Funding projects that promise broader impacts and benchmarking progress require checklists, not wish lists. This should be an enabling national priority. If education and human resources are the lifeblood of science, then experts, too, must learn how to recognize and reward peers who simultaneously enrich knowledge and have the capacity to teach, invent, and consume science.

So is the glass half full or half empty? A 2006 report by the National Academies (elaborated below) puts the last decade into sharp perspective by analyzing what we know from research on gender and how we act (or fail to act) on this evidence of residual bias and blunted opportunity. With the power of the purse, federal agencies can spur at least two kinds of significant action—*besides research*—on bias and efforts to reduce its pernicious effects on science: the provision of technical assistance to individuals and organizations, and advocacy that keeps issues of policy and practice in front of stakeholders, especially lawmakers and federal administrators.

Technical Assistance: An Exemplar

Typically, federal agencies award project monies on a competitive basis to "performers" who pursue programmatic goals. One co-sponsored example focused on gender in science is the Committee on the Advancement of Women Chemists, or COACh, an organization devoted to accelerating the slow progress toward reaching gender equity in academia in the chemical sciences. COACh was formed in 1998 with seed funding from the Camille and Henry Dreyfus Foundation. From its Web site (http://coach.uoregon.edu/), we learn that

> since 2000 its efforts have been jointly funded by grants from NSF, NIH [the National Institutes of Health], and the Department of Energy. COACh activities and programs are developed by an Advisory Board consisting of senior women chemists and chemical engineers, mainly in academia. This group, which represents a cross-section of institutions and ethnic backgrounds, has been meeting for the past six years in its capacity as the governing body of the organization, planning and implementing the programs described herein.

The goals of COACh, a membership organization of over 300, are concrete and measurable. The programs "are designed to increase the number of women chemists entering academic chemistry departments, succeeding up the ranks and achieving leadership roles. Both women chemists themselves and departments and research centers are targeted with these programs" (http://coach .uoregon.edu/).

Indeed, COACh's aspirations reach beyond discipline and sector to offer professional skills workshops that help women scientists, especially women of color, achieve their full career potential as they progress from undergraduate to graduate to faculty status. Ultimately, these faculty would work to effect change in institutions to provide an inclusive and supportive environment for all underrepresented groups, as well as networking and mentoring activities. COACh also seeks to evaluate the impact of programs and disseminate the results beyond the chemical sciences. The need for research on factors that slow the careers of women in the academic sciences is ongoing, serving to fuel other efforts and organizations concerned with gender equity (Fox, Johnson, and Rosser 2006).

A major reference point for many of these activities is the chief professional association for U.S.-based chemists, the American Chemical Society. For the record, chemistry lags other disciplines among the physical sciences in the hiring, promoting, tenuring, and advancing Ph.D.-holding women in academe (Marzabadi et al. 2006). Disciplines alone, however, should not grapple with these issues. There remain formidable challenges to *measuring* gender inequities even at the institutional level (Bailyn 2003; Jaschik 2006a).

Advocacy (Research-Based)

The National Academies (Committee on Women in Science and Engineering 2006) recently catalogued gender differences in careers by state and institution. The report exhorts the federal agencies and Congress to use the "bully pulpit." One can identify at least four ways in which the federal government figures prominently:

1. Federal agencies and private foundations could collaborate with professional societies in organizing national meetings to educate university department chairs, agency program officers, and members of review panels on ways to minimize the effects of gender bias in performance evaluations. These sponsors should support administrative assistance for researchers who are on leave because of caregiving responsibilities.
2. Federal enforcement agencies—including the U.S. Equal Employment Opportunity Commission (EEOC); U.S. departments of Education, Justice, and Labor; and various federal civil rights offices—could provide technical assistance in helping universities pursue their diversity goals in employment and programs.
3. Federal agencies should also conduct periodic compliance reviews at higher education institutions to monitor whether federal antidiscrim-

ination laws are being upheld and discrimination complaints promptly investigated.

4. To ensure that laws are being enforced by various agencies (Agriculture, Defense, Education, Energy, and Labor; EEOC; and science agencies, including the National Institutes of Health, the National Science Foundation, the National Institute of Standards and Technology, and the National Aeronautical and Space Administration [NASA]), Congress could routinely hold oversight hearings (Committee on Maximizing the Potential 2006).

Clearly, we are getting a better empirical handle on how gender influences the inputs to and outcomes of science. After all, just as allegiance to discipline competes with allegiance to institution and teaching with research, so does gender as a variable—often unspoken—influence decisions about hiring, promotion, and advancement. That evidence of bias in faculty composition persists indicates how deep cultural biases and institutional practices run (Nelson 2005).

The federal government has a substantial role—as sponsor and "client"— in what happens on campus and in the technical workforce. Similarly, professional associations for the science and engineering disciplines provide authoritative judgment of quality and progress, both of its knowledge base and its practitioners. Performers (both individuals and organizations) can ill afford to ignore those judgments. What, then, should be the posture of the federal government toward changing culture, if not individual behavior, to increase participation in science?

Federal Enforcement—Passive or Aggressive?

Institutional change is, by definition, slow and often imperceptible. For those fomenting, advocating, and documenting change at a department, college, or whole institution level, progress registers as a tweaked policy, a modified practice, or perhaps a trend indicating tangible improvements in the participation of those traditionally underrepresented: new hires, promotion and tenure decisions, advancement to leadership positions, recognition by one's institution, discipline, or professional association.

Starting in the summer of 2006, the U.S. Education Department began to conduct in-depth investigations of whether selected colleges and universities are complying with federal antibias laws in their treatment of women in math and science. The investigations were undertaken by the Education Department's Office for Civil Rights (OCR) as full "compliance reviews," which look broadly at institutional policies and practices—and tend to be much more thorough and sometimes last much longer than investigations of a specific complaint.

Of course, all federal agencies have enforcement responsibilities under Title IX. All federal agencies, including Education, the Department of Energy, NASA, and NSF, are responsible for handling Title IX enforcement of their own grantees and may refer complaints against educational institutions to Education's OCR and employment-related sex discrimination complaints to EEOC. OCR plays a key role in ensuring compliance with Title IX because it has primary responsibility to investigate most types of complaints at educational institutions, including complaints referred from other federal agencies.

As far as one can tell, investigations are ongoing. Progress is not reported in the usual media outlets, though *Science* (Bhattajarchee 2007) recently noted that DOE and NASA compliance reviews continue for months, while NSF's review is now the responsibility of an interagency group within the White House Office of Science and Technology Policy (OSTP). The reviews fall under the OCR's authority to enforce Title IX of the Education Amendments of 1972, which bars sex discrimination in education programs receiving federal funds. Such reviews end when institutions agree to change certain policies and with policy guidance that is broadened to apply to colleges that were not reviewed.

These investigations on how women are treated in science mark a huge expansion of federal enforcement activities on behalf of women in science. A Government Accountability Office (2004) report, which criticized enforcement as inadequate, found that in the previous 11 years the Education Department had conducted a total of three compliance reviews of how colleges and universities handled science and gender equity.

Most observers realize that the discrimination women face as students or faculty members in mathematics, engineering, and science may be subtle and not involve written rules. Nonetheless, barriers in the form of access to laboratory facilities, amount of lab space and type of equipment, expression of doubt about capabilities, and outright harassment are quite real. Department reviews examine policies that result in women feeling unwelcome, encountering "glass ceiling" assumptions that exclude them from consideration for certain kinds of positions, or having to contest apparent placement on a "Mommy track." In the words of Jocelyn Samuels, vice president for education and employment at the National Women's Law Center, compliance reviews are welcome because historically Title IX enforcement in math and science "has not been a priority" (Jaschik 2006b).

Although EEOC does not have any authority under Title IX, it does have authority under Title VII of the Civil Rights Act of 1964 to investigate sex-based complaints of employment discrimination, including sex discrimination against faculty and scientists. Arguably, the federal government has been too passive in investigating gender bias in science. But the outlook is one of more aggressive enforcement. Stay tuned. . . .

Using Policy Levers within a Federal R&D Agency: Two Cases

Could the federal government withhold research funding from universities that oppose or are indifferent to advancing the careers of women in science? There is no question that this falls within the policy purview of a federal funding agency. What one *can* do, however, differs from what one *dares* to do.

The director of the Office of Research on Women's Health at the National Institutes of Health, Vivian Pinn, says that stricter scrutiny of NIH-funded institutions for gender bias is a possibility to examine. "If you're in academia, you don't want the government dictating what you do," she said. But as the only woman and the only African American in her 1962 medical school class, "I know many doors were opened to me . . . because someone had to make sure that opportunities were made available to everyone."

Pinn's office ensures the inclusion of women in NIH-funded clinical trials, serves as the focal point for research in women's health issues, and helps advance the careers of women in science and medicine. There's much work to do. And NIH (2007) has announced the creation of an NIH Working Group on Women in Biomedical Careers "to examine issues raised in the recent National Academies report, *Beyond Bias and Barriers* . . . and to respond to the challenges issued to government funding agencies to maximize the potential of women scientists and engineers." NIH director Elias Zerhouni and Dr. Pinn will co-chair the Working Group.

Statistics from the Association of American Medical Colleges show that while women account for 47 percent of all medical school graduates, they hold few senior positions. For instance, women make up just 15 percent of those with the rank of full professor. Of the 1,971 clinical department chairs at U.S. medical schools, women occupy 176 of those positions. And the percentage of women on medical faculties has been increasing by about 1 percent a year, meaning that women aren't likely to hit the 50 percent mark until around 2025 (Ipaktchian 2006).

Gender differences in rank and salary across university campuses have indeed begun to be documented (*AAUP Faculty Gender Equity Indicators* 2006). It is essential that institutions keep score, monitoring what can reflect both overall performance and particular hot spots. Such indicators also depersonalize what can be excused as "personality conflict," "isolated incidents," and "anomalies" to expose biases deeply ingrained in departmental and faculty treatments. Again, this is culture change, that is, change of behavior, perception, and professional practice.

A second NIH-centered example draws on research to modify the ground rules for a grant competition and change agency practice in the process. A new study focuses on NIH's Clinical and Translational Science Award, a prestigious award that will fund principal investigators (PIs) at academic health centers. Annual budgets will exceed $10 million. Given the finding from controlled studies that both men and women preferentially select men for leadership positions, even when credentials of men and women are comparable, concern that unconscious stereotypes will result in the selection of male leaders is well founded.

To mitigate the impact of this bias and broaden the pool of potential leaders for this NIH initiative, Carnes and Bland (2007) recommend that academic health centers specify the skills they seek, constitute a search committee that is at least one third women, and increase awareness of the impact of unconscious gender bias on women's advancement. The authors also recommend that NIH institute a multiple PI rule, include in the request for applications a statement encouraging diversity among PIs, call attention to the importance of work-life balance for young investigators, and constitute study sections that are at least one third women. The aforementioned NIH Working Group on Women, it seems, has another item for its action agenda.

Conclusion

Reports by now have amply documented the disadvantages that federal programs inflict on women competing for scarce resources, notably compliance of NSF, NIH, and USDA with Title IX (Hosek et al. 2005). Title IX continues to be seen as a policy lever underutilized outside of college athletics. But the burden of proof of discrimination makes this more a public policy issue and a consciousness-raising tool than a legal remedy. Science, despite policy injunctions, remains a collegial activity. On a case-by-case basis, informal norms are still likely to trump formal sanctions.

In the end, leadership—and the *will* to enforce—are critical for change, especially since time has only hardened perceptions on all sides. As we approach the end of the first decade of the 21st century, we scientists should remember that

> in a diverse community that has long welcomed citizens of foreign nationality, there is great consciousness, reinforced by census categories and requests for self-identification, about who is participating and who is not—with the inevitable search for explanations that range from individual differences in interest and aptitude [a foreshadowing of Larry Summers] to structural barriers of prejudice and discrimination. (Chubin and Pearson 2001, 88)

Citizens of a democracy expect their government to craft solutions, not perpetuate problems. Given the federal apparatus for monitoring, investigating, and enforcing the laws of equal opportunity and treatment in the workplace, we would hope gender inequities to be little more than a historical footnote. Alas, that is not the case, even in the merit-based communities that scientists inhabit and claim to honor. Sensitivity and vigilance may be organizational imperatives, but human judgment allows gender to persist as an analytical, career, and federal issue. (*See also* Chemistry; Discrimination; Professional Societies)

References and Further Reading

AAUP Faculty Gender Equity Indicators 2006. Washington, DC: American Association of University Professors, 2006. http://www.aaup.org/NR/rdonlyres/63396944–44BE-4ABA-9815–5792D93856F1/0/AAUPGenderEquityIndicators2006.pdf.

Bailyn, Lotte. "Academic Careers and Gender Equity: Lessons Learned from MIT." *Gender, Work & Organization* 10 (March 2003): 137–153.

Bhattajarchee, Yudhijit. "Gender Equity: U.S. Agencies Quiz Universities on the Status of Women in Science." *Science* 315 (March 30, 2007): 1776.

Carnes, Molly, and Carole Bland. "A Challenge to Academic Health Centers and the National Institutes of Health to Prevent Unintended Gender Bias in the Selection of Clinical and Translational Science Award Leaders." *Academic Medicine* 82 (February 2007): 202–206.

Chubin, D. E., and W. Pearson Jr. "Postscript." In *Scientists and Engineers for the New Millennium: Renewing the Human Resource,* 87–93. Washington, DC: Commission on Professionals in Science and Technology, March 2001.

Commission on the Advancement of Women and Minorities in Science, Engineering, and Technology Development (CAWMSET). *Land of Plenty: Diversity as America's Competitive Edge in Science, Engineering and Technology.* Washington DC: CAWMSET, September 2000.

Committee on Maximizing the Potential of Women in Academic Science and Engineering. *Beyond Bias and Barriers: Fulfilling the Potential of Women in Academic Science and Engineering.* Washington, DC: National Academies Press, 2006.

Fox, Mary Frank, Deborah Johnson, and Sue Rosser, eds. *Women, Gender, and Technology.* Urbana: University of Illinois Press, 2006.

Government Accountability Office. *Gender Issues: Women's Participation in the Sciences Has Increased, but Agencies Need to Do More to Ensure Compliance with Title IX.* July 2004, GAO-04–639. http://www.gao.gov/new.items/d04639.pdf.

Hosek, Susan G., Amy G. Cox, Bonnie Ghosh-Dastidar, Aaron Kofner, Nishal Ramphal, Jon Scott, and Sandra H. Berry. *Gender Differences in Major Federal External Grant Programs.* Rand Corporation: Santa Monica, CA, 2005. http://www.rand.org/pubs/technical_reports/TR307/.

Ipaktchian, Susan. "Women Bioscientists Still Face Challenges to Upward Mobility, Top NIH Official Says in Campus Talk." *Stanford Report*, October 25, 2006. http://news-service.stanford.edu/news/2006/october25/med-pinn–102506.html.

Jaschik, Scott. "Federal Inquiry on Women in Science." *InsideHigherEd.com*, March 28, 2006a. http://www.insidehighered.com/news/2006/03/28/women.

Jaschik, Scott. "New Measures for Gender Inequities." *InsideHigherEd.com*, October 26, 2006b. http://insidehighered.com/layout/set/print/news/2006/10/26/salaries.

Marzabadi, Cecilia H., Valerie J. Kuck, Susan A. Nolan, and Janine P. Buckner, eds. *Dissolving Disparity, Catalyzing Change: Are Women Achieving Equity in Chemistry?* American Chemical Society, ACS Symposium Series No. 929, March 2006.

National Academies, Committee on Women in Science and Engineering. "Gender Differences in Careers of Science, Engineering, and Mathematics Faculty." http://www7.nationalacademies.org/cwse/gender_faculty_links.html#P234_9013. (Accessed April 13, 2007.)

National Institutes of Health. "NIH Leads Effort to Help Women in Science and Medicine Fulfill Potential. NIH news release, January 29, 2007. http://www.nih.gov/news/pr/jan20007/od–29.htm.

National Science Foundation. *Women & Science: Celebrating Achievements, Charting Challenges.* Conference Report, March 1997. http://www.nsf.gov/pubs/1997/nsf9775/start.htm.

National Science Foundation. "Merit Review Broader Impacts Criterion: Representative Activities." 2002. www.nsf.gov/pubs/2002/nsf022/bicexamples.pdf.

Nelson, Donna J. "A National Analysis of Diversity in Science and Engineering Faculties at Research Universities." Norman, OK, January 2005. http://cheminfo.chem.ou.edu/~djn/diversity/briefings/Diversity%20Report%20Final.pdf.

Industry

Suzanne Gage Brainard

Historically, men have traditionally dominated the fields of science and particularly engineering. However, the civil rights movement in the 1960s and Title IX in the early 1970s made possible the increase in women pursuing careers in the science and engineering professions during the early 1970s (Selby 1999). In the 1980s the National Science Foundation (NSF) projected a serious shortfall of scientists and engineers (National Research Council 1994). In order to keep the United States' competitive edge, the rationale followed with the need to target other pools of talent such as women and minorities to meet the demands of the workforce. Coupled with the legislative policies of the 1960s and 1970s, the idea that women and minorities are an untapped source for the scientific and engineering workforce became a driving argument to fuel policy initiatives in the 1980s. The 1990s cast doubt on the accuracy of those NSF projections. Regardless, by the middle of the 1990s both the science community and the industrial sector began to see the advantages of diversity in the science community as well as the workforce.

In many ways, the industrial sector was quicker to see the advantages of diversity. Since corporations were facing shortages of traditional male employees, they became aware that the workforce of the future was either not going to exist or it would need to look very different from the workforce of today. Recognizing the need to build a workforce as diverse as possible, global corporations began to think in different ways and to take serious steps to create a diverse, well-trained, and multicultural workforce. Faced with a decrease of general interest in science and engineering careers and an increase in demand for scientists and engineers, companies worldwide began to look beyond the traditional pool of talent (largely men) and target the other half of the population, women. To do this, companies implemented recruitment and retention strategies to increase the participation of women and minorities. Some of these included affinity groups (for women, minorities, people with different sexual orientations, and so on), mentoring programs, and career development seminars. Many of these are still highly successful.

Among those college educated in the science and engineering (S&E) work-force in 2003, 27 percent were women (CPST, specially derived analysis 2007). If the social sciences are removed, 24 percent were women of the S&E work-force. However, when one looks closely at the data, it is clear that women are often found in some but not all subspecialties. For example, if one looks only at the engineering occupations, 11 percent were women, whereas in science occupations, 31 percent were women. Finally, among scientists and engineers within industry, 38 percent were women. This is an increase from 28 percent in 1993.

Furthermore, occupational segregation exists horizontally in the top leader-ship of women in corporations. Proportionately, very few women are in top leadership positions in corporations. Top leadership positions could include the chief executive officer, vice presidents of marketing or research, general managers, or directors. Within the corporate environment, there are barriers that inhibit women's progress at every stage. As noted in the National Acad-emy of Sciences Report (National Research Council 1994), these include

- Recruitment and hiring practices that create de facto entry barriers for women
- Allegations of reverse discrimination
- Sexual harassment
- Different standards for women and men
- Disparities in the distribution of high-quality job assignments
- Salary discrepancies based on sex
- Failure of corporations to accommodate work-family issues
- Difficulty for women to advance into management

To some extent, each of these barriers noted in 1994 still exists today. How-ever, legislation to protect women and minorities from discrimination and provide equal opportunities has helped to ease some of these—but not com-pletely. Plus, corporations have begun to recognize the benefits of diversity, issues of balancing family and career, issues of childbearing, different sexual orientations, and the importance of a friendly corporate climate. By making strides to change the corporate culture to one that is friendly for women and minorities, the culture also becomes equally effective for all employees.

In closing, not one country in the world can boast of gender and racial eq-uity in its academic institutions or employment sectors. Some countries have mobilized their efforts to establish initiatives to effect change in the academic infrastructure, yet most of these are marginal rather than systemic initiatives and flounder when funding is curtailed. With almost two decades of initiatives in the United States to increase the participation of women and minorities in engineering, some progress has been made. Enrollments alone for women have increased from 2 percent in the early 1960s to slightly less than 20 percent and to less than 10 percent for minorities in 2006. And women engineers and scientists in the industrial sectors of the workforce fluctuate between 8 and 10 percent (NSF 2006).

The United States is still facing declines in science and engineering enrollments and demographic shifts, a call from industry to better prepare scientists and engineers for the workforce, a backlash against affirmative action programs, and a public outcry for quality education and accountability from corporations and educational institutions. However, the cry for diversity in the educational system, the corporate world, and the other sectors is stronger than ever before and is making changes in the ways that people think and act. (*See also* Discrimination)

References and Further Reading

Commission on Professionals in Science and Technology (CPST). *Employed Scientists and Engineers in the US by Employment Sector, Sex and Level of Highest Degree, 1993 to 2003.* Data derived from the National Science Foundation, SESTAT Database.

National Research Council Committee on Women in Science and Engineering, Office of Scientific and Engineering Personnel. *Women Scientists and Engineers Employed in Industry: Why So Few?* Washington, DC: National Academies Press, 1994.

National Science Foundation. *Science and Engineering Indicators 2006.* Arlington, VA: National Science Foundation, 2006.

Selby, Cecily C. *Women in Science and Engineering: Choices for Success. Annals of the New York Academy of Sciences,* Vol. 869. New York: New York Academy of Sciences, 1999.

Sonnert, Gerhard. "Women in Science and Engineering: Advances, Challenges, and Solutions." In *Women in Science and Engineering: Choices for Success. Annals of the New York Academy of Science,* Vol. 869, 34–57. New York: New York Academy of Sciences, 1999.

Professional Societies

DARYL E. CHUBIN

Validation and Participation

Professional societies play a unique role in the lives of scientists and engineers. As nonprofits or NGOs (nongovernmental organizations), "scientific societies" augment, mediate, enhance, and reward behavior that flows from collegial relations and validates professional contributions and status. Such validation extends beyond what employing institutions can offer. Scientists, after all, work in communities. Those communities tend to focus on separate aspects of the academic life: research, teaching, and service. Professional societies promote all three. They value the feedback from various quarters of the community—be it from sponsors, journals, collaborators, or competitors—and remind their members that a world beyond one's employing institution seeks to consume the knowledge, skills, advice, and just plain presence of "citizen-scientists." These consumers include local schools, community organizations, companies, and government agencies concerned about the next generation of skilled workers educated and trained in science and engineering.

Gender intersects with professional societies in predictable ways. Science, being merit based, should be gender and race blind in the evaluation of contributions to knowledge and the production of new professionals. But advantages accumulate in ways that "the rich get richer and the poor poorer." In the aggregate, women and persons of color have had fewer opportunities, less access, modest resources, uneven mentoring, and so on (Shaywitz and Hahm 2004). The result, disaggregated and displayed over time in Bell, Di Fabio, and Frehill (2006), is higher attrition at the baccalaureate and graduate levels, less ascendance through the faculty ranks, and fewer professionals from these underrepresented groups in leadership positions throughout the science and technology (S&T) workforce and, indeed, in American society.

Professional societies recognize these dynamics. Until the mid-20th century, it has been alleged that they too, at least in the physical sciences, practiced gender discrimination (Byers and Williams 2006). Unfortunately, "glass ceil-ings" and "mommy tracks" have not receded completely into the past.

In recent decades, scientific societies have often been at the forefront of exposing education and workplace disadvantage and reducing inequities. As the public-private partnership, Building Engineering and Science Talent (BEST) writes (2004, 15),

> As symbols of achievement and leadership, scientific and professional societies can play a major role in expanding opportunities for women and minorities in the science and engineering workforce. Through their basic activities, they en-sure that women and minority scientists share in the professional rewards of their discipline and are given prominence as role models. . . .
>
> For example, giving an invited talk at a national meeting is an important sign of being a recognized expert in a field, yet women and minorities have often been overlooked. Professional societies can help correct this by appointing or electing balanced program committees . . . and seek[ing] nominations from the broadest candidate pool. . . .
>
> Most professional societies have educational programs aimed at their mem-bers or students who may become future members. Working to increase di-versity should be an explicit part of whatever type of educational program is offered. . . . But just as professional societies can help increase the diversity within a field, so can they retard it. If the honors and recognitions they confer are narrowly distributed by and to members of an "old-boys club," the careers of women and minorities will be hindered in many ways. The field will look less attractive to the next generation, recruitment will suffer and the field will lose talent.

This is an apt description of computer science and engineering, which has seen a downward trend in women's enrollment and degree-taking at all levels over the last 20 years (American Association for the Advancement of Science 2005; Chubin, Malcom, and Babco 2005). Regardless of interest or academic preparation, students will not go where they do not feel welcome. So the "IT revolution," as it were, continues without the contributions of a large segment of talent, mostly women.

Scientific Societies as Change Agents

There are several varieties of scientific societies: multidisciplinary (American Association for the Advancement of Science, or AAAS; Sigma Xi—the Scien-tific Research Society), disciplinary (American Chemical Society, or ACS; Amer-ican Physical Society, or APS; Federation of American Societies for Experimental

Biology, or FASEB), and targeted (Society of Women Engineers, or SWE; Women in Engineering Programs and Advocates Network, or WEPAN; Association for Women in Science, or AWIS). Among these are 30 with "women" and "science," "technology," or "engineering" in their name. Many are international as well (see "Women-Related Web Sites in Science/Technology" 2007). These societies are voluntary organizations that reinforce professional identity, provide forums for face-to-face interaction, and represent a special kind of "club" for those who elect to join.

Scientific societies can be advocates and watchdogs, too. Not to be underestimated is the power of the policy statements issued by their boards of directors (typically sage scientists and engineers recruited from the membership ranks). For example, a notable statement issued in 1974 by the AAAS Board on "Equal Opportunity in the Sciences and Engineering" recognized "that complex social, economic, and political forces have combined in the past to discourage women . . . from entering the sciences and engineering, and to deny those who do enter equal access to positions of respect and authority." In response, AAAS transformed its own governance to achieve greater diversity among officers, board, and senior staff and sought to raise awareness of these issues at the highest policy levels. Twenty years later, AAAS issued a "Statement on Discrimination in the Workplace," and in the wake of Larry Summers's uninformed remarks at Harvard about women's "intrinsic aptitude" for science reaffirmed its policies to promote the participation of women, minorities, and persons with disabilities, observing that academe lags behind industry and government in achieving a diverse workforce (American Association for the Advancement of Science 2005).

Some scientific societies serve a scholarly function as well by sponsoring symposia and publishing as a way of keeping gender equity in the forefront of their members' consciousness. In December 1975, AAAS hosted a conference, funded by the National Science Foundation (NSF), on a phenomenon that had received little attention in the science community—*The Double Bind: The Price of Being a Minority Woman in Science* (Malcom, Hall, and Brown 1976). This landmark examination of the combined effects of gender, race, and ethnicity on career development showed that what awaits minority women who pursue a pathway in science is not pretty. As a reflection on the science community, it was an indictment of how ascribed characteristics seemed to subvert opportunity and achievement for those who had earned credentials but (in the prefatory words of AAAS Executive Officer William D. Carey) "are excluded from the mainstream."

If we fast-forward 30 years, the prospects are brighter but the picture remains dim. For example, an American Chemical Society (2006) collection features 10 chapters on the reasons for "underrepresentation of women in academic science," examining the factors "hindering women from attaining and advancing in these positions." Virtually every science and engineering society has produced similar volumes over the last decade. Such "self-study" is both vital and therapeutic, celebrating progress while grappling with those forces within disciplines and institutions that resist efforts to enhance participation by all.

What should not escape our notice from these examples is that professional societies are at the forefront of efforts to probe for evidence of "chilly climates" and to inspire scholars to explain why gender inequities persist (e.g., Davis et al. 1996), especially as they intersect with race, ethnicity, and class (e.g., Leggon 2006). They also serve as rallying cries for society members and as pressure points for others to exploit.

Title IX—A Public Policy Case Study

The voice of scientific societies can become a drumbeat of advocacy for actions to be taken by the very organizations that employ or fund. A recent example is the application of Title IX, a law implemented over 30 years ago in athletics, to women in science. The issue is not the absence of policy to induce change but rather the enforcement of existing policy.

The report also urges higher education organizations to consider forming a collaborative, self-monitoring body that would recommend standards for faculty recruitment, retention, and promotion; collect data; and track compliance across institutions.

The Society for Women Engineers has dedicated its public policy apparatus to Title IX. By positioning itself as a resource for government and policy makers, it seeks to educate its members on the legislative process and provide them with the tools they need to become more involved in public policy advocacy. This approach is instructive, providing Web access (Society of Women Engineers 2007) to the following types of information:

- The Legislative Process. Being effective on Capitol Hill requires reviewing the legislative process. Thus, we provide an overview of the legislative process and how a bill becomes a law.
- Communicating with Congress. Your members of Congress want to hear from you, but congressional offices receive thousands of e-mails and letters daily. Therefore, it is very important to send your e-mail/letter in such a way that it does not get lost in the masses.
- Roles of Congressional Staff. Each member of Congress has staff to assist him or her during a term in office. To be most effective in communicating with Congress, you should know the titles and principal

functions of key staff. They will be your primary contacts in the congressional office.

- Guidelines for Congressional Visits. While your member of Congress or his or her staff would like to meet with you, meetings typically only last 15–20 minutes. It is important to plan out your meeting ahead of time, especially if more than one constituent is present.
- Summary and Legislative Status on Legislation of Interest to SWE. While there are numerous education-related bills introduced each Congress, only a handful of these bills proceed past the committee level of the legislative process.
- Representing SWE. To date, the SWE Board of Directors has approved two general Society position statements: one on the need to improve science, technology, engineering, and mathematics (STEM) education in America's schools and the other regarding the application of Title IX to STEM fields.

Access and Recruitment

Professional societies are integral to a world closed to those neither credentialed nor employed in an organization valued in that world. This is one outcome of professionalization in which experts prefer to interact with like-experts. So how does one negotiate this world, internalize its norms, and learn "what matters" to excel professionally? How, for instance, does one become informed about employment opportunities? Further, how does one become a real candidate instead of treated as a token or mere window dressing to comply with federal and state "fairness doctrines"?

Women in science and engineering have long endured *faux* searches. *The Chronicle of Higher Education* occasionally publishes essays on the experiences women have had in the search process. Professional societies can be potent antidotes to access inequality and the mischief one might encounter in academic recruitment and hiring. Many societies have caucuses, registries, and databases, in addition to committees, to aid in faculty or other searches.

Today there are well-known strategies for conducting inclusive searches that afford women and underrepresented minorities an opportunity to join the pool of eligibles and compete for late-stage campus visits and interviews (Smith et al. 2004). Ethnic-affiliated and women's professional societies exist in science and engineering disciplines to act as resources for such searches, to promote networking, and to offer career assistance for prospective candidates. Such assistance can take many forms: programs, mentoring, professional development seminars. All are intended to convey a simple reality: you are not alone and are not the only individual experiencing the "chill" that a life in science sometimes—indeed, more often than not for women—brings. The problem is typically "out there" in the workplace environment, not "in here"— between the scientist's ears or as a figment of her imagination.

Advancement—The Meaning of Full Participation

The playing field is hardly level. As Joseph McGrath, a MentorNet mentor at Los Alamos National Laboratory, observes, "Through all my years since 1969, men have outnumbered women in engineering and scientific fields by a huge margin. It is clear that much more work is required to achieve complete equality in the workplace." But there is good news, too, courtesy of a kind of professional organization known as MentorNet (http://www.mentornet.net/). Studies suggest that women engineering and science students who are involved in mentoring relationships with either women or men mentors are more committed to and more likely to persist in their fields of study and are also more likely to earn degrees in engineering, related sciences and technology, and mathematics.

MentorNet is an award-winning nonprofit e-mentoring network that positively affects the retention and success of those in engineering, science, and mathematics, particularly but not exclusively women and others underrepresented in these fields. Founded in 1997, MentorNet provides highly motivated protégés from many of the world's top colleges and universities with positive, one-on-one, e-mail-based mentoring relationships with mentors from industry, government, and higher education. In addition, the MentorNet Community provides opportunities to connect with others from around the world who are interested in diversifying engineering and science.

To appreciate the reach of MentorNet and the role of "connectedness" that a professional association can create even at a distance, it is important to review the 2005–2006 MentorNet demographics (see Table 1).

Through voluntary disclosure, MentorNet also knows the ethnic diversity of its mentors and students that have been matched and are currently participating in one role or the other. For example, more than half of the students (55 percent) and almost three in four mentors (72 percent) are White. Yet there are twice as many Asian (30 percent) and African American (10 percent) students, respectively, as mentors (17 percent Asian, 4 percent African American). Hispanics/Latinos represent equal proportions of the student (6 percent) and mentor (5 percent) pools. The same holds, though at more modest levels, for American Indians (1 percent students, 2 percent mentors).

These similarities and differences hint at various issues. Most MentorNet mentoring occurs predominantly at the undergraduate level, with engineering

Table 1. MentorNet Demographics, 2005–2006

New Community Members	6,905
Total Community Members	16,524
Matched Pairs	2,523
Participating Colleges and Universities	111
Number of Companies Represented by Mentors	1,045
Companies with Largest Numbers of Mentor Volunteers	
IBM	335
HP	246
3M	175
Texas Instruments	76
Cisco Systems	48
Schlumberger	42
Résumés Posted during Fiscal Year	375

Countries Represented (Matched) Students 8 Mentors 41

Nationalities (Citizenships) Represented (Matched) Students 97 Mentors 67

Mentors by Gender (Matched)
- 61% Female
- 39% Male

Students by Gender (Matched)
- 76% Female
- 24% Male

Students by Degree Program (Matched)
- 3% Associates
- 65% Undergraduates (34% freshman/sophomore; 31% junior/senior)
- 12% Master's
- 16% Ph.D.
- 4% Postdoc
- 1% Untenured Faculty

Students by Fields of Study (Matched)
- 4% Business
- 17% Computer Sciences/Computer Engineering (CS/CE)
- 55% Engineering (See separate listing for CS/CE)
- 2% Environmental Sciences (including Geology, Earth Sciences)
- 13% Life Sciences (including Agricultural and Biological Sciences) and Mathematical Sciences (including Chemistry, Physics, Math, Astronomy)

Source: http://www.mentornet.net/documents/about/results/0506stats.aspx, reprinted with permission of Carol B. Muller.

far and away the dominant field. Three of five mentors and three of four students are women. Mentors from information technology companies are the most common. Overall, the number of participating companies exceeds faculty mentors at universities almost by an order of magnitude. Over its decade of existence, MentorNet has raised the profile of mentoring and fostered relationships that deliver advice to women in science and engineering regardless of discipline or physical location. Though effectiveness is an elusive quality to measure, evaluation of MentorNet's approach indicates high satisfaction of mentors and protégés and valuable professional socialization of protégés (Muller 2007). Surely, these relationships reduce the learning curve and sense of isolation by introducing students into networks that form within specialized communities.

It is important to begin harvesting the lessons of MentorNet participants as their careers evolve. A mentored scientist recognizes that every successful professional needs assistance at critical junctures: you give what you get. This is an intergenerational responsibility that builds trust and confidence, clarifies expectations, and rewards giver and receiver alike.

Symbolism and Conclusions on What's Possible

In our iconic "American Idol" culture, symbols matter. Who competes to win is increasingly decided by popular vote. Who sponsors or sanctions the competition imparts credibility—on one's candidacy, talent, and performance. So it is with the National Academies' report, *Beyond Bias and Barriers* (Committee on Maximizing the Potential of Women in Academic Science and Engineering 2006), which suggests a role for professional societies in conjunction with higher education associations to monitor progress toward gender equity in science. The American Council on Education is named as convenor of other relevant groups—for example, the Association of American Universities and the National Association of State Universities and Land-Grant Colleges—to discuss formation of a monitoring body.

In addition, the report urges honorary societies to review their nomination and election procedures to address the underrepresentation of women in their memberships. The committee calls on scientific and professional societies to assist in setting professional and equity standards; collect and disseminate data; provide professional development training that addresses evaluation bias; develop guidelines to ensure diversity of invited speakers at society events; ensure "reasonable representation of women on editorial boards and in other significant leadership positions"; nominate women for awards and leadership positions; and "provide child-care and elder-care grants or subsidies so that their members can attend work-related conferences and meetings."

Juxtapose this recommendation against one made at the 1995 NSF-hosted Women & Science Conference (National Science Foundation 1997): "Strengthen connections between organizations that have a stake in the participation of women in the sciences and engineering, such as the corporate and academic worlds, the formal and informal education sectors, associations of women and associations of sciences, and between higher education and K-12 schools."

Not much has changed: we know what to do, but can institutions be moved to act? Scientific societies can supply the clue to make symbolic actions stick: who runs for society offices, who interacts with leaders from the political arena, who brands efforts as being progressive and worthy of broad support? In the symbiotic world of science and engineering, the professional societies can do—relentlessly—what others cannot. But organizations age like people. Will the change agent become stodgy and sedentary? Can societies compel their constituencies to put gender in its proper place in the 21st century? For the future of science, if not society, let us—in the name of excellence, equity, and self-interest—hope so. (*See also* Discrimination; Federal Agencies; Gender and Occupational Interests)

References and Further Reading

American Association for the Advancement of Science. "AAAS Board Statement on Women in Science and Engineering," February 5, 2005. www.aaas.org/news/releases/2005/0208board.shtml.

American Association for the Advancement of Science. *Preparing Women and Minorities for the IT Workforce: The Role of Nontraditional Educational Pathways.* Washington, DC: American Association for the Advancement of Science and the Commission on Professionals in Science and Technology, 2005.

American Chemical Society. *Dissolving Disparity, Catalyzing Change: Are Women Achieving Equity in Chemistry?* Washington, DC: ACS Symposium Series 929, March 2006.

Bell, Nathan E., Nicole M. Di Fabio, and Lisa M. Frehill. *Professional Women and Minorities: A Total Human Resources Data Compendium.* 16th ed. Washington DC: CPST, November 2006.

Building Engineering and Science Talent. *A Bridge for All: Higher Education Design Principles to Broaden Participation in Science, Technology, Engineering, and Mathematics,* February 2004. www.bestworkforce.org.

Byers, Nina, and Gary Williams, eds. *Out of the Shadows: Contributions of Twentieth-Century Women to Physics.* New York: Cambridge University Press, 2006.

Chubin, Daryl E., Shirley M. Malcom, and Eleanor L. Babco. "Gender and STEM Disciplines: Beyond the Barriers." AAC&U *On Campus with Women,* 34, October 2005. www.aacu.org/ocww/volume34_4/feature.cfm?section=2.

Committee on Maximizing the Potential of Women in Academic Science and Engineering. *Beyond Bias and Barriers: Fulfilling the Potential of Women in Academic Science and Engineering.* Washington, DC: National Academies Press, 2006.

Davis, Cinda-Sue, Angela Ginorio, Carol Hollenshead, Barbara Lazarus, Paula Rayman, and associates. *The Equity Equation: Fostering the Advancement of Women in the Sciences, Mathematics, and Engineering.* San Francisco: Jossey-Bass, 1996.

Leggon, Cheryl B. "Gender, Race/Ethnicity, and the Digital Divide." In *Work, Gender, and Technology,* ch. 5. Edited by Mary Frank Fox, Deborah G. Johnson, and Sue V. Rosser. Champaign: University of Illinois Press, 2006.

Malcom, Shirley Mahaley, Paula Quick Hall, and Janet Welsh Brown. *The Double Bind: The Price of Being a Minority Woman in Science.* April 1976, Publication 76-R-3. Washington, DC: American Association for the Advancement of Science.

Muller, Carol B. Highlights of MentorNet Evaluation/Research Studies, 1998–2005, personal communication, April 13, 2007.

National Science Foundation. *Women & Science: Celebrating Achievements, Charting Challenges.* Conference Report, March 1997. http://www.nsf.gov/pubs/1997/nsf9775/start.htm.

Shaywitz, Sally, and Jong-on Hahm, eds. *Achieving XXcellence in Science: Role of Professional Societies in Advancing Women in Science.* Proceedings of a 2002 Workshop Committee on Women in Science and Engineering, Washington DC: National Research Council, 2004.

Smith, Daryl G., C. S. V. Turner, N. Osei-Kofi, and S. Richards. "Interrupting the Usual: Successful Strategies for Hiring Diverse Faculty." *Journal of Higher Education* 75 (March/April 2004): 133–160.

Society of Women Engineers. "Public Policy Toolbox for SWE Members Launched." http://www.swe.org/stellent/idcplg?IdcService=SS_GET_PAGE&ssDocName=swe_005256&ssSourceNodeId=227. (Accessed April 13, 2007.)

"Women-Related Web Sites in Science/Technology." www.research.umbc.edu/~korenman/wmst/links_sci.html. (Accessed March 26, 2007.)

Discrimination

Discrimination

SUE V. ROSSER

Influence of Notions of Male Superiority/Female Inferiority on Scientific Theories

Discrimination against women in science has a lengthy history intertwined with beliefs about masculinity, femininity, and their association with science. As suggested by the entries on antiquity and the medieval era, views of women's inferiority led to flawed scientific "facts" that reinforced prevailing gender notions. Aristotle "counted" fewer teeth in the mouths of women than in those of men—adding this dentitional inferiority to all the others. Galen, having read the book of Genesis, "discovered" that men had one less rib on one side than women did. Clearly, observation of what would appear by today's standards to be easily verifiable facts were seen incorrectly because of the expectations and paradigms under which the scientists operated.

The roots of the bias of women's inferiority on theories of human reproduction can be traced back through the preformationists to Aristotle. Nancy Tuana argues that "adherence to a belief in the inferiority of the female creative principle biased scientific perception of the nature of woman's role in human generation" (Tuana 1989, 147), thereby illustrating ways in which the gender/science system informs the process of scientific investigation.

Scientists today recognize numerous flaws in Aristotle's biology. Certainly his ideas that women are colder than men and therefore less developed and that women are "not the parent, just a nurse to a seed" (Aeschylus 1975, 666–669) are not acceptable to modern biologists. His ideas about woman's inferiority and man's providing the form and motion of the fetus were not only perpetuated in one form or another until the 11th century but they also influenced the notion of preformation. While looking at "systematic animalcules" under the microscope, Van Leeuwenhoek claimed to observe two kinds of spermatozoa, one from which the male developed and the other from which the female developed (Tuana 1989, 165). Clearly an example of androcentric bias influencing observation, Van Leeuwenhoek's "seeing" the preformed homunculus in the sperm makes sense in light of the basic belief in the primacy of the male and his active role in reproduction, which fit with social stereotypes regarding the passivity and inferiority of women for the previous 2,000 years.

Notions of gender roles continue to influence descriptions of natural phenomena in modern science. As early as 1948, Ruth Herschberger wrote a most amusing account of fertilization. By reversing the sexes, she drew attention to the extreme activity and importance assigned to the sperm as contrasted with passivity and insignificance given to the role of the egg in fertilization. Developmental biologists have suggested that these same stereotypes of female inferiority and passivity may influence current reproductive and developmental theories. Anthropologist Emily Martin (1991) reviewed the language that science used to describe fertilization in "The Egg and the Sperm: How Science has Constructed a Romance Based on Stereotypical Male-Female Roles" to explore how the gendered language continues to permeate theories of reproduction.

Work on Bacon helped to untangle the role of gender as well as class at the birth of modern science in the 17th century. Nature was deemed female and knowable; the task of the scientist was male domination over nature. Only men could be members of the Royal Society and serve as valid witnesses for scientific experiments. Even when women were allowed to be present during an experiment, their vote did not "count" (Potter 2001). The modern mechanistic notion of science represents a masculine approach to the world by which men are given the authority to dominate and control both women and nature, including discriminating against women scientists by preventing them from receiving a scientific education and training, prohibiting their obtaining posts in laboratories and universities, blocking their admission to professional scientific societies, and defining their work as nonscience and/or not worthy of recognition and reward.

Individuals Who Became Scientists despite Discrimination

Although women have always been in science, all too frequently the work of women scientists has been credited to others, brushed aside and misunderstood, or classified as nonscience. Demonstrating that women have been successful in traditional science is important as it documents that women can do science despite extreme barriers and obstacles.

Ann Sayre's (1975) biography of Rosalind Franklin underscores the fact that the "discovery" of the double helix by Watson and Crick could not have occurred had they not used, without her authorization or knowledge, Franklin's x-ray diffraction picture of DNA. Sayre also revealed, by cleverly emphasizing

Watson's own words from his account of the discovery in *The Double Helix* (1969), the sexist behavior of Watson toward Franklin. Not only did he use her work without her knowledge but he also falsely assumed that she had been brought into the lab to assist Wilkins. In fact, she had been invited to join the group as an equal to Wilkins and held superior experience to his in x-ray diffraction. Sayre records the disparaging comments made by Watson about Franklin's personality and physical and sexual attractiveness. The lack of recognition of Franklin's significant contribution to the double helical model was aided by her discrediting at the hands of a male colleague. He emphasized her unmarried state as an indicator of her difficult personality and sexual unattractiveness rather than as a signal that she wished to pursue a serious career in science.

H. Patricia Hynes (1989) found that Rachel Carson's unmarried status and emphasis on her personal characteristics were also used by her male colleagues to undermine the significance of her work. Hynes chronicles Carson's recognition that pesticides developed for chemical warfare during World War II and marketed as necessary for crop production after the war were biocides harmful to people and animals, although profitable for the chemical industry. Despite the extensive efforts of agribusiness and the chemical industry to discredit Carson's work, her book *Silent Spring* made the public aware of the problem and led ultimately to the establishment of the Environmental Protection Agency (EPA). Hynes's account of Carson reveals a woman whose life was inspired and fulfilled by both her work and her strong friendships with women. Although they rejected the propaganda painted by government and pesticide-industry officials that her work was flawed and exaggerated, Carson's previous male biographers had accepted the negative image of Carson as a lonely spinster.

Despite Barbara McClintock's work in 1931 with Harriet Creighton in which they provided the evidence for crossing over between chromosomes that firmly established her reputation as a geneticist, her work on genetic transposition was neither understood nor accepted. When McClintock finally received the Nobel Prize in Physiology or Medicine in 1983 for the theory, several aspects of her and her work appealed to the scientific and popular media: McClintock's work represented significant discoveries in basic research that had enormous practical applications not anticipated initially; the importance of her work was ignored and misunderstood by her colleagues for almost 40 years; she worked alone without the benefit of sophisticated equipment or substantial funding; and McClintock was a woman scientist who embodied other unusual personal characteristics such as a lack of interest in material personal possessions and a status of being single.

Franklin, Carson, and McClintock exemplify individual women who received recognition as scientists despite having their work devalued or credited to others and not holding secure positions of the type traditionally held by male scientists of their stature. Scholars studying each of these individuals brought to light the particularities of appropriation of Franklin's work by Watson and Crick (Sayre 1975), undermining and discrediting of Carson's work by agribusiness and the chemical industry (Hynes 1989), and failure to understand the significance of McClintock's work on the genetics of complex organisms (Keller 1983). The case studies of these individuals—how the discrimination they experienced prevented them and their research from achieving rewards and the potential they might have—provide an important mechanism for revealing the impact of discrimination against individual women scientists and their careers at a time when discrimination against women scientists was not illegal.

Challenges to Institutional Discrimination against Women as Scientists

Arising from the civil rights movement in the 1960s, the women's movement used legal means to challenge quotas and other forms of institutional and structural discrimination against women. Unlike the professional schools such as law and medicine that had stated quotas limiting the numbers of Jews and women, the admissions criteria and numbers of women, Jews, and racial/ethnic minorities for U.S. graduate schools in science remained vague.

Pieces of legislation such as the Equal Pay Act of 1963 and Title VII of the 1964 Civil Rights Act directly impacted women scientists. Title IX, passed in 1972, applied to all aspects of higher education, not just athletics, as many believe today. Title IX not only made quotas for admission against women in medicine and law illegal but it also led to scrutiny of applications and admissions practices in other parts of the university, including science departments. The finding that the nepotism rules common at most universities—preventing married couples from both holding tenure-track positions—were illegal greatly enhanced the careers of many women scientists. Overnight, many prominent women Ph.D.s who had been relegated to lifetime roles as permanent lecturers or research scientists because they were married to tenured men became tenured full professors.

Removal of nepotism rules especially impacted women scientists since some 60 percent of women scientists are married to men scientists. Obviously, the reverse is not the case or few male scientists would be married. Often these scientific couples meet in graduate school and work in the same subfield. Although removal of nepotism rules lifts the legal prohibition against scientific couples holding tenured positions in the same institution, subtle forms of discrimination continue to serve as barriers to married women seeking these positions. If married couples work and publish on the same problems, the woman's name is usually placed in an inferior position on the paper; this is a result of conventions in the profession or the man's role as head of the laboratory or family decision making, ensuring that he receives credit and promotion.

In some cases, the wife who worked with her husband as a scientist may not have had her name on the publication. The recent controversy surrounding the role of Einstein's first wife, Mileva, in his famous four papers published in 1905 demonstrates the no-name and no-credit phenomenon faced by women scientists who worked with their husbands. Mileva Maric Einstein was the first wife of Albert Einstein and mother of his two sons. Despite the fact that he worked six days per week as a civil servant, during a seven-month time span in 1905, Einstein published four articles in the top European physics journal, *Annalen der Physik*, that provided the framework for 20th-century physics. The first focuses on quantum of light and photoelectric effect, which led to his Nobel Prize in 1921. The second paper gave reasons for Brownian motion and evidence for atomic theory. The third proved the special theory of relativity, and the fourth demonstrated the equivalence of mass and energy, the famous $E = mc^2$ (www.pbs.org/opbeinsteinswife/science/1905htm; retrieved 8/29/06).

Several credible scientists believe that Mileva may have collaborated on some of these papers; Soviet scientist Abram Joffe claims to have seen her name as well as that of Einstein on the 1905 papers. Einstein gave Mileva the money from the Nobel Prize, although they were already divorced. Both the editors of *The Collected Papers of Albert Einstein* and a group from American Association for the Advancement of Science (AAAS) who debated Mileva's contribution failed to definitively weigh in on her role in the 1905 papers. The editors of his papers stated, "We have found no documentary evidence that would demonstrate her active participation in his scientific work, but we do not endorse the view that she took no part in it. We simply do not know" (www.pbs.org/opbeinsteinswife/science/1905htm; retrieved 8/29/06).

Role of the Equal Opportunities Act and National Science Foundation (NSF)

Similar lack of knowledge of their contributions continued to plague women scientists even in the wake of the legislation of the 1960s and 1970s. The intertwining of the gender myths that only men had the ability to become scientists, coupled with the myth of meritocracy for the selection of graduate students and scientists, required data to demonstrate that discrimination existed. The Science and Technology Equal Opportunities Act of 1980 mandated that the NSF collect and analyze data and report to Congress on a biennial basis on the status of women and minorities in the science and engineering professions. Starting in 1982, these biennial reports on women and minorities in science and engineering, to which persons with disabilities were added in 1984, provided the data documenting that science and engineering have lower representation of men of color and women than their proportions in the U.S. population overall. These reports laid the statistical foundation for NSF officials to plan program initiatives to address these underrepresentations.

NSF funded several initiatives targeting various segments of the science and engineering pipeline. Graduate Fellowships for Women provided an incentive for women graduate students to remain in graduate school and complete their Ph.D.s. These fellowships provided support for individual women and their individual research in science and engineering. Career Advancement Awards (CAA), initiated in 1986, focused on advancing the careers of individual women by providing them funds to pursue their own research agendas. By targeting junior women, CAA used a combination of release from teaching and recognition of potential to make a significant research contribution to place these women on a fast track to academic success in science or engineering research.

Visiting Professorships for Women (VPW), initially established in late 1982, sought to retain women who already had faculty appointments in science and engineering and to provide them with research opportunities and exposure to further their careers. The primary thrust of VPW underwrote the research goals and projects of individual women scientists. VPW facilitated women's exposure to new equipment, new approaches, and the different environment of another institution as mechanisms to boost their research and/or provide new exposure.

Although support of research of individual women scientists and engineers served as the predominant focus for the VPW during most of its 14-year history, each VPW was required to spend approximately 30 percent of her time and effort attracting and retaining women scientists and engineers at the institutions they were visiting. VPWs engaged in activities such as forming chapters of the Society of Women Engineers (SWE), establishing mentor networks among women graduate students, and teaching women in science courses jointly with women's studies programs.

Recognizing that efforts to target minorities and White women would not work as long as the system remained unchanged, the Directorate of Education and Human Resources at NSF began to focus on systemic initiatives. NSF established the Program for Women and Girls (PWG) in 1993 to explore comprehensive factors and climate issues that may systematically deter women from science and engineering. In addition to dissemination projects, PWG included two other initiatives for women and girls: Model Projects for Women and Girls (MPWG), short-term highly focused activities that will improve the access to and/or retention of females in science, engineering, and mathematics education and careers, and Experimental Projects for Women and Girls (EPWG), large-scale projects requiring a consortium effort with multiple target populations.

In 1996, NSF replaced VPW with Professional Opportunities for Women in Research and Education (POWRE), giving the first POWRE awards in fiscal year 1997. POWRE was conceived in the wake of the November 1994 Republican sweep of Congress that resulted in cuts in federal spending, with programs that had gender and/or race as their central focus under particular scrutiny. CAA also was subsumed by POWRE in fiscal year 1998. POWRE became a cross-directorate program, with objectives of providing visibility for, encouraging, and providing opportunities for further career advancement, professional growth, and increased prominence of women in engineering and in the disciplines of science supported by NSF. Despite threats against affirmative action, the approach to achieving these objectives came through individual research grants to support science and engineering research of individual women researchers. POWRE did not retain from VPW the concept of committing 30 percent of time devoted to infrastructure to attracting and retaining women in science and engineering.

In 1998, NSF decided to organize a workshop of NSF program directors and scientists and engineers from the professional community to study POWRE and provide recommendations. One recommendation that emerged from the workshop was that "NSF should develop long-term strategies to encourage institutional transformation" (Rosser and Zieseniss 1998, 9).

21st-Century Institutional Transformation

At the dawn of the 21st century, several promising developments indicated the willingness of the scientific and engineering professions and the academy to address the underrepresentation of women in academic ranks that had continued for decades, despite federally and foundation-funded programs to increase the number of female faculty members. In March 1999 the Massachusetts Institute of Technology released "A Study on the Status of Women Faculty in Science at MIT," creating a stir that spread far beyond the boundaries of that institution. Five years earlier, senior biology professor Nancy Hopkins initiated the collection of evidence documenting that the 15 tenured women faculty in science had received lower salaries and fewer resources for research than their male colleagues. Dean Robert Birgeneau recognized that in addition to salary disparities, the data in the report revealed systemic, subtle biases in space, startup packages, and access to graduate students and other resources that inhibited the careers of women scientists relative to their male counterparts. Release of the report struck a nerve with administrators and women faculty on campuses across the nation, fueling questions about the status of women scientists at other academic institutions and in the broader profession.

More than one year later, MIT President Charles Vest hosted a meeting of the presidents, chancellors, provosts, and 25 women scientists from Cal Tech, MIT, University of Michigan, Princeton, Stanford, Yale, University of California at Berkeley, Harvard, and Penn. For the first time, in public and in print, the leaders of the nation's most prestigious research universities suggested that institutional barriers have prevented women scientists and engineers from having a level playing field and that science and engineering might need to change to accommodate women.

In fiscal year 2001, NSF launched the ADVANCE initiative to succeed POWRE. Initially funded at $17 million, ADVANCE encouraged institutional solutions at nine institutions because of "increasing recognition that the lack of women's full participation at the senior level of academe is often a systemic consequence of academic culture" (NSF 2001, 2). Under ADVANCE, Institutional Transformation Awards, as much as $750,000 per year for up to five years, promote the increased participation and advancement of women. Now in its third round of institutional awards, ADVANCE promises to go beyond individual research projects of women scientists and engineers that initiatives such as POWRE, FAW, CAA, and VPW supported to solve problems with broader systemic and institutional roots, such as balancing career and family.

On January 14, 2005, at a conference at the National Bureau of Economic Research at Harvard University, President Larry Summers delivered an infamous speech in which he provided hypotheses for the small number of women holding tenured positions in science and engineering, especially at top universities and research institutions. The transcript of his speech, www .president.harvard.edu/speeches/2005/nber.html, allows individuals to assess the logic and quality of research that he used to support his three primary hypotheses for the paucity of women scientists and engineers: (1) women are unwilling or unable to work the 80-hour weeks required for success in science at top-flight academic institutions; (2) innate or biological factors, rather than socialization, probably account for sex differences in mathematical aptitude and also in adult preferences for choice of academic study and occupational field; (3) discrimination, which he defined as a "taste" for hiring people like oneself, does not exist in academia because that would be eliminated through market forces by lesser institutions hiring highly qualified women and minorities, thereby gaining a competitive advantage. Although President Summers used some questionable and older research studies buttressed with examples from his personal experiences to support his "hypo-theticals," his speech drew national attention to the small number of women who hold tenured positions in science and engineering, especially in "top universities and research institutions." The reports of his resignation in February 2006 focused on Summers's discrimination against women in science as one of the factors leading to the votes of no confidence in him and his ultimate downfall.

In addition to efforts toward institutional transformation to remove discrimination, women scientists and senators have pushed to apply Title IX to women in science and engineering. Chemist Debra Rolison called on the federal government and convinced Senator Wyden of Oregon to hold hearings to investigate the scarcity of women in science and engineering. Violation of Title IX could lead to denial and removal of federal funding, without which no major scientific institution could function.

Conclusion

The current movement to apply Title IX legislation stands as the latest strategy to overcome gender discrimination in science. Notions of women's inferiority have infected scientific observation, leading to inaccurate theories and conclusions drawn from data since antiquity. Such notions prohibited women from serving as witnesses at the birth of early modern science. Since women could not witness science, the discoveries that individual women made were often discredited, attributed to others, or ignored. Notions of inability to witness also provided the legal basis for discrimination against women in academia, especially in science and engineering, until the legislation of the 1960s and 1970s.

Removal of the overall legal barriers to women's participation in science has allowed access and success for many individual women scientists: 199 of the 2,013 active members of the National Academy of Sciences are now women. As this number of less than 10 percent suggests (www.awis.org/pubs/wireArchive/wire), science is still strongly associated with men and masculinity.

It is too early to evaluate the efforts of the current approaches to change the climate, culture, and structure of scientific institutions. Will these institutional transformations result in more women becoming scientists? More importantly, will the absence of discrimination and inclusion of women and other diversity in the pool of scientists lead to the exploration of new questions, different approaches, and ultimately to better science? (*See also* Antiquity; Ecofeminism; Federal Agencies; Nobel Laureates; Universities)

References and Further Reading

Aeschylus. *The Oresteia*. Translated by R. Fagles. New York: Viking Press, 1975.

Association for Women in Science (AWIS). "NRC Releases a New Report on Women in Science and Engineering." http://www.awis.org/pubs/wireArchive/wire. (Accessed May 4, 2006.)

Harvard University. "President's Speeches." http://www.president.harvard.edu/speeches/2005/nber.html. (Accessed May 12, 2005.)

Hynes, H. Patricia. *The Recurring Silent Spring*. Elmsford, NY: Pergamon Press, 1989.

Keller, Evelyn Fox. *A Feeling for the Organism: The Life and Work of Barbara McClintock*. New York: W. H. Freeman, 1983.

Martin, Emily. "The Egg and the Sperm: How Science Has Constructed a Romance Based on Stereotypical Male-Female Roles." *Signs* 16 (3) (1991): 485–501.

National Science Foundation. *ADVANCE Program Solicitation*. Arlington, VA: National Science Foundation, 2001.

Potter, Elizabeth. *Gender and Boyle's Law of Gases*. Bloomington: Indiana University Press, 2001.

Public Broadcasting Service (PBS). "Einstein's Wife." http://www.pbs.orga/opbein stenswife/science/1905. (Accessed August 29, 2006.)

Rosser, Sue V., and Mireille Zieseniss. *Final Report on Professional Opportunities for Women in Research and Education (POWRE) Workshop*. Gainesville, FL: Center for Women's Studies and Gender Research, 1998.

Sayre, Anne. *Rosalind Franklin and DNA*. New York: W. W. Norton, 1975.

Tuana, Nancy. "The Weaker Seed: The Sexist Bias of Reproductive Theory." *Feminism and Science*. Edited by Nancy Tuana. Bloomington: Indiana University Press, 1989.

Watson, James. *The Double Helix*. New York: Atheneum, 1969.

Women Scientists as Leaders

Suzanne Gage Brainard

Despite years of progress that have resulted in increased enrollments, a larger number of degrees granted to women in all fields, and larger percentages of women in the workforce, women still remain a small percentage of those in top leadership positions in any sector of the U.S. workforce. The purpose of this chapter is to highlight women scientists and engineers who are in top leadership positions in educational institutions, federal agencies, and industry. Prior to this, however, it is important to summarize a set of antidiscrimination laws that have enabled these women to succeed.

From the mid-1960s through the 1990s, a series of antidiscrimination laws were implemented that greatly facilitated the career paths of both women and minorities (National Academies 2006). First, Title VII of the Civil Rights Act of 1964 banned discrimination based on sex, race, national origin, and religion by all organizations that employed 15 or more people, regardless of whether these employers received federal funds. Title VII is enforced by the Equal Employment Opportunity Commission, which investigates and resolves discrimination complaints and can bring lawsuits on behalf of claimants. Second, Title IX bans sex discrimination in education for any institutions of higher education that receive federal funds. Third, Executive Order 11246 bans discrimination and requires federal contractors (including universities) to maintain affirmative action plans that set goals and timetables for increasing the representation of women and underrepresented minorities in their workforces. Finally, the Equal Pay Act made it illegal to pay higher salaries to men than to women doing "equal work" or in jobs that require substantially "equal skill, effort, and responsibilities . . . under equal working conditions." Each of these laws, coupled with additional laws in 1990 and early 2000, has substantially helped to level the playing field, but the United States still has a long way to go.

Three reports in the last few years have examined the barriers that women interested in science and engineering face at various stages of their careers. The first of these was a result of the congressional Commission on the Advancement of Women and Minorities in Science, Engineering, and Technology (CAWMSET). CAWMSET investigated the barriers that still exist for women, underrepresented minorities, and persons with disabilities at different stages of the pipeline, and in September 2000, the Commission issued its report, *Land of Plenty: Diversity as America's Competitive Edge in Science, Engineering and Technology* (National Science Foundation). Building on the recommendations of CAWMSET, the Building Engineering and Science Talent (BEST) initiative began in September 2001, and three years later it issued three reports that identified the best practices across the country to develop the technical talent of underrepresented groups in primary, secondary, and higher education and in the workplace (Building Engineering and Science Talent 2004). In 2006, the National Academies issued its report titled *Beyond Bias and Barriers: Fulfilling the Potential of Women in Academic Science and Engineering* (National Academies 2006).

In addition, three indicators of the challenges still facing women in science and engineering (S&E) fields are the numbers of science and engineering doctoral recipients, salaries of women compared to men, and representation in different workforce sectors. Women receive 30.3 percent of all science and engineering doctorates (Commission on Professionals in Science and Technology [CPST] 2004); yet, women receive only 15.9 percent of engineering doctorates. Employed female scientists and engineers with doctorates are represented in four different sectors of the workforce: two-year and four-year institutions, four-year colleges and universities and research universities, government, and business and industry (CPST 2003). Respectively, 15.5 percent of women are employed in two-year institutions, 9.5 percent in four-year and research institutions, 12.7 percent in government, and 62.4 percent in business and industry. Women total 35.6 percent of the entire S&E workforce (CPST 2003).

Finally, there is a significant differential in the median salaries of men and women (CPST 2004) across science and engineering disciplines (see Table 2).

Table 2. Average Salaries of Men and Women in Various Scientific Fields in 2003

	Biological and Related Fields	Computer Information Sciences	Mathematics	Physical Sciences	Engineering Occupations
Men	$75,000	$91,800	$77,000	$83,100	$94,000
Women	$65,000	$80,000	$64,000	$70,000	$85,000

Source: Data derived by CPST from the NSF Foundation/SRS, SESTAT Database System 2003.

Women Scientists as Academic Leaders

Women, especially minority women, are underrepresented in both tenure-track faculty positions in science and engineering and in top leadership positions (Handelsman et al. 2005). Further, women have lower salaries (Trower and Chait 2002), are awarded less grant money (Hosek et al. 2005), and perceive the workplace as unwelcoming and hostile (Olsen, Maple, and Stage 1995). In addition, they are challenged with barriers that most men do not face, such as balance of family and career, hostile department and workplace environment, quality of office and laboratory space, unequal research support, lack of mentoring and collaboration, concerns about spouse or partner hiring, finding childcare options, and other issues. Nevertheless, an increasing number of women are moving into top-level leadership positions in academic institutions, and brief summaries of their career paths follow, all of which are excerpted from their biographies available online.

Mary Sue Coleman (1943–), President, University of Michigan

In August 2002, Mary Sue Coleman was appointed the 13th president of the University of Michigan. At the university, she also holds the appointments of professor of biological chemistry in the medical school and professor of chemistry in the College of Literature, Science, and the Arts. She built a distinguished research career through her work on the immune system and malignancies during 19 years. Dr. Coleman is a national spokesperson for the educational value of affirmative action and diverse perspectives in the classroom.

Drew G. Faust (1947–), President, Harvard University

On July 1, 2007, Drew G. Faust became the 28th and first female president of Harvard University. Her appointment follows the controversy that ensued after Lawrence Summers, Harvard's previous president, suggested that the gender gap in science might be a function of innate differences between men and women (*Washington Post* 2007). She is an expert on the Civil War and the American South. Since 2001, she has served as the founding dean of the Radcliffe Institute for Advanced Study, which has emerged as one of the nation's foremost centers of scholarly and creative enterprise.

Alice P. Gast (1958–), President, Lehigh University

In August 2006, Alice P. Gast became the 13th president of Lehigh University. Dr. Gast earned a bachelor's degree in chemical engineering from the

University of Southern California followed by a master's and doctorate in chemical engineering from Princeton University. After completing her doctorate, she spent a postdoctoral year on a NATO fellowship at the École Supérieure de Physique et de Chimie Industrielles in Paris. Afterward, she spent 16 years as a professor of chemical engineering at Stanford University and at the Stanford Synchrotron Radiation Laboratory. In 2001, she began her tenure at the Massachusetts Institute of Technology as vice president for research and associate provost.

Susan E. Hockfield (1951–), President, Massachusetts Institute of Technology

Since December 2004, Susan E. Hockfield has served as the 16th president of the Massachusetts Institute of Technology and is the first life scientist to hold the position. A noted neuroscientist, she also holds a faculty appointment as professor of neuroscience in the Department of Brain and Cognitive Sciences at MIT. She is a strong advocate for the vital role that science, technology, and the research university play in the world and has worked to extend MIT's long tradition of international engagement through initiatives in education and scholarship with partners around the world.

Karen A. Holbrook (1942–), President, The Ohio State University

In October 2002, Karen A. Holbrook became the 13th president of The Ohio State University. Since she took office, Dr. Holbrook has received wide recognition for her leadership in strengthening relationships with the Columbus community. She spent the majority of her academic career as a professor of biological structure and medicine at the University of Washington and gained a national reputation for her expertise in human fetal skin development and genetic skin disease. After her tenure at the University of Washington, during which time she also served as associate dean for scientific affairs, Dr. Holbrook became vice president for research and dean of the graduate school, as well as professor of anatomy, cell biology, and medicine, at the University of Florida (Gainesville). After that, she was provost at the University of Georgia.

Shirley Ann Jackson (1946–), President, Rensselaer Polytechnic Institute

In July 1999, Shirley Ann Jackson became the 18th president of Rensselaer Polytechnic Institute, the first African American woman to lead a national research university, and the first African American woman elected to the National Academy of Engineering. She is the first African American woman to receive a doctorate from MIT in any subject and is one of the first two African American women to receive a doctorate in physics in the United States. In 1995, President Clinton appointed Dr. Jackson to serve as chairman of the U.S. Nuclear Regulatory Commission (NRC), a position she held until 1999. She is a distinguished scientist and an advocate for education, science, and public policy whose career has encompassed senior positions in government, industry, research, and academe. As a theoretical physicist, she specializes in theoretical condensed matter physics and is best known for her work on polaronic aspects of electrons in two-dimensional systems.

Maria Klawe (1951–), President, Harvey Mudd College

In July 2006, Maria Klawe became the fifth president of Harvey Mudd College. Dr. Klawe has made significant research contributions in several areas of mathematics and computer science, including functional analysis, discrete mathematics, theoretical computer science, human-computer interaction, gender issues in information technology, and interactive multimedia for mathematics education. Her current research focuses on the development and use of multimodal applications to assist people with aphasia and other cognitive impairments. Dr. Klawe spent eight years with IBM Research and two years at the University of Toronto. She then went to the University of British Columbia, where she served as dean of science, vice president of student and academic services, and head of the Department of Computer Science. Dr. Klawe then became the dean of engineering and professor of computer science at Princeton University.

Carolyn W. Meyers (1946–), President, Norfolk State University

In 2007, Carolyn W. Meyers became the fourth president of Norfolk State University. Previously, she served as provost and vice chancellor for academic affairs and a tenured professor in the College of Engineering at North Carolina Agricultural & Technical State University. She holds a bachelor's degree in mechanical engineering from Howard University, a master's in mechanical engineering, and a Ph.D. in chemical engineering from Georgia Tech. She served as the first chair of the board of directors of the National Institute of Aerospace, served as the first associate dean of research for the College of Engineering at Georgia Tech, and was later appointed professor and dean of the College of Engineering at North Carolina A&T University.

Karen W. Morse (1940–), President, Western Washington University

In 1993, Karen W. Morse became the 12th chief executive of Western Washington University. Dr. Morse earned her bachelor's degree from Denison University and a master's and doctorate degree from the University of Michigan. Prior to joining Western, she was provost at Utah State University after serving as a professor of chemistry, head of the Chemistry and Biochemistry Department, and dean of the College of Science. In addition, she is a fellow of the American Association for the Advancement of Science.

Zorica Pantic (1951–), President, Wentworth Institute of Technology

In 2005, Zorica Pantic became the fourth and first female president of the Wentworth Institute of Technology. Dr. Pantic is the only female engineer to lead an institute of technology in the United States. She earned her bachelor's, master's, and doctoral degrees in electrical engineering from the University of Nis in Serbia. She began her career on the faculty of the University of Nis. After receiving a Fulbright scholarship and visiting scientist post at the University of Illinois, she moved to the Division of Engineering at San Francisco State University. She served as a professor of electrical engineering and director of the School of Engineering at SFSU and then became dean of the School of Engineering at the University of Texas–San Antonio.

Donna E. Shalala (1941–), President, University of Miami

In June 2002, Donna E. Shalala became professor of political science and president of the University of Miami. A leading scholar on the political economy of state and local governments, Dr. Shalala has more than 25 years of experience as an accomplished scholar, teacher, and administrator. She also is the longest serving secretary of Health and Human Services (HHS) in United States history. Dr. Shalala received her bachelor's degree in history from Western College for Women and her doctorate from the Maxwell School of Citizenship and Public Affairs at Syracuse University. She has held tenured professorships at Columbia University, the City University of New York, and the University of Wisconsin–Madison. Prior to becoming president of Hunter College in 1980, she served in the Carter administration as assistant secretary for Policy Development and Research at the U.S. Department of Housing and Urban Development. In 1987, Dr. Shalala became chancellor of the University of Wisconsin–Madison and in 1993, President Clinton appointed her U.S.

Political scientist Donna Shalala was appointed president of the University of Miami in 2002, after serving as secretary of the Department of Health and Human Services (HSS) under President Bill Clinton. (U.S. Department of Health and Human Services)

secretary of Health and Human Services (HHS) where she served for eight years.

Shirley M. Tilghman (1946–), President, Princeton University

In May 2001, Shirley M. Tilghman was elected Princeton University's 19th president. She is an exceptional teacher and a world-renowned scholar in the field of molecular biology. During postdoctoral studies at the National Institutes of Health, she made a number of groundbreaking discoveries while participating in cloning the first mammalian gene. She continued to make scientific breakthroughs at the Institute for Cancer Research in Philadelphia at the University of Pennsylvania. In 1986, she came to Princeton as a professor in the life sciences and joined the Howard Hughes Medical Institute two years later. In 1998, she became the founding director of Princeton's multidisciplinary Lewis-Sigler Institute for Integrative Genomics.

Women Scientists as CEOs

Large corporations did not seek out women leaders until the early 1970s and they did so then only as a result of federal laws that were put in place to assure women and minorities equal opportunities in employment. As such,

Table 3. Female CEOs of Fortune 500 Companies, 2007

Name	Company	Rank
Patricia A. Woertz	Archer Daniels Midland	56
Brenda C. Barnes	Sara Lee	111
Mary F. Sammons	Rite Aid	129
Anne Mulcahy	Xerox	142
Patricia F. Russo	Lucent	255
Susan M. Ivey	Reynolds American	280
Andrea Jung	Avon	281
Marion O. Sandler	Golden West Financial	326
Paula G. Rosput Reynolds	Safeco	339
Margaret C. Whitman	eBay	458

Source: CNN (2007).

the profile of the workforce in the late 1960s and early 1970s is much different from that of today. Women make up almost half of the workforce, yet only 20 Fortune 1,000 companies have women in the top position and only 67 of the top 500 companies have any women corporate officers. In addition, only 10 Fortune 500 companies have women CEOs or presidents (see Table 3). It is interesting that among the women in current and past top positions, three were appointed in times of crisis: Carly Fiorina, previous CEO of Hewlett-Packard, Anne Mulcahy of Xerox, and Patricia Russo of Lucent Technologies. As there is little information about the process by which these women became CEOs, the conditions under which they were appointed force us to ask whether they were being set up as scapegoats.

Although the numbers are still low, data from Catalyst, a New York–based not-for-profit research organization, do indicate positive change over the last 10 years. For instance, in 1995, 8.7 percent of corporate officers in Fortune 500 companies were women, a number that had increased to 16.4 percent by 2005. Also, more women are running Fortune 500 companies in 2007 than in 2006. Two of these women, Margaret Whitman and Brenda Barnes, have undergraduate degrees in economics and MBAs, while the others hold MBAs (see Table 3).

Brenda Barnes (1953–), CEO, Sara Lee

Brenda C. Barnes is chairman and CEO of Sara Lee Corporation. She has been a member of the board of directors of Sara Lee since joining the company as president and CEO in July 2004. She was appointed to her current position in

October 2005. She earned a bachelor's degree in economics from Augustana College in 1975 and received a master of business administration degree from Loyola University Chicago in 1978.

Meg Whitman (1957–), President and CEO, eBay

As president and CEO of eBay since March 1998, Meg Whitman has led the company to become an unparalleled global e-commerce engine. Whitman's expertise in brand building, combined with her consumer technology experience, has helped eBay evolve into a leading company that is reshaping online commerce, payments, and communications around the world. She received a bachelor's degree in economics from Princeton University and a master's in business administration from Harvard Business School.

Women Scientists as Leaders of Federal Agencies

The federal government was among the first in all sectors of the workforce to implement Equal Employment Opportunity programs to assure women and minorities fair and just assessment of their skills. As a result, many women and minorities are employed in federal agencies and have been since the early 1960s. However, few women scientists are or have been in the mid- and top-level cabinet positions, such as Joycelyn Elders, M.D., former U.S. surgeon general. Following are biographies of these few women.

Rita R. Colwell (1934–), Ph.D., Director, National Science Foundation

Dr. Colwell was appointed the 11th director of the National Science Foundation on August 4, 1998, and resigned in 2004. Under her leadership, the Foundation received significant budget increases, and its funding reached more than $5.3 billion. Before coming to NSF, Dr. Colwell was president of the University of Maryland Biotechnology Institute, 1991–1998. She remains professor of microbiology and biotechnology at the University of Maryland. She was also a member of the National Science Board from 1984 to 1990. She is the recipient of numerous awards, including the Medal of Distinction from Columbia University, the Gold Medal of Charles University in Prague, the UCLA Medal from the University of California, and the Alumna Summa Laude Dignata from the University of Washington, Seattle.

Elaine L. Chao (1953–), Secretary of Labor

Elaine Chao is the 24th secretary of labor and the first Asian American woman appointed to a president's cabinet in the United States. Prior to joining the U.S. cabinet, she was president and chief executive officer of the United Way of America and director of the Peace Corps. Her government service includes terms as deputy secretary of the U.S. Department of Transportation, chairman of the Federal Maritime Commission, and deputy maritime administrator in the U.S. Department of Transportation. Chao has an M.B.A. from the Harvard Business School and an undergraduate degree in economics from Mount Holyoke College.

Julie Louise Gerberding (1955–), M.D., M.P.H., Director of Centers for Disease Control

Director Julie Louise Gerberding, M.D., M.P.H., has been head of the Centers for Disease Control and Prevention (CDC) and administrator of the Agency for Toxic Substances and Disease Registry (ATSDR) since July 2002. She also serves as an associate clinical professor of medicine at Emory University and an associate professor of medicine at the University of California at San Francisco.

Cynthia A. Glassman, Ph.D., Under Secretary for Economic Affairs, Department of Commerce

Dr. Glassman was appointed by President Bush in October 2006 as under secretary for economic affairs in the Department of Commerce. Prior to her nomination, she served as commissioner on the U.S. Securities and Exchange Commission from January 2002 until 2006. She received her M.A. and Ph.D. in economics from the University of Pennsylvania and her B.A. in economics from Wellesley College.

Women Scientists as Leaders in Associations and Private Foundations

Several women scientists have played significant leadership roles in professional associations and private foundations by helping to change federal policy.

Shirley Malcom (1946–), Head, Directorate for Education and Human Resources at AAAS

Shirley Malcom is head of the Directorate for Education and Human Resources Programs of the American Association for the Advancement of Science (AAAS), where she leads programs in education, activities for underrepresented groups, and public understanding of science and technology. Dr. Malcom is a former trustee of the Carnegie Corporation of New York. She served on the National Science Board from 1994 to 1998 and on the President's Committee of Advisors on Science and Technology from 1994 to 2001. Dr. Malcom received her doctorate in ecology from Pennsylvania State University; her master's degree in zoology from the University of California, Los Angeles; and her bachelor's degree with distinction in zoology from the University of Washington.

Maxine Singer (1931–), Ph.D., President, Carnegie Institution

A product of the New York City public schools, Maxine Frank Singer graduated from Swarthmore College (A.B., 1952, with high honors) and Yale University (Ph.D., biochemistry, 1957). She joined the National Institutes of Health as a postdoctoral fellow in 1956 and received a research staff appointment two years later. She was chief, Laboratory of Biochemistry, National Cancer Institute, 1980–1987, where she led 15 research groups engaged in various biochemical investigations. She became president of the Carnegie Institution in 1988 and retains her association with the National Cancer Institute as scientist emeritus. Throughout her career, Singer has taken leading roles influencing and refining the nation's science policy, often in realms having social, moral, or ethical implications.

References and Further Reading

Building Engineering and Science Talent. "The Talent Imperative: Diversifying America's Science and Engineering Workforce." April 2004. http://www.bestworkforce .org/PDFdocs/BESTTalentImperative_FullReport.pdf. (Accessed March 13, 2007.)

CNN. "Women CEOs for FORTUNE 500 Companies." http://money.cnn.com/ magazines/fortune/fortune500/womenceos/. (Table was compiled with information from the CNN Study for 2006; accessed March 13, 2007.)

Commission on the Advancement of Women and Minorities in Science, Engineering, and Technology Development. *Land of Plenty: Diversity as America's Competitive Edge in Science, Engineering and Technology*. Washington, DC: National Science Foundation, 2000.

Commission on Professionals in Science and Technology (CPST). "Employed Scientists & Engineers by Field of Highest Degree Attained, Employment Sector, Sex, and Race/Ethnicity, October 1, 2003." Data derived from National Science Foundation/ SRS, SESTAT Database System.

Commission on Professionals in Science and Technology (CPST). "Median Annual Salaries of Full-Time Employed Doctoral Scientists and Engineers by Sector of Employment, Broad Occupation and Sex, 2003." Data derived from the National Science Foundation, 2003 Survey of Doctorate Recipients.

Commission on Professionals in Science and Technology (CPST). "Doctorates by Broad Field, Decade and Sex, 1920 to 2004." Data derived from the National Research Council, *A Century of Doctorates and Doctorate Records Files,* and the National Science Foundation, *Science and Engineering Degrees: 1950–80,* and *Science and Engineering Doctorate Awards, 2004* and earlier editions.

Department of Commerce. "Cynthia A. Glassman Sworn in as Commerce Department's Under Secretary for Economic Affairs." http://www.commerce.gov/opa/ press/Secretary_Gutierrez/2006_Releases/December/04_Glassman_Sworn_In_rls .htm. (Accessed March 13, 2007.)

Handelsman, J., N. Cantor, M. Carnes, D. Denton, E. Fine, B. Grosz, V. Hinshaw, C. Marrett, S. Rosser, D. Shalala, and J. Sheridan. "More Women in Science." *Science* 309 (2005): 1190–1191.

Hosek, S. D., A. G. Cox, B. Ghosh-Dastiar, A. Kofner, N. Ramphal, J. Scott, and S. H. Berry. *Gender Differences in Major Federal External Grant Programs.* Washington, DC: Rand, 2005.

National Academies. *Beyond Bias and Barriers: Fulfilling the Potential of Women in Academic Science and Engineering.* Edited by Donna E. Shalala et al. Washington, DC: National Academies Press, 2006.

Olsen, D., S. A. Maple, and F. K. Stage. "Women and Minority Faculty Job Satisfaction: Professional Role Interests, Professional Satisfactions, and Institution Fit." *Journal of Higher Education* 66 (1995): 267–293.

Trower, Cathy A., and Richard P. Chait. "Faculty Diversity: Too Little for Too Long." *Harvard Magazine,* March–April 2002. http://www.harvardmagazine.com/on-line/ 030218. (Accessed March 13, 2007.)

Washington Post. "Harvard Chief's Comments on Women Assailed" http://www .washingtonpost.com/wp-dyn/articles/A19181–2005Jan18.html. (Accessed March 14, 2007.).

Nobel Laureates

Joyce Tang

Introduction

Since its inception in 1901, the Nobel Prize has been awarded to 33 women and 735 men in recognition of their contributions to science, literature, and humanitarian causes. Women constitute 4 percent of the Nobel laureates. Twelve of the 34 awards that women received were in science (35 percent): Marie Curie (received the Prize twice), Gerty Cori, Irene Joliot-Curie, Barbara McClintock, Maria Goeppert-Mayer, Rita Levi-Montalcini, Dorothy Hodgkin, Gertrude Elion, Rosalyn Yalow, Christiane Nusslein-Volhard, and Linda Buck. On average, one award has gone to a female scientist every nine years (see Table 4).

The small number of women among the laureates does not allow conclusions to be drawn about the relative influences of various forces underlying the (lack of) success of women in science, but clearly there is no typical female laureate. The experiences of these women reveal flaws in the biological, economical, and cultural myths about gender differences in science performance.

This essay highlights the similarities and differences in this elite group of female scientists by examining their backgrounds, upbringing, and support mechanisms. It highlights common themes in their lives and work using a life course approach, and concludes with a brief discussion of the implications for research and policy making.

Most of the books about female scientists tell us that women are not doing as well as men in science (Tang 2006). The arguments for women's relatively lackluster performance in science range from biological causes to individual choice to structural elements. These explanations for gender differences in science can be discouraging to the large numbers of female students who have already enrolled in science and mathematics courses.

Three explanations have been proposed to address the important question of why women have a difficult time excelling in science compared to men. The biological explanation stresses women's lack of abilities to pursue intellectual

Table 4. Female Nobel Laureates in Science, 1901–2006

Name	Field	Year of Birth	Country of Birth (adopted country)	Year Nobel Prize Awarded (age received prize)	Area(s)	Prize Co-recipient(s) and Relationship
Marie Curie	Physicist, Radiochemist	1867–1934	Poland (France)	1903 (36)	Physics	Henri Becquerel, Pierre Curie (husband)
Marie Curie				1911 (44)	Chemistry	n/a
Gerty Cori	Biochemist	1896–1957	Czech/Austria (U.S.)	1947 (51)	Physiology or Medicine	Carl Cori (husband)
Irene Joliot-Curie	Radiochemist	1897–1956	France	1935 (38)	Chemistry	Frederic Joliot Curie (husband)
Barbara McClintock	Geneticist	1902–1992	United States	1983 (81)	Physiology or Medicine	n/a
Maria Goeppert-Mayer	Mathematical Physicist	1906–1972	Germany (U.S.)	1963 (57)	Physics	J. H. D. Jensen
Rita Levi-Montalcini	Neuroembryologist	1909–	Italy (U.S.)	1986 (77)	Physiology or Medicine	Stanley Cohen
Dorothy Hodgkin	Crystallographer	1910–1994	Britain	1964 (54)	Chemistry	n/a
Gertrude Elion	Biochemist	1918–1999	United States	1988 (70)	Physiology or Medicine	James W. Black, George Hitchings
Rosalyn Yalow	Medical Physicist	1921–	United States	1977 (56)	Physiology or Medicine	n/a
Christiane Nusslein-Volhard	Developmental Biologist	1942–	Germany	1995 (53)	Physiology or Medicine	Eric Wieschaus, Edward B. Lewis
Linda Buck	Neuroscientist	1947–	United States	2004 (57)	Physiology or Medicine	Richard Axel

Source: Nobel Foundation (2007).

tasks. According to the individual choice explanation, women express a general preference for nonscience careers. The structural explanation attributes the virtual absence of women in science to institutional obstacles. None of these views encourages young women aspiring to science careers. But the life, work, and career histories of female Nobel laureates in science reveal another side of the story.

Who Are These Women Nobel Laureates in Science?

Not only are these women pioneers in research but they are also "the" first women to receive almost every prestigious honor and recognition from the scientific establishment. In many ways, they are the lady version of Albert Einstein. Trained in the principles and practices of science, these female laureates demonstrated the drive, discipline, and energy to test new ideas continuously. Their discoveries saved lives or transformed the direction of a particular line of research, resulting in substantial recognition for their contributions to society. They emerge as role models for young scientists.

The female laureates overcame numerous (yet different) barriers at different stages of their careers. They lived very different lives, in different times and places. The educational, governmental, and social structures (such as marriage and family) vary tremendously among Poland, France, England, Germany, and the United States, and between the 1860s (when Marie Curie was born) and the 1940s (when Christiane Nusslein-Volhard and Linda Buck were born). In addition to their passion for science, they share many qualities considered essential in doing pioneering work:

1. Very early in the lives and careers of these women, their actions reflected intelligence, courage, discipline, enthusiasm, competitiveness, ability to focus and concentrate, ambition, confidence, risk-taking, assertiveness, and creative thinking and work styles.
2. Many showed exceptional academic abilities in childhood.
3. They were persistent and consistent in expressing their purposes and values of life.
4. They always took initiatives to improve themselves through training and development.
5. They had the ability to adapt to changes and deal with adversity and setbacks in a positive way.
6. Willing to take risk and face loss, they were prepared to make significant personal and professional sacrifices in pursuit of science.

Although these qualities would help almost anyone to overcome obstacles in life and work, these intangible and nonlinear attributes take on greater significance for women for overcoming many obstacles with family, school, and work.

Marie Curie

Despite and because of her humble background, physicist and radiochemist Marie Curie had an optimistic outlook on life and work. She viewed adversity and barriers in life as challenges and opportunities for growth and demonstrated bold ambitions. Instead of giving up any hope for higher education, she supported her older sister Bronya through medical school in Paris. Bronya in turn later helped to support Curie's university education.

Curie chose radioactivity as the subject of her doctoral dissertation and the focus of her future research. Henri Becquerel's discovery of the release of rays from uranium had drawn little attention from the scientific community. Curie seized the opportunity to study this neglected topic. Her discovery of radioactivity (with her husband Pierre Curie) broke new ground for research in the field of physics, bringing fame in 1903 when she became the first woman Nobel laureate. She received her second Nobel Prize in chemistry for her discovery of radium eight years later; she remains the only female to win two Nobel Prizes. Challenges Curie faced included studying in the intimidating environment of a private school in Russian-controlled Poland, being a widow and a single parent for two young daughters, exclusion from the most prestigious scientific institution in France, and denial of adequate support for research. She estimated that a properly equipped laboratory would have allowed her and Pierre to compress four years of work into one, minimizing their exposure to radiation (Curie 1937; Curie 1923).

Marie Curie grew up in an impoverished but professional home. Her mother was the principal of a private girls' school; her father was a physics teacher at a secondary school for boys in Warsaw. Her parents took the education of their children very seriously. She named her father as the most important figure in her life (Quinn 1995, 74). Curie's brother, Josef, observed that none of his three sisters (Helena, Bronya, and Marie) seemed to fit the role of a young girl typical for that time. They all prepared to postpone marriage or remain single to acquire higher education, and they planned to have independent careers.

Even someone as reclusive as Marie Curie had a great deal of support. Her supporters included American men and East European women. The Radium Institute became her professional base. She enjoyed an egalitarian scientific partnership with her husband Pierre Curie. After his death in an accident, her father-in-law Dr. Eugene Curie moved into the household and helped raise his

Polish-born French physicist Marie Curie. Curie shared the 1903 Nobel Prize in physics with her husband, Pierre, and Antoine Henri Becquerel for their discovery of radioactivity. She was also the sole winner of the 1911 Nobel Prize in chemistry. (Library of Congress)

granddaughters, Irene and Eve. His generosity allowed Marie Curie to study and research with little interruption. Though she shunned publicity and politicking in France, Curie had successful fund-raising tours in the United States spearheaded by an American journalist, Marie Meloney. In addition to running the Radium Institute, she became more active in public and professional communities later in life. Curie participated in war efforts and was also involved in the League of Nations' International Committee on Intellectual Cooperation. She always kept her ties with Albert Einstein and other leading figures in the scientific community.

Gerty Cori

Biochemist Gerty Cori, the first female laureate in medicine or physiology, shared striking similarities with Marie Curie. Both set an example of successful scientific partnerships with their husbands while also raising families. Both suffered the humiliation of being ignored or overlooked by the scientific establishment but demonstrated the stamina and perseverance required for a woman to succeed in a man's enterprise. Both helped produce the next generation of Nobel winners. Marie Curie groomed her daughter Irene Joliot-Curie and indirectly her son-in-law Frederic Joliot to be potential laureates. Cori's laboratory, a major center for biochemical research, was home to five future Nobel laureates: Severo Ochoa (1958 Nobel Prize in medicine), Arthur Kornberg (1958 Nobel Prize in medicine), Earl W. Sutherland Jr. (1971 Nobel Prize in medicine), Christian deDuve (1974 Nobel Prize in medicine), and Luis Leloir (1970 Nobel Prize in chemistry).

Cori overcame numerous obstacles in life and work. She had to take remedial required courses such as Latin, science, and mathematics to qualify as one of the few women entering medical school. Antinepotism rules prevented her from obtaining employment commensurate with her education and experience, resulting in underemployment for most of her life and strong resistance from employers and colleagues. The numerous appointments, recognitions, and honors that went solely to her husband and scientific partner Carl Cori for their collaborative work did not stop her and her husband from making joint discoveries with implications for the treatment of diabetes and other diseases. She was recognized belatedly with appointments to full professorships and other scientific honors for significant study of enzymes and hormones. In 1947, Gerty and Carl Cori shared the Nobel Prize for their discovery of the course of the catalytic conversion of glycogen. Even after being diagnosed with bone marrow disease requiring numerous blood transfusions, she maintained a grueling work schedule (McGrayne 1998).

Gerty Cori came from a relatively wealthy family and was the eldest of three daughters. Her father managed several sugar refineries. She was tutored at home until the age of 10 when she entered a private girls' school. Born in Prague, she was educated at the medical school of the German University of Prague (Carl Ferdinand University) where she met her future husband and lifelong collaborator Carl Cori. They moved to Vienna upon graduation. When Vienna could not house their ambition, they took up employment in New York. They eventually settled in Missouri. Her maternal uncle, a professor of pediatrics, encouraged Cori to attend the university, specializing in medicine. It was unusual at the time in American higher education for her to work with her husband side-by-side as an equal partner. She was among the first group of women to break this rule. With Carl Cori, she ran a productive laboratory while running a household and raising her son.

Gerty Cori worked in institutions throughout her life. First, she held an assistant position at the Karolinen Children's Hospital in Vienna. Second, she joined her husband Carl Cori at the State Institute for the Study of Malignant Diseases in Buffalo as an assistant pathologist and later as assistant biochemist. Carl Cori turned down several job offers when the universities refused to hire his wife. Finally, when the couple moved to Washington University in St. Louis, Missouri, she first was appointed as a research fellow and then research associate. She became associate professor of research in 1942 and full professor in 1947, the year she won the Nobel Prize. Her (under)employment at various institutions gave her resources (laboratory, equipment, library, personnel) to do research, the opportunity to build up her publication record, and the forum for intellectual exchanges with peers and scholars.

Irene Joliot-Curie

Marie Curie shared similarities with her daughter, radiochemist Irene Joliot-Curie. Like her mother, Joliot-Curie also studied mathematics and physics, worked in the same field (radioactivity), studied alpha rays of polonium (an element discovered by her mother) for her doctoral topic, and married, collaborated, and had children with a scientific spouse. She worked her entire career at the Radium Institute founded by her mother, was rejected repeatedly for admission into the French Academy of Sciences, and received a Nobel Prize with her husband Frederic Joliot, a protégé handpicked by her mother. Brought up in a scientific family, Joliot-Curie demonstrated early scientific talent. Despite her privileged childhood, her life was not easy. At the age of nine, she lost her father, forcing her to cope with the stress of her widowed mother's grief and subsequently, the public's criticism of her mother's relationship with fellow scientist Paul Langevin. For most of her adult life, while a leading scientist, wife, and mother she suffered a life-threatening case of tuberculosis (Crossfield 1997; McGrayne 1998).

Irene Joliot-Curie came from a scientific dynasty. Her grandfathers were highly educated, and she was the eldest daughter of the recipients of three Nobel prizes, Marie and Pierre Curie. She grew up with the children of prominent scientists, many of whom were her parents' colleagues or close friends. Joliot-Curie, along with her younger sister Eve, was educated in a private cooperative (secondary school) set up by her mother and colleagues. Thus, she learned every day from the most distinguished scholars and scientists in their fields. She expected and received support from her parents' friends and colleagues. As mentor and collaborator, her widowed mother was the most critical person in Joliot-Curie's career. Like her mother, Joliot-Curie intended to have a family and scientific career in her life. The second most important figure for Joliot-Curie was her grandfather who helped shape her moral and intellectual development.

The Radium Institute served as the training ground as well as professional home for Irene Joliot-Curie. She had two successful scientific partnerships. The first one, a maternal partnership with her widowed mother, lasted for decades. The second, a spousal partnership with her protégé, future husband, and later co-winner of the Nobel Prize in chemistry in 1935, lasted for about five years, after which they took positions at different institutions. In the former, Joliot-Curie was the apprentice and successor of Marie Curie; a role reversal took place in the latter when she became the master of a novice scientist Frederic Joliot. Her first and only experience of being excluded from the scientific establishment was her unsuccessful nomination for the French Academy of Sciences.

Barbara McClintock

Geneticist Barbara McClintock did not show early promise as an outstanding academic. She earned an overall B average as an undergraduate at Cornell University in Ithaca, New York. Her risk-taking and persistence became evident when she focused on maize, an unusual research subject. Her passion for science and commitment to work are notorious in the scientific community, making her brilliance and capacity to see what no one else saw hard to ignore (Fedoroff 1996, 591). Before making Cold Spring Harbor in Long Island, New York, her professional home, McClintock had many unpleasant experiences at the University of Missouri and other academic institutions.

The mother of Barbara McClintock was an amateur painter and poet. Her father was a medical doctor. Compared to the parental influence of other female laureates, the McClintocks played a strong but less direct role in their daughter's education. Being afraid that her daughter would become a professor, her mother had reservations about her daughter attending college. She reluctantly yielded to her husband's decision that Barbara McClintock would go to Cornell University. McClintock did not think that her parents had directly supported her intellectual pursuits. In fact, she did not consider them, or anyone else, as role models. From the beginning, her parents raised McClintock as a boy. They changed her original name, "Eleanor," to "Barbara" for they considered the former a feminine and delicate name and the latter a more masculine name, which seemed to fit their daughter better. Her mother did not stop her from ice-skating, roller skating, bicycling, and playing basketball with boys. Her father gave her a set of boxing gloves when she was four. When she lived with her relatives in Massachusetts as a toddler, her uncle taught McClintock to repair machinery and nurtured her love for nature (McGrayne 1998). All this helped develop and strengthen McClintock's need for freedom and independence throughout her life and career.

Even independent Barbara McClintock also needed continuous support for her pioneering research on maize. As a Carnegie Institute employee, she did not need to apply for federal grants, but her professional home was Cold Spring Harbor, a research and conference center on Long Island, New York. McClintock's approach to research and scholarship provides a stark contrast to that of most female laureates. Fiercely independent and never married, she enjoyed working alone. She was selective in cultivating formal and informal ties for career advancement. Relying on lifelong friendships with a few male

The sole winner of the 1983 Nobel Prize in physiology or medicine, Barbara Mc-Clintock is considered one of the most important geneticists of the 20th century. (Barbara McClintock Papers, American Philosophical Society)

colleagues such as Marcus Rhoades and George Beadle, she was able to tap into the scientific community's resources. Rollins A. Emerson, a renowned maize geneticist and head of the breeding plant department, brought Rhoades and Beadle to Cornell. When others were lukewarm to McClintock's research, these two talented graduate students found her cytological work exciting. Together, this trio formed a formidable cross-sex research team, and they all benefited from their professional kinship (Rhoades became a leading geneticist and Beadle shared a Nobel Prize in physiology in 1958). Despite the idiosyncrasies of her personality, McClintock had her cheerleaders. Lewis Stadler, a colleague of Emerson at Cornell, found her an assistant professor position at the University of Missouri. Support from Carnegie President Vannevar Bush solidified her research position at Cold Spring Harbor. She became the third woman to be an elected member of the prestigious National Academy of Sciences when both Stadler and Emerson held membership there. Besides having regular contacts with her male friends, she consulted extensively with Harriet Creighton, a fellow graduate student and lifelong friend.

Maria Goeppert-Mayer

Few in the scientific community would see mathematical physicist Maria Goeppert-Mayer as a formidable rival. Her unassuming style won her friends and loyal supporters as well as respect from colleagues. A late bloomer, Goeppert-Mayer learned nuclear physics from scratch and worked with renowned figures in the field such as Enrico Fermi and Edward Teller. Of all the female laureates, she worked the longest without pay and formal recognition. Due to antinepotism rules since she was married to Joseph Mayer, who was on the faculty at Johns Hopkins, then Columbia, and then the University of Chicago, for decades she became a "serial volunteer researcher/teacher." The knowledge and skills she acquired from learning and working with a group of leading scientists at top research institutions facilitated her award-winning work on the shell model of the nucleus. In addition to being a woman physicist, wife, and mother, who worked without pay or recognition, she was frequently second-guessed, partly because of her tendency to procrastinate (Dash 1973; McGrayne 1998).

As Maria Goeppert-Mayer was the only child in a well-educated upper-class family, her parents expected her to receive a good education and eventually to be economically independent. Her mother taught French and piano before marriage, and her father was a professor of pediatrics at the University of Gottingen in Germany. Goeppert-Mayer was brought up in an intellectual environment very similar to that of Irene Joliot-Curie. She grew up in a university town populated by distinguished scholars and scientists. Many close family friends were prominent mathematicians and physicists. Very early in life, her father made it clear that his daughter should "never become just a woman." She adopted her father's low opinion of women. Her parents encouraged her to be curious and adventurous. Her father took her on science walks. On her father's side, she was the seventh generation of a family of university professors.

Maria Goeppert-Mayer had a paid job as a senior physicist at Argonne National Laboratory outside Chicago. Before landing a job at the University of Chicago's Fermi Institute and later at the University of California in La Jolla, she was a volunteer researcher or lecturer at two other top research universities— Johns Hopkins and Columbia. Like Irene Joliot-Curie, Goeppert-Mayer was used to seeing and interacting with intellectuals and their offspring. Besides having her father as her strongest supporter from childhood to young adulthood, she stayed extremely well connected throughout her career. In fact, Goeppert-Mayer's champions were among the who's who in physics. For example, three Nobel laureates sat on her doctoral examining committee (James Frank received the 1925 Nobel Prize in physics, Adolf Windaus was awarded the 1928 Nobel Prize in chemistry, and mentor Max Born received the 1954

Maria Goeppert-Mayer won the Nobel Prize in physics in 1963 for developing a nuclear shell model. (Nobel Foundation)

Nobel Prize in physics). Robert Oppenheimer, Victor Weisskopf, Max Delbruck, and Harold Frey were her friends. She was a member of Enrico Fermi's research team at Chicago (Fermi was a co-recipient of the Nobel Prize in 1963 with Eugene Wigner), and his innocent probing—What about spin-orbit couple?—helped her solve the mystery of the nuclear shell structure problem.

Similar to Marie Curie's situation, her scientific husband, Joseph Mayer, was the most important supporter in her professional life. Joe Mayer supported Goeppert-Mayer to continue her work in physics. However, unlike Pierre Curie, Joe Mayer played the role of a facilitator instead of collaborator.

Rita Levi-Montalcini

Despite very limited resources and little support, neuroembryologist Rita Levi-Montalcini also accomplished significant scientific research. She conducted experiments in a makeshift laboratory set up in her tiny bedroom (Liversidge 1988, 73). This clandestine bedroom experimental laboratory served as a springboard for the discovery of nerve growth factor. Levi-Montalcini described herself as having "just average intelligence," but she attributed her success in science to her ability to underestimate the difficulties of present tasks. Levi-Montalcini encountered racial and gender barriers. Anti-Semitism against Jews in Italy during the war caused Levi-Montalcini to lose her research assistant job, to be prohibited from practicing medicine, and to find no scientific journals in Italy that would publish her work (Levi-Montalcini 1988).

Rita Levi-Montalcini was born into an educated middle-class family. Her father was an engineer by training. Unlike McClintock's mother, Levi-Montalcini's mother fully supported her decision to study medicine. It was her father who had early reservations about her academic ambition because of difficulties for women in combining family and career. Nonetheless, he hired tutors to prepare her for university entrance examinations. Like Barbara McClintock, Levi-Montalcini unequivocally rejected the traditional gender roles for women. She did not want to be a wife and mother. She showed a passion for trains as a child and had no interest in feminine pursuits. Levi-Montalcini acknowledged the enduring influence of her father on her personal development (Levi-Montalcini 1988, 16–17), but her mother urged Levi-Montalcini to accept the invitation from embryologist Viktor Hamburger to go to Washington University in St. Louis, her professional home for almost three decades.

While she was still in Europe, she studied under Giuseppe Levi (no relation) at the Institute of Anatomy of the Turin Medical School. He was a role model for Levi-Montalcini, one of his three students who received Nobel Prizes in medicine (Salvador Edward Luria in 1969 and Renato Dulbecco in 1975).

Her networking strategies bear striking resemblance to those of McClintock. Levi-Montalcini formed lifelong friendships and later partnerships with a few influential male scientists. She sought advice from Luria and Dulbecco about her projects. They introduced her to up-and-coming and renowned scientists such as James Watson. Her correspondence with Luria paid off with a flattering recommendation that led to an invitation from Viktor Hamburger in St. Louis for Levi-Montalcini in Italy to reconcile apparently different findings of Hamburger's and Levi-Montalcini's experiments. Her work with Hamburger at Washington University laid the foundation for her prize-winning research on the nerve growth factor. Another close friend and colleague was Stanley Cohen, a postdoctoral research fellow at Washington University who later shared the Nobel Prize with Levi-Montalcini in 1986 for their discoveries of growth factors. Throughout her career, she continued to cultivate ties within and outside the United States. Later in her career, she commuted between St. Louis and Rome every six months to run research laboratories set up in both countries.

Dorothy Hodgkin

A master of making minute observations as well as synthesizing divergent information, crystallographer Dorothy Hodgkin helped discover penicillin,

Vitamin B_{12}, and insulin. Like other female laureates, she chose research topics no one else had tackled (Wolpert and Richards 1988, 72). While Joliot-Curie battled tuberculosis throughout her life, Hodgkin dealt with constant pain and discomfort in her hands crippled by arthritis in childhood. Considerably behind in arithmetic in secondary school, she worked hard to catch up. Excluded from the chemistry club and weekly research talks at Oxford, Hodgkin made holiday visits to mentor and collaborator Desmond Bernal to keep up with the latest developments in the field of crystallography in his laboratory. Since her husband Thomas Hodgkin did not have stable employment, Dorothy Hodgkin supported the family (Ferry 1998).

The families of Dorothy Hodgkin's parents were relatively well off. Her grandfather studied classics at Oxford before serving as a missionary in India. Her parents were archaeologists. As a result, family dislocations and separations from her parents were a fact in Hodgkin's childhood and adolescence. As a child, she traveled to the countryside with her younger sisters, all by themselves, to explore nature. She carried out simple chemical experiments in the attic laboratory at home. As Dorothy was the oldest in a family of three girls with no sons, her father decided to educate her the same way as a son. In addition to tutoring her daughters at home whenever possible, her mother sparked Hodgkin's interest in science. For example, she gave Hodgkin a children's book by William Henry Bragg. Bragg and his son were co-recipients of the 1915 Nobel Prize in physics for their contribution to the study of crystal structures by x-rays. At home, her mother also taught Hodgkin and her sister all the subjects she knew. Her father was instrumental in getting Hodgkin into Oxford to study chemistry in 1928. Hodgkin followed the example of her parents as well as Marie Curie, Irene Joliot-Curie, and Maria Goeppert-Mayer in having both a marriage and a scientific career.

Dorothy Hodgkin pursued her postdoctoral work at Cambridge under the supervision of John Desmond Bernal, a leading figure in the field of crystallography. Her whole career was built on her position at Somerville College, a women's college. Hodgkin succeeded in building extensive global contacts that were related to her interests in science, education, and world peace. Similar to Levi-Montalcini, word of mouth resulted in Hodgkin's working in Bernal's laboratory in 1932. As her mentor, Bernal gave Hodgkin free rein in his laboratory. He put her name on his papers to which she had made some contribution. This enabled her to build her publishing record and attract attention from the scientific community. Through Bernal, she met many interesting people from other fields. As director of studies at Somerville College for science students at Oxford, she had the opportunity to develop ties with scientists across disciplines. She continued to enlist the help of others throughout her career. Support from her husband in child rearing and other family matters allowed Hodgkin to concentrate on her work.

Gertrude Elion

Inspired by Marie Curie, other discoverers, and the deaths of her grandfather
and fiancée, biochemist Gertrude Elion became a chemical researcher to save
lives. Elion proved the most versatile female laureate in overcoming hurdles
in life and work. The huge financial loss her father experienced as a result of
the Great Depression substantially impacted her educational goals. Discrimination from higher educational institutions and employers forced Elion into
marginal and temporary jobs to support her graduate studies; she left graduate school before finishing her doctorate. For the discoveries of new drugs
that saved lives, she shared the 1988 Nobel Prize in physiology or medicine
with George Hitchings and Eric Wieschaus. Because her fiancée statistician
Leonard Canter died of bacterial infection in 1941, Elion was never married.
She led an active social life, surrounded by her nieces, nephews, and children
of her colleagues. Unlike Levi-Montalcini, Elion held the view that women
can have a family and career (McGrayne 1988).

Gertrude Elion grew up in a middle-class immigrant family in New York
City. Her mother came from a scholarly family; her father was a dentist. She
accompanied her grandfather (a biblical scholar) to the park and listened to
his stories. Her father regularly took her to Metropolitan Opera performances.
Elion's close relationship with her grandfather was very similar to Joliot-Curie's
relationship with her grandfather Eugene Curie. Elion and her younger brother
Herbert were expected to go to college. Her mother encouraged Elion to have
a career and be economically independent. Her father's bankruptcy during
the Great Depression did not lower Elion's academic aspirations. She graduated from Hunter College with highest honors in chemistry in 1937. Despite
having good grades, lack of money in the family and failure to receive financial assistance from 15 graduate schools prompted Elion to suspend her
plan for graduate training. For years, she worked odd jobs and tried to save
enough money to pay for graduate education. In 1941, she obtained her master's degree from New York University. However, she chose to keep her job
and quit her part-time doctoral studies at Brooklyn Polytechnic Institute when
the school told Elion to give up her job and go full-time with her studies.

The Burroughs Wellcome research laboratory in New York and later in
North Carolina served as the professional base for Gertrude Elion for nearly
half a century. Acting on her father's advice, she approached Burroughs Wellcome, a British medical research company, and started working as an assistant
for Harvard-educated biochemist George Hitchings in its American subsidiary
in Tuckahoe, New York. Elion's career in research took off at this research
facility. From 1944 to 1983, she rose through the ranks of research chemist,
senior research chemist, department head, scientist emerita, and consultant.
Under George Hitchings's sponsorship, Elion met prominent scientists at pro-

fessional meetings, published hundreds of scientific papers, and had several dozen U.S. patents relating to drugs for cancer treatment, organ transplant, and AIDS. Upon retirement from Burroughs Wellcome, Elion became a research professor at Duke University to train the next generation of scientists.

Rosalyn Yalow

Medical physicist Rosalyn Yalow wanted to follow in Marie Curie's footsteps as a wife, mother, and successful scientist. Among female laureates, Yalow was the most combative and aggressive in terms of her approach to problem solving (Straus 1998, 42). Although she was considered more masculine than her elder brother, Allie, this toughness and assertiveness served Yalow well academically and professionally. With the help of influential professors at Hunter College (Herbert Otis, Duand Roller, and Jerrold Zacharias), she was the first woman to hold a graduate assistantship in physics as a Ph.D. student at the University of Illinois. When her research partner Solomon Berson died, she carried on the research and eventually received the Nobel Prize for their discovery of the radio-immunoassay procedure. Yalow is also unique among female Nobel laureates in that she prides herself on being the "professional mother" who produced scores of successful young scientists. She accomplished this while doing research, running a lab, and keeping a home. She was the first among female laureates to hold and express the unorthodox view that work, marriage, and family are compatible for men and women in science. She espoused the view that women scientists should marry and have children, that mothers who have career aspirations should not stay home to take care of children, and that society should provide quality childcare to working mothers (Straus 1998).

Compared to other female laureates, Rosalyn Yalow probably had the most humble beginnings. She grew up in a poor, less-educated family. Her mother quit school after sixth grade and did garment work at home. Her father left school after eighth grade and became a streetcar conductor before opening a paper-and-twine business. However, they both valued education. Rosalyn learned to read before she began kindergarten. Like other female laureates, she grew up in an environment that encouraged her to follow her own inclination rather than those considered suitable only for women. Her father urged her to do whatever boys did. As a child, she learned the virtue of fighting back.

The Bronx Veterans Administration (VA) Hospital was Rosalyn Yalow's professional home as a researcher and administrator for three decades. Edith Quimby was her strongest female ally and gave her good career advice, even when the Hunter College female professors did not. Yalow found women a hindrance to achieving her goals and men a resource for her career advancement. Yalow married a supportive scientific spouse, Aaron Yalow, a graduate student in nuclear physics whom she met at the University of Illinois. Like Joseph Mayer, Aaron Yalow played the role of facilitator of his wife's career. Yalow studied with eminent scientists like Maurice Goldhaber, who became her thesis adviser and mentor. Aside from her husband, Solomon Berson was the second most important person in Yalow's career. Berson teamed up with female scientist Yalow to do research that eventually led to her receipt of the Nobel Prize. Yalow continued to form new partnerships with young scientists.

Christiane Nusslein-Volhard

In many respects, developmental biologist Christiane Nusslein-Volhard and Barbara McClintock shared commonalities. They had similar approaches to the study of nature. Interested in plants and animals, they conducted genetic research to understand complex developmental processes. As a high school senior, Nusslein-Volhard tried to develop a new theory about evolution. Curiosity and ambition led Nusslein-Volhard to do postdoctoral work at laboratories in Germany and Switzerland where she teamed with an American fruit fly expert and future co-winner of the Nobel Prize Eric Wieschaus for groundbreaking research on fruit flies. Both McClintock and Nusslein-Volhard conducted experimental research at a top research institute instead of holding faculty appointments at a research university. Nusslein-Volhard remained in Europe, unlike Gerty Cori, Maria Goeppert-Mayer, and Rita Levi-Montalcini. Her quest for understanding the development of a single cell into a complex being was rewarded by receipt of the Nobel Prize in medicine with Eric Wieschaus and Edward Lewis in 1995 for their discoveries concerning the genetic control of early embryonic development. Their work on mutations in fruit fly embryos has implications for detecting birth defects in humans. Compared to the earlier generation of female scientists, Nusslein-Volhard has encountered less overt discrimination but more subtle gender discrimination in German science. She has been taken less seriously in the scientific community compared to her male counterparts in competition for jobs and first authorship on scientific publications (McGrayne 1998; Nobel Foundation 2007).

The second oldest in a family of five children, Christiane Nusslein-Volhard was born into a modest household. Due to economic necessities, she learned to make things herself instead of buying them, or to learn from books by herself. Similar to her parents, she enjoys music and likes painting. Her father was an architect and a son of a professor of medicine and heart and kidney specialist; her mother stayed home to take care of the children. A painter, her maternal grandmother's strong discipline and character inspired Nusslein-Volhard. The books from parents and tales and theories from siblings sustained her lifelong interest in science. Her father expected good academic performance from the children. Nusslein-Volhard is a rarity among female laureates in that she enjoys the feminist activities that others shunned while also recognizing the conflict between work and family for women. Like Yalow, Nusslein-Volhard is a strong advocate for providing childcare for working mothers. She took action to set up daycare facilities at her workplace and gave part of her money to support childcare for women scientists.

The Max Planck Institute in Germany has served as the professional home for Christiane Nusslein-Volhard since 1985. Support from the top research powerhouse in Germany gave her a chance to be in charge of her own research. Heinz Schaller was her thesis adviser for the master's and doctoral degrees. She received her doctorate in 1973 and obtained the permanent position of director of the Department of Developmental Biology at the Max Planck Institute in 1985. Despite recognition for her originality and brilliance, for the most part, Nusslein-Volhard sustained her research through a series of hard-won fellowships. Had she been more geographically mobile like other female European laureates, Nusslein-Volhard might have garnered more support for her work.

Linda Buck

Neuroscientist Linda Buck, the most recent female winner of the Nobel Prize, had never thought of being a scientist as a child. Like Nusslein-Volhard, Buck liked music and enjoyed doing the things that girls do, such as playing with dolls. She also learned from her father how to use tools and build things. Although Buck thought she wanted to have a career as a psychotherapist to help others, after taking a course in immunology as an undergraduate at the University of Washington in Seattle, she wanted to be a biologist. Buck learned how to be a scientist when she was a graduate student in the microbiology department at the University of Texas Medical Center in Dallas. When she underwent postdoctoral training at Columbia University in Richard Axel's laboratory, Buck learned the recently developed techniques of molecular biology. Her first introduction to neuroscience led to Buck's fascination with the brain's cellular and connectional diversity. Like other female laureates, she found experimenting with different ways to study the nervous system "a great source of creative enjoyment." A paper published by Sol Snyder's group in 1985 on odor detection made her determined to solve the puzzles of how humans and mammals could detect over 10,000 odorous chemicals and how identical chemicals could generate different odor perceptions. Buck conducted her

Neuroscientist Dr. Linda Buck was awarded the Nobel Prize in medicine in 2004 (with Richard Axel) for research related to the sense of smell. (Fred Hutchinson Cancer Research Center/ Roland Morgan)

award-winning research at Harvard Medical School over a period of 10 years as a faculty member in the neurobiology department. In 2004, she shared the Nobel Prize in medicine with Richard Axel for their discoveries of odorant receptors and the organization of the olfactory system (Nobel Foundation 2007).

Born and raised in Seattle, Washington, Linda Buck is the middle child of three girls in a professional family. Her mother was a homemaker and her father was an electrical engineer. She attributed her scientific curiosity to her parents' interest in puzzles and inventions. Her mother taught Buck "not to settle for something mediocre." Like Nusslein-Volhard, Buck enjoyed spending time with her maternal grandmother from Sweden. The lessons of Buck's parents for their daughter strike a similar chord among female laureates: "I was given considerable independence. . . . I was fortunate to have wonderfully supportive parents who told me that I had the ability to do anything I wanted with my life. They taught me to think independently and to be critical of my own ideas, and they urged me to do something worthwhile with my life" (Nobel Foundation 2007).

Buck seemed to have a career trajectory typical of a male scientist. Her career development and advancement were smooth sailing compared to those of other female laureates. After graduating from college with co-majors in psychology and microbiology in 1975, Buck completed her graduate study in five years, followed by a decade-long stint as a postdoctoral fellow and later an associate at Columbia University. At Harvard, she rose through the ranks of assistant, associate, and full professor from 1991 to 2001. In 2002, Buck returned to her hometown of Seattle to take up a position as a full member at the Fred Hutchinson Cancer Research Center while being an affiliate pro-

fessor at her alma mater. Buck has not been critical of the scientific establishment. On the contrary, she seems to be very grateful for the support she
received from her thesis adviser, supervisors of her postdoctoral work, and
peers.

Sources of Nurture and Support for the Laureates

These descriptions confirm that the family has a decisive influence as an important agent of socialization on the academic and/or career choices of the
female laureates. These winners share several themes in their upbringing.
Most came from middle-class, academic, or professional backgrounds. They
grew up with a family tradition of emphasis on learning. Family figures such
as (grand)parents were instrumental in nurturing and developing their intellectual interests. Usually their upbringing was inconsistent with the gender
role expectations at the time. Most of the parents of female laureates did not
raise their children according to the gender role expectations. They expected
their children to choose subjects of their own interest instead of the academic
or career interests typical for women in society. Many of them had "tinker-
ing" experience in childhood and saw the practice of science firsthand. For
some, engaging in science was part of their childhood. They had female role
models who questioned or broke gender rules. They learned early that contrary to societal expectations, being a woman and learning science were
compatible.

Science is a social activity. Female laureates needed laboratory space and
assistance for research activities. They surrounded themselves with people
who were also committed to science and were willing to work with them to
achieve their goals. Organizations and gatekeepers of science saw these talented women as resources rather than as threats. Large institutions and those
with significant power on the lookout for great ideas are not afraid to invite
"newcomers" (including women) to join them and work on their projects. Female laureates used the institution of science to their advantage. They were
also employed (in)directly by the private or public sector. In addition to being
a part of the "old-boys club," some female laureates used limited individual ties
with women to seek career advancement.

How Do Laureates Deal with Gender Discrimination?

In this essay, gender discrimination is broadly defined as being treated differently because of one's biological makeup. Men are generally considered
superior to women in intellectual and physical abilities. Gender stratification

is the outcome of this ideology. It often results in differential evaluation of social worth based on biological sex and unequal distribution of power, prestige, and wealth between men and women. The outstanding accomplishments of the female laureates are counterintuitive to the cultural and political barriers that they faced. Many had extensive administrative or leadership experience:

> Marie Curie founded and became the head of the Radium Institute in Paris. She also directed a large-scale radiology service in France during World War I (1914–1919).
>
> Gerty Cori ran the Cori's laboratory at Washington University in St. Louis, Missouri, for decades when her husband Carl Cori focused on writing and other administrative tasks.
>
> Irene Joliot-Curie served as the under secretary of state for Scientific Research (1936) and commissioner for Atomic Energy (1946–1951) in France. She succeeded her mother and became director of the Radium Institute (1946–1956).
>
> Rita Levi-Montalcini was a co-director of two research laboratories: the laboratory at Washington University in St. Louis and the Center for Neurobiology in Rome (1961–1979).
>
> Gertrude Elion was head of the Department of Experimental Therapy at Burroughs Wellcome Research Laboratories (1967–1983).
>
> Rosalyn Yalow directed the Solomon A. Berson Research Laboratory at the Bronx VA Medical Center (1973–1992).
>
> Christiane Nusslein-Volhard directed the Department of Genetics (1986–1990) and the Department of Developmental Biology (1990–present) at the Max Planck Institute in Tubingen, Germany.

These examples document that the success of female laureates is not limited to making discoveries. They are also shrewd managers or leaders of their organizations. As for gender discrimination or unwelcoming workplaces, their responses range from refusing to admit its existence through ignoring its presence to downplaying its significance for career advancement. Finding a job at a department or institution with a culture of collegiality may provide the most sensible solution. Whether acknowledging or denying discrimination, they learned to deal with it as the "lone girl" and through networking with the "old boys" instead of calling for or initiating collective actions. A review of those who expressed their views on this issue is enlightening:

> Marie Curie: Life is not easy for any of us. But what of that? We must have perseverance and above all confidence in ourselves. We must believe

that we are gifted for something, and that this thing, at whatever cost, must be attained (Curie 1937, 121).

Barbara McClintock: When a person gets to know you well, they forget that you are a woman. . . . The matter of gender drops away (Keller 1983, 76).

Rita Levi-Montalcini: I do not believe my career has been affected by being a woman. A woman's career may be hampered in two ways: by her feeling of responsibility to her family and by professional discrimination. In my case, I had no family obligations because I am single and did not have that problem to face. As for the second difficulty, I have never felt, either in Italy or in the United States, any professional hostility because of being a woman (Wasserman 2000, 42–43).

Dorothy Hodgkin: No, I think it is because I did not really notice it very much, that I was a woman amongst so many men and the other thing is . . . that I am a little conscious that there were moments when it was to my advantage . . . and at the time just after the war, when there was an air of liberalism abroad and the first elections of women to the Royal Society that were made, that probably got me in earlier than one might have as a man, just because one was a woman (Wolpert and Richards 1988, 77).

Gertrude Elion: I hadn't been aware that any doors were closed to me until I started knocking on them. . . . So when I got out and found that they didn't want women in the laboratory, it was a shock. . . . I almost fell apart. That was the first time that I thought being a woman was a real disadvantage. It surprises me to this day that I didn't get angry. I got very discouraged (McGrayne 1998, 287).

Rosalyn Yalow: Personally, I have not been terribly bothered by it. I have understood that it exists, and it's just one other thing that you have to take into account what you're doing. . . . Women, even now, must exert more effort than men do for the same degree of success [even though] there was something wrong with the discriminators, not something wrong with me (McGrayne 1998, 338, 341–342). I didn't pay any price for working so hard, and I never felt any gender bias. . . . I'd like to think that I serve as a symbol of the fact that women can make it in what was once a man's world (Straus 1998, 256).

Christiane Nusslein-Volhard: As grad students, we didn't talk about being discriminated against, though in retrospect I probably had more difficulties [than men] (McGrayne 1998, 389).

Linda Buck: The Hutchinson Center has a reputation for cutting edge science as well as a high level of collegiality, both of which were important to me. . . . As a woman in science, I sincerely hope that my

receiving a Nobel Prize will send a message to young women everywhere that the doors are open to them and that they should follow
their dreams (Nobel Foundation 2007).

As for family demands, there is no uniformity in the patterns of their life.
A few handled the conflict between family and work by remaining single and
not having parenting responsibilities at all (e.g., McClintock, Levi-Montalcini).
Elion stayed unmarried after her fiancée died. Nusslein-Volhard was married
but divorced later without having any children. But most of them married or
had a scientific partner (e.g., Buck) and many had children (e.g., Curie, Cori,
Joliot-Curie, Goeppert-Mayer, Hodgkin, Yalow).

Conclusion

No specific career path leads to scientific success. Female Nobel laureates have
followed both linear and nonlinear paths to reach the top. The majority hold
the unconventional view that marriage is compatible with careers for women,
although some do not.

Female laureates have political acumen. They overcame the odds by themselves along with the help of others. With the exception of Rosalyn Yalow
and Christiane Nusslein-Volhard, they did not call for or work for collective
changes in the practices and policies in science and society. For them, the
best way to do better (or to overcome obstacles) was to be more qualified
than men. Their actions legitimized the "Marie Curie Strategy," the strategy of
deliberate overqualification when competing with their male counterparts
(Rossiter 1982, 130, 158–159). One can then argue that their defense mechanisms undermine rather than promote women's progress in science and imply that women have themselves to blame for their disadvantaged status. The
career success of these exceptional women might actually hurt other women's
prospects in science.

Support for the structural explanation for the production of female laureates exists. All have relied disproportionately on the old boy network in career development and advancement. They collaborated primarily with men
(with the exception of Marie Curie, who worked closely with her daughter
Irene Joliot-Curie after the death of her husband Pierre Curie). Seven female
laureates shared their Nobel Prize with either their scientific husband or male
collaborators. Many obtained jobs (teaching or research) the old-fashioned
way—through networks. By conventional standards in science, they are not
deviants (Cottrell 1962). Women need and seek the support of men to make
it in a man's world, a dilemma that female scientists generally face.

Female laureates subscribe to the male culture of science and help to perpetuate the traditional scientific role model. First, they are intensely dedicated to achieving success in science. Second, rather than criticizing or changing the structure of science, they adapt to the male culture of science. Third, they show that women can make contributions to science within a male domain without changing the existing norms that measure excellence.

Policy makers should explore particular problems that women may have at this elite level of the scientific establishment. The scientific community will not be able to attract and retain the best and brightest if individuals with high performance are not properly rewarded. (*See also* Discrimination; Professional Societies)

References and Further Reading

Cottrell, A. H. "Scientists: Solo or Concerted?" In *The Sociology of Science*. Edited by Bernard Barber and Walter Hirsch, 388–393. New York: Free Press, 1962.

Crossfield, E. Tina. "Irene Joliot-Curie: Following in Her Mother's Footsteps." In *A Devotion to Their Science: Pioneer Women of Radioactivity*. Edited by M. F. Rayner-Canham and G. W. Rayner-Canham, 97–123. Philadelphia: Chemical Heritage Foundation and Montreal: McGill-Queen's University Press, 1997.

Curie, Eve. *Madame Curie*. New York: Doubleday, 1937.

Curie, Marie. *Pierre Curie*. New York: Macmillan, 1923.

Dash, Joan. "Maria Goeppert-Mayer." In *A Life of One's Own: Three Gifted Women and the Men They Married*, 229–346. New York: Harper and Row, 1973.

Fedoroff, Nina V. "Two Women Geneticists." *American Scholar* 65(4) (1996): 587–592.

Ferry, Georgina. *Dorothy Hodgkin: A Life*. Cold Spring Harbor, NY: Cold Spring Harbor Laboratory Press, 1998.

Keller, Evelyn Fox. *A Feeling for the Organism: The Life and Work of Barbara McClintock*. New York: W. H. Freeman, 1983.

Levi-Montalcini, Rita. *In Praise of Imperfection: My Life and Work*. New York: Basic Books, 1988.

Liversidge, Anthony. "Interview: Rita Levi-Montalcini." *Omni* 10(6) (1988): 70–74, 102–105.

McGrayne, Sharon Bertsch. *Nobel Prize Women in Science: Their Lives, Struggles, and Momentous Discoveries*. 2nd ed. Secaucus, NJ: Carol Publishing Group, 1998.

Nobel Foundation. Official Web Site of the Nobel Foundation. 2007. http://NobelPrize.org.

Quinn, Susan. *Marie Curie: A Life*. Cambridge, MA: Perseus Books, 1995.

Rossiter, Margaret W. *Women Scientists in America: Struggles and Strategies to 1940*. Baltimore, MD: Johns Hopkins University Press, 1982.

Straus, Eugene. *Rosalyn Yalow: Nobel Laureate: Her Life and Work in Medicine*. New York: Plenum, 1998.

Tang, Joyce. *Scientific Pioneers: Women Succeeding in Science*. Lanham, MD: University Press of America, 2006.

Wasserman, Elga. *The Door in the Dream: Conversations with Eminent Women in Science*. Washington, DC: Joseph Henry Press, 2000.

Wolpert, Lewis, and Alison Richards. *A Passion of Science*. New York: Oxford University Press, 1988.

Gender and Occupational Interests

Sue V. Rosser

Strong associations exist between particular occupations and the gender of individuals associated with that occupation. For example, in the United States, the occupations of elementary school teacher or nurse evoke images and associations with women in the minds of most individuals. Engineer and mechanic link closely with men.

The association of occupations with a particular gender occurs across cultures, but the sex/gender associated with a specific occupation varies among cultures and countries. For example, in the 1970s in the United States, most people paired doctor or physician with men, while in the former Soviet Union at that time, physicians were assumed to be women. The statistical reality formed the basis for this difference in the two countries. In the United States at that time, 93 percent of physicians were men whereas in the Soviet Union over 90 percent of physicians were women. Although the connection of a particular sex with a specific occupation varies among cultures, one factor remains constant: in most societies, occupations dominated by men hold more prestige and command higher salaries than occupations dominated by women.

In the United States, women currently earn more of the bachelor's and master's degrees than men. In 2004, women earned 57.6 percent of the bachelor's degrees in all fields (NSF 2007) and 59.1 percent of all master's degrees. Beginning in 2000, women also earned more of the bachelor's degrees in science and engineering (S&E) (50.4% in 2004), although they earn only 43.6 percent of the master's degrees in science and engineering. In 2004, women earned 60 percent of the Ph.D.s in nonscience and engineering fields, but only 44 percent of the Ph.D.s in science and engineering received by U.S. citizens and permanent residents.

The major gender differences occur in distribution of the genders across the disciplines. Overall, at the bachelor's level, women earn the majority (61.1%) of the degrees in the nonscience and engineering fields such as humanities, education, and fine arts, and in the science and engineering fields of psychology (77.8%), the social sciences (54.2%), agricultural sciences (52.2%), and biological sciences (62.5%). Men earn most of the degrees in the physical sciences (57.9%); earth, atmospheric, and ocean sciences (57.8%); mathematics and statistics (54.1%); computer sciences (74.9%); and engineering (79.5%) (NSF 2007).

Factors Impacting Career Choice

Why are girls and women not choosing careers in science and engineering, since these represent some of the most prestigious and well-paying careers in our increasingly technological society? Many studies have explored the contributions of parents in their choice of toys, differential expectations for boys and girls, and interactions with their sons and daughters in shaping this choice. Other work has examined the impact of teachers, counselors, and curriculum as well as peers in the school environment as significant forces in the decision. Some work has emphasized biological differences between the sexes in terms of genes (Benbow and Stanley 1984), brain, and hormones that might lead to differences in visuospatial abilities, cognitive pathways, and aggression that might influence career choice.

Even when girls and women do choose careers in science, the particular disciplinary areas they choose and the reasons for their choices seem to differ from those of boys and men. What accounts for the reasons most women choose some disciplines in science and engineering while more men choose others? Why did women earn 67.3 percent of the Ph.D.s in psychology in 2004 while they earned only 11.1 percent of the Ph.D.s in mechanical engineering? Why did women receive almost half (46.3%) of the Ph.D.s in the biological sciences but only 20.5 percent of the Ph.D.s in computer science (NSF 2007)?

Eccles (1994) has examined the factors significant in career choices and achievement goals. Her studies on gifted students reveal that females tend to be less confident of success than males in science-related professions, and males are less confident of their success than females in health-related professions, even those that involve extensive scientific training. Gifted girls rated biological science and both medical and social service occupations and training higher than the boys did, while boys expressed more interest in both higher status and business-related occupations in general, and in the physical sciences, engineering, and the military in particular. Females desired jobs that were people-oriented while males placed a higher interest in jobs that allowed for work with machinery, math, or computers.

Female high school seniors place more value than males on the importance of making occupational sacrifices for their families and on the importance of having a job that allows them to help others and do something worthwhile for society. These data also revealed that gifted women desired a more varied, or multifaceted, type of life than men. This desire for variety, coupled with the tendency of women, more than men, to be involved in and to value competence in several activities simultaneously, may suggest why scientifically competent women are especially interested in biology, chemistry, medicine, and health rather than physics, computer sciences, and engineering. Physics, computer sciences, and engineering may be perceived as having a narrower focus and lacking orientation toward people.

Helping others and doing something worthwhile for society serve as powerful motivators in attracting women to science in general and to the biosciences and health in particular. Studies of first-year college students' majors show that students who switch from physical science majors to other sciences tend to choose biology. This trend is particularly true for females. Rarely do these women switch because of problems with grades or achievement in the physical sciences; more typically they become restive with the absence of people orientation and/or because of their attraction to other fields. In addition to biology, women leaving physical science majors switched to psychology, education, and the humanities while men who left switched to the social sciences and business.

Men and women may change majors for different reasons. College women gave "non-science, mathematics, and engineering ME major offers interest" as the most frequent reason for switching, while college men ranked that reason as fifth. Instead, the men ranked "lack of/loss of interest in SME: 'turned off science'" as the most frequent reason; women ranked that as their second most frequent reason (Seymour and Hewitt 1994). These studies also strongly suggest that women leave science because of their service orientation to help others in difficulty. Understanding how science helps people may retain women.

Different Employment and Advancement Opportunities

Those women who persist through graduate school, receive the Ph.D., and become scientists and engineers have different experiences, hold different ranks, and earn different salaries than their male counterparts. Although men and women have similar educational qualifications, women with degrees in science and engineering have higher unemployment rates, lower job status, smaller salaries, and greater unemployment in science and engineering than their male counterparts (NSF 2007).

Why are women who choose careers in science excluded from the higher positions in science? Women scientists have fewer opportunities for networking and mentoring and experience gender discrimination in recruitment and

A medical student makes up a solution in a laboratory. (Laurence Gough)

promotion, both of which may stall their careers. Women in fields such as computer science and engineering report that the low numbers of women in these fields lead them to have a feeling of isolation and lack of camaraderie. Since women, including women in science, are more people-oriented than men, this isolation may bother them more. Women also report difficulties in gaining credibility and respectability from peers and superiors, especially in the more male-dominated fields (Rosser 2004).

The major career issue reported by most women scientists and engineers is balancing career and family (Rosser 2004). Childbearing and childcare rank as very significant issues that conflict with pursuing a scientific career. In addition, dual career difficulties may more frequently confront women scientists than women pursuing other careers because 62 percent of women scientists are married to men scientists (Sonnert and Holton 1995). Given the relatively small numbers of women scientists, most men scientists are not married to other scientists.

Impact of Masculine Domination on Science

Some have argued that science and masculinity have been conjoined since the birth of early modern science and are mutually reinforcing. Women have historically been relegated to lower-level positions in science because of their perceived failure to behave in ways that follow the male traditions of science. These traditions include toughness, rigor, rationality, impersonality, competition, and lack of emotionality. These traditions continue to attract men to science and exclude women, creating a type of science that reflects these characteristics. Science is a masculine province not only because it is populated mostly by men but also because of the choice of experimental topics, use of male subjects for experimentation, interpretation and theorizing from data, and the practice and applications of science undertaken by the scientists. Evelyn Fox Keller (1982) suggests that since the scientific method stresses objectivity, rationality, distance, and autonomy of the observer from the object of study, individuals who feel comfortable with independence, autonomy, and distance will be most likely to become scientists. Since these characteristics of the scientific method overlap considerably with characteristics associated with masculinity, more men will feel drawn to science while more women will feel excluded from it.

Building on the work in object relations theory, Keller (1982) suggested that in our society where most of the primary caretakers are women, boys are pushed to be independent, distant, and autonomous from their female caretakers, whereas girls are permitted to be more dependent, more intimate, and less individuated from their mothers or female caretakers. She explored how the gender identity proposed by object relations theory with women as caretakers might lead more men to choose careers in science since individuals who feel comfortable with independence, autonomy, and distance will be most likely to become scientists and in turn create a science that reflects those same characteristics of independence, distance, and autonomy. Clearly, having men play a more prominent role as caretakers of children might lead to more women choosing science.

Policy Conclusions

In the interim, solving some of the more practical issues of balancing career and family by providing adequate daycare, including care for sick children, would improve the lives and possibly the careers of women scientists and engineers. Strong government policies encouraging women to obtain education and participate in careers in science and engineering can also be effective. In the former East Germany, in keeping with the official political goal of gender equality, women were directed into the sciences and vocational training in technical fields. A generous childcare infrastructure also existed. This resulted in relatively high participation of East German women in the labor force (78%) compared to women in West Germany (39%). In East Germany,

46 percent of the students in the sciences were women; in West Germany during the same time women were 32 percent of science students. In engineering, the relative numbers were 25 percent versus 12 percent (Grimm and Meier 1994). Since reunification, the percentages of women in the overall labor force and in science and engineering in the former East Germany have dropped. These figures suggest that policies and infrastructure contribute significantly to the choice and numbers of women in scientific and technical occupations. (*See also* Appendix Tables; Cognitive Abilities; Critiques of Science; Nature/Nurture)

References and Further Reading

Benbow, Camilla, and J. Stanley. "Gender and the Science Major: A Study of Mathematically Precocious Youth." In *Women in Science*. Edited by M. W. Steinkamp and M. L. Maehr, 3–29. Greenwich, CT: JAI Press, 1984.

Eccles, Jacquelynne. "Understanding Women's Educational and Occupational Choices." *Psychology of Women Quarterly* 11 (1994): 3–29.

Grimm, S., and U. Meier. "On the Disparity of the Sexes in German Universities." In *The Gender Gap in Higher Education: World Yearbook of Education*. Edited by Suzanne Stiver Lie, Linda Malik, and Duncan Harris. London: Kogan Page, 1994.

Keller, Evelyn F. "Feminism and Science." *Signs* 7(3) (1982): 589–602.

National Science Foundation (NSF). *Women, Minorities, and Persons with Disabilities in Science and Engineering*. 2007. http://www.nsf.gov/statistics/wmpd. (Accessed April 5, 2007.)

Rosser, Sue V. *The Science Glass Ceiling: Academic Women Scientists and Their Struggle to Succeed*. New York: Routledge, 2004.

Seymour, Elaine, and Nancy Hewitt. *Talking about Leaving: Factors Contributing to High Attrition Rates among Science, Mathematics, and Engineering Undergraduate Majors*. Boulder, CO: Ethnography and Assessment Research, Bureau of Sociological Research, 1994.

Sonnert, Gerhardt, and Gerald Holton. *Who Succeeds in Science? The Gender Dimension*. New Brunswick, NJ: Rutgers University Press, 1995.

Other Perspectives on Gender and Myths and Beliefs in Scientific Research

Feminist Philosophy of Science

Lynn Hankinson Nelson

Feminist philosophy of science emerges at the intersections of feminist science studies and the philosophy of science. Its core research questions and developments are significantly influenced by each tradition. Nowhere is this influence clearer than in its origins. Philosophical engagements with the sciences from feminist perspectives arose in direct response to the internal science critiques feminist scientists leveled in the 1970s and 1980s. These critiques focused on remaining informal barriers to women's full participation in science and on the role of male-centered or androcentric beliefs and values in shaping the directions, methods, and content of various sciences.

From the outset, there was considerable interest in the epistemological implications of these critiques: what they suggested about the nature of scientific reasoning and practices and the objectivity or unbiased nature of scientific knowledge. There was also considerable disagreement about them. Were the cases in which feminist scientists had documented the role and consequences of androcentrism simply cases of *bad* science and thus without implications for science itself? When many feminists answered no, they drew hostile reactions from many philosophers and scientists. Should *feminism* be credited with enabling scientists to recognize androcentrism in various sciences that had previously gone unrecognized? Affirmative answers to this question were also received with hostility, with many traditionalists arguing that the recognition of androcentrism was just typical of science's ability and tendency to self-correct. Any suggestion of a relationship between the content of science and the social identities and/or contextual beliefs and values of individual scientists as feminists or nonfeminists was condemned as embracing relativism. An important source of these reactions was a picture of science developed in the philosophy of science.

Foundations of the Philosophy of Science

The philosopher W. V. Quine described the philosophy of science as "science gone self-conscious." From the 1930s, when philosophy of science emerged as a distinct and vibrant area of philosophical inquiry, philosophers sought to understand the nature of scientific reasoning, the nature and strength of the evidence that supported scientific theories, and the sources of scientific success in explaining and predicting natural and social phenomena. Their analyses sought to demonstrate that observation provides a firm foundation against which scientific theories and hypotheses were rigorously tested and that science's objectivity was a function of its value freedom and intersubjectivity or replicability for verification. This cluster of commitments is often termed *objectivism*.

For philosophers and scientists whose views were influenced by these arguments, it was difficult to conceive of ways in which gender (either that of individual scientists or a scientist's assumptions about gender) could have any impact on the content of good science. A long-held distinction between "the context of discovery" and "the context of justification" allowed for contextual beliefs and values (i.e., personal, social, cultural, and historical beliefs and values) to have a role in the context in which hypotheses are formulated or discovered but not in the context in which hypotheses are tested and either confirmed or falsified (the context of justification). In the context of justification, philosophers had maintained that logical relationships between hypotheses and data and the role of data in determining the fate of hypotheses ensure scientific intersubjectivity, value freedom, and the acceptance of only those theories that accurately reflect nature.

Feminists also disagreed about the epistemological implications of feminist internal science critiques. Evelyn Fox Keller stressed the need to find "a middle ground" between viewing science as irredeemably masculinist and/or as simply "politics by other means," as some early feminist analyses suggested, and the objectivism, summarized above, which traditionally minded philosophers and scientists took to be the only alternative to relativism (Keller in Tuana 1987, 37–50). Keller argued that just as feminist analyses of scientific theories about purported sex differences had required reconceptualizing gender as a complex and pliable construct rather than a fixed and independently real set of characteristics, feminist analyses of science must also incorporate insights emerging in a variety of disciplines that the sciences are historical, contingent, and thoroughly human undertakings (Tuana 1987).

Challenges of Feminism to Science

Keller's article appeared in a special double issue of *Hypatia* on the topic "Feminism and Science" (Tuana 1987, 1988). The themes, issues, and arguments of these volumes shaped feminist philosophy of science for the next decade and a half. Three themes, in particular, constituted points of departure for many efforts to understand the epistemological implications of feminist engagements with science. First, contributors concurred with Keller that there was a need for more adequate and comprehensive theories of science. Although their approaches differed, many argued that these theories must reconceptualize objectivity in ways to disentangle it from value freedom and explore how a scientist with explicit value commitments, such as feminism, might "still do 'good' science" (Longino in Tuana 1987, 56). Reflecting evidence from science studies that scientific objects can be partly a function of human construction as well as of an independent reality, contributors also argued that feminist theories of science must take social constructivist insights seriously "without sacrificing" the ability to explain how science can be "a reliable, though not foolproof process" (Alcoff in Tuana 1987, 122). In these and other ways, contributors rejected relativism.

Second, a number of contributors recommended a thorough and social naturalism: "We need to look and see what assumptions scientists actually hold when they decide between conflicting generalizations" (Potter in Tuana 1988, 30). Several also saw the need for close study of the specifics of research practice to avoid the false universalizing that had led philosophers to highly idealized accounts of such practice (e.g., Harding in Tuana 1987, 29–32).

A third theme was a strong commitment to a *symmetry thesis:* that taking gender into account is relevant for understanding bad science and good science, perhaps even the best science (Potter in Tuana 1988, 19–33). In their arguments for this thesis, many contributors noted relatively recent developments in the philosophy of science that reflected a shift from efforts of earlier generations to "justify" science to a more "naturalistic" approach that studied historical and contemporary science as *actually* practiced. Work motivated and characterized by naturalism, both in philosophy of science and fields such as sociology of science, was revealing the role of contextual and contingent factors in scientific practice. Contributors drew directly on this body of work, as would feminist philosophers and scientists in the years that followed.

Role of Assumptions

In the philosophy of science of the 1960s and 1970s, empiricists such as Carl Hempel argued that models of the context of justification that took hypotheses and data as the only factors involved in the testing of hypotheses are inadequate. Hempel demonstrated a ubiquitous and unavoidable role for auxiliary assumptions in linking specific hypotheses to relevant data. He also used historical cases to demonstrate that faulty auxiliary assumptions can lead to the rejection of a good hypothesis. Conversely, he showed that the apparent confirmation of a hypothesis might not be a function of *its* adequacy but rather reflect one or more auxiliary assumptions that, together with the hypothesis, yielded the prediction.

Hempel's argument provided feminists with a methodological approach to studying precisely how and when contextual assumptions enter scientific reasoning as auxiliary assumptions. For example, Helen E. Longino cited cases she and Ruth Doell had earlier investigated in research undertaken in endocrinology into the role of prenatal hormones in fetal brain development. They found that sociocultural assumptions about gender played a significant role in the formation of hypotheses, design of experiments, and interpretations of experimental results. Longino used this and similar cases to strongly defend the symmetry thesis: "One can't give an *a priori* specification of [the logic of justification] that effectively eliminates the role of *value-laden/contextual assumptions* in legitimate scientific inquiry," she argued, "without eliminating auxiliary [assumptions] *altogether*" (Longino in Tuana 1987, 55, emphasis added). That is to say, there is no legitimate (empirically based) way to deny any role for auxiliary assumptions that reflect social and cultural beliefs without denying the role of all auxiliary assumptions, and Hempel had demonstrated that this was not possible.

Investigating the role of contextual and value-laden assumptions in helping to forge the relationship between a hypothesis and data became a major component of feminists' analyses of science in the 1990s. In *Science as Social Knowledge,* Longino developed "constructive empiricism," a theory of scientific practice that sought to explain the role and consequences of the auxiliary assumptions feminists criticized and the role of feminist values in the construction of alternative hypotheses and methods (Longino 1990). An example on which many feminists focused was the "Man, the Hunter" theory of human evolution that credited the evolution of humans' large brains, language, and social evolution to hunting engaged in by our male hominid ancestors. The only data available were chipped stones found near the remains of early hominids. On the basis of auxiliary assumptions linking males with tool use and hunting, the stones were taken as evidence of a "hunting adaptation" that required and led to the development of language, cooperation, and social structures. Demonstrating that the auxiliary assumption was unwarranted, feminists in anthropology advanced an alternative. This "Woman, the Gatherer" theory, according to which the stones were evidence of tool making for gathering typically associated with women, credited mother/child bonds with the evolution of language, cooperation, and social structures (Longino 1990; Nelson 1990).

Symmetry Thesis

Contributors also used positions advanced by W. V. Quine to support the symmetry thesis. They appealed to Quine's holism: his argument that theories of science, common sense, and philosophy form a network and are *radically interdependent*. Quine argued against foundationalism, that there is a "nontheoretical" foundation for science in observation or anything else, and against the possibility of anything like an Archimedean standpoint or "view from nowhere." We work, he argued, as scientists, philosophers, and lay persons *from within a body of theories we inherit and seek to improve*. Coherence with experience and coherence with the network of theories we currently accept are the appropriate (and only) criteria for evaluating beliefs, hypotheses, and theories.

Some contributors cited holism as demonstrating, by example, that there are alternatives to objectivism and relativism, since holism dictates that we cannot presume access to an unmediated reality (Alcoff in Tuana 1987, 107–129) and that the world we theorize about is the world we are already in (Heldke in Tuana 1987, 129–141). Linda Alcoff also suggested that the interrelationships Quine posited between all "levels" of theories and theorizing and the value attributed to intertheoretical coherence might prove useful in explaining the relationships between science and commonsense assumptions about gender. Such relationships might also explain and justify the alternative hypotheses and research questions feminists in the social sciences were advocating. Although holism itself might not be sufficient to feminist efforts to develop more adequate theories of science, holism challenges the boundary traditionalists claimed to obtain between the sciences and "commonsense" beliefs and values.

Underdetermination

Contributors also appealed to Quine's underdetermination thesis: the thesis that *all* theories, even the most successful, are underdetermined by all the evidence there is. There is "slack," Quine argued, between any theory and all the evidence we have or ever will have for it. Numerous theories, including those conflicting with those currently accepted, might be *equally compatible with all available evidence*.

That all theories, not just those feminists criticized, are underdetermined by all available evidence was seen to provide additional support for the symmetry thesis. The gap between theories and evidence is yet another avenue by which contextual beliefs and values can come to inform good science. Elizabeth Potter argued that in choosing between two formulations of the Ideal Gas Law, both compatible with all the relevant phenomena, Robert Boyle was simultaneously choosing between two metaphysics: one that nature is inert; the other that nature is active. At the time, Potter documented social and cultural assumptions about women linking them to nature and passivity. Potter suggested that Boyle's socially conservative beliefs about women and other groups may have had a role in his choice of an inert nature, although the data supported either theory (Potter in Tuana 1988, 19–34).

Taxonomy of Feminist Epistemologies

In *The Science Question in Feminism,* Sandra Harding provided a taxonomy of feminist epistemologies, which included feminist empiricism, feminist standpoint theory, and feminist postmodernism. The least promising appeared to be feminist empiricism (Harding 1986). But in 1990, two books appeared outlining neo-empiricist theories of science commensurate with feminist science critiques and with the constructive alternatives feminist scientists were developing: Longino's *Science as Social Knowledge* and Lynn Hankinson Nelson's *Who Knows: From Quine to Feminist Empiricism* (Nelson 1990). Each appealed directly and extensively to holism and underdetermination. While the details of their models of science differed, both used these positions to argue that scientific knowledge is fundamentally social (i.e., the product of social and contingent processes) and that social beliefs and values can and do inform legitimate science.

Two other developments revealed contextual and contingent aspects of scientific practice and further supported the symmetry thesis. Philosophers of science had come to recognize the role of values in scientific practice; these were limited to so-called epistemic values—values thought to be truth-conducive (i.e., theories that had such values were more likely to be true). They used these when choosing between theories equally compatible with available evidence. Thomas Kuhn's list of epistemic values included simplicity, generality of scope, and internal and external consistency, among others. It closely resembled other such lists. But Kuhn cited cases in historical and contemporary science to argue that since epistemic values cannot be attained simultaneously, scientists must and do engage in trade-offs (between, for example, simplicity and generality of scope). Such trade-offs often reflect the contingent values of particular research traditions.

The role of epistemic and nonepistemic values in scientific practices led to promising developments in feminist philosophy of science. Longino juxtaposed a list of traditionally recognized epistemic values with the epistemic values she found as criteria of theory choice in the work of feminist scientists (Longino in Nelson and Nelson 1996). While "empirical adequacy" appeared on both lists, there were clear distinctions between the two lists in terms of other values. In contrast to the traditional value attributed to simplicity, Longino identified "ontological heterogeneity" and "complexity of relationships" as among the features feminist scientists value. Recognizing differences and complexities was often important in not allowing gender to "disappear," as Longino illustrated with specific cases. For example, instead of focusing virtually exclusively on the role of the Y chromosome and forms of testosterone in directing male fetal development, as generations of scientists had done to simplify their accounts of fetal development, feminists argued that any model that treated female fetal development as simply the "default" trajectory would fail to provide an accurate account of *human* fetal development (Wylie and Nelson 2007). Here simplicity was not a virtue; ontological heterogeneity, the recognition of difference, was. Drawing another contrast, Longino identified "novelty" as a virtue valued by feminist scientists as opposed to "conservatism" (or external consistency) on traditional lists. After all, feminists argued, conservatism—coherence with other accepted theories—seemed to function to entrench androcentric assumptions across a variety of sciences.

The last development mentioned here that proved useful in defending the symmetry thesis was the recognition of how theories help to shape what is observed. In the 1950s, N. R. Hanson demonstrated that what observers "see" is not solely determined by the physical processes at work, including the light rays given off by an object independent of an observer that impact the eye, etch impressions on the retina, and so forth. Rather, what observers "see" in the sense of visual experience is as much a function of their conceptual schemes, background knowledge, prior experience, and expectations as it is of their retinal images. Kuhn used Hanson's arguments and cases in the history of science to argue that scientists who have undergone a scientific revolution are able to observe what the earlier theory prohibited, and do so using the same instruments and looking in places they have looked before. An implication of Hanson's and Kuhn's arguments is that although partly a function of physical processes, observation does not constitute the "firm foundation" earlier generations of philosophers and scientists had assumed.

Translation to Research Practice

Feminist scientists cited many cases as suggesting that observations in their field were shaped by assumptions about gender. Contributors appealed to the theory-ladenness of observation to explore how such assumptions helped to shape observations of reproductive systems and processes (Tuana 1988, 35–60) and the process of fertilization (Biology and Gender Study Group in Tuana 1988, 61–76). They also noted observations *not made* (e.g., of women's contributions to various aspects of public life, including science, or female dominance hierarchies within primate groups) because contextual beliefs or values suggested they did not exist (e.g., Alcoff in Tuana 1987; Harding 1987). Contributors also cited examples in which observations not shaped by andro- centric assumptions were more accurate (e.g., Biology and Gender Study Group in Tuana 1988, 61–76).

Later feminist analyses would continue to explore the role of theories and assumptions in shaping observation. For example, Emily Martin cited both the theory-ladenness of observation and gender stereotypes in her critique of the ways in which the process of fertilization was described as a romantic fairy tale in which the sperm/male had the primary role in awakening the passive egg (Keller and Longino 1996); and Elisabeth A. Lloyd analyzed how "pre-theoretical assumptions" linking females' sexuality with reproduction led researchers to fail to observe, or choose to ignore, females in a variety of species achieving orgasm with each other (Keller and Longino 1996).

The need to reconceptualize objectivity so as to disentangle it from value freedom also contributed to significant developments. Feminist standpoint theorists (e.g., Harding 1991; Wylie 2003) and postmodern theorists (e.g., Har- away 1991) emphasized that all inquirers are "situated" and their perspectives necessarily "partial." Sandra Harding developed the notion of "strong objec- tivity," which called for "reflexivity"—for seeking to understand the limits of one's own perspective through active efforts to take on the perspective of others (Harding 1991). Donna Haraway related objectivity directly to recog- nizing the particularity, partiality, and embodied nature of one's vision (Har- away 1991). Advocating a sophisticated neo-empiricism, Longino attributed objectivity to the kinds of processes that should characterize the knowledge- seeking practices of science communities. These processes would allow a diverse and equally respected group of scientists to identify unwarranted aux- iliary assumptions and contribute to better (more warranted) hypotheses and theories (Longino 1990).

Since 1987–1988, an even greater number of philosophers of science have come to accept and adopt the naturalism and contextualism that began to emerge in the 1970s and served as resources for feminists' engagements in the philosophy of science. Feminists no longer must argue for many of the con- textualizing insights for which they had to argue in the 1980s. Instead, they can concentrate on substantive case studies that reveal the relationships between gender and other socially salient categories and specific research programs and hypotheses.

A recent double issue of *Hypatia* devoted to feminism and science illustrates this and the growth of interdisciplinary approaches in feminist theorizing about and within science (Nelson and Wylie 2004). Many contributors adopt a naturalistic stance to undertake substantive analyses of areas of empirical science, focusing on a broad range of disciplines. These include analyses and critiques of reproductive endocrinology and molecular biology (Roy in Nelson and Wylie 2004, 255–279) and of historical and contemporary research on female sexuality and anatomy (Tuana in Nelson and Wylie 2004, 194–232). One contributor interrogates the role of race and gender in biomedical uses and understandings of the HeLa cell line (Weasel in Nelson and Wylie 2004, 183–193); another offers a gendered reworking of colonial and postcolonial science (Schiebinger in Nelson and Wylie 2004, 233–254). In keeping with an increasingly constructive, not simply critical, approach to the sciences, contributors propose feminist alternatives to the models they criticize and explore how feminist perspectives can lead to advances in both the sciences and our historical and philosophical understanding of them.

A number of contributors also cite feminist analyses of the 1990s as influencing their work as scientists. Cell and molecular biologist Lisa Weasel cites the influence of the work of Sandra Harding and Donna Haraway on "situatedness" and "the privilege of partial vision" as motivating her engagements with the HeLa cell line as a study of "what a critical feminist practice of science looks like from within the science laboratory, from within the scientific research process" (Weasel in Nelson and Wylie 2004, 184–185). Reproductive neuroendocrinologist Deboleena Roy cites the arguments of Harding concerning feminist methods of gathering evidence and conducting research as motivating her own search for what a feminist method within a science might be (Roy in Nelson and Wylie 2004, 259). She also cites Longino's arguments—that "feminist science" is best conceived, not in terms of the content of science, but rather as "practicing science as a feminist" (Longino in Tuana 1987, 51–65)—as motivating her search for how feminism, as a methodology and epistemology, might transform her practice as a scientist. Both scientists note some difficulties they encounter trying to put feminists' philosophical recommendations into practice and what their own experiences suggest for other feminist scientists and for feminist philosophy of science.

Current Situation

When contributors to the second *Hypatia* volume turned to broader philosophical issues, it was now in the context of an epistemic terrain structured by several decades of feminist exploration. They were able to work with a number of more finely delineated positions than were available in 1987–1988. They called for a more thoroughgoing feminist naturalism by turning to under-used resources (Clough in Nelson and Wylie 2004, 102–118); they argued for ways to improve and refine feminist empiricism (Anderson in Nelson and Wylie 2004, 1–24; Sobstyl in Nelson and Wylie 2004, 119–141) and feminist standpoint theories (Harding in Nelson and Wylie 2004, 25–47; Ruetsche in Nelson and Wylie 2004 73–101); and they substantially extended earlier and influential analyses of the nature and role of nonepistemic values in scientific practice (Anderson in Nelson and Wylie 2004, 1–24).

Collectively, contributors undertook an extended exploration of a number of epistemic and ethical issues important to feminist science studies in the last decades. They are concerned with understanding the precise nature of the values that inform science and the ways these values shape scientific content and practice; they further scrutinize the "situatedness" of scientists *and* science studies scholars; they attend to the ways the dynamics of gender, race, class, and culture inform scientific practice; and they ask what implications their emphasis on the contingency and sociality of science has for philosophical debates about objectivism and relativism. (*See also* Critiques of Science; Feminist Science Studies)

References and Further Reading

Haraway, Donna. "Situated Knowledges: The Science Question in Feminism and the Privilege of Partial Perspective." In *Simians, Cyborgs, and Women*. New York: Routledge, 1991.

Harding, Sandra. *The Science Question in Feminism*. Ithaca, NY: Cornell University Press, 1986.

Harding, Sandra. *Whose Science? Whose Knowledge? Starting Thought from Women's Lives*. Ithaca, NY: Cornell University Press, 1991.

Keller, Evelyn Fox, and Helen E. Longino, eds. *Feminism and Science*. Oxford: Oxford University Press, 1996.

Longino, Helen E. *Science as Social Knowledge*. Princeton, NJ: Princeton University Press, 1990.

Nelson, Lynn Hankinson. *Who Knows: From Quine to Feminist Empiricism*. Philadelphia: Temple University Press, 1990.

Nelson, Lynn Hankinson, and Jack Nelson, eds. *Feminism, Science, and the Philosophy of Science*. Dordrecht: Kluwer Academic Press, 1996.

Nelson, Lynn Hankinson, and Alison Wylie, eds. *Hypatia* 19(1) (2004): Special Issue, Feminist Science Studies.

Tuana, Nancy, ed. *Hypatia* 2(3) (1987): Special Issue, Feminism and Science.

Tuana, Nancy, ed. *Hypatia* 3(1) (1988): Special Issue, Feminism and Science.

Wylie, Alison. "Why Standpoint Matters." In *Science and Other Cultures: Issues in Philosophies of Science and Technology*. Edited by R. Figueroa and S. Harding. New York: Routledge, 2003.

Wylie, Alison, and Lynn Hankinson Nelson. "Coming to Terms with the Values of Science: Insights from Feminist Science Scholarship." In *Value-Free Science: Ideal or Illusion?* Edited by H. Kincaid et al., 58–86. Oxford: Oxford University Press, 2007.

Biologists Who Study Gender/Feminism

MARY WYER

In the heyday of the women's liberation movement in the 1970s, professors and students at universities challenged major assumptions and paradigms of academic disciplines that had marginalized and/or excluded women's lives as valid subjects of study. These challenges pointed to an "invisible curriculum" that reinforced the social, economic, and political power of men over women. In tandem with these efforts, a small cadre of biologists began to explore the ways in which scientific perspectives promoted the inequality of women by fostering myths about women's abilities and interests. Seven women have been especially important to the development of feminist perspectives on science inside and outside of academia. These seven biologists identified and articulated in scholarly detail the myths upon which the "invisible curriculum" rested, targeting in particular the claim that biological sex differences in intellectual ability and interests favor men and disadvantage women. By the 1980s, these scientists had combined their commitments to objectivity and feminism to provide a uniquely informed perspective on scientific research that launched a major national debate about objectivity in science. Though each author has offered a distinct theoretical perspective and scope of work, their collective contribution has been to demonstrate that biological knowledge about humans—women's bodies, health and medicine, neurobiology, reproduction, sexuality, and sex differences—is shaped by, and shapes, society (Longino 1990; Rose 1994). Pioneering contributors to this approach include Linda Birke, Ruth Bleier, Anne Fausto-Sterling, Ruth Hubbard, Evelyn Fox Keller, Sue Rosser, and Bonnie Spanier. More recently, Patricia Gowaty has made significant contributions. Many other scholars from inside and outside of biology have developed theory and research in feminist science studies. However, this small group of women are notable as biologists who applied their scientific expertise to elaborating specific topics, approaches, and arguments about women's biology, intellectual abilities, experiences, and education.

Linda Birke (1948–)

Linda Birke earned degrees in the biological sciences and animal behavior from the University of Sussex, United Kingdom, with a focus on hormones and animal behavior. Her earliest work on women/gender emerged from a discussion group in the 1970s, the Brighton Women and Science Group, where she and her colleagues sought to bridge the seemingly intractable divide between feminist perspectives and scientific ones. Birke critiqued both feminist theory and biological theory about sex differences. In her first major book, *Women, Feminism, and Biology* (1986), she analyzed early feminist theory about the origins of women's oppression, arguing that by focusing exclusively on patriarchal power as a transhistorical force in gender relations, feminist theory unwittingly reinforced the idea that women's biology determined social arrangements. She also challenged the concept of biological determinism, arguing that research in this vein depended on experimental designs that reduced complex phenomena to a simple one-way relationship, precluding more dynamic models of the nature/culture relationship. "Our biology," she said, "does not determine anything" (106). As a biologist, Birke's objective has been to advance an understanding of scientific inquiry as feminist inquiry, to develop a "feminist science." In her definition, a feminist science would be one in which scientists recognize that they are social agents, that the human/nature relationship is one of cooperation rather than exploitation and domination, that research practices should be humane and egalitarian, and that research goals should be directed at human well-being and liberation. She reflected on her experiences in the laboratory with animal experiments in "On Keeping a Respectful Distance" (Birke and Hubbard 1995).

Ruth Bleier (1923–1988)

Ruth Bleier was a leading expert on neuroanatomy and the hypothalamus in animals. She received an M.D. from the Woman's Medical College of Pennsylvania in 1949 and practiced general medicine before beginning her research career at the Johns Hopkins School of Medicine in 1957. She was active in the peace and civil rights movements, affirmative action and salary equity initiatives, and the founding of the Women's Studies Program at the University of Wisconsin–Madison, which she chaired from 1982 to 1986. By her account, her book *Science and Gender* (1984) was the first book-length feminist critical analysis of science by a scientist. It was followed by her edited collection, *Feminist Approaches to Science* (1986), which included a series of groundbreaking essays describing the ideological content of modern science, the possibilities of feminist perspectives as a corrective, and the implications of these insights for the university curriculum. Bleier's writings reveal her deep commitment to objectivity and the scientific method in her energetic challenges to theories of human evolution, research on sex differences, and studies of hormones, behavior, and the brain. Her template for analyzing flawed scientific assumptions, methods, and conclusions is a classic demonstration of scientific rigor, as useful today as when it first appeared in *Science and Gender*. For Bleier, feminist perspectives are revolutionary and transforming, offering the sciences a path to a more complete, holistic, and complex understanding of the natural world.

Anne Fausto-Sterling (1944–)

Anne Fausto-Sterling earned her doctorate in developmental genetics at Brown University in 1970; her current research interests are in molecular and developmental genetics. Her widely read first book, *Myths of Gender* (1985), launched her career as a public scholar, lecturer, and educator about the oppressive, distorted, and destructive themes of research on sex/gender differences. In the years since, Fausto-Sterling's work has consistently asserted that scientists' claims to hold rational and value-free perspectives are undercut by an unrecognized and unarticulated ideology of male dominance in conventional content, priorities, and methods. In particular, Fausto-Sterling has revealed the ways in which this ideological content informs multiple generations of scientific research. She has elaborated her arguments with persuasive detail on topics such as menopause and menstruation, cognitive abilities and intelligence, brain function and organization (famously the corpus callosum), genes and gender, sex hormones, and human sexualities. Her book, *Sexing the Body* (2000), received numerous awards, including an American Library Association award (2000) for outstanding academic book, the Robert K. Merton award (2000) from the American Sociological Association, and the distinguished publication award (2000) from the Association for Women in Psychology. In addition to her research, Fausto-Sterling sparked a debate within women's studies programs about the marginalization of scientific perspectives in their degree requirements and courses (Fausto-Sterling 1992). Fausto-Sterling's call for "building two-way streets" between women's studies and the sciences has prompted a variety of programmatic efforts to utilize women's studies in the science curriculum and vice versa.

Patricia Gowaty

Patricia Gowaty received her doctorate in zoology from Clemson University in 1980. Her current research focuses on the intersections of ecology, evolution, and behavior in theories about sexual conflict, mate choice, and reproduction. As a scientist, she is perhaps best known for her behavioral research on Eastern bluebirds. Gowaty has contributed a unique perspective to feminist science studies by embracing some of the general premises of sociobiology and evolutionary psychology while advancing significant critiques of conclusions about sex roles and parental investment. For instance, she has argued that mate choices are subject to social and ecological pressures as well as evolutionary ones, so that male and female sex roles may be at once flexible and yet predictable when all of the parameters are known and measured. In her important *Signs* article, "Sexual Natures: How Feminism Changed Evolutionary Biology," Gowaty (2003) challenges universalizing evolutionary theories that characterize females' mate choice strategy as choosy and males' mate choice as indiscriminate. Like other biologists with feminist perspectives, Gowaty critiques research that is "bad science" about sex role differences in mating strategies and parental investment—that is, research that utilizes untested theories to generate inadequate evidence for explanations that are poorly explored. Gowaty argues that her feminist perspective made it possible for her not only to see the limitations of earlier research but also to imagine the experiments that could adequately test the theories at play and offer alternate explanations for the phenomena.

Ruth Hubbard (1924–)

Ruth Hubbard was born in Austria and emigrated to the United States with her parents in 1938 to escape Nazi Germany. She received her Ph.D. in biology from Radcliffe College in 1950. She is the first woman to have been tenured as a professor of biology at Harvard University. Her scientific research focused on the photochemistry of vision in vertebrates and invertebrates, and in 1967, she won the University of Zurich Paul Karrer Medal with her husband, George Wald, for their work on this topic. Hubbard's fearless and vocal political commitments in the 1960s and 1970s placed her in the forefront of feminist challenges to biological explanations for women's inequality. Hubbard's essay, "Have Only Men Evolved?" (1979), broke new ground in calling attention to the ways in which discredited ideas from 19th-century social Darwinism had been reformulated as sociobiology. Her 1979 edited collection, *Genes and Gender* (co-editor Marian Lowe) is perhaps the first volume to critically examine contemporary biological theories about women. Over 30 years of writings consistently champion the necessity of demystifying scientific research in order to see that scientists work within social and political contexts. The cultural authority of science, she argues, is implicated in providing "factual" evidence to legitimate race, class, and gender inequalities. For Hubbard, the pretense that science is objective, value-neutral, and apolitical masks the complicity of scientists in supporting the status quo of power relations. She has thus presented feminists (women and men) in science with the challenge of integrating their political vision with their working lives. Recent work extends this challenge to rethinking exploitive relations with plant and animal life in research, including the Human Genome Project.

Evelyn Fox Keller (1936–)

Evelyn Fox Keller received a Ph.D. in physics from Harvard University in 1963. She developed a successful research and teaching career in theoretical physics and molecular biology. Then, as an associate professor of mathematics at SUNY-Purchase, in 1977 she launched her career as a gender and science theorist with the publication of "The Anomaly of a Woman in Physics," her autobiographical account of sexism in graduate school. The following year, she published the essay "Gender and Science," in which she explored the psychosocial dynamics of objectivity in relation to behavioral norms for masculinity and femininity. From the foundation of these early works, she

Biologist Evelyn Fox Keller. (Photograph by Marleen Wynants)

developed a series of essays and books that identified a new frontier of knowledge about the formative influence of beliefs about women and men in the history, philosophy, and contemporary practices of Western science. Keller has, perhaps more than any other, mapped the terrain by which the cultural authority, language, subjects, models, and methods of Western science have a reciprocal relationship with social constructions of gender. She has argued that the exclusion from science of qualities associated with women (emotion, empathy, subjectivity) has emerged in tandem with the construction of scientific reasoning as masculine (rational, detached, and objective). As a result, she says, science has not yet embraced the full range of human abilities to understand the natural world. She has not advocated a "feminist science" but rather a more fully human science. Keller was awarded a MacArthur Fellowship in 1992 for the originality of her work.

Sue V. Rosser (1947–)

Sue Rosser received a Ph.D. in zoology from the University of Wisconsin in 1973. Rosser is recognized as the national leader in curriculum transformation efforts in the sciences to promote the participation of women. She was an early and energetic advocate for integrating women's studies research and pedagogy into the science curriculum, particularly into biology courses. Though she published widely in the 1980s, it was in her *Female-Friendly Science* (1990) that she presented a consolidated vision for innovation in the reformulation of science education and training. Rosser argues that conventional course contents (textbooks, activities, and illustrations) marginalize issues of interest to women and girls, underrepresent the accomplishments of women scientists, favor images of males over those of females, and tap skills and abilities to which women and girls are seldom socialized. After two decades of work developing curriculum initiatives in the sciences, in *Re-Engineering Female-Friendly Science* (1997) Rosser reexamined her strategies, their outcomes, and the feminist theories upon which she and others have relied. She found that curriculum projects are successful in motivating individual faculty members to improve their teaching, that inclusive teaching approaches increase the retention and performance of all students, but that institutional change to promote these outcomes remains a distant goal. In later work, she has elaborated these themes in several arenas, including health, medicine, and reproductive technologies, to emphasize the institutional forms and forces that systematically privilege a few men and exclude the talents and abilities of the majority. Rosser is a clear and consistent proponent of the theory that women will not be fully represented in the sciences until they are fully represented in the content of science teaching and research.

Bonnie Spanier (1946–)

Bonnie Spanier received a PhD. in microbiology and molecular genetics from Harvard University in 1975. Spanier was an early advocate for incorporating material about women into the curriculum and in 1980 was appointed director of an initiative at Wheaton College. Her examination of hidden biases about gender, sexuality, race, and class in molecular biology, *Im/Partial Science: Gender Ideology in Molecular Biology* (1995), is a classic application of feminist science theory to a specific field. In this book, Spanier details a host of organizing principles, theories, and representations of basic biological processes that deploy the ideological touchstones of a White, masculinist, elitist, heterosexist culture. She argues that the covert ideological content discourages the participation of underrepresented groups in molecular biology, and that alternative language, concepts, and paradigms would provide more accurate descriptions of the natural world. In her later work, Spanier has focused on the science and politics of breast cancer as a founding member of the activist organization, Capital Region Action against Breast Cancer (CRAAB).

These scientists have engaged feminist theory about women and gender in the context of biological theory and research. Their work has resonated with scholars in a variety of disciplines who proposed developing a successor science project that reimagines scientific research as a fully inclusive and fully human activity with liberatory goals. This idea emerged from and is grounded in debates about epistemology within feminist scholarship, reflecting the interdisciplinary reach of women's and gender studies. For the earliest formulations, see Flax (1983), Hartsock (1983), and Rose (1983). For a review of successor science debates, see Harding (1986).

A second generation now seeks to institutionalize research about women/gender within the sciences. This new work falls into four categories: research into new topics, methods, and theories about women/gender in the sciences (Mayberry, Subramaniam, and Weasel 2001); faculty development initiatives to address scientists' interests in scholarship on women/gender (Musil 2001); educational innovations to incorporate material about women/gender into courses and curriculum in the sciences (Rosser 1995); and educational research about the effects of the new material on students' knowledge about women/gender in science and on their persistence in science majors and scientific careers (Damschen et al. 2005; Wyer et al. 2007). (*See also* Biology; Feminist Science Studies)

References and Further Reading

Birke, L. *Women, Feminism, and Biology: The Feminist Challenge.* Brighton, UK: Harvester Press, 1986.

Birke, L., and J. Barr. *Common Science? Women, Science and Knowledge*. Bloomington: Indiana University Press, 1998.

Birke, L., S. Himmelweit, and G. Vines. *Tomorrow's Child: Reproductive Technologies in the Nineties*. London: Virago, 1990.

Birke, L., and R. Hubbard, eds. *Reinventing Biology: Respect for Life and the Creation of Knowledge*. Bloomington: Indiana University Press, 1995.

Bleier, R. *Science and Gender: A Critique of Biology and Its Theories on Women*. New York: Pergamon, 1984.

Bleier, R., ed. *Feminist Approaches to Science*. New York: Pergamon, 1986.

Damschen, E., K. Rosenfeld, M. Wyer, D. Murphy-Medley, T. Wentworth, and N. Haddad "Visibility Matters: Increasing Student Knowledge of Women's Contributions to Ecology." *Frontiers in Ecology and the Environment* 3 (2005): 212–219.

Fausto-Sterling, A. *Myths of Gender: Biological Theories about Women and Men*. New York: Basic Books, 1985; 1992.

Fausto-Sterling, A. "Society Writes Biology, Biology Constructs Gender." *Daedelus* 116 (1987): 61–76.

Fausto-Sterling, A. "Life in the XY Corral." *Women's Studies International Forum* 12(3) (1989): 319–331.

Fausto-Sterling, A. "Building Two-Way Streets: The Case of Feminism and Science." *NWSA Journal* 4(3) (1992): 336–349.

Fausto-Sterling, A. *Sexing the Body: Gender Politics and the Construction of Sexuality*. New York: Basic Books, 2000.

Fausto-Sterling, A. "Bare Bones of Sex: Part I, Sex & Gender." *Signs: Journal of Women in Culture and Society* 30(2) (2005): 1491–1528.

Flax, J. "Political Philosophy and the Patriarchal Unconscious: A Psychoanalytic Perspective on Epistemology and Metaphysics." In *Discovering Reality: Feminist Perspectives on Epistemology, Metaphysics, Methodology and Philosophy of Science*. Edited by S. Harding and M. B. Hintikka. Dordrecht: D. Reidel, 1983.

Gowaty, P. A. "Evolutionary Biology and Feminism." *Human Nature* 3(3) (1992): 217–249.

Gowaty, P. A. "What if within-sex Variation Is Greater than between-sex Variation?" Invited peer commentary on R. Thornhill and N. W. Thornhill, "The Evolutionary Psychology of Men's Coercive Sexuality." *Behavioral and Brain Sciences* 15 (1992): 393–394.

Gowaty, P. A., ed. *Feminism and Evolutionary Biology: Boundaries, Intersections, and Frontiers*. New York: Chapman Hall, 1997.

Gowaty, P. A. "Sexual Natures: How Feminism Changed Evolutionary Biology." *Signs: Journal of Women in Culture and Society* 28(3) (2003): 901–921.

Harding, S. "The Instability of the Analytic Categories of Feminist Theory." *Signs: Journal of Women in Culture and Society* 11(4) (1986): 645–664.

Hartsock, N. "The Feminist Standpoint: Developing the Ground for a Specifically Feminist Historical Materialism." In *Discovering Reality: Feminist Perspectives on Epistemology, Metaphysics, Methodology and Philosophy of Science*. Edited by S. Harding and M. B. Hintikka. Dordrecht: D. Reidel, 1983.

Hubbard, R. "Have Only Men Evolved?" In *Women Look at Biology Looking at Women*. Edited by R. Hubbard, M. S. Henifin, and B. Fried. Cambridge, MA: Schenkman, 1979.

Hubbard, R. *The Politics of Women's Biology*. New Brunswick, NJ: Rutgers University Press, 1990.

Hubbard, R., and L. Birke, eds. *Respect for Life and the Creation of Knowledge*. Bloomington: Indiana University Press, 1995.

Hubbard, R., and M. Lowe. *Genes and Gender*. Staten Island, NY: Gordian Press, 1979.

Hubbard, R., and E. Wald. *Exploding the Gene Myth: How Genetic Information Is Produced and Manipulated by Scientists, Physicians, Employers, Insurance Companies, Educators, and Law Enforcers*. Boston: Beacon Press, 1993.

Keller, E. F. "The Anomaly of a Woman in Physics." In *Working It Out*. Edited by S. Ruddick and P. Daniels. New York: Pantheon, 1977.

Keller, E. F. "Gender and Science." *Psychoanalysis and Contemporary Thought* 1(3) (1978): 409–433.

Keller, E. F. *A Feeling for the Organism: The Life and Work of Barbara McClintock*. San Francisco: W. H. Freeman, 1983.

Keller, E. F. *Reflections on Gender and Science*. New Haven, CT: Yale University Press, 1985.

Keller, E. F. *Secrets of Life, Secrets of Death: Essays on Language, Gender, and Science*. New York: Routledge, 1992.

Keller, E. F. *Refiguring Life: Metaphors of Twentieth Century Biology*. New York: Columbia University Press, 1995.

Longino, H. *Science as Social Knowledge*. Princeton, NJ: Princeton University Press, 1990.

Lowe, M., and R. Hubbard. *Woman's Nature: Rationalizations of Women's Inequality*. Oxford: Pergamon, 1983.

Mayberry, M., B. Subramaniam, and L. Weasel, eds. *Feminist Science Studies: A New Generation*. New York: Routledge, 2001.

Musil, C. M., ed. *Gender, Science, and the Undergraduate Curriculum: Building Two-Way Streets*. Washington, DC: Association of American Colleges and Universities, 2001.

Rose, H. "Hand, Brain, and Heart: A Feminist Epistemology for the Natural Sciences." *Signs: Journal of Women in Culture and Society* 9(1) (1983): 73–90.

Rose, H. *Love, Power and Knowledge: Towards a Feminist Transformation of the Sciences*. Bloomington: Indiana University Press, 1994.

Rosser, Sue V. *Female-Friendly Science: Applying Women's Studies Methods and Theories to Attract Students to Science*. New York: Pergamon, 1990.

Rosser, Sue V. *Feminism and Biology*. New York: Twayne/Macmillan, 1992.

Rosser, Sue V. *Women's Health: Missing from U.S. Medicine*. Bloomington: Indiana University Press, 1994.

Rosser, Sue V., ed. *Teaching the Majority: Science, Mathematics, and Engineering Teaching that Attracts Women*. New York: Teachers College Press, 1995.

Rosser, Sue V. *Re-Engineering Female-Friendly Science*. New York: Teachers College Press, 1997.

Rosser, Sue V. *Women, Science, and Society: The Crucial Union*. New York: Teachers College Press, 2000.

Rosser, Sue V. *The Science Glass Ceiling: Academic Women Scientists and the Struggle to Succeed*. New York: Routledge, 2004.

Spanier, B. "Biological Determinism and Homosexuality." *NWSA Journal* 7 (1995): 54–72.

Spanier, B. *Im/Partial Science: Gender Ideology in Molecular Biology*. Bloomington: Indiana University Press, 1995.

Spanier, B. "'Your Silence Will Not Protect You': Feminist Science Studies, Breast Cancer, and Activism." In *Feminist Science Studies: A New Generation*. Edited by M. Mayberry, B. Subramanian, and L. Weasel. New York: Routledge, 2001.

Wyer, M., D. Murphy-Medley, E. Damschen, K. Rosenfeld, and T. Wentworth. "No Quick Fixes: Adding Women to Ecology Course Content." *Psychology of Women Quarterly* 31 (2007): 96–102.

Historians of Science and Technology Who Focus on Feminism

Erika Lorraine Milam

Origins of the History of Science and Technology and the Feminist Critique of "Pure" Science

During the 1950s and 1960s, most academics with an interest in the history and philosophy of science were trained first in the sciences and then gained an interest in the history of their field. As a discipline, the history and philosophy of science was designed to produce well-rounded citizens in two ways. First, historians and philosophers hoped to educate nonscientists about how science really worked and thus bridge the two cultures of science and humanities. Second, they sought to teach future scientists about the history and ethics of their field, thereby preventing them from repeating the mistakes of their predecessors. Both of these goals were predicated on the idea that good science was inherently free of ideologies that corrupt true knowledge of the world, like socialism or communism. Good science was democratic and a potential source of international cooperation and peace. By understanding the history of science and technology, educators could produce better future citizens. As U.S. politicians became increasingly concerned that Americans were falling behind the Soviets scientifically and technologically, federal funding of science and engineering increased exponentially, as did the opportunities to study the history and philosophy of science.

By the late 1960s, the rise of the women's health movement, sexual liberation, radical civil rights, anti-Vietnam war protests, and ecological concern over pesticides and the environment combined to provide a nexus of highly visible new perspectives within society. No longer could one claim to speak for the general "American public." Social divisions based on ethnicity, class, and gender brought this fractionated American society into view for anyone with access to a radio, newspapers, or television. This view of American society as irretrievably divided contributed to scholarly and popular reactions to scientific, technological, and medical research, not only through "externalist" critiques of the military-industrial complex but also from within the scientific community itself.

As second-wave feminism continued to gather steam throughout the 1970s, feminist scholars challenged the prevailing stereotype that science and engineering were disciplines for intelligent young boys and erudite adult men. At the core of the feminist critique of science was the contention that scientists did not have the authority, foresight, or expertise to speak for all social constituencies affected by the conclusions of the scientific and technological elite. This push against the presumed authority of science as a universal way to true knowledge built on existing tensions at university campuses over the traditional canon of great white men assigned in philosophy, literature, and history classes.

Feminist scholars turned their gaze to analyzing not only highly contentious issues within science (like Edward O. Wilson's *Sociobiology*) but also the normal processes of science and engineering. They asked how do we "know" things, and how do different cultures produce scientific or technological knowledge in different ways? Feminist historians of science and technology were further interested in how cultures of science had changed over time and when the study of the natural, physical world had become a predominantly male activity. For these scholars, biological definitions of gender, sex, race, and femininity were constantly negotiated in society and had changed drastically in recent centuries. Gender identities were not fixed but malleable, and modern science provided only the most recent means of reifying cultural definitions of social identity by repositioning them in a biological, scientific framework.

The debate over the relative importance of natural and cultural causes of status quo erupted on the pages of newspapers, magazines, and on television, with both scientists and nonscientists on either side. In the following decades, similar debates over the values and social agendas embedded in scientific research became polarized as cultures of scientists and humanists developed specialized vocabularies and frameworks for discussing the similar issues.

Feminism and the Science Culture Wars

In the 1980s and 1990s, feminist historians of science and technology found academic homes within departments of history, history of science, philosophy, and women's studies. The avenues by which feminist historians of science and technology enter the field have continued to vary serendipitously. While some scholars obtained graduate training in history, philosophy, sociology, anthropology, or other social science disciplines, others began their graduate training in the sciences or engineering and subsequently became interested in the history of their field. This diversity of training and perspective among feminist historians of science and technology has helped invigorate the field and has also contributed to the variety of strategies women have used to reform the practice and conclusions of the scientific community.

In the 1970s and 1980s, feminist historians of science and technology approached their research with at least four goals in mind. The first was to demonstrate that cultural conceptions of gender were separate from scientific conceptions of sex and that women's gender roles were not fixed but were constantly negotiated. Second, feminist historians sought to acknowledge and understand the ways in which women were framed as subjects of scientific research and consumers of technology and the inequality of access to the products of science, technology, and medicine. Third, they additionally strove to increase the visibility of women as producers of technological and scientific knowledge. Fourth, feminist historians of science and technology also worked to demonstrate how claims of scientific and technological expertise and definitions of knowledge were culturally situated. The feminist critique of scientific and technological enterprises thus extended beyond merely differentiating between "good science" and "bad science" to understanding the social forces constructing all scientific claims.

Not all scientists took this in stride. To many scientists, science was about observations of the natural and physical world, and the questions raised by feminists were beyond the purview of science. Feminist approaches to science and technology were synonymous with the social construction of science and technology and missed what scientists felt was truly important about science and engineering as powerful ways of knowing and manipulating the natural world. Feminists questioned the processes by which the scientific community came to accept observations as facts or made decisions about scientific or technological policy, and they concerned themselves with environmental and social justice in regard to pesticides, pollutants, and radiation disproportionately affecting those people in the United States and around the world who lacked strong political voices; to some scientists these issues had no bearing on what scientists knew about the natural world. For many feminists, such criticisms missed the point; they argued that it was possible to believe both that the natural world investigated by scientists was real and that scientific communities are social, political cultures. Yet many scientists remained convinced that feminist historians of science and technology sought to undermine the power and legitimacy of science and engineering as ways of knowing. This reaction from the scientific community was by no means universal, yet nonetheless it became extremely important within the politics of academia by creating a sense of antagonism between feminist studies of science and technology and the scientific community in the last decades of the 20th century.

Effects of Feminism on the Practice of Science and Technology

Today, feminist approaches to the history of science and technology sit at the intersection of several scholarly disciplines: history, certainly, but also sociology, anthropology, ethics, philosophy, and public policy. This interdisciplinary set of analytical tools has proved both analytically and politically powerful in reforming scientists' ideas about the skills, rituals, and conventions inherent to scientific practice.

Scientists have become increasingly interested in the methods of feminist analyses of scientific and technological systems as inherently social networks as mounting critiques of science from outside academic communities have taken the shape of popular disbelief in global climate change, carbon dating, and evolutionary biology (evolution is "just a theory" not a "fact"). As a result, scientists, especially biologists and climatologists, are looking to feminist analyses of how ideas are spread through a community of peers, what kinds of authority are more convincing than others, and how to demarcate science and pseudo-science in an attempt to make their conclusions more accessible to a popular audience. Part of learning to participate in the scientific community, they argue, is learning about the culture and norms of communication within that community. Similarly, part of being a responsible scientist is to understand the social networks in which your research exists as a way of gauging the short- and long-term effects of science and technology in society. These trends have been especially pronounced in both science education and science policy.

The scientific community has emphasized multi-inter-cross-disciplinary approaches to understanding the relationships among scientific, technological, and social endeavors, including feminism. Each discipline within science and technology studies (anthropology, sociology, history, philosophy, cultural studies, women's studies, etc.) utilizes a different set of tools that provide complementary kinds of information about the nexus of the natural, physical, and social world in which we live.

Influential Feminist Historians of Science and Technology

Cynthia Cockburn entered the field of feminist studies of science and technology through her job as a research assistant at University College, London's Bartlet School of Architecture and later at the Center of Environmental Studies. Already in her thirties, she learned how to conduct research and analyze data about current social issues. Although her work has been more sociologically than historically oriented, her books have been very influential in helping historians frame the gendered modes of production and marketing of everyday technologies (especially Cockburn and Ormrod 1993). More recently, Cockburn has turned her attention to the conjunction of feminism and peace/conflict studies. She is active in Women in Black, a worldwide network of women committed to peace with justice and actively opposed to injustice, war, militarism and other forms of violence, and seeks to highlight the effects of war on women's lives and ultimately to promote peaceful resolutions in conflict-ridden areas of the world. She currently lives in London and works as a visiting professor of sociology at City University London.

Ruth Schwartz Cowan earned her Ph.D. from Johns Hopkins University in 1969, with a thesis on Francis Galton and the history of eugenics. However, her first faculty position at SUNY–Stony Brook fundamentally changed her research interests. After student riots on campus in 1968 and 1969, the administration asked professors to volunteer for an experimental teaching project. Faculty would teach classes on topics with which they had no prior experience—the professor and the students would then learn the material together. Cowan volunteered to teach a course on "Technological Determinism," which quickly led to a new research project on "labor-saving" devices in U.S. households. In 1973, she presented the results of her research at the annual meeting of the Society of the History of Technology (SHOT): new domestic technologies actually increased the amount of time the average woman spent on housework and were not, in fact, labor saving. This research became her first book, *More Work for Mother* (Cowan 1983), which won the 1984 Dexter Prize awarded by SHOT. In later work, she elucidated the ways in which technological change occurs as a result of behavioral changes in many different people, all of whom are joined together through a social network. Cowan has also published an incredibly successful textbook on the social history of American technology. In 2002, she moved to Philadelphia as the Janice and Julian Bers Professor of History and Sociology of Science at the University of Pennsylvania.

After earning a dual bachelor's degree in physics and electrical engineering and while working on a master's degree in physics from the Massachusetts Institute of Technology, Evelynn Hammonds discovered her passion for the history of science and medicine. Staying in Cambridge, she completed her Ph.D. in the history of science at Harvard University in 1993. Hammonds's research has centered on the devastating effects of race in the 19th and 20th centuries. She argues that because ideas of race are socially constructed, they have phenomenal power in American society and have been used to justify gross inequities in access to medical treatment, education, and environmental quality (Hammonds 1999). Currently, Hammonds is a professor of the history of science and of African and African American affairs at Harvard; after serving as senior vice provost for faculty development and diversity, she was named dean of Harvard College in 2008.

Historian Donna Haraway. (Rusten Hogness)

Donna Haraway is famous for her statement that she'd "rather be a cyborg than a goddess." Born in Denver, Colorado, Haraway also began her academic training in the sciences, earning a Ph.D. in cell biology from Yale in 1972. After her first position at Johns Hopkins University in Baltimore, she moved to California where she is now professor of the Program in the History of Consciousness and Women's Studies at the University of California–Santa Cruz. It is hard to underestimate Haraway's importance to feminist theory's engagement with science, gender, race, and technology. She argues that we are all cyborgs, products of and actors in a technological web. We no longer can separate our self-identity from the technologies of our lives, from the running shoes in which we go jogging to our cell phones and the computers on which we check our e-mail. The coalitions we build through our technology give us the power to define our identity through kinship with communities of our choosing. Thus, Haraway's vision of cyborg identity is at once liberating and community oriented. Her most historical book, *Primate Visions* (Haraway 1989), created a huge ruckus when it was published because of her contention that primates have served as mirrors of humanity. She contended that throughout the 20th century, American popular culture projected current images of human society into the narratives they told about primates. She used images and stories about primates in museums, magazines, television, and science fiction to uncover American social narratives of gender and race. In 2000, Haraway was awarded the J. D. Bernal Prize by the Society for the Social Studies of Science for her distinguished contribution to science studies.

Evelyn Fox Keller entered graduate school at Harvard in the 1950s intending to study theoretical physics. Despite the hostile climate of the department faculty and her fellow graduate students, she earned her Ph.D. in 1963 by writing a thesis in molecular biology, where the climate was a little friendlier. Her intellectual journey from physics to molecular biology to the history and epistemology of the life sciences appears at first to have been quite long, but her curiosity about how we know what we know about the natural world has run through all of her research. This trajectory from science and/or engineering to the history of science and technology is shared by many feminists with technoscience interests, although Keller's journey from one to the other was at least partly driven by the social attitudes of her peers in graduate school, who maintained that theoretical physics was hard, certainly too hard for any woman to understand, much less to provide insightful and novel research in. Keller has published several important books in the history of the life sciences, most notably *A Feeling for the Organism,* a biography of Barbara McClinock and her research on maize (Keller 1983). Her personal, psychoanalytic style interrogates the effects of social assumptions about masculinity, femininity, and science on the life of a scientist. Keller has held faculty positions at Northeastern University, SUNY-Purchase, New York University, and the University of California–Berkeley. For the last 25 years she has been a professor in the Science, Technology, and Society Program at the Massachusetts Institute of Technology.

Following a path that is more common now than it was in the 1960s, Sally Gregory Kohlstedt began her academic training in the history of science, earning her Ph.D. in history from the University of Illinois–Urbana in 1972. Over the course of her career, both her research and her institutional service reflect her interests in feminism and the history of science. Her research has explored the institutional boundaries to professional science that women have faced in the United States as well as expanded our vision of how women participated in the scientific enterprise, from laboratory technicians to nature study in the home (Kohlstedt et al. 1996). In Kohlstedt's work, feminism became a useful tool for reevaluating what counts as "doing" science and in opening our vision as historians to the great many people who are required to make the scientific enterprise succeed. The history of science is not just about a few great White men who had brilliant ideas; it concerns the entire intellectual and practical effort required to conduct scientific research and to convince the scientific community of its validity and importance.

In her philosophical analyses of evolutionary explanations of female orgasm, Elisabeth Lloyd made visible a persistent male bias in the approach of biologists to women's sexuality. Lloyd earned her Ph.D. in philosophy at Princeton University in 1984, spending a year of her graduate training working with Stephen Jay Gould at Harvard. Using philosophical and statistical evidence to substantiate her claims, Lloyd argues that sufficient evidence does not yet exist to demonstrate that female orgasm is adaptive. Although her work has been criticized by feminists, who suggest Lloyd must be antifeminist because her claim that female orgasm is not an adaptation implies it is devoid of worth, Lloyd sees her work as liberating for women. Lloyd argues that because female orgasm is an unexpected bonus and completely unconnected to fertility or reproductive success in women, then women should be free to explore as many avenues to achieving orgasm as they desire.

Judith McGaw became interested in the history of American technology as a graduate student working with Brooke Hindle at New York University. After earning her Ph.D., she accepted a position at the University of Virginia but quickly moved to join the Department of History and Sociology of Science at the University of Pennsylvania. McGaw's research sat at the intersection of American history, the history of technology, and gender studies, and her first book, *Most Wonderful Machine,* won the 1989 Edelstein Prize from SHOT (McGaw 1987). In subsequent publications she has argued that everyday, mundane technologies were critically important in defining nationhood in the early American republic and in demarcating gender roles within society. McGaw has now retired to Portland, Oregon, where she teaches meditation.

Carolyn Merchant's vision of the earth in peril has served as a clarion call to a burgeoning community of ecofeminists interested in environmental justice. Merchant earned her Ph.D. in the history of science at the University of Wisconsin–Madison and subsequently moved west to join the department of history at the University of California–Berkeley, where she has been a faculty member for over 20 years. Merchant became interested in environmental studies after reading Rachel Carson's indictment of pesticides in *Silent Spring* (1962) and in feminism because of Betty Friedan's *Feminine Mystique* (1963). Merging these environmentalist and feminist perspectives, Merchant wrote *The Death of Nature* as an indictment of the modern mechanical vision of inert nature arising during the scientific revolution of the 16th and 17th centuries (Merchant 1980). This vision, she argued, replaced an older conception of nature as an active, organic, feminine entity. As natural philosophers viewed matter as passive, they naturalized dominion over the mechanized nature through objective technological and scientific research. Merchant's more recent work has continued to interrogate both the metaphorical relationships of women to the environments in which they live and the practical effects of gender, race, and class on women's access to and relationship with nature.

As Margaret W. Rossiter earned her Ph.D. in history from Yale in 1971, she began to wonder why there were so few women in the standard history of science. Did this lack of female role models illustrate how impossible it was for women to get a foot in the door of professional science or reflect historians' lack of interest in the contributions of the female scientists who did exist? Rossiter's two-volume answer implicated both the systematic institutional barriers to women in science and the lack of historical attention to women in science (Rossiter 1982). The books are not entirely bleak, however, as Rossiter also explored the ways in which women succeeded in overcoming the barriers they faced, whether by confronting discriminatory policies directly, establishing prizes and fellowships for fellow women scientists, or by accepting low status and/or low-paying jobs simply to continue the work they loved. Rossiter currently holds the Marie Underhill Professorship of the History of Science in the Department of Science and Technology Studies at Cornell University.

Earning her Ph.D. in history from Harvard in 1984, Londa Schiebinger has quickly become one of the most visible feminist historians of science in the United States. Her first book, *The Mind Has No Sex?* investigated Enlightenment conceptions of femininity and masculinity in nature (Schiebinger 1989). She suggested that during the 18th century, with the development of public and private spheres of social influence, men and women were constructed as biologically suited to different kinds of labor. The pursuit of "science" became a public, democratic enterprise based on the presumed intellectual equality of peers; women were thereby restricted from participating in the scientific enterprise except where cultures of science intersected with the domestic sphere (parlor science and children's education). Schiebinger's historical work analyzes the metaphorical underpinnings of scientific analysis of sexed and gendered public identities and the effects of assumptions about sex and gender on the current inequality of women's access to professional careers in science and engineering. Schiebinger now works at Stanford University as a professor in the history of science and as director of the Institute for Gender Research.

Effects of Feminism on the History of Science and Technology

The conceptual tools and analytical questions of feminism have effected profound change in academic conceptions of the history of science and technology. Feminists have sought ways to change what they identified as a male-biased social structure by pointing out the systemic ways in which it was difficult for women to forge successful careers in science and to remedy the effects of science on socially disadvantaged populations. Feminist approaches to science and technology have also helped to rediscover and revive traditional technologies of domestic life that were previously invisible to the scholarly community. In doing so, they have enriched our understanding of science and technology as cultures and processes, expanded our definitions of what kinds of activities are central to the scientific-technological enterprise, and enlarged our roster of who counts as performing scientific and technological research. (*See also* Critiques of Science; Feminist Philosophy of Science; Feminist Science Studies; Technology)

References and Further Reading

Cockburn, Cynthia, and Susan Ormrod. *Gender and Technology in the Making*. London: Sage, 1993.

Cowan, Ruth Schwartz. *More Work for Mother: The Ironies of Household Technology from the Open Hearth to the Microwave*. New York: Basic Books, 1983.

Hammonds, Evelynn. *Childhood's Deadly Scourge: The Campaign to Control Diphtheria in New York City, 1880–1930*. Baltimore, MD: Johns Hopkins University Press, 1999.

Haraway, Donna. *Primate Visions: Gender, Race, and Nature in the World of Modern Science*. New York: Routledge, 1989.

Keller, Evelyn Fox. *A Feeling for the Organism: The Life and Work of Barbara McClintock*. San Francisco: Freeman, 1983.

Kohlestedt, Sally Gregory, Barbara Laslett, Helen Longino, and Evelyn Hammonds, eds. *Gender and Scientific Authority*. Chicago: University of Chicago Press, 1996.

Lloyd, Elisabeth. *The Case of the Female Orgasm: Bias in the Science of Evolution*. Cambridge, MA: Harvard University Press, 2005.

McGaw, Judith A. *Most Wonderful Machine: Mechanization and Social Change in Berkshire Paper Making, 1801–1885*. Princeton, NJ: Princeton University Press, 1987.

Merchant, Carolyn. *The Death of Nature: Women, Ecology, and the Scientific Revolution*. San Francisco: Harper & Row, 1980.

Rossiter, Margaret. *Women Scientists in America: Struggles and Strategies to 1940*. Baltimore, MD: Johns Hopkins University Press, 1982.

Schiebinger, Londa L. *The Mind Has No Sex? Women in the Origins of Modern Science*. Cambridge, MA: Harvard University Press, 1989.

Primatologists Who Focus on Females/Gender

Linda Marie Fedigan

Primatology is today, for several reasons, arguably a gender-inclusive science. First, the discipline includes a large and growing proportion of women practitioners. Second, leading figures of the discipline consider themselves feminists (e.g., Jeanne Altmann, Sarah Hrdy, Jane Lancaster). Third, primatology is widely recognized by science studies scholars as a feminist science (e.g., Schiebinger 2003). And finally, this science has shown itself to be responsive to prior criticism of gender bias and highly inclusive of issues relevant to women, females, and feminists.

Following earlier considerations of *why* this might be the case (e.g., Fedigan 2001), the present essay describes *how* this came to be the case only over time as the discipline of primatology amended early biases. Two heuristic devices are used to focus this essay: historical stages and transformation phases.

1. Primatologists at different stages of the discipline's history have addressed the enduring issue: "what is the social role of female primates?" In the 1990s, Shirley Strum and Linda Fedigan constructed a history of North American field primatology (e.g., Fedigan and Strum 1999) that characterized the science as having occurred in four distinctive stages, to which this essay now adds a fifth, more recent one:
   Stage 1 1950–1965. The Natural History Phase
   Stage 2 1965–1975. The Discovery and Enigma of Variability
   Stage 3 1975–1985. The Sociobiological Era
   Stage 4 1985–1995. Behavioral Ecology
   Stage 5 1995–2005. Comparative Socioecology
2. A transformation model originally developed to characterize phases in the growing incorporation of women into the curriculum is also applied. Several scholars have proposed models to categorize steps in the transformation of curriculum. Rosser (1990) has expanded upon these models and shown how a recognizable set of phases can be

applied to the transformation of research and teaching about gender in the sciences.

Phase 1 The Womanless Curriculum

Phase 2 Women as an Addition to the Curriculum

Phase 3 Women as a Problem, Anomaly

Phase 4 Women as the Focus of Study

Phase 5 A Gender-balanced Curriculum

This essay explores how a curriculum transformation model can be applied to the scheme of historical stages in primatology, with the goal of better understanding the steps in scientific transformation and the effects of changing gender beliefs on the discipline of primatology, a science that is widely recognized as gender inclusive. In the following adaptation of the transformation model, the word "females" is substituted for "women" and "science of primatology" for "curriculum."

1950–1965: Stage/Phase 1. Natural History/The Female-less Science

According to Rosser's adaptation of transformation models, the absence of women ("females") is simply not noted during the first phase of a science. This was arguably the case during Stage 1 of primatology from 1950 to 1965. Although a few attempts at scientific observation of nonhuman primates in the wild were made in the early part of the 20th century, primate field studies only flowered in the 1950s, after World War II. In this decade, the influential American anthropologist, Sherwood Washburn, promulgated the view that insight into human social evolution would be achieved through delineation of a universal "primate pattern" and sent his graduate students to Africa and Asia to observe the social lives of monkeys. Simultaneously in Japan, Kenji Imanishi established a collaborative, descriptive method of studying sociality in primates and sent his students out to observe chimpanzees and macaques. In Britain, Robert Hinde recognized that studies of primates would shed light on the psychology of human behavior, particularly infant development and mother-infant relations. In Kenya, Louis Leakey pursued his hunch that clues to early hominid behavior would be revealed through the study of great ape behavior in nature and proposed that women would make better, more patient observers of animals. He recruited women, such as Jane Goodall and Dian Fossey, to go to Africa (and later Birute Galdikas to go to Borneo) to establish long-term field sites for the study of chimpanzees, gorillas, and orangutans.

Washburn, Imanishi, Hinde, and Leakey mentored most of the early field primatologists, all of them dedicated to better understanding human behavior. Many of these scientists, at least in the West, were women who became the

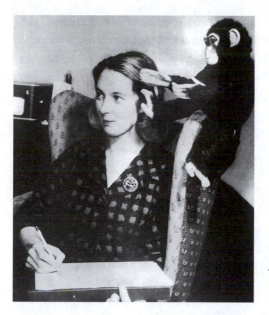

Scientist and conservationist Jane Goodall with a stuffed chimpanzee in 1962. Famous for her groundbreaking work with chimpanzees in East Africa, Goodall became a passionate advocate for the humane treatment of animals used in biomedical studies. (Library of Congress)

founding mothers of the discipline, such as Phyllis Dolhinow, Jane Lancaster, Thelma Rowell, and Jane Goodall. Another group of early primatologists (e.g., Stuart and Jeanne Altmann, Alison Jolly, and Alison Richard) were trained as field biologists. Whatever their disciplinary backgrounds and countries of origin, one theme common to field workers during this first period was the collection of as much natural history data as possible on the social lives of the primates they studied.

During the first and all subsequent stages of primatology, there was no debate about whether women were capable of arduous field research in the physically demanding, politically difficult conditions of Third World, tropical countries and remote habitats, far from the conveniences of modern life. It has always been assumed among primatologists that women are as capable of fieldwork as men, and sometimes that women are more so. This is not true in other disciplines with a large fieldwork component, such as geology, archaeology, and botany, where women have often been excluded from field projects, tacitly or otherwise. Perhaps because primatology is a disciplinary offshoot of anthropology, psychology, and ethology and because there was an established tradition of women field anthropologists (e.g., Margaret Mead), the problem of "women in the field" simply did not arise in the minds of even this first generation of primatologists.

A great irony of this stage is that the female primates being studied were almost exclusively portrayed in their roles as mothers who did not participate in group leadership, predator and resource defense, dominance hierarchies, or intergroup encounters. It was generally assumed that the role of females was to gestate, lactate, and rear the young and do little else of social significance.

Females were viewed as resources over which males would compete and that males would defend. There seems to have been a "disconnect" between the actual gender roles of scientists studying these animals and portrayal of their subjects. This was a postwar era that idealized mothers who stayed home to raise children while their husbands were out earning an income. The prevailing gender myth of the time had a greater influence on how primate sex roles were perceived than did the reality of what women and men were doing in this era. Alison Jolly (2000) has argued that this stage's emphasis on males as the primary social actors and females as behind-the-scenes players was a case of "gender unconsciousness," which certainly fits the theme of the first phase of transformation: absence of females not noted.

1965–1975: Stage/Phase 2. The Enigma of Variability/Finding the Missing Females

In Rosser's transformation model, it is during the second phase that researchers start to notice the absent females and to add females to the mix but without any serious change to the traditional framework. During this stage of primatology, a second wave of field studies occurred such that the same species (e.g., baboons, langurs, chimpanzees) were studied at different field sites. This research brought back unexpected news that the same species often behaved distinctively in different places and that newly studied species behaved much differently than expected on the basis of previously studied species. Thus Washburn's idea of a universal primate pattern collapsed and scientists began to search for sources of variability in social behavior. One source was recognized as the environment (e.g., langurs behave differently in crowded urban habitats versus rural, forest parks); another newly recognized source of variation was how the data were collected for each study (e.g., observer bias). In 1974, Jeanne Altmann published her classic paper codifying the sampling methods used in observational studies, which continues to be the most cited paper in animal behavior research. She demonstrated that all individuals (males, females, juveniles) must be observed for equal periods of time for any valid comparisons of behavioral patterns.

A further source of variation was change over time. During the prior stage, all field studies lasted less than a year. During the second stage, we began to reap the benefits of longer term studies. Japanese primatologists, following in Imanishi's collaborative tradition, were particularly tenacious and cooperative in their research, handing down their data and knowledge of the animals to the next researcher. From their studies, scientists realized that in many African and Asian monkey species, the adult males come and go, but the females remain in their social groups for life, forming matrilines and stable dominance hierarchies and maintaining years of knowledge about resources in their home ranges.

Even in species where females disperse and males stay in the natal area (e.g., chimpanzees), the vital social role of females beyond that of motherhood began to be recognized. In 1973, Jane Lancaster wrote a prescient article, entitled "In Praise of the Achieving Female Monkey," in which she articulated the many important social and ecological functions performed by female primates beyond that of mother. By the end of this stage, female primates were emerging from the wings of the social theater and moving onto central stage.

1975–1985: Stage/Phase 3. Sociobiology/Females as Anomalies

During the third phase of curriculum transformation, people begin to ask why there are not more females represented and why female experiences do not fit the prevailing models.

In primatology, by the end of Stage 2, many observations of behaviors had accumulated that resisted understanding through the currently available explanatory models of group selection; these included behaviors such as occasional killing of infants by adult males, conflict between mothers and infants during weaning, and infidelity by both male and female partners. Sociobiological theory did a remarkable job of formulating scientifically satisfying answers to these behavioral riddles. Sociobiology, which is actually a body of theories (e.g., kin selection, parental investment, and reciprocal altruism) shifted the unit of selection in evolutionary models from the group to the individual and ultimately to the gene. Behaviors that had previously been interpreted as altruistic were now interpreted as fundamentally competitive. The sociobiological approach to understanding behavior had such a revolutionary impact on animal behavior research during this era that it qualifies as a "scientific revolution" in the Kuhnian sense.

Although some social scientists and feminist critics of science were appalled at the implication of sociobiological theory that all behavior is ultimately, selfishly, directed toward improving the reproductive success of the individual/gene, the irony is that sociobiological thinking played a large role in the growing conceptualization of female primates as social strategists rather than pawns in male games. Initially in good part through the work of Sarah Hrdy (e.g., 1981), primatologists came to recognize that female animals are proactive, reproductive strategists rather than passive recipients of male initiatives. As noted by Rosser, Hrdy's early work certainly fits the "female as anomaly" theme for this phase of the transformation model. It was during this stage that Hrdy began to ask why the theories she had learned in graduate school did not fit her observations of female monkeys.

Indeed, during the latter part of this stage, many women primatologists became "gender conscious" and several influential works appeared that fleshed out the picture of how important female primates are in their societies. Jeanne Altmann wrote of baboon females as "dual career mothers"; Meredith Small edited a volume of studies on female primates by women primatologists. Thelma Rowell led a critique of the "male dominance model," and Adrienne Zihlman produced the "Woman, the Gatherer" model of human evolution based in part on primate data. Linda Fedigan wrote the first edition of *Primate Paradigms*, which pulled together data to show that the roles of female primates are far more powerful and wide-ranging than previously assumed. It is not a coincidence that growing focus on female primates between 1975 and 1985 occurred simultaneously with the second wave of Western feminism, which urged women scientists to take account of the female point of view.

1985–1995: Stage/Phase 4. Behavioral Ecology/Females as a Focus of Study

As formulated by Rosser, it is in the fourth phase of transformation that females become the focus of study. In primatology, this had already begun during the third stage, in part through the advent of sociobiology. One of the criticisms of sociobiological theory as initially applied in the previous stage is that it was deterministic and gave too much weight to the power of genes to directly control behavior. It is true that in the first rush of enthusiasm and defense against critics, sociobiological models of behavior were too simplistic, reductionist, and all-encompassing. Although sociobiological explanations are here to stay in the field of animal behavior, during Stage 4, primatologists moderated the deterministic explanations of the prior era and began to explore multicausal analyses. In particular, they worked on a more holistic approach that integrates environmental, social, and genetic processes.

It was also during this stage of primatology that many scientists produced theoretical insights that remade the understanding of female behavior. For example, during this era the reasons why many lemurs live in female-dominated societies, why adult males in monogamous societies show extensive parental care, why female baboons develop friendships with particular males, and why female monkeys are as competitive as males were explained.

During this stage, it was no longer necessary to keep pointing out that female primates are significant players in social life—that becomes one of the assumptions. Female behavior and relations with their kin, their young, and their mates were increasingly seen as highly variable combinations of cooperation and competition.

1995–2005: Stage/Phase 5. Socioecology/A Gender-Inclusive Science

In Rosser's transformation model, Phase 5 is the era when a science has been wholly redesigned and reconstructed to include everyone. It is a fully transformed, "balanced" science, an ideal phase that is almost impossible to achieve. Is this description typical of Stage 5 in primatology?

It is doubtful that a completely successful docking on this phase in the transformation of any discipline could be reached. The current stage of primatology, being closest in time, is the most difficult to characterize and to distinguish from the prior one. Nonetheless, primatology appears now as a "gender-balanced" science. Overtly female-focused studies and volumes are not so common in this stage as in the previous one. This could either be a sign that females are fully integrated and recognized in our science or an indicator that the interest in female perspectives was short-lived and faddish. One hopes for the former.

During the current stage of primatology, there has been much emphasis on testing socioecological models, in particular a model of the evolution of female social relationships and primate social systems proposed by Elisabeth Sterck. Accumulation of a sufficient amount of data on a variety of primates makes it possible to conduct informed, comparative analyses of the factors that affect female relations and how these relations among females in turn affect the overall social system of different primates. The assumption that female relations (with each other, with males, and with their environment) have a determining effect on male behavior has become so commonplace that it is no longer debated or remarked on. Female counterstrategies to male attempts at dominance are now so widely studied that "intersexual conflict" is a thriving area of research. Feminist theorists might prefer that cooperation between the sexes be an equally thriving area of research, but nonetheless, "sexual conflict" is a model of social behavior in which females play a role equal to that of males.

Conclusion

Rosser's adaptation of curriculum transformation models to an understanding of how a science can change over time toward a more gender-balanced perspective proves to be a useful way to think about the history of field primatology in North America. It would be too much to expect that every phase in the transformation model would correspond entirely to each of the stages in our previously reported history of primatology. Nonetheless, the progressive steps in the transformation model (e.g., from "gender unconsciousness" to "search for the missing females," to "focus on females," to a more "balanced approach") can all be easily detected in the historical scheme of our discipline. This brief history of the progression through which primatology achieved its current gender-balanced status can be instructive as a model for the viability of transformation in other scientific disciplines. (*See also* Conclusion; Feminist Science Studies)

References and Further Reading

Altmann, Jeanne. "Observational Study of Behavior: Sampling Methods." *Behavior* 49 (1974): 227–265.

Fedigan, Linda M. "The Paradox of Feminist Primatology: The Goddess's Discipline?" In *Feminism in Twentieth Century Science, Technology and Medicine*. Edited by Angela N. H. Creager, Elizabeth Lunbeck, and Londa Schiebinger, 46–72. Chicago: University of Chicago Press, 2001.

Fedigan, Linda M., and Shirley C. Strum. "A Brief History of Primate Studies: National Traditions, Disciplinary Origins, and Stages in North American Field Research." In *The Nonhuman Primates*. Edited by Phyllis Dolhinow and Agustin Fuentes, 258–269. Mountain View, CA: Mayfield Publishing, 1999.

Hrdy, Sarah B. *The Woman that Never Evolved*. Cambridge, MA: Harvard University Press, 1981.

Jolly, Alison. "The Bad Old Days of Primatology?" In *Primate Encounters. Models of Science, Gender and Society*. Edited by Shirley C. Strum and Linda M. Fedigan, 71–84. Chicago: University of Chicago Press, 2000.

Lancaster, Jane B. "In Praise of the Achieving Female Monkey." *Psychology Today* 7 (1973): 30–36, 99.

Rosser, Sue V. *Female-friendly Science. Applying Women's Studies Methods and Theories to Attract Students*. New York: Pergamon Press, 1990.

Schiebinger, Londa. "Primatology, Archaeology and Human Origins: Feminist Interventions." In *Equal Rites, Unequal Outcomes: Women in American Research Universities*. Edited by Lilli S. Hornig, 247–256. New York: Kluwer Academic/Plenum, 2003.

Critiques of Science

Chris Cuomo

Feminist critiques of science evaluate sexist and male-centered biases in scientific methods, practices, and institutions; trace the deep roots of those biases in misguided beliefs about the nature of knowledge and knowers; and develop alternative models for improved science that would better serve the interests of diverse human societies and ecological communities. In opposition to the image of science as a value-neutral zone, feminists show that masculinist values deeply inform scientific disciplines that systematically exclude or discriminate against female practitioners and that far too regularly produce research that is ignorant of or harmful to the interests of women and other marginalized groups. Such exclusions and harms are not merely the result of direct discrimination—they are also consequences of conceptual assumptions that characterize science as a purely rational, emotionless, masculine, elite domain and knowledge as the result of a universal "view from nowhere" that needs not take the particulars of its own social and historical contexts into account.

Work in feminist science criticism includes historical and sociological interrogations of scientific cultures and practices as well as philosophical investigations of underlying epistemologies and ethics. Primary concerns include the roots of detrimental biases in conceptions of knowledge, the damaging persistence of masculinist and positivist values, the meanings of and myths surrounding the ideal of objectivity, and the problem of false universalisms. Overall, feminist criticism highlights the tendency of Western science to serve domination rather than liberation and to reduce its objects of inquiry to their use value. Yet feminists also remain hopeful that scientific tools and methods can be revised and redeployed for more life-affirming ends.

Epistemology

Epistemology refers to theories of knowledge, which include theories about the nature, scope, and sources of human knowledge and what it means to say that we actually know anything. Western philosophy has been particularly fixated on epistemological topics, and theorists in that tradition have focused on questions about truth and belief, the nature of minds, the role reason plays in knowing, and the structures and limits of human knowledge. Such inquiries typically begin with several assumptions: that the "perfect knower" is a universal ideal (rather than a culturally specific ideal), that all knowing is cognitive (rather than also embodied), that knowers are independent individuals (rather than social beings or communities), and that the production of knowledge is politically neutral (rather than inevitably biased). Those assumptions are deeply questioned by feminist theorists, who argue that androcentrism and cultural imperialism are often at the root of supposedly universal ideals and paradigms of knowledge. Feminists broaden the field of inquiry in epistemology because they acknowledge and explore the extent to which knowledge is embodied, emotional, socially situated, and informed by specific experiences and interests. They therefore shift the philosophical framework and raise new questions about epistemic agency, cognitive authority, and ideals such as objectivity and rationality.

While the principal task of most Anglo-American epistemology has been to refute skepticism and determine the conditions for objective knowledge, feminist epistemologies focus on the social and historical circumstances that determine knowledge in particular contexts, on assumptions about ideal knowers, and on the relationships between knowledge production and other forms of power. Perhaps most important, feminists have emphasized that all knowledge is social and that knowers are deeply social and ecological beings rather than starkly independent individuals. Feminist epistemology has therefore been described as a branch of social epistemology, which describes scientific knowledge as possessed and enacted by communities. Knowledge, including scientific knowledge, is not discovered by exceptional individuals but produced by complex social systems, and so all knowledge is situated and incomplete, or partial. Furthermore, that situatedness is political and closely linked to existing systems of power, including gender, race, nation, and capital.

Feminist critics also emphasize that modern and postmodern science and epistemology are social practices engaged in primarily by elite professionals in academic settings where authority is almost always aligned with race, gender, and class privilege. In contexts of dominance and subordination, oppressive power relations may be reinforced by epistemological theories and methods. It is therefore crucial to identify the relationships between particular theories and the forms of social power they propagate. Feminists argue that attention to those dimensions will inevitably strengthen epistemology as a practice that aims to better understand and enable human knowledge.

Objectivity

Feminists expose the image of science as value free as a smokescreen hiding its own deep and pervasive hierarchical, power-laden values. Because all perspectives are socially and historically situated, all knowledge is partial and biased in ways that are often not readily apparent to knowers themselves. The inevitability of bias therefore should be acknowledged and negotiated rather than denied. "Value-neutral" accounts of objectivity ignore the powerful cultural background beliefs that shape any inquiry. In response, feminist philosophers of science acknowledge the importance of the scientific ideals captured by the concept of objectivity (integrity, reproducibility, avoidance of confirmation bias) but argue that those ideals are best served by including multiple relevant perspectives, making the politics behind epistemic and scientific projects more visible, and using methodologies that are rationalized, transparent, and self-reflexive (Nelson 1990; Harding 1991; Haraway 1991). Sandra Harding has argued that "strong objectivity," which includes multiple standpoints, actually fosters a better empiricism, generates a more rigorous objectivity, and produces more accurate results.

Feminist critical examinations of traditional theories of science and rationality and their relationships to canonical views on sex and gender have drawn clear connections between Enlightenment ideals of rationality, objectivity, and intellectual detachment, and the masculinist ideals that organize most scientific and epistemological inquiries (Lloyd 1984; Bordo 1987). In one influential account, Susan Bordo offered a psychosocial analysis of René Descartes' well-known *Meditations on First Philosophy,* diagnosing the masculine anxieties beneath Descartes' strategy for achieving objective certainty. She argues that the Cartesian epistemic position, which conceives of the ideal "thinker" of "I think therefore I am" as detached from the natural world, is an expression of male anxiety that results from separation from mothers and from their own femininity, a rift that is necessary for the reproduction of male dominance. The Cartesian promise of absolute epistemic objectivity is therefore a flight from the material feminine toward a masculine epistemic stance that pursues knowledge as pure thought and perception and that takes knowers to be transcendent and disembodied subjects.

The common ideal of a disembodied subject engaging in "pure thought" shows how thoroughly emotions and feelings have been ignored or dismissed in influential theories of knowledge. This is because science often takes reason and emotion to be opposites, with reason, the faculty that supposedly generates knowledge, associated with male competence, and emotion, which allegedly distracts from knowledge, linked to the uncontrollable feminine. Along with its misogynist underpinnings, that dichotomy relies on a rather naïve view of what emotions even are. In response, feminists have developed alternative accounts of emotion and have argued that appropriate integration of emotional responses is vital for reason, perception, and systematic knowledge (Jaggar 1989). Eschewing an emphasis on the need for detached objectivity, feminist theorists instead focus on the diverse and complex qualities of subjectivities and intersubjectivities. Knowledge is quite embedded in the material world, not detached from it.

Masculinity

The fact that science, the ultimate site of knowledge production, has been characterized as an elite masculine domain feeds other assumptions that put scientific inquiry at odds with the interests and well-being of women and other disenfranchised groups and that compromise scientific integrity. Androcentric perspectives create scientific models and symbolic systems that conform to privileged masculine experience but alienate or exclude others. If scientific communities are far more welcoming to and concerned about privileged men, their perspectives and prejudices will shape research projects, methods of inquiry, and institutional cultures. When upper-class male bodies and experiences are taken as paradigmatic of human reality, research generates results that are most useful to them and characterizes others as intellectually capable, or as suitable only as objects of study.

The masculinist qualities of Western science emerge from a worldview that characterizes reality according to dualistic patterns and hierarchies, draws sharp distinctions between elements characterized as either masculine or feminine, and bestows masculinity with the power to conquer and control. To be associated with femininity (or deficient masculinity) is to be subject to that control, and so women, men of color, sexual minorities, the disabled, children, and nonhuman animals have often been the unwitting victims of science's drive toward knowledge-as-mastery. Women scientists have documented the deep and long-standing influence of sexism in biological, psychological, sociological, and evolutionary accounts of female bodies and experiences. Others have chronicled the chilling history and present realities of racist science, including gross patterns of dangerous and nontherapeutic medical experimentation without consent on women and people of color (Washington 2006).

Positivism

Positivist traditions take scientific knowledge to be simple descriptions of sensory phenomena and articulation of laws and theories verifiable through observation. Positivism also asserts a stark fact/value dichotomy and excludes from the scientific domain all reference to values, contexts, and anything else not directly related to sensory evidence. But as many critics of positivism have pointed out, our observations are themselves theory laden, for the world does not dictate the concepts and categories we use to describe it. Rather, scientific descriptions of the world—and questions about it—are shaped by underlying conceptual frameworks and background fields of knowledge that are specific to particular contexts and cultures. Theories that focus only on the logic and justifiability of scientific laws ignore the wider contexts that determine what sorts of processes are considered, which topics and questions are legitimate, and whose interests and concerns are at the heart of inquiry. History, identity, culture, and context can determine legitimate methods of hypothesis formation, ideas about what counts as evidence, and beliefs about what is reasonable or justified.

In contrast with positivist traditions, a major contribution of feminism has been the development of "feminist standpoint theory," which is rooted in the Marxist observation that the epistemic locations of marginalized groups who are intimately involved in material production and reproduction can often yield more comprehensive and accurate questions, observations, and analyses of the world than those of dominant groups who are distanced from material relations. Science that begins from feminist standpoints raises questions and includes data that are relevant to real lives and needs. However, it is important to note that standpoint is a form of understanding that results from collective political struggle and analysis, not knowledge that one has simply by virtue of having a particular identity or type of body. Certainly, women everywhere do not share the same concerns or priorities, and so there is not one feminist perspective or standpoint. Different cultural priorities shape different versions of feminism and therefore different conceptions of what feminist knowledge and politics entail. Integrating different perspectives into research programs is thus a primary challenge for feminist researchers. For example, it is important that feminists not romanticize the perspectives of marginalized groups but instead recognize the high price women, people of color, and the poor often must pay for living the complex realities that give rise to their unique ways of perceiving and knowing (Narayan 1989).

Universalism

Although there are clear patterns of exclusion and discrimination in science, transparency, peer review, and reproducibility are considered scientific virtues, and so some would say that in theory science is "open" to all. Western science tends to cast its claims in universally applicable terms and to believe itself to be universally relevant. But as feminist and multicultural critics have shown, the openness and universal aspirations of Western science are predicated on a refusal to ask difficult questions about the actual practice of science in elitist and male-dominated contexts and about the specific but very powerful cultural assumptions behind its supposedly "universal" claims and methods. Furthermore, because science often wields significant power to define, diagnose, and distribute, categorical or universal claims about its objects of inquiry can be catastrophic when they are not really universally true. For example, coercive importation of First World agricultural models to rural communities in India had devastating effects when diverse ecosystems were transformed into monocultural plantations that were profitable for some but that turned subsistence conditions into conditions of extreme poverty for many more (Shiva 1988).

Along with the appropriate humility that comes with recognizing the limits of one's own epistemic position and understanding the importance of multiple standpoints, the cultural and historical specificity of scientific values and the inevitability of bias in the construction of knowledge lead feminists to relinquish the modern Western dream of a universal unified science. Because of severe differences of social and economic power, any movement to transfer knowledge should be approached with caution and care. For feminists, questions about whose interests are served or harmed by any form of science or knowledge are absolutely fundamental. Furthermore, because any knowledge is partial, there can be no complete and unified theory that captures all relevant truths. Instead, there is a permanent plurality of perspectives that might communicate and collaborate in relation to common interests and concerns but whose integrity may also depend on maintaining their unique and irreducible differences. (*See also* Biologists Who Study Gender/Feminism; Feminist Philosophy of Science)

References and Further Reading

Bordo, Susan. *The Flight to Objectivity: Essays on Cartesianism and Culture*. Albany: State University of New York Press, 1987.

Haraway, Donna. *Simians, Cyborgs, and Women: The Reinvention of Nature*. New York: Routledge, 1991.

Harding, Sandra. *Whose Science, Whose Knowledge? Thinking from Women's Lives*. Ithaca, NY: Cornell University Press, 1991.

Jaggar, Alison. "Love and Knowledge: Emotion in Feminist Epistemology." In *Gender/ Body/Knowledge: Feminist Reconstructions of Being and Knowing*. Edited by Alison Jaggar and Susan Bordo. New Brunswick, NJ: Rutgers University Press, 1989.

Lloyd, Genevieve. *The Man of Reason: "Male" and "Female" in Western Philosophy*. Minneapolis: University of Minnesota Press, 1984.

Narayan, Uma. "The Project of Feminist Epistemology: Perspectives from a Non-western Feminist." In *Gender/Body/Knowledge: Feminist Reconstructions of Being and Knowing.* Edited by Alison Jaggar and Susan Bordo. New Brunswick, NJ: Rutgers University Press, 1989.

Nelson, Lynn Hankinson. *Who Knows: From Quine to a Feminist Empiricism.* Philadelphia, PA: Temple University Press, 1990.

Shiva, Vandana. *Staying Alive: Women, Ecology, and Development.* London: Zed Press, 1988.

Washington, Harriet A. *Medical Apartheid: The Dark History of Medical Experimentation on Black Americans from Colonial Times to the Present.* New York: Doubleday, 2006.

Marxism/Socialism and Feminism/Gender

SUE V. ROSSER

Marxist theory and its successor and practical implementation as socialism emphasized economics, placing the class struggle as the central focus determining human oppression, behaviors, and power struggles. Marxists/socialists viewed the dominance of men over women and gender oppression as results of class inequality. They believed that equality of income distribution and absence of class differentials would also result in the disappearance of gender inequity.

Because of its emphasis upon collectivism, Marxism rejects individualism and positivism as approaches to knowledge. Since positivism and individualism form cornerstones of the scientific method, Marxists believe that knowledge, including scientific knowledge, cannot be solely individualistic. Instead, as a productive activity of human beings, whose basic categories are shaped by human purposes and values, knowledge cannot be objective and value free. Marxists purport that the prevailing mode of production determines the problems studied, approaches, and funding for scientific research. In the 21st century, United States capitalism determines scientific knowledge and science reflects the interests of the dominant class who hold power under capitalism.

Marxist/Socialist Feminist Critiques of Science

Although feminists have criticized Marxism for decades (Goldman 1931) about its shortcomings on the woman question, the Marxist critique of science opened the door to three insights shared by feminist theories and methodologies:

1. It proposed that scientific knowledge was socially constructed and could not be dichotomized from other human values a scientist holds. Beginning with the work of Thomas Kuhn (1970) and his followers, historians and philosophers of science have pointed out that the scientific paradigms acceptable to the mainstream of practicing scientists

are convincing precisely because they reinforce or support the historical, economic, social, racial, political, and gender policies of the majority of scientists at that particular time.

Socialist feminists (Rose and Rose 1980, 28) underscore the reason that Darwin's theory of natural selection was acceptable to 19th-century England: it was laden with the values of the upper classes of that Victorian period—competition of the species, the struggle for existence, and survival of the fittest. These metaphors reflected Victorian society and were acceptable to it because they, and the social Darwinism quickly derived from them, seemed to ground their norms solidly in a biological foundation.

The use of craniometry in the 19th century provides another example. Incorrect biological measurements and false conclusions drawn from accurate measurements were accepted because the biological "fact" provided a justification for the inferior social position of colonials (especially Blacks) and women.

Feminist critics have discussed the extent to which the emphasis on sex differences research (when, in fact, for most traits there are not differences or only very small mean differences characterized by a large range of overlap between the sexes) in the neurosciences and endocrinology and on the search for genetic bases to justify sex role specialization and the division of labor originate from the desire to find a biological basis for the social inequality between the sexes. One can imagine that a society free from inequality between the sexes would not view sex differences research as a valid scientific endeavor. The fact that our society supports such research indicates the extent to which the values of the society and the scientists influence scientific inequity and "objectivity."

2. By emphasizing the social construction of knowledge, Marxism implies that dichotomies such as nature/culture, subjective/objective might not be the only or even appropriate ways to categorize knowledge. Interdisciplinary methods that study disease processes such as cardiovascular disease, cancer, and menopause based on interactions between genetic and environmental factors would be more in tune with Marxist approaches.

3. Marxism also suggests that methods distancing the observer from the object of study and/or placing the experimenter in a different plane from the subject are seen as more scientific only when the social construction of knowledge is not recognized. The privileging of double-blind studies and quantitative methods may no longer seem as valid when knowledge is recognized as socially constructed. Active partici-

pation of subjects in research and qualitative methods may then be viewed as a superior way to study health problems.

Marxist/Socialist Feminist Critiques of Technology

Just as capitalism, the prevailing mode of production in the 21st-century United States, determines the basic scientific research undertaken, capitalism also determines the technologies transferred from basic research. These technologies favor the interests of the dominant class. Numerous scholars of technology use Marxist/socialist theory as a foundation for their research on "the social shaping of technology." This phrase suggests that technology and society co-evolve, with technology as a social product made up of human activities and "know-how." Technology also helps to form social interactions among individuals from different social classes under capitalism.

As Webster (1995, 4) points out, most scholars of technology have been men and have thought about the social shaping of technology in ways that tend to exclude women from creation, design, and use of technology. Sometimes women are included as consumers of technology. In contrast, socialist feminist critiques include women. Placing gender on equal footing with class is referred to as the dual systems approach (Hartmann 1981). In this approach, capitalism and patriarchy function as mutually reinforcing parts of a system. Both wage labor and the sexual division of labor stand as central features of capitalism. Failure to count contributions of women to reproduction and child rearing as "productivity" combine with gender differences in wages outside the home in a capitalist economy to reinforce patriarchy and power differentials in the home.

Socialist feminism's dual system provides information useful for analyzing the technology wage labor market. For example, women hold jobs in the worst-paid, most tedious, and most health-destroying segment of the labor market in electronics assembly. Analyses by class and gender have documented that for seven to 10 hours each day, it is women who etch circuits onto wafers of silicon, dip circuits into vats of carcinogenic solvents, and peer through microscopes to bond wires to silicon chips. Because these women receive poor pay and because they cannot easily move to different cities or states, their jobs are less likely to be automated than those held by men. The relatively higher pay and geographic mobility of men motivates management to automate men's jobs, even though they may be less menial and more difficult to automate than those held by women. Similar analyses may suggest why men dominate the creation of new technologies. Men have more access to venture capital, greater geographic mobility, and the ability to work longer hours

Near Jones Beach in New York about 1931. The Wantagh Spur Parkway passes under Sunrise Highway. (Library of Congress)

than women. These factors may be as critical as is technological expertise for the success of start-ups.

The class relations that emerge under capitalism and gender relations under patriarchy help to explain much about the technological labor force. The intertwining of military and masculinity drives much technological innovation in this country and explains the choices made to develop technologies in a certain way. For example, engineering decisions often favor the wealthy few over relatively less expensive technologies (such as devices for the home) that aid many people, especially women.

Robert Caro's work revealed that Robert Moses, the master builder of New York's roads, parks, bridges, and other public works from the 1920s to the 1970s, had overpasses built to specifications that discouraged buses on parkways. White upper- and middle-class car owners could use the parkways, such as Wantagh Parkway, for commuting and for accessing recreation sites, including Jones Beach. Because the 12-foot height of public transit buses prohibited their fitting under the overpasses, Black and poor people dependent on public transit did not have access to Jones Beach (Winner 1980).

Technology Transfer

Many of the current intellectual property rights agreements and laws provide opportunities for choices in technology development that transfer rights and money from the public to the hands of private individuals or corporations. Patents become the mechanism for transferring to the private sector technologies developed using public monies. Many ideas from research that was paid for by federal grants funded by taxpayer dollars are patented. Capitalist interests in potential profits determine which products are developed from patents. The intellectual property rights agreements surrounding technology transfer permit decisions of product development to occur in the private rather than the public realm. This means that capitalist interests in the bottom line rather than public needs and interests determine which "products" are developed. The result is that the intellectual property rights (and profits) are transferred from the public who paid for the research with their tax dollars to the private company, start-up dot.com, institution, or individual who controls the patent. This transfer from the pockets of the working class, who pay the taxes to underwrite federal research, to the patent holders in the private sector, who will reap massive profits, might be viewed by socialist feminists as serving the interests of the upper class and capitalism. New technologies in computer science and engineering represent prime examples of such transfer because the basic research underpinning the technologies is often developed using federal grants (paid for by taxes).

Because middle- and upper-class men create and design most new technologies, it is not surprising that such technologies are more likely to meet their needs and appeal to their aesthetics of design. Not only are more engineers and computer scientists men, but the primary sources of money for design and creation of technology also come from men. If women were creators and designers, as well as users, of technology, more technologies might meet the needs of women and be adapted for the spaces where women spend time. In the 19th century, an article in *New Ideas* magazine (1896, 214) said, "It is due to the inventive faculty of women that we owe the majority of devices which lighten and perfect labor in their own domain." More recently, Frances Gabe attempted to eliminate the drudgeries of housework by designing a patented house that cleans itself, using 68 separate devices (Macdonald 1992). Although the self-cleaning house is likely to remain a white, upper-middle-class suburban solution that would not necessarily improve the lives of lower income women (and might, in fact, eliminate the employment of some), it does hold the potential to improve the lives of many women by reducing housework.

Using the rule of providing the greatest benefit for the common good would result in a very different allocation of resources for technology development.

Application of such a socialist feminist rule would cause a sort of reversal of the Robert Moses overpasses to Jones Beach example. Instead of a road that was accessible only to cars and not buses, highest priority would go to development of technologies that would redistribute resources to mass transit and provide greater access for the poor.

With the expense of sophisticated equipment, maintenance of laboratory animals and facilities, and salaries for qualified technicians and researchers, virtually no scientific, technological, or medical research is undertaken today without federal or foundation support. Gone are the days when individuals had laboratories in their homes or made significant discoveries working in isolation using homemade equipment. The choice of problems for study in research is substantially determined by a national agenda that defines what is worthy of study—that is, funding. As Marxist, socialist, and feminist critics have pointed out, the research that is undertaken reflects the societal bias toward the powerful, who are overwhelmingly white, middle- to upper-class, and male in the United States. The majority of members of Congress who appropriate the funds for the federal agencies such as the National Science Foundation and National Institutes of Health fit this description; the same descriptors tend to characterize the individuals in the theoretical and decision-making positions within the scientific, medical, and engineering establishment. These individuals are more likely to vote funds or make research decisions they view as significant and beneficial as defined from their perspective, which includes the class and gender biases revealed by socialist feminist critics. The patents emerging from such research and particularly decisions of technology transfer and development further exacerbate these class and gender biases. (*See also* Critiques of Science; Gender and Occupational Interests; Technology)

References and Further Reading

Goldman, Emma. *Living My Life*. 2 vols. 1931. Reprint, New York: Dover, 1970.
Hartmann, Heidi. "The Unhappy Marriage of Marxism and Feminism: Towards a More Progressive Union." In *Women and Revolution: A Discussion of the Unhappy Marriage of Marxism and Feminism*. Edited by L. Sargent, 1–41. Boston: South End Press, 1981.
Kuhn, Thomas. *The Structure of Scientific Revolutions*. 2nd ed. Chicago: University of Chicago Press, 1970.
Macdonald, Anne. *Feminine Ingenuity: Women and Invention in America*. New York: Ballantine Books, 1992.
New Ideas Women's Magazine. New York: New Idea Publishing, 1896.

Rose, Hilary, and Steven Rose. "The Myth of the Neutrality of Science." In *Science and Liberation*. Edited by Rita Arditti, Pat Brennan, and Steve Cavrak. Boston: South End Press, 1980.

Webster, Juliet. *Shaping Women's Work: Gender, Employment and Information Technology*. New York: Longman, 1995.

Winner, Langdon. "Do Artifacts Have Politics?" *Daedalus* 109 (1980): 121–136.

Ecofeminism

BARBARA L. WHITTEN

Introduction

Ecofeminism means many different things to different people, ranging from completely apolitical goddess worship to highly academic analysis to grass-roots political activism. I will use the term to mean any feminist analysis of environmental issues, though I will briefly discuss some of the different threads of ecofeminism.

Founding Mothers and Founding Texts

Rachel Carson and Silent Spring

Feminists and environmentalists and ecofeminists all claim Rachel Carson, although she died before the women's or environmental movements began. There are good reasons to think of her as an ecofeminist; she lived a very woman-centered life, and her appreciation for the natural world was expressed in her early work. She used all her gifts: her scientific training, her deep love of nature, and her extraordinary eloquence to write the book that defines her—one of the most important books of the 20th century. When it was published in 1962, *Silent Spring* and its quiet retiring author were widely praised and as widely reviled. Attacks by conservative politicians and chemical industry officials were highly gendered; she was called unscientific (despite her master's degree from Johns Hopkins), overemotional (despite her careful marshaling of scientific information), and a spinster who cared more for birds than people. She made use of her fame to speak out to groups all over the country and to testify before Congress and the president's Science Advisory Council. Many believe that *Silent Spring* was the trigger for the environmental movement. The first Earth Day was in 1970, and the Environmental Protection Agency was formed the same year. Rachel Carson did not live to

Rachel Carson was a noted biologist and ecology writer whose books played a major role in launching the modern environmental movement. Carson's book Silent Spring, *published in 1962, became a best seller and touched off a controversy that led to a fundamental shift in the public's attitudes toward the use of pesticides.* (Library of Congress)

see these consequences of her work; she was struggling with breast cancer during the writing of *Silent Spring* and the publicity following its publication, and she died in 1964.

Carolyn Merchant *and* The Death of Nature

The first important book firmly in the ecofeminist tradition is *The Death of Nature,* which analyzed negative effects for women and the natural world that resulted from the Enlightenment and the Scientific Revolution. Medieval Europe had an organizing vision of a benevolent Mother Earth presiding over an organic natural world in which all beings, including people, have their place. The Scientific Revolution replaced this with an image of a Newtonian world machine that men could understand, dominate, and use for their own purposes. The identification of women and nature meant that the denigration of nature was accompanied by the denigration of women; many female healers were punished as witches. Merchant has applied this analysis to the European colonization and westward expansion of North America.

Vandana Shiva and Staying Alive

Vandana Shiva's work has forced ecofeminists to look beyond Europe and the United States to the Third World and to consider colonization and globalization as important factors in the oppression of women and the environment. Shiva argued that indigenous women of the Third World have a more complete understanding of their ecosystems than First World men with their "scientific" worldview. When Indian peasant women look at a forest, they see food and medicine and firewood for their families, fodder for their livestock, and stabilization of soil and water and climate cycles. A masculinist forester, in contrast, sees only "economic" trees and "waste" trees. Shiva is one of the most prominent Indian intellectuals and activists in the world. She has continued to write about the effects of globalization on poor women of India, and in 1993 she won the Right Livelihood Award, often called the Alternative Nobel Prize.

Women and Nature

One of the thorniest issues for ecofeminists is the historical Western identification of women and nature. Carolyn Merchant (1980) documents the horrifying metaphors of rape and subjugation used by Francis Bacon and others to describe the scientific exploitation of the natural world. Some women, whom Merchant (1992) calls liberal ecofeminists, argue that the identification of women and nature should be abandoned as an outdated artifact of Western culture. Women are as rational and logical as men, with no special connection to the natural world. In contrast, cultural, or radical, ecofeminists believe that women's biological nature gives them a deep affinity for the natural world that should be celebrated. Social (often Marxist) ecofeminists argue that identifying women with nature is essentialist and dangerous. They suggest that any identification of women with the natural world comes from women's socialization and gender roles and that it differs for women in different social locations. However, environmental degradation and the oppression of women, people of color, and the Third World all derive from the same will to domination, and it is vital to see these issues as linked. The different conclusions reached by these different schools of thought suggest that the connection between women and the natural world remains unresolved.

Women and the Environmental Movement

Joni Seager (1993) has written an important feminist analysis of the environmental movement. She points out that the mainstream environmental groups like the Sierra Club and the Audubon Society grew out of wealthy White male groups of hunters and fishermen and that these organizations have been more interested in "protecting" and "managing" the wilderness than in the health of poor women and children. They have historically been dominated by White men, although they have made efforts in recent years to include women and people of color. The mainstreaming of environmental issues in the 1980s and 1990s resulted in greatly increased power and influence for these groups. But as they gained influence they also became more professionalized, with lobbyists in Washington and slick publicity campaigns and corporate contributions. They have increasingly taken on the style of the politicians and corporate executives with whom they interact and have perhaps lost touch with the grassroots environmentalists who had originally been their constituency.

As mainstream environmental organizations became more corporate, more radical deep ecology groups like Greenpeace or Earth First! were formed. Deep ecologists borrowed from radical ecofeminists (without attribution) a good deal of their rhetoric of honoring the earth. But they failed to incorporate feminist analysis into their approach to environmental issues. On the contrary, they are as male dominated as the mainstream groups and often display a macho misogynist attitude. They focus on heroic men "protecting" the wilderness and "saving" charismatic threatened species like pandas and whales. The rhetoric of "ecocentrism" all too easily becomes antihuman. Calls for significant reductions of the human population barely bother to disguise their racism and sexism, as exemplified by the appalling letter of Miss Ann Thropy (1987), hailing AIDS as a "necessary solution" that will provide a "respite for endangered wildlife" by reducing the human population (though not that of the author or her friends).

Grassroots Activism and Environmental Justice

In contrast to the male-dominated mainstream and radical environmental groups, women are often leaders in grassroots organizations that focus on human-centered environmental issues like toxic waste dumps, lead poisoning, and other threats to human health. Some notable examples are Katsi Cook and the Mohawk mothers, who are monitoring PCBs in the St. Lawrence Seaway and in mothers' milk; the Chipko movement of India documented by Vandana Shiva, in which Indian peasant women literally hugged the trees on which their lives depend to prevent them from being logged by international companies; and the Greenbelt movement in Kenya, founded by Wangari

Maathai to restore indigenous forests by paying rural women to plant trees. These projects are exemplified by Lois Marie Gibbs, a working-class house-wife who almost single-handedly forced government officials to abandon Love Canal and reimburse the people living there. Like Rachel Carson and virtually every female environmental activist, Gibbs was derided in very gen-dered terms. Chemical company executives and government officials treated her as an uneducated and ignorant, "hysterical housewife" and discarded her carefully prepared maps of deaths, birth defects, cancer, and other serious ill-nesses as "useless." Gibbs persisted, finding volunteer scientists to dress up her epidemiological studies with "all the pi squareds and all that junk" (Sea-ger 1993, 265), and she ultimately prevailed. She went on to found the Toxic Waste Clearing House to provide resources to other grassroots groups.

Ecofeminists claim these and similar women involved in grassroots move-ments, although often the women themselves do not identify as feminists. Many believe that the women's movement is for White, upper-middle-class, educated Western women and identify more strongly with their own less-privileged communities and with the environmental justice movement. Many, however, also feel disrespected by their male relatives and other community members, and some have become feminists under this pressure.

But ecofeminists are deeply indebted to grassroots activists, whether or not they can be claimed as part of the community. These activists raise important questions, for example, about authority in environmental issues. And they al-low ecofeminists to be critical of masculinist science and to begin to formulate some ideas about what feminist science might be. Joni Seager, for example, is skeptical of an overemphasis on science in the environmental movement, claiming that it downgrades other equally important evidence; she believes that the uncertainty associated with science tends to aid skeptics and delay action, as we have seen in the global warming debate in recent years.

How Ecofeminist Analysis Affects Environmental Understanding

Ecofeminists, along with other women and people of color, have significantly changed our understanding of important environmental issues. Mainstream and radical environmental groups often argued that people of color just don't care about the environment. Environmental justice groups have helped us see that human communities are also environments and that human health issues are environmental issues. Practically speaking, whales and redwood trees do not vote; unless a large percentage of people see environmental causes as their causes, the movement will have limited impact.

Joni Seager exposes the misogyny behind campaigns that focus on eliminating disposable diapers (2% of garbage) or that blame women for wearing fur when the fur-bearing industry is almost exclusively male and most furs are bought by men. Feminist environmentalists have also focused attention on the enormous environmental damage caused by the military, an issue largely ignored by mainstream groups.

Human population growth is the most important issue to benefit from an ecofeminist analysis. During the 1980s, mainstream environmental groups talked uncritically about the "population bomb" and were complimentary of China's cruel and coercive one-child policy. The thinly disguised racism and sexism of this fear of too many brown women having too many brown babies went unnoticed. It is ecofeminists who are teaching environmentalists to see that the size of the human population is only one facet of a problem that includes maldistribution of resources and overconsumption among the rich. New research shows that programs designed to enhance the position of women in the Third World through, for example, education or microcredit, are a much more effective way of reducing population growth in poor countries than coercive and dangerous family planning programs. Programs to increase the status of Third World women also need to be linked to efforts to provide secure sources of food, water, and shelter to the world's poor and to decrease overconsumption in the First World.

At the beginning of the 21st century, environmental issues are some of the most critical facing the human race. Ecofeminists are contributing to our understanding of an environmental analysis that includes humanity in environmental protection and shows that the environment is indeed a women's issue. (*See also* Discrimination)

References and Further Reading

Carson, Rachel. *Silent Spring*. New York: Houghton Mifflin, 1962.

Gibbs, Lois Marie. *Love Canal: The Story Continues (20th Anniversary Edition)*. Stony Creek, CT: New Society Publishers, 1998.

Lear, Linda. *Rachel Carson: Witness for Nature*. New York: Henry Holt, 1997.

Merchant, Carolyn. *The Death of Nature: Women, Ecology, and the Scientific Revolution*. New York: HarperCollins, 1980.

Merchant, Carolyn. *Radical Ecology: The Search for a Livable World*. New York: Routledge, 1992.

Seager, Joni. *Earth Follies: Coming to Feminist Terms with the Global Environmental Crisis*. New York: Routledge Press, 1993.

Shiva, Vandana. *Staying Alive: Women, Ecology, and Development*. London: Zed Books, 1989.

Thropy, Miss Ann. "Population and AIDS." First published in *Earth First!*, 1987. http://www.off-road.com/green/ef_aids_wish.html. (Accessed February 5, 2007.)

Cyberfeminism

REBECCA K. SCHECKLER

Cyberfeminism is an attempt by feminists to own a part of the computer revolution, where the field of computer science has established a resistant, male center of power. In part, cyberfeminism has been very successful in enacting feminisms in cybersphere. However, it is currently a marginal part of the computer revolution and will remain so until it becomes engaged in two related goals. One is to recognize the deeply embedded values in the layers of software and layers of hardware comprising computer tools that cyberfeminism utilizes but did not create. The second, a related project, is to engage with and join mainstream women, including the few women and supporting men in the field of computer science, in order to work with allies who are able to deconstruct and reconstruct computer tools to include feminisms. These projects require (1) knowledge of the research on gender in computer science that has revealed the myth that computers are gender neutral and (2) an understanding of the creativity and energy that has already been generated by cyberfeminism.

In this essay I begin by describing and giving examples of cyberfeminism. I cannot call this a definition since the term has evaded being defined. This lack of definition is congruent with a postmodernist concept of gender as a process that is enacted and reenacted on a daily basis. In addition, the lack of a definition has also been a goal of the women who began cyberfeminism and who are not about to be captured in the rigidity of definitions and disciplinary boundaries. I then describe in greater detail the two projects that cyberfeminism has yet to achieve and that hinder its ability to accomplish feminist reform in design and usage of computers.

What Is Cyberfeminism?

Cyberfeminism was begun in Australia by four artists as a reaction to the male domination of computers that were taking over the world. The VNS Matrix (pronounced Venus matrix), a Web site, was the result of these first efforts and established a high level of creativity, bodily reference, and use of the World Wide Web in cyberfeminism (Rimini et al. 1991). Drawing on French postmodern theory, these women wrote the cyberfeminist manifesto (http://www .obn.org/reading_room/manifestos/html/cyberfeminist.html). Since then there have been several international cyberfeminist forums and many Web sites exploring the World Wide Web as a medium for art and literature. Art and literature became the main focus of cyberfeminism (Cyberfeminism—special issue of ArtWomen.org 2001).

Many women involved in cyberfeminism are cyber utopians who see cyberspace as a new, open, and egalitarian frontier where anything is possible. The postmodern view of gender is as a process, not an identity, and playing with gender online enhances this view of gender. Online, anyone can be anything he or she wishes to be and physical realities do not need to hinder cyber transformations. Avatars are sometimes used as a representation of physical bodies in the cybersphere.

However, limitations to gender playfulness and physical transformation exist in software. Avatar construction is limited by choices embedded in the software. If the software designers recognized only heterosexuality and traditional gender norms, then the users of the software were likewise limited.

Cyberfeminists use the Internet to be outspoken and expressive with computers (e.g., see http://grrrlmeetworld.com and http://www.hot-topic.org/ riotgrrrl) and often to fiercely fight images in popular culture that objectify women. Women are finding their way to be politically active, creative, and forthcoming with computers. In the process, some are getting hurt by abuse and many are fighting back. The Internet as a free space also allows repression, misogyny, and sexual harassment without control. As the Internet developed, women found that they needed to band together and protect one another against intentional acts to disrupt women's spaces.

Researchers, particularly Susan Herring, have shown that the social construction of gender involves language that is so ingrained it persists in cyberspace where the physical body cannot be seen (Herring, Johnson, and DiBenedetto 1995). This research on gender confronts the desire of cyberfeminists to perform gender on the Internet.

Donna Haraway expanded cyberfeminism with her "Cyborg Manifesto," which suggested among other things that the computer could blur the dualistic boundaries of person/machine, person/animal, and man/woman (Haraway 1991). She sees the necessity of cyborg formations of women and machines, another way of recognizing that women must actively take their place in a technological world. Some, but not many, women have taken up this project. Unfortunately, much of what cyberfeminism creates remains in the genre of "using the computer" rather than "creating the computer." The next two sections briefly explain why this is a problem and suggest ways that cyberfeminists might expand their projects.

Revealing the Value-laden Nature of Computer Tools

Cyberfeminists are using tools that are imbued with value in layer on layer of hardware and software. For instance, all computers rely on Boolean logic, in which values can only be true or false, to utilize switches that have only two positions: on and off. Boolean logic sets up a basic duality in all computer-based logic. A Boolean logic certainly does not support plasticity and change. All one can do is add binary rule upon binary rule to try to reach the impossible goal of covering all contingencies.

Imagery on Web sites and within software tools constitutes another example of valuation in computers. The limitations of avatars represent examples of such imagery. A program designer and programmer have already embedded in software the choices that the avatar user may access. If white skin and straight blonde hair are the choices, then users cannot represent themselves as dark-skinned and dark curly haired or as having purple skin or hair.

Cyberfeminists must recognize and overcome the valuation of hardware and software. They must interrogate the black boxes that hide from view the valuation that design and programming produce. Some cyberfeminists manage to do this by imaginative use of software. They create Web sites and zines very rich in graphic representations that are certainly innovative in the realm of graphics and Web originality. Women in the computer science field still need to ask: Where are the women? Why are they not in the field reinventing the computer rather than using the androcentric computer in other ways?

Forming an Alliance of Cyberfeminism with the Feminists in Computer Science

Another side of cyberfeminism exists: the women who work in the field of computer science creating and who wonder periodically where the rest of the women are. Discussion forum sites, such as systers.org, periodically ask how to get more girls into the field. Female computer science professionals, along with researchers in sociology, women's studies, education, and science and technology studies view cyberfeminism as a way of reallocating the power structures that currently favor male control of computers and computing.

In my experience, the feminists in computer science do not normally communicate with cyberfeminists. They have different professional meetings, different listservs and blogs, and different projects. The insiders in computer science constantly deal with a male hierarchy and thus are often stymied about the changes they can make to support women. The socialization of these women into an androcentric environment potentially makes them less sensitive to a feminist viewpoint. On the other hand, the outsiders to computer science mainly use the machine rather than creating the machine. They often represent a hyperfeminized view of individuals who are sensitive, artistic, and creative. These two groups rarely talk to each other. In fact, these two groups may not even see each other as part of the same milieu. The women inside computer science keep asking: Where are the women? The women outside computer science use the products of a male-dominant field without questioning the source and reified values of their tools.

These two groups need to merge and work together. The insiders fight beliefs that computer science is gender neutral or genderless. The outsiders hold the belief that gender is plastic and can be reformed and reimagined at will. These two groups need to agree on conceptualizations of both gender and digital tools to be truly effective.

In a 1997 paper following the first Cyberfeminist International Conference, Faith Wilding recommended that cyberfeminism form alliances with technically skilled women (Wilding 1997). Donna Haraway promoted cyborg imagery for feminists. Women within computer science continue to do "men's" work. Cyberfeminists continue to be oblivious to "deep" technology. It is past time for technologically proficient women to use the creativity of cyberfeminism to design feminist hardware and software.

Where Can We Go from Here?

Right now cyberfeminists are swimming on the surface of a great abyss of male-dominated and infiltrated software and hardware. It is not even a case of trying to "dismantle the master's house with the master's tools." It is a case of not knowing the master or his tools and the tools remaining hidden within many unreachable black boxes. The myths of gender and cyberfeminisms hold that somehow computer hardware and software design occurred without use of gendered values and that somehow they are neutral and ready for exploitation by any interested user. Cyberfeminists today need to understand computer design and programming or to form alliances with those who do. (*See also* Computer Science; Technology)

References and Further Reading

Cyberfeminism—special issue of ArtWomen.org. 2001. Edited by M. J. Aagerstoun. http://www.artwomen.org/cyberfems/index-intro.htm. (Accessed July 23, 2007.)

Haraway, Donna J. "A Cyborg Manifesto: Science, Technology, and Socialist-Feminism in the Late Twentieth Century." In *Simians, Cyborgs, and Women: The Reinvention of Nature*. London: Routledge, 1991.

Herring, Susan, Deborah A. Johnson, and Tamara DiBenedetto. "'This Discussion Is Going too Far!': Male Resistance to Female Participation on the Internet." In *Gender Articulated, Language and the Socially Constructed Self*. Edited by K. Hall and M. Bucholtz. New York: Routledge, 1995.

Rimini, Francesca da, Josephine Starrs, Julianne Pierce, and Virginia Barratt. *VNS Matrix*. 1991. http://lx.sysx.org/vnsmatrix.html.

VNS Matrix Web page. sysx.apana.org.au/artists/vns.

Wilding, Faith. *Where Is Feminism in Cyberfeminism?* 1997. http://www.andrew.cmu.edu/user/fwild/faithwilding/wherefem.html. (Accessed July 23, 2007.)

Race, Postcolonial Gender, and Science

JOSEPHINE BEOKU-BETTS

Feminist discourse on race, postcolonial (particularly after 1940–1960 when European colonization of non-White societies ended) gender, and science accommodates a vast array of disciplines and contesting perspectives. Essentially, the interconnectedness of racism, colonialism, and globalization, along with their impact on women and gender, set a context for understanding the concerns, priorities, and contributions of feminist scholarship on the subject. Drawing on Black, postcolonial, and postcolonial science feminist studies, this paper discusses the meanings and understandings they bring to the subject and briefly reviews the contributions of key theorists within each category. None of these perspectives is mutually exclusive. They all share the common epistemological goal of integrating the experiential with the analytical and of developing a transformative scholarship and political agenda.

Underlying much of the discourse on postcolonial gender and science are notions of racial difference that are embedded in Eurocentric beliefs about the biological, intellectual, and cultural inferiority of formerly colonized non-White peoples. While there is no scientific validity to these beliefs, representations of race difference based on binary divisions were used by Western scientists, particularly in the 19th century, to legitimize colonization of non-White societies. These beliefs are still prevalent in the ways popular culture portrays people of color, in the racial and cultural biases inherent in measurements used for intelligence testing, and in race and gender discrimination experienced by women and men of color who pursue training in the sciences. Black feminist theorists challenge the historical impact that such racist notions have had on non-White—especially Black—women since the beginning of colonialism. A noted example of scientific racism is the case of Sarah Bartman. A South African woman of Khoi Khoi descent, her body was denigrated in displays of her genitalia and buttocks in numerous exhibitions in Europe during the 19th century. Dehumanized and objectified, she was used to exemplify the racial, sexual, and physical inferiority of Africans and to normalize the White female body. Under slavery and colonialism, Black women

were represented as sexually promiscuous or asexual beasts of burden to justify their exploitation as productive and reproductive labor and their physical
and sexual abuse. Today, Black feminists criticize White feminists for margin-
alizing Black women's sexuality in discourses on the female body, such as in
the debate on reproductive choice, which did not address the unequal relationships structuring how women of color define and respond to the right to
choose based on societal constructions of race, ethnicity, class, and sexuality.
Implicit therefore in Black feminist conceptions of race in the colonial and
postcolonial context are constructs of race, class, sexuality, and gender as interlocking systems of oppression shaping Black women's experiences. While
numerous scholars have written about these issues, this entry focuses on
selected writings of Evelynn Hammonds and Patricia Hill Collins, Black feminist scientists whose works have done much to transform feminist theorizing
by politicizing Black women's sexuality and by developing knowledge construction based on intersectional analysis of women's lived experiences.

The feminist historian of science, Evelynn Hammonds, has used her experiences as a student and scholar to draw the attention of the academy to
race and gender discrimination in the sciences. Her work compels feminists
to reframe the discourse on women's sexuality, understanding that it is based
on cultural constructions that differentially locate women on the basis of race,
gender, class, and sexuality. Her seminal article, "Toward a Genealogy of Black
Female Sexuality" (1997), argues that dominant discourses of women's sexuality have historically rendered Black women invisible while applying binary
divisions to characterize their sexuality—in contrast to that of White women—
as pathological, immoral, and impure. Black women have reacted to this de-
valuation of their bodies with a culture of silence. Hammonds suggests that
Black feminist theorists have avoided exploring the agency of Black women's
sexuality because of their own sexual objectification that can be used by others to discredit the intellectual knowledge they produce on the subject. This
silence has had a negative impact on how the experiences and needs of Black
women have been addressed with respect to the AIDS epidemic, in the failure
to address Black lesbian sexuality, and in the potential development of a
Black feminist community that is inclusive of separate and common interests.

In *Black Feminist Thought* (1990), arguably the most widely acclaimed theoretical work on Black feminism, feminist sociologist Patricia Hill Collins challenges the discourse on feminist epistemology by putting Black women at
the very center of analysis. As producers of scientific knowledge, Black women
intellectuals have seen their work made invisible by the dominant Eurocentric
male paradigm that disregards it. Hill Collins urges them to create their own
intellectual knowledge informed by their own lived experience. Such experiences bring to scientific knowledge production a self-defined and alternative
vantage point that is unavailable to those who do not share them. In "Mov-

Sociologist Patricia Hill Collins. (Courtesy Patricia Hill Collins)

ing beyond Gender: Intersectionality and Scientific Knowledge" (1999), Hill Collins applies the concept of intersectionality to feminist discourse on gender and scientific knowledge. She argues that feminist critiques of gender and science have been complicit in failing to address the politics of gender, race, class, ethnicity, sexuality, and nationality. These interlocking systems of oppression are historically constituted and have shaped the framework within which scientific knowledge has been produced and articulated. Hill Collins posits that intersectionality analysis will significantly transform understandings of scientific knowledge when applied to feminist discourse on science.

Postcolonial feminist theories apply a feminist lens to the postcolonial critique of racism, colonialism, and globalization and to analysis of how these processes have pervaded the construction of knowledge, identity, laws, and policies in formerly colonized societies. They challenge the privileging of Euro-American feminism over other feminisms, which they view as a replication of colonial hegemony. They express frustration in having to conform with, while being excluded from, the dictates of shared intellectual space in feminist theoretical frameworks, some of which cannot adequately explain situated differences or complex social arrangements that shape Third World women's experiences. Thus, much of what is known about women in the Third World/ Global South is based on essentialized notions of the "Third World woman" as a monolithic analytical category. Western feminists have also been challenged for their inattention to the gendered dimensions of racism, colonialism, and globalization in analyses of processes that shape differences among women in colonized and postcolonial societies. They have ignored or overlooked the culturally and politically distinctive struggles of colonized women to resist, overcome, and transform oppressive patriarchal practices in their societies. Postcolonial feminists see all this as being complicit with the historical and contemporary legacies of colonialism and global economic expansionism. While various postcolonial feminists have discussed this issue, selected contributions from the works of Gayatri Spivak and Chandra Talpade Mohanty raise issues that have triggered considerable debate and reshaped feminist understandings of the impact of race, class, and gender on knowledge production in postcolonial societies.

Gayatri Spivak (1988) is best known for her essay, "Can the Subaltern Speak?' in which she addresses the representation of Third World women as the marginalized "other" in Western discourse. She describes as "epistemic violence" the subjugation and disqualification of the Third World woman's situated knowledge under colonialism because of race and class oppression as well as indigenous and colonial state patriarchy, which deny her access to education, the law, and a voice of authority. Spivak draws on the historical Hindu practice of Sati to illustrate how the Hindu woman was portrayed as a victim to be rescued from "backward" and "traditional" Indian customs, unable to articulate her own oppression. Although Spivak suggests that postcolonial feminist intellectuals can give a voice to the subaltern, some others contend that subaltern voices are not necessarily silent and that evidence of that agency must be recovered, articulated, and validated.

Chandra Talpade Mohanty is a trailblazer in postcolonial feminist studies in that she has reframed scholarship on Third World women epistemologically and pedagogically, helping to transform thinking about transnational feminist activism. Focusing on the social sciences, Mohanty's path-breaking paper, "Under Western Eyes" (1991), challenges Western feminist constructs of gender and patriarchy as universal and ahistorical, and the objectification of Third World women as a homogeneous and unitary group—irrespective of diversities across class, race, ethnicity, and nationality. She deconstructs the objectification of Third World women as poor, uneducated, traditional, and powerless in contrast to their White and middle-class and Western counterparts. She exposes the political underpinnings of these analytical strategies by showing historical continuities in Western hegemonic control over global economic, political, scientific, and cultural knowledge production, and she analyzes the exploitative effects of this process on Third World women. In her article, "Women Workers and Capitalist Scripts" (1997), she examines the sexual politics of gender and race under global capitalism and the specific ways in which women workers are exploited under this process. Her vision of transnational feminist scholarship and activism is that both must reflect the shared economic and political realities of women's lives under global capitalism and provide a more comparative and relational analytical framework. This forms a basis for forging self-defined common interests, political solidarity, and ideological transformation among women workers across race, ethnicity, class, sexuality, and nationality. Mohanty's most recent work argues that transnational feminist theorizing and activism in the 21st century must focus on antiglobalization struggles, making the experiences and struggles of marginalized women of color in the Third World/Global South and First World/Global North the center of analysis. In her view, this will provide a stronger and more inclusive understanding of the politics of knowledge production and embedded power relations, thereby providing a means to demystify, resist, and engender transformative processes.

Postcolonial feminist science sees the postcolonial science agenda from a feminist standpoint, which means that it is the historically constituted relationship among racism, sexism, and science that becomes the focal point. Postcolonial science theories take the perspective of non-European cultures and especially the most marginalized within those societies. This vantage point makes it possible to identify differing priorities and concerns in science and technology that are not usually considered legitimate by the dominant masculinist and Eurocentric scientific community. A key issue is the importance of understanding differences between First World/Global North and other worldviews and the influence of these differences on the production and application of scientific knowledge. In sum, postcolonial feminist science aims to challenge and transform the prevailing knowledge base of science and to promote a democratic and socially responsible science that is historically situated and aware of the effects of interlocking relations of domination of race, gender, class, sexuality, and nation. Selected contributions of Sandra Harding brought the feminist voice to discourse in postcolonial science.

In the fields of feminist science and postcolonial science, feminist philosopher Sandra Harding has been instrumental in establishing the case for a more culturally diverse and democratic science that is historically situated and rooted in the lives of women and other economically and politically marginalized groups in the Third World/Global South and First World/Global North. Thinking from these distinctive standpoints provides a starting point from which new questions can be asked about existing social arrangements and conventional knowledge claims concerning nature and society. It allows for "strong objectivity," that is, more innovative, accurate, and unbiased scientific knowledge and policy initiatives that will benefit the most vulnerable in society. In her book, *Is Science Multicultural?* (1998), Harding argues that postcolonial feminist standpoints have been bypassed in the construction of postcolonial science and Global North science, including feminist science studies. Yet they broaden understanding of ways in which race, ethnicity, class, colonialism, sexuality, and gender intersect to construct scientific agendas of the Global North. They also provide a lens through which to assess the impact of science and technology policies and practices on the marginalized, among which women and their dependents are often severely affected. In other words, post-colonial feminist science studies help us envision what Harding describes as a "world of sciences." (*See also* Feminist Science Studies; Marxism/Socialism and Feminism/Gender; Race)

References and Further Reading

Hammonds, Evelynn, M. "Toward a Genealogy of Black Female Sexuality: The Problematic of Silence." In *Feminist Genealogies, Colonial Legacies, Democratic Futures.* Edited by M. Jacqui Alexander and Chandra Talpade Mohanty, 170–182. New York: Routledge, 1997.

Harding, Sandra. *Is Science Multicultural? Postcolonialisms, Feminisms, and Epistemologies.* Bloomington: Indiana University Press, 1998.

Hill Collins, Patricia. *Black Feminist Thought: Knowledge, Consciousness, and the Politics of Empowerment.* Boston: Unwin Hyman, 1990.

Hill Collins, Patricia. "Moving beyond Gender: Intersectionality and Scientific Knowledge." In *Revisioning Gender.* Edited by Myra Marx Ferree, Judith Lorber, and Beth B. Hess, 261–284. Thousand Oaks, CA: Sage, 1999.

Mohanty, Chandra Talpade. "Under Western Eyes: Feminist Scholarship and Colonial Discourses." In *Third World Women and the Politics of Feminism.* Edited by Chandra Talpade Mohanty, Ann Russo, and Lourdes Torres, 51–80. Bloomington: Indiana University Press, 1991.

Mohanty, Chandra Talpade. "Women Workers and Capitalist Scripts: Ideologies of Domination, Common Interests, and the Politics of Solidarity." In *Feminist Genealogies, Colonial Legacies, Democratic Futures.* Edited by M. Jacqui Alexander and Chandra Talpade Mohanty, 3–29. New York: Routledge, 1997.

Mohanty, Chandra Talpade. "Under Western Eyes" Revisited: Feminist Solidarity through Anticapitalist Struggles." In *Feminism without Borders: Decolonizing Theory, Practicing Solidarity.* Edited by Chandra Talpade Mohanty, 221–251. Durham, NC: Duke University Press, 2003.

Spivak, Gayatri Charkravotry. "Can the Subaltern Speak?" In *Marxism and the Interpretation of Culture.* Edited by Cary Nelson and Lawrence Grossberg, 271–313. Urbana: University of Illinois Press, 1988.

Feminist Science Studies

Mary Wyer

The emergence of scholarship about women and gender in the 1970s and 1980s sparked a feminist critique of gender bias in the theories, methods, language, and interpretations of scientific research (e.g., Linda Birke, Ruth Bleier, Anne Fausto-Sterling, Ruth Hubbard, Evelyn Fox Keller, Sue Rosser, and Bonnie Spanier). The resulting firestorm launched a multidisciplinary debate about the strengths and limitations of commitments to objectivity in scientific research. Feminists pointed out that women had been excluded from science as professionals and as subjects of study and that this exclusion was based on inaccurate and biased information about the scope of women's scientific abilities, interests, and accomplishments. This insight led some to question whether scientific inquiry could be objective within a culture that dismissed and marginalized women, since scientists had contributed to these biases through the conventions and authority of science. Others argued that scientific knowledge was a social construction, that scientists could not "discover" nature but rather could only build best-approximate models of nature, inevitably contained by historical and social context. Still others maintained that the roots of Western science were inextricably linked to patriarchal, post-colonial, and/or capitalist domination and that much of contemporary scientific knowledge rested on the appropriation and exploitation of knowledge from colonized peoples of Africa and Asia.

Contributing to the debate were philosophers (e.g., Sandra Harding, Helen Longino), sociologists (e.g., Harriet Zuckerman, Hilary Rose), psychologists (e.g., Carol Gilligan, Nancy Chodorow), historians (e.g., Margaret Rossiter, Londa Schiebinger), anthropologists (e.g., Adrienne Zihlman, Sharon Traweek), primatologists (e.g., Donna Haraway, Linda Fedigan), and a host of others to explore how, if, when, and why social processes and practices have grounded, inspired, and shaped scientific knowledge. This body of work has been known variously under titles such as "women and science," "gender and science," and "feminist critiques of science." In recent years, contemporary feminist scholars of/in science have adopted the term *feminist science studies* to indicate that the field includes studies of both progressive and oppressive elements of scientific values, perspectives, and institutions. Feminist science studies as a field emphasizes the intersections of multiple social identities, practices, and processes in science, including gender, race, ethnicity, class, and sexualities (Mayberry, Subramaniam, and Weasel 2001). An important new focus within feminist science studies emphasizes "successor science" projects, that is, developing theory, methods, and topics that embrace feminist values and perspectives and then teaching that new approach within the university curriculum.

Studies that tap feminist perspectives in/on the sciences fall broadly into five categories of work: (1) biographical or autobiographical accounts of experiences with invisibility, marginalization, and exclusion; (2) explorations of the use of science in the perpetuation of gender inequality; (3) analyses of science as socially produced and embedded; (4) successor science projects; and (5) education and public policy initiatives. These efforts are characteristically multidisciplinary and interdisciplinary—that is, they have emerged from within several disciplines and they integrate themes, perspectives, and methods across disciplines. Though a wide variety of work falls under the umbrella of "feminist science studies," all share an underlying commitment to uncovering and challenging systematic and systemic social, economic, and political oppressions of women.

Biographical, Autobiographical, and Historical Accounts

Because women have been excluded from, or marginalized within, scientific fields, many researchers have focused on recovering knowledge about women scientists and their experiences. Major biographical studies of exceptional women in science chronicle lives filled with determination in the face of discrimination and bias that contained, diverted, and seldom recognized their abilities and achievements. For instance, longevity appears to be an additional criterion necessary for women to win a Nobel Prize in science, indicating that women must be brilliantly productive for a lifetime to be awarded a prize while men are awarded the prize earlier in their careers. First-person accounts and autobiographical studies have detailed the ways in which women scientists' teachers, colleagues, friends, and family have discouraged or encouraged their commitment to a scientific career. Stories about explicit insults and exclusion, intellectual sabotage, and institutional discrimination reveal the hardships and resistance that women faced (and still face) in male-dominated fields of study (Weisstein 1977; Wayne 2000). For many readers, such accounts are their first encounter with the harsh educational realities of becoming a woman in science. Some theorists have argued that scientific practices are predicated on the exclusion of women so that women must abandon their gender identity to become a scientist (Keller 1977). Others maintain that women do science in distinctive ways (Eisenhart and Finkel 1998). First-person accounts most often reveal a host of educational and social processes that are endemic to broader cultural beliefs about women, men, and science, as people testify to the challenges they have overcome. Histories of women in the sciences have elaborated the broader contexts of educational opportunities and working conditions of women scientists as well as the legal, political, economic, and scientific challenges that confronted them in the United States, Great Britain, and Europe (Rossiter 1982, 1995).

The Use of Science in the Perpetuation of Inequality

Though women and people of color have made significant and often overlooked contributions to scientific knowledge, in general the scientific professions have been dominated by White males. This stark fact has given rise to questions about the degree to which the scientific method can produce objective results in research about women and about sex and gender differences. Research about the emergence and application of medical knowledge about women, for instance, documents the ways in which male physicians have understood women's bodies almost exclusively in terms of reproduction rather than as fully human and physiologically complex (Martin 1992). Research about sex difference has been particularly contested since its emergence in 19th-century Great Britain and Europe in debates about human evolution. Because lawyers, educators, economists, employers, and policy makers often drew on biased science to explain why women should be denied constitutional rights, access to higher education, fair wages, employment, and political representation, sex difference research has few advocates among feminist scientists. Sex difference research is critiqued by many contemporary scholars as thoroughly flawed by its origins in efforts to legitimate and naturalize the oppression and exploitation of women and people of color by elite White males (Connell 2002). Most contemporary researchers emphasize that differences between women and men in social status and power cannot be linked scientifically to physiological sex differences (Rose and Rose 2000).

Science as Socially Produced and Embedded

Though some have argued that research about sex differences is an example of "biased" science that can become objective through a process of review, critique, and revision, others have argued that all science is a product of human activity and as such is limited by the social and historical contexts of discovery. Human activity is never "value free" since all that people do and say is interpreted and given meaning within social life. Which research topics are deemed worthy of study, how research questions are formulated, how the resulting data are gathered and interpreted, and the language that is used in all of the above often depend on when; in what social, economic, and political environment; and by whom the work is done. Science is thus a social activity that is constructed and constrained by the shared practices of a community of highly trained specialists (Harding 1991; Traweek 1988). Feminist science studies grounded in this perspective have explored, in particular, the subtle ways in which the language of science at once reveals and reinforces cultural practices and politics in the grounding assumptions, methods, interpretations of data, and theories utilized by scientists (Haraway 1991). The language that scientists use is not transparent—it does not function simply as a passive vehicle through which scientists gather and relate knowledge of the natural world. Rather, language both represents and creates the shared meanings that a scientific community attaches to the concepts, metaphors, and images that scientists use (Keller 1992). Specialized vocabularies develop in fields as a consequence of this process, but scientists (and all specialists) use concepts, metaphors, and images from the culture at large as well (e.g., Cohn 1987).

Successor Science Projects

Feminist science researchers have confronted a dilemma: scientific research can be a powerful tool with which to challenge and correct knowledge about women and gender. But the scientific method has not only failed to eradicate social biases, it has sometimes been used in the service of them. Women and men who are highly trained scientists committed to fully inclusive, liberatory, and empirically persuasive research have begun to explore how to reimagine and reinvigorate science with insights gained from feminist theory. There are several components of such work: understanding how sex and gender differences matter (or do not matter) for a research question, accepting that theories and hypotheses are not transparently unbiased and apolitical, avoiding reductionist methods, viewing nature as a phenomenon that should be understood but not dominated, and working with a diverse community of researchers (Longino 1989). Because success in contemporary scientific laboratory research demands a high degree of conformity to social arrangements based on a set of opposing components (neutrality, reductionism, and hierarchy, for instance), laboratory-based successor science projects are rare or rarely reported. Some argue that primatology, as a field, is a successor science because it has been fundamentally changed by an increase in the participation of women and the influence of feminist ideas (Fedigan 2001).

Education and Public Policy

There is a substantial body of research that focuses on educational and public policy concerns related to the underrepresentation of women in scientific training and employment. In contrast, feminist science studies emphasizes the content of science curriculum and the goals and commitments of the scientific profession. Advocates promote educational innovation to underscore the systematic and institutionalized exclusion and marginalization of women and gender as subjects that matter in scientific education, training, and research (Rosser 1995; Mayberry, Subramaniam, and Weasel 2001). This emphasis distinguishes feminist science studies as an effort to encourage changes in the values, priorities, and goals of the scientific community—changes that will need to be represented in the curriculum to be effective in reeducating the next generation of scientists. There is experimental evidence that students benefit educationally from the course revisions advocated (Wyer et al. 2007). The national Women's Health Initiative is one example that demonstrates how including women changes scientific knowledge for the benefit of women. It was launched in 1991 as a public health policy initiative in response to criticisms that medical research used the male body as the biological norm for all human medical research. As a consequence of relying on this norm, medical professionals had received too little training about women's bodies and gender dynamics in the conditions of their lives, impairing the health care that women receive. Through the Women's Health Initiative, and in conjunction with reforms at the National Institutes of Health, research and medical training about the general health of women have expanded significantly. Though this growth is important, within feminist science studies there is a continued press to extend such work to include health issues related to ethnicity, sexuality, and class. (*See also* Biologists Who Study Gender/Feminism; Critiques of Science; Discrimination; Feminist Philosophy of Science; Marxism/Socialism and Feminism/Gender; Race, Postcolonial Gender, and Science; Women's Health Movement)

References and Further Reading

Cohn, C. "Sex and Death in the Rational World of Defense Intellectuals." *Signs: Journal of Women in Culture and Society* 12(4) (1987): 687–718.

Connell, R. W. *Gender.* Cambridge, UK: Polity, 2002.

Eisenhart, M. A., and E. Finkel. *Women's Science: Learning and Succeeding from the Margins.* Chicago: University of Chicago Press, 1998.

Fausto-Sterling, A. *Myths of Gender: Biological Theories about Women and Men.* 2nd ed. New York: Basic Books, 1992.

Fedigan, L. "The Paradox of Feminist Primatology." In *Feminism in 20th Century Science, Technology, and Medicine.* Edited by A. Creager, E. Lunbeck, and L. Schiebinger, 46–72. Chicago: University of Chicago Press, 2001.

Gould, S. *The Mismeasure of Man.* New York: W. W. Norton, 1981.

Haraway, D. *Simians, Cyborgs, and Women: The Reinvention of Nature.* New York: Routledge, 1991.

Harding, S. *Whose Science, Whose Knowledge? Thinking from Women's Lives.* Ithaca, NY: Cornell University Press, 1991.

Harding, S., ed. *The Racial Economy of Science.* Bloomington: Indiana University Press, 1993.

Keller, E. F. "The Anomaly of a Woman in Physics." In *Working It Out.* Edited by S. Ruddick and P. Daniels. New York: Pantheon Books, 1977.

Keller, E. F. *Secrets of Life, Secrets of Death: Essays on Language, Gender, and Science.* New York: Routledge, 1992.

Keller, E. F., and H. Longino, eds. *Feminism and Science.* New York: Oxford University Press, 1996.

Longino, Helen. "Can There Be a Feminist Science?" In *Feminism and Science.* Edited by Nancy Tuana, 45–57. Bloomington: Indiana University Press, 1989.

Longino, H. *Science as Social Knowledge.* Princeton, NJ: Princeton University Press, 1990.

Martin, Emily. *The Woman in the Body.* Boston: Beacon Press, 1992.

Mayberry, M., B. Subramaniam, and L.Weasel. *Feminist Science Studies: A New Generation.* New York: Routledge, 2001.

Rose, H., and S. Rose, eds. *Alas, Poor Darwin: Arguments against Evolutionary Psychology.* New York: Harmony Books, 2000.

Rosser, Sue V., ed. *Teaching the Majority: Science, Mathematics, and Engineering Teaching that Attracts Women.* New York: Teachers College Press, 1995.

Rossiter, M. *Women Scientists in America: Struggles and Strategies to 1940.* Baltimore, MD: Johns Hopkins University Press, 1982.

Rossiter, M. *Women Scientists in America: Before Affirmative Action, 1940–1972.* Baltimore, MD: Johns Hopkins University Press, 1995.

Traweek, Sharon. *Beamtimes and Lifetimes: The World of High Energy Physics.* Cambridge, MA: Harvard University Press, 1988.

Wayne, M. "Walking a Tightrope: The Feminist Life of a *Drosophila* Biologist." *NWSA Journal* 12(3) (2000): 139–150.

Weisstein, N. "'How Can a Little Girl Like You Teach a Great Big Class of Men?' the Chairman Said, and Other Adventures of a Woman in Science." In *Working It Out: Twenty-three Writers, Scientists, and Scholars Talk about Their Lives.* Edited by S. Ruddick and P. Daniels. New York: Pantheon Books, 1977.

Wyer, M., D. Murphy-Medley, E. Damschen, K. Rosenfeld, and T. Wentworth. "No Quick Fixes: Adding Women to Ecology Course Content." *Psychology of Women Quarterly* 31 (2007): 96–102.

Women's Health Movement

SUE V. ROSSER

Historically, myths surrounding gender and sexuality meant that the health of all—men, women, and children—fell into the hands of women. Because of their experience with pregnancy and childbirth, midwives knew about the anatomy of the body, evolved knowledge of herbs and their medicinal properties to cure disease, and understood variations in reproductive cycles and life stages of healthy women. Most women had at least a rudimentary knowledge of herbs and medicinal properties of plants, which they used to cure disease and maintain health within their families.

Colonial Era to Mid-1950s

In the Colonial era, in the United States, most physicians freely used the title doctor, although most were self-taught. Two thirds of New England medical practitioners did not have college, apprentice training, access to safe pharmaceutical preparations, or antiseptic surgical procedures. By the 18th century, male physicians gradually began to take over the practices of midwives. In *Witches, Midwives, and Nurses,* Ehrenreich and English (1974) document the struggle by male physicians to wrest health care from midwives in the late 19th century as they sought credibility and a base of economic security for their practice as physicians. The end of the 19th century and particularly the early part of the 20th century witnessed increasing medicalization of pregnancy, childbirth, and lactation. Concurrently, there was a shift from female support and guidance during these normal reproductive events occurring in the home to male authority and control over events that were seen as requiring hospitalization and physician intervention. In the 1940s for women giving birth, U.S. physicians began to use the drug scopolamine or "twilight sleep," first introduced in Germany in the 1930s, increasing the incidence of hospital births under total anesthesia (Leavitt 1986). At approximately the same time, bottle feeding on schedule replaced breast feeding on demand. By the middle of the 20th century, the male medical establishment had gained almost complete control over childbirth in the United States; for example, in 1983, 99 percent of births in the United States "occurred in hospitals, and 98 percent of these were attended by physicians" (Sullivan and Weitz 1988, 1).

Women physicians channeled their work into community-focused educational activities and collaborative work with nurses, practicing in community schools, orphanages, and voluntary health agencies. They initiated well-child clinics and mothers' milk banks and urged humane laws to restrict child labor. In the late 19th century, excluded from practicing in most hospitals, women physicians opened hospitals for women and children. Because male physicians tended to ignore the working classes and poor and because too many children too closely space imperiled the health of poor women, reproductive issues became significant in the first wave of feminism—at the beginning of the 20th century and in the rise of public health in the United States. Margaret Sanger spearheaded the birth control movement in the 1910s and 1920s, opening the first birth control clinic in the United States in Brooklyn in 1916 (Tone 1996). Joined by hundreds of organizations and individuals in a collec-

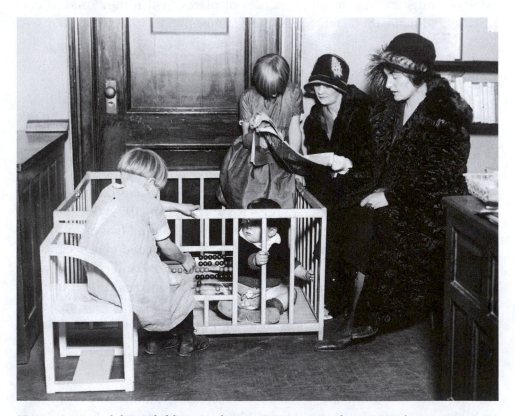

Two women and three children in clinic waiting room, about 1920. (Margaret Sanger Papers collection/Library of Congress)

tive struggle, Sanger led the fight against the Comstock Act passed in 1873 prohibiting distribution of contraceptives or information preventing conception, and her publicizing and popularizing birth control created public consciousness around the need for women to control their bodies. Although Sanger became somewhat discredited after World War II because of her association with the eugenics movement, in the early 20th century in the United States, she stands out as the individual who crusaded for safe, legal contraception.

After the American Civil War, most states passed laws overturning the traditional right of girls and women to abort during the first trimester of pregnancy. These laws, passed in the late 19th century, allowed licensed physicians to perform abortions only when the pregnant woman's life was in danger due to a medical condition. Until about 1950, most hospitals performed legal abortions frequently and routinely for a number of medical conditions, including severe psychiatric disorders. Beginning in the 1950s and extending until *Roe v. Wade* made abortion legal in all states in the United States in 1973, medical-technological advances and improvements in obstetrics divided the medical profession over abortions. Thinking of pregnancy as an added burden that women with certain diseases and mental conditions could not withstand became more difficult as improvements in technology and medicine decreased the situations in which the pregnant woman's life was clearly in danger. Abortion rates in the 1950s and 1960s decreased significantly over the rates earlier in the 20th century (Solinger 1992).

The 1960s

As in the first wave of feminism, a motivating force begun in the 1960s was women's health concerns. Women sought the right to control their own bodies through access to safe birth control, abortion, and information about their physiology and anatomy; to define their own experiences as a valid aspect of their health needs; and to question the androcentric bias found in the hierarchy of the male-dominated health care system and its approach to research and practice.

Activist individuals, encouraged partially by the women's movement in the late 1960s, brought legal challenges, including class action suits, against medical schools that had quotas limiting the admission of women as well as men of racial and ethnic minorities. Their legal challenge of the quota system was a first of many critiques women presented to the medical profession. Women activists can claim responsibility for initiating a demographic shift within the medical profession that increased the percentage of women medical school graduates from about 7 percent in the mid-1960s to almost 50 percent today.

Much of the impetus for women's health arose from the women's movement in the 1960s and from community activists. In 1970, the U.S. Senate held hearings on the contraceptive pill, organized in response to Barbara Seaman's 1969 book, *The Doctor's Case against the Pill*. In 1972, Belita Cowan created *Her-Self,* the leading newspaper of feminist health, and Phyllis Chesler wrote *Women and Madness,* critiquing sexism in the mental health system. These individuals, along with Mary Howell, the first female dean at Harvard Medical School and author of *Why Would a Girl Go into Medicine?* became founding members of the National Women's Health Network in 1975 in Washington, DC (Pearson and Seaman 1998).

Consumer, community-based organizations such as the National Women's Health Network (NWHN), the National Breast Cancer Coalition (NBCC), and the Boston Women's Health Book Collective (BWHBC) remain very active today. As women's health becomes institutionalized within the profession and academy, leaders such as Adrienne Fugh-Berman, president of the National Women's Health Network, epitomize and facilitate connections among women's health consumers, activists, and health care professionals to understand new issues and ethical dilemmas in women's health; they also ensure that women's health continues to address the practical concerns of the lives of real women. The NBCC played an instrumental role in bringing together activists, consumers, politicians, and researchers to increase funding for research into breast cancer. In 2005, the BWHBC published a new edition of *Our Bodies, Ourselves,* written by over 400 women based on their experiences and knowledge. *Our Bodies, Ourselves* has sold over 4 million copies since it was written over 30 years ago.

Not until a substantial number of women had entered the professions of biology and medicine could biases from androcentrism be exposed. Once the possibility of androcentric bias was discovered, the potential for distortion on a variety of levels of research and theory was recognized: the choice and definition of problems to be studied, the exclusion of females as experimental subjects, bias in the methodology used to collect and interpret data, and bias in theories and conclusions drawn from the data. Since the practice of modern medicine uses a biomedical approach based in positivist research in biology and chemistry and depends heavily on clinical research, any flaws and ethical problems in this research are likely to result in poorer health care and inequity in the medical treatment of disadvantaged groups (Rosser 1994).

This realization uncovered gender bias that had distorted some medical research. Women's health had become synonymous with reproductive health and obstetrics/gynecology. This meant that many diseases that occurred in both sexes had been studied in males only and/or used a male-as-norm approach. Cardiovascular diseases are a case in point. Research protocols for large-scale studies of cardiovascular diseases conducted in the early 1990s—such as the

Multiple Factor Risk Intervention Trial, the Physicians' Health Study, and the study of coffee and cardiovascular disease (Rosser 1994)—failed to assess gender differences. Women were excluded from clinical trials of drugs because of fear of litigation from possible teratogenic effects on fetuses. Exclusion of women from clinical drug trials was pervasive: a meta-analysis, published in September 1992 in the *Journal of the American Medical Association,* surveyed the literature from 1960 to 1991 on clinical trials of medications used to treat acute myocardial infarction; the results showed that women were included in less than 20 percent and the elderly in less than 40 percent of those studies (Gurwitz, Nananda, and Avorn 1992). A 1996 study included all prospective treatment and intervention studies published in the *New England Journal of Medicine,* the *Journal of the American Medical Association,* and the *Annals of Internal Medicine* between January and June in 1990 and 1994; it revealed that only 19 percent of the 1990 studies and 24 percent of the 1994 studies reported any data analysis by gender, despite the fact that 40 percent of the subjects were female (Charney and Morgan 1996).

Excessive focus on male research subjects and definition of cardiovascular diseases as "male" led to underdiagnosis and undertreatment of the disease in women. Studies demonstrated that women were significantly less likely than men to undergo coronary angioplasty, angiography, or surgery when admitted to the hospital with a diagnosis of myocardial infarction, unstable or stable angina, chronic ischemic heart disease, or chest pain. This significant difference remained even when variables such as race, age, economic status, and other chronic diseases such as diabetes and heart failure were controlled. Similarly, women experienced angina before myocardial infarction as frequently as, and with more debilitating effects than, men; yet women were referred for cardiac catheterization only half as often. These and similar studies led Bernadine Healy, a cardiologist and first woman director of the National Institutes of Health (NIH), to characterize the diagnosis of coronary heart disease in women as the Yentl syndrome: "Once a woman showed that she was just like a man, by having coronary artery disease or a myocardial infarction, then she was treated as a man should be" (Healy 1991, 274). The male-as-norm approach in research and diagnosis, unsurprisingly, was translated into bias in treatments for women. Women exhibited higher death rates from angioplasty and coronary bypass surgery because the techniques had been pioneered using male subjects (Rosser 1994).

Women scientists, consumers, physicians, and politicians brought these revelations and other examples of bias and gaps in research and practice to the attention of the health community. After the 1985 U.S. Public Health Service survey recommended that the definition of women's health be expanded beyond reproductive health, the Government Accountability Office (GAO) reported that the NIH expended only 13.5 percent of its budget on women's health issues. In 1990, the GAO criticized the NIH for inadequate representation of women and minorities in federally funded studies and the Congressional Caucus for Women's Issues introduced the Women's Health Equity Act. In 1991, Bernadine Healy established the Office of Research on Women's Health and announced plans for the Women's Health Initiative. The Women's Health Initiative is designed to collect baseline data and look at interventions to prevent cardiovascular disease, breast cancer, colorectal cancer, and osteoporosis; it seeks to fill the gaps in research and practice.

Expanding the Definition of Women's Health

The interdisciplinary nature of most issues in women's health and disease formed the raison d'etre for health care professionals and researchers from diverse specialties, professions, and disciplines to interact. They recognized that the traditional territory of obstetrics/gynecology failed to include much of women's health beyond the defined limits of reproductive issues such as pregnancy, childbirth, menopause, ovarian hormones, menstrual cycles, and contraception. They expanded women's health to include differences in frequency, symptoms, and effects of diseases found in both sexes, such as differences in cardiovascular diseases, many lung diseases (such as primary pulmonary hypertension), sexually transmitted diseases, gastrointestinal disorders (such as gallstones), neurological disorders (such as multiple sclerosis and migraine headaches), urinary tract disorders (such as incontinence), and psychiatric and behavioral problems (such as depression, anxiety, substance abuse, and eating disorders). Women's health encompasses sex differences at the molecular level of metabolism of drugs, including their interactions with hormones, exposure to environmental toxins, and absorption of food, vitamins, and minerals. This expanded definition extends throughout women's life span from before adolescence through aging, including end-of-life issues and dying; it encompasses all facets of women's life, recognizing sociocultural issues such as domestic violence, rape, child abuse, and poverty as primary health issues for women and their families.

This expanded definition also requires linkages with researchers in liberal arts to understand women's health. Behavioral and social sciences, particularly psychology, sociology, anthropology, and women's studies, provided basic research theories for domestic violence, eating disorders, and sexual and/or physical abuse, now recognized as central to women's health.

Acquired immune deficiency syndrome (AIDS) in women also exemplifies why an understanding of social factors and power/gender interactions need to be understood to effectively combat the disease. Much as with cardiovascular disease, androcentric bias led to the definition of AIDS as a male dis-

National Women and Girls HIV/AIDS Awareness Day poster, an event sponsored by the Office on Women's Health at the U.S. Department of Health and Human Services. (U.S. Department of Health and Human Services)

ease in the United States. Although for some time women infected with the human immunodeficiency virus (HIV) had demonstrated higher rates of abnormal Pap smears and cervical cancer, increased incidence of pelvic inflammatory disease resistant to treatment, and severe vaginal yeast infections resistant to cure, until 1993 these conditions were not included in the revised Centers for Disease Control (CDC) case definition of AIDS. Immediately when the definition changed, the numbers of cases of AIDS increased dramatically because women were included in the statistics (Rosser 1994). Furthermore, statements by women that their only possible risk behavior might have been heterosexual intercourse with a male who had said he was not HIV-positive were not taken seriously by most researchers until they were corroborated by a study of men in which 35 percent admitted that they would lie to a potential sex partner about their HIV status, and 20 percent said they had lied about having been tested. Similarly, most of the education and advertising campaigns about condom use initially were directed toward women, despite reports by some women that requiring condom use increased battering by their partners. Little research has focused on the information given to health care practitioners to address complications that women face with their own AIDS illness because they also serve as caretakers to their male partners or children with the disease (Rosser 1994).

Impact upon Curriculum and Research

Part of the impetus initiating the women's health movement was women's desire to have access to information about their physiology and anatomy as part of the need to control their own bodies. In an attempt to respond to that desire, women's health courses sprang up in women's studies, nursing, sociology, and a variety of places in the curriculum, beginning in the early 1970s.

Once understanding began to emerge about the pervasiveness of women's exclusion from research designs and curricula and the bias that exclusion introduces into research, teaching, and practice, women became a new focal point for research and curricula. A substantial group of investigators, lecturers, and practitioners committed their efforts and careers to studying women. These individuals designed experiments that not only included women as experimental subjects but for which women's health, diseases, and issues also served as the central topic of study. The topics led to the development of experimental methods particularly appropriate for the female body and life cycle and the experiences of women. Understanding also grew that race and class were interlocked with gender in the health and disease of women and that these issues must be integrated into research design, teaching, and practice. In many respects, this awareness represents the current phase of research on women's health. The Women's Health Initiative and other studies are collecting data on cardiovascular diseases, using the female body as the norm.

The ultimate goal is to integrate the information on women's health into research in all specialties and to transform all aspects of the health curriculum to include women and their health. This would aid other disciplines and specialties in understanding the importance of including women in research and teaching while simultaneously providing trained specialists to undertake more focused research in this interdisciplinary field.

Diversities among Women

Demographic projections reveal that the current racial "minorities" will soon constitute the majority of the U.S. population; as the baby boom generation ages, the elderly population, predominantly female, will increase dramatically. Research on health of lesbians, women of color, women from non-U.S. cultures/countries, and elderly women has remained underfunded, understudied, and overlooked (Rosser 1994). Disabled women remain largely invisible to both the U.S. population at large and the health research agenda in particular. To rectify this dearth of research and avoid problems from failing to consider the comprehensive health of the majority of U.S. women, research and needs of diverse women must become a central focus of women's health education.

Racism intertwines with sexism and economics to move health care issues for women of color to the far margins or to move them entirely out of the national agenda for clinical research. Gender and color doubly remove these women from the White male, from whose perspective the research agenda is formulated and whose body serves as the norm from which deviations are calculated. When included, women of color too often become misused as subjects in experiments that either lend credence to racial stereotypes or fail to distinguish true health problems among races.

Many of the health and disease concerns of women of color overlap with those of White women, which have only recently begun to be a focus of the national research agenda—with the establishment of the Office of Women's Health Research in 1990. Women of color also face many of the same problems with health and disease as do the men of their racial and ethnic groups. Men of color have not shared the central spotlight for research with White men. The Office for Minority Health Affairs was not established until 1991.

Racism and sexism have combined to severely limit advances in health care for women of color. The dearth of research in general and the often delimitative nature of this research have yielded only meager, and in many cases unreliable, data regarding frequency and cause of diseases, exacerbation of illness by environmental factors, and effective treatments for promoting health and preventing disease in women of color. Some complications of racism and sexism have effectively invalidated such research in the past. A major problem has been that the phrase "women of color" is too often taken to mean a coherent group when in fact it includes women of extremely diverse racial and ethnic backgrounds who are not closely related to each other genetically or culturally. They may, therefore, differ more from each other than they do from White women. Another controversy focuses on the appropriateness and reliability of undertaking race-based research, diagnosis, and treatment, since race is not a biological category. Considerable diversity exists within each group. For example, Asians and Pacific Islanders in the United States include more than 25 subgroups—Chinese, Filipinos, Japanese, Indians, Koreans, Vietnamese, Hawaiians, Samoans, Guamanians, Burmese, Cambodians, Laotians, Thais, and others. Although they share an origin in Asia and the Pacific Islands, they have different cultures, languages, and probably gene pools. Since many of the Asians and Pacific Islanders in the United States today are first-generation immigrants, virtually no baseline data exist on the health of these women. Less explicable is the fact that even for those whose ancestors immigrated to this country more than a century ago, only limited baseline data exist.

The Hispanic population also does not represent a homogeneous ethnic group. Mexican Americans, Puerto Ricans, Cubans, and individuals from 16 other Latin American countries and Spain speak Spanish but have their origins in very different cultures and countries. Since many Chicanas and those from other Latin American cultures are also first-generation Americans, there is little history of research and few baseline data for Hispanic women, either.

For American Indian and Alaskan Native women—the first female Americans, predating not only White women but also White men—short tenure in the United States cannot be used to explain the absence of research (and their poor health). Similarly, the African American population, originally transported to the United States against its will, is the oldest and most stable nonindigenous minority group. Yet little good research has explored Black women's health, even though in many ways Black women are the most vulnerable of all minority women. For example, the breast cancer rates for African American women are lower than for White women but higher than for Latinas. However, five-year survival rates are lower and death rates are higher for African American women than for either White women or Latinas with breast cancer. Some of the reasons for these statistics are that African American women have higher rates of poverty, are more likely to be diagnosed later, and are often undertreated when compared to their White and Latina counterparts (Kasper 2000). Inclusion of social, psychological, and public health perspectives are needed for a more comprehensive research base to also explore why poor women and women of color have higher death rates from breast cancer. Epidemiological approaches include these perspectives; they reveal factors important for disease prevention. Because the poor, in general, have a 20 to 25 percent lower cancer survival rate regardless of race, research that relies on biology alone and ignores socioeconomic factors will be unlikely to uncover the best way to remove this survival differential. Interdisciplinary approaches, including coupling methods from the social sciences with those of biomedicine, may tease apart the relative effects of more exposure to workplace and environmental carcinogens and less access to high-quality medical care, nutritious food, and decent living conditions on the higher incidence and lower survival rates experienced by African Americans with regard to breast cancer.

In the rare cases where women of color have been the focus of research, at best the results have yielded little or inadequate information about health and disease processes. At worst, the women have served as guinea pigs for clinical trials of unsafe drugs, such as the use of Puerto Rican women for testing birth control pills without informed consent or for experiments to document possible biological bases for social ills. Studies have revealed that Black women are almost 10 times more likely to be tested and reported for drug use during pregnancy than White women, and 80 percent of cases brought against women for drug use during pregnancy have been against women of color (Pattrow 1990). This research illuminated the overall health of pregnant women of color, who may avoid prenatal care if they use drugs or alcohol. Researchers agree that it is safer for a baby to be born to a drug-abusing, anemic, or diabetic mother who visits the doctor than to be born to a "normal" women who does not (Pattrow 1990). Access to health care may be defined as the controlling factor for health and disease in the lives of minority women.

As women and as nonheterosexuals, lesbians are doubly distanced from the heterosexual male norm focus of health research and care. When lesbians are recognized, they are often subsumed as a subset of women or homosexuals, where heterosexual females or homosexual males become the respective norms against which lesbians are measured. The implicit assumptions underlying this failure to recognize the health care issues of lesbians are that lesbians do not exist, that they have precisely the same health care issues as heterosexual females, or in rare cases that they share the same health care issues as male homosexuals.

Ignoring or lumping together lesbian health care issues becomes exacerbated by homophobia among health care professionals. Not only does homophobia discourage lesbians from seeking necessary health care, but it also prevents health care workers from tying appropriate diagnoses and treatments to risk behaviors.

Until the Women's Health Initiative, very little research on women's menopausal experience existed. As the baby boom generation ages, the pharmaceutical companies have developed an extreme interest in capturing the market of consuming women approaching menopause. These companies redefined menopause as a disease that required hormones to cure it and made large amounts of money by selling hormone replacement therapy (HRT) to women before, during, and after menopause.

Until the Women's Health Initiative, very little research compared the health of menopausal women who took HRT with those who did not take HRT. With the revelation that hormone replacement therapy did not prevent heart disease or Alzheimer's but increased the risk of stroke, blood clots, breast cancer, and incontinence, over 6 million women stopped taking hormones and demanded to know more about the research and policies that had encouraged them to do so (Pearson 2006). A primary reason that little comparative research had been undertaken was the general dearth of research on menopausal women.

For elderly women, a recognized clinical specialty, gerontology, should address some of their health needs. Gerontology remains a relatively new, emerging field without a clear research agenda. It has already demonstrated androcentrism by excluding women from its most comprehensive longitudinal study; the Baltimore Longitudinal Study on Aging, the largest longitudinal study to assess the geriatric population, was begun in 1958 and included no women subjects for the first 20 years (Johnson 1992). This omission delayed the discovery of the link among osteoporosis, calcium, estrogen, and progesterone.

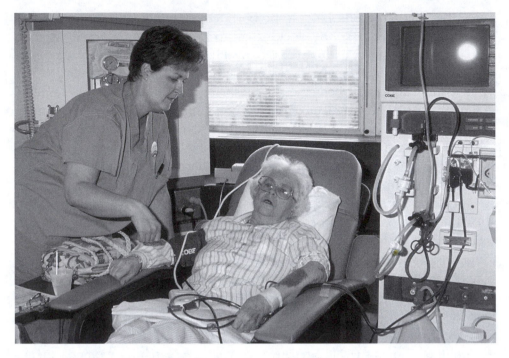

An elderly woman receives medical treatment. (Corel)

Recent census data projections completed by the Administration on Aging underscore the dramatic increase in the elderly population in the United States. In 2030, one fifth of the total population will be 65 or older; the number of women 85 and older was 2.3 million in 2000 and is expected to reach 6.3 million by 2030, since women reaching 65 have an average additional life expectancy of 19.5 years. Elderly women outnumber elderly men by a ratio of 2:1. Because women live longer than men, they accumulate more acute, chronic diseases that tend to result in greater disability before death and greater out-of-pocket expenses than do the acute illnesses suffered more commonly by men. Women's greater longevity also means that most women who serve as care-takers for a spouse when his health fails must rely on the support of health services, extended family, and friends during their own health care crises.

This information strongly suggests that elderly women will become an increasingly significant proportion of the population who will need a dispro-portionately large amount of health care. Research on diseases; maintenance of health and well-being; and successful, cost-efficient health care practices appropriate for elderly women should be accorded high priority on the na-tional health care agenda.

Although women with disabilities typically differ from their able-bodied sisters because of mental or physical health issues that may lead them to fre-quent encounters with the health care system, in many ways they remain the most marginalized and invisible of women. In most ways, the issues of disabled women overlap with those of nondisabled women. Excluded as research subjects, absent from clinical trials of drugs, compared with male norms, and out of central focus for research agendas are all descriptors for both disabled and nondisabled women concerning their health issues. Many women with disabilities are also women of color, lesbians, and/or elderly.

For many disabled women, issues of access, poverty, and environment become especially significant. Because of the relatively small numbers of women experiencing a particular disability, coupled with different manifestations of the disability, garnering research attention and funding may be especially difficult and acute. In addition to the bias, ignoring, overlooking, and understudy of health issues faced by all women, disabled women experience additional, different issues. Disabled women are compared not only to the male norm but also to the nondisabled female norm.

Women's health has experienced many successes over the last three decades, making it a major component of the current public agenda. Resources for research in women's health have multiplied, and with these successes have come increased competition and co-optation by those who are primarily interested in controlling women's health in their own interests. With women now the majority of medical students, the possibility opens for increasing influence of women on health care delivery and practice. Whether prevailing ideas about gender roles and who can and should do science will allow women to control the research agenda in health remains an open question. Health care delivery and research to understand what works to maintain health and prevent disease appear to return control of health to the pre-19th-century situation when women controlled health. Today, of course, business forces in the form of insurance and pharmaceutical industries, controlled primarily by men, now dominate the health care industry. (*See also* Women's Health Movement; Medicine)

References and Further Reading

Charney, Pamela, and Carole Morgan. "Do Treatment Recommendations Reported in the Research Literature Consider Differences between Women and Men?" *Journal of Women's Health* 5(6) (1996): 579–584.

Ehrenreich, Barbara, and Deirdre English. *Witches, Midwives, and Nurses: A History of Women Healers*. Old Westbury, NY: Feminist Press, 1974.

Gurwitz, J. H, F. C. Nananda, and J. Avorn. "The Exclusion of the Elderly and Women from Clinical Trials in Acute Myocardial Infarction." *Journal of the American Medical Association* 268(2) (1992): 1417–1422.

Healy, Bernadine. "The Yentl Syndrome." *New England Journal of Medicine* 325(4) (1991): 274–276.

Johnson, Karen. "Pro: Women's Health: Developing a New Interdisciplinary Specialty." *Journal of Women's Health* 2 (1992): 101.

Kasper, Anne. "Barriers and Burdens: Poor Women Face Breast Cancer." In *Breast Cancer: Society Shapes an Epidemic*. Edited by Anne Kasper and Susan Ferguson. New York: St. Martin's Press, 2000.

Leavitt, Judith. *Brought to Bed: Childbearing in America 1750–1950*. New York: Oxford University Press, 1986.

Pattrow, Lynn M. "When Becoming Pregnant Is a Crime." *Criminal Justice Ethics* (Winter/Spring 1990): 41–47.

Pearson, Cynthia. "Menopause Hormone Therapy and Age of Initiation: Reasonable Theory or Marketing Hoax?" *The Women's Health Activist*. Washington, DC: National Women's Health Network, March/April 2006.

Pearson, Cynthia, and Barbara Seaman. "When Were We Founded? And Just What Were We Doing Back Then Anyway?" *Network News* 3, 1998.

Rosser, Sue V. *Women's Health: Missing from U.S. Medicine*. Bloomington: Indiana University Press, 1994.

Solinger, Rickie. "Race and 'Value': Black and White Illegitimate Babies in the U.S.A., 1945–1965." *Gender and History* 4 (1992).

Sullivan, Deborah, and Rose Weitz. *Labor Pains: Modern Midwives and Home Birth*. New Haven, CT: Yale University Press, 1988.

Tone, Andrea. "Birth Control in the 1930s." *Journal of Social History* 29 (1996): 485–506.

Science Fiction

Lisa Yasek

Women write science fiction (SF) for many reasons: to dramatize scientific theories, to explore the development of new technologies, and even to speculate about the future of social and political relations. Indeed, this latter reason is often the most pressing of all. Americans have long treated sex and gender as immutable categories arising from natural laws. These categories seem to justify a division of labor that equates women's work with housekeeping and family maintenance and men's work with economic and political activity. Although such equations acknowledge the centrality of feminine labor to modern society, especially in the private sphere of the home, they exclude women from key areas of influence in the public sphere and thus the creation of those narratives used to justify contemporary social and political arrangements. Writing SF enables women to imaginatively intervene in these arrangements. More specifically, it enables women to critically assess "commonsense" understandings of sex and gender while imagining new and more egalitarian futures grounded in their own experience of the world. Therefore, it is not surprising that the history of women's writing about sex and gender in SF parallels the history of American feminism itself.

This history begins with the Seneca Falls Convention of 1848, where American women lodged their first formal protests again taxation without representation. The "first wave" of feminist activity inspired by this convention culminated in 1920 with the passage of the Nineteenth Amendment, which guaranteed the right to vote for all Americans. Throughout this period, women generally used one of two strategies to argue for universal suffrage. Activists allied with the conservative Woman Movement invoked the rhetoric of "republican motherhood" to propose that women, with their innate morality and special talent for domestic organization, were ideally suited to political service as "municipal housekeepers." Meanwhile, liberal-to-radical feminists lobbied political leaders to embrace democracy, reject sexual stereotypes, and grant the vote to all people. Whether they emphasized women's duties or women's rights, first-wave feminists made their arguments for political equality by challenging simple distinctions between women's work in the private home and men's work in the public sphere.

Women writing utopian fiction at this time incorporated both aspects of first-wave feminism into their storytelling. This is particularly apparent in Mary E. Bradley Lane's *Mizora: A Prophecy* (1881) and Charlotte Perkins Gilman's *Herland* (1915), both of which depict single-sex societies organized around mothering, homemaking, and community building. The women of Mizora and Herland enjoy unprecedented standards of living because they apply the principles of municipal housekeeping on the widest scale possible, abolishing the distinction between the public and private spheres and treating the entire nation as one family. Significantly, these utopian heroines are also scientists who make fantastic advances in psychology and genetics as well as engineers who transform their arctic and jungle homes into fertile paradises. Thus, Lane and Gilman combined the differing feminist ideals of their time to illustrate how women who traverse the private and public spheres might initiate the next stage of human evolution.

Utopian dreams also permeate the first generation of women's SF stories. SF emerged as a distinct genre with its own readers, writers, and publications in the 1920s, 1930s, and early 1940s. Although speculation about the future of science and technology was perceived to be a masculine activity, the dozens of women who helped establish SF used their chosen genre to speculate about the future of sex and gender as well. Such authors generally connected women's liberation to science and technology. For example, the protagonists of Lilith Lorraine's "Into the 28th Century" (1930) enjoy labor-free banquets of jeweled food flakes and sparking beverages, while the women of Leslie F. Stone's "Women with Wings" (1930) delegate housework to autonomous robots. Meanwhile, in Sophie Wenzel Ellis's "Creatures of the Light" (1930), the dangers of childbirth are eliminated by the perfection of glass wombs, and in Stone's "Men with Wings" (1929) women are free to pursue careers outside the home because children are raised by trained professionals. Much like Lane and Gilman before them, early women SF authors made feminist ideas about women's work central to their storytelling practices. However, while pre-suffrage authors used these ideas to illustrate why women deserved the vote, their post-suffrage counterparts used them to remind readers that political reform must be accompanied by scientific and social reform as well.

The period from 1945 to 1966 was one of transition for women in both politics and SF. Initially, cold war politicians glorified women as "domestic patriots" who could best serve their country through housekeeping and child rearing in the suburbs. This new gender role was justified by the rhetoric of "the feminine mystique," which suggested that women were naturally evolved to choose family over career. But by the late 1950s, new government agencies including the National Manpower Council and the National Aeronautics and

Space Administration (NASA) argued that the United States could not win the space race unless it followed the Soviet practice of training women for careers in math and science. The real domestic patriots, then, were those women who sacrificed hearth and home—at least for a while—to join the workforce and help ensure worldwide democracy.

Meanwhile, women in the postwar SF community proposed that women's domestic lives might be inspiration for, rather than impediments to, scientific and political progress. The stories written by these authors tend to fall in one of two broad categories. Some equated the forced choice between family and career with disaster. For example, in Marion Zimmer Bradley's "The Wind People" (1959), a medical officer is abandoned on an isolated planet with her newborn son after refusing to euthanize him and return to service; this choice saves her child but leads Bradley's protagonist to madness and death. Meanwhile, in Judith Merril's "Dead Center" (1954), Earth Space Agency officials replace their veteran female rocket designer with an inexperienced male engineer. This choice initiates a string of tragedies including the death of the designer's astronaut husband and six-year-old son, the designer's subsequent suicide, and the end of Earth's space program.

SF authors also imagined women might combine their professional and personal lives in startling new ways. Stories in this vein include Katherine MacLean's "And Be Merry . . ." (1950), in which a scientist unlocks the secret of immortality in her kitchen-turned-laboratory; Merril's "Daughters of Earth" (1952), in which the death of their husbands inspires two generations of space-faring women to develop new exploration techniques; and Doris Pitkin Buck's "Birth of a Gardner" (1961), in which a bad marriage inspires yet another woman to perfect multidimensional travel. In all these tales women are compassionate and consummate professionals who lead their people to the stars.

Such stories anticipated both the revival of American feminism and the emergence of an overtly feminist SF in the late 1960s and 1970s. Extending the efforts of their first-wave predecessors, second-wave feminists challenged simple equations between femininity and domesticity as they sought to ensure equal rights for women in all areas of public life. New political groups such as the National Organization for Women (NOW) were instrumental in this respect. Such groups worked to enforce laws derived from the Civil Rights Act of 1964, which guaranteed equal access to jobs regardless of race or gender. At the same time, they lobbied for new legislation such as Title IX of the Education Amendment Acts of 1972, which banned sex discrimination in all federally funded education programs.

Second-wave feminists also set out to reform gender relations in the private sphere. Many formed consciousness-raising groups where women could productively channel anger with the patriarchal status quo into new plans for their daily lives. Others imagined new programs by which women might

Author and feminist Marge Piercy.
(Robert Shapiro/Library of Congress)

reorganize the entire world. For example, radical feminist Shulamith Firestone proposed that cultural patriarchy stems from the biological dependency women experience during pregnancy, childbirth, and child rearing. To end their oppression, she argued, women must seize the means of reproduction and develop new modes of technologically enhanced propagation. Only then could women and men alike explore new gender roles and develop new social and political relations.

Firestone's vision powerfully influenced feminist SF. Some authors, such as Ursula K. Le Guin in *The Left Hand of Darkness* (1969), used anthropology and sociology to demonstrate how androgynous cultures might distribute childbearing responsibilities and thus power relations more equitably. Others, like Marge Piercy in *Woman on the Edge of Time* (1976) and Joanna Russ in *The Female Man* (1975), looked to new reproductive technosciences instead. In Piercy's novel, babies gestate in mechanical wombs while both men and women use hormone therapy to produce breast milk and experience mothering. Meanwhile, the technosciences of Russ's single-sex utopia liberate women to engage in activities ranging from farming to dueling. Much like the utopian writers who preceded them, feminist SF authors challenged conventional ideas about gender by doing away with distinctions between the public and private spheres. Rather than telling stories about saintly, super-feminine heroines, however, this new generation of writers told stories about flawed protagonists who were distinctly human.

Feminist authors also used SF to express the anger that women felt when they were denied equality. In both Piercy's and Russ's novels, individual characters gladly turn the weapons of science against patriarchy to ensure the creation of better worlds, even at the cost of their own lives. In other stories, entire societies of women are defined by their anger. This is particularly apparent in Suzy McKee Charnas's Holdfast series (1974–1999), where women must literally fight men to prevent their own enslavement. And finally, still other novelists displaced women's anger onto the feminized body of the earth itself. In Sally Miller Gearhart's *Wanderground: Stories of the Hill Women* (1980), women roam the world in perfect harmony with nature while men retreat to walled cities because technology no longer works on open ground. By imagining worlds where women turn science against men, transforming it for their own political ends and abandoning it when it no longer works for them, feminist SF authors dramatize the different strategies that political activists used to combat the patriarchal status quo.

While the quest for sex and gender equality continues today, the development of new information and communication technologies and the advent of global capitalism have brought new issues to the attention of activists and authors. In contrast to earlier feminists who saw science as one locus of discrimination among many, the third-wave feminists who first emerged in the 1980s propose that thinking carefully about the relations of science, society, and gender should be a central priority for all women. Led by science historian Donna Haraway and U.S. Third World scholar Chela Sandoval, contemporary feminists insist that we must recognize not just that new sciences and technologies have transformed women's lives but also that women experience what Haraway calls the "integrated circuit" of capitalism differently based on economic, racial, and national distinctions.

Other feminist science studies scholars including Evelyn Fox Keller, Hilary Rose, and Sandra Harding propose that progressive people might transform the relations of science, society, and gender more effectively by exploring the impact of patriarchal values on science itself. To overcome masculinist bias in science, feminists must recover the scientific practices of women and other people who have been left out of history, and they must identify the gendered metaphors that structure scientific thinking and writing. Finally, scientists themselves must practice what Harding calls "standpoint epistemology" by acknowledging how their social positions influence their practices. Taken together, these analytic activities might make science more truly objective by accounting for all the different factors informing it.

Insights derived from feminist science studies are central to the imaginative practices of contemporary SF authors. For example, feminist writers often use the SF subgenre of cyberpunk to dramatize the gendered implications of life in the integrated circuit of high-tech capitalism. Novels including Pat Cadigan's *Synners* (1991) and Melissa Scott's *Trouble and Her Friends* (1994) predict that the dream of a future in which people use new technologies to escape the messy problems of the material world will eventually trigger information apocalypse and social destruction. But these authors also imagine that people who recognize why bodies still matter in the world of computation might transform bad futures into better ones where women can pursue satisfying politics, work, and even romance.

Like their cyberpunk counterparts, feminist writers of color intervene in contemporary narratives of science, society, and gender in provocative ways. This is particularly true of African American author Octavia E. Butler. Nearly every story Butler published between her literary debut in 1976 and her death in 2006 uses the classic SF theme of "the encounter with the alien other" to complicate readers' thinking about science, technology, and the racial other. Most notably, "Blood Child" (1984) and the Xenogenesis trilogy (1987–1998) imagine that humans and aliens might use science and technology to breed the new, hybrid races that are both species' only hope for survival. Significantly, the offspring of these new races experience both sadness about the passing of old ways and anxiety about their uncertain futures. And yet Butler's stories are ultimately imbued with great hope because her characters look forward to truly new futures that do not simply repeat the past but come with challenges and triumphs all their own.

Finally, women writing postmodern SF critique the Eurocentric, patriarchal bias inherent in science as it is currently practiced while retaining an overall faith in the possibility of progress. This is particularly apparent in Marge Piercy's *He, She, and It* (1991), which follows three generations of female computer scientists as they strive to transform the dystopic near future in which they live. Whether they are corporate workers, independent scientists, or revolutionaries, Piercy's protagonists remain bound together by the desire to create a better world for their children. Meanwhile, Caribbean-Canadian author Nalo Hopkinson's *Brown Girl in the Ring* (1998) and *The Midnight Robber* (2000) revolve around women of color who embrace the practices of their African and Caribbean ancestors to better combat the deadliest aspects of Western science while extending its beneficial tendencies. Like their counterparts in feminist science studies, Piercy and Hopkinson insist that women can reform both patriarchal science and patriarchal society by mapping the complex and sometimes contradictory interactions of power, knowledge, and love. (*See also* Discrimination; Feminist Philosophy of Science; The 19th Century; Early 20th Century)

References and Further Reading

Donawerth, Jane L. *Frankenstein's Daughters: Women Writing Science Fiction*. Syracuse, NY: Syracuse University Press, 1997.

Flanagan, Mary, and Austin Booth, eds. *Reload: Rethinking Women + Cyberculture*. Cambridge, MA: MIT Press, 2002.

Holden, Rebecca. "Shifting Worlds: Visions and Re-Visions of Feminism in Science Fiction Narrative." Unpublished dissertation, Madison: University of Wisconsin, 1998.

Lefanu, Sarah. *Feminism and Science Fiction*. Bloomington: Indiana University Press, 1989.

Roberts, Robin. *A New Species: Gender and Science in Science Fiction*. Urbana: University of Illinois Press, 1993.

Yaszek, Lisa. *Galactic Suburbia: Gender, Technology, and the Creation of Women's Science Fiction*. Columbus: Ohio State University Press, 2007.

Conclusion

SUE V. ROSSER

The introduction to *Women, Science, and Myth* discussed the interrelationship between gender and scientific research, including how gender and science have co-evolved over time. Many entries in the volume provided rich examples of how notions of gender roles have shaped both who can or should do science as well as what questions are asked, the methods chosen for scientific observation, the actual data collected, and the theories and conclusions drawn from the data. Simultaneously, science has been used to explore and study gender, especially gender differences, and support social constructs of appropriate gender roles and behavior that may have changed over time.

The 19th-century entry written by Narin Hassan exemplifies both how the gender and beliefs of who did the science determined the theories and how the theories themselves reinforced and shaped gender roles of the period. She describes how science was a domain open to the privileged "gentlemen of science." She also underlines how John Stuart Mill's arguments in "The Subjection of Women" (1869) suggesting that gender was largely a social category, not a biological category, spurred Charles Darwin's strong emphasis, buttressed by observations from the animal kingdom, that male and female nature were rooted in biology in *The Descent of Man* (1871). Although controversial, Darwin's theories of natural selection and of sexual selection were accepted by his contemporaries because they represented paradigms laden with the values of 19th-century England. Rose and Rose (1980) underline the congruence between the values expressed in Darwin's theory of natural selection and those of the upper classes of Victorian England. "Its central metaphors drawn from society and in their turn interacting with society were of the competition of species, the struggle for existence, the ecological niche, and the survival of the fittest" (Rose and Rose 1980, 28). These metaphors reflected Victorian society and were acceptable to it because they, and the "social Darwinism" quickly derived from them, seemed to ground their norms solidly in a biological foundation.

The theory of sexual selection, demonstrated over time to be increasingly problematic and riddled with error, reflected and reinforced Victorian social norms of separate spheres regarding the sexes. What seems to have struck Darwin most when he observed males and females of species throughout the natural world was the tremendous difference between them: "how enormously these sometimes differ in the most important characters is known to every naturalist" (Darwin 1967, 424). What amazed him was that such different beings belong to the same species. When viewing the human world in the light of other natural realms, he was even surprised to note that even greater differences still had not evolved. "It is, indeed, fortunate that the law of equal transmission of characters to both sexes prevails with mammals; otherwise it is probable that man would have become as superior in mental endowment to woman, as the peacock is in ornamental plumage to the peahen" (Darwin 1871, 565).

These 19th-century examples illustrate the co-evolution of gender and science. The gender of the scientist coupled with the cultural norms of the era surrounding gender roles may impact the questions asked, observations and data collected, and theories and conclusions drawn. Concurrently, scientific data are used to reinforce and buttress social and cultural notions of gender.

The co-evolution of both science and gender over time raises several questions: How should we read and understand these changing myths and beliefs over time? Should we read this as a progressive narrative in which the role of women in science has steadily improved over time in a linear fashion from no women in science to equity today? If the role of women in science has increased over time, has this led to a concurrent improvement in science itself? What role have scientific knowledge and understanding played in shaping changing notions of gender roles throughout the centuries? Are the findings of gender differences in fMRI scans, rates of depression and alcoholism, and scores on the visuospatial portions of the SAT really valid, or will people in the 23rd century laugh at these findings of 21st-century science the way we are amused by Aristotle's finding fewer teeth in the mouths of women, the findings of craniometry, or the early 20th-century notion that the new technology known as the automobile could not be driven by women?

Evaluation of changes in gender and science over a lengthy chronological period is difficult. Even a superficial knowledge of the history of both suggests that the change has been uneven, with major increases at some periods and less at others. Times of rapid change in scientific knowledge may or may not have corresponded with expansion of gender roles. For example, while the Renaissance fostered the flourishing of the arts, letters, and science, as Joan Kelly (1984) suggests, it may have diminished the roles held by women in the medieval period.

If evaluation of change over the chronological periods represented in the first part of this volume presents a challenge, evaluation of change in the thematic portion of the volume is even more difficult. Different disciplines, different types of institutions, knowledge of the brain and body, discrimination and leadership, critiques of science, and feminism have all influenced women's participation in science, notions of gender, and science itself over time. The impact and influence of each has varied, depending upon and interacting with other factors. Does a schema or theory exist that might help to distinguish patterns or ways to think about the co-evolution of gender and science both chronologically and thematically?

Several entry authors such as Linda Fedigan, Rebecca Scheckler, and Mary Wyer either applied or referred to my work on phase theory in science. Although in the past, it typically has been applied to assess curriculum transformation (Rosser 1993, 1995, 1997), because it has been used to assess the status of a department or discipline, applying it to both the chronological and thematic portions of *Women, Science, and Myth* seemed possible.

Phase Theory Models

Models for gender integration grew out of projects, primarily during the 1980s and 1990s, for gender transformation of the curriculum. They reflected the idea that integrating information about women into the curriculum is a process occurring in phases. The first phase constitutes the situation in which women are absent from the curriculum; the gender-balanced curriculum represents the final phase.

First, the model developed by Peggy McIntosh (1984) from the Wellesley Center for Research on Women will be outlined here, using history as an example.

Phase I. The Womanless Curriculum: This represents a traditional approach to history in which the absence of women is not noted. Great events and men such as wars and presidents form the structure for the periods and presentation of history.

Phase II. Women as an Add-on: Heroines, exceptional women, or an elite few who are seen to have been of benefit to culture as defined by the traditional (male) standards of history are included. Individuals such as Joan of Arc, Abigail Adams, Sojourner Truth, or Hillary Clinton would be stirred into historical accounts at this phase.

Phase III. Women as a Problem, Anomaly, or Absence: At this phase, women are studied as victims, as deprived or defective variants of men, or as protestors, with critical issues. At this phase, historians begin to

ask why there have been no women presidents, but the categories of
historical analysis are still derived from those who had the most power.

Phase IV. Women as the Focus: Women become the center of focus in
this phase, as exemplified by women's/gender studies. The categories
for analysis shift and become racially inclusive, multifaceted, and filled
with variety; they demonstrate and validate plural versions of reality.
Because women have had half of the world's lived experience, this
phase centers on asking what that experience has been and whether
it should constitute half of history, forcing people to use nontraditional sources and evidence to discover that history and experience.

Phase V. Redefinition and Reconstruction to Include All: This phase represents the ultimate goal of transformation. It creates more usable and
inclusive constructs that validate a wider sample of life and demonstrate that women are both part of and alien to the dominant culture.
It does not replace the absence of women not noted with the absence
of men not noted. Instead, it is inclusive and reflective of the diversity
of experiences, roles, and achievements of all people in history.

In 1995, I modified the five-stage model that I had developed previously
for the sciences (1993), based on the McIntosh model. The six-stage model
that I developed for sciences follows:

Phase I: Absence of Women Is Not Noted: Because most scientists accept
the positivist notion that science is objective, they assume that gender does not influence either who becomes a scientist or the science
produced by scientists. They are unaware of the absence of women
scientists, especially in the theoretical and decision-making positions
of the scientific establishment. To the extent that they think about gender, they assume that science is gender neutral and could not influence the theories, data collection, subjects chosen for experimentation,
or questions asked.

*Phase II. Recognition that Most Scientists are Male and that Science May
Reflect a Masculine Perspective:* Exposure to the data collected bien-
nially by the National Science Foundation or to media coverage makes
most people aware that women are underrepresented in most scientific fields, particularly in the physical sciences and engineering and
especially in the theoretical and decision-making levels of the profession. Influenced by the scholarship in women's studies, the philosophy and history of science, and psychology, some scientists recognize
that gender may influence science. Accepting the work of Keller (1982),
they realize that the absence of women from the decision-making
levels of science has produced a science that views the world from

a male perspective that is represented in theories, practices, and approaches reflecting a masculine approach to the natural, physical world.

Phase III. Identification of Barriers that Prevent Women from Entering Science: Scientists who reach phase II and recognize that science reflects masculine approaches to the world begin to realize that these approaches may constitute a barrier to women's entering science. They also begin to identify other problems, such as absence of women, especially in leadership positions, as barriers to attracting other women.

Phase IV. Search for Women Scientists and Their Unique Contributions: Often in an attempt to overcome the barriers of the large numbers of men and masculine approaches, scientists search for examples of role models and successful women scientists. Women Nobel laureates and outstanding examples from the history of science document that women have been successful in doing excellent traditional science despite extreme barriers.

Phase V. Science Done by Feminists and Women: Comparison of the work currently done by women scientists to that done by men scientists as well as comparisons from the history of science reveal possible subtle gender differences in questions asked, approaches, and theories and conclusions drawn from the data. Questioning of language such as dominance hierarchies and explorations of behavior in different species undertaken by women primatologists illustrate the expansion and improvement of research that may result when gender becomes a major focus.

Phase VI. Science Redefined and Reconstructed to Include Us All: At this phase, science would no longer reflect solely a masculine province, with the limitations imposed by that perspective, in numbers of scientists or in the science itself. Nor would science reflect solely a feminine province. Instead, science would be inclusive in terms of the gender distribution among scientists and awareness of the impact and interrelationship between gender and science.

Application of Phase Theory to This Volume

Can this phase theory be applied to chronological periods and the thematic issues described in this book? In one sense, application of phase theory reveals a major reason for this book: to understand the co-evolution of gender and science. Applying the phase theory to the broad time frame from antiquity to the present suggests that currently we have moved beyond the stage where the absence of women is not noted (phase I), but have not yet reached phase VI of a reconstructed, inclusive science. Simplistically, it appears that we are somewhere in phases II, III, IV, and V; these phases constitute the focus of this book. Governments, educational institutions, and individual scientists recognize that having most scientists as men impacts science in various ways (phase II); professional societies, granting agencies, and individuals seek ways to overcome the barriers that prevent women from entering science (phase III) and examples of successful women scientists and their unique contributions to science (phase IV). Many believe that science done by feminists and women provides a significant critique to the business of science as traditionally done, correcting potential bias in science (phase V).

In the United States, scientists, policy makers, government officials, and the general public have become aware of the absence of women in science. Media coverage of events such as the debates that ensued in the wake of Harvard President Larry Summers's remarks and the need for increased H1-B visas to fill the shortage in the technologically and scientifically trained American workforce in the wake of September 11, 2001, have helped to create this awareness. This awareness creates a demand for books such as *Women, Science, and Myth* that include information about how the problem might be solved.

Internationally, many countries, especially in Western Europe and Japan, have few women in science and engineering. As Table 7 in the appendix shows, Great Britain, Germany, Sweden, and Japan have even smaller percentages of women participating in the science and engineering workforce than does the United States. Ironically, many of the countries considered more traditional regarding gender roles such as Israel, Italy, and Spain have higher percentages of women scientists and engineers. These data raise the very interesting question of whether more barriers exist (phase III) for women in science and technology in countries where science and technology provide keys to economic leadership. Does science become more of a masculine province in such countries? Are women scientists making more and unique contributions (phases IV and V) in the countries with more traditional gender roles?

Just as international data provide a backdrop that surprises and makes interpretation of the U.S. data more complex, examination of specific periods in history suggests that often proportionally fewer women appear to be in science at a later date than in earlier periods. For example, more women appeared to "do" what was defined as "science" in the medieval period than in the Renaissance. In the United States, the early 20th century had a higher percentage of women scientists than did the 1950s (see Table 5 in the appendix). A decrease in women scientists often occurs when a major change or paradigm shift in science itself happens; this was the case during the Renaissance when rebirth led to the beginnings of experimentation and dissection, as well as after World War II with the rise of the military-industrial complex and "big science." These examples suggest that "fits and starts," rather than linear increases, illustrate the progress of women in science chronologically.

Application of phase theory to the thematic subjects discussed in this volume reveals even more variety than its application to the chronological historical portions.

Using the phase theory as a lens through which to examine different disciplines both for percentages of women scientists and for the integration of gender into the research of the discipline itself exemplifies this variety.

Disciplines such as psychology and biology currently have large percentages of women. As Table 5 documents, 67 percent of the Ph.D. degrees in psychology now go to women; women received 44 percent of the Ph.D.s in biological and agricultural sciences in 2000–2004 (phase V or even VI). However, examination of the higher ranks and leadership positions (see Table 8) in those disciplines reveals continued domination by men, suggesting some continuing barriers (phase III).

Because of their focus on living beings and humans, the relevance of gender to biology and psychology was not questioned. In psychology, as in sociology, political science, and other social sciences, much early research did include gender as a variable. Emphasis on gender differences research resulted in women being cast as deviant from the norm, an anomaly, or a problem because of the assumption of the male as the norm. Although the psychology of women emerged as a significant field of study in the 1960s (phase V), substantial portions of experimental psychology and neuroscience still ignore gender or consider only gender differences research.

Linda Fedigan's entry chronicles very well the integration and transformation of gender into primatology; the situation in many of the biological sciences parallels that transformation from phase I to phase V. Similarly, in the health sciences, the Women's Health Initiative illustrates a clear recognition of the need to rectify the masculine perspective and focus on women. The April 2001 Institute of Medicine publication, *Exploring the Biological Contributions to Human Health: Does Sex Matter?* (Wizemann and Pardue 2001), validated the study of basic biologic and molecular bases for sex and gender difference in disease, including "sex-based biology as an integral part" of research conducted by the National Institutes of Health.

In the physical sciences and engineering, women scientists lag in parity with their male peers. Although the percentages of women obtaining degrees in chemistry, geosciences, and astronomy has increased substantially since the 1960s (see Tables 3–5), as discussed in the entries on those disciplines, barriers remain to translation of these percentages into the workforce, particularly at high-level and decision-making positions (phase III). In engineering, the percentages of women have remained relatively flat for more than a decade. In computer science, the percentages dropped precipitously after their mid-1980s peak; beginning in 2001, the percentages of women in computer science in developed countries have plummeted further. Currently, considerable time, money, effort, and discussion center on how to remove barriers to attract and retain women in the physical sciences and technology (phase III).

Most physical scientists and engineers remain at phase I when considering whether gender might impact physical science or technology itself. Unaware of the work of historians described by Amy Bix and Barbara Whitten in their entries on technology and physics/astronomy, they assume that gender impacts neither questions asked, data gathered, or conclusions drawn in the physical sciences nor the design or use of technology.

Institutions also fall at a variety of phases along the process of gender integration. Most educational institutions moved through several phases during the 1980s and 1990s to recognize barriers to women in science and engineering. Many universities have women in science and engineering (WISE) programs or other supports to lower barriers (phase III). Working with women's studies, some science faculty have explored feminist critiques of science (phase V). Through National Science Foundation (NSF) ADVANCE funding, some have attempted institutional transformation to reconstruct the institution as more inclusive.

The official position of most government agencies toward the science and engineering workforce centers on promoting equity and lowering barriers to participation (phase III). NSF, through ADVANCE and NIH, through its gender-based medicine approaches, promote efforts at the level of phase V with the goal of reaching phase VI.

As Suzanne Brainard underlines in her entry on industry, legislative changes in the 1970s forced most corporations to begin to remove barriers to level the playing field for women (phase III). Discrimination law passed through a series of changes that parallel phase theory in its attempts to achieve racial and gender integration of the workforce. In the 21st century, some of these gains have been challenged, resulting in prohibitions on gender or racial preferences in contracts, hiring, and even college admissions.

The most prestigious scientific and technological professional societies remain male provinces (phase II). As Joyce Tang points out, only 3 percent of the Nobel Prizes in science or medicine have gone to women. Although the National Academies in the United States have issued reports about bias and barriers to women (phase III), women still constitute only about 10 percent of their members in 2007 (phase II). Muriel Lederman underlines the convergence of science and religion in her entry. Conservative institutions, such as the Catholic and evangelical Protestant churches that fight against current scientific advances such as stem cell research and evolutionary theory, also advocate limited roles for women, excluding them as priests and scientists.

Most of the entries that focused on biological or psychological processes such as the cognitive abilities, menstruation/menopause/PMS, or nature/nurture reveal subtle differences in questions asked, approaches, and theories and conclusions drawn from the data when gender becomes the central focus (phase V). Many of the critiques such as Marxist/socialist, postcolonial, or science fiction reveal other social factors that, when coupled with gender, may distort or bias science (phase II). Feminist critiques such as ecofeminism, cyberfeminism, and feminist science studies compare the research done by feminists to that done by traditional male scientists and engineers to reveal biases and to improve science for the benefit of all (phase V).

In sum, application of phase theory to both the chronological and thematic entries in *Women, Science, and Myth* underlines the dynamic nature of the co-evolution of gender and science. While the absence of women from science has certainly been noted, full integration of women, particularly in the physical sciences and engineering, has definitely not yet occurred. Critiques of science, especially feminist critiques, underscore the very obvious and more subtle ways that the results from scientific research buttress the social status quo regarding gender roles.

References and Further Reading

Darwin, Charles. *On the Origin of the Species* (1859): *A Facsimile of the First Edition.* New York: Atheneum, 1967.

Darwin, Charles. *The Descent of Man and Selection in Relation to Sex.* London: John Murray, 1871.

Keller, E. F. "Feminism and Science." *Signs: Journal of Women in Culture and Society* 7(3) (1982): 589–602.

Kelly, Joan. "Did Women Have a Renaissance?" *Women, History, and Theory: The Essays of Joan Kelly.* Chicago: University of Chicago Press, 1984.

McIntosh, P. "The Study of Women: Processes of Personal and Curricular Re-vision." *Forum for Liberal Education* 6(5) (1984): 2–4.

Mill, J. S. "The Subjection of Women." In *Essays on Sex Equality,* by John Stuart Mill and Harriet Taylor Mill. Edited by Alice S. Rossi, 123–242. Chicago: University of Chicago Press, 1970.

Rose, H., and S. Rose. "The Myth of the Neutrality of Science." In *Science and Liberation.* Edited by R. Arditti, P. Brennan, and S. Cavrak. Boston: South End Press, 1980.

Rosser, Sue. *Female-friendly Science.* Elmsford, NY: Pergamon Press, 1993.

Rosser, Sue V. *Teaching the Majority: Breaking the Gender Barrier in Science, Mathematics, and Engineering.* New York: Teachers College Press, 1995.

Rosser, Sue V. *Re-engineering Female-friendly Science.* Elmsford, NY: Pergamon Press, 1997.

Wizemann, T. M., and M. Pardue, eds. *Exploring the Biological Contributions to Human Health: Does Sex Matter?* Washington, DC: National Academies Press, 2001.

Appendix of Statistical Tables

Table 1. Percentage of Public High School Graduates Taking Selected Mathematics and Sciences in 2000

Courses	Women	Men
Any Math	99.9	99.8
Algebra I	63.4	60.0
Geometry	81.4	74.9
Algebra II	70.5	64.8
Trigonometry	7.7	7.3
Analysis/Pre-Calculus	27.9	25.4
Stats/Probability	5.6	5.8
Calculus	11.1	12.2
AP Calculus	7.3	8.5
Any Science	99.7	99.3
Biology	93.3	89.0
AP/Honors Biology	18.5	13.8
Chemistry	65.7	58.0
AP/Honors Chemistry	5.7	5.8
Physics	29.0	34.2
AP/Honors Physics	2.5	5.4
Engineering	3.5	4.3
Astronomy	2.6	3.0
Geo/Earth Sciences	16.6	18.4

Source: Data excerpted from Commission on Professionals in Science and Technology (CPST). *Professional Women and Minorities: A Total Human Resources Data Compendium.* 16th ed. Washington, DC: CPST, 2006, Table 1-11, p. 14.

Table 2. SAT Score Averages by Sex for College-Bound Seniors

Year	Verbal		Math	
	Women	Men	Women	Men
1975	509	515	479	518
1980	498	506	473	515
1985	503	514	480	522
1990	496	505	483	521
1995	502	505	490	525
2000	504	507	498	533
2005	505	513	504	538

Source: Data excerpted from Commission on Professionals in Science and Technology (CPST). *Professional Women and Minorities: A Total Human Resources Data Compendium.* 16th ed. Washington, DC: CPST, 2006, Table 1-13, p. 16.

Table 3. Percentage of Women Receiving Bachelor's Degrees by Decade

	All Fields	Total Science & Engineering	Engineering	Physical/ Environmental Science	Math/ Computer Science	Biological & Agricultural Sciences	Psychology	Social Sciences	Nonscience & Engineering
1950–59	9.8	14.8	0.3	11.6	28.6	15.3	41.6	26.3	39.9
1960–69	11.6	23.0	0.5	13.6	32.8	23.1	41.4	33.1	49.3
1970–79	45.2	32.0	3.4	17.7	36.1	29.7	52.0	38.6	51.9
1980–89	51.0	39.0	13.7	27.3	38.0	44.0	67.8	45.7	56.7
1990–99	55.0	46.4	17.0	35.2	34.7	50.5	73.4	49.7	59.0
2000–04	57.5	50.0	20.5	41.8	30.9	58.3	77.4	54.6	60.8

Source: Data excerpted from Commission on Professionals in Science and Technology (CPST). *Professional Women and Minorities: A Total Human Resources Data Compendium.* 16th ed. Washington, DC: CPST, 2006, Table 3-15, pp. 125–126.

Table 4. Percentage of Women Receiving Master's Degrees by Decade

	All Fields	Total Science & Engineering	Engineering	Physical/ Environmental Science	Math/ Computer Science	Biological & Agricultural Sciences	Psychology	Social Sciences	Nonscience & Engineering
1950–59	32.0	10.3	0.3	7.8	18.8	13.0	28.2	17.5	39.2
1960–69	33.7	13.1	0.5	10.3	21.0	19.8	31.6	19.9	41.9
1970–79	44.5	21.9	2.9	15.1	25.7	27.4	44.9	28.2	51.0
1980–89	50.5	31.3	10.6	23.1	30.4	38.7	62.8	39.7	56.5
1990–99	55.3	38.1	16.4	30.5	31.3	48.2	71.5	48.5	60.5
2000–04	58.7	43.6	21.0	37.4	34.6	54.9	76.4	54.5	62.7

Source: Data excerpted from Commission on Professionals in Science and Technology (CPST). *Professional Women and Minorities: A Total Human Resources Data Compendium.* 16th ed. Washington, DC: CPST, 2006, Table 3-22, pp. 136–137.

Table 5. Percentage of Women Receiving Doctorates by Decade

	All Fields	Total Science & Engineering	Engineering	Physical/ Environmental Science	Earth	Math/ Computer Science	Biological & Agricultural Sciences	Psychology	Social Sciences	Nonscience & Engineering
1920–29	15.3	12.2	0.9	6.9	4.8	14.5	15.9	29.3	10.8	21.0
1930–39	14.7	11.0	0.7	5.8	3.5	14.8	15.0	26.0	11.1	21.1
1940–49	13.4	8.9	0.5	4.2	5.7	10.7	12.7	24.1	10.1	21.4
1950–59	9.8	6.3	0.2	3.8	2.1	5.3	8.3	13.7	8.3	15.3
1960–69	11.6	7.9	0.4	4.8	1.6	5.9	11.4	20.4	10.2	18.0
1970–79	20.7	14.8	1.4	7.7	6.3	10.1	18.2	32.1	18.6	28.8
1980–89	33.9	25.5	5.9	15.1	16.3	14.8	29.1	49.4	30.8	46.7
1990–99	39.2	31.2	11.2	21.5	22.9	19.3	38.1	63.4	37.8	53.3
2000–04	44.7	37.0	16.9	25.8	31.9	23.5	43.6	67.1	43.8	57.5

Source: Data excerpted from Commission on Professionals in Science and Technology (CPST). *Professional Women and Minorities: A Total Human Resources Data Compendium.* 16th ed. Washington, DC: CPST, 2006, Table 3-26, p. 144.

Table 6. Percentage of Women by Field of Highest Degree and Employment Sector in 2003

Field of Degree	Total Employed	2-Year College and Pre-College Institutions	4-Year Colleges/ Universities, Medical Schools, Research	Government	Business/Industry
All Degree Fields	42.1	16.0	9.9	11.8	62.3
All Science & Engineering	35.3	15.5	9.5	12.7	62.4
Total Sciences	43.6	13.6	10.3	13.0	63.0
Health-Related	63.7	8.6	13.4	9.6	68.4
Computer & Math Science	32.7	13.2	7.1	7.9	71.8
Life Sciences	43.1	10.0	17.1	11.9	60.9
Chemistry Except Biochemistry	32.8	9.4	14.6	7.0	69.1
Physics & Astronomy	14.4	22.5	23.2	12.5	41.8
Other Phys.-Related Science	24.1	9.3	17.9	20.4	52.4
Social Sciences	42.5	12.0	8.6	14.7	64.6
Psychology	66.7	18.8	7.6	15.1	58.6
Engineering	11.6	4.7	5.1	14.3	75.8

Source: Data excerpted from Commission on Professionals in Science and Technology (CPST). *Professional Women and Minorities: A Total Human Resources Data Compendium.* 16th ed. Washington, DC: CPST, 2006, Table 4-9, pp. 311–312.

Table 7. Percentage of Women Obtaining Doctoral Degrees by Continent and for Selected Countries by Field 2002 or Most Recent Year

Continent/Country	All Fields	Nonscience & Engineering	All Science & Engineering	Physical/Biological Sciences	Math/Computer Science	Agricultural Sciences	Sociology/Behavioral	Engineering
Asia	24.9	32.6	17.2	20.3	20.8	22.7	29.9	10.9
Japan	24.9	32.2	17.1	15.9	n/a	25.2	30.0	10.1
Taiwan	23.3	43.1	13.3	24.3	13.4	21.5	32.6	6.1
Middle East	34.9	40.7	30.5	37.7	25.7	31.1	31.4	28.1
Iran	34.1	40.0	16.7	19.2	21.2	6.1	23.7	5.3
Israel	47.4	58.3	42.8	47.2	24.1	40.9	46.8	25.5
Africa	22.1	20.1	26.6	13.4	0.0	19.7	53.1	12.8
Europe	40.4	45.8	34.3	39.0	23.8	42.2	35.6	32.2
Austria	37.6	45.2	29.8	34.4	18.0	28.3	49.4	19.1
Croatia	46.7	42.3	47.9	54.8	50.0	46.2	55.8	27.1
Estonia	51.7	66.7	28.8	26.3	66.7	50.0	50.0	0.0
Finland	45.9	58.5	33.9	43.9	15.8	33.3	51.5	21.1
France	42.7	51.1	38.4	42.8	21.7	56.5	45.2	26.8
Germany	37.9	47.0	27.5	32.7	22.1	33.9	33.5	9.2
Hungary	44.8	52.4	31.7	27.6	25.8	20.5	48.6	32.1
Italy	51.9	58.2	45.5	49.4	0.0	55.6	51.7	35.9
Norway	36.8	35.6	40.7	0.0	0.0	44.1	47.4	16.0
Russia	38.1	47.2	31.3	37.2	32.0	43.5	17.6	47.2
Spain	45.4	47.6	42.8	49.3	30.8	41.8	47.4	25.3
Sweden	40.6	54.2	31.5	40.8	16.7	41.2	37.6	24.9
United Kingdom	41.4	47.7	37.0	40.2	24.0	44.8	54.0	17.8
North America	44.8	56.1	38.8	41.6	22.5	32.0	54.5	16.9
Canada	41.9	56.6	35.8	34.2	0.0	28.0	58.5	12.5
United States	45.3	56.9	39.4	42.4	23.6	34.1	55.1	17.1
Australia/New Zealand	44.4	52.4	38.1	41.3	23.7	33.0	54.6	22.0

Source: Data excerpted from Commission on Professionals in Science and Technology (CPST). *Professional Women and Minorities: A Total Human Resources Data Compendium.* 16th ed. Washington, DC: CPST, 2006, Table 5-7, pp. 385–386.

Table 8. Percentage of Women Doctoral Scientists and Engineers Employed in Academic Institutions by Field and Rank, 2003

	All Fields	Computer Information	Psychology	Social Sciences	Biology/Life Sciences	Physical Sciences	Engineering	Math & Statistics
Assistant Professor	41.0	23.3	63.1	48.4	38.4	24.5	16.0	29.2
Associate Professor	31.1	19.9	52.5	35.5	29.4	19.2	11.9	15.9
Full Professor	17.6	12.3	30.8	21.4	19.0	6.8	3.8	9.2
Total (Includes Instructor/Lecturer)	29.8	18.3	50.0	32.8	32.1	14.8	10.3	17.1

Source: Data excerpted from Commission on Professionals in Science and Technology (CPST). *Professional Women and Minorities: A Total Human Resources Data Compendium.* 16th ed. Washington, DC: CPST, 2006, Table 4-50, p. 350.

Glossary

actor network theory
idea originating in science studies that the people, equipment, ideas, and institution all influence and cannot be separated from scientific experiments and theories with which they are involved

ADVANCE
National Science Foundation (NSF) grant initiative begun in 2001 for institutional transformation to encourage women to attain academic leadership positions in science and engineering

agency
the capacity to make choices, often linked to stereotypes of masculinity characterized as focused on a concern about one's own interests and success

agoraphobia
anxiety disorder consisting of the fear of experiencing an embarrassing situation that can't be escaped that leads to fear of going out of the house, particularly into crowded, unknown places

alchemy
an early form of the investigation of nature and an early philosophical and spiritual discipline that combined elements of chemistry, metallurgy, physics, medicine, astrology, semiotics, and art; mystical and cultlike traditions often surrounded it

androcentrism
worldview that is male-centered, or focused on using the male as the norm

androgen insensitivity (testicular feminization)
set of disorders of sexual differentiation resulting from mutations of the gene encoding the androgen receptor; mostly individuals who are genetic males

(XY) with testes but who develop female genitalia due to failure to respond to testosterone

antinepotism
descriptive of rules that forbid employment of spouses or family members in the same department, unit, university, government agency, or corporation

apothegm
a terse, witty, instructive saying; a maxim

attributional style
refers to how people explain the events of their lives; whether individuals tend to blame themselves or others for events that happen

autism spectrum disorders
five pervasive developmental disorders that result in inability to relate appropriately in social interactions or to communicate properly and result in restricted, repetitive, and stereotyped behavioral patterns

auxiliary assumptions
connections made by researchers to propose theories when the experimental evidence is lacking

avatars
virtual identity or representation that individuals use as their representations when on the Internet

aversion therapy
psychiatric or psychological treatment in which conditioning attempts to associate a stimulus with something very unpleasant or painful, so that the individual turns away from the behavior—for example, shocking a person when he or she has a sexual desire for someone of the same sex

"bad science"
research that utilizes untested theories to generate inadequate evidence for explanations that are poorly explored

belief
acceptance of the truth or actuality of anything without certain proof; something held to be true or actual; acceptance with or without proof or strong emotional feelings

"Big Science"
increase in size of research groups and facilities associated with the increase in funding during and after World War II resulting from the rise of the military-industrial complex

bioinformatics
interdisciplinary field that combines computing with biology in ways such as using computers to process and analyze large DNA sequences and solve biological problems

biological determinism
use of biological differences in anatomy, hormones, and genes among races, sexes, classes, and species to justify social, behavioral, and psychological inequalities

biomedical
descriptive of the practice of modern medicine founded on basic research in biology, chemistry, and clinical research relying on double-blind studies

bipolar disorder
mental disorder in which the individual alternates between periods of depression and euphoria; manic-depressive illness

Black Death
a form of bubonic plague that arrived in Europe around 1350, spreading to kill about one third of the European population

Boolean logic
binary; everything is 0 or 1; the basis of computing

brain imaging
techniques to determine the structure or function of the brain that depict brain activity (e.g., functional magnetic resonance imaging [fMRI]) or anatomy (e.g., computed axial tomography [CAT scans]) that provide pictures depicting brain activity and anatomy

broader impacts criterion
one of two major criteria, the other being intellectual merit, used by review panels to judge whether a proposal should receive National Science Foundation (NSF) funding

"Canary Girls"
women who worked in chemical plants during World War I whose skin turned yellow from working with the toxic compound TNT

Cartesian duality
the idea of René Descartes of the separation of the nonphysical mind and the body, with the mind being superior

cathedral schools
schools introduced near the beginning of the High Middle Ages open only to men training for the clergy, thereby excluding women from mainstream education

chilly climate
the less than encouraging climate many women experience in academia, especially in science and engineering classes and professions; the term was coined by Bernice Sandler in the article "The Classroom Climate: A Chilly One for Women," published in 1982

Civil Rights Act of 1964
act of Congress guarantees equal access to jobs regardless of race or gender

COACh (Committee on the Advancement of Women Chemists)
membership organization with programs to increase the number of women chemists entering and advancing through the ranks to leadership roles in academic chemistry departments

co-evolution
situation in which two or more concepts or processes change over time, with the interaction or change in one affecting or causing a change in the other

cognitive neuroscience
academic field that studies the relationship between human cognition and activities with the anatomy and functioning of the brain and nervous system

cognitive style
the way individuals think, perceive, and remember information

colonial hegemony
privilege and power of Euro-Americans over colonized people in Africa, Asia, and Latin America

"common school" movement
movement led by Horace Mann in the early 19th century that promulgated widespread education in tuition-free public schools

compliance review
investigation by federal agency as to whether universities or other organizations receiving federal funds are adhering to federal laws in a particular area such as antibias situations

Comstock Act of 1873
U.S. congressional acts that banned mailing of obscene materials, including information on contraception and abortion

congenital adrenal hyperplasia (CAH)
condition in which exposure of female fetuses to high levels of androgens results in masculinized external genitalia

constructive empiricism
a theory of scientific practice to explain the role and consequences of auxiliary assumptions and the role of feminist values in the construction of alternative hypotheses and methods

context of justification
circumstances in which hypotheses are tested and either falsified or confirmed

contextual beliefs
personal, social, cultural, and historical factors that underpin and influence beliefs

contextual extrapolation
a method used, in the absence of direct evidence, to make assumptions about the likelihood of a person's participating in an event, given the social and cultural milieu of the historical period in which a person or event existed

corpus callosum
brain structure that links the left and right cerebral hemispheres of the brain

cosmology
quantitative study of the universe, including humanity's place in it

craniometry
19th-century study of the size, weight, and shape of the skull used to provide biological bases for differences among races, sexes, and classes

crystallography
study of the crystal structure of compounds or the arrangement of atoms in solids

"Cult of Domesticity"
also known as the Cult of True Womanhood; part of the 19th-century notion of separate spheres, where women were confined to the private sphere of home and children

cultural imperialism
practice of promoting, distinguishing, separating, or artificially injecting the culture or language of one nation onto another

cyberpunk
science fiction subgenre that explores the relationship between technology, capitalism, and society; focuses on high tech and low life

cybersphere
the space and power dominated by computers and software, especially the Internet

Cyberutopians
people who see the Internet and virtual space as ideal and better than real society

cyborg
an organism that has self-regulating integration of artificial and natural systems; an organism with enhanced abilities due to technology

death of nature
phrase used by ecologist Carolyn Merchant to describe the change in conceptualization of nature from an active female principle to something that was inert and could be exploited by humans and scientists

deconstruct
analyze each piece and how it is put together to understand the whole better and to reveal the unspoken and implicit assumptions, ideas, and frameworks that form the basis for thought and belief

deep ecology
idea that all living things should have the equal right to live and flourish; humans should not exploit the earth, plants, and animals for their own survival

"deep" technology
the theory and mathematics that underpin, determine, and structure what the technology can ultimately do—for example, Boolean logic for computing

dependence
the capacity to make connections often linked to stereotypes of femininity, characterized as representing a connectedness to others

dimorphic
descriptive of two forms or types, such as male and female

"dismantle the master's house with the master's tools"
a phrase used by African American lesbian feminist Audre Lorde to suggest that approaches, new and different from the ones used in constructing something, may be needed to tear it down and build a better structure

domestic economy or domestic science
19th-century term for home economics

double blind study
study in which neither the researcher nor the subject in the experiment knows whether the subject is receiving the drug being tested or a placebo; favored method for clinical testing of drugs in the United States and Western Europe

DSM (Diagnostic and Statistical Manual of Mental Disorders)
handbook of the American Psychiatric Association that is the authoritative basis for categorization and diagnosis of mental illnesses in the United States

dual systems approach
suggestion of socialist feminists that gender should be placed on equal footing with class because patriarchy and capitalism function as mutual reinforcements for the place of women in society

ecocentrism
philosophy that recognizes the ecosphere, rather than any individual organism, as the source and support of all life

emotional decoding
examination of the feelings that individuals ascribe to others

endogenous
internal or intrinsic, as opposed to exogenous, meaning external

Enlightenment
philosophy of the 18th century that emphasized rationality, universality, equality, and objectivity

environmental justice
idea that all living things should be treated in ways that allow them to thrive and grow; White, powerful men should not dominate

epidemiological approaches
statistical methods used to study the health and illness of populations; may reveal impact of race, gender, class, socioeconomic class, and other factors in addition to biomedical causes

epistemic agency
entity that has the authority to decide what is known and true

epistemology
theories of knowledge

Equal Pay Act
1963 law that makes it illegal to pay higher salaries to men than to women working in the same establishment who are performing under similar working conditions

essentialism
philosophical view that for any entity, there is a set of characteristics, all of which any entity of that kind must have; notion that maleness and femaleness are completely biologically determined

ethnicity
population of humans whose members identify with each other on the basis of presumed ancestry; often used interchangeably with race

eugenics
social philosophy that advocates improvement of human hereditary traits through forms of intervention

Executive Order 11246
bans discrimination and requires federal contractors, including universities, to maintain affirmative actions plans to increase numbers of women and minorities in their workforce

existentialism
philosophy associated with 20th-century philosophers such as Jean Paul Sartre that claims individual human beings create meaning in their own lives; human existence is defined by free choice or a leap of faith, correlated with responsibility

feminist empiricism

notion that scientific knowledge is social and that social beliefs and values, including those about gender, can and do inform legitimate science

feminist science studies

interdisciplinary field that emphasizes the intersections of multiple social identities, practices, and processes in science, including gender, race, ethnicity, class, and sexualities

first-wave feminism

U.S. feminist movement from 1848 Seneca Falls Convention to passage of the Nineteenth Amendment; focused on women's suffrage

fMRI (functional magnetic resonance imaging)

a type of neuroimaging that identifies sites of mental activity by increased blood flow in the brain

frontal lobes

anterior part of the cerebral hemispheres of the brain thought to be the site of intelligence

gay

originally, male homosexuals; more recently, both male homosexuals and many lesbians identify as gay

gay rights movement

political organization of homosexuals to obtain civil, legal, and religious rights denied them because of their sexual orientation; it arose in the late 1960s and early 1970s and continues through the present time

gender

socially constructed roles, behaviors, and expectations associated with masculinity and femininity; usually masculine gender is consonant with the male biological sex and feminine gender with that of the female biological sex, although this need not be so

gender blind

descriptive of activities undertaken and services provided without regard to the gender of those who participate; equally accessible to males and females

gender discrimination

being treated differently because of one's perceived sex or biological makeup

gender neutral

neither reveals nor implies the gender or sex of the person; neither male nor female, masculine nor feminine

gender stratification

unequal distribution of power, prestige, and property between men and women based on their sex; cuts across all aspects of social life and all social classes

genderless

free of gender; gender is not part of it

gestational motherhood

pregnancy in which the woman who carries the baby for another woman may or may not be the genetic mother

GI Bill

legislation passed by the U.S. government in 1944 that provided funds for veterans to receive higher education

glass ceiling

barrier to reaching the higher career levels, which can be seen, but not attained; the limitation is usually based on some form of discrimination such as gender or race

hermaphrodite

an individual with both ovaries and testes

Hermetical tradition

tradition from the Renaissance claiming that humans could use their bodies to regulate all things under their intellect

holism

philosopher Quine's notion that theories of science, common sense, and philosophy form a dependent network

Holy Grail

according to Christian mythology, the dish, plate, or cup used by Jesus at the Last Supper, said to possess miraculous powers. The quest for the Holy Grail is part of the myth about King Arthur and the Knights of the Roundtable

homophobia

fear of homosexuality and homosexuals

homunculus
"little man" that Van Leeuwenhoek claimed he had seen in each sperm cell using the microscope

HRT
hormone replacement therapy, usually either estrogen and/or progesterone, given to women to alleviate symptoms of menopause

Human Genome Project
project, funded by the National Institutes of Health, undertaken by the scientific community in the 1990s and completed in 2003 to sequence and map all of the genes in humans

humanists
scholars of the Renaissance who recovered and revived the ideas, practices, and technologies of the classical age, appropriating Greek and Latin learning with a focus on grammar, rhetoric, and poetics

humors
blood, phlegm, yellow bile, and black bile; Hippocrates, the father of medicine, in the fourth century BC, believed that good health was dependent on having a natural balance of the four humors

hypothalamus
part of the brain that links the nervous system to the endocrine system via the pituitary gland

hysteria
Victorian notions of women's fragility during menstruation and links to mental imbalances; derived from the Greek word for uterus

immaterial
not embodied; not consisting of matter

impartiality
notion that science should be objective and value free

industrial medicine
study of diseases associated with particular occupations and/or workplace environments; initiated by Alice Hamilton in the early 20th century

Industrial Revolution
shift of technological, socioeconomic, and cultural conditions from agrarian, rural to industry, urban-based society in the late 18th and 19th centuries in Western Europe and North America; led to the rise of the middle class

intellectual property rights
an umbrella term for legal entitlements to written and recorded media and inventions; determine who "owns" the income and profits resulting from the products when basic research is translated into drugs, technology, or other socially useful commodities

intellectual sabotage
destruction or misrepresentation of ideas, data, or research

interlocking systems of oppression
interactions among racism, sexism, classism, and heterosexuality that reinforce the power of the White, heterosexual, middle- to upper-class male; also known as intersectionality

intersexual conflict
struggles between males and females of the same species

"invisible curriculum"
exclusion of women's lives, perspectives, and interests from courses and studies so that the social, economic, and political power of men over women is reinforced in knowledge learned in a subtle manner

IT (information technology) revolution
profound changes in society, culture, and the way of doing business brought about by information technologies and their availability and utility

kin selection
behavior of living beings that results in increasing the chances of survival of their genes in their offspring and relatives, even at a cost to their own survival and/or reproduction

Kinsey Reports
two books that represented the first comprehensive, scientific series of studies on the sexual behavior of the American population, carried out by Alfred Kinsey and students from Indiana University and published in the mid-20th century

Kleinianism
theories of psychologist Melanie Klein

lack of camaraderie
absence of mentoring or collegiality

late luteal phase dysphoria
label given to premenstrual syndrome in the *Diagnostic and Statistical Manual of Mental Disorders (DSM)*

lateralization
refers to whether certain activities and functions such as speech are confined to one half of the brain (more lateralized) or are distributed evenly between both hemispheres

laureates
individuals who have won the Nobel Prize

leaky pipeline
metaphor used to describe the loss of women and minority scientists as they progress through the stages of education and up the career ladder

left-brain thinking
supposed to emphasize reason, critical thinking, and verbal abilities

lesbian
female homosexual or woman loving women

male-as-norm approach
androcentrism; man is assumed to be the standard for comparison

"Marie Curie Strategy"
deliberate overqualification of women when competing with male counterparts

masculinist values
ideas, beliefs, and behaviors associated with men and masculinity such as power, money, competition, and control

maternal discourse
idea of Sara Ruddick that the practice of motherhood is a discipline that combines preservative love, nurturance, and training

mechanization of nature
Enlightenment notion that the universe and nature function like a machine

meritocracy
belief that science and who succeeds in science are based solely on intrinsic worth of the ideas and hard work, and not affected by social structures and politics

meta-analysis
statistical technique that combines the results of a large number of studies that address a related research hypothesis

Middle Ages
period in European history between classical antiquity (late fifth century) and the Renaissance (around 1350); also known as the medieval era

misogyny
hatred of or strong prejudice against women

MIT Report
A Study on the Status of Women Faculty at the Massachusetts Institute of Technology released in 1999 documenting that 15 tenured women received lower salaries and fewer resources for research than their male colleagues

"mommy tax"
loss of income estimated to be around $1 million dollars on a woman's lifetime earnings from having and rearing a child

mommy track
a separate, unofficial, slower career track that many corporations, professions, and universities establish for women who leave the workforce to pursue childbearing and caregiving and then return; these women are perceived as not giving as much time to their careers as men or as women without children

myth
a traditional story focusing on the deeds of gods or heroes, often in explanation of some natural phenomenon such as the origin of the sun; a false opinion, belief, or idea

natural philosopher
scientist of the 16th, 17th, or 18th centuries who engaged in objective study of nature and the physical universe that preceded modern or natural science

natural theology
attempt to find evidence of God in an intelligent designer without recourse to any special or supposedly supernatural revelation

Nature
very prestigious, weekly, peer-reviewed journal that covers many areas of science

NGO (nongovernmental organization)
private institution, independent of the government; usually focuses on a specific issue or the interests of a particular set of individuals

niches
reduced positions in areas outside the mainstream, in which women were allowed to excel

objectify
treat a living being as if it were an object, denying the person's feelings, consciousness, and agency

objectivity
a neutral, unbiased position that is free of personal values or situations for observation of natural phenomena; universally true

Paracelsian tradition
use of chemistry, especially mineral therapies, as a new approach to natural philosophy and medicine, proposed by Paracelsus and prominent in the late 16th and 17th century in Europe

parental investment
time, effort, and resources that parents put into ensuring that their biological offspring survive and reproduce, at the expense of investing in other components of fitness

parietal lobes
lobes in the brain behind the frontal lobes and above the occipital lobes; integrate sensory information

patriarchy
structuring of the society on the basis of family units in which fathers have primary responsibility and rule the welfare of these units; the dominance of men over women and reinforcement of that dominance through social and cultural institutions

"perform gender"
phrase used by Judith Butler to demonstrate that gender is socially, not biologically, constructed and can be created through what one wears and how one acts

perspective
viewpoint from which something is understood; scientific perspective is traditionally associated with objectivity

phase theory
developmental scheme that explains how change occurs in curriculum, institutions, and personal awareness

phrenology
19th-century notion that mental functions, character, and personality traits could be assessed by measurement of the size and shape of the head

physiognomy
19th-century study of the facial features to predict personality traits or intelligence

PI (principal investigator)
the primary individual who has applied for a grant or award and is responsible for the project

positivism
philosophy that the only authentic knowledge is scientific knowledge obtained through the strict scientific method using a simple description of sensory phenomena that are verifiable and replicable by observation

postcolonial
descriptive of theories in philosophy, film, and literature that grapple with the legacy of colonial rule, particularly after the time of European colonization of non-White societies, roughly from the late 1940s through the 1960s

postdoctoral
after receiving the Ph.D.

postmodern
associated with style and form of global late capitalism and seen as superseding modernism; questions assumptions of the Enlightenment such as universality, singular truth, and rational human progress

primary sex characteristics
ovaries in females; testes in males

"principle of sympathy"
belief from antiquity that lasted into the 18th century that a disease could be expelled if it were transferred from the body to other objects

psychopathology
mental illness

queer
homosexual or gay

race
socially constructed means of dividing people into groups on the basis of various sets of characteristics and beliefs about common ancestry; these groups may share elements of a particular physical appearance or originate from a particular location; the construct does not have a biological basis

radically interdependent
fundamentally dependent on each other

"Radium Girls"
women who painted radium onto the face of watch dials during World War I; many developed lip and mouth cancers from ingesting radium by licking the tips of the paintbrushes to get a fine line on the watch face

reciprocal altruism
one organism provides benefit to another without expecting immediate payment or compensation but with the expectation that the other will reciprocate in the future

reflexivity
seeking to understand the limits of one's own perspective through active efforts to take on the perspective of others

reify
turn social relations into a thing; treat an abstraction as if it were a real thing

relativism
notion that objectivity and absolute truth do not exist but are influenced by the social, political, and cultural contexts of individuals and communities; often associated with postmodernism

republican motherhood
idea that women's innate morality and talents as housekeepers suited them for political service as "municipal housekeepers"; 19th-century argument emanating from the notion of separate spheres

research university
category used by the Carnegie Classification of Institutions of Higher Education for universities receiving the highest amounts of federal science research funding and graduating the most Ph.D. students

reverse discrimination
discrimination against the majority or against those who traditionally had access or held certain positions

right-brain thinking
supposed to involve emotions, intuitions, creativity, imagination, and mathematical brilliance

Romanticism
artistic, literary, and intellectual movement that originated in 18th-century-Western Europe during the Industrial Revolution and focused on understanding nature and the proper relationship of humans to nature; counter-movement to the Enlightenment

Rosie the Riveter
woman portrayed on a poster used to encourage women to support the war effort by working in shipyards and in airplane manufacturing during World War II in the United States

salons
discussion groups in which intellectual ideas, including science and mathematics, might be considered; often meeting in the homes of wealthy individuals during the 17th and 18th centuries in Europe

schizophrenia
severe mental disorder in which the individual experiences periods of hallucinations and being out of touch with reality

Scholasticism
the system of thought that integrated philosophy and theology with emphasis on dialectical reasoning during the Middle Ages, from 1100 to 1500, especially during the 13th century

Science

the very prestigious, weekly, peer-reviewed journal published by the American Association for the Advancement of Science

Science and Technology Equal Opportunities Act of 1980

mandated the National Science Foundation to collect and analyze data and report to Congress on a biennial basis on the status of women and minorities in the science and engineering professions

scientific racism

use of scientific data to reinforce notions of inferiority of race and gender to justify exploitation, abuse, and maltreatment of targeted individuals

Scientific Revolution

change in approach from emphasis on books to observation and experimentation to study the physical, natural world; occurred in the mid-16th and early 17th centuries, promulgated by Nicolaus Copernicus and Andreas Vesalius.

scopolamine

a drug derived from plants that was combined with morphine and known as "twilight sleep" because it induced amnesia; introduced in the United States in the 1930s from Germany for use during childbirth in hospitals, it is now considered dangerous

second-wave feminism

feminist movement beginning in the 1960s focused on gaining equal rights for women in all areas of public life

secondary sex characteristics

characteristics that develop at puberty such as breasts, beards, and change in vocal cords that distinguish the two sexes

separate spheres

19th-century belief that men and women were fundamentally different, resulting in women's superiority in the private sphere of the home and men's superiority in the public sphere

sex

biological male or female; biological sex is determined by chromosomal, hormonal, internal anatomical, and external anatomical components that are usually concordant with each other and with the gender, although they need not be. For example, usually an individual with a genetic XX will produce more estrogen and progesterone, have ovaries, a uterus, and a vagina and labia, and identify as feminine

sexual inversion
term for homosexuality used by 19th-century sexologist Havelock Ellis

sexual orientation
preference or desire to have sex with individuals of the same sex (homosexuality) or of the opposite sex (heterosexuality)

situated
idea that all knowledge, including science, comes from, or is embedded in, a particular position or set of social, political, and cultural circumstances

social construction of science and technology
idea that social forces may influence all steps of science from questions asked, through observation and data collection, to theories and conclusions drawn from the data

social constructivist
descriptive of a notion that social, cultural, and political forces, as opposed to biological forces, underpin a factor

social epistemology
a branch of philosophy that describes the social dimensions of knowledge, including scientific knowledge, as possessed and enacted by communities, not by exceptional individuals

social identities
features associated with caring, friendly, and emotional characteristics

social naturalism
close observation by philosophers of historical and contemporary science and research as actually practiced

social shaping of technology
the idea that technology and society co-evolve, with technology as a social product developed by human activities and know-how

sociobiology
study of the biological bases of behavior

sodomy
all sexual acts other than coital sex between a male and female; homosexual male intercourse

somatoform disorders
individual complaints of a physical problem in the absence of a medical or physical explanation

standpoint epistemology
idea that race, class, gender, sexual orientation, and other factors influence one's observation of reality and knowledge, including scientific knowledge; those from nondominant positions have a more comprehensive picture of reality

Stanford-Binet test
popularly known as an IQ test, although originally developed as an indicator to predict student success in the classroom

stem cell research
research done using primal embryo cells that are capable of division and differentiation into a variety of cell types

Stonewall Riots
uprising that occurred in Greenwich Village, New York, in 1969 that marked the beginning of the gay rights movement

strong objectivity
philosopher Sandra Harding's idea that including multiple relevant perspectives, making the politics behind scientific projects more visible, and using self-reflexive, transparent methodologies are superior to the supposedly neutral, unbiased objectivity traditionally associated with the scientific method

STS (science and technology studies)
study of how social, political, and cultural values affect scientific research and technology

subaltern
used in postcolonial theory to refer to individuals whose class, race, gender, and indigenous status have denied them access to education, the law, and voice of authority

successor science projects
an approach within the university curriculum that develops theory, methods, and topics in science that embrace feminist values and perspectives

suffrage movements
movements in late 19th- and early 20th-century Europe and North America advocating the right for women to vote

survival of the fittest
notion derived from Darwin's theory of evolution that those best suited to the environment will reproduce and their offspring will survive

tenure
lifetime employment commitment from a college or university to ensure academic freedom; awarded to a faculty member, typically after a six-year trial period of proven teaching and research

teratogenic effects
birth defects caused by exposure to drugs or other environmental toxins during pregnancy

third-wave feminism
feminist movement that emerged in the early 1990s that seeks to challenge any universal definition of femininity; response to failures of second-wave feminism

Title IX
part of the Education Acts of 1972 that bans sex discrimination in all federally funded education programs

Title VII
part of the Civil Rights Act of 1964 that bans discrimination based on sex, race, national origin, and religion by all organizations employing 15 or more people

"Top 10"
one of the top departments in a particular field, usually as determined by National Research Council rankings

transformation model
a method of changing an institution, curriculum, or structure in phases

transgender
assuming a gender identity that is different or opposite from the biological sex without undergoing transsexual surgery—that is, an XX individual assuming masculine gender identity

transsexual surgery
surgeries undertaken to make the physical appearance of individuals congruent with their socially constructed gender identity

transvestite
individuals who cross-dress or wear clothing typically associated with the opposite sex/gender in a particular culture

"two cultures"
an idea that science and the humanities have very different methods, vocabularies, and communities that have led to a breakdown in communication; originally popularized by C. P. Snow in the 1950s

underdetermination
the thesis of the philosopher Quine that there is slack between any theory and all the evidence for it

uniformitarianism
idea propagated by 19th-century geologist Charles Lyell that the natural processes operating in the past can be observed operating in the present

universal
the idea, first emerging in the Enlightenment, that science is open to all and that scientific ideas can be applied to all

utopia
an ideal, fictional, positive world

value freedom
free from biases or perspectives of individuals or contexts

vernacular science
popular understandings of science; lay comprehension; the type of training acquired by apprenticeship rather than at the university, such as the training of some midwives

visuospatial ability
capacity to visualize a three-dimensional structure from two-dimensional diagrams or drawings; important in engineering, architecture, and mathematics

voice
form of power given to or constructed by women within relationships that is in opposition to the "silencing" of women's perceptions and perspectives by men

woman question in Marxism
challenge of the Marxist notion that disappearance of class because of equality of income distribution would also correct inequities between the sexes

Yentl syndrome
based on the movie *Yentl* in which a woman obtained entrance into exclusively male Jewish culture by dressing and acting like a man; once a woman shows she is like a man, she is treated like one

zines
abbreviation of the word fanzine that originated from magazine; writings and drawings with a magazine-like format published and distributed by individuals

Bibliography

Abir-Am, Pnina G., and Dorinda Outram, eds. *Uneasy Careers and Intimate Lives. Women in Science 1789–1979.* New Brunswick, NJ: Rutgers University Press, 1987.

Adam, Alison. *Artificial Knowing: Gender and the Thinking Machine.* London: Routledge, 1998.

Aisenberg, N., and M. Harrington. *Women of Academe: Outsiders in the Sacred Grove.* Washington, DC: Joseph Henry Press, 1988.

Alic, Margaret. *Hypatia's Heritage: A History of Women in Science from Antiquity through the Nineteenth Century.* Boston: Beacon Press, 1986.

Ambrose, Susan, Kristin Dunkle, Barbara Lazarus, Indira Nair, and Deborah Harkus. *Journeys of Women in Science and Engineering: No Universal Constants.* Philadelphia: Temple University Press, 1997.

American Association for the Advancement of Science. *Preparing Women and Minorities for the IT Workforce: The Role of Nontraditional Educational Pathways.* Washington, DC: American Association for the Advancement of Science and the Commission on Professionals in Science and Technology, 2005.

American Association of University Professors. *AAUP Faculty Gender Equity Indicators 2006.* Washington, DC: American Association of University Professors, 2006. http://www.aaup.org/NR/rdonlyres/63396944–44BE-4ABA-9815–5792D93856F1/0/AAUPGenderEquityIndicators2006.pdf.

American Association of University Women. *How Schools Shortchange Girls.* Washington, DC: AAUW Educational Foundation, 1992.

American Association of University Women. *Tech-Savvy: Educating Girls in the New Computer Age.* Washington, DC: AAUW Educational Foundation, 2000.

American Chemical Society. *Dissolving Disparity, Catalyzing Change: Are Women Achieving Equity in Chemistry?* ACS Symposium Series No. 929. Washington, DC: American Chemical Society, March 2006.

Arditti, Rita. "Feminism and Science." In *Science and Liberation.* Edited by Rita Arditti, P. Brennan, and Steve Cavrak. Boston: South End Press, 1981.

Badinter, Elisabeth. *Mother Love.* New York: Macmillan, 1982.

Barker-Benfield, G. J. *The Horrors of the Half-Known Life.* New York: Harper and Row, 1976.

Belenky, Mary F., B. M. Clinchy, N. R. Goldberger, and J. M. Tarule. *Women's Ways of Knowing: The Development of Self, Voice, and Mind*. New York: Basic Books, 1986.

Bell, N. E., N. M. Di Fabio, and L. M. Frehill. *Professional Women and Minorities: A Total Human Resources Data Compendium*. 16th ed. Washington, DC: Commission on Professionals in Science and Technology, November 2006.

Bem, Sandra L. *The Lenses of Gender: Transforming the Debate in Sexual Inequality*. New Haven, CT: Yale University Press, 1993.

Benbow, Camilla Persson, and Julian C. Stanley. "Sex Differences in Mathematical Ability: Fact or Artifact?" *Science* 210 (1980): 1262–1264.

BEST. *A Bridge for All: Higher Education Design Principles to Broaden Participation in Science, Technology, Engineering, and Mathematics*. www.bestworkforce.org. (Accessed February 2004.)

The Biographical Dictionary of Women in Science. Pioneering Lives from Ancient Times to the Mid-20th Century. Edited by Marilyn Ogilvie and Joy Harvey. 2 vols. New York: Routledge, 2000.

Birke, Lynda. *Women, Feminism, and Biology: The Feminist Challenge*. New York: Methuen, 1986.

Blackwell, Elizabeth. *Pioneer Work in Opening the Medical Profession for Women*. New York: E. P. Dutton, 1895.

Bleier, Ruth. *Science and Gender. A Critique of Biology and Its Theories on Women*. New York: Pergamon Press, 1984.

Bordo, Susan. *The Flight to Objectivity: Essays on Cartesianism and Culture*. Albany: State University of New York Press, 1987.

Boserup, Ester. *Women's Role in Economic Development*. New York: St. Martin's Press, 1970.

Brizendine, Louann. *The Female Brain*. New York: Morgan Rood Books, 2006.

Brush, Stephen G. "Women in Science and Engineering." *American Scientist* 79 (1991): 404–419.

Bryson, Mary, and Suzanne de Castell. "En/gendering Equity: Paradoxical Consequences of Institutionalized Equity Policies." In *Radical In<ter>ventions*. Edited by S. de Castell and M. Bryson. Albany: State University of New York Press, 1997.

Butler, Judith. *Gender Trouble: Feminism and the Subversion of Identity*. New York: Routledge, 1990.

Byers, Nina, and Gary Williams, eds. *Out of the Shadows: Contributions of Twentieth-Century Women to Physics*. New York: Cambridge University Press, 2006.

Caplan, P. J., and J. B. Caplan. *Thinking Critically about Research on Sex and Gender*. New York: HarperCollins, 1994.

Carson, Rachel. *Silent Spring*. New York: Houghton Mifflin, 1962.

Ceci, S., and W. Williams. *Why Aren't More Women in Science?* Washington, DC: American Psychological Association, 2007.

Chakravorty Spivak, Gayatri. "Can the Subaltern Speak?" In *Marxism and the Interpretation of Culture*. Edited by Cary Nelson and Lawrence Grossberg, 271–313. Urbana: University of Illinois Press, 1988.

Chodorow, Nancy. *The Reproduction of Mothering: Psychoanalysis and the Sociology of Gender*. Berkeley: University of California Press, 1978.

Chubin, Daryl E., and Willie Pearson Jr. "Postscript." *Scientists and Engineers for the New Millennium: Renewing the Human Resource,* 87–93. Washington, DC: Commission on Professionals in Science and Technology, March 2001.

Clarke, A., and V. Olesen. *Revisioning Women, Health, and Healing.* New York: Routledge, 1999.

Clewell, Beatriz, and Angela Ginorio. "Examining Women's Progress in the Sciences from the Perspective of Diversity." In *The Equity Equation.* Edited by C. S. Davis, A. B. Ginorio, B. Lazarus, and P. Rayman. San Francisco: Jossey-Bass, 1996.

Cockburn, Cynthia. *Brothers: Male Dominance and Technological Change.* London: Pluto Press, 1983.

Cockburn, Cynthia. *Machinery of Dominance: Women, Men and Technical Know-How.* London: Pluto Press, 1985.

Cockburn, Cynthia, and Susan Ormrod. *Gender and Technology in the Making.* London: Sage, 1993.

Cohn, C. "Sex and Death in the Rational World of Defense Intellectuals." *Signs: Journal of Women in Culture and Society* 12(4) (1987): 687–718.

Cohoon, J. McGrath, and William Aspray, eds. *Women and Information Technology: Research on Underrepresentation.* Boston: MIT Press, 2006.

Commission on the Advancement of Women and Minorities in Science, Engineering, and Technology Development (CAWMSET). *Land of Plenty: Diversity as America's Competitive Edge in Science, Engineering and Technology.* Report of the Commission on the Advancement of Women and Minorities in Science, Engineering, and Technology Development. Washington, DC: National Science Foundation, September 2000.

Cowan, Ruth S. *More Work for Mother: The Ironies of Household Technology from the Open Hearth to the Microwave.* New York: Basic Books, 1981.

Creager, Angela N. H., Elizabeth Lunlock, and Londa Schiebinger, eds. *Feminism in Twentieth Century Science, Technology, and Medicine.* Chicago: University of Chicago Press, 2001.

Crittenden, Ann. *The Price of Motherhood: Why the Most Important Job in the World Is Still the Least Valued.* New York: Metropolitan Books, 2001.

Curie, Marie. *Pierre Curie.* New York: Macmillan, 1936.

Curie, Eve. *Madame Curie.* New York: Doubleday, 1937.

Dash, Joan. "Maria Goeppert-Mayer." *A Life of One's Own: Three Gifted Women and the Men They Married.* New York: Harper and Row, 1973.

Davis, Cinda-Sue, Angela B. Ginorio, Carol S. Hollenshead, Barbara B. Lazarus, Paula M. Rayman, eds. *The Equity Equation: Fostering the Advancement of Women in the Sciences, Mathematics, and Engineering.* San Francisco: Jossey-Bass, 1996.

De Beauvoir, Simone. *The Second Sex.* Edited and translated by H. M. Parshley. New York: Vintage Books, 1947.

Dear, Peter. *Revolutionizing the Sciences: European Knowledge and Its Ambitions, 1500–1700.* Princeton, NJ: Princeton University Press, 2001.

Donawerth, Jane L. *Frankenstein's Daughters: Women Writing Science Fiction.* Syracuse, NY: Syracuse University Press, 1997.

Duster, Troy. "Buried Alive: The Concept of Race in Science." In *Genetic Nature/ Culture: Anthropology and Science beyond the Two-Culture Divide*. Edited by A. H. Goodman et al. Berkeley: University of California Press, 2003.

Ehrenreich, Barbara, and Deirdre English. *Witches, Midwives, and Nurses: A History of Women Healers*. Old Westbury, NY: Feminist Press, 1972.

Ehrenreich, Barbara, and Dierdre English. *Complaints and Disorders: The Sexual Politics of Sickness*. New York: Feminist Press, 1973.

Eisenhart, M. A., and E. Finkel. *Women's Science: Learning and Succeeding from the Margins*. Chicago: University of Chicago Press, 1998.

Etzkowitz, H., et al. *Who Will Do Science? Educating the Next Generation*. Baltimore, MD: Johns Hopkins University Press, 1994.

Fausto-Sterling, A. *Myths of Gender: Biological Theories about Women and Men*. 2nd ed. New York: Basic Books, 1992.

Fausto-Sterling, A. *Sexing the Body: Gender Politics and the Construction of Sexuality*. New York: Basic Books, 2000.

Fedigan, Linda M. "The Paradox of Feminist Primatology: The Goddess's Discipline?" In *Feminism in Twentieth Century Science, Technology and Medicine*. Edited by Angela N. H. Creager, Elizabeth Lunbeck, and Londa Schiebinger, 46–72. Chicago: University of Chicago Press, 2001.

Feinberg, Leslie. *Transgender Warriors: Making History from Joan of Arc to Dennis Rodman*. Boston: Beacon Press, 1996.

Ferry, Georgina. *Dorothy Hodgkin: A Life*. Cold Spring Harbor, NY: Cold Spring Harbor Laboratory Press, 1998.

Figueroa, R., and S. Harding, eds. *Science and Other Cultures: Issues in Philosophies of Science and Technology*. New York: Routledge, 2003.

Fischer, Agnetta H., and Anthony S. R. Manstead. "Gender Differences in Emotion across Cultures." In *Gender and Emotion: Social Psychological Perspectives*. Edited by Agnetta H. Fischer, 91–97. London: Cambridge University Press, 2000.

Fissell, Mary. *Vernacular Bodies: The Politics of Reproduction in Early Modern England*. Oxford: Oxford University Press, 2004.

Fivush, Robyn, and Janine P. Buckner. "Constructing Gender and Identity through Autobiographical Narratives." In *Autobiographical Memory and the Construction of a Narrative Self: Developmental and Cultural Perspective*. Edited by Robyn Fivush and Catherine Haden, 140–168. Hillsdale, NJ: Erlbaum, 2003.

Flanagan, Mary, and Austin Booth, eds. *Reload: Rethinking Women + Cyberculture*. Cambridge, MA: MIT Press, 2002.

Flax, J. "Political Philosophy and the Patriarchal Unconscious: A Psychoanalytic Perspective on Epistemology and Metaphysics." In *Discovering Reality: Feminist Perspectives on Epistemology, Metaphysics, Methodology and Philosophy of Science*. Edited by S. Harding and M. B. Hintikka. Dordrecht: D. Reidel, 1983.

Flexner, Eleanor. *Mary Wollstonecraft*. Baltimore, MD: Penguin Books, 1972.

Foucault, Michel. *The History of Sexuality*. Vol. 1. New York: Vintage Books, 1978.

Fox, Mary, Deborah Johnson, and Sue Rosser, eds. *Women, Gender and Technology*. Champaign: University of Illinois Press, in press.

Gallagher, A., and J. Kaufmann. *Gender Differences in Mathematics*. New York: Cambridge University Press, 2005.

Gibbs, Lois Marie. *Love Canal: The Story Continues*. 20th anniversary ed. Stony Creek, CT: New Society Publishers, 1998.

Gilligan, Carole. *In a Different Voice*. Cambridge, MA: Harvard University Press, 1982.

Glazer, P., and M. Slater. *Unequal Colleagues*. New Brunswick, NJ: Rutgers University Press, 1987.

Gould, S. *The Mismeasure of Man*. New York: W. W. Norton, 1981.

Gould, Stephen Jay. *The Mismeasure of Man*. 2nd ed. New York: W. W. Norton, 1996.

Griffin, Susan. *The Death of Nature*. New York: Harper and Row, 1978.

Hacker, Sally. "The Culture of Engineering: Woman, Workplace, and Machine." *Women's Studies International Quarterly* 4 (1981): 341–353.

Hacker, Sally. *Pleasure, Power and Technology*. Boston: Unwin Hyman, 1989.

Hall, R. M., and B. R. Sandler. *The Classroom Climate: A Chilly One for Women*. Washington, DC: Association of American Colleges, 1982.

Haller, John S., and Robin M. Haller. *The Physician and Sexuality in Victorian America*. Champaign: University of Illinois Press, 1974.

Hammonds, Evelynn. *Childhood's Deadly Scourge: The Campaign to Control Diphtheria in New York City, 1880–1930*. Baltimore, MD: Johns Hopkins University Press, 1999.

Handelsman, J., N. Cantor, M. Carnes, D. Denton, E. Fine, B. Grosz, V. Hinshaw, C. Marrett, S. Rosser, D. Shalala, and J. Sheridan. "More Women in Science." *Science* 309 (2005): 1190–1191.

Haraway, Donna. *Primate Visions: Gender, Race, and Nature in the World of Modern Science*. New York: Routledge, 1989.

Haraway, Donna. *Simians, Cyborgs, and Women: The Reinvention of Nature*. New York: Routledge, 1991.

Haraway, Donna. *Modest_Witness@Second_Millenium.Female_Man©Meets_Oncomouse™: Feminist and Technoscience*. New York: Routledge, 1997.

Harding, Sandra. *The Science Question in Feminism*. Ithaca, NY: Cornell University Press, 1986.

Harding, Sandra. *Whose Science, Whose Knowledge? Thinking from Women's Lives*. Ithaca, NY: Cornell University Press, 1991.

Harding, Sandra, ed. *The Racial Economy of Science*. Bloomington: Indiana University Press, 1993.

Harding, Sandra. *Is Science Multicultural? Postcolonialisms, Feminisms, and Epistemologies*. Bloomington: Indiana University Press, 1998.

Harth, Erica. *Cartesian Women*. Ithaca, NY: Cornell University Press, 1992.

Hartmann, Heidi. "The Unhappy Marriage of Marxism and Feminism: Towards a More Progressive Union." *Women and Revolution: A Disc*. Edited by L. Sargent. Boston: South End Press, 1981.

Hawthorne, S., and R. Klein. *Cyberfeminism*. Sydney, Australia: Spinifex Press, 1999.

Hays, Sharon. *The Cultural Contradictions of Motherhood*. New Haven, CT: Yale University Press, 1996.

Herring, Susan, Deborah A. Johnson, and Tamara DiBenedetto. *Gender Articulated, Language and the Socially Constructed Self*. Edited by K. Hall and M. Bucholtz. New York: Routledge, 1995.

Herzenberg, Caroline L. *Women Scientists from Antiquity to the Present: An Index.* West Cornwall, CT: Locust Hill Press, 1986.

hooks, bell. *Race and Representation.* London: Turnaround Press, 1992.

Hill Collins, Patricia. *Black Feminist Thought: Knowledge, Consciousness, and the Politics of Empowerment.* Boston: Unwin Hyman, 1990.

Hornig, Lilli S. *Equal Rites, Unequal Outcomes: Women in American Research Universities.* New York: Kluwer Academic/Plenum Publishers, 2003.

Horowitz, Roger, and Arwen Mohun, eds. *His and Hers: Gender, Consumption, and Technology.* Charlottesville: University Press of Virginia, 1998.

Hosek, Susan G., Amy G. Cox, Bonnie Ghosh-Dastidar, Aaron Kofner, Nishal Ramphal, Jon Scott, and Sandra H. Berry. *Gender Differences in Major Federal External Grant Programs.* Santa Monica, CA: Rand Corporation, 2005. http://www.rand.org/pubs/technical_reports/TR307/.

Høyrup, Elise. *Women of Science, Technology, and Medicine: A Bibliography.* Roskilde, Denmark: Roskilde University Library, 1987.

Hrdy, Sarah B. *The Woman that Never Evolved.* Cambridge, MA: Harvard University Press, 1981.

Hrdy, Sarah Blaffer. *Mother Nature: Maternal Instincts and How They Shape the Human Species.* New York: Ballantine, 1999.

Hubbard, Ruth. *The Politics of Women's Biology.* New Brunswick, NJ: Rutgers University Press, 1990.

Hurd-Mead, Kate Campbell. *A History of Women in Medicine: From the Earliest Times to the Beginning of the Nineteenth Century.* Haddom, CT: Haddom Press, 1938.

Hyde, J. S., and M. C. Linn. "Gender Similarities in Mathematics and Science." *Science* 314 (2006): 599–600.

Hynes, H. Patricia. *The Recurring Silent Spring.* Elmsford, NY: Pergamon Press, 1989.

Ivie, Rachel, and Kim Nies Ray. "Women in Physics and Astronomy, 2005." AIP report R-430.02. (2005). http://www.aip.org/statistics/trends/gendertrends/html. (Accessed November 15, 2006.)

Jaggar, Alison. "Love and Knowledge: Emotion in Feminist Epistemology." In *Gender/Body/Knowledge: Feminist Reconstructions of Being and Knowing.* Edited by Alison Jaggar and Susan Bordo. New Brunswick, NJ: Rutgers University Press, 1989.

Jordanova, Ludmilla. *Sexual Visions. Images of Gender in Science and Medicine between the Eighteenth and Twentieth Centuries.* Madison: University of Wisconsin Press, 1989.

Katz, Jay. *Gay American History: Lesbians and Gay Men in the USA.* New York: Meridien, 1992.

Keller, E. F. "The Anomaly of a Woman in Physics." In *Working It Out: Twenty-three Writers, Scientists, and Scholars Talk about Their Lives.* Edited by S. Ruddick and P. Daniels, 77–91. New York: Pantheon Books, 1977.

Keller, Evelyn F. *A Feeling for the Organism: The Life and Work of Barbara McClintock.* New York: W. H. Freeman, 1983.

Keller, Evelyn F. *Reflections on Gender and Science.* New Haven, CT: Yale University Press, 1985.

Keller, E. F. *Secrets of Life, Secrets of Death: Essays on Language, Gender, and Science.* New York: Routledge, 1992.

Keller, E. F., and H. Longino, eds. *Feminism and Science*. New York: Oxford University Press, 1996.

Kelly-Gadol, Joan. "Did Women Have a Renaissance?" *Women, History, and Theory: The Essays of Joan Kelly*. Chicago. University of Chicago Press, 1984.

King, Margaret. *Women in the Renaissance*. Chicago: University of Chicago Press, 1991.

Kohlestedt, Sally Gregory, Barbara Laslett, Helen Longino, and Evelyn Hammonds, eds. *Gender and Scientific Authority*. Chicago: University of Chicago Press, 1996.

Latour, Bruno. *Science in Action*. Cambridge, MA: Harvard University Press, 1987.

Leavitt, Judith. *Brought to Bed: Childbearing in America 1750–1950*. New York: Oxford University Press, 1986.

Lefanu, Sarah. *Feminism and Science Fiction*. Bloomington: Indiana University Press, 1989.

Leggon, Cheryl B. "Gender, Race/Ethnicity, and the Digital Divide." *Women, Gender, and Technology*. Edited by Mary Frank Fox, Deborah G. Johnson, and Sue V. Rosser, 98–110. Champaign: University of Illinois Press, 2006.

Lerman, Nina E., Ruth Oldenziel, and Arwen P. Mohun, eds. *Gender and Technology: A Reader*. Baltimore, MD: Johns Hopkins University Press, 2003.

Levi-Montalcini, Rita. *In Praise of Imperfection: My Life and Work*. New York: Basic Books, 1988.

Lloyd, Elisabeth. *The Case of the Female Orgasm: Bias in the Science of Evolution*. Cambridge, MA: Harvard University Press, 2005.

Lloyd, Genevieve. *The Man of Reason: "Male" and "Female" in Western Philosophy*. Minneapolis: University of Minnesota Press, 1984.

Longino, Helen. *Science as Social Knowledge*. Princeton, NJ: Princeton University Press, 1990.

Lubbock, Constance A. *The Herschel Chronicle: The Life-Story of William Herschel and His Sister Caroline Herschel*. Cambridge: Cambridge University Press, 1933.

Maccoby, E. E., and C. N. Jacklin. *The Psychology of Sex Differences*. Stanford, CA: Stanford University Press, 1974.

Macdonald, Anne. *Feminine Ingenuity: Women and Invention in America*. New York: Ballantine Books, 1992.

Madden, T. E., L. F. Barrett, and P. R. Pietromonaco. "Sex Differences in Anxiety and Depression: Empirical Evidence and Methodological Questions." In *Gender and Emotion: Social Psychological Perspectives*. Edited by Agnetta H. Fischer, 277–298. London: Cambridge University Press, 2000.

Maddox, Brenda. *Rosalind Franklin: The Dark Lady of DNA*. New York: Harper Collins, 2002.

Malcom, Shirley Mahaley, Paula Quick Hall, and Janet Welsh Brown. *The Double Bind: The Price of Being a Minority Woman in Science*. AAAS publication 76-R-3. Washington, DC: American Association for the Advancement of Science, April 1976.

Martin, Emily. *The Woman in the Body*. Boston: Beacon Press, 1987.

Martin, Emily. "The Egg and the Sperm: How Science Has Constructed a Romance Based on Stereotypical Male-Female Roles." *Signs: Journal of Women in Culture and Society* 16 (1991): 485–501.

Martin, Emily. *Flexible Bodies: Tracking Immunity in American Culture from the Days of Polio to the Days of AIDS*. Boston: Beacon Press, 1994.

Mason, M. A., and M. Goulden. "Do Babies Matter (Part II). Closing the Baby Gap." *Academe* (November–December 2004).

Mayberry, M., B. Subramaniam, and L. Weasel, eds. *Feminist Science Studies: A New Generation.* New York: Routledge, 2001.

Matlin, M. W. *The Psychology of Women.* 5th ed. Belmont, CA: Wadsworth, 2004.

McGrayne, Sharon Bertsch. *Nobel Prize Women in Science: Their Lives, Struggles, and Momentous Discoveries.* 2nd ed. Secaucus, NJ: Carol, 1998.

McIlwee, J., and J. G. Robinson. *Women in Engineering: Gender, Power and Workplace Culture.* Albany: State University of New York Press, 1992.

Merchant, Carolyn. *The Death of Nature: Women, Ecology, and the Scientific Revolution.* San Francisco: Harper and Row, 1980.

Microsysters. *Not over Our Heads: Women and Computers in the Office.* London: Microsysters, 1988.

Mill, John Stuart, and Harriet Taylor Mill. *Essays on Sex Equality.* Edited by Alice S. Rossi. Chicago: University of Chicago Press, 1970.

Millar, Melanie. *Cracking the Gender Code: Who Rules the Wired World?* Toronto: Second Story Press, 1998.

Miller, Jean B. *Toward a New Psychology of Women.* Boston: Beacon Press, 1976.

Miller, Neil. *Out of the Past: Gay and Lesbian History from 1869 to the Present.* New York: Alyson Books, 2006.

MIT. "A Study on the Status of Women Faculty in Science at MIT." *MIT Faculty Newsletter* 11(4) (March 1999). http://web.mit.edu/fnl/women/women.html#The%20Study. (Accessed November 15, 2006.)

Mohanty, Chandra Talpade. "Women Workers and Capitalist Transcripts: Ideologies of Domination, Common Interests, and the Politics of Solidarity." In *Feminist Genealogies, Colonial Legacies, Democratic Futures.* Edited by M. Jacqui Alexander and Chandra Talpade Mohanty, 3–29. New York: Routledge, 1997.

Mohanty, Chandra Talpade. "Under Western Eyes Revisited: Feminist Solidarity through Anticapitalist Struggles." In *Feminism without Borders: Decolonizing Theory, Practicing Solidarity.* Edited by Chandra Talpade Mohanty, 221–251. Durham, NC: Duke University Press, 2003.

Morantz-Sanchez, Regina. *Sympathy and Science: Women Physicians in American Medicine.* Oxford: Oxford University Press, 1985.

Morantz-Sanchez, Regina. "The Many Faces of Intimacy: Professional Options and Personal Choices among Nineteenth and Early Twentieth Century Women Physicians." In *Uneasy Careers and Intimate Lives. Women in Science 1789–1979.* Edited by Pnina G. Abir-Am and Dorinda Outram. New Brunswick, NJ: Rutgers University Press, 1987.

Moss, Kary, ed. *Man Made Medicine. Women's Health, Public Policy, and Reform.* Durham, NC: Duke University Press, 1996.

Mozans, H. J. *Women in Science.* 1913. Reprint, Notre Dame, IN: University of Notre Dame Press, 1991.

Musil, C. M., ed. *Gender, Science, and the Undergraduate Curriculum: Building Two-Way Streets.* Washington, DC: Association of American Colleges and Universities, 2001.

National Council for Research on Women. *Balancing the Equation: Where Are Women and Girls in Science, Engineering, and Technology?* New York: National Council for Research on Women, 2001.

National Science Board. *Science and Engineering Indicators 2004.* NSB 04–1, Vol. 1. Arlington, VA: National Science Foundation, 2004.

National Science Foundation. *Women and Science: Celebrating Achievements, Charting Challenges.* Conference Report, March 1997. http://www.nsf.gov/pubs/1997/nsf9775/start.htm.

National Science Foundation. *Science and Engineering Indicators 2006.* Arlington, VA: National Science Foundation, 2006.

Neeley, Kathryn A. *Mary Somerville. Science, Illumination, and the Female Mind.* Cambridge: Cambridge University Press, 2001.

Nelson, Lynn Hankinson. *Who Knows: From Quine to Feminist Empiricism.* Philadelphia: Temple University Press, 1990.

Nelson, Lynn Hankinson, and Jack Nelson, eds. *Feminism, Science, and the Philosophy of Science.* Dordrecht: Kluwer Academic Press, 1996.

Nobel Foundation. Official Web site of the Nobel Foundation, 2007. http://Nobel Prize.org.

Noble, David F. *A World without Women: The Christian Clerical Culture of Western Science.* New York: Oxford University Press, 1993.

Nolen-Hoeksema, S. *Sex Differences in Depression.* Stanford, CA: Stanford University Press, 1990.

O'Brien, Mary. *The Politics of Reproduction.* Boston: Routledge and Kegan Paul, 1981.

Ogilvie, Marilyn Bailey. *Women in Science. Antiquity through the Nineteenth Century. A Biographical Dictionary with Annotated Bibliography.* Cambridge, MA: MIT Press, 1986.

Ogilvie, Marilyn Bailey, and Joy Harvey, eds. *The Biographical Dictionary of Women in Science. Pioneering Lives from Ancient Times to the Mid-20th Century.* New York: Routledge, 2000.

Oldenziel, Ruth. *Making Technology Masculine: Men, Women, and Modern Machines in America, 1870–1945.* Amsterdam: Amsterdam University Press, 1999.

Ormrod, Susan. "Feminist Sociology and Methodology: Leaky Black Boxes in Gender/Technology Relations." In *The Gender-Technology Relation: Contemporary Theory and Research.* Edited by K. Grint and R. Gill. London: Taylor and Francis, 1995.

Pomeroy, Sarah B. *Goddesses, Whores, Wives, and Slaves. Women in Classical Antiquity.* New York: Schocken Books, 1975.

Potter, Elizabeth. *Gender and Boyle's Law of Gases.* Bloomington: Indiana University Press, 2001.

Pratt, Mary Louise. *Imperial Eyes: Travel Writing and Transculturation.* New York: Routledge, 1992.

Quinn, Susan. *Marie Curie: A Life.* Cambridge, MA: Perseus Books, 1995.

Rapp, Rayna. "One New Reproductive Technology, Multiple Sites: How Feminist Methodology Bleeds into Everyday Life." In *Revisioning Women, Health, and Healing.* Edited by Adele Clarke and Virginia Olesen. New York: Routledge, 1999.

Raymond, Janice. *The Transsexual Empire: The Making of the She-male*. Boston: Beacon Press, 1979.

Rayner-Canham, Marelene F., and Geoffrey W. Rayner-Canham. *Women in Chemistry. Their Changing Roles from Alchemical Times to the Mid-Twentieth Century*. Philadelphia: American Chemical Society and Chemical Heritage Foundation, 1998.

Rich, Adrienne. *Of Women Born: Motherhood as Experience and Institution*. New York: W. W. Norton, 1978.

Rimini, Francesca da, Josephine Starrs, Julianne Pierce, and Virginia Barratt. *VNS Matrix*. http://lx.sysx.org/vnsmatrix.html. (Accessed 1991.)

Roberts, Robin. *A New Species: Gender and Science in Science Fiction*. Urbana: University of Illinois Press, 1993.

Rose, H. *Love, Power and Knowledge: Towards a Feminist Transformation of the Sciences*. Bloomington: Indiana University Press, 1994.

Rose, Hilary, and Steven Rose. "The Myth of the Neutrality of Science." In *Science and Liberation*. Edited by Rita Arditti, Pat Brennan, and Steve Cavrak. Boston: South End Press, 1980.

Rose, H., and S. Rose, eds. *Alas, Poor Darwin: Arguments against Evolutionary Psychology*. New York: Harmony Books, 2000.

Rosser, Sue V. *Female-friendly Science*. Elmsford, NY: Pergamon Press, 1990.

Rosser, Sue V. *Feminism and Biology*. New York: Twayne/Macmillan, 1992.

Rosser, Sue V. *Women's Health: Missing from U.S. Medicine*. Bloomington: Indiana University Press, 1994.

Rosser, Sue V. *Teaching the Majority: Breaking the Gender Barrier in Science, Mathematics, and Engineering*. New York: Teachers College Press, 1995.

Rosser, Sue V. *Re-engineering Female-friendly Science*. Elmsford, NY: Pergamon Press, 1997.

Rosser, Sue V. *The Science Glass Ceiling: Academic Women Scientists and the Struggle to Succeed*. New York: Routledge, 2004.

Rossiter, Margaret W. *Women Scientists in America: Struggles and Strategies to 1940*. Baltimore, MD: Johns Hopkins University Press, 1982.

Rossiter, Margaret. *Women Scientists in America: Before Affirmative Action*. Baltimore, MD: Johns Hopkins University Press, 1995.

Rubens, Jack. *Karen Horney: Gentle Rebel of Psychoanalysis*. New York: Dial Press, 1978.

Rubin, Gayle. "The Traffic in Women: Notes on the 'Political Economy' of Sex." In *Toward an Anthropology of Women*. Edited by Rayna Reiter, 157–210. New York: Monthly Review Press, 1975.

Ruddick, Sara. *Maternal Thinking*. Boston: Beacon Press, 1989.

Russett, Cynthia Eagle. *Sexual Science: The Victorian Construction of Womanhood*. Cambridge, MA: Harvard University Press, 1989.

Sadker, M., and D. Sadker. *Failing at Fairness: How America's Schools Cheat Girls*. New York: Charles Scribner's Sons, 1994.

Sayers, Janet. *Biological Politics*. New York: Tavistock, 1982.

Sayre, Anne. *Rosalind Franklin and DNA: A Vivid View of What It Is Like to Be a Gifted Woman in an Especially Male Profession*. New York: W. W. Norton, 1975.

Scharff, Virginia. *Taking the Wheel: Women and the Coming of the Motor Age.* New York: Free Press, 1991.

Schiebinger, Londa L. *The Mind Has No Sex? Women in the Origins of Modern Science.* Cambridge, MA: Harvard University Press, 1989.

Schiebinger, Londa. *Has Feminism Changed Science?* Cambridge, MA: Harvard University Press, 1999.

Seager, Joni. *Earth Follies: Coming to Feminist Terms with the Global Environmental Crisis.* New York: Routledge Press, 1993.

Selby, Cecily C. "Women in Science and Engineering: Choices for Success." *Annals of the New York Academy of Sciences.* Vol. 869. New York: New York Academy of Sciences, 1999.

Seymour, E., and N. Hewitt. *Talking about Leaving: Factors Contributing to High Attrition Rates among Science, Mathematics, and Engineering Undergraduate Majors.* Final Report to the Alfred P. Sloan Foundation. Boulder: University of Colorado, 1994.

Shaywitz, B. A., S. E. Shaywitz, K. R. Pugh, R. T. Constable, et al. "Sex Differences in the Functional Organization of the Brain for Language." *Nature* 373 (1995): 607–609.

Shaywitz, Sally, and Jong-on Hahm, eds. *Achieving Excellence in Science: Role of Professional Societies in Advancing Women in Science.* Proceedings of a 2002 Workshop Committee on Women in Science and Engineering, Washington, DC: National Research Council, 2004.

Shilts, Randy. *And the Band Played On: Politics, People and the AIDS Epidemic.* New York: St. Martin's Press, 1987.

Shiva, Vandana. *Staying Alive: Women, Ecology, and Development.* London: Zed Books, 1989.

Sicherman, Barbara. *Alice Hamilton: A Life in Letters.* Cambridge, MA: Harvard University Press, 1984.

Smith-Doerr, L. *Women's Work: Gender Equality vs. Hierarchy in the Life Sciences.* Boulder, CO: Lynne Rienner, 2004.

Solomon, B. M. *In the Company of Educated Women.* New Haven, CT: Yale University Press, 1985.

Sonnert, G., and G. Holton. *Gender Differences in Science Careers.* New Brunswick, NJ: Rutgers University Press, 1995.

Spencer, S. J., C. M. Steele, and D. M. Quinn. "Stereotype Threat and Women's Math Performance." *Journal of Experimental Social Psychology* 35 (1999): 4–28.

Stanley, Autumn. *Mothers and Daughters of Invention: Notes for a Revised History of Technology.* New Brunswick, NJ: Rutgers University Press, 1995.

Straus, Eugene. *Rosalyn Yalow: Nobel Laureate: Her Life and Work in Medicine.* New York: Plenum, 1998.

Sullivan, Deborah, and Rose Weitz. *Labor Pains: Modern Midwives and Home Birth.* New Haven, CT: Yale University Press, 1988.

Tang, Joyce. *Scientific Pioneers: Women Succeeding in Science.* Lanham, MD: University Press of America, 2006.

Tannen, Debra. *You Just Don't Understand. Women and Men in Conversation.* New York: HarperCollins, 1990.

Traweek, Sharon. *Beamtimes and Lifetimes: The World of High Energy Physics*. Cambridge, MA: Harvard University Press, 1998.

Tuana, Nancy, ed. *Hypatia* 2(3) (1987). Special Issue: Feminism and Science,.

Tuana, Nancy. *Feminism and Science*. Bloomington: Indiana University Press, 1989.

Valian, Virgina. *Why So Slow? The Advancement of Women*. Cambridge, MA: MIT Press, 1998.

Wajcman, Judy. *Feminism Confronts Technology*. University Park: Pennsylvania State University Press, 1991.

Wasserman, Elga. *The Door in the Dream: Conversations with Eminent Women in Science*. Washington, DC: Joseph Henry Press, 2000.

Watson, James. *The Double Helix*. New York: Atheneum, 1969.

Webster, Juliet. *Shaping Women's Work: Gender, Employment and Information Technology*. New York: Longman, 1995.

Weisstein, N. "'How Can a Little Girl like You Teach a Great Big Class of Men?' the Chairman Said, and Other Adventures of a Woman in Science." In *Working It Out: Twenty-three Writers, Scientists, and Scholars Talk about Their Lives*. Edited by S. Ruddick and P. Daniels. New York: Pantheon Books, 1977.

Wilding, Faith. *Where Is Feminism in Cyberfeminism?* 1997. http://www.andrew.cmu .edu/user/fwild/faithwilding/wherefem.html. (Accessed July 23, 2007.)

Williams, Patricia. *The Alchemy of Race and Rights*. Cambridge, MA: Harvard University Press, 1991.

Winner, Langdon. "Do Artifacts Have Politics?" *Daedalus* 109 (1980): 121–136.

Wolpert, Lewis, and Alison Richards. *A Passion of Science*. New York: Oxford University Press, 1988.

Women Chemists' Committee, Committee on Economic and Professional Affairs. *Women Chemists 2000*. Washington DC: American Chemical Society, 2001.

Women Scientists and Engineers Employed in Industry: Why So Few? Washington, DC: National Academies Press, 1994.

Wosk, Julie. *Women and the Machine: Representations from the Spinning Wheel to the Electronic Age*. Baltimore, MD: Johns Hopkins University Press, 2001.

Wyer, M., D. Murphy-Medley, E. Damschen, K. Rosenfeld, and T. Wentworth. "No Quick Fixes: Adding Women to Ecology Course Content." *Psychology of Women Quarterly* 31 (2007): 96–102.

Wyer, M., and Alison Wylie, eds. *Hypatia* 19(1) (2004). Special Issue: Feminist Science Studies.

Xie, Y., and K. Shauman. *Women in Science*. Boston: Harvard University Press, 2003.

Yaszek, Lisa. *Galactic Suburbia: Gender, Technology, and the Creation of Women's Science Fiction*. Columbus: Ohio State University Press, 2007.

Zinsser, Judith P. *La Dame d'Esprit. A Biography of the Marquise Du Châtelet*. New York: Viking, 2006.

Zuckerman, H., J. Cole, and J. Bruer. *The Outer Circle: Women in the Scientific Community*. New York: W. W. Norton, 1991.

Index

About the Editor

Sue V. Rosser received her Ph.D. in zoology from the University of Wisconsin–Madison in 1973. Since July 1999, she has served as dean of Ivan Allen College, the liberal arts college at Georgia Institute of Technology, where she is also professor of public policy and of history, technology, and society. She holds the endowed Ivan Allen Dean's Chair of Liberal Arts and Technology. From 1995 to 1999, she was director of the Center for Women's Studies and Gender Research and professor of anthropology at the University of Florida (Gainesville). In 1995, she was senior program officer for women's programs at the National Science Foundation. From 1986 to 1995, she served as director of women's studies at the University of South Carolina, where she also was a professor of family and preventive medicine in the medical school.

She has edited collections and written approximately 120 journal articles on the theoretical and applied problems of women, science, technology and women's health. She is author of 10 books: *Teaching Science and Health from a Feminist Perspective: A Practical Guide* (1986), *Feminism within the Science and Health Care Professions: Overcoming Resistance* (1988), *Female-friendly Science* (1990) from Pergamon Press, *Feminism and Biology: A Dynamic Interaction* (1992) from Twayne Macmillan, *Women's Health: Missing from U.S. Medicine* (1994) from Indiana University Press, and *Teaching the Majority* (1995), *Re-engineering Female-friendly Science* (1997), *Women, Science, and Society: The Crucial Union* (2000) from Teachers College Press, and *The Science Glass Ceiling: Academic Women Scientists and Their Struggle to Succeed* (2004). Her latest book is *Women, Gender, and Technology* (2006), co-edited with Mary Frank Fox and Deborah Johnson. She also served as the Latin and North American co-editor of *Women's Studies International Forum* from 1989 to 1993 and currently serves on the editorial boards of *NWSA Journal, Journal of Women and Minorities in Science and Engineering,* and *Transformations.* She has held several grants from the National Science Foundation, including "A USC System Model for Transformation of Science and Math Teaching to Reach Women in Varied Campus Settings" and "POWRE

Workshop"; from 2001 to 2006 she served as co-principal investigator on a $3.7 million ADVANCE grant from NSF. She currently serves as principal investigator on "InTEL: Interactive Toolkit for Engineering Learning," a $900,000 NSF grant. During the fall of 1993, she was Visiting Distinguished Professor for the University of Wisconsin System Women in Science Project. During the spring of 2008, she was a Clayman Fellow at Stanford University.